DEFINING DOCUMENTS
IN AMERICAN HISTORY

Dissent & Protest
(1635–2017)

DEFINING DOCUMENTS
IN AMERICAN HISTORY

Dissent & Protest
(1635–2017)

Editor

Aaron Gulyas

Volume 1

SALEM PRESS
A Division of EBSCO Information Services
Ipswich, Massachusetts

GREY HOUSE PUBLISHING

Publisher's Cataloging-In-Publication Data
(Prepared by The Donohue Group, Inc.)

Names: Gulyas, Aaron John, 1975- editor.
Title: Dissent & protest (1635-2017) / editor, Aaron Gulyas.
Other Titles: Dissent and protest (1635-2017) | Defining documents in American history (Salem Press)
Description: [First edition]. | Ipswich, Massachusetts : Salem Press, a division of EBSCO Information Services ; [Amenia, New York] : Grey House Publishing, [2017] | Includes bibliographical references and index.
Identifiers: ISBN 978-1-68217-289-6 (set) | ISBN 978-1-68217-291-9 (v. 1) | ISBN 978-1-68217-292-6 (v. 2)
Subjects: LCSH: Protest movements--United States--History--Sources. | Social movements--United States--History--Sources. | Dissenters--United States--History--Sources. | United States--Social conditions--Sources.
Classification: LCC HM881 .D57 2017 | DDC 303.484/0973--dc23

FIRST PRINTING
PRINTED IN THE UNITED STATES OF AMERICA

Table of Contents

Volume 1

FROM COLONIES TO NATION   1

SLAVERY AND ABOLITION   81

SECTIONAL CONFLICT, CIVIL WAR, AND RECONSTRUCTION 225

NATIVE AMERICAN DISSENT 287

Volume 2

AFRICAN-AMERICAN CIVIL RIGHTS 355

WOMEN'S RIGHTS
481

POLITICAL AND SOCIAL PROTEST
533

ANTI-WAR ACTIVISM   621

APPENDIXES   663

Publisher's Note

Defining Documents in American History series, produced by Salem Press, consists of a collection of essays on important historical documents by a diverse range of writers on a broad range of subjects in American history. This established series offers twenty-three titles ranging from *Colonial America* to *The 1970s* and *Immigration* to *Environment & Conservation*.

This two-volume set, *Defining Documents in American History: Dissent & Protest (1635-2017)*, offers in-depth analysis of a broad range of historical documents and historic events that make up the vibrant and ever-evolving story of dissent and protest in the United States. It beings with testimony from the Massachusetts Bay Colony trial against Anne Hutchinson in which she defends herself and her break from the Church of England and continues Angela's Davis's speech at the Women's March on Washington in January 2017, the day following the inauguration of the forty-fifth president of the United States. Dissent and protest is, to many, one of the defining characteristics of the American way of life. The speeches, articles, essays, petitions, editorials, even laws and court orders over the span of this nation's history demonstrate the ways in which its citizens have exercised the right to free speech. The ninety-three articles in this two-volume title are organized into eight sections:

- **From Colonies to Nation,** beginning with Anne Hutchinson's testimony and continuing to a petition against the Excise Tax;
- **Slavery and Abolition** which includes such powerful documents as *The Confessions of Nat Turner* and *Twelve Years a Slave*;
- **Sectional Conflict, Civil War, and Reconstruction,** focusing on the great conflict over the continued practice of slavery in both the South and in new states including Kansas and Nebraska, the cessation of the southern states from the Union, and the Reconstruction era, that led to the Jim Crow era;
- **Native American Dissent,** which includes editorials concerning the Battle of Sand Creek and letters to the Army Corps of Engineers, asking for a reconsideration of the Dakota Pipeline;

- **African American Civil Rights** featuring the words of such inspirational writers and speakers as Ida B. Wells, W. E. B. Du Bois, James Lawson, Jr., Stokely Carmichael, Martin Luther King, Jr. and Malcom X;
- **Women's Rights** from the Seneca Falls convention and the Declaration of Sentiments to Angela Davis's speech at the Women's March on Washington;
- **Political and Social Protest,** with calls to action for those seeking social justice for the poor and underprivileged, laborers, and gays; and
- **Anti-War Activism,** with speeches against conscription during the World War I, John Kerry's 1971 testimony to Congress about atrocities during the Vietnam War, and Senator Robert Byrd's speech concerning the war in Iraq.

Historical documents provide a compelling view of dissent and protest, an important aspect of American history. Designed for high school and college students, the aim of the series is to advance historical document studies as an important activity in learning about history.

Essay Format

Dissent & Protest contains ninety-three primary source documents—many in their entirety. Each document is supported by a critical essay, written by historians and teachers, that includes a Summary Overview, Defining Moment, Author Biography, Document Analysis, and Essential Themes. Readers will appreciate the diversity of the collected texts, including treaties, letters, speeches, political and religious sermons, laws, pamphlets, diplomatic communications, government reports, and trial notes, among other genres. An important feature of each essay is a close reading of the primary source that develops evidence of broader themes, such as the author's rhetorical purpose, social or class position, point of view, and other relevant issues. In addition, essays are organized by section themes, listed above, highlighting major issues of the period, many of which extend across eras and continue to shape life as we know it around the world. Each section begins with a brief introduction that defines questions and problems underlying the subjects in the historical documents. Each essay also includes a Bibliography and Additional Reading section for further research.

Appendixes

- **Chronological List** arranges all documents by year.
- **Web Resources** is an annotated list of websites that offer valuable supplemental resources.
- **Bibliography** lists helpful articles and books for further study.

Contributors

Salem Press would like to extend its appreciation to all involved in the development and production of this work. The essays have been written and signed by scholars of history, humanities, and other disciplines related to the essays' topics. Without these expert contributions, a project of this nature would not be possible. A full list of contributor's names and affiliations appears in the front matter of this volume.

Editor's Introduction

The United States is, in many ways, a nation founded on both the ideal and the reality of dissent. This is particularly true of the English colonies. Religious dissent drove the Calvinists (both Pilgrims and Puritans) to New England, Catholics to Maryland, and the Society of Friends to Pennsylvania. Economic dissent or, at least, a desire to opt-out of a system that had no place for them led discharged soldiers, second-born sons of nobility, and indentured servants to Virginia. Political dissidents, such as those who fought for King Charles on the losing side of the English Civil War, the Scotch-Irish, and others came later. From the beginning, the colonies where the United States developed were a haven for those whose ideas were suppressed and those who did not, in some way, fit in. As the new nation emerged following the Revolutionary War, new debates rose and new points of resistance began to form. As dissent against theocracy and British tyranny faded, they were replaced with arguments over the nature of the new American state, protests against the existence and spread of slavery, and a new movement for women's political and economic independence. In the late nineteenth and into the twentieth centuries, the plight of the poor and laboring classes would become a subject of debate and protest as well, with permutations of these and other civil and economic rights issues dominating the twentieth century.

This collection of historical documents gathers a wide variety of examples of dissent and protest throughout American history. It is our goal that the depth and breadth of the sources we selected gives readers a sense of the variety of American opposition to the political, social, cultural, or economic status quo. While the documents we present here stretch across the seventeenth to the twenty-first centuries, they are all similar as examples of resistance to entrenched power structures. From the tyranny of Parliament to that of the slave owner, and from the faceless cruelty of corporate greed to that of the military industrial complex, these documents present a broad array of American responses to oppression. We have organized the documents topically, with the intention of illustrating how different facets of American dissent and protest have changed over time.

From Colonies to Nation
This section contains documents from the era of the British American colonies, through the Colonial crises and War for Independence, and into the earliest years of the new American Republic. The documents collected here illustrate the religious conflicts in the colonial era, as dissenters from the Church of England found themselves facing the issue of dissent in their own midst. The evolution of the American protest over British taxation policy and the move toward independence is another key component of this section. These documents also reflect the struggles of national unity as the United States established itself in the 1780s and 1790s.

Slavery and Abolition
From the colonial era of the late 1600s to the eve of the Civil War in the 1850s, the debate over African American slavery and its abolition played a crucial role in the formation of American identity and the development of American ideals of liberty and equality. The documents in this section represent a number of different strands of abolitionist thought from a variety of viewpoints including white opponents of slavery, African American abolitionists, examples of slave narratives, and accounts of slave rebellions and uprisings. Taken together, these documents provide a window into how changes in American politics and culture shaped the development of the abolition movement and the movement's thinking about race in America.

Sectional Conflict, Civil War, and Reconstruction
As the nation's population grew and its borders expanded westward, divisions over the spread of slavery to new western territories overwhelmed political debate, becoming nearly all-consuming by the 1850s. The powers of individual states tested the sovereignty of the federal government leading, eventually, to the secession of southern states and four years of Civil War. The period of national reconstruction after the war, from 1865 to 1877 saw the rise of African-American political influence in the south. This influence, however, would fade in the face of oppression and violence. The documents in this section address the debate over slavery in the west, secession and the creation of the Confederacy, and the resistance of African-American political leaders resisting the resurgent white supremacy at the end of the reconstruction era.

Native American Dissent

From Tecumseh's attempts unify the Native American tribes of the west to fight white settlement to the Indians of All Tribes' occupation of Alcatraz in 1969, the documents in this section illustrate Native American response to nearly two centuries of changing Federal policy and unrelenting oppression. Included here are the Cherokee response to the encroachment of Americans in Georgia, documents reflecting the White conquest of the Trans-Mississippi West and the development of policies aiming to "civilize" Native Americans, as well as Native perspectives on American military atrocities. The recent stand-offs over the building of the Dakota pipeline, which could impact tribal lands, was still a significant issue at the time of publication.

African-American Civil Rights

The story of African-American civil rights presented through these documents begins in the late nineteenth century, in the Jim Crow era of segregation that arose in the decades following the end of Reconstruction. Starting with Booker T. Washington's thoughts on economic uplift, continuing through the foundation of the Niagara movement and the ideas of W. E. B. Du Bois, on through the 1950s and the emergence of leaders like Martin Luther King Jr., and the 1960s emergence of Malcolm X, Stokely Carmichael, leaders continue to emerge for each new generation.

Women's Rights

From its roots in the mid-nineteenth century, the organized women's rights movement in the United States was intently focused on suffrage (the right to vote) until the passage of the nineteenth amendment in 1920. Different proponents of women's suffrage advanced different arguments for why the right to vote should be extended to women around the country. The documents in this section reflect those different arguments as well as they way these arguments differed based on the intended audiences. The women's movement in the 1960s, like many other aspects of the civil rights movement during that time focused on political and economic opportunity in addition to the right to cast a ballot. As a movement, it continues to shape the national dialogue with events such as the Women's March on Washington in 2017.

Political and Social Protest

The documents on political and social protest, dating from the late nineteenth to the late twentieth centuries, address a number of concerns form a variety of points on the political spectrum. From left of center, the collection includes class conscious labor activists like Eugene V. Debs and Samuel Gompers as well as pioneers of social welfare and reform movements such as Jane Addams and Jacob Riis. From the right, the words figures like Henry Cabot Lodge and the anti-integration signers of the Southern Manifesto illustrate that political and social developments do not exist in isolation but, rather, are part of an often complex and passionate political dialogue.

Anti-War Activism

While the twentieth century did not see the first anti-war sentiments in American history, it did see larger anti-war movements than ever before. As the documents in this section demonstrate, often the anti-war movements were one aspect of a broader social or political trend that was manifesting itself at the time. In the case of American entry into the First World War, anti-war activists identified with political radicalism brought a class-conscious argument against military conflict. Protests against the Vietnam War presented here fit within the wider context of the "new left" movements of the 1960s.

The documents in this collection represent a variety of materials, such as petitions to legislative bodies, manifestos and public declarations, excerpts from book chapters, legislation and newspaper articles. While many are presented in full, some have been edited for reasons of space. Each document is accompanied by commentary that helps the reader gain a deeper understanding of the document, its author, and the historical context of its creation. The Summary Overview gives the reader a bird's-eye view of the document and its significance in American History. The Defining Moment section provides the historical and cultural background necessary to fully understand the document and the brief biography of the document's author (or authors) is intended not only to provide an overview of their life and work but also to provide additional context and background to the document itself. In cases where the author is unknown, or a group of people, the biography discusses a representative member of the group (if known) and the movement or cause that produced the document. Each document is followed by a glossary that provides definitions for four to ten archaic words or usages that may be unfamiliar to modern readers. We did not define terms that have alternative spellings, unless those spellings were so different as to impede understanding. The Analysis section is an in-depth look at the document which examines, in detail, the intricacies of the author's argument. It also will provide additional historical context, clarify and explain obscure references, and ensure that readers have the tools necessary to fully comprehend and appreciate the significance of the source. It is followed by the Essential Themes section, which emphasizes the one or two most significant aspects of the document and reiterates the most fundamentally important things readers should take away from their study of it. The documents' bibliography provides a number of sources—including books, journal articles, or websites—that inform the analytical materials and provide opportunities for additional study

and understanding. Websites listed were operational when this volume was published but, given the nature of the Internet, may eventually be unavailable or their addresses might change.

We hope this collection provides readers, whether they are students or others with a more general interest in history, a broader and deeper insight into the history of those who pushed back against the political, religious, economic, gendered, or racial power structures of their times. These documents represent an important part of centuries-long, and still ongoing, conversation.

Aaron Gulyas

Contributors

David Gray Adler, PhD
Idaho State University

John K. Alexander, PhD
University of Cincinnati

Angela M. Alexander
University of Georgia

L. Diane Barnes, PhD
Youngstown State University

Kirk H. Beetz
Professor Emeritus

W. Lewis Burke, PhD
University of Southern Carolina

C. Ellen Connally, JD
Cleveland-Marshall College of Law

Allan L. Damon
Amherst College

Christine Dee, PhD
Fitchburg State University

Mark R. Ellis, PhD
University of Nebraska at Kearney

Tim Alan Garrison, PhD
Portland State University

G. Mehera Gerardo, PhD
University of South Florida

Aaron Gulyas, MA
Mott Community College

Michael Allen Holmes
Independent Scholar, Burlington, VT

Micah Issitt, MA
Independent Scholar, Philadelphia, PA

Daniel R. Mandell, PhD
Truman University

Richard Newman, PhD
Rochester Institute of Technology

Michael J. O'Neal, PhD
Independent Scholar, Moscow, ID

Martha Pallante, PhD
Youngstown State University

Carl Rollyson, PhD
Baruch College

Peggy A. Russo, PhD
Pennsylvania State University, Mont Alto

Keith E. Sealing, JD
Widener University

Mitchell Snay, PhD
Denison University

James Brewer Stewart, PhD
Macalester College

Kristin Teigen
Portland State University

Wendy Thowdis, MA
San Jose State University

Zachery Williams, PhD
University of Akron

Christopher J. Young, PhD
Indiana University Northwest

DEFINING DOCUMENTS
IN AMERICAN HISTORY

Dissent & Protest
(1635-2017)

FROM COLONIES TO NATION

The establishment of the English colonies in North America and their development throughout the seventeenth and eighteenth centuries provide a number of examples of dissent and protest. The nature of the dissent is rooted in the background and context of the different colonies. Each of the English colonies had a distinct origin and the inhabitants of the different colonies—at least initially—often had somewhat common backgrounds and world views. When members of these colonial societies deviated from the norms of their community, there were often consequences. That was certainly the case in Anne Hutchinson's situation. Testimony from the 1637 Massachusetts Bay Colony Trial against Anne Hutchinson illustrates the limits of religious and social ideas that did not conform to strict Puritan ideas in colonial Massachusetts. The testimony also provides a window into the intricacies of gender relations within Massachusetts society. Religious differences and questions of political power were also at the heart of 1689's Declaration of Protestant Subjects in Maryland. This justification for an armed force of Protestant Marylanders' toppling of the Roman Catholic government was rooted in animosity for the Catholics in power but also criticized the arbitrary and tyrannical behavior of the colony's governing officials. This declaration's presentation of arguments about the nature of English government and the rights of Englishmen not only echoed political developments in England but also presaged concerns and philosophical principles that would divide the colonies from their mother country.

The French and Indian War (1754-1763) marked a turning point in the relationship between Great Britain and its North American colonies. The war marked the end of a period often termed "salutary neglect." This was an era typified by the British government taking a hand-off approach to governing the colonies. During this time, the colonies developed robust local and colonial governmental structures. Following the war, Britain kept troops on colonial soil and imposed taxes on its American subjects. In 1764, Massachusetts lawyer James Otis, in his essay The Rights of the British Colo-

nies Asserted and Proved, argued for American representation in the British Parliament, claiming this was the only way its taxation would be legitimate. A year later, the Declaration of Rights of the Stamp Act Congress reiterated this point, insisting that the rights of British subjects in the colonies were the same as the rights of subjects living in Britain itself. Britain repealed the Stamp Act but other laws, such as the Quartering Act, were seen by colonists such as John Dickinson, as equally insidious. Dickinson, in his Letters from a Farmer in Pennsylvania, argued that resistance to unjust and tyrannical measures was necessary. Dickinson's call for resistance resulting in actions such as boycotts of British manufactured goods, such as declared in the 1768 Boston Non-Importation Agreement.

Relations between Great Britain and the colonies worsened during the 1770s. Samuel Adams, in his 1771 essays and letters signed with the pen name Candidus, warns his fellow colonists against complacency regarding British actions. Benjamin Franklin, in 1774, cautioned Britain with a satirical essay detailing the Rules by Which a Great Empire May Be Reduced to a Small One and John Hancock delivered his Boston Massacre Oration, reminding his fellow Bostonians of the violence British soldiers perpetrated against their own countrymen. When events in Massachusetts broke out into armed conflict between colonial militia and the British Army, the other British colonies debated whether or not to come to the New Englanders' assistance. Virginia's Patrick Henry, in his 1775 "Liberty or Death" Speech, lays out the reasons why the colonies should stand together against Britain. The next year, as the war between colonies and mother land raged, Thomas Paine proclaimed that it was *Common Sense* for the colonies to become their own independent nation. This section concludes with evidence that protest against an overbearing government did not end with the establishment of the United States. In 1792, Albert Gallatin spoke for the farmers of western Pennsylvania in their Petition against the Excise Tax by Inhabitants of Western Pennsylvania.

Excerpts from the Massachusetts Bay Colony Trial against Anne Hutchinson

Date: 1637
Author: Anne Hutchinson
Genre: Court transcript

Summary Overview

Anne Hutchinson remains one of the most well known and significant figures in 17ᵗʰ century American colonial history and almost certainly the most well-known woman. What many usually know of her is that she was a women who got in trouble for teaching men and, for this crime, was exiled from the Massachusetts Bay colony. While this is true, it is hardly the whole story. As the transcript from Hutchinson's trial shows, she was at the center of a highly complex and contention political and religious controversy in the young colony. Her crime was not simply that she was a women who was teaching men—she was a woman whose teachings were prohibited because they threatened to undermine the religious—and, by extension, political—power structure of the colony.

One thing in particular to watch out for when reading these selections from her trial transcript is the high level of determination and logic that Hutchinson expresses in arguing her case with the governor and deputy governor of the colony. A no point does she acquiesce to their power. Rather, she forces them to lay out, explicitly, the charges against her which she then proceeds to refute. Note, also, the point at which she claims personal revelation from God.

Defining Moment

The trial of Anne Hutchinson came amidst a wider conflict within the Massachusetts Bay colony known awn the Antinomian Controversy (also sometimes known as the "Free Grace" Controversy). The colony had been founded in 1630 by Puritans from England and the government of the colony was tightly intertwined with the religious hierarchy. There was no freedom of religion in Massachusetts Bay. In order to possess political authority it was necessary to be in good standing with the church. Thus, controversies over religious doctrine had an effect on the civil government and heterodox or heretical ideas were prosecuted and punished as civil crimes.

The controversy itself revolved around several issues. One was the believe that God's grace (or unmerited favor) was the only thing necessary for salvation, aside from any good behavior ("works") on the part of a Christian. The Puritans often viewed these good works as an outward sign that a person had received God's grace. The Antinomians believed that the Puritan preachers overemphasized such works. Just as troubling to the religious establishment was the idea among Antinomians, including Anne Hutchinson, that once saved, a Christian was literally inhabited by the Holy Spirit and could receive direct revelation from God. In England, John Cotton and William Wheelwright were prominent preachers of these ideas. When they came to Massachusetts Bay Colony in the 1630s, they brought their teaching with them. Hutchinson became a popular and charismatic teacher at this time as well. A petition was circulated in support of the preachers but in 1637, Wheelwright was exiled from the colony, but Cotton was permitted to stay.

Author Biography

Anne Marbury Hutchinson was born in July of 1591. While we do not know her exact date of birth, she was baptized on July 20 in Lincolnshire, England. As the daughter of a priest and teacher, she received a thorough education and, after her marriage to William Hutchinson, began following the work of John Cotton, a popular preacher. In 1634, Anne and William, along with their eleven children, migrated to the Massachusetts Bay colony, settling in Boston.

While she worked as a midwife, she also held religious meetings for other women in her home. Soon men began to attend as well. The preaching of John Cotton (who had come to Massachusetts as well) and John Wheelwright began to take root. Still being a follower of Cotton and Wheelwright (her husband's brother-in-law), she began to share their ideas with others in the community, leading to the trial transcript here.

After her conviction, she and her fellow exiles established a settlement at Portsmouth, in Rhode Island. She later, after her husband's death, moved outside English territory completely, settling in the Dutch colonies to the south. In 1643, an attack by local Native Americans from the Siwanoy tribe killed Hutchinson and the six of the children who had moved with her. A daughter, nine year old Susanna survived but was taken captive.

HISTORICAL DOCUMENT

Gov. John Winthrop: Mrs. Hutchinson, you are called here as one of those that have troubled the peace of the commonwealth and the churches here; you are known to be a woman that hath had a great share in the promoting and divulging of those opinions that are the cause of this trouble, and to be nearly joined not only in affinity and affection with some of those the court had taken notice of and passed censure upon, but you have spoken divers things, as we have been informed, very prejudicial to the honour of the churches and ministers thereof, and you have maintained a meeting and an assembly in your house that hath been condemned by the general assembly as a thing not tolerable nor comely in the sight of God nor fitting for your sex, and notwithstanding that was cried down you have continued the same. Therefore we have thought good to send for you to understand how things are, that if you be in an erroneous way we may reduce you that so you may become a profitable member here among us. Otherwise if you be obstinate in your course that then the court may take such course that you may trouble us no further. Therefore I would intreat you to express whether you do assent and hold in practice to those opinions and factions that have been handled in court already, that is to say, whether you do not justify Mr. Wheelwright's sermon and the petition.

Mrs. Anne Hutchinson: I am called here to answer before you but I hear no things laid to my charge.

Gov. John Winthrop: I have told you some already and more I can tell you.

Mrs. Anne Hutchinson: Name one, Sir.

Gov. John Winthrop: Have I not named some already?

Mrs. Anne Hutchinson: What have I said or done?

Gov. John Winthrop: Why for your doings, this you did harbor and countenance those that are parties in this faction that you have heard of.

Mrs. Anne Hutchinson: That's matter of conscience, Sir.

Gov. John Winthrop: Your conscience you must keep, or it must be kept for you.

Mrs. Anne Hutchinson: Must not I then entertain the saints because I must keep my conscience.

Gov. John Winthrop: Say that one brother should commit felony or treason and come to his brother's house, if he knows him guilty and conceals him he is guilty of the same. It is his conscience to entertain him, but if his conscience comes into act in giving countenance and entertainment to him that hath broken the law he is guilty too. So if you do countenance those that are transgressors of the law you are in the same fact.

Mrs. Anne Hutchinson: What law do they transgress?

Gov. John Winthrop: The law of God and of the state.

Mrs. Anne Hutchinson: In what particular?

Gov. John Winthrop: Why in this among the rest, whereas the Lord doth say honour thy father and thy mother.

Mrs. Anne Hutchinson: Ey Sir in the Lord.

Gov. John Winthrop: This honour you have broke in giving countenance to them.

Mrs. Anne Hutchinson: In entertaining those did I entertain them against any act (for there is the thing) or what God has appointed?

Gov. John Winthrop: You knew that Mr. Wheelwright did preach this sermon and those that countenance him in this do break a law.

Mrs. Anne Hutchinson: What law have I broken?

Gov. John Winthrop: Why the fifth commandment.

Mrs. Anne Hutchinson: I deny that for he (Mr. Wheelwright) saith in the Lord.

Gov. John Winthrop: You have joined with them in the faction.

Mrs. Anne Hutchinson: In what faction have I joined with them?

Gov. John Winthrop: In presenting the petition.

Mrs. Anne Hutchinson: Suppose I had set my hand to the petition. What then?

Gov. John Winthrop: You saw that case tried before.

Mrs. Anne Hutchinson: But I had not my hand to [not signed] the petition.

Gov. John Winthrop: You have councelled them.

Mrs. Anne Hutchinson: Wherein?

Gov. John Winthrop: Why in entertaining them.

Mrs. Anne Hutchinson: What breach of law is that, Sir?

Gov. John Winthrop: Why dishonouring the commonwealth, Mrs. Hutchinson.

Mrs. Anne Hutchinson: But put the case, Sir, that I do fear the Lord and my parents. May not I entertain them that fear the Lord because my parents will not give me leave?

Gov. John Winthrop: If they be the fathers of the commonwealth, and they of another religion, if you entertain them then you dishonour your parents and are justly punishable.

Mrs. Anne Hutchinson: If I entertain them, as they have dishonoured their parents I do.

Gov. John Winthrop: No but you by countenancing them above others put honor upon them.

Mrs. Anne Hutchinson: I may put honor upon them as the children of God and as they do honor the Lord.

Gov. John Winthrop: We do not mean to discourse with those of your sex but only this: you so adhere unto them and do endeavor to set forward this faction and so you do dishonour us.

Mrs. Anne Hutchinson: I do acknowledge no such thing. Neither do I think that I ever put any dishonour upon you.

Gov. John Winthrop: Why do you keep such a meeting at your house as you do every week upon a set day?

Mrs. Anne Hutchinson: It is lawful for me to do so, as it is all your practices, and can you find a warrant for yourself and condemn me for the same thing? The ground of my taking it up was, when I first came to this land because I did not go to such meetings as those were, it was presently reported that I did not allow of such meetings but held them unlawful and therefore in that regard they said I was proud and did despise all ordinances. Upon that a friend came unto me and told me of it and I to prevent such aspersions took it up, but it was in practice before I came. Therefore I was not the first.

Gov. John Winthrop:...By what warrant do you continue such a course?

Mrs. Anne Hutchinson: I conceive there lies a clear rule in Titus that the elder women should instruct the younger and then I must have a time wherein I must do it.

Gov. John Winthrop: All this I grant you, I grant you a time for it, but what is this to the purpose that you Mrs. Hutchinson must call a company together from their callings to come to be taught of you?

Mrs. Anne Hutchinson: If you look upon the rule in Titus it is a rule to me. If you convince me that it is no rule I shall yield.

Gov. John Winthrop: You know that there is no rule that crosses another, but this rule crosses that in the Corinthians. But you must take it in this sense that elder women must instruct the younger about their business and to love their husbands and not to make them to clash Mrs. Hutchinson....

Mrs. Anne Hutchinson: Will it please you to answer me this and to give me a rule for then I will willingly submit to any truth, Mrs. Hutchinson If any come to my house to be instructed in the ways of God what rule have I to put them away?....Do you think it not lawful for me to teach women and why do you call me to teach the court?

Gov. John Winthrop: We do not call you to teach the court but to lay open yourself....

[The argument over the broken rule continues.]

Gov. John Winthrop: Your course is not to be suffered for. Besides that we find such a course as this to be greatly prejudicial to the state. Besides the occasion that it is to seduce many honest persons that are called to those meetings and your opinions and your opinions being known to be different from the word of God may seduce many simple souls that resort unto you. Besides that the occasion which hath come of late hath come from none but such as have frequented your meetings, so that now they are flown off from magistrates and ministers and since they have come to you. And besides that it will not well stand with the commonwealth that families should be neglected for so many neighbors and dames and so much time spent. We see no rule of God for this. We see not that any should have authority to set up any other exercises besides what authority hath already set up and so what hurt comes of this you will be guilty of and we for suffering you.

Mrs. Anne Hutchinson: Sir, I do not believe that to be so.

Gov. John Winthrop: Well, we see how it is. We must therefore put it away from you or restrain you from maintaining this course.

Mrs. Anne Hutchinson: If you have a rule for it from God's word you may.

Gov. John Winthrop: We are your judges, and not you ours and we must compel you to it.

Mrs. Anne Hutchinson: If it please you by authority to put it down I will freely let you for I am subject to your authority....

Deputy Gov. Thomas Dudley: I would go a little higher with Mrs. Hutchinson. About three years ago we were all in peace. Mrs. Hutchinson, from that time she came hath made a disturbance, and some that came over with her in the ship did inform me what she was as soon as she was landed. I being then in place dealt with the pastor and teacher of Boston and desired them to enquire of her, and then I was satisfied that she held nothing different from us. But within half a year after, she had vented divers of her strange opinions and had made parties in the country, and at length it comes that Mr. Cotton and Mr. Vane were of her judgment, but Mr. Cotton had cleared himself that he was not of that mind.

But now it appears by this woman's meeting that Mrs. Hutchinson hath so forestalled the minds of many by their resort to her meeting that now she hath a potent party in the country. Now if all these things have endangered us as from that foundation and if she in particular hath disparaged all our ministers in the land that they have preached a covenant of works, and only Mr. Cotton a covenant of grace, why this is not to be suffered, and therefore being driven to the foundation and it being found that Mrs. Hutchinson is she that hath depraved all the ministers and hath been the cause of what is fallen out, why we must take away the foundation and the building will fall.

Mrs. Anne Hutchinson: I pray, Sir, prove it that I said they preached nothing but a covenant of works.

Dep. Gov. Thomas Dudley: Nothing but a covenant of works. Why a Jesuit may preach truth sometimes.

Mrs. Anne Hutchinson: Did I ever say they preached a covenant of works then?

Dep. Gov. Thomas Dudley: If they do not preach a covenant of grace clearly, then they preach a covenant of works.

Mrs. Anne Hutchinson: No, Sir. One may preach a covenant of grace more clearly than another, so I said....

Dep. Gov. Thomas Dudley: When they do preach a covenant of works do they preach truth?

Mrs. Anne Hutchinson: Yes, Sir. But when they preach a covenant of works for salvation, that is not truth.

Dep. Gov. Thomas Dudley: I do but ask you this: when the ministers do preach a covenant of works do they preach a way of salvation?

Mrs. Anne Hutchinson: I did not come hither to answer questions of that sort.

Dep. Gov. Thomas Dudley: Because you will deny the thing.

Mrs. Anne Hutchinson: Ey, but that is to be proved first.

Dep. Gov. Thomas Dudley: I will make it plain that you did say that the ministers did preach a covenant of works.

Mrs. Anne Hutchinson: I deny that.

Dep. Gov. Thomas Dudley: And that you said they were not able ministers of the New Testament, but Mr. Cotton only.

Mrs. Anne Hutchinson: If ever I spake that I proved it by God's word.

Court: Very well, very well.

Mrs. Anne Hutchinson: If one shall come unto me in private, and desire me seriously to tell them what I thought of such an one, I must either speak false or true in my answer.

Dep. Gov. Thomas Dudley: Likewise I will prove this that you said the gospel in the letter and words holds forth nothing but a covenant of works and that all that do not hold as you do are in a covenant of works.

Mrs. Anne Hutchinson: I deny this for if I should so say I should speak against my own judgment....

Mrs. Anne Hutchinson: If you please to give me leave I shall give you the ground of what I know to be true. Being much troubled to see the falseness of the constitution of the Church of England, I had like to have turned Separatist. Whereupon I kept a day of solemn humiliation and pondering of the thing; this scripture was brought unto me—he that denies Jesus Christ to be come in the flesh is antichrist. This I considered of and in considering found that the papists did not deny him to be come in the flesh, nor we did not deny him—who then was antichrist? Was the Turk antichrist only? The Lord knows that I could not open scripture; he must by his prophetical office open it unto me. So after that being unsatisfied in the thing, the Lord was pleased to bring this scripture out of the Hebrews. he that denies the testament denies the testator, and in this did open unto me and give me to see that those which did not teach the new covenant had the spirit of antichrist, and upon this he did discover the ministry unto me; and ever since, I bless the Lord, he hath let me see which was the clear ministry and which the wrong.

Since that time I confess I have been more choice and he hath left me to distinguish between the voice of my beloved and the voice of Moses, the voice of John the Baptist and the voice of antichrist, for all those voices are spoken of in scripture. Now if you do condemn me for speaking what in my conscience I know to be truth I must commit myself unto the Lord.

Mr. Nowel (assistant to the Court): How do you know that was the spirit?

Mrs. Anne Hutchinson: How did Abraham know that it was God that bid him offer his son, being a breach of the sixth commandment?

Dep. Gov. Thomas Dudley: By an immediate voice.

Mrs. Anne Hutchinson: So to me by an immediate revelation.

Dep. Gov. Thomas Dudley: How! an immediate revelation.

Mrs. Anne Hutchinson: By the voice of his own spirit to my soul. I will give you another scripture, Jeremiah 46: 27–28—out of which the Lord showed me what he would do for me and the rest of his servants. But after he was pleased to reveal himself to me I did presently, like Abraham, run to Hagar. And after that he did let me see the atheism of my own heart, for which I begged of the Lord that it might not remain in my heart, and being thus, he did show me this (a twelvemonth after) which I told you of before....

Therefore, I desire you to look to it, for you see this scripture fulfilled this day and therefore I desire you as you tender the Lord and the church and commonwealth to consider and look what you do.

You have power over my body but the Lord Jesus hath power over my body and soul; and assure yourselves thus much, you do as much as in you lies to put the Lord Jesus Christ from you, and if you go on in this course you begin, you will bring a curse upon you and your posterity, and the mouth of the Lord hath spoken it.

Dep. Gov. Thomas Dudley: What is the scripture she brings?

Mr. Stoughton (assistant to the Court): Behold I turn away from you.

Mrs. Anne Hutchinson: But now having seen him which is invisible I fear not what man can do unto me.

Gov. John Winthrop: Daniel was delivered by miracle; do you think to be deliver'd so too?

Mrs. Anne Hutchinson: I do here speak it before the court. I look that the Lord should deliver me by his providence....[because God had said to her] though I should meet with affliction, yet I am the same God that delivered Daniel out of the lion's den, I will also deliver thee.

Mr. Harlakenden (assistant to the Court): I may read scripture and the most glorious hypocrite may read them and yet go down to hell.

Mrs. Anne Hutchinson: It may be so....

Gov. John Winthrop: I am persuaded that the revelation she brings forth is delusion.

[The trial text here reads:] All the court but some two or three ministers cry out, we all believe it—we all believe it.

[Mrs. Hutchinson was found guilty.]

Gov. John Winthrop: The court hath already declared themselves satisfied concerning the things you hear, and concerning the troublesomeness of her spirit and the danger of her course amongst us, which is not to be suffered. Therefore if it be the mind of the court that Mrs. Hutchinson for these things that appear before us is unfit for our society, and if it be the mind of the court that she shall be banished out of our liberties and imprisoned till she be sent away, let them hold up their hands.

[All but three did so.]

Gov. John Winthrop: Mrs. Hutchinson, the sentence of the court you hear is that you are banished from out of our jurisdiction as being a woman not fit for our society, and are to be imprisoned till the court shall send you away.

Mrs. Anne Hutchinson: I desire to know wherefore I am banished?

Gov. John Winthrop: Say no more. The court knows wherefore and is satisfied.

GLOSSARY

commonwealth: the Massachusetts Bay colony

elders: non-clergy leaders of the church congregation.

intreaty: noun form of "intreat" or "entreat": to plead strongly

saints: members of the Puritan church

sepratist: contemporary term for Puritan; someone who rejected the teachings and practice of the Church of England

wherefore: the reason for something;

Document Analysis

The testimony begins with an exchange between Governor Winthrop and Hutchinson. Winthrop informs Hutchinson that she is well known to be a divisive figure in the colony, particularly in the churches. This is because her connection with others who have been censured (condemned) but the court and also her own words against the church and its leaders. More seriously, she has "maintained a meeting and an assembly" in her home, teaching in ways that are not allowed for both doctrinal reasons and because she is a woman and forbidden to teach men. Winthrop asks her whether or not she agrees with the Wheelwright's opinions. After this lengthy preamble, Hutchinson responds that she does not hear an actual charge against her. She and Winthrop trade questions and answers, with Hutchinson forcing Wintrhop to provide specific charges, that she associated and agreed with the "faction" whose theological views were at odds with the church of Massachusetts Bay. Hutchinson defends herself with the claim that such associations are a matter of "conscience" rather than law.

She explains that she must associate with them ("entertain the saints") because he conscience wills it, dismissing Winthrop's analogy that what she did was the same as harboring a felon or traitor. This is because, according to Hutchinson, Wheelwright and the others did not, in fact, break any law. Discussion of this point follows, but Winthrop's argument that she associated with the condemned faction led by Wheelwright is difficult for him to fully prove since she did not publicly speak out on the matter and did not sign her name to a petition in support of them.

Eventually, Winthrop moves on to the charge that Hutchinson led religious meetings in her home. Hutchinson asserts that whatever teaching she did was in accordance with the Bible, citing Titus chapter 2, verses 3 and 4, which instruct "aged women" to instruct "younger women." This argument continues for some time.

Eventually, Winthrop moves onto the charge the Hutchinson's actions were "prejudicial to the state" in that her actions would "seduce many honest persons that are called to those meetings and your opinions and your opinions being known to be different from the word of God" and that the some people have been listening to Hutchinson's teachings rather than that of their own ministers. Hutchinson replies that she doesn't think that's what's happening and if the court has a "a rule for it from God's word" they can condemn her. Winthrop points out that she is not the judge.

On the second day of Hutchinson's trial, the Deputy Governor, Thomas Dudley, took over the questioning. He begins by accusing Hutchinson of disruption the peace of the colony, almost from the moment she arrived. She began discussing her "strange opinions. She continued to spread these opinions at the meetings she held at her house, disparaging all the ministers in the colony, accusing them of teaching "a covenant of works" where as John Cotton preached "a covenant of grace." Her words, Dudley asserts, threaten the entire colony. Hutchinson asks Dudley to provide proof that she ever accused the ministers of preaching wrongly.

In the final section of the transcript presented here, Hutchinson testifies on her own behalf, detailing her separation from the Church of England. She then explains that, with regard to her religious learning, "The Lord knows that I could not open scripture; he must by his prophetical office open it unto me." She claims that the Spirit of God spoke to her. When Nowel, a court assistant, asks how she knew this voice was God's she responds by asking how Abraham in the book of Genesis, knew that he heard the voice of God and affirms that she received direct revelation from God just as figures in the Bible had.

Hutchinson goes on to explain that she has no fear of the court, saying "I look that the Lord should deliver me by his providence. ... [because God had said to her] though I should meet with affliction, yet I am the same God that delivered Daniel out of the lion's den, I will also deliver thee." The court erupts into commotion at this point, as Winthrop claims Hutchinson is delusional. Hutchinson is found guilty and the court declares her "unfit" for the community. She is sentenced to exile. The court then declines to answer her question about why ("wherefore") she should be banished.

Essential Themes

As discussed above, Anne Hutchinson's case was part of the wider context of religious and political conflict in the Massachusetts Bay colony between 1636 and 1637. Her testimony reflects this, but also shows the distinct status she had not only as a perceive heretic but as a woman. The charge, for example, that she held meetings in her home in which improper teachings were discussed is supplemented by the fact this was also "not

fitting" for a woman. While the leaders of the Puritan church and government of the colony would not, of course, looked kindly on a woman teaching anyone but other women even the most orthodox and correct of teachings, the fact that Hutchinson was thought to be involved with theological troublemakers like John Cotton and John Wheelwright place Anne Hutchinson in a more severe criminal category. This is one important thematic element of this testimony—in many ways, Anne Hutchinson's case was not an isolated one. She was part of a movement deemed by the colony's leadership to be dangerous and that threatened to undermine their authority.

The other aspect of Hutchinson's testimony that stands out is her claim, near the end, to have received direct revelations from God in the same manner as had the supposedly divinely-inspired figures who composed the books of the Bible. This took Hutchinson beyond even someone who consorted with heretics or someone who persisted in a misinterpretation of doctrine. Rather, she was, in the eyes of the authorities, placing he views and actions on the same level as the prophets an apostles of the old and new testaments.

——Aaron Gulyas, MA

Bibliography and Additional Reading

Battis, Emery. *Saints and Sectaries: Anne Hutchinson and the Antinomian Controversy in the Massachusetts Bay Colony*. (Chapel Hill: University of North Carolina Press, 1962).

Ditmore, Michael G. (2000). "A Prophetess in Her Own Country: an Exegesis of Anne Hutchinson's 'Immediate Revelation". *William and Mary Quarterly*. 57 (2): 349–392.

Gura, Philip F. *A Glimpse of Sion's Glory: Puritan Radicalism in New England, 1620–1660*. (Middletown, Connecticut: Wesleyan University Press, 1984).

LaPlante, Eve. *American Jezebel: The Uncommon Life of Anne Hutchinson, the Woman Who Defied the Puritans*. (New York: HarperOne, 2004).

Williams, Selma R. *Divine Rebel: The Life of Anne Marbury Hutchinson*. (New York: Henry Holt, 1981).

Winship, Michael Paul. *Making Heretics: Militant Protestantism and Free Grace in Massachusetts, 1636–1641*. (Princeton, New Jersey: Princeton University Press, 2002).

■ Declaration of Protestant Subjects in Maryland

Date: 1689
Author: Various
Genre: Petition

Summary Overview

The late 1680s and 1690s were a time of tremendous upheaval in England and its American colonies. A transition of power from King James II to King William and Queen Mary led to international conflict and, in several of the American colonies, a breakdown of colonial government control as the regimes shifted. Incidents occurred such as Leisler's rebellion in New York and the power vacuum in Massachusetts that opened the door for the Salem witch hunts. In Maryland, the Catholic leadership of the colony, under the control of Charles Calvert, the third Lord Baltimore had faced resistance from protestants for several years. In 1689, an armed mass of Protestant Marylanders seized control of the government.

This declaration is the statement of the protestors (who would, eventually, call themselves the Protestant Associators) describing the causes for their armed insurrection. The reasons for the rebellion have their roots in both the religious conflicts that had long existed in the colony between Roman Catholics and Protestants as well as established principles of English government and law with which the colonial government, according to the rebels, refused to conform. In addition to broad principles of political philosophy and religious oppression, the declaration provides specific examples of the perceived abuses of power by the Calvert-controlled government. It also illustrates the ways in which the English colonies were sometimes profoundly affected by political issues in the mother country.

Defining Moment

The roots of the Maryland's Protestant Revolution of 1689—and of the document presented here—lie in three intersecting contexts.

The first is the religious background and makeup of Maryland. The colony of Maryland had, since its beginnings, been something of an anomaly among England's North American possessions. Established in 1632, Maryland was a proprietary colony. This meant that its colonial charter (the royal "permission" for the colony to exist) was granted to an private proprietor rather than being directly controlled by the crown. While the

Kings of England often granted proprietary charters to joint-stock companies, which managed the colony via a board of directors, others went to individual proprietors who did not have to answer to a board or investors. Maryland's first proprietor was Cecilius Calvert, the 2nd Lord Baltimore. Calvert wished to establish a haven for English Catholics in North America. Despite its Catholic origins, a large number of Protestants were among the earliest settlers of Maryland and the colony's "Act Concerning Religion" established toleration for Christians of differing sects or denominations.

The second factor was the nature of government in colonial Maryland. The initial charter issued by King Charles I granted broad powers to the Calvert family as proprietors. They could declare war, collect taxes and establish a formal nobility or aristocratic class within the colony. In most cases, the proprietor or his appointed governor would have final say on laws and regulation as well as their enforcement in the colony.

The final factor contributing to this crisis was the Glorious Revolution of 1688. This was the largely peaceful overthrow of English King James II by a cabal of members of Parliament and the installation of William of Orange as King William III and his wife Mary (James II's daughter) as Queen Mary II. James II had increasing tolerated Catholicism in England, to the point of changing succession laws so his Catholic son would inherit the throne. In Maryland, Protestant rebels, led by John Coode, fearing that the Catholic government of the colony was not loyal to the new Protestant regime in London, seized control of the colonial government.

Author Biography

While the declaration of the Protestant rebels is unsigned, one of the most prominent leaders the leader of their 1689 revolution was John Coode, who had long-standing conflicts with the Calvert regime and their policies. It is likely that his conflicts and complaints were representative of many of the rebels and reflected in their declaration.

Coode was born in Cornwall, England around 1648 and educated at Oxford University. After becoming a priest in the Church of England, Coode migrated to Maryland in 1672. He left the priesthood to marry a Maryland woman, Susannah Slye, whose father was embroiled in longstanding disputes with the Calvert family. Coode became increasing involved in leadership roles in the colony, including service as a militia captain, representative in the legislative assembly and as a judge. In 1681, he was convicted of playing a role in a plot against he government and removed from office. This placed him firmly within the ranks of the enemies of the Calvert regime.

In April of 1689, concern that the colonial government had not yet publicly recognized William and Mary as the rightful monarchs of England combined with longstanding complaints about the ruling cabal of Roman Catholics resulted in an armed uprising led by Coode and others. Coode led an army of about 700 soldiers against the colonial government and forced the surrender of Deputy Governor Henry Darnall. Coode took political control of the colony as its governor (although he used the title Commander-in-Chief) from August 1, 1689 to July 27, 1691, when a new Royal Governor arrived to take control.

HISTORICAL DOCUMENT

The Declaration of the Reasons and Motives for the Present Appearing in Arms of Their Majesties Protestant Subjects in the Province of Maryland.

Licens'd, November 28th 1689. J. F.

Although the Nature and State of Affairs relating to the Government of this Province is so well and notoriously known to all Persons any way concerned in the same, as to the People and Inhabitants here, who are more immediately Interested, as might excuse any Declaration or Apology for this present inevitable Appearance: Yet forasmuch as (by the Plots, Contrivances, Insinuations, Remonstrances, and Subscriptions, carried on, suggested, extorted, and obtained by the Lord Baltemore, his Deputies, representatives, and Officers here) the Injustice and Tyranny under which we groan is palliated, and most if not all the Particulars of our Grievances shrouded from the Eye of Observation and the Hand of Redress, We thought fit for general Satisfaction, and particularly to undeceive those that may have a sinister Account of our Proceedings, to Publish this Declaration of the Reason and Motives inducing us thereunto.

His Lordship's Right and Title to the Government is by Virtue of a Charter to his Father Cecilius, from King Charles the First, of Blessed Memory. How his present Lordship has managed the Powers and Authorities given and granted in the same, We could Mourn and Lament only in silence, would our Duty to God, our Allegeance to his Vicegerent, and the Care and Welfare of our Selves and Posterity, permit us.

In the First Place, In the said Charter, is a Reservation of the Faith and Allegeance due to the Crown of England (the Province and Inhabitants being immediately subject thereunto) but how little that is manifested, is too obvious to all unbiassed Persons that ever had any thing to do here; The very name and owning of that Soveraign Power is sometimes Crime enough to incur the Frowns of our Superiors, and to render our Persons obnoxious and suspected to be Ill Affected to the Government.

The Ill Usage and Affronts to the King's Officers belonging to the Customs here, were a sufficient Argument of this; We need but instance the Business of Mr. Badcock and Mr. Rousby, of whom the former was forcibly detained by his Lordship from going home to make his just Complaints in England, upon which he was soon taken Sick, and 'twas more than probably conjectured that the Conceit of his Confinement was the chief Cause of his Death, which soon after happened. The other was Barbarously Murthered upon the Execution of his Office, by one that was an Irish Papist and our Chief Governor.

Allegeance here, by these Persons under whom We Suffer, is little talk'd of, other then what they would have done and sworn to his Lordship, the Lord Proprietary; for it was very lately owned by the President himself, openly enough in the Upper House of Assembly, That Fidelity to his Lordship was Allegeance, and that the denial of the one was the same thing with refusal or denial of the other. In that very Oath of Fidelity that was then imposed under the Penalty and Threats of Banishment, there is not so much as the least word or intimation of any Duty, Faith, or Allegeance to be reserved to Our Soveraign Lord the King of England.

How the Jus Regale is improved here, and made the Prerogative of his Lordship, is too sensibly felt by us all in that absolute Authority exercised over us, and by the greatest part of the Inhabitants in the Seizure of their persons, Forfeiture and Loss of their Goods, Chattels, Freeholds and Inheritances.

In the next place, Churches and Chappels (which by the said Charter should be Built and Consecrated according to the Ecclesiastical Laws of the Kingdom of England) to our great Regret and Discouragement of our Religion are erected and converted to the use of Popish Idolatry and Superstition. Jesuits and Seminary Priests are the only Incumbents (for which there is a Supply provided by sending our Popish Youth to be Educated at St. Omers) as also the chief Advisers and Councellors in Affairs of Government, and the Richest and most Fertile Land set apart for their Use and Maintenance; while other Lands that are piously intended, and given for the Maintenance of the Protestant Ministry, become Escheat, and are taken as Forfeit, the Ministers themselves discouraged, and no care taken for their Subsistance.

The Power to Enact Laws is another branch of his Lordship's Authority; but how well that has been Executed and Circumstanced is too notorious. His present Lordship upon the Death of his Father, in order thereunto, sent out Writs for Four (as was ever the usuage) for each County to serve as Representatives of the People; but when Elected, there were Two only of each Respective Four pick'd out and summoned to that Convention, Whereby many Laws were made, and the greatest Levy yet known, laid upon the Inhabitants.

The next Session, the House was filled up with the remaining Two that was left out of the former, in which there were many and the best of our Laws Enacted, to the great Benefit and Satisfaction of the People. But his Lordship soon after Dissolved and Declared the best of those Laws, such as he thought fit, null and void by Proclamation; notwithstanding they were Assented to in his Lordship's Name by the Governor, in his absence, and he himself sometime Personally Acted and Governed by the same; so that the Question in our Courts of Judicature, in any point that relates to many of our Laws, is not so much the relation it has to the said Laws, but whether the Laws themselves be agreeable to the Approbation and Pleasure of his Lordship? Whereby our Liberty and Property is become uncertain, and under the Arbitrary Disposition of the Judges and Commissioners of our Courts of Justice.

The said Assembly being sometime after Dissolved by Proclamation, another was Elected and met, consisting only of Two Members for each County, directly opposite to an Act of Assembly for Four, in which several Laws, with his Lordship's Personal Assent, were Enacted: Among the which, one for the Encouragement of Trade and Erecting of Towns. But the Execution of that Act was soon after, by Proclamation from his Lordship out of England, suspended the last Year, and all Officers Military and Civil severely prohibited executing or inflicting the Penalties of the same. Notwithstanding which suspension, being in effect a dissolution and abrogating the whole Act, the Income of Three Pence to the Government by the said Act, payable for every Hogshead of Tobacco Exported, is carefully Exacted and Collected.

How Fatal, and of what Pernicious Consequence, that Unlimited and Arbitrary pretended Authority may be to the Inhabitants, is too apparent, but by considering, That by the same Reason, all the rest of our Laws, whereby our Liberty and Property subsists, are subject to the same Arbitrary Disposition, and if timely Remedy be not had, must stand or fall according to his Lordship's Good Will and Pleasure.

Nor is this Nullifying and Suspending Power the only Grievance that doth perplex and burthen us, in relation to Laws; but these Laws that are of a certain and unquestioned acceptation are executed and countenanced, as they are more or less agreeable to the good liking of our Governours in particular; One very good Law provides, That Orphan Children should be disposed of to Persons of the same Religion with that of their deceased Parents. In direct opposition to which, several Children of Protestants have been committed to the Tutelage of Papists, and brought up in the Romish Superstition. We could instance in a Young Woman, that has been lately forced, by Order of Council, from her Husband, committed to the Custody of a Papist and brought up in his Religion. 'Tis endless to enumerate the particulars of this nature, while on the contrary those Laws that enhance the Grandeur and Income of his said Lordship are severely Imposed and Executed; especially one that against all Sense, Equity, Reason, and Law Punishes all Speeches, Practices, and Attempts relating to his Lordship and Government, that shall be thought Mutinous and Seditious by the Judges of the Provincial Court, with either Whipping, Branding, Boreing through the Tongue, Fine, Imprisonment, Banishment, or Death; all or either of the said Punishments, at the Discretion of the said Judges; who have given a very recent and remarkable Proof of their Authority in each particular Punishment aforesaid, upon several of the good People of this Province, while the rest are in the same danger to have their Words and Actions liable to the Constructions and Punishment of the said Judges, and their Lives and Fortunes to the Mercy of their Arbitrary Fancies, Opinions, and Sentences.

To these Grievances are added,

Excessive Officers Fees, and that too under Execution, directly against the Law made and provided to redress the same; wherein there is no probability of a Legal Remedy, the Officers themselves that are Parties and culpable being Judges.

The like Excessive Fees imposed upon and extorted from Masters and Owners of Vessels Trading into this Province, without any Law to Justifie the same, and directly against the plain Words of the Charter, that say, there shall be no Imposition or Assessment without the Consent of the Freemen in the Assembly: To the great Obstruction of Trade, and Prejudice of the Inhabitants.

The like excessive Fees Imposed upon and extorted from the Owners of Vessels that are Built here, or do really belong to the Inhabitants; contrary to an Act of Assembly, made and provided for the same: Wherein, Moderate and Reasonable Fees are assertained, for the Promoting and Encouragement of Shipping and Navigation amongst our selves.

The frequent Pressing of Men, Horses, Boats, Provisions, and other Necessaries, in time of Peace; and often to gratifie private Designs and Occasions, to the great Burthen and Regret of the Inhabitants, contrary to Law and several Acts of Assembly in that Case made and provided.

The Seizing and Apprehending of Protestants in their Houses, with Armed Force consisting of Papists, and that in time of Peace; then- hurrying them away to Prisons without Warrant or Cause of Commitment, there kept and Confined with Popish Guards, a long time without Trial.

Not only private but publick Outrages and Murthers committed and done by Papists upon Protestants without any Redress, but rather connived at and Tollerated by the chief in Authority; and indeed it were in vain to desire or expect any help or measures from them, being Papists and Guided by the Counsels and Instigations of the Jesuits, either in these or any other Grievances or Oppression. And yet these are the Men that are our Chief Judges, at the Common Law, in Chancery, of the Probat of Wills, and the Affairs of Administration, in the Upper House of Assembly, and the Chief Military Officers and Commanders of our Forces; being still the same Individual Persons, in all these particular Qualifications and Places.

These and many more, even Infinite Pressures and Calamities, we have hitherto with Patience lain under and submitted too; hoping that the same Hand of Providence, that hath sustained us under them, would at length in due time release us; and now at length, For as much as it has pleased Almighty God, by means of the great Prudence and Conduct of the best of Princes, Our most gracious King William, to put a Check to the great Innundation of Slavery and Popery, that had like to overwhelm Their Majesties Protestant Subjects in all their Territories and Dominions (of which none have suffered more, or are in greater Danger than our selves) we hope[d] and expected in our particular Stations and Qualifications, a proportionable Share of so great a Blessing. But to our great Grief and Consternation, upon the first News of the great Overture and happy Change in England, we found our selves surrounded with Strong and Violent Endeavours from our Governours here, being the Lord Baltemore's Deputies and Representatives, to defeat us of the same.

We still find all the means used by these very Persons and their Agents, Jesuits, Priests, and lay Papists, that Art or Malice can suggest, to divert the Obedience and Loyalty of the Inhabitants from Their Most Sacred Majesties, to that heighth of Impudence, that solemn Masses and Prayers are used (as we have very good Information) in their Chappels and Oratories, for the prosperous Success of the Popish Forces in Ireland, and the French Designs against England, whereby they would involve us in the same Crime of Disloyalty with themselves, and render us Obnoxious to the Insupportable Displeasure of Their Majesties.

We every where hear, not only Publick Protestation against Their Majesties Right and Possession of the Crown of England, but their most Illustrious Persons villified and aspers'd with the worst and most Traiterous Expressions of Obloquy and Detraction.

We are every day threatned with the Loss of our Lives, Liberties, and Estates, of which we have great Reason to think our selves in Imminent Danger, by the Practices and Machinations that are on foot to betray us to the French, Northern, and other Indians, of which some have been dealt withal, and others Invited to Assist in our Destruction; well remembring the Incursion and Inrode of the said Northern Indians, in the Year 1681, who were conducted into the Heart of the Province by French Jesuits, and lay sore upon us, while the Representatives of the Country, then in the Assembly, were severely press'd upon by our Superiors, to yield them an Unlimited and Tiranical Power in the Affairs of the Militia. As so great a Piece of Villany cannot be the Result but of the worst of Principles; so we should with the greatest Difficulties believe it to be true, if Undeniable Evidence and Circumstances did not convince us.

Together with the Promises, we have, with all due Thinking and Deliberation, considered the Endeavours that are making to Disunite us among our selves, to make and Inflame Differences in our Neighbour Colony of Virginia, from whose Friendship, Vicinity, great Loyalty and Sameness of Religion, we may expect Assistance in our greatest Necessity.

We have considered, that all the other Branches of Their Majesties Dominions in this Part of the World (as well as we could be informed) have done their Duty in Proclaiming and Asserting their undoubted Right in these, and all other Their Majesties Territories and Countries.

But above all, with Due and Mature Deliberation, we have reflected upon that vast Gratitude and Duty incumbent likewise upon us, To our Sovereign Lord and Lady, the King and Queen's most Excellent Majesties, in which, as it would not be safe for us, so it will not suffer us to be Silent, in so great and General a Jubile, withal considering and looking upon our selves Discharged, Dissolved, and Free from all manner of Duty, Obligation, or Fidelity, to the Deputies, Governours, or Chief Magistrates here, as such: They having Departed from their Allegiance (upon which alone our said Duty and Fidelity to them depends) and by their Complices and Agents aforesaid endeavoured the Destruction of our Religion, Lives, Liberties, and Properties, all which they are bound to Protect.

These are the Reasons, Motives, and Considerations, which we do Declare, have induced us to take up Arms, to Preserve, Vindicate, and Assert the Sovereign Dominion, and Right, of King William and Queen Mary to this Province: To Defend the Protestant Religion among us, and to Protect and Shelter the Inhabitants from all manner of Violence, Oppression, and Destruction, that is Plotted and Designed against them; which we do Solemnly Declare and Protest, we have no Designs or Intentions whatsoever.

For the more Effectuate Accomplishments of which, We will take due Care that a Free and full Assembly be Called, and Convened with all Possible Expedition, by whom we may likewise have our Condition and Circumstances and our most Dutifull Addresses represented and rendered to Their Majesties: From whose great Wisdom, Justice, and especial Care of the Protestant Religion, We may Reasonably and Comfortably hope to be Delivered from our present Calamities, and for the Future be secured under a Just and Legal Administration, from being evermore subjected to the Yoke of Arbitrary Government, Tyrany and Popery.

In the Conduct of this, We will take Care, and do Promise, That no Person now in Arms with us, or that shall come to Assist us, shall commit any Outrage, or do any Violence to any Person whatsoever, that shall be found Peaceable and Quiet, and not oppose us in our said Just and necessary Designs: And that there shall be Just and due Satisfaction made for Provision, and other Necessaries had and Received from the Inhabitants: And the Soldiers punctually and duely Paid, in such Ways and Methods as have been formerly accustomed, or by Law ought to be.

And we do, Lastly, Invite and Require all manner of Persons whatsoever, Residing or Inhabiting in this Province, as they tender their Allegiance, the Protestant Religion, their Lives, Fortunes and Families, to Aid and Assist us in this our Undertaking.

Given under our Hands in Mary Land, the 25th Day of July, in the First Year of Their Majesties Reign, Annoque Domini 1689.

GLOSSARY

aspers'd: harshly criticized

assertained: in this context, meaning assessed or determined, as in the government deciding the amount of a fee.

innundation: a flood or huge amount

Jus Regale: Latin for the "Royal Right," political or legal powers that belong to the King.

murthers: murders

popish; popery; Romish: derogatory references to Catholicism

Document Analysis

Following the formal title and "license" information establishing the date of the declaration, the petitioners begin by explaining that despite the "State of Affairs relating to the Government of this Province" being well known to those in the colony, it is important for others elsewhere to understand the conditions that led to Maryland's Protestants taking up arms. The reason for this, they explain, is that "most if not all the Particulars" of their suffering is not readily visible or understandable to those in power who might assist them. The declaration, then, is a list of their grievances. This is especially important because people outside the colony might have been misled about the situation; the authors of this document which to "undeceive" them.

In the second paragraph, the petitioners explain the origins of Lord Baltimore's powers, being inherited from his father and embodied in a charter from King Charles I. This charter places Baltimore and the colony under "allegeance" [sic] to the Crown of England but no such obedience is evident. In fact, loyalty to the Crown is considered to be a suspicious activity and in the following paragraph, the petitioners recount the story of two colonists who wished to complain about conditions in Maryland and were forcibly prevented from doing so. One was imprisoned (leading to his death) and the other was murdered by an Irish Catholic ("and our Chief Governor"). Here we have the appearance of fears based on nationality and religion. As we will see, fear of foreign and Catholic subversion and oppression is a recurring theme in the document. The next two paragraphs expand on this theme, alleging that Lord Baltimore had set himself as the supreme authority in the colony with no allegiance to the royal government, requiring an "oath of authority" to the colonial government rather than to the King. Lord Baltimore and his people on the scene had taken royal authority (Jus Regale) for himself and ruled in an absolute and arbitrary manner.

The next six paragraphs provide detailed examples of the ways in which Baltimore and his ruling cabal exercised their authority. The first example is religious in nature, explaining that the government has illegally repurposed Protestant churches to be Roman Catholic ones ("converted to the use of Popish Idolatry and Superstition"). They also express concern about the fact that Jesuit priests are especially prominent as clergy, teachers, and advisers to government officials. These Catholic figures also receive the best farmland while lands belonging to Protestant groups are seized and Protestant clergy are destitute. The colonial government has also manipulated the legislative assembly, allowing only two of the allowed four representatives to be part of the assembly. When the assembly passed laws that were "to the great Benefit" of the people, Baltimore "dissolved" the laws he did not like. A new assembly was called, again not seating as many representatives as the law required. Once more, the petitioners accuse, Baltimore refused to enforce laws he did not like. The tax on tobacco, however, was "carefully Exacted and Collected." The petitioners fear that these examples of "arbitrary" enforcement of the laws will continue and the entire legal basis of the colony may collapse. They are also concerned with the domination of Roman Catholicism, citing cases in which orphaned Protestant children were placed with Catholic families. This section concludes with the example of people facing horribly punishments for the crime of speaking out against the abuses committed by the government.

The petitioners, up to this point, have discussed their concerns about the government of Maryland in a fairly reasonable way, pointing out where Lord Baltimore and his followers had violated established law and precedent in the colony. The remainder of the petition shifts to a more conspiratorial tone, complaining not only about excessive fees (often to the point of extortion) placed on merchants and the seizure of labor and goods for the leadership's personal benefit but also allege "publick Outrages and Murthers" that are committed by Catholics against Protestants without any penalty or punishment, and being actively promoted by those in charge of the colony as well as by Jesuits. The petitioners call upon King William to intervene on their behalf. They are also careful to explicitly declare how happy they are with the results of the shift in royal power from James II to William—indicating that they are loyal subjects of the rightful King. The final paragraphs of the petition detail the many ways in which the Baltimore regime were not loyal to William and request that they be "delivered" from their suffering and troubles. In the meantime, however, the petitioners have armed themselves and will assert control of the colony to restore proper, lawful government, promising to not do violence to anyone who is "peaceable and quiet" and calling on all other Protestants to come to their aid.

Essential Themes

The Declaration of the Reasons and Motives for the Present Appearing in Arms of Their Majesties Protestant Subjects in the Province of Maryland speaks to two key issues. The first of these is the danger of one religious group dominating the political, social, and cultural life of the colony. While the rebels complaints about the Roman Catholics among them occasionally veer into conspiratorial areas, there is a strong sense that the rebels are concern not only about the political power of Roman Catholic leaders but also the way that Catholicism is displacing the various Protestant religions. This is true not only of their churches but also in their concerns about the educational system and, significantly, the placement of orphaned protestant children with Catholic families.

The other issue the rebels raise is one that would echo across the coming century in English North America: concerns over the arbitrary use of government power. The government of Maryland had, according to the rebels imposed fines, fees, and committed other acts that were "directly against the Law" and were not subject to legal dispute. Acts of the legislature had been ignored and the colonial legislature itself had been manipulated and marginalized by colonial authorities. One of the key issues in the events leading up the Glorious Revolution had been the primacy of Parliament. Here, the Maryland Protestants assert the importance of their own legislatures in a similar fashion. In less than one hundred years, colonial rebels from across English North America would raise similar concerns about arbitrary power and the abuse of their colonial legislatures by the government of Great Britain.

———*Aaron Gulyas, MA*

Bibliography and Additional Reading

Brugger, Robert J., *Maryland, a Middle Temperament 1634-1980* (Baltimore: Johns Hopkins University Press, 1988).

Carr, Lois Green and David William Jordan. *Maryland's Revolution of Government*, 1689-1692. (Ithaca, New York: Cornell University Press, 1974).

Hoffman, Ronald, *Princes of Ireland, Planters of Maryland: A Carroll Saga, 1500-1782* (Chapel Hill: University of North Carolina Press, 2000).

■ The Rights of the British Colonies Asserted and Proved

Date: 1764
Author: James Otis
Genre: Pamphlet

Summary Overview

For those who are even only slightly familiar with the history of the United States, the cry of "no taxation without representation" is synonymous with the colonial crises of the 1760s and 1770s and the subsequent American Revolution. James Otis of Massachusetts was the man who crafted the political argument that launched this catchphrase of independence. Otis's *The Rights of the British Colonies Asserted and Proved* had its roots in the increasingly draconian measures taken by the British government against the colonies beginning in the early 1760s and responds to them with a detailed explanation of the origins of government, the importance of legislative bodies, particularly the "subordinate" legislatures, such as the Massachusetts General Court or other colonial law-making assemblies.

Otis, in this pamphlet, also promoted the argument that the colonies should have representation in the British Parliament. His reasoning for this—thoughts that would be taken up by other revolutionary-era thinkers and writers—was that the British subjects born on the colonies were equal to those subjects born in Britain itself. The vast distance separating the colonists from their mother country was immaterial to their legal and political standing. They were entitled to the same rights, privileges and representation as any other British citizen.

Defining Moment

From the founding of England's North American colonies in the early 17th century, there existed something of a parallel governmental structure. Each colony had a legislature that regulated its internal taxes and laws along with a royal governor appointed by the government in London to ensure that these laws conformed with those of the motherland. In the mid 1600s, a series of laws called the Navigation Acts attempted to regulate commerce between the colonies and mother country. The colonists were notorious for subverting these laws and, eventually, enforcement began to slacken. England treated the colonies with what historians have termed "salutary neglect," a policy to let enforcement of many regulations slide.

However, during the French and Indian War and, especially after its end in 1763, the relationship between the North American British colonies and their mother country fundamentally changed. The war and its aftermath brought the two entities into much closer and more frequent contact than ever before. During the war, thousands of British troops flooded into the colonies. Other policies, such as the use of "writs of assistance," which allowed for warrantless searches and seizures by authorities began as an effort to control smuggling but would continue to exist after the wars end. At the close of the war, in an effort to prevent conflict between Native American tribes and acquisitive westward moving settlers, Britain issued the Proclamation of 1763 which prohibited colonial settlement west of the Appalachian mountains and required those already living there to move back east.

In 1764, the year in which Otis wrote this essay, the British government would embark on the first of its many attempts to raise revenue from the American colonies. The political and philosophical concepts presented here by Otis would form the foundation of the arguments that colonists raised about the legality and constitutionality of these measures.

Author Biography

James Otis Jr. was born on February 5, 1725 in West Barnstable, Massachusetts. Otis attended Harvard University, graduating in 1743. He practiced law in Boston and, in the 1760s, began to challenge the British use of "writs of assistance." These gave the authorities the right to enter a home or business and search for unspecified contraband and smuggled goods. In 1761 he resigned in protest from his position as an attorney in the vice admiralty court and turned his efforts to the defense of merchants against renewal of writs of assistance. Otis lost the case, but he brought the matter to public attention, became something of an instant celebrity.

Soon after, Otis was elected to the Massachusetts General Court (that is, the colonial legislature), where he became an outspoken opponent of onerous British rule. After writing *The Rights of the British Colonies Asserted and Proved*, he became a member of the Massachusetts Committee of Correspondence (which communicated with other legislatures) and of the Stamp Act Congress. Although not as radical as Samuel Adams, the two worked together to lead the resistance to the Townshend Revenue Act of 1767. Sadly, Otis endured a vicious beating in 1769 at the hands of a British tax offi-

cial, leaving him mentally unstable until his death from a lightning strike on May 23, 1783. During the years between 1769 and his death, his efforts in support of American independence were largely forgotten, despite figures like John Adams promoting Otis's pamphlets as being foundational to the revolutionary cause.

HISTORICAL DOCUMENT

...Let no Man think I am about to commence advocate for *despotism*, because I affirm that government is founded on the necessity of our natures; and that an original supreme Sovereign, absolute, and uncontroulable, *earthly* power *must* exist in and preside over every society; from whose final decisions there can be no appeal but directly to Heaven. It is therefore *originally* and *ultimately* in the people. I say this supreme absolute power is *originally* and *ultimately* in the people; and they never did in fact *freely*, nor can they *rightfully* make an absolute, unlimited renunciation of this divine right. It is ever in the nature of the thing given in *trust*, and on a condition, the performance of which no mortal can dispense with; namely, that the person or persons on whom the sovereignty is conferred by the people, shall *incessantly* consult *their* good. Tyranny of all kinds is to be abhorred, whether it be in the hands of one, or of the few, or of the many. And though "in the last age a generation of men sprung up that would flatter Princes with an opinion that *they* have a *divine right* to absolute power;" yet "slavery is so vile and miserable an estate of man, and so directly opposite to the generous temper and courage of our nation, that it is hard to be conceived that an *Englishman*, much less a *gentleman*, should plead for it:" Especially at a time when the finest writers of the most polite nations on the continent of *Europe*, are enraptured with the beauties of the civil constitution of *Great Britain*; and envy her, no less for the *freedom* of her sons, than for her immense *wealth* and *military* glory.

But let the *origin* of government be placed where it may, the *end* of it is manifestly the good of *the whole*. *Salus populi suprema lex esto*, *is* of the law of nature, and part of that grand charter given the human race (though too many of them are afraid to

assert it) by the only monarch in the universe, who has a clear and indisputable right to *absolute* power; because he is the *only* ONE who is *omniscient* as well as *omnipotent*....

The British constitution in theory and in the present administration of it, in general comes nearest the idea of perfection, of any that has been reduced to practice, and if the principles of it are adhered to, it will, according to the infallible prediction of *Harrington*, always keep the *Britons* uppermost in *Europe*, 'till their *only* rival nation shall either embrace that perfect model of a commonwealth given us by that author, or come as near it as *Great Britain is*. Then indeed, and not till then, will that rival and our nation either be eternal confederates, or contend in greater earnest than they have ever yet done, till one of them shall sink under the power of the other, and rise no more....

Every British Subject born on the continent of America, or in any other of the British dominions, is by the law of God and nature, by the common law, and by act of parliament, (exclusive of all charters from the crown) entitled to all the natural, essential, inherent and inseparable rights of our fellow subjects in Great-Britain.

1st. *That the supreme and subordinate powers of legislation should be free and sacred in the hands where the community have once rightfully placed them.*

2dly. *The supreme national legislative cannot be altered justly till the commonwealth is dissolved, nor a subordinate legislative taken away without forfeiture or other good cause.* Nor then can the subjects in the subordinate government be reduced to a state of slavery, and subject to the despotic rule of others. A state has no right to make slaves of the conquered. Even when the subordinate right of legislature is forfeited, and so declared, this cannot effect the natural persons either of those who were invested with it, or the inhabitants, so far as to deprive them of the rights of subjects and of men. The colonists will have an equitable right, notwithstanding any such forfeiture of charter, to be represented in parliament, or to have some new subordinate legislature among themselves. It would be best if they had both. Deprived, however, of their common rights as subjects, they cannot lawfully be, while they remain such.

Representation in Parliament from the several colonies, since they are become so large and numerous, as to be called on not only to maintain provincial government, civil and military, among themselves, for this they have chearfully done, but to contribute towards the support of a national standing army, by reason of the heavy national debt, when they themselves owe a large one, contracted in the common cause, cannot be thought an unreasonable thing, nor if asked, could it be called an immodest request) *Qui sentit commodum sentire debet et onus*, has been thought a maxim of equity. But that a man should bear a burthen for other people, as well as himself, without a return, never long found a place in any law-book or decrees, but those of the most despotic princes. Besides the equity of an American representation in parliament, a thousand advantages would result from it. It would be the most effectual means of giving those of both countries a thorough knowledge of each others interests; as well as that of the whole, which are inseparable.

Were this representation allowed; instead of the scandalous memorials and depositions that have been sometimes, in days of old, privately cooked up in an inquisitorial manner, by persons of bad minds and wicked views, and sent from America to the several boards, persons of the first reputation among their countrymen, might be on the spot, from the several colonies, truly to represent them. Future ministers need not, like some of their predecessors, have recourse for information in American affairs, to every vagabond stroller, that has run or rid post *through* America, from his creditors, or to people of no kind of reputation from the colonies; some of whom, at the time of administering their sage advice, have been as ignorant of the state of this country, as of the regions in Jupiter and Saturn.

No representation of the colonies in parliament alone, would, however, be equivalent to a subordinate legislative among themselves; nor so well answer the ends of increasing their prosperity and the commerce of Great Britain. It would be impossible for the parliament to judge so well of their abilities to bear taxes, impositions on trade, and other duties and burthens, or of the local laws that might be really needful, as a legislative here.

3dly. *No legislative, supreme or subordinate, has a right to make itself arbitrary.*

GLOSSARY

omnipotent: All powerful

omniscient: All knowing

Salus populi suprema lex esto: Latin phrase meaning "Let the good of the people be the supreme law"

Qui sentit commodum sentire debet et onus: Latin phrase meaning "He who enjoys the benefit, ought also to bear the burden"

Document Analysis

In these excerpts from *The Rights of the British Colonies Asserted and Proved*, Otis begins by taking a very eighteenth-century Enlightenment view of the nature of government. He asserts that the nature of man makes government necessary and that this government needs to be "an original supreme Sovereign, absolute, and uncontroulable, *earthly* power." He immediately makes clear, though, that he is not advocating despotism. This power, he says, is "*originally* and *ultimately* in the people." Thus, the "person or persons on whom the sovereignty is conferred by the people, shall *incessantly* consult *their* good." He goes on to argue that the end of government "is manifestly the good of *the whole*" and that the "law of nature" is *Salus populi suprema lex esto,* or "Let the good of the people be the supreme law" (incidentally, the state motto of Missouri). In this way, Otis appeals to principles of natural law and natural rights. These ideas were almost a commonplace among political philosophers during this era of the Enlightenment, which thrived in Britain and France during the late seventeenth and eighteenth centuries. British writers such as John Locke (1632-1704) and French writers like Jean-Jacques Rousseau (1712-1776) promoted the idea that government was based, in some way, in the sovereignty of the people themselves.

Otis extols the British constitution, referring to the political philosopher James Harrington and his prediction in *The Commonwealth of Oceana* (1656) that the British constitutional form of government would reign supreme in Europe. He also expresses the opinion that the people of the "polite" nations of Europe are as jealous of Britain's form of government as they are of Britain's wealth or military strength. He then makes a clear—and what to some would have been a controversial—assertion: "Every British Subject born on the continent of America, or in any other of the British dominions, is by the law of God and nature, by the common law, and by act of parliament, (exclusive of all charters from the crown) entitled to all the natural, essential, inherent and inseparable rights of our fellow subjects in Great-Britain." It should be remembered the colonies were formed by charters from the Crown, and many colonists tried to assert their rights by appealing not to Parliament but to the king. This notion would become a critical part of colonial arguments against Parliamentary attempts to tax the colonists. Otis then states three arguments about the nature of legislative bodies.

First, he asserts that he power to legislate must be placed in the hands of the people. In his second point, the longest, he asserts that the legislature cannot be dissolved unless the "commonwealth," or the entire nation is dissolved. He also states that subordinate legislatures (like the colonial legislative assemblies) cannot be "taken away" without justification. In later years, this concern would prove to be somewhat prophetic as the British government limited the powers of the Massachusetts General Court. Otis, on the basis of this argument, calls for representation of the American colonies in the British Parliament. He cites the Latin maxim *Qui sentit commodum sentire debet et onus* ("He who enjoys the benefit, ought also to bear the burden") and turns it around to argue that a people should not be required to bear a burden without enjoying a corresponding right. At the same time, Otis recognizes that Parliament might not be the best judge of what is good for the colonies. He argues, therefore, for the sovereignty of the "subordinate legislatures" he mentioned earlier by stating: "It would be impossible for the parliament to judge so well of their abilities to bear taxes, impositions on trade, and other duties and burthens, or of the local laws that might be really needful, as a legislative here." His third, and final, point is that no legislative body—whether the "supreme" one or a lower body—is allowed to "make itself arbitrary." That is to say, it must operate within the bounds of established law and precedent.

Essential Themes

James Otis's ideas drew heavily on the ideas of political philosophers and theorists whose names would become synonymous with the Enlightenment era. Otis explicitly rejects the notion of arbitrary government and, while he believes that government is necessary, he does not accept that government must be tyrannical to be effective. One of the important themes that shines through in these excerpts from Otis's work is the primary position of representative legislative bodies in his vision of just government. The power of these legislatures must be, in Otis's words "free and sacred." Otis's assertions about the importance of "subordinate" legislatures represents a distinctive colonial view of the British system of government. The colonial assemblies were closer to the people they represented and, because of this, would have greater insight into the needs of those people.

Another important aspect of Otis's work that is a bit less obvious but is no less significant. Otis, at least in 1764 when he wrote this pamphlet, is not a radical or a revolutionary. Not only does he proclaim the British constitution to be close to "perfection" in theory but also "in the present administration of it." The British system of legislative government and the political philosophy that underlies it are not the problem. The problem, according to Otis, is that the American colonists are not fully able to enjoy the benefits of this near-perfect political system. That second-class status leads to abuses like the writs of assistance that Otis fought in court and, in months and years to come, would lead to conflicts over taxation and, eventually, war.

———*Michael J. O'Neal, PhD*

Bibliography and Additional Reading

Breen, T. H. "Subjecthood and Citizenship: The Context of James Otis's Radical Critique of John Locke," *New England Quarterly* (Sep., 1998) 71 #3, 378–403.

Farrell, James M. "The Writs of Assistance and Public Memory: John Adams and the Legacy of James Otis," *New England Quarterly* (2006) 79 #4 533–556.

Ferguson, James R. "Reason in Madness: The Political Thought of James Otis," *William and Mary Quarterly,* (1979): 36:194–214.

Samuelson, Richard A. "The Constitutional Sanity of James Otis: Resistance Leader and Loyal Subject," *Review of Politics* (Summer, 1999), 61 #3 493–523.

■ Declaration of Rights of the Stamp Act Congress

Date: 1765
Author: Delegates to the Stamp Act Congress
Genre: Public statement

Summary Overview

The Stamp Act Congress was convened on October 7, 1765, to address the passage of the Stamp Act by Parliament on March 8, 1765. The delegates responded to the act on October 19 by issuing the Declaration of Rights of the Stamp Act Congress, which included fourteen resolutions and was accompanied by several petitions denying Parliament's authority to tax the thirteen colonies. The Stamp Act Congress and its Declaration of Rights helped lead to the Stamp Act's repeal in March 1766. They also led the colonists to focus on the idea of constitutional limitations on parliamentary authority, a concept that contributed to the American Revolution.

The Stamp Act required that anything formally written or printed must appear on stamped paper dispensed by English agents. This was a visible and pervasive tax, which was imposed by Parliament to help pay the great debts the English incurred while protecting their colonies during the French and Indian War (1754–1763). The stamp duties triggered outrage among the American colonists. They maintained that taxes were gifts to the king that could be offered only through a body that represented them. Since the colonists were not represented in Parliament, either actually or virtually, they believed that Parliament had no authority to impose the stamp tax on the colonies. In their minds, the stamp duties represented a confiscation of their property, since they had not given their consent to a parliamentary power to lay taxes.

Defining Moment

Faced with massive debts incurred in the French and Indian War, Great Britain sought means of raising revenue in the American colonies, which, in their view, were the beneficiary of England's generous military action. In 1763 George Grenville, the first lord of the treasury and the chancellor of the exchequer, began hatching a series of legislative measures that would impose taxes on the colonists to satisfy England's financial needs. These laws included the Sugar Act (1764). The American colonists were still seething over the Sugar Act, which they considered an illegal tax, when they were hit with the Stamp Act duties in 1765. At the same time, the British expanded the jurisdiction of the vice admiralty courts to try those who interfered with revenue laws. These courts did not employ juries. Colonists saw this as a violation of their ancient rights as Englishmen to trial by jury.

The American colonists sniffed conspiracy against their liberties. They resented the Stamp Act as a violation of their rights as Englishmen. Those who lived in England, the colonists explained, could be taxed by Parliament because they enjoyed representation. But those in the American colonies were not represented in Parliament. Thus they were being taxed without their consent, a violation not only of their rights as subjects of the Crown but also of their natural rights as men.

The Massachusetts Assembly, at the suggestion of James Otis, sent an invitation to the other colonial assemblies to meet in New York City and discuss the colonies' options. The resulting Stamp Act Congress determined to issue a Declaration of Rights and to petition the king and Parliament seeking repeal of the act.

The Stamp Act Congress, caught in the clutches of a great national crisis, was forced to choose between acquiescence or confrontation. It chose confrontation. In this, it gave vent to ideas and concepts that had lain dormant, awaiting an occasion for articulation. When the chance came, the congress rejected Parliament's authority to tax the American colonists. This assertion of the colonists' rights placed the colonies on a path that changed history.

Author Biography

The journal of the Stamp Act Congress provides no hint as to the delegate or delegates who wrote the initial draft of the convention's Declaration of Rights, the document that provided the foundation for the petitions to the king and Parliament in which the colonists sought relief from the Stamp Act. This was by design; as it was determined that discussions and debates among the twenty-seven delegates could be more candid if their remarks were not published, and, given the sensitive nature of the deliberations, the delegates preferred anonymity. The assertion of limits on parliamentary authority, including denial of authority to levy taxes, might invite retribution.

(279)

Anno quinto

Georgii III. Regis.

C A P. XII.

An Act for granting and applying certain Stamp
Duties, and other Duties, in the *British* Colonies and Plantations in *America*, towards
further defraying the Expences of defending,
protecting, and securing the same; and for
amending such Parts of the several Acts of
Parliament relating to the Trade and Revenues of the said Colonies and Plantations,
as direct the Manner of determining and re-
covering the Penalties and Forfeitures therein mentioned.

WHEREAS by an Act made in
the last Session of Parliament,
several Duties were granted,
continued, and appropriated, towards defraying the Expences
of defending, protecting, and
securing, the British Colonies
and Plantations in America:
And whereas it is just and necessary, that Provision be made
for raising a further Revenue
within Your Majesty's Domi-
nions in America, towards defraying the said Expences:
We, Your Majesty's most dutiful and loyal Subjects,
the Commons of Great Britain in Parliament assembled,
have

4 A 2

5

Knowledge of the congress's work is drawn mainly from fragmentary accounts in diaries, the delegates' letters, newspaper accounts and pamphlets that bear close resemblance to the petitions, and resolves issued by the convention. It is a safe bet that John Dickinson, a brilliant pamphleteer and an acute theorist from Pennsylvania, produced the first draft of the resolutions. The collection of his papers includes a paper in his handwriting that provides "the original Draft of the Resolves of the first Congress held at New York in the year 1765."

HISTORICAL DOCUMENT

The members of this Congress, sincerely devoted, with the warmest sentiments of affection and duty to His Majesty's Person and Government, inviolably attached to the present happy establishment of the Protestant succession, and with minds deeply impressed by a sense of the present and impending misfortunes of the British colonies on this continent; having considered as maturely as time will permit the circumstances of the said colonies, esteem it our indispensable duty to make the following declarations of our humble opinion, respecting the most essential rights and liberties of the colonists, and of the grievances under which they labour, by reason of several late Acts of Parliament.

I. That His Majesty's subjects in these colonies, owe the same allegiance to the Crown of Great-Britain, that is owing from his subjects born within the realm, and all due subordination to that august body the Parliament of Great Britain.

II. That His Majesty's liege subjects in these colonies, are entitled to all the inherent rights and liberties of his natural born subjects within the kingdom of Great-Britain.

III. That it is inseparably essential to the freedom of a people, and the undoubted right of Englishmen, that no taxes be imposed on them, but with their own consent, given personally, or by their representatives.

IV. That the people of these colonies are not, and from their local circumstances cannot be, represented in the House of Commons in Great-Britain.

V. That the only representatives of the people of these colonies, are persons chosen therein by themselves, and that no taxes ever have been, or can be constitutionally imposed on them, but by their respective legislatures.

VI. That all supplies to the Crown, being free gifts of the people, it is unreasonable and inconsistent with the principles and spirit of the British Constitution, for the people of Great-Britain to grant to His Majesty the property of the colonists.

VII. That trial by jury is the inherent and invaluable right of every British subject in these colonies.

VIII. That the late Act of Parliament, entitled, An Act for granting and applying certain Stamp Duties, and other Duties, in the British colonies and plantations in America, etc., by imposing taxes on the inhabitants of these colonies, and the said Act, and several other Acts, by extending the jurisdiction of the courts of Admiralty beyond its ancient limits, have a manifest tendency to subvert the rights and liberties of the colonists.

IX. That the duties imposed by several late Acts of Parliament, from the peculiar circumstances of these colonies, will be extremely burthensome and grievous; and from the scarcity of specie, the payment of them absolutely impracticable.

X. That as the profits of the trade of these colonies ultimately center in Great-Britain, to pay for the manufactures which they are obliged to take from thence, they eventually contribute very largely to all supplies granted there to the Crown.

XI. That the restrictions imposed by several late Acts of Parliament, on the trade of these colonies, will render them unable to purchase the manufactures of Great-Britain.

XII. That the increase, prosperity, and happiness of these colonies, depend on the full and free enjoyment of their rights and liberties, and an intercourse with Great-Britain mutually affectionate and advantageous.

XIII. That it is the right of the British subjects in these colonies, to petition the King, Or either House of Parliament.

Lastly, That it is the indispensable duty of these colonies, to the best of sovereigns, to the mother country, and to themselves, to endeavour by a loyal and dutiful address to his Majesty, and humble applications to both Houses of Parliament, to procure the repeal of the Act for granting and applying certain stamp duties, of all clauses of any other Acts of Parliament, whereby the jurisdiction of the Admiralty is extended as aforesaid, and of the other late Acts for the restriction of American commerce.

GLOSSARY

burthensome: burdensome; creating an unnecessary hardship

courts of Admiralty: courts that exercise jurisdiction over all maritime matters, including shipping of goods

liege: subordinate

specie: money

Document Analysis

Resolutions I and II speak of the duties of the colonists as subjects of the Crown. The first resolution recognizes of Parliament's authority to make laws governing the entire empire, but that sweeping authority is limited, according to the colonists, who contend that the power to legislate does not include the power to tax, a point emphasized in the sixth resolution.

The assertion in the second resolution that the colonists are "entitled" to the rights and liberties enjoyed by "natural born subjects" aims at reminding English readers that their rights are the same as those of their peers in the kingdom. Implicit in this reminder is the concept that taxes may be imposed only by a body that represents the taxpayer. Since the colonists are not represented in Parliament, that body may not levy taxes upon them. In addition, all of the other rights possessed by English subjects, including trial by jury, are enjoyed by the colonists.

In the third resolution, the Stamp Act Congress provides that "it is inseparably essential to the freedom of a people" that taxes may not be levied without their consent. This resolution emphasizes two key points. First, taxes are a gift, founded on the willingness and approval of the people. Second, the right to grant one's consent is essential to a free people. The third resolution, then, broadens the argument about Parliament's taxing power and denies it in terms that are universal.

These themes of representation and consent color the fourth and fifth resolutions. The congress emphasizes in the fourth resolution that the colonists "are not" and "cannot be" represented in Parliament. The dispute between the two sides centered on the issue of whether the colonies enjoyed *virtual* representation. Great Britain maintained that even though the colonists did not elect their own representatives, they were nonetheless virtually represented, since Parliament represents everyone within the empire. Accordingly, the colonists were represented and could be taxed.

Having established in the fourth resolution that the colonists are not represented in Parliament, the congress asserts in the fifth resolution that "no taxes" may be "constitutionally imposed on them, but by their respective legislatures." The concept of consent, the sheet anchor of the Declaration of Independence and republicanism itself, is repeatedly brandished by the congress. Without the consent of the governed, taxation is illegitimate and unconstitutional.

The Stamp Act Congress draws a distinction between legislation and taxation. In the sixth resolution, the congress complains that Parliament may not tax the colonists, since taxes are a gift that may be granted by the representatives of the people who offer the gift. Since Parliament does not represent the colonists, it would be "unreasonable" and in violation of the British Constitution for Parliament to assume it may give the property of the colonists to the king.

England's decision to extend the jurisdiction of the vice admiralty courts to prosecutions of acts that violated the revenue laws, including the Stamp Act, generated great anxiety and anger among the colonists. In the seventh and eighth resolutions, the Stamp Act Congress reiterates the right to trial by jury and the threat that the admiralty courts pose to that right. The right to trial by jury was regarded as an ancient liberty. The right to be tried by one's peers plumbed the depths of English legal history. In the admiralty courts, there was no jury. As a consequence, the congress asserts that trial in the admiralty courts deprives colonists of an "inherent and invaluable right" guaranteed to every British subject.

To make matters worse, the Stamp Act duties were enforceable by the vice admiralty courts, which were originally established to handle disputes between merchants and seamen. In these courts, there was no trial by jury, so a refusal to abide by the Stamp Act provisions could result in a prosecution in which a colonist would not be tried by his peers. This feature, the colonists maintained, would violate their right under the British Constitution to a jury trial. As the colonists surveyed these programs and policies, it became increasingly clear to them that their liberty was being threatened.

The remaining resolutions reflect the assertions of the Stamp Act Congress that the stamp duties, like other revenue laws, threaten the livelihood, the financial well-being, and the liberty, security, and happiness of the colonists. The congress was clever and correct in observing that the Stamp Act would hurt British merchants as well, since, as explained in the eleventh resolution, the restrictions would hinder the ability of the colonists to purchase goods manufactured in England. The implied threat, backed by nonimport agreements in various colonies, was aided by British merchants' appeals to the House of Commons to repeal the Stamp Act for the reasons asserted by the congress.

The Stamp Act Congress's combination of legal and constitutional arguments, supported by eminently practical concerns that reflected the impact of the stamp duties on the colonies, created a powerful and persuasive case for repeal. The innovative thinking that colors the resolutions invited further exploration among the colonists and paved the way for additional claims of violations of constitutional rights, which resounded throughout the colonies in the run-up to the Revolutionary War.

Essential Themes

The legal and political notions of "consent" and "representation" are critical to understanding the work of the Stamp Act Congress and, indeed, the entire Revolutionary period. If the people are not represented in Parliament, which the colonists contend they are not, then they cannot give their consent to be taxed. Rather, the tax imposed by Parliament represents a confiscation of their property. In this declaration the congress also draws on the idea of the "rights of men," or "natural rights." The appeal to natural rights became a powerful weapon and motivating argument for the colonists, a commonplace in their battles with Great Britain over the next decade.

It should be clear to all, who read the Declaration that the colonists did not enjoy any actual representation in Parliament; they did not vote for candidates who stood for election. The colonists rejected the concept of virtual representation, which was asserted by Parliament as a justification for their ability to tax the colonies. The colonists continued to emphasize actual representation, which could occur only if they had the opportunity to elect their representatives. For a time, some leading thinkers, including James Otis, considered the idea of pushing for actual representation in Parliament, but this pursuit was wisely discouraged by others. It was observed that even if the colonists sent delegates to London, they would be outnumbered, outmaneuvered, and unable to assert any real influence. They also would be at the mercy of Parliament's taxing power because they would be unable to argue that they were being taxed without representation or their consent. It was more effective, the members of the congress believed, to be in a position to argue that the Stamp Act was unconstitutional because the colonists were not represented.

———David Gray Adler, PhD

Bibliography and Additional Reading

Gipson, Lawrence Henry. "The Great Debate in the Committee of the Whole House of Commons on the Stamp Act, as Reported by Nathaniel Ryder." *Pennsylvania Magazine of History and Biography* 86, no. 1 (1962): 10–41.

Laprade, William T. "The Stamp Act in British Politics." *American Historical Review* 35, no. 4 (1930): 735–757.

Morgan, Edmund S. *TheBirth of the Republic, 1763–1789*. Chicago: University of Chicago Press, 1977.

Morgan, Edmund S., and Helen M. Morgan. *The Stamp Act Crisis: Prologue to Revolution*. New York: Collier Books, 1963.

Vaughan, Alden T., ed. *Chronicles of the American Revolution*. New York: Grosset and Dunlap, 1965.

Weslager, Clinton A. *The Stamp Act Congress*. Newark: University of Delaware Press, 1976.

■ Letters from a Farmer in Pennsylvania

Date: 1767–1768
Author: John Dickinson
Genre: Essay

Summary Overview

John Dickinson's twelve *Letters from a Farmer in Pennsylvania*, published under the pseudonym of "A Farmer" in 1767 and 1768 were one of the fundamental pieces of writing that galvanized American colonists in their protests against British policies in the era between the French and Indian War and the outbreak of the American Revolution. The letters presented here, the first and third, concern two key ideas.

The first letter discusses the dangers to the American colonies (and colonists) not only from the well-published and widely-denounced Stamp Act but also from laws like the Quartering Act and punitive British actions taken against colonial legislatures—in this case that of New York—that did not fully comply with the law. Dickinson argues that Colonists should be at least as concerned about this attack on their liberties as they are about the Stamp Act.

In the third letter, Dickinson addresses the bigger picture of the dangers the colonists currently face as well as a defense of colonial resistance to British policies that infringe on the rights and liberties of the colonists and their institutions. Here, Dickinson outlines the basic justification for firm (but peaceful) resistance such policies. While Dickinson prefers peaceful solutions he also acknowledges that "riots and tumults" are part and parcel of attempting to persuade Britain to redress the grievances of the colonies.

Defining Moment

The end of the French and Indian War in 1763 saw the British Empire come into possession of a vast amount of territory in North America but acquiring this territory was one of the factors which led to Britain also acquiring a great deal of debt. The war had brought the mother country into closer contact with its North American colonies and, since much of the fighting had been the result of events that took place in those colonies, British officials sought ways to raise revenue in those colonies, including through taxation.

One of these attempts, the Stamp Act of 1765, had led to a widespread uproar in the colonies and, eventually, an attempted boycott of British goods in response.

Parliament repealed the Act, but issued the Declaratory Act of 1766, in which they declared to have sovereignty over the colonies "in all cases." Less noticed was the Quartering Act of 1765, which provided for British soldiers to be housed in American barracks but, if there were more soldiers than barracks, they could be quartered in taverns, stables, barns, and uninhabited houses. Colonial government were required to pay for the cost of housing the troops as well as feeding them. In 1766, the Provincial Assembly of New York (the colonial legislative body) did not comply with the law when 1500 troops came to the city. In retaliation, Parliament formally suspended the governor and assembly during 1767 as well as in 1769. While this suspension was not implemented, the only thing that prevented it was New York's agreement to pay part of the cost of supporting the British troops.

Dickinson wrote his *Letters from a Farmer in Pennsylvania* in 1767 and 1768 in the midst of this crisis and the ongoing colonial debate on the the best way to effectively protest British taxation policies.

Author Biography

Born in November, 1732, John Dickinson was one of the most significant figures in the American revolutionary era, even if he is not as known to the public as Jefferson, Paine, Adams, Franklin, Washington, or others. Born and raised in Pennsylvania. Dickinson studied law, passing the Pennsylvania Bar in 1757. During the early years of the colonial crisis in the 1760s, he composed his *Letters from a Farmer in Philadelphia* and s the crisis escalated in the 1770s, he served as a representative to the First Continental Congress, which met in September and October of 1774 to consider action in response to the Intolerable Acts—a series of punitive actions against Boston and the colony of Massachusetts as punishment for the destruction that resulted from the Boston Tea Party. As a delegate to this body, Dickinson helped draft the petition to King George III asking for the acts to be repealed. He also signed the "Continental Association" which called for a colonies-wide boycott of British manufactured goods.

As the crisis devolved into open warfare in 1775, Dickinson was also a delegate to the Second Continental Congress. Here, he composed the so-called "Olive Branch Petition" which was the final attempt at peace between the colonies and the British government. However, Dickinson also contributed edits and additions to the "Declaration of the Causes and Necessity of Taking up Arms," including one of the key lines that, for a long time, was attributed to Thomas Jefferson: "Our cause is just. Our union is perfect. Our internal resources are great, and, if necessary, foreign assistance is undoubtedly attainable." While Dickinson was firmly in support of the American cause, he was reluctant to embrace independence. When that decision came, however, he supported it wholeheartedly, helping to craft the Articles of Confederation, the initial governing document of the new United States.

HISTORICAL DOCUMENT

Letter I

My dear Countrymen,

I am a *Farmer*, settled, after a variety of fortunes, near the banks of the river *Delaware*, in the province of *Pennsylvania*. I received a liberal education, and have been engaged in the busy scenes of life; but am now convinced, that a man may be as happy without bustle, as with it. My farm is small; my servants are few, and good; I have a little money at interest; I wish for no more; my employment in my own affairs is easy; and with a contented grateful mind, undisturbed by worldly hopes or fears, relating to myself, I am completing the number of days allotted to me by divine goodness.

Being generally master of my time, I spend a good deal of it in a library, which I think the most valuable part of my small estate; and being acquainted with two or three gentlemen of abilities and learning, who honor me with their friendship, I have acquired, I believe, a greater knowledge in history, and the laws and constitution of my country, than is generally attained by men of my class, many of them not being so fortunate as I have been in the opportunities of getting information.

From my infancy I was taught to love *humanity* and *liberty*. Enquiry and experience have since confirmed my reverence for the lessons then given me, by convincing me more fully of their truth and excellence. Benevolence toward mankind, excites wishes for their welfare, and such wishes endear the means of fulfilling them. *These* can be found in liberty only, and therefore her sacred cause ought to be espoused by every man on every occasion, to the utmost of his power. As a charitable, but poor person does not withhold his *mite*, because he cannot relieve *all* the distresses of the miserable, so should not any honest man suppress his sentiments concerning freedom, however small their influence is likely to be. Perhaps he "may touch some wheel," that will have an effect greater than he could reasonably expect.

These being my sentiments, I am encouraged to offer to you, my countrymen, my thoughts on some late transactions, that appear to me to be of the utmost importance to you. Conscious of my own defects, I have waited some time, in expectation of seeing the subject treated by persons much better qualified for the task; but being therein disappointed, and apprehensive that longer delays will be injurious, I venture at length to request the attention of the public, praying, that these lines may be *read* with the same zeal for the happiness of *British America*, with which they were *wrote*.

With a good deal of surprise I have observed, that little notice has been taken of an act of parliament, as injurious in its principle to the liberties of these colonies, as the *Stamp Act* was: I mean the act for suspending the legislation of *New York*.

The assembly of that government complied with a former act of parliament, requiring certain provisions to be made for the troops in *America*, in every particular, I think, except the articles of salt, pepper and vinegar. In my opinion they acted imprudently, considering all circumstances, in not complying so far as would have given satisfaction, as several colonies did: But my dislike of their conduct in that instance, has not blinded me so much, that I cannot plainly perceive, that they have been punished in a manner pernicious to *American* freedom, and justly alarming to all the colonies.

If the *British* parliament has legal authority to issue an order, that we shall furnish a single article for the troops here, and to compel obedience to *that* order, they have the same right to issue an order for us to supply those troops with arms, clothes, and every necessary; and to compel obedience to *that* order also; in short, to lay *any burthens* they please upon us. What is this but *taxing* us at a *certain sum*, and leaving to us only the *manner* of raising it? How is this mode more tolerable than the *Stamp Act*? Would that act have appeared more pleasing to *Americans*, if being ordered thereby to raise the sum total of the taxes, the mighty privilege had been left to them, of saying how much should be paid for an instrument of writing on paper, and how much for another on parchment?

An act of parliament, commanding us to do a certain thing, if it has any validity, is a *tax* upon us for the expense that accrues in complying with it; and for this reason, I believe, every colony on the continent, that chose to give a mark of their respect for *Great Britain*, in complying with the act relating to the troops, cautiously avoided the mention of that act, lest their conduct should be attributed to its supposed obligation.

The matter being thus stated, the assembly of *New York* either had, or had not, a right to refuse submission to that act. If they had, and I imagine no *American* will say they had not, then the parliament had *no right* to compel them to execute it. If they had not *this right*, they had *no right* to punish them for not executing it; and therefore *no right* to suspend their legislation, which is a punishment. In fact, if the people of *New York* cannot be legally taxed but by their own representatives, they cannot be legally deprived of the privilege of legislation, only for insisting on that exclusive privilege of taxation. If they may be legally deprived in such a case, of the privilege of legislation, why may they not, with equal reason, be deprived of every other privilege? Or why may not every colony be treated in the same manner, when any of them shall dare to deny their assent to any impositions, that shall be directed? Or what signifies the repeal of the *Stamp Act*, if these colonies are to lose their *other* privileges, by not tamely surrendering *that* of taxation?

There is one consideration arising from this suspension, which is not generally attended to, but shows its importance very clearly. It was not *necessary* that this suspension should be caused by an act of parliament. The crown might have restrained the governor of *New York*, even from calling the assembly together, by its prerogative in the royal governments. This step, I suppose, would have been taken, if the conduct of the assembly of *New York* had been regarded as an act of disobedience *to the crown alone*; but it is regarded as an act of "disobedience to the authority of the British Legislature." This gives the suspension a consequence vastly more affecting. It is a parliamentary assertion of the *supreme authority* of the *British* legislature over these colonies, in *the point of taxation*, and is intended to Compel *New York* into a submission to that authority. It seems therefore to me as much a violation of the liberties of the people of that province, and consequently of all these colonies, as if the parliament had sent a number of regiments to be quartered upon them till they should comply. For it is evident, that the suspension is meant as a *compulsion*; and the *method* of compelling is totally indifferent. It is indeed probable, that the sight of redcoats, and the hearing of drums, would have been most alarming; because people are generally more influenced by their eyes and ears, than by their reason. But whoever seriously considers the matter, must perceive that a dreadful stroke is aimed at the liberty of these colonies. I say, of these colonies; for the cause of *one* is the cause of *all*. If the parliament may lawfully deprive *New York* of any of *her* rights, it may deprive any, or all the other colonies of *their* rights; and nothing can possibly so much encourage such attempts, as a mutual inattention to the interests of each other. *To divide, and thus to destroy*, is the first political maxim in attacking those, who are powerful by their union....

With concern I have observed, that *two* assemblies of this province have sat and adjourned, without taking any notice of this act. It may perhaps be asked, what would have been proper for them to do? I am by no means fond of inflammatory measures; I detest them. I should be sorry that anything should be done which might justly displease our sovereign, or our mother country: But a firm, modest exertion of a free spirit, should never be wanting on public occasions. It appears to me, that it would have been sufficient for the assembly to have ordered our agents to represent to the King's ministers their sense of the suspending act, and to pray for its repeal. Thus we should have borne our testimony against it; and might therefore reasonably expect that, on a like occasion, we might receive the same assistance from the other colonies.

Concordia res parvae crescunt.

Small things grow great by concord.

A Farmer

Letter III

My dear Countrymen,

I rejoice to find that my two former letters to you have been generally received with so much favor by such of you, whose sentiments I have had an opportunity of knowing. Could you look into my heart you would instantly perceive a zealous attachment to your interests, and a lively resentment of every insult and injury offered to you, to be the motives that have engaged me to address you.

I am no further concerned in anything affecting *America*, than any one of you; and when liberty leaves it, I can quit it much more conveniently than most of you: But while Divine Providence, that gave me existence in a land of freedom, permits my head to think, my lips to speak, and my hand to move, I shall so highly and gratefully value the blessing received as to take care that my silence and inactivity shall not give my implied assent to any act, degrading my brethren and myself from the birthright, wherewith heaven itself *"hath made us free."*

Sorry I am to learn that there are some few persons who shake their heads with solemn motion, and pretend to wonder, what can be the meaning of these letters. *"Great Britain,"* they say, "is too powerful to contend with; she is determined to oppress us; it is in vain to speak of right on one side, when there is power on the other; when we are strong enough to resist we shall attempt it; but now we are not strong enough, and therefore we had better be quiet; it signifies nothing to convince us that our

rights are invaded when we cannot defend them; and if we should get into riots and tumults about the late act, it will only draw down heavier displeasure upon us."

What can such men design? What do their grave observations amount to, but this—"that these colonies, totally regardless of their liberties, should commit them, with humble resignation, to *chance, time,* and the tender mercies of *ministers.*"

Are these men ignorant that usurpations, which might have been successfully opposed at first, acquire strength by continuance, and thus become irresistible? Do they condemn the conduct of these colonies, concerning the *Stamp Act?* Or have they forgot its successful issue? Should the colonies at that time, instead of acting as they did, have trusted for relief to the fortuitous events of futurity? If it is needless "to speak of rights" now, it was as needless then. If the behavior of the colonies was prudent and glorious then, and successful too; it will be equally prudent and glorious to act in the same manner now, if our rights *are* equally invaded, and may be as successful. Therefore it becomes necessary to inquire whether "our rights are invaded." To talk of "defending" them, as if they could be no otherwise "defended" than by arms, is as much out of the way, as if a man having a choice of several roads to reach his journey's end, should prefer the worst, for no other reason, but because it *is* the worst.

As to "riots and tumults," the gentlemen who are so apprehensive of them, are much mistaken, if they think that grievances cannot be redressed without such assistance.

I will now tell the gentlemen, what is "the meaning of these letters." The meaning of them is, to convince the people of these colonies that they are at this moment exposed to the most imminent dangers; and to persuade them immediately, vigorously, and unanimously, to exert themselves in the most firm, but most peaceable manner, for obtaining relief.

The cause of *liberty* is a cause of too much dignity to be sullied by turbulence and tumult. It ought to be maintained in a manner suitable to her nature. Those who engage in it, should breathe a sedate, yet fervent spirit, animating them to actions of prudence, justice, modesty, bravery, humanity and magnanimity.

To such a wonderful degree were the ancient *Spartans*, as brave and free a people as ever existed, inspired by this happy temperature of soul, that rejecting even in their battles the use of trumpets and other instruments for exciting heat and rage, they marched up to scenes of havoc, and horror, with the sound of flutes, to the tunes of which their steps kept pace—"exhibiting," as *Plutarch* says, "at once a terrible and delightful fight, and proceeding with a deliberate valor, full of hope and good assurance, as if some divinity had sensibly assisted them."

I hope, my dear countrymen, that you will, in every colony, be upon your guard against those who may at any time endeavor to stir you up, under pretenses of patriotism, to any measures disrespectful to our Sovereign, and our mother country. Hot, rash, disorderly proceedings, injure the reputation of the people as to wisdom, valor, and virtue, without procuring them the least benefit. I pray GOD that he may be pleased to inspire you and your posterity, to the latest ages, with a spirit of which I have an idea, that I find a difficulty to express. To express it in the best manner I can, I mean a spirit that shall so guide you that it will be impossible to determine whether an *American's* character is most distinguishable for his loyalty to his Sovereign, his duty to his mother country, his love of freedom, or his affection for his native soil.

Every government at some time or other falls into wrong measures. These may proceed from mistake or passion. But every such measure does not dissolve the obligation between the governors and the governed. The mistake may be corrected; the passion may subside. It is the duty of the governed to endeavor to rectify the mistake, and to appease the passion. They have not at first any other right, than to represent their grievances, and to pray for redress, unless an emergency is so pressing as not to allow time for receiving an answer to their applications, which rarely happens. If their applications are disregarded, then that kind of *opposition* becomes justifiable which can be made without breaking the laws or disturbing the public peace. This conflicts in the *prevention of the oppressors reaping advantage from their oppressions*, and not in their punishment. For experience may teach them what reason did not; and harsh methods cannot be proper until milder ones have failed.

If at length it becomes Undoubted that an inveterate resolution is formed to annihilate the liberties of the governed, the *English* history affords frequent examples of resistance by force. What particular circumstances will in any future case justify such resistance can never be ascertained till they happen. Perhaps it may be allowable to say generally, that it never can be justifiable until the people are Fully Convinced that any further submission will be destructive to their happiness.

When the appeal is made to the sword, highly probable is it, that the punishment will exceed the offense; and the calamities attending on war outweigh those preceding it. These considerations of justice and prudence, will always have great influence with good and wise men.

To these reflections on this subject, it remains to be added, and ought for ever to be remembered, that resistance, in the case of colonies against their mother country, is extremely different from the resistance of a people against their prince. A nation may change their king, or race of kings, and, retaining their ancient form of government, be gainers by changing. Thus *Great Britain*, under the illustrious house of *Brunswick*, a house that seems to flourish for the happiness of mankind, has found a felicity unknown in the reigns of the *Stuarts*. But if once we are separated from our mother country, what new form of government shall we adopt, or where shall we find another *Britain* to supply our loss? Torn from the body, to which we are united by religion, liberty, laws, affections, relation, language and commerce, we must bleed at every vein.

In truth—the prosperity of these provinces is founded in their dependence on *Great Britain*; and when she returns to her "old good humor, and her old good nature," as Lord *Clarendon* expresses it, I hope they will always think it their duty and interest, as it most certainly will be, to promote her welfare by all the means in their power.

We cannot act with too much caution in our disputes. Anger produces anger; and differences, that might be accommodated by kind and respectful behavior, may, by imprudence, be enlarged to an incurable rage. In quarrels between countries, as well as in those between individuals, when they have risen to a certain height, the first cause of dissension is no longer remembered, the minds of the parties being wholly engaged in recollecting and resenting the mutual expressions of their dislike. When feuds have reached that fatal point, all considerations of reason and equity vanish; and a blind fury governs, or rather confounds all things. A people no longer regards their interest, but the gratification of their wrath. The sway of the *Cleons and Clodiuses*, the designing and detectable flatterers of the *prevailing passion*, becomes confirmed. Wise and good men in vain oppose the storm, and may think themselves fortunate, if, in attempting to preserve their ungrateful fellow citizens, they do not ruin themselves. Their *prudence* will be called *baseness*; their *moderation* will be called guilt; and if their virtue does not lead them to destruction, as that of many other great and excellent persons has done, they may survive to receive from their expiring country the mournful glory of her acknowledgment, that their counsels, if regarded, would have saved her.

The constitutional modes of obtaining relief are those which I wish to see pursued on the present occasion; that is, by petitions of our assemblies, or where they are not permitted to meet, of the people, to the powers that can afford us relief.

We have an excellent prince, in whose good dispositions toward us we may confide. We have a generous, sensible and humane nation, to whom we may apply. They may be deceived. They may, by artful men, be provoked to anger against us. I cannot believe they will be cruel and unjust; or that their anger will be implacable. Let us behave like dutiful children who have received unmerited blows from a beloved parent. Let us complain to our parent; but let our complaints speak at the same time the language of affliction and veneration.

If, however, it shall happen, by an unfortunate course of affairs, that our applications to his Majesty and the parliament for redress, prove ineffectual, let us then take *another step*, by withholding from *Great Britain* all the advantages she has been used to receive from us. Then let us try, if our ingenuity, industry, and frugality, will not give weight to our remonstrances. Let us all be united with one spirit, in one cause. Let us invent—let us work—let us save—let us, continually, keep up our claim, and incessantly repeat our complaints—But, above all, let us implore the protection of that infinitely good and gracious being, "by whom kings reign, and princes decree justice."

Nil desperandum.

Nothing is to be despaired of.

A Farmer

GLOSSARY

benevolence: kindness and generosity

"Cleons and Clodiuses": A reference to Cleon, an Athenian general presented in classical histories as an opponent of democracy and Clodius, a populist politician during the last years of the Roman Republic.

design: to plan

"In vain": hopeless

Plutarch (45 CE-120 CE): Greek biographer who lived

prince: the King

Document Analysis

Dickinson begins the first letter describing his background and current situation, emphasizing his broad education and describing his economic position. Dickinson is careful to present himself as having sufficient wealth and being "undisturbed by worldly hopes or fears." He is cultivating an image of being "disinterested" in the sense that he has no real financial stake in the debates over colonial policy and taxation, unlike merchants or business owners. Thus, he is setting himself up to the reader as someone who can approach these issues from a philosophical viewpoint rather than an opinion shaded by monetary concerns. He also establishes that he values "humanity and liberty" and believes that "any honest man" should present his opinions about political issues concerning threats to liberty. Even though that person may think they have little influence, their words may have a greater effect than they can imagine.

All of that is a prelude to the fourth paragraph, in which Dickinson declares he is offering his opinions on the recent controversies, in part because he has been unsatisfied with the writings that have appeared from those who he thought to be "much better qualified" to comment on current events. He then, in the next paragraph, moves into the main issue of this letter. Despite all the colonial concern over the Stamp Act, Dickinson is surprised that the same attention was not paid to Parliament suspending the colonial legislature of New York. Dickinson recounts the events surrounding New York's reaction to the Quartering Act of 1765. He acknowledges that he thinks New York should have complied more more fully with the law (as other colonies did) but regardless of New York's actions, Parliament's response is "pernicious to American freedom."

Dickinson explains the position taken by the New York legislature. If Parliament does have the authority to force compliance with the quartering act, then it is indeed a form of "tax." He then asks how this is any different from the Stamp Act, which produced such more opposition from American colonists. The only difference, he explained, is that the Quartering Act required colonists to spend money to support troops rather than paying a direct tax to the government. Dickinson then addresses the question of whether or not New York had the right to "refuse submission to that act." If they had the right to do so (and, in Dickinson's words "no American" would disagree with that right) then Parliament, logically, had no right to force them to comply with it. Parliament, however, did punish New York by suspending its "privilege of legislation. If Parliament can do this, Dickinson basically asks, is there nothing than they can do?

Dickinson then notes that an additional concern is that it was Parliament that suspended the legislature of New York, not the King. The idea that the colonies are subject to the authority of Parliament rather than the King that issued the charters creating the colonies

is a new and troubling development for Dickinson. It is just as alarming as if soldiers had been placed on the streets to compel obedience. He closes this first letter by noting that two colonial assemblies have completely ignored this situation. While he does not want "inflammatory measures," it would be appropriate for more Americans to voice their concerns about what happened to the political rights of the people of New York.

Letter III begins with Dickinson expressing gratitude for the positive reaction to his previous letters and asserts that he knows that he knows other Americans are as concerned as he is about the current state of the American colonies. He is, however, worried about those who thing that Britain is "too powerful to contend with" and that it is hopeless to express those concerns about the relationship between the colonies and the motherland and warn against "riots and tumults" that might lead to a losing confrontation with Britain. Dickinson, however, argues that if violations of the colonies rights and liberties are not opposed whenever they occur, they can never be opposed. This might, unfortunately, involve the "assistance" of "riots and tumults."

At this point, Dickinson turns to the broader "meaning of these letters." It is, simply that, regardless of what some colonists may think, the actions of Parliament against the colonies—such as the suspension of the New York legislature—are serious violations and need to be resisted as in a firm, but "peaceable" way. At the same time, Dickinson warns his readers to be wary of those who would stir up ideas and actions that are actually treasonable ("disrespectful to our Sovereign and out mother country"). These will do more harm than good. Liberty, he explains, is virtuous and dignified and must be " be maintained in a manner suitable to her nature." Every government, Dickinson argues, makes mistakes. These mistakes do not "dissolve the obligation" of subjects to the government. Instead, everyone must work together to fix these mistakes until that is no longer possible. Dickinson does acknowledge that the history of England has several examples of "resistance by force" to tyranny. However, that should not be the first step—the consequences are too great.

In the closing paragraphs, Dickinson reiterates that he believes the peaceful, "constitutional modes of obtaining relief" are sufficient at the moment. He praises the king and the mother country but also asserts that the citizens of the colonies have a duty to present their concerns.

Essential Themes

These two letters lay out the arguments that would be part and parcel of the American colonial cause throughout the crises of the 1760s and 1770s. Here, Dickinson makes the case for the sovereignty and independence of the colonial legislative assemblies, drawing attention to Parliamentary attacks on these institutions at a time when most colonial activists were most concerned with the more overtly financial repercussions of taxes like the Stamp Act. Dickinson argues that the Quartering Act was just as much a tax as the Stamp Act and warns that if Parliament took upon itself the authority to coerce New York to comply with the "tax," what else would it feel empowered to do?

In the third letter, Dickinson presented the justification not only for alarm and concern over Britain's actions but also the need for and appropriateness of resistance to those actions. Dickinson walks a fine line as he promotes the importance of peaceful, rational protest and the inevitability and utility of "riot and tumult" in these proceedings. Dickinson's deep understanding of and respect for the supremacy of legislative bodies—particularly the legislative assemblies of the colonies—underlay both of these letters and prefigure the coming conflict with Britain over Parliament's increasingly overbearing policies.

——*Aaron Gulyas, MA*

Bibliography and Additional Reading

Calvert, Jane E. (July 2007). "Liberty Without Tumult: Understanding the Politics of John Dickinson". *The Pennsylvania Magazine of History and Biography*. Philadelphia: Historical Society of Pennsylvania. CXXXI (3): 233–62.

——. *Quaker Constitutionalism and the Political Thought of John Dickinson*. (Cambridge and New York: Cambridge University Press, 2008).

Flower, Milton E. *John Dickinson – Conservative Revolutionary*. (Charlottesville, Virginia: University Press of Virginia, 1983).

Munroe, John A. *Philadelawareans*. (Newark, Delaware: University of Delaware Press, 2004).

■ Boston Non-Importation Agreement

Date: 1768
Authors: Merchants and Traders of Boston
Genre: Public Declaration

Summary Overview

On August 1, 1768, some sixty merchants signed the Boston Non-Importation Agreement in opposition to Parliament's ongoing attempts to levy taxes on the American colonies. In a town meeting in Boston, merchants and traders agreed to boycott goods that were subject to England's Townshend Revenue Act until the duties (taxes) imposed on those goods were repealed. Some critical supplies, such as salt, hemp, and duck, were exempt from the boycott. Within two weeks, all but sixteen of Boston's shopkeepers, traders, and merchants had joined the effort. Tradesmen and craftsmen soon followed, since the protest would encourage their business. Within weeks and months, most of the major cities and many of the colonies subscribed to the non-importation movement. As in other areas, Boston led the way in fomenting opposition and protest to Parliament's taxing measures. The Boston Non-Importation Agreement of 1768 reflected the heated debate between the American colonists and Great Britain over the issue of Parliament's authority to tax the colonies. Initially an effort undertaken by merchants and traders to protest the passage by Parliament of the Townshend Revenue Act, which imposed new duties on goods imported by the colonists, the agreement to refuse to import those items until the duties were repealed ignited similar protests up and down the eastern seaboard.

Defining Moment

The Townshend Revenue Act, which imposed duties on a variety of goods, including tea, paper, glass, salt, coal, and fishhooks, among many others, represented an exercise of this broad authority. Unlike the Stamp Act, which triggered outrage in the colonies with its stated goal of raising revenue to pay the debt incurred during the French and Indian War, the purpose of the Townshend Revenue Act was to raise funds to provide for the maintenance and salaries of judges and governors. The act was met initially with acquiescence, but it soon produced a storm of protest and indignation among the colonists.

The implementation of the Townshend Revenue Act on November 20, 1767, drew virtually no criticism in the colonies. Some observed that the colonists could hardly protest these duties when they had acquiesced in the duties imposed a year earlier by the Molasses Act. Benjamin Franklin tried to maintain the distinction between the authority of Parliament to levy external taxes, though not internal ones, which would dictate acquiescence. In the end, the absence of objection was likely attributable to the fact that the Townshend duties applied to a relatively small number of colonists, principally merchants and traders, unlike the Stamp Act taxes, which applied to tens of thousands of people.

The Townshend Act was merely the most recent affront. The Stamp Act had triggered significant resistance because of its threats to the colonists' cherished right of consent. The Declaratory Act, passed on the heels of the rescission of the Stamp Act, renewed Parliament's claim to tax the colonists, a claim that the colonists bitterly rejected. The New York Restraining Act suspended the authority of the New York Assembly until it appropriated funds to support the Quartering Act, which required the colonies to provide money to support English troops quartered in America. The colonists resented these measures as encroaching on their rights to representation and consent and to tax themselves.

Author Biographies

It is not possible to identify the author or authors of the Boston Non-Importation Agreement of August 1, 1768. Some sixty merchants and traders signed the agreement on the day of its adoption. The agreement was perhaps inspired by the widely read and influential newspaper letters authored by a "Farmer," known to be John Dickinson, a lawyer in Pennsylvania, whose powers of analysis exposed the frailties of the Townshend Revenue Act duties, which were the object of protest. Opposition and protest, particularly in the form of non-importation agreements, might never have emerged had it not been for the fiery writings of John Dickinson and his famous "Letters from a Farmer." Dickinson's letters to newspapers, each signed "A Farmer," were possibly more influential than any contemporary political document other than Thomas Paine's *Common Sense*. In reaction to the Townshend Revenue Act, Dickinson penned twelve weekly letters that were published initially in the *Pennsylvania Chronicle* in early December of 1767 and in more than two dozen additional papers throughout the colonies. He argued that the duties were unconstitutional because Parliament lacked authority to tax the colonists, who were not represented in that body and, consequently, had not consented to be taxed. After authoring the first of his protest letters, he wrote to James Otis, a member of the Massachusetts House of Representatives, to complain about the violation of colonial liberties wrought by the Townshend Act. Otis was moved to act and led the assembly in the passage of a petition to the king to protest the Townshend duties. That petition persuaded other colonial assemblies to follow suit, and soon the city of Boston approved the Non-Importation Agreement.

HISTORICAL DOCUMENT

August 1, 1768

The merchants and traders in the town of Boston having taken into consideration the deplorable situation of the trade, and the many difficulties it at present labours under on account of the scarcity of money, which is daily increasing for want of the other remittances to discharge our debts in Great Britain, and the large sums collected by the officers of the customs for duties on goods imported; the heavy taxes levied to discharge the debts contracted by the government in the late war; the embarrassments and restrictions laid on trade by several late acts of parliament; together with the bad success of our cod fishery, by which our principal sources of remittance are like to be greatly diminished, and we thereby rendered unable to pay the debts we owe the merchants in Great Britain, and to continue the importation of goods from thence; We, the subscribers, in order to relieve the trade under those discouragements, to promote industry, frugality, and economy, and to discourage luxury, and every kind of extravagance, do promise and engage to and with each other as follows:

First, That we will not send for or import from Great Britain, either upon our own account, or upon commission, this fall, any other goods than what are already ordered for the fall supply.

Secondly, That we will not send for or import any kind of goods or merchandize from Great Britain, either on our own account, or on commissions, or any otherwise, from the 1st of January 1769, to the 1st of January 1770, except salt, coals, fish hooks and lines, hemp, and duck bar lead and shot, woolcards and card wire.

Thirdly, That we will not purchase of any factor, or others, any kind of goods imported from Great Britain, from January 1769, to January 1770.

Fourthly, That we will not import, on our own account, or on commissions or purchase of any who shall import from any other colony in America, from January 1769, to January 1770, any tea, glass, paper, or other goods commonly imported from Great Britain.

Fifthly, That we will not, from and after the 1st of January 1769, import into this province any tea, paper, glass, or painters colours, until the act imposing duties on those articles shall be repealed.

In witness whereof, we have hereunto set our hands, this first day of August, 1768.

GLOSSARY

card wire: very fine steel wire used in a brush for the purpose of combing cotton wool

duck bar lead and shot: a bar of lead converted into shot for hunting ducks

hemp: the tough, coarse fiber of the cannabis plant used to make cordage or ropes, especially for ropes used in the rigging of ships

woolcards: wire-toothed brushes, similar to a dog brush, used to disentangle textile fiber; especially used for carding woo

Document Analysis

The Boston Non-Importation Agreement is a relatively brief, straightforward statement of intent to boycott goods and products subject to duties imposed by the Townshend Revenue Act. An understanding of the audience for this brief, but significant document, is crucial to understanding its approach. The Boston Non-Importation Agreement was aimed directly at Parliament. The purpose of the agreement was to persuade Parliament to repeal the Townshend Act duties, and until members did repeal the act, the many goods that were subjected to its taxes would not be imported by Boston merchants and traders. The Boston businessmen were, of course, shrewd enough to believe that their English counterparts would have an interest in persuading Parliament to repeal the act as a means of preventing damage to colonial trade, which was an important facet of their economic welfare. As such, the traders, merchants, and shopkeepers in England formed a target of the Non-Importation Agreement.

The American population represented an audience for the Boston agreement as well. The announcement of a boycott of British goods would enjoy a greater prospect for success if the boycott were embraced not only in Boston but also in New England and throughout the colonies. As a business document, the agreement was intended to engender support among merchants, traders, shopkeepers, craftsmen, and others who would, in one way or another, enjoy the fruits of a successful boycott. As a political document, its aim was wide, and it was intended to be a model worthy of emulation by leaders throughout the colonies who harbored the same interests and concerns that motivated those who signed the agreement.

The agreement, signed by sixty "Merchants and Traders in the Town of Boston," signals the intention of its signers to refrain from purchasing various products and supplies until the duties are repealed by Parliament. The bold authors stated that "we will not, from and after the 1st of January 1769, import into this province any tea, paper, glass, or painters colours, until the act imposing duties on those articles shall be repealed." Further, the signers agreed not to import "any kind of goods or merchandize from Great Britain...from the 1st of January 1769, to the 1st of January 1770, except salt, coals, fish hooks and lines, hemp, and duck bar lead and shot, woolcards and card wire."

It is difficult to imagine a more lean statement of a city's policy. Unadorned by moving, passionate, and transcendent lines like those found in the Declaration of Independence, and lacking the fiery rhetoric of works from the pens of writers such as Patrick Henry and James Otis, the Non-Importation Agreement is marked by its simplicity. It was, in a word, a business agreement and, as such, it did not require elegance and peroration. Its aim was emphatic.

The decision to employ a boycott, a time-tested method of obtaining changes and concessions, reflected several factors. First, it expressed the views of the Boston signers that the duties were burdensome. The taxes did not impose a burden on tens of thousands of colonists, as had the Stamp Act, but it was a burden nonetheless on merchants, traders, and shopkeepers. Second, it gave vent to the increasing frustration of businessmen caused by the increased restrictions on colonial trade. Third, the restrictions were snuffing out the prospects of merchants to enjoy prosperity. In short, they viewed the restrictions as harassing and intended, by design, to shackle colonial aspirations. Fourth, it reflected the emphatic belief, among a growing number of colonists, and most recently given persuasive articulation by John Dickinson, that Parliament lacked authority to tax the colonists. Indeed, as Dickinson and others had argued, the imposition of taxes violated the constitutional rights of the American colonists as English subjects. Fifth, the offense against their rights, not merely in the form of taxation but also manifested in the threat to their independence to determine the support and salaries of local judges and governors, suggested a broad conspiracy against their liberties.

Essential Themes

The statement in the Non-Importation Agreement that the boycott would endure until the Townshend duties were repealed marks a firm intent to redraw the terms of trade between Great Britain and the American colonies. In a word, it represented a new contract. The Boston Non-Importation Agreement reflected the boiling anger of colonists, offended by what they perceived to be deep threats to their political and economic liberties. The agreement, if not always faithfully followed, provided an occasion for intercolonial union in opposing and protesting Great Britain's measures. They reflected earlier boycott efforts aimed at the effects of the Stamp Act. As a consequence, the non-importation agreements represented a continuation of resistance tactics, and they afforded an opportunity to the colonists to contemplate their loss of confidence in English rule. Great Britain's colonial policy was under siege, and the opportunities for repairing the strained relations became more and more remote. The willingness of the colonists to assert their interests and their rights in a more assertive manner was likely to continue. And the level of assertion, sparked by the writings of men like John Dickinson, was likely to embolden others and, eventually, a nation.

———*David Gray Adler, PhD*

Bibliography and Additional Reading

Knollenberg, Bernhard. *Growth of the American Revolution: 1766–1775.* (New York: Free Press, 1975).

Maier, Pauline. *From Resistance to Revolution: Colonial Radicals and the Development of American Opposition to Britain, 1765–1776.* (New York: Alfred A. Knopf, 1972).

Miller, John C. *Origins of the American Revolution.* (Stanford, California: Stanford University Press, 1959).

Morgan, Edmund S. *The Birth of the Republic, 1763–89,* rev. ed. (Chicago: University of Chicago Press, 1977).

Thomas, Peter D. G. *The Townshend Duties Crisis: The Second Phase of the American Revolution, 1767–1773.* (Oxford: Oxford University Press, 1987).

■ Samuel Adams Writing as Candidus

Date: 1771
Author: Samuel Adams
Genre: Pamphlet

Summary Overview

Samuel Adams's emergence as a prominent crafter of political documents began in 1764, when Britain placed direct taxes on Americans. From 1764 on, Adams consistently labored to persuade his fellow colonists to resist Britain's efforts to reshape the empire. He supported using economic boycotts to oppose the Stamp Act (1765) and the Townshend duties (1767). He seethed when Britain introduced troops into Boston in 1768 and soon decided that only independence could protect Americans' rights. Once the Revolutionary War began in 1775, Adams gave special attention to fashioning and defending central and state governments that were approved by the people and that protected their liberties. In his fifth "Candidus" essay, written for the *Boston Gazette* in 1771, Adams specifically decries the Stamp Act, which required that anything formally written or printed must appear on stamped paper dispensed by English agents, and urges his fellow citizens to take action against it.

Defining Moment

Responding to the colonists' economic boycott, Parliament repealed the Stamp Act on March 18, 1766. Parliament, however, passed the Declaratory Act the same day. It said that Parliament had and always had had the right to bind the colonies in all cases whatsoever. By 1766 the issue was less about the government's need for revenue than it was about establishing a clear precedent for such taxation. If the colonists voluntarily paid *any* tax it levied, Parliament could cite that tax as precedent, as justification for placing additional taxes on the colonists. That is why Adams applauded using an economic boycott against the 1768 Townshend duties. The effort was partially successful. In March 1770, Parliament decided to repeal every Townshend duty except one. By retaining the tea duty, Parliament effectively issued a second Declaratory Act. Given his concern about precedents, Adams wanted the boycott continued until *all* the taxes were repealed.

In the spring of 1770 there was reason to believe that Americans would be particularly concerned about protecting their rights. Responding to Boston's resistance to its imperial policies, in 1768 Britain sent soldiers to police, not protect, Boston. From the day troops arrived on October 1, Bostonians feared they would kill civilians. It happened on March 5, 1770, when British soldiers fired into a crowd. Three civilians were killed; eight were wounded, and two of them later died. Although it seemed that resistance to Britain would escalate in the wake of this "Boston Massacre," just the opposite happened. The boycott collapsed; the resistance movement withered.

Adams employed newspapers, the American media of the eighteenth century, to try to awaken his fellow colonists from their political lethargy. He adopted the clever pen name "CANDIDUS" for one of the many series of essays he produced for the *Boston Gazette*. The fifth "CANDIDUS" essay appeared on August 19, 1771.

Author Biography

Samuel Adams was born in Boston on September 16, 1722. He entered the Massachusetts House of Representatives in 1765. He became a member of the Continental Congress in 1774, signed the Declaration of Independence, and was an architect of the Articles of Confederation. He helped draft Massachusetts's 1780 Constitution. Upon retiring from Congress in 1782, he served as a state senator until becoming Massachusetts lieutenant governor in 1789. He attended the 1788 Massachusetts convention that ratified the proposed U.S. Constitution. Adams became governor upon the death of John Hancock in 1793 and was elected governor in his own right in 1794. He served as governor until 1797, when he retired from public life. He died in Boston on October 2, 1803.

Adams's lengthy political career demonstrates that eighteenth-century American politicians need not be great orators. It was his 1764 written instructions to Boston's representatives, not speeches, that helped propel Adams into the Massachusetts House. There he became famous for crafting powerful documents. The documents that Adams fashioned to attack British policies reveal a skilled politician using language to try to awaken people to what Adams once called the threat of the lurking serpent. His writings, especially those dealing with American government, show a pragmatic politician at work. Adams accepted the old adage that "politics is the art of compromise." He embraced compromise in part because he believed humans are fallible; thus, even their best political formulations will be flawed. Nevertheless, his pragmatism was always tempered by a guiding principle: One must steadfastly defend the people's natural and constitutional rights.

HISTORICAL DOCUMENT

For my own part, I cannot but at present be of the opinion, and "*I have reason to believe*" that my opinion is well founded, that the measures of the British administration of the colonies, are still as disgustful and *odious* to the inhabitants of this respectable metropolis in general, as they ever have been: And I will venture further to add, that nothing, in my opinion, can convey a more unjust idea of the spirit of a true American, than to suppose he would even compliment, much less make an *adulating address* to any person sent here to trample on the Rights of his Country; or that he would ever condescend to kiss the hand which is ready prepared to rivet his own fetters—There are among us, it must be confess'd, needy expectants and dependents; and a few others of sordid and base minds, form'd by nature to bend and crouch even to *little* great men:—But whoever thinks, that by the most refined art and assiduous application of the most ingenious *political* oculist, the "public eye" can yet look upon the chains which are forg'd for them, or upon those detestable men who are employ'd to put them on, without abhorrence and indignation, are very much mistaken—I only wish that my Countrymen may be upon their guard against being led by the artifices of the tools of Administration, into any indiscreet measures, from whence they may take occasion to give such a coloring. …

We cannot surely have forgot the accursed designs of a most detestable set of men, to destroy the Liberties of America as with one blow, by the Stamp-Act; nor the noble and successful efforts we then made to divert the impending stroke of ruin aimed at ourselves and our posterity. The Sons of Liberty on the 14th of August 1765, a Day which ought to be for ever remembered in America, animated with a zeal for their country then upon the brink of destruction, and resolved, at once to save her, or like *Samson*, to perish in the ruins, exerted themselves with such distinguished vigor, as made the house of *Dogon* to shake from its very foundation; and the hopes of the *lords of the Philistines* even while *their hearts were merry*, and when they were anticipating the joy of plundering this continent, were at that very time buried in the pit they had digged. The *People* shouted; and their shout was heard to the distant end of this Continent. In each Colony they deliberated and resolved, and every *Stampman* trembled; and swore by his Maker, that he would never execute a commission which he had so *infamously* received.

We cannot have forgot, that at the very Time when the stamp-act was repealed, another was made in which the Parliament of Great-Britain declared, that they had right and authority to make any laws whatever binding on his Majesty's subjects in America— How far this declaration can be consistent with the freedom of his Majesty's subjects in America, let any one judge who pleases—In consequence of such right and authority claim'd, the commons of Great Britain very soon fram'd a bill and sent it up to the Lords, wherein they pray'd his Majesty to accept of *their grant* of such a part as they were then pleas'd, by virtue of the right and authority *inherent* in them to make, of the property of his Majesty's subjects in America, by a duty upon paper, glass, painter's colours and tea. And altho' these duties are in part repeal'd, there remains enough to answer the purpose of administration, which was *to fix the precedent*. We remember the policy of Mr. Grenville, who would have been content for the present with *a pepper corn establish'd as a revenue in America*: If therefore we are voluntarily silent while the single duty on tea is continued, or do any act, however innocent, *simply considered*, which may be construed by the tools of administration, (some of whom appear to be fruitful in invention) as an acquiescence in the measure, we are in extreme hazard; if ever we are so distracted as to consent to it, we are undone.

Nor can we ever forget the indignity and abuse with which America in general, and this province and town in particular, have been treated, by the servants & officers of the crown, for making a manly resistance to the arbitrary measures of administration, in the representations that have been made to the men in power at home, who have always been dispos'd to believe every word as infallible truth. For opposing a *threatned Tyranny*, we have been not only called, but in effect adjudged *Rebels & Traitors* to the best of Kings, who has sworn to maintain and defend the *Rights* and *Liberties* of his Subjects—We have been represented as inimical to our fellow subjects in Britain, because we have boldly asserted those Rights and Liberties, wherewith they, as Subjects, are made free.—When we complain'd of this injurious treatment; when we petition'd, and remonstrated our grievances: What was the Consequence? Still further indignity; and finally a formal invasion of this town by a fleet and army in the memorable year 1768.

GLOSSARY

acquiescence in the measure: the act of giving in to a policy

Candidus: a pen name making reference to a Latin word meaning "clear"

Dogon: a deity, sometimes known as Dagon, worshipped by enemies of Israel in the Old Testament

duty: tax

Mr. Grenville: the British prime minister George Grenville (1712–1770)

a pepper corn establish'd as revenue: a very small tax

rivet: fasten or attach

Samson: judge or leader of Israel, known for his physical strength, whose story is told in the biblical book of Judges

sordid and base: scandalous and low-minded

Stampman: tax collector for the British in colonial America

Document Analysis

Adams begins "CANDIDUS" by asserting that the actions of the British government toward its colonies—particularly Massachusetts—are "as disgustful and odious" to the people as at any other time. He goes on to question the "spirit" of those American people who would "complement" or "make an adulating address" to British officials whose goal is to "trample on the Rights of his Country." He ends the first paragraph by lamenting that his fellow colonists are 'on their guard" against efforts to limit their freedoms.

He continues, in the second paragraph, to remind colonists of the the British officials (a "detestable set of men") who had arrived to enforce the Stamp Act (and, in Adams's words, "destroy the Liberties of America") and the efforts undertaken by groups us as the Sons of Liberty to fight them. August 14, 1765 refers to the day on which members of the Sons of Liberty gathered at the so-called "liberty tree" Boston Common and on it hung an effigy of Andrew Oliver, the tax commissioner for Boston. Following this display a mob assaulted Oliver's home as well as his office and, eventually, decapitated and burned the effigy. He compares these actions to those of Biblical heroes such as Samson and equates the activities of the Sons of Liberty to being the will of the populace at large ("the People shouted"). This display of public anger struck fear into the hearts of the officials, Adams claims.

In the next paragraph, he reminds readers that even though Parliament repealed the Stamp Act, the Declaratory Act indicated their contempt for American freedoms. Following this, Parliament levied taxes on a number of taxes on items such as tea, paper, glass, and paint ("painter's colors"), collectively known as the Townshend Duties. Even though some of the taxes had been repealed, Adams asserts that if colonists "are voluntarily silent" on the issue of the remaining tax (on tea), if they consent to pay it, then the cause of freedom would be "undone."

In the final paragraph, Adams points out the many ways in which British officials have assaulted "America in general, and this province and town in particular" because they have resisted Britain's "arbitrary measures." He takes issue with those who protest "threatened tyranny" as being treasonous or rebellions. Rather, the Americans were defending their rights and liberties—something the King himself had sworn to do. He closes by lamenting that their efforts to defend their rights were answered not with recognition of their liberties but, rather, with a invasion of troops and naval forces.

Essential Themes

One of the key themes in Adams's writing is his enthusiasm for and promotion of direct action by the colonists. He praises an influential Boston crowd action of August 14, 1765, that forced the resignation of the man scheduled to distribute stamps in Massachusetts under the Stamp Act. "The *People* shouted; and their shout was heard to the distant end of this Continent." All true Americans should, says Adams, remember that these heroes were "animated with a zeal for their country then upon the brink of destruction, and resolved,

at once to save her." The message is clear: People can protect their rights by taking bold, direct action.

Adams also underscores the importance of precedent. If the people "are voluntarily silent while the single duty on tea is continued," then "we are in extreme hazard; if ever we are so distracted as to consent to it, we are undone." By alluding to Britain's responses to earlier petitions, Adams calls for bolder action than petitioning: "When we petition'd, and remonstrated our grievances: What was the Consequence? Still further indignity; and finally a formal invasion of this town by a fleet and army in the memorable year 1768." In spite of such arguments and Adams's continuing efforts, the resistance movement did not again gain real strength until Parliament made the mistake of passing the Tea Act of May 1773, which raised the specter that Great Britain would destroy American business through the creation of monopolies.

———*John K. Alexander, PhD,*
with additional material by Aaron Gulyas, PhD

and Additional Reading

Fowler, William M., Jr. *Samuel Adams: Radical Puritan.* (New York: Longman, 1997).

Puls, Mark. *Samuel Adams: Father of the American Revolution.* (New York: Palgrave Macmillan, 2006).

Stoll, Ira. *Samuel Adams: A Life.* (New York: The Free Press, 2008).

Thomas, Peter D. G. *The Townshend Duties Crisis: The Second Phase of the American Revolution, 1767–1773.* (New York: Oxford University Press, 1987).

■ Rules by Which a Great Empire May Be Reduced to a Small One

Date: 1773
Author: Benjamin Franklin
Genre: Essay

Summary Overview

Benjamin Franklin had many facets to his life, of which writing was only one. For most of his lifetime he was physically strong and fit. On sea voyages he would swim in the ocean, circumnavigating the ship on which he was sailing and taking the opportunity to observe sharks and other mysteries of the sea. He was an outdoorsman who had a vigorous life on city streets and in the countryside. But his writings outlived him, and it is through them that he is now best known. He valued clarity in his writing, which has resulted in some misunderstandings about his artistry. Some critics have foolishly insisted that he lacked a poetic sensibility or that he sacrificed art for plainness. A reading of his texts proves both charges to be incorrect. Instances of sharp, powerful metaphorical imagery may be found even in his essays of persuasion, and they are abundant in his writings about the friction between America and Great Britain as well as in those about his hopes for a unified America with a republican government emerging from the Revolutionary War.

Franklin did not always favor an independent America. For many years he urged colonists to remain terms with Great Britain. By 1751 his views had shifted, as evidenced in his satirical essay "Exporting of Felons to the Colonies." In the ensuing years, he worked as a member of the Pennsylvania Assembly and became deeply involved in Revolutionary-era politics. His essay "Rules by Which a Great Empire May Be Reduced to a Small One," published in the journal *Public Advertiser* in September 1773, highlighted the grievances that would be fundamental to provoking the American Revolution.

Defining Moment

In 1773, when Franklin wrote this essay, Great Britain and its thirteen American colonies had been experiencing a contentious relationship for a decade. The British victory in the French and Indian War led to a drastic change in the governance and management of the colonies. Britain levied a series of taxes and import duties on staple goods such as tea, glass, sugar, and other materials in order to reduce the debt incurred during the war (a war which, at least in some British circles, was blamed partially on the colonists). Colonial leaders—particularly those whose business interests were negatively affected by these policy changes—protested in the form of petitions and established boycotts of British goods. In addition to taxation, large numbers of British troops remained quartered in American cities such as Boston. Friction between troops and residents was frequent and, as in the case of the "Boston Massacre" of 1770, sometime led to violence.

At the heart of this conflict was a question of where the British colonies fit within the governmental structure of the Empire. They had been established by charters granted by the monarch, had developed their own forms of representative government and—in their view at least—had survived and thrived with minimal assistance from the mother country. The post 1763 situation saw Parliament (the legislative body of the United Kingdom of Great Britain and Ireland) imposing laws on the colonies without those colonies being directly represented. In response to complaints about this lack of representation, Parliament responded in 1766 with the Declaratory Act, which proclaimed the colonies subject to acts of Parliament "in all cases whatsoever."

Author Biography

Benjamin Franklin (1706-1790) was born in Boston, the son of a candle and soap maker. Franklin claimed to have mastered writing through independent effort of his own as a child; he had only about two years of formal schooling. In his autobiography he often mentions reading and writing as essential to an individual person's success in American society. In his descriptions of his countrymen, he creates an image of them as self-made successes who as early settlers, through their own hard work and risk taking, built a strong society in which even those born into poverty could have a chance to become prosperous. He indeed seems to have believed it his duty to participate in social causes, as he helped

found a fire department, a lending library, and other institutions. He dutifully, though sometimes reluctantly, accepted posts that he had not sought, such as postmaster and delegate to Pennsylvania's legislature.

By the 1750s he was well aware that he was famous and admired, and he took his status seriously, believing that it put him under obligations to sacrifice his leisure time for the sake of public service. When he wrote for publication, he did so knowing that what he wrote would be read in part because it was written by the widely admired Ben Franklin. He also knew that much of the world would judge Americans on the basis of what he himself said and achieved. To the learned peo-ple and political leaders of Europe, he represented the surprises of America and of Americans and was a living example that Americans could equal and even exceed Europeans in learning, in genius, and in achievement.

Within a few years of penning this essay, Franklin would be called upon to represent Pennsylvania at the Second Continental Congress and was instrumental in the debate over declaring independence from Great Britain. During the Revolutionary war he represented the nation-to-be in France, seeking financial, diplomatic, and military aid. Following the war, he was the elder statesman present at the Constitutional Convention in 1787.

HISTORICAL DOCUMENT

I address myself to all ministers who have the management of extensive dominions, which from their very greatness are become troublesome to govern, because the multiplicity of their affairs leaves no time for fiddling.

I. In the first place, gentlemen, you are to consider, that a great empire, like a great cake, is most easily diminished at the edges. Turn your attention, therefore, first to your remotest provinces; that, as you get rid of them, the next may follow in order.

II. That the possibility of this separation may always exist, take special care the provinces are never incorporated with the mother country; that they do not enjoy the same common rights, the same privileges in commerce; and that they are governed by severer laws, all of your enacting, without allowing them any share in the choice of the legislators. By carefully making and preserving such distinctions, you will (to keep to my simile of the cake) act like a wise gingerbread baker, who, to facilitate a division, cuts his dough half through in those places where, when baked, he would have it broken to pieces....

IV. However peaceably your colonies have submitted to your government, shewn their affection to your interests, and patiently borne their grievances; you are to suppose them always inclined to revolt, and treat them accordingly. Quarter troops among them, who by their insolence may provoke the rising of mobs, and by their bullets and bayonets suppress them. By this means, like the husband who uses his wife ill from suspicion, you may in time convert your suspicions into realities.

V. Remote provinces must have Governors and Judges, to represent the Royal Person, and execute everywhere the delegated parts of his office and authority. You ministers know, that much of the strength of government depends on the opinion of the people; and much of that opinion on the choice of rulers placed immediately over them. If you send them wise and good men for governors, who study the interest of the colonists, and advance their prosperity, they will think their King wise and good, and that he wishes the welfare of his subjects. If you send them learned and upright men for Judges, they will think him a lover of justice. This may attach your provinces more to his government. You are therefore to be careful whom you recommend for those offices. If you can find prodigals, who have ruined their fortunes, broken gamesters or stockjobbers, these may do well as governors; for they will probably be rapacious, and provoke the people by their extortions....

VIII. If, when you are engaged in war, your colonies should vie in liberal aids of men and money against the common enemy, upon your simple requisition, and give far beyond their abilities, reflect that a penny taken from them by your power is more honourable to you, than a pound presented by their benevolence; despise therefore their voluntary grants, and resolve to harass them with novel taxes. They will probably complain to your parliaments, that they are taxed by a body in which they have no representative, and that this is contrary to common right. They will petition for redress. Let the Parliaments flout their claims, reject their petitions, refuse even to suffer the reading of them, and treat the petitioners with the utmost contempt. Nothing can have a better effect in producing the alienation proposed; for though many can forgive injuries, none ever forgave contempt....

X. Possibly, indeed, some of them might still comfort themselves, and say, "Though we have no property, we have yet something left that is valuable; we have constitutional liberty, both of person and of conscience. This King, these Lords, and these Commons, who it seems are too remote from us to know us, and feel for us, cannot take from us our Habeas Corpus right, or our right of trial by a jury of our neighbours; they cannot deprive us of the exercise of our religion, alter our ecclesiastical constitution, and compel us to be Papists, if they please, or Mahometans." To annihilate this comfort...And, lest the people should think you cannot possibly go any farther, pass another solemn declaratory act, "that King, Lords, Commons had, hath, and of right ought to have, full power and authority to make statutes of sufficient force and validity to bind the unrepresented provinces IN ALL CASES WHATSOEVER." This will include spiritual with temporal, and, taken together, must operate wonderfully to your purpose; by convincing them, that they are at present under a power something like that spoken of in the scriptures, which can not only kill their bodies, but damn their souls to all eternity, by compelling them, if it pleases, to worship the Devil....

XV. Convert the brave, honest officers of your navy into pimping tide-waiters and colony officers of the customs. Let those, who in time of war fought gallantly in defence of the commerce of their countrymen, in peace be taught to prey upon it. Let them learn to be corrupted by great and real smugglers; but (to shew their diligence) scour with armed boats every bay, harbour, river, creek, cove, or nook throughout the coast of your colonies; stop and detain every coaster, every wood-boat, every fisherman, tumble their cargoes and even their ballast inside out and upside down; and, if a penn'orth of pins is found unentered, let the whole be seized and confiscated....

XIX. Send armies into their country under pretence of protecting the inhabitants; but, instead of garrisoning the forts on their frontiers with those troops, to prevent incursions, demolish those forts, and order the troops into the heart of the country, that the savages may be encouraged to attack the frontiers, and that the troops may be protected by the inhabitants. This will seem to proceed from your ill will or your ignorance, and contribute farther to produce and strengthen an opinion among them, that you are no longer fit to govern them.

GLOSSARY

common right: natural rights, or good behavior according to common sense

despise therefore their voluntary grants: look down on the things they give you freely

ecclesiastical constitution: religious practices

gamesters or stockjobbers: gamblers or corrupt stockbrokers

garrisoning: placing troops in a permanent or semipermanent location

if a penn'orth of pins is found unentered: if a penny's worth of pins (or any other insignificant item) has not been accounted for

Mahometans: Muslims

Papists: Catholics

pimping tide-waiters: dishonest sailors who simply wait for the easiest opportunities to go out to sea

the Royal Person: the king or queen

savages: a reference to Native Americans

shewn: shown

Document Analysis

This satire's itemization of American grievances toward Great Britain is among the best such elaborations written prior to the Declaration of Independence. A comparison of the two documents suggests that the United States owed much to Benjamin Franklin's identifying and explaining why the American colonies were effectively being driven out of the British Empire. Rarely did the author achieve a more powerful phrasing of exactly what angered Americans. The logical consequence of all that Franklin enumerates is revolution. When he wrote this document, presented in the *Public Advertiser* in September 1773, his hopes for a great empire in which Americans were equal to the English still lingered in him, but as a pragmatic man he had come to see himself and other Americans as a people separate from the English.

The satire imagines that there were a set of instructions given to the Earl of Hillsborough (Wills Hill, first Marquess of Downshire), Great Britain's minister in charge of affairs with the American colonies, at the moment he took office. The voice of "Rules by Which a Great Empire May Be Reduced to a Small One" is distinctly Franklin's, written in a robust, direct manner that he may have intended to represent the way liberated Americans should speak. In its bitterness and anger, it echoes "Exporting of Felons to the Colonies." In its detailed accounts of injustices, every American could see expressed with clarity what he or she had in common with other Americans in their desire for liberty and fairness.

Franklin itemizes the Americans' grievances, assigning them Roman numerals from one to twenty. The result is a nuanced work that defies quick reading. The first point is simple enough: To diminish an empire, begin by alienating the outer fringes of the empire. The second point strikes at the heart of Franklin's disap-

pointments with Great Britain. He had long harbored a vision of the British Empire as greater than it was; in this vision the colonies of Great Britain would become integral, equal parts of the empire, with a parliament elected by English subjects equally from former colonies that had become as much a part of the homeland as England itself. He saw in Great Britain's behavior a failure of foresight that was leading to catastrophe, as the colonists were made to feel like aliens rather than fellow countrymen. In the third and fourth points, Franklin notes reasons why colonists are deserving of the respect of the motherland, having built a society themselves, at their own expense and risk, even while showing love and friendship toward Great Britain.

In the fifth through twentieth points, Franklin notes the conduct of Great Britain's government that has pushed Americans into reluctantly believing that their best interests would be served by being a people independent of Great Britain. He notes the broad perception that the justice system imposed by the British government is unfair, with foreign judges, many incompetent or criminals themselves, running the trials of Americans; he notes the misrule and corruption of governors imposed on colonies; he notes the injustice of taxes imposed by a parliament in which the colonies are not represented (and in point ten, in particular, he refers to the Declaratory Act of 1766); he notes that the American people had given much willingly to the defense of the realm.

That the ideas that would be embodied in the Bill of Rights were being promulgated prior to America's Declaration of Independence is well demonstrated in the tenth point, in which Franklin writes that while Americans thought they should be protected by the English constitution, they were being denied such rights as habeas corpus and freedom to choose one's own religion. The phrase "that they are at present under a power something like that spoken of in the scriptures, which can not only kill their bodies, but damn their souls to all eternity, by compelling them, if it pleases, to worship the Devil" draws deeply from American anger and typifies the power of the satire as a whole. The eleventh through fourteenth points expand on the ways in which tax collection has been made odious and the mother country has actively thwarted justice in the colonies. The foolish conduct of Great Britain's government has made Americans an oppressed people.

Essential Themes

A consistent theme in "Rules by Which a Great Empire May Be Reduced to a Small One" is that the rift between the British government and its colonial subjects is largely of Britain's doing. His satirical advice that Britain, if it wants to lose its empire, should ensure that "the provinces are never incorporated with the mother country; that they do not enjoy the same common rights, the same privileges in commerce; and that they are governed by severer laws, all of your enacting, without allowing them any share in the choice of the legislators" succinctly states the political and constitutional issue.

Franklin goes further, however, when he connects this inequitable treatment as being insulting to the honor of colonial troops who fought, died, or otherwise sacrificed to serve the empire in its wars of acquisition (point VIII) and criticizing the increasing presence of British troops on American streets. Britain is treating the American colonies, Franklin seems to imply, more as conquered territory than as a far-flung—but vital—part of the British realm.

Taxation, the enforcement of laws, the fairness of the judicial system, the use of military troops as a police force, and the consistent application of constitutional principles (such as representation in Parliament) are among the most crucial issues, in fact, that would be cited in 1776 as sufficient to justify the separation of the 13 British colonies and the formation of the United States of America. That this declaration did not come until after more than a year of military conflict between motherland and colony only illustrates the depth of the connection between the two lands.

———*Kirk H. Beetz, Professor Emeritus*

Bibliography and Additional Reading

Bailyn, Bernard. *The Ideological Origins of the American Revolution*, Enlarged Edition (New York: Belknap Press, 1992).

Mathews, L. K. "Benjamin Franklin's Plans for a Colonial Union, 1750–1775." *American Political Science Review* 8 (August 1914): 393–412.

Reid, John Phillip. *Constitutional History of the American Revolution, II: The Authority to Tax.* (Madison: University of Wisconsin Press, 1987)

Sheridan, R. (1960). The British Credit Crisis of 1772 and The American Colonies. *The Journal of Economic History*, 20 (2), 161-186.

■ Boston Massacre Oration

Date: 1774
Author: John Hancock
Genre: Speech

Summary Overview

John Hancock's fiery Boston Massacre Oration of 1774, marking the anniversary of the Boston Massacre, reflects the mood of a people transitioning from protesters to Revolutionaries. Four years earlier, British troops stationed in Boston to protect and support colonial agents of the Crown had fired on an angry mob, killing five civilians. In December of 1773, protesters against the British government's monopoly on tea had boarded British ships and thrown their cargo of tea into Boston Harbor. The colonists were painfully distancing themselves from Britain and dissociating being American from being English. It was in this context that Hancock delivered his address. Prefiguring portions of the Declaration of Independence, Hancock characterizes the purpose of government as ensuring the security of the governed and maintaining that the British administration was not abiding by its first principles. He urges the colonists to exert themselves for the "public weal" and to deliver the "oppressed from the iron grasp of tyranny."

Defining Moment

Before two of the Intolerable Acts of 1774 closed the port of Boston and changed the government of Massachusetts, the Boston Tea Party on December 16, 1773, had been one of the most dramatic moments yet in a period filled with drama. Just under three months after the Boston Tea Party, John Hancock, one of the richest men in North America, was scheduled to speak at the annual commemoration of the Boston Massacre. Bostonians had been marking the anniversary with a speech by a leading member of the community since that fateful day of March 5, 1770, when British regulars opened fire on those gathered around them, leaving five dead (including Crispus Attucks, the first African American casualty of the American Revolution). In March 1774, with people still aroused from the Boston Tea Party and waiting the inevitable response from Great Britain, Hancock gave the most important speech of his life up to that time. The speech was to take place at Faneuil Hall, but the immense crowd forced a move to the Old South Meeting House. There

Hancock delivered a riveting speech that was universally recognized as a success.

It was a successful speech, but it was not unique as far as American Revolutionary rhetoric goes. Like others in Massachusetts and throughout the rebellious colonies, Hancock had to deal with the issue of separating himself from a long-standing and proud association with Great Britain. Historians have pointed out that speeches and sermons of the period were characterized by this need to disassociate the colonies from England and being American from being English. This was problematic, since there had been great pride in being English, in contributing to the empire, and in perpetuating English political traditions.

Author Biography

John Hancock was born on January 12, 1737, in Braintree (now Quincy), Massachusetts. In 1745, after his father's death, Hancock moved in with his affluent uncle, Thomas, who lived in Boston. This decision set Hancock's life on a course of wealth and privilege that afforded him the opportunity to be a generous public servant. His wealth and popularity in Boston made him a central figure in the American Revolutionary cause.

Hancock began to work for his uncle in the mid-1750s. He spent the year 1760–1761 in England establishing business networks that no doubt helped when he took over his uncle's business a few years later. As a private businessman, Hancock was at the center of the growing struggle between colonies and Parliament during the 1760s and early 1770s over taxation and trade restrictions and provided funds when necessary. He also served as a leader in an official capacity at both the local and state levels. When the Massachusetts General Court defiantly transformed itself into the Provincial Congress (1774), they chose John Hancock as its president.

Hancock's name seemed always to be part of the Revolutionary controversy, whether it was when the British seized his ship *Liberty* in the late 1760s or when he became a target of British troops on that fateful April day in 1775 when the battles of Lexington and Concord became etched permanently in history, or when he sat as president of the Second Continental Congress and was the first person to sign the Declaration of Independence. In fact, the British monarch perceived Hancock's role to be so central that King George III named him as one of only a few that the king would not pardon when or if the colonists came to their senses.

In 1780 Massachusetts approved its state constitution, and Hancock was elected the first governor of the Commonwealth. Hancock resigned the governorship in 1785 but was reelected to that position two years later and remained in it until his death on October 8, 1793.

HISTORICAL DOCUMENT

The attentive gravity; the venerable appearance of this crowded audience; the dignity which I behold in the countenances of so many in this great assembly; the solemnity of the occasion upon which we have met together, joined to a consideration of the part I am to take in the important business of this day, fill me with an awe hitherto unknown....

I have always, from my earliest youth, rejoiced in the felicity of my fellow-men; and have ever considered it as the indispensable able duty of every member of society to promote, as far as in him lies, the prosperity of every individual, but more especially of the community to which he belongs; and also, as a faithful subject of the State, to use his utmost endeavors to detect, and having detected, strenuously to oppose every traitorous plot which its enemies may devise for its destruction. Security to the persons and properties of the governed is so obviously the design and end of civil government, that to attempt a logical proof of it would be like burning tapers at noonday, to assist the sun in enlightening the world; and it cannot be either virtuous or honorable to attempt to support a government of which this is not the great and principal basis; and it is to the last degree vicious and infamous to attempt to support a government which manifestly tends to render the persons and properties of the governed insecure. Some boast of being friends to government; I am a friend to righteous government, to a government founded upon the principles of reason and justice; but I glory in publicly avowing my eternal enmity to tyranny. Is the present system, which the British administration have adopted for the government of the Colonies, a righteous government—or is it tyranny?... They have declared that they have ever had, and of right ought ever to have, full power to make laws of sufficient validity to bind the Colonies in all cases whatever. They have exercised this pretended right by imposing a tax upon us without our consent; and lest we should show some reluctance at parting with our property, her fleets and armies are sent to enforce their mad pretensions. The town of Boston, ever faithful to the British Crown, has been invested by a British fleet; the troops of George III have crossed the wide Atlantic, not to engage an enemy, but to assist a band of traitors in trampling on the rights and liberties of his most loyal subjects in America—those rights and liberties which, as a father, he ought ever to regard, and as a king, he is bound, in honor, to defend from violation, even at the risk of his own life....

Let not the history of the illustrious house of Brunswick inform posterity that a king, descended from that glorious monarch George II, once sent his British subjects to conquer and enslave his subjects in America. But be perpetual infamy entailed upon that villain who dared to advise his master to such execrable measures; for it was easy to foresee the consequences which so naturally followed upon sending troops into America to enforce obedience to acts of the British Parliament, which neither God nor man ever empowered them to make. It was reasonable to expect that troops, who knew the errand they were sent upon, would treat the people whom they were to subjugate, with a cruelty and haughtiness which too often buries the honorable character of a soldier in the disgraceful name of an unfeeling ruffian. The troops, upon their first arrival, took possession of our Senate House, and pointed their cannon against the judgment hall, and even continued them there whilst the supreme court of judicature for this province was actually sitting to decide upon the lives and fortunes of the King's subjects. Our streets nightly resounded with the noise of riot and debauchery; our peaceful citizens were hourly exposed to shameful insults, and often felt the effects of their violence and outrage. But this was not all: as though they thought it not enough to violate our civil rights, they endeavored to deprive us of the enjoyment of our religious privileges, to vitiate our morals, and thereby render us deserving of destruction. Hence, the rude din of arms which broke in upon your solemn devotions in your temples, on that day hallowed by heaven, and set apart by God himself for his peculiar worship. Hence, impious oaths and blasphemies so often tortured your unaccustomed ear. Hence, all the arts which idleness and luxury could invent were used to betray our youth of one sex into extravagance and effeminacy, and of the other to infamy and ruin....Did not our youth forget they were Americans, and, regardless of the admonitions of the wise and aged, servilely copy from their tyrants those vices which finally must overthrow the empire of Great Britain?... When virtue has once erected her throne within the female breast, it is upon so solid a basis that nothing is able to expel the heavenly inhabitant. But have there not been some few, indeed, I hope, whose youth and inexperience have rendered them a prey to wretches, whom, upon the least reflection, they would have despised and hated as foes to God and their country? I fear there have been some such unhappy instances, or why have I seen an honest father clothed with shame; or why a virtuous mother drowned in tears?

But I forbear, and come reluctantly to the transactions of that dismal night, when in such quick succession we felt the extremes of grief, astonishment, and rage; when heaven in anger, for a dreadful moment, suffered hell to take the reins; when Satan, with his chosen band, opened the sluices of New England's blood, and sacrilegiously polluted our land with the dead bodies of her guiltless sons! Let this sad tale of death never be told without a tear; let not the heaving bosom cease to burn with a manly indignation at the barbarous story, through the long tracts of future time; let every parent tell the shameful story to his listening children until tears of pity glisten in their eyes, and boiling passions shake their tender frames; and whilst the anniversary of that ill-fated night is kept a jubilee in the grim court of pandemonium, let all America join in one common prayer to heaven that the inhuman, unprovoked murders of the fifth of March, 1770, planned by Hillsborough, and a knot of treacherous knaves in Boston, and executed by the cruel hand of Preston and his sanguinary coadjutors, may ever stand in history without a parallel. But what, my countrymen, withheld the ready arm of vengeance from executing instant justice on the vile assassins? Perhaps you feared promiscuous carnage might ensue, and that the innocent might share the fate of those who had performed the infernal deed. But were not all guilty? Were you not too tender of the lives of those who came to fix a yoke on your necks? But I must not too severely blame a fault, which great souls only can commit. May that magnificence of spirit which scorns the low pursuits of malice, may that generous compassion which often preserves from ruin, even a guilty villain, forever actuate the noble bosoms of Americans! But let not the miscreant host vainly imagine that we feared their arms. No; them we despised; we dread nothing but slavery. Death is the creature of a poltroon's brains; 'tis immortality to sacrifice ourselves for the salvation of our country. We fear not death. That gloomy night, the pale-faced moon, and the affrighted stars that hurried through the sky, can witness that we fear not death. Our hearts which, at the recollection, glow with rage that four revolving years have scarcely taught us to restrain, can witness that we fear not death; and happy it is for those who dared to insult us, that their naked bones are not now piled up an everlasting lasting monument of Massachusetts' bravery. But they retired, they fled, and in that flight they found their only safety. We then expected that the hand of public justice would soon inflict that punishment upon the murderers, which, by the laws of God and man, they had incurred. But let the unbiased pen of a Robertson, or perhaps of some equally famed American, conduct this trial before the great tribunal of succeeding generations.

And though the murderers may escape the just resentment of an enraged people; though drowsy justice, intoxicated by the poisonous draught prepared for her cup, still nods upon her rotten seat, yet be assured such complicated crimes will meet their due reward. Tell me, ye bloody butchers! ye villains high and low! ye wretches who contrived, as well as you who executed the inhuman deed! do you not feel the goads and stings of conscious guilt pierce through your savage bosoms? Though some of you may think yourselves exalted to a height that bids defiance to human justice, and others shroud yourselves beneath the mask of hypocrisy, and build your hopes of safety on the low arts of cunning, chicanery, and falsehood, yet do you not sometimes feel the gnawings of that worm which never dies? Do not the injured shades of Maverick, Gray, Caldwell, Attucks, and Carr attend you in your solitary walks, arrest you even in the midst of your debaucheries, and fill even your dreams with terror?

Ye dark designing knaves, ye murderers, parricides! how dare you tread upon the earth which has drunk in the blood of slaughtered innocents, shed by your wicked hands? How dare you breathe that air which wafted to the ear of heaven the groans of those who fell a sacrifice to your accursed ambition?... The eye of heaven penetrates the darkest chambers of the soul, traces the leading clue through all the labyrinths which your industrious folly has devised; and you, however you may have screened yourselves from human eyes, must be arraigned, must lift your hands, red with the blood of those whose death you have procured, at the tremendous bar of God!

But I gladly quit the gloomy theme of death, and leave you to improve the thought of that important day when our naked souls must stand before that Being from whom nothing can be hid. I would not dwell too long upon the horrid effects which have already followed from quartering regular troops in this town. Let our misfortunes teach posterity to guard against such evils for the future. Standing armies are sometimes (I would by no means say generally, much less universally) composed of persons who have rendered themselves unfit to live in civil society; who have no other motives of conduct than those which a desire of the present gratification of their passions suggests; who have no property in any country; men who have given up their own liberties, and envy those who enjoy liberty; who are equally indifferent to the glory of a George or a Louis; who, for the addition of one penny a day to their wages, would desert from the Christian cross and fight under the crescent of the Turkish Sultan. From such men as these, what has not a State to fear?... These are the men whom sceptred robbers now employ to frustrate the designs of God, and render vain the bounties which his gracious hand pours indiscriminately upon his creatures. By these the miserable slaves in Turkey, Persia, and many other extensive countries, are rendered truly wretched, though their air is salubrious, and their soil luxuriously fertile. By these, France and Spain, though blessed by nature with all that administers to the convenience of life, have been reduced to that contemptible state in which they now appear; and by these, Britain,—but if I were possessed of the gift of prophesy, I dare not, except by divine command, unfold the leaves on which the destiny of that once powerful kingdom is inscribed.

But since standing armies are so hurtful to a State, perhaps my countrymen may demand some substitute, some other means of rendering us secure against the incursions of a foreign enemy.... Will not a well-disciplined militia afford you ample security against foreign foes? We want not courage; it is discipline alone in which we are exceeded by the most formidable troops that ever trod the earth. Surely our hearts flutter no more at the sound of war than did those of the immortal band of Persia, the Macedonian phalanx, the invincible Roman legions, the Turkish janissaries, the gens d'armes of France, or the well-known grenadiers of Britain. A well-disciplined militia is a safe, an honorable guard to a community like this, whose inhabitants are by nature brave, and are laudably tenacious of that freedom in which they were born. From a well-regulated militia we have nothing to fear; their interest is the same with that of the State. When a country is invaded, the militia are ready to appear in its defense; they march into the field with that fortitude which a consciousness of the justice of their cause inspires; they do not jeopardy their lives for a master who considers them only as the instruments of his ambition, and whom they regard only as the daily dispenser of the scanty pittance of bread and water. No; they fight for their houses, their lands, for their wives, their children; for all who claim the tenderest names, and are held dearest in their hearts; they fight *pro aris et focis*, for their liberty, and for themselves, and for their God. And let it not offend if I say that no militia ever appeared in more flourishing condition than that of this province now cloth; and pardon me if I say, of this town in particular. I mean not to boast; I would not excite envy, but manly emulation. We have all one common cause; let it, therefore, be our only contest, who shall most contribute to the security of the liberties of America. And may the same kind Providence which has watched over this country from her infant state still enable us to defeat our enemies! I cannot here forbear noticing the signal manner in which the designs of those who wish not well to us have been discovered. The dark deeds of a treacherous cabal have been brought to public view....But the representatives of the people have fixed a mark on these ungrateful monsters, which, though it may not make them so secure as Cain of old, yet renders them, at least, as infamous. Indeed, it would be effrontive to the tutelar deity of this country even to despair of saving it from all the snares which human policy can lay....

Remember, my friends, from whom you sprang. Let not a meanness of spirit, unknown to those whom you boast of as your fathers, excite a thought to the dishonor of your mothers I conjure you, by all that is dear, by all that is honorable, by all that is sacred, not only that ye pray, but that ye act; that, if necessary, ye fight, and even die, for the prosperity of our Jerusalem. Break in sunder, with noble disdain, the bonds with which the Philistines have bound you. Suffer not yourselves to be betrayed, by the soft arts of luxury and effeminacy, into the pit digged for your destruction. Despise the glare of wealth. That people who pay greater respect to a wealthy villain than to an honest, upright man in

poverty, almost deserve to be enslaved; they plainly show that wealth, however it may be acquired, is, in their esteem, to be preferred to virtue.

But I thank God that America abounds in men who are superior to all temptation, whom nothing can divert from a steady pursuit of the interest of their country, who are at once its ornament and safeguard. And sure I am...if I paid a respect, so justly due to their much-honored characters, in this place. But when I name an Adams, such a numerous host of fellow-patriots rush upon my mind, that I fear it would take up too much of your time, should I attempt to call over the illustrious roll. But your grateful hearts will point you to the men; and their revered names, in all succeeding times, shall grace the annals of America. From them let us, my friends, take example; from them let us catch the divine enthusiasm; and feel, each for himself, the godlike pleasure of diffusing happiness on all around us; of delivering the oppressed from the iron grasp of tyranny; of changing the hoarse complaints and bitter moans of wretched slaves into those cheerful songs, which freedom and contentment must inspire. There is a heartfelt satisfaction in reflecting on our exertions for the public weal, which all the sufferings an enraged tyrant can inflict will never take away; which the ingratitude and reproaches of those whom we have saved from ruin cannot rob us of. The virtuous asserter of the rights of mankind merits a reward, which even a want of success in his endeavors to save his country, the heaviest misfortune which can befall a genuine patriot, cannot entirely prevent him from receiving.

I have the most animating confidence that the present noble struggle for liberty will terminate gloriously for America. And let us play the man for our God, and for the cities of our God; while we are using the means in our power, let us humbly commit our righteous cause to the great Lord of the Universe, who loveth righteousness and hateth iniquity. And having secured the approbation of our hearts, by a faithful and unwearied discharge of our duty to our country, let us joyfully leave our concerns in the hands of him who raiseth up and pulleth down the empires and kingdoms of the world as he pleases; and with cheerful submission to his sovereign will, devoutly say: "Although the fig tree shall not blossom, neither shall fruit be in the vines; the labor of the olive shall fail, and the field shall yield no meat; the flock shall be cut off from the fold, and there shall be no herd in the stalls; yet we will rejoice in the Lord, we will joy in the God of our salvation."

GLOSSARY

fifth of March, 1770: date of the Boston Massacre

George II: English king (1683–1760) and grandfather of George III

a George or a Louis: a reference to the kings of England and France, respectively

Hillsborough: Lord Hillsborough, parliamentary minister for American affairs

house of Brunswick: the family, also known as the House of Hanover, who controlled the English throne from 1714 to 1901

Maverick, Gray, Caldwell, Attucks, and Carr: the five civilians who died as a result of the Boston Massacre: Samuel Maverick, Samuel Gray, James Caldwell, Crispus Attucks, and Patrick Carr

Preston: British captain Thomas Preston, who was charged with giving his soldiers the order to fire on the Boston crowd

pro aris et focis: in Latin, literally, "for altars and firesides," meaning "for God and country"

Document Analysis

After a brief introduction, Hancock explains to his audience that the purpose of government is to provide "security to the persons and properties of the governed" and that this is so obviously true that to attempt to logically prove it would be pointless. He then asserts that to support a government that does not abide by these first principles is unacceptable. He maintains that he is a friend of government that protects person and properties, but he is an enemy of tyranny and then rhetorically asked the crowd if the British control over the colonies is "a righteous government—or is it tyranny?" He points to the Declaratory Act of 1766, which asserted parliamentary authority over the colonies, and charges the king (who, Hancock argues, was given bad advice by his ministers) with failing to fulfill his protective duties while branding as traitors those colonials who aided the British in destroying American liberty.

Hancock and his fellow Bostonians, who had been at the center of political tensions and Revolutionary activity since the mid-1760s, believed that the British government had become tyrannical. A point of reference for Hancock and his audience alike was the presence and behavior of a standing army in their midst. Their shared experience created a bond and a common language. Hancock's discussion of the effect of the British troops stationed among them in Boston contrasted the crude and un-Christian behavior of the troops with the peaceful and virtuous way of life of Bostonians.

Hancock pays particular attention to the negative effect that the troops' presence was having on Boston's youth. Males, Hancock observed, were acquiring bad habits from the soldiers as well as becoming less industrious—a hallmark of societal decline for many eighteenth-century Americans—while females were vulnerable to seduction and becoming victims of rape. Hancock laments that the innocence of youth has made them "prey to wretches" who were enemies to both God and country. Clearly these evil instances have taken place—why else, Hancock asks, is "an honest father clothed with shame; or why a virtuous mother drowned in tears?"

Hancock continues by comparing the standing army with the New England militia. His critique draws on his classical republican worldview, in which duty to community is more virtuous than personal enrichment for one's own sake. Between 1720 and 1723, John Trenchard and Thomas Gordon had written a series of articles called *Cato's Letters*—subtitled "Essays on Liberty, Civil and Religious, and Other Important Subjects"—that had had a tremendous influence on the way Americans viewed their relationship to government. One important feature of those letters was a stern warning regarding standing armies in peacetime. Standing armies in times of peace could mean only one thing—tyranny. Knowing that his audience was just as cognizant as he of the dangers of a such a permanent army of paid soldiers, Hancock continues to distinguish the differences between the Americans and the British by contrasting the motives of a standing army with those of a militia.

The soldiers of a standing army, Hancock contends, are uncivilized and are driven by a quest to gratify neither God nor country but only themselves. They work for the highest bidder—no matter the king or the religious symbol depicted on a standard. Unlike other fighting forces in history, the American militias, he claims, are motivated by a love of country, of community, of family, and of God. To an approving audience, Hancock cries that the militia "fight for their houses, their lands, for their wives, their children; for all who claim the tenderest names, and are held dearest in their hearts; they fight pro aris et focis, for their liberty, and for themselves, and for their God." In short, the militia is a strong, virtuous, and effective fighting force. The Americans, as intrepid and virtuous citizens, have no need for a standing army.

Hancock publicly worries that the emulation of the poor behavior of the British army by the youth of Boston could bring destruction upon the community—a sentiment quite similar to that of John Winthrop, the colony's first governor. Hancock's audience of Puritan descendants would not have blinked when Hancock fused heritage and religion in his rallying cry: "Let not a meanness of spirit, unknown to those whom you boast of as your fathers, excite a thought to the dishonor of your mothers I conjure you, by all that is dear, by all that is honorable, by all that is sacred, not only that ye pray, but that ye act; that, if necessary, ye fight, and even die, for the prosperity of our Jerusalem."

Essential Themes

In keeping with the occasion and topic of his address to Boston—commemorating the deaths of Bostonian civilians at the hands of Britain's professional soldiers—Hancock wisely spends a great deal of time in this speech emphasizing the growing and dangerous presence and influence of a standing army in Boston. As discussed above, writings such as *Cato's Letters* had firmly implanted in the minds of many American colonists that standing armies in time of pease equated to tyranny—that they were a tool of oppression just waiting to be utilized by an unscrupulous state.

In drawing a comparison between Britain's standing military forces in the colony and the colony's own citizen militia forces, Hancock was, perhaps, making a larger point about the differences between the mother country and her American colonies. The theme of new world virtue versus old world corruption was a common one in Revolutionary-era rhetoric. Also important to note is the way in which Hancock refers to himself and his fellow citizens as Americans, which had become increasingly common since the 1750s. Unlike earlier uses—and periods—the moment had arrived when a sense of identity divorced from the British Empire and from the rights of the English needed to be forged. Hancock's speech commemorating the Boston Massacre contributed mightily to creating a sense of national American identity.

———*Christopher J. Young, PhD*

Bibliography and Additional Reading

Nobles, Gregory. "Yet the Old Republicans Still Persevere: Samuel Adams, John Hancock, and the Crisis of Popular Leadership in Revolutionary Massachusetts, 1775–90". In Hoffman, Ronald; Albert, Peter J. *The Transforming Hand of Revolution: Reconsidering the American Revolution as a Social Movement*. (Charlottesville: University Press of Virginia, 1995). pp. 258–85.

Ritter, Kurt W (1977). "Confrontation as Moral Drama: the Boston Massacre in Rhetorical Perspective". *Southern Speech Communication Journal* (Volume 42, No. 1): 114–136.

Tyler, John W. *Smugglers & Patriots: Boston Merchants and the Advent of the American Revolution*. (Boston: Northeastern University Press 1986).

Unger, Harlow Giles. *John Hancock: Merchant King and American Patriot*. (New York: Wiley & Sons, 2000).

York, Neil Longley (2009). "Rival Truths, Political Accommodation, and the Boston 'Massacre'". *Massachusetts Historical Review* (Volume 11): 57–95.

——— *The Boston Massacre: a History with Documents*. (New York: Taylor & Francis, 2010).

■ "Liberty or Death" Speech

Date: 1775
Author: Patrick Henry
Genre: Speech

Summary Overview

On March 23, 1775, Patrick Henry delivered his famous "Liberty or Death" Speech to a meeting of the Virginia House of Burgesses being held at St. John's Church in Richmond. A renowned orator, Henry was speaking out of more than a decade of opposition to the British Crown, which he viewed as usurping the rights of American colonists. As he arose to speak, he understood that several of his fellow burgesses were not yet prepared to accept the idea of revolution. While acknowledging their reservations about such a drastic course of action, he framed the debate as a question of freedom or slavery. It was too late to talk of peace when the war, in his view, had already begun with the Crown's massing of its military forces. Henry's frustration, anger, and passion poured forth in his most famous speech. Warning that men were grasping at the "illusions of hope" while Britain prepared for war, an exasperated Henry declared that "war is actually begun!"

His speech elevated public discourse far beyond mere protests against the British Crown or even the upholding of the colonists' rights as British subjects. Henry's words became famous because he suggested that what was at stake was the very identity of free citizens and demanded that Virginia support its New England brethren who were facing British guns.

Defining Moment

In May 1774, Lord Dunmore,the British governor of the Virginia, dissolved the colonial assembly because of its participation in the Committees of Correspondence (groups organized by colonists to obtain advance knowledge of acts of Parliament that had an impact on the American colonies). Believing that the governor's act was an effort to curb colonial self-government, Henry began in November 1774 to organize a volunteer militia in his home county of Hanover, moving toward a position of armed opposition to the British Crown. Both Governor Dunmore and Henry also were responding to the actions of other colonies, especially Massachusetts, which as early as 1773 had initiated its own Committee of Correspondence.

Some members of the Virginia House of Burgesses considered Henry's views extreme. They were prepared to defend colonial rights, but believed that a negotiated settlement could be reached with the mother country. To Henry, this position weakened the rights he was attempting to preserve. While caution and prudence might seem the wisest course, in fact it would doom the colonies to servitude. Great Britain was already taking measures that showed it had little interest in recognizing colonial rights, Henry pointed out to the burgesses. He believed the moderates were no longer responding to the reality of the situation, which was one of crisis.

It was time for immediate and decisive action. Henry's powerful speech in March 1775 acknowledged his colleagues' concerns about the consequences of open resistance to royal authority, but he was asserting that the time for compromise had already elapsed and that the threat to liberty was so grave that calls for conciliation were no longer beneficial. The choice he described was stark: The colonists had to assert their rights with force. To do otherwise would result in nothing less than slavery. Henry believed that moderation was not an option because colonial self-government had already eroded to a point that made it impossible for the colonists to retrieve their rights from royal authority.

Author Biography

Patrick Henry was born in Hanover County, Virginia, on May 29, 1736. After working in a store, then farming, he studied law and began practicing in 1760. One of Henry's early court cases challenged the English Crown's authority to overturn a law passed by the Virginia assembly. Although he lost his case, Henry became a popular colonial leader.

He was elected to the Virginia House of Burgesses in 1765, gaining a reputation for good speechmaking and strong defense of Virginian rights. He became so outraged over the Stamp Act that he proposed that the Virginia Assembly should declare itself independent. The incensed Henry even issued a threat to the British monarchy, warning King George III to heed the examples of previous rulers who had lost their lives to usurpers.

By *the* LION *&* UNICORN, Dieu & mon droit, *their Lieutenant-Generals, Governours, Vice Admirals, &c. &c. &c. &c.*

A HUE *&* CRY.

WHEREAS I have been informed, from undoubted authority, that a certain PATRICK HENRY, of the county of Hanover, and a number of *deluded followers*, have taken up arms, chosen their officers, and, ftyling themfelves an *independent company*, have marched out of their county, encamped, and put themfelves in a poflure of war; and have written and defpatched letters to divers parts of the country, exciting the people to join in thefe *outrageous* and *rebellious* practices, to the *great terrour* of all his Majefty's *faithful* fubjects, and in *open defiance* of *law* and *government*; and have *committed other acts of violence*, particularly in *extorting* from his Majefty's *Receiver-General* the fum of 330 l. under *pretence* of *replacing the powder* I *thought proper* to order from the magazine; whence it undeniably appears, there is *no longer* the leaft fecurity for the *life* or *property* of any man: Wherefore, I have *thought proper*, *with the advice of his Majefty's Council*, and *in his Majefty's name*, to iffue this *my* proclamation, ftrictly charging *all perfons*, upon their *allegiance*, not to *aid*, *abet*, or *give countenance* to the faid PATRICK HENRY, or *any other perfons* concerned in *fuch unwarrantable combinations*; but, on the contrary, to oppofe *them*, and *their defigns*, by *every means*, which defigns muft otherwife inevitably involve the *whole country* in the *moft direful calamity*, as they will call for the *vengeance of offended Majefty*, and the *infulted laws*, to be *exerted here*, to vindicate the *conftitutional* authority of government.

Given, &c. this 6th day of May, 1775.

D****.

G** d*** the P****.

Now aligned with a radical faction that included Thomas Jefferson, Henry joined a number of burgesses calling for a Virginia constitutional convention and a continental congress—his response to the royal governor's dissolution of the colonial assembly in 1774. As a delegate to the First and Second Continental Congresses (1774–1775), he called for the arming of a militia—the first step, he openly announced, in a war he deemed inescapable.

Henry's passionate commitment to individual liberty made him a keen supporter of the American Revolution and the Articles of Confederation, a document that ceded sovereign authority to the states but opposed the ratification of the U.S. Constitution, arguing that it granted the federal government too much power, and made the states subordinate. Henry rejected efforts to make him part of the newly formed U.S. government, although in 1799 he consented in deference to President George Washington's request to run as a Federalist for a Virginia state senate seat. Henry won but died on June 6, 1799, before taking office.

HISTORICAL DOCUMENT

No man thinks more highly than I do of the patriotism, as well as abilities, of the very worthy gentlemen who have just addressed the house. But different men often see the same subject in different lights; and, therefore, I hope it will not be thought disrespectful to those gentlemen if, entertaining as I do opinions of a character very opposite to theirs, I shall speak forth my sentiments freely and without reserve. This is no time for ceremony. The question before the house is one of awful moment to this country. For my own part, I consider it as nothing less than a question of freedom or slavery; and in proportion to the magnitude of the subject ought to be the freedom of the debate. It is only in this way that we can hope to arrive at the truth, and fulfill the great responsibility which we hold to God and our country. Should I keep back my opinions at such a time, through fear of giving offense, I should consider myself as guilty of treason towards my country, and of an act of disloyalty toward the Majesty of Heaven, which I revere above all earthly kings.

Mr. President, it is natural to man to indulge in the illusions of hope. We are apt to shut our eyes against a painful truth, and listen to the song of that siren till she transforms us into beasts. Is this the part of wise men, engaged in a great and arduous struggle for liberty? Are we disposed to be of the numbers of those who, having eyes, see not, and, having ears, hear not, the things which so nearly concern their temporal salvation? For my part, whatever anguish of spirit it may cost, I am willing to know the whole truth, to know the worst, and to provide for it.

I have but one lamp by which my feet are guided, and that is the lamp of experience. I know of no way of judging of the future but by the past. And judging by the past, I wish to know what there has been in the conduct of the British ministry for the last ten years to justify those hopes with which gentlemen have been pleased to solace themselves and the House. Is it that insidious smile with which our petition has been lately received?

Trust it not, sir; it will prove a snare to your feet. Suffer not yourselves to be betrayed with a kiss. Ask yourselves how this gracious reception of our petition comports with those warlike preparations which cover our waters and darken our land. Are fleets and armies necessary to a work of love and reconciliation? Have we shown ourselves so unwilling to be reconciled that force must be called in to win back our love? Let us not deceive ourselves, sir. These are the implements of war and subjugation; the last arguments to which kings resort. I ask gentlemen, sir, what means this martial array, if its purpose be not to force us to submission? Can gentlemen assign any other possible motive for it? Has Great Britain any enemy, in this quarter of the world, to call for all this accumulation of navies and armies? No, sir, she has none. They are meant for us: they can be meant for no other. They are sent over to bind and rivet upon us those chains which the British ministry have been so long forging. And what have we to oppose to them? Shall we try argument? Sir, we have been trying that for the last ten years. Have we anything new to offer upon the subject? Nothing. We have held the subject up in every light of which it is capable; but it has been all in vain. Shall we resort to entreaty and humble supplication? What terms shall we find which have not been already exhausted? Let us not, I beseech you, sir, deceive ourselves. Sir, we have done everything that could be done to avert the storm which is now coming on. We have petitioned; we have remonstrated; we have supplicated; we have prostrated ourselves before the throne, and have implored its interposition to arrest the tyrannical hands of the ministry and Parliament. Our petitions have been slighted; our remonstrances have produced additional violence and insult; our supplications have been disregarded; and we have been spurned, with contempt, from the foot of the throne! In vain, after these things, may we indulge the fond hope of peace and reconciliation.

There is no longer any room for hope. If we wish to be free—if we mean to preserve inviolate those inestimable privileges for which we have been so long contending—if we mean not basely to abandon the noble struggle in which we have been so long engaged, and which we have pledged ourselves never to abandon until the glorious object of our contest shall be obtained—we must fight! I repeat it, sir, we must fight! An appeal to arms and to the God of hosts is all that is left us! They tell us, sir, that we are weak; unable to cope with so formidable an adversary. But when shall we be stronger? Will it be the next week, or the next year? Will it be when we are totally disarmed, and when a British guard shall be stationed in every house? Shall we gather strength but irresolution and inaction? Shall we acquire the means of effectual resistance by lying supinely on our backs and hugging the delusive phantom of hope, until our enemies shall have bound us hand and foot? Sir, we are not weak if we make a proper use of those means which the God of nature hath placed in our power. The millions of people, armed in the holy cause of liberty, and in such a country as that which we possess, are invincible by any force which our enemy can send against us. Besides, sir, we shall not fight our battles alone. There is a just God who presides over the destinies of nations, and who will raise up friends to fight our battles for us. The battle, sir, is not to the strong alone; it is to the vigilant, the active, the brave. Besides, sir, we have no election. If we were base enough to desire it, it is now too late to retire from the contest. There is no retreat but in submission and slavery! Our chains are forged! Their clanking may be heard on the plains of Boston! The war is inevitable—and let it come! I repeat it, sir, let it come.

It is in vain, sir, to extenuate the matter. Gentlemen may cry, Peace, Peace—but there is no peace. The war is actually begun! The next gale that sweeps from the north will bring to our ears the clash of resounding arms! Our brethren are already in the field! Why stand we here idle? What is it that gentlemen wish? What would they have? Is life so dear, or peace so sweet, as to be purchased at the price of chains and slavery? Forbid it, Almighty God! I know not what course others may take; but as for me, give me liberty or give me death!

GLOSSARY

awful: enormously important, extremely shocking, or so impressive as to inspire awe

extentuate: to lessen the seriousness of a mistake or wrongdoing

insidious: slowly and subtly harmful or destructive

irresolution: the state of being unsure and unable to make decisions

remonstrated: reasoned or pleaded forcefully

supplicated: begged

Document Analysis

Henry's first sentence directs a compliment at his opposition, admiring their patriotism. Henry, with a well-known reputation for radicalism, begins his speech in the mildest, most engaging way to address the concerns of those dissenting from his views.

The topic of Henry's speech is his craving for liberty, which he emphasizes by using the word *freely* and discussing the notion that a man should be able to speak "without reserve." Henry's speech thus becomes the personification of his ideas: a free man speaking freely who means no disrespect to those who think otherwise. The first two sentences exhibit a man keenly desirous of maintaining the decorum of the assembly, taking issue with certain opinions by expressing his own, as is inevitable among groups of different men. The final sentence in the first paragraph concludes by putting the British monarch in his place by reminding Henry's fellow burgesses that their ultimate loyalty must be to the Creator, the first cause of all life. Henry suggests that his radicalism is founded on universal principles that cannot be overturned by any lesser authority than God.

In Henry's second, shorter paragraph, he cautions against being blind to the truth of British tyranny. As difficult as it may be, it needs to be faced. The short second paragraph is followed by two paragraphs in which Henry gathers up the experience of the colony's last decade (beginning in 1765, when he delivered his defiant attack on the Stamp Act). The only way to gauge the future is by assessing the past, which leads Henry to reject the counsel of those who believe they can negotiate better terms with the British ministry. At this point, presenting old arguments to Britain would only be a form of self-deception. Then, in two hammer-blow sentences, Henry dispatches the efforts of a decade: No amount of pleading, begging, and bowing has moved the king to intervene on the colonists' behalf; indeed, the monarch has spurned their love. Henry works up a scene of shame in which the colonists have allowed themselves to be the victims of a tyrannical government. They can recover their dignity only by abandoning spurious reasons to hope. Henry reaches the crescendo of this paragraph when he boldly declares his solution to all these years of shame: In order to be free, the colonists must fight.

Having declared his support for war, Henry now confronts in the fifth paragraph the concern that the colonies do not have the strength to fight an empire. He argues that the colonists can only become weaker if they delay their declaration of war. Hope has become a phantom, which Henry pictures as the colonists lying supinely on their backs, unable to take decisive action. Liberty, Henry assures his fellow burgesses, is a "holy cause" and will draw millions to its defense. The idea of freedom is invincible, Henry asserts. God is just, and right is on the colonists' side. They will be fighting for the destiny of their nation, and there will be friends to help, perhaps an allusion to American hopes that the French would side against the British. The coming battle will reward the brave and the watchful—those who have given up hope in British fairness and integrity. It is too late for any other choice: Any retreat at this point would mean submitting to the Crown's power and thus to slavery. Shifting again to vivid imagery, Henry announces, "Our chains are forged! Their clanking may be heard on the plains of Boston! The war is inevitable—and let it come! I repeat it, sir, let it come." From initially expressing due deference to his opponents, Henry has moved to an uncompromising, radical, and vehement call for war, rousing his fellow burgesses to embrace the inevitable conflict and to do so with enthusiasm.

He concludes by saying there is no point in pursuing the matter, as the time for excusing or rationalizing British actions is over. Some still cry for peace, but the war has actually begun, Henry insists, returning to his vehemence. Colonists are already on the field of battle, he notes, alluding to the clashes between the royal government and colonists in Boston. Henry asks his fellow burgesses: Is life precious at any cost, at the cost of freedom? Is a life of slavery preferable to death? Then, shifting the responsibility from them to himself, Henry concludes in one of the most powerful and famous declarations in American history: "I know not what course others may take; but as for me, give me liberty or give me death!"

Essential Themes

When Patrick Henry began speaking on March 23, 1775, he understood that while his calls for militant action against the British Crown enjoyed considerable support, many of his fellow burgesses still questioned the wisdom of a direct confrontation with the king and Parliament. Quite aside from a sense of loyalty to the mother country, which many of the burgesses continued to espouse with diminishing enthusiasm, Virginia and the other colonies faced the world's greatest empire. Great Britain had vanquished France in the Seven

Years' War (1756–1763), and the idea of a band of colonists emerging victorious from a war with a world power seemed doubtful to a considerable number of Virginians. How other colonies would react to a call to arms also remained a problem. Certainly Massachusetts could be counted on, but Pennsylvania, for example, continued to be dominated by a political elite that resisted demands for direct and immediate action against the royal government.

In his speech, Henry does not side-step the considerable challenges faced by Virginia and other colonies who chose to stand against what they perceived to be Britain's tyranny. He does, however, use vivid imagery combined with a sharp indictment of the past decade of British-Colonial relations to argue, persuasively, that the conflict moderate Virginians wish to avoid has been thrust upon them. Since the first assaults against liberty in the 1760s, the choices that face colonists have dwindled to two: liberty or death.

———*Carl Rollyson, PhD*

Bibliography and Additional Reading

Beeman, Richard R. *Patrick Henry: A Biography.* (New York: McGraw-Hill, 1974).

Mayer, Henry. *A Son of Thunder: Patrick Henry and the American Republic.* (New York: Franklin Watts, 1986).

Mayo, Bernard. *Myths and Men: Patrick Henry, George Washington, Thomas Jefferson.* (Athens: University of Georgia Press, 1959).

Meade, Robert D. *Patrick Henry.* 2 vols. (Philadelphia: Lippincott, 1957–1969).

Willison, George F. *Patrick Henry and His World.* (Garden City, N.Y. Doubleday, 1969).

■ *Common Sense*

Date: 1776
Author: Thomas Paine
Genre: Pamphlet

Summary Overview

By the close of 1775, after years of antagonism between the American people and the British government, not a single patriot had stepped forth to passionately argue the case for refusing the control of the empire centered across the Atlantic Ocean. The first patriot to speak out for this cause was Thomas Paine, who presented his ideas in the pamphlet *Common Sense*. The pamphlet was first published and distributed in Philadelphia, Pennsylvania, on January 9, 1776—nine months after the first clash between American and British soldiers in Lexington and Concord, Massachusetts. Six months after the publication of *Common Sense*, the Continental Congress formally issued Thomas Jefferson's Declaration of Independence, and the Revolutionary War officially began.

Paine was, in fact, an Englishman who had been in North America for only about a year when he wrote *Common Sense*. As such he was perhaps in a good position to understand the illegitimacy and absurdity of his home country's rule in the New World. Americans were angered by excesses in taxation; extensive restriction on trade; and the many recent atrocities inflicted on them by British troops ("Redcoats"), such as the slaying of five civilians in the Boston Massacre of 1770. Nevertheless, separation from Britain simply was not widely discussed as an option until the publication of *Common Sense*.

Defining Moment

With the end of the Seven Years' War in 1763, antagonism between the American colonies and their governing nation across the Atlantic gradually grew too great to be ignored. Perhaps the most widespread grievance among colonists was that they did not enjoy the same general rights as did the citizens who lived in Great Britain. When Patrick Henry famously demanded either "liberty" or "death" in 1775, after the incidents at Lexington and Concord, he wished for his fellow colonists not independence but simply equal rights as English citizens. In July of that year, the Continental Congress tried to end hostilities and seek reconciliation by extending the Olive Branch Petition to the king

of England. The king, however, declined to receive the petition, and to demonstrate his authority he issued a Proclamation for the Suppression of Rebellion and Sedition against the colonies.

Thus, frustration with and resentment over the rule of the British was nearly universal in America by 1776, but a consensus regarding the most appropriate way for the colonies to proceed was not. There had been conflicts, occasionally violent, but the majority of the American population desired only greater liberty within the existing political structure, not a complete dismantling of it. Most Americans saw England as a loving, if stern and unfair, parent, and many colonists rejected the notion of independence for fear of demonstrating ingratitude and irrationality.

The citizens of the various colonies, meanwhile, found themselves in a range of circumstances. While Virginia and Massachusetts, in particular, were suffering economically because of imperial policies, other colonies—such as New York, Pennsylvania, and South Carolina—were flourishing. Certain colonies even bore rivalries with each other, such as over the delineations of borders. Many people believed that only the continued oversight of the "mother" country could sustain any unity among the religiously and socially diverse American populace. Indeed, few people had envisioned any alternate form of government; in some circles *democracy* was simply another word for "mob rule."

Author Biography

Thomas Paine was born in Thetford, England, in 1737. He served for two years aboard one of the many privateers operating as both merchant and pirate ships during the Seven Years' War with France. Upon returning to England, Paine began his own corset-making business and attempted to start a family, but his first wife died after only a year of marriage, perhaps while giving birth to the couple's premature infant. Paine remarried but separated from his second wife after several years.

While traveling in England's dissident circles, Paine made the acquaintance of the American statesman Benjamin Franklin, who wrote him letters of introduction to take with him upon his eventual move to America. Paine reached America on November 30, 1774. Paine wrote for the *Pennsylvania Magazine*, through which he became moderately known after penning a polemic against slavery. Benjamin Rush, another antislavery advocate, suggested that Paine write something that could stir the colonists to consider separation from the mother country. Paine set to work on such a project and published *Common Sense* on January 9, 1776. Just six months later, America declared its independence.

Paine, meanwhile, would spend his remaining years engaged in many pursuits, and would receive mixed reviews from critics. Through the Revolutionary War he served in various political offices while bolstering national morale by producing some sixteen *Crisis* papers and a number of other publications. (The first issue of *Crisis*, published in December 1776, opens with the legendary words, "These are the times that try men's souls.") Afterward, moved to France, writing on the condition of workers in England and on philosophical topics. Paine finally returned to America in 1802, moving to a farm awarded him by New York State for his wartime services. Lacking family and abusing alcohol, he died with few remaining assets to his name on June 8, 1809.

HISTORICAL DOCUMENT

Of the Origin and Design of Government in General, with Concise Remarks on the English Constitution

Some writers have so confounded society with government, as to leave little or no distinction between them; whereas they are not only different, but have different origins. Society is produced by our wants, and government by our wickedness; the former promotes our happiness *positively* by uniting our affections, the latter *negatively* by restraining our vices. The one encourages intercourse, the other creates distinctions. The first is a patron, the last a punisher.

Society in every state is a blessing, but Government, even in its best state, is but a necessary evil; in its worst state an intolerable one: for when we suffer, or are exposed to the same miseries *by a government*, which we might expect in a country *without government*, our calamity is heightened by reflecting that we furnish the means by which we suffer. Government, like dress, is the badge of lost innocence; the palaces of kings are built upon the ruins of the bowers of paradise. For were the impulses of conscience clear, uniform and irresistibly obeyed, man would need no other lawgiver; but that not being the case, he finds it necessary to surrender up a part of his property to furnish means for the protection of the rest; and this he is induced to do by the same prudence which in every other case advises him, out of two evils to choose the least. Wherefore, security being the true design and end

of government, it unanswerably follows that whatever form thereof appears most likely to ensure it to us, with the least expense and greatest benefit, is preferable to all others.

In order to gain a clear and just idea of the design and end of government, let us suppose a small number of persons settled in some sequestered part of the earth, unconnected with the rest; they will then represent the first peopling of any country, or of the world. In this state of natural liberty, society will be their first thought. A thousand motives will excite them thereto; the strength of one man is so unequal to his wants, and his mind so unfitted for perpetual solitude, that he is soon obliged to seek assistance and relief of another, who in his turn requires the same. Four or five united would be able to raise a tolerable dwelling in the midst of a wilderness, but one man might labour out the common period of life without accomplishing any thing; when he had felled his timber he could not remove it, nor erect it after it was removed; hunger in the mean time would urge him to quit his work, and every different want would call him a different way. Disease, nay even misfortune, would be death; for, though neither might be mortal, yet either would disable him from living, and reduce him to a state in which he might rather be said to perish than to die.

Thus necessity, like a gravitating power, would soon form our newly arrived emigrants into society, the reciprocal blessings of which would supercede, and render the obligations of law and government unnecessary while they remained perfectly just to each other; but as nothing but Heaven is impregnable to vice, it will unavoidably happen that in proportion as they surmount the first difficulties of emigration, which bound them together in a common cause, they will begin to relax in their duty and attachment to each other: and this remissness will point out the necessity of establishing some form of government to supply the defect of moral virtue.

Some convenient tree will afford them a State House, under the branches of which the whole Colony may assemble to deliberate on public matters. It is more than probable that their first laws will have the title only of Regulations and be enforced by no other penalty than public disesteem. In this first parliament every man by natural right will have a seat.

But as the Colony encreases, the public concerns will encrease likewise, and the distance at which the members may be separated, will render it too inconvenient for all of them to meet on every occasion as at first, when their number was small, their habitations near, and the public concerns few and trifling. This will point out the convenience of their consenting to leave the legislative part to be managed by a select number chosen from the whole body, who are supposed to have the same concerns at stake which those have who appointed them, and who will act in the same manner as the whole body would act were they present. If the colony continue encreasing, it will become necessary to augment the number of representatives, and that the interest of every part of the colony may be attended to, it will be found best to divide the whole into convenient parts, each part sending its proper number: and that the *elected* might never form to themselves an interest separate from the *electors*, prudence will point out the propriety of having elections often: because as the *elected* might by that means return and mix again with the general body of the *electors* in a few months, their fidelity to the public will be secured by the prudent reflection of not making a rod for themselves. And as this frequent interchange will establish a common interest with every part of the community, they will mutually and naturally support each other, and on this, (not on the unmeaning name of king,) depends the *strength of government, and the happiness of the governed*.

Here then is the origin and rise of government; namely, a mode rendered necessary by the inability of moral virtue to govern the world; here too is the design and end of government, viz. Freedom and security. ...

I know it is difficult to get over local or long standing prejudices, yet if we will suffer ourselves to examine the component parts of the English Constitution, we shall find them to be the base remains of two ancient tyrannies, compounded with some new Republican materials.

First. — The remains of Monarchical tyranny in the person of the King.

Secondly. — The remains of Aristocratical tyranny in the persons of the Peers.

Thirdly. — The new Republican materials, in the persons of the Commons, on whose virtue depends the freedom of England.

The two first, by being hereditary, are independent of the People; wherefore in a *constitutional sense* they contribute nothing towards the freedom of the State.

To say that the constitution of england is an *union* of three powers, reciprocally *checking* each other, is farcical; either the words have no meaning, or they are flat contradictions.

First. — That the King it not to be trusted without being looked after; or in other words, that a thirst for absolute power is the natural disease of monarchy.

Secondly. — That the Commons, by being appointed for that purpose, are either wiser or more worthy of confidence than the Crown.

But as the same constitution which gives the Commons a power to check the King by withholding the supplies, gives afterwards the King a power to check the Commons, by empowering him to reject their other bills; it again supposes that the King is wiser than those whom it has already supposed to be wiser than him. A mere absurdity!

There is something exceedingly ridiculous in the composition of Monarchy; it first excludes a man from the means of information, yet empowers him to act in cases where the highest judgment is required. The state of a king shuts him from the World, yet the business of a king requires him to know it thoroughly; wherefore the different parts, by unnaturally opposing and destroying each other, prove the whole character to be absurd and useless.

...

How came the king by a power which the people are afraid to trust, and always obliged to check? Such a power could not be the gift of a wise people, neither can any power, *which needs checking*, be from God; yet the provision which the constitution makes supposes such a power to exist.

...

Though we have been wise enough to shut and lock a door against absolute Monarchy, we at the same time have been foolish enough to put the Crown in possession of the key.

The prejudice of Englishmen, in favour of their own government, by King, Lords and Commons, arises as much or more from national pride than reason. Individuals are undoubtedly safer in England than in some other countries: but the will of the king is as much the law of the land in Britain as in France, with this difference, that instead of proceeding directly from his mouth, it is handed to the people under the formidable shape of an act of parliament

...

Wherefore, laying aside all national pride and prejudice in favour of modes and forms, the plain truth is that *it is wholly owing to the constitution of the people, and not to the constitution of the government* that the crown is not as oppressive in England as in Turkey.

...

Of Monarchy and Hereditary Succession

...

There is another and great distinction for which no truly natural or religious reason can be assigned, and that is the distinction of men into *kings* and *subjects*. Male and female are the distinctions of nature, good and bad the distinctions of Heaven; but how a race of men came into the world so exalted above the rest, and distinguished like some new species, is worth inquiring into, and whether they are the means of happiness or of misery to mankind.

...

To the evil of monarchy we have added that of hereditary succession; and as the first is a degradation and lessening of ourselves, so the second, claimed as a matter of right, is an insult and imposition on posterity. For all men being originally equals, no one by birth could have a right to set up his own family in perpetual preference to all others for ever, and tho' himself might deserve some decent degree of honours of his contemporaries, yet his descendants might be far too unworthy to inherit them. One of the strongest natural proofs of the folly of hereditary right in Kings, is that nature disapproves it, otherwise she would not so frequently turn it into ridicule, by giving mankind an *ass for a lion*.

...

Most wise men in their private sentiments have ever treated hereditary right with contempt; yet it is one of those evils which when once established is not easily removed: many submit from fear, others from superstition, and the more powerful part shares with the king the plunder of the rest.

...

But it is not so much the absurdity as the evil of hereditary succession which concerns mankind. Did it ensure a race of good and wise men it would have the seal of divine authority, but as it opens a door to the *foolish*, the *wicked*, and the *improper*, it hath in it the nature of oppression. Men who look upon themselves born to reign, and others to obey, soon grow insolent. Selected from the rest of mankind, their minds are early poisoned by importance; and the world they act in differs so materially from the world at large, that they have but little opportunity of knowing its true interests, and when they succeed in the government are frequently the most ignorant and unfit of any throughout the dominions.

...

The nearer any government approaches to a Republic, the less business there is for a King. It is somewhat difficult to find a proper name for the government of England. Sir William Meredith calls it a Republic; but in its present state it is unworthy of the name, because the corrupt influence of the Crown, by having all the places in its disposal, hath so effectually swallowed up the power, and eaten out the virtue of the House of Commons (the Republican part in the constitution) that the government of England is nearly as monarchical as that of France or Spain. Men fall out with names without understanding them. For 'tis the Republican and not the Monarchical part of the Constitution of England which Englishmen glory in, viz. the liberty of choosing an House of Commons from out of their own body—and it is easy to see that when Republican virtues fail, slavery ensues. Why is the constitution of England sickly, but because monarchy hath poisoned the Republic; the Crown hath engrossed the Commons.

...

Thoughts on the Present State of American Affairs

Volumes have been written on the subject of the struggle between England and America. Men of all ranks have embarked in the controversy, from different motives, and with various designs; but all have been ineffectual, and the period of debate is closed.

Arms as the last resource decide the contest; the appeal was the choice of the King, and the Continent has accepted the challenge.

...

The Sun never shined on a cause of greater worth. 'Tis not the affair of a City, a County, a Province, or a Kingdom; but of a Continent—of at least one-eighth part of the habitable Globe. 'Tis not the concern of a day, a year, or an age; posterity are virtually involved in the contest, and will be more or less affected even to the end of time, by the proceedings now. Now is the seed-time of Continental union, faith and honour. The least fracture now will be like a name engraved with the point of a pin on the tender rind of a young oak; the wound would enlarge with the tree, and posterity read in it full grown characters.

By referring the matter from argument to arms, a new era for politics is struck—a new method of thinking hath arisen.

...

It hath lately been asserted in parliament, that the Colonies have no relation to each other but through the Parent Country, i.e. that Pennsylvania and the Jerseys and so on for the rest, are sister Colonies by the way of England; this is certainly a very roundabout way of proving relationship, but it is the nearest and only true way of proving enmity (or enemyship, if I may so call it.) France and Spain never were, nor perhaps ever will be, our enemies as *Americans*, but as our being the *subjects of Great Britain*.

But Britain is the parent country, say some. Then the more shame upon her conduct. Even brutes do not devour their young, nor savages make war upon their families. Wherefore, the assertion, if true, turns to her reproach; but it happens not to be true, or only partly so, and the phrase *parent or mother country* hath been jesuitically adopted by the King and his parasites, with a low papistical design of gaining an unfair bias on the credulous weakness of our minds. Europe, and not England, is the parent country of America. This new World hath been the asylum for the persecuted lovers of civil and religious liberty from *every part* of Europe. Hither have they fled, not from the tender embraces of the mother, but from the cruelty of the monster; and it is so far true of England, that the same tyranny which drove the first emigrants from home, pursues their descendants still.

In this extensive quarter of the globe, we forget the narrow limits of three hundred and sixty miles (the extent of England) and carry our friendship on a larger scale; we claim brotherhood with every European Christian, and triumph in the generosity of the sentiment.

...

I challenge the warmest advocate for reconciliation to show a single advantage that this continent can reap by being connected with Great Britain. I repeat the challenge; not a single advantage is derived. Our corn will fetch its price in any market in Europe, and our imported goods must be paid for buy them where we will.

But the injuries and disadvantages which we sustain by that connection, are without number; and our duty to mankind at large, as well as to ourselves, instruct us to renounce the alliance: because, any submission to, or dependance on, Great Britain, tends directly to involve this Continent in European wars and quarrels, and set us at variance with nations who would otherwise seek our friendship, and against whom we have neither anger nor complaint. As Europe is our market for trade, we ought to form no partial connection with any part of it. It is the true interest of America to steer clear of European contentions, which she never can do, while, by her dependance on Britain, she is made the makeweight in the scale of British politics.

Europe is too thickly planted with Kingdoms to be long at peace, and whenever a war breaks out between England and any foreign power, the trade of America goes to ruin, *because of her connection with Britain.* ...

It is the good fortune of many to live distant from the scene of present sorrow; the evil is not sufficiently brought to their doors to make them feel the precariousness with which all American property is possessed. But let our imaginations transport us a few moments to Boston; that seat of wretchedness will teach us wisdom, and instruct us for ever to renounce a power in whom we can have no trust. The inhabitants of that unfortunate city who but a few months ago were in ease and affluence, have now no other alternative than to stay and starve, or turn out to beg. Endangered by the fire of their friends if they continue within the city and plundered by the soldiery if they leave it, in their present situation they are prisoners without the hope of redemption, and in a general attack for their relief they would be exposed to the fury of both armies.

Men of passive tempers look somewhat lightly over the offences of Great Britain, and, still hoping for the best, are apt to call out, "Come, come, we shall be friends again for all this." But examine the passions and feelings of mankind: bring the doctrine of reconciliation to the touchstone of nature, and then tell me whether you can hereafter love, honour, and faithfully serve the power that hath carried fire and sword into your land? If you cannot do all these, then are you only deceiving yourselves, and by your delay bringing ruin upon posterity. Your future connection with Britain, whom you can neither love nor honour, will be forced and unnatural, and being formed only on the plan of present convenience, will in a little time fall into a relapse more wretched than the first. But if you say, you can still pass the violations over, then I ask, hath your house been burnt? Hath your property been destroyed before your face? Are your wife and children destitute of a bed to lie on, or bread to live on? Have you lost a parent or a child by their hands, and yourself the ruined and wretched survivor? If you have not, then are you not a judge of those who have. But if you have, and can still shake hands with the murderers, then are you unworthy the name of husband, father, friend or lover, and whatever may be your rank or title in life, you have the heart of a coward, and the spirit of a sycophant.

...

As Britain hath not manifested the least inclination towards a compromise, we may be assured that no terms can be obtained worthy the acceptance of the continent, or any ways equal to the expense of blood and treasure we have been already put to.

The object, contended for, ought always to bear some just proportion to the expense. The removal of North, or the whole detestable junto, is a matter unworthy the millions we have expended. A temporary stoppage of trade, was an inconvenience, which would have sufficiently ballanced the repeal of all the acts complained of, had such repeals been obtained; but if the whole continent must take up arms, if every man must be a soldier, it is scarcely worth our while to fight against a contemptible ministry only. Dearly, dearly, do we pay for the repeal of the acts, if that is all we fight for; for in a just estimation, it is as great a folly to pay a Bunker-hill price for law, as for land. As I have always considered the independancy of this continent, as an event, which sooner or later must arrive, so from the late rapid progress of the continent to maturity, the event could not be far off....No man was a warmer wisher for reconciliation than myself, before the fatal nineteenth of April 1775, but the moment the event of that day was made known, I rejected the hardened, sullen tempered Pharaoh of England for ever; and disdain the wretch, that with the pretended title of *Father of His People,* can unfeelingly hear of their slaughter, and composedly sleep with their blood upon his soul.

But admitting that matters were now made up, what would be the event? I answer, the ruin of the continent. And that for several reasons.

First. The powers of governing still remaining in the hands of the king, he will have a negative over the whole legislation of this continent. And as he hath shewn himself such an inveterate enemy to liberty, and discovered such a thirst for arbitrary power; is he, or is he not, a proper man to say to these colonies, *"You shall make no laws but what I please."* And is there any inhabitant in America so ignorant, as not to know, that according to what is called the *present constitution*, that this continent can make no laws but what the king gives it leave to; and is there any man so unwise, as not to see, that (considering what has happened) he will suffer no law to be made here, but such as suit *his* purpose. We may be as effectually enslaved by the want of laws in America, as by submitting to laws made for us in England. After matters are made up (as it is called) can there be any doubt, but the whole power of the crown will be exerted, to keep this continent as low and humble as possible? ...

America is only a secondary object in the system of British politics, England consults the good of *this* country, no farther than it answers her *own* purpose....Reconciliation and ruin are nearly related.

Secondly. That as even the best terms, which we can expect to obtain, can amount to no more than a temporary expedient, or a kind of government by guardianship, which can last no longer than till the colonies come of age, so the general face and state of things, in the interim, will be unsettled and unpromising. Emigrants of property will not choose to come to a country whose form of government hangs but by a thread, and who is every day tottering on the brink of commotion and disturbance; and numbers of the present inhabitants would lay hold of the interval, to dispose of their effects, and quit the continent.

But the most powerful of all arguments, is, that nothing but independance, i. e. a continental form of government, can keep the peace of the continent and preserve it inviolate from civil wars. I dread the event of a reconciliation with Britain now, as it is more than probable, that it will followed by a revolt somewhere or other, the consequences of which may be far more fatal than all the malice of Britain.

...

The colonies have manifested such a spirit of good order and obedience to continental government, as is sufficient to make every reasonable person easy and happy on that head. No man can assign the least pretence for his fears, on any other grounds, that such as are truly childish and ridiculous, viz. that one colony will be striving for superiority over another.

Where there are no distinctions there can be no superiority, perfect equality affords no temptation. The republics of Europe are all (and we may say always) in peace. Holland and Swisserland are without wars, foreign or domestic: Monarchical governments, it is true, are never long at rest; the crown itself is a temptation to enterprizing ruffians at *home*; and that degree of pride and insolence ever attendant on regal authority, swells into a rupture with foreign powers, in instances, where a republican government, by being formed on more natural principles, would negotiate the mistake.

If there is any true cause of fear respecting independance, it is because no plan is yet laid down. Men do not see their way out—Wherefore, as an opening into that business, I offer the following hints; at the same time modestly affirming, that I have no other opinion of them myself, than that they may be the means of giving rise to something better. Could the straggling thoughts of individuals be collected, they would frequently form materials for wise and able men to improve into useful matter.

Let the assemblies be annual, with a President only. The representation more equal. Their business wholly domestic, and subject to the authority of a Continental Congress.

...

The members of Congress, Assemblies, or Conventions, by having had experience in national concerns, will be able and useful counsellors, and the whole, being impowered by the people, will have a truly legal authority.

The conferring members being met, let their business be to frame a *continental charter*, or Charter of the United Colonies; (answering to what is called the Magna Charta of England) fixing the number and manner of choosing members of Congress, members of Assembly, with their date of sitting, and drawing the line of business and jurisdiction between them: (Always remembering, that our strength is continental, not provincial:) Securing freedom and property to all men, and above all things, the free exercise of religion, according to the dictates of conscience; with such other matter as is necessary for a charter to contain. Immediately after which, the said Conference to dissolve, and the bodies which shall be chosen comfortable to the said charter, to be the legislators and governors of this continent for the time being: Whose peace and happiness, may God preserve, Amen.

...

But where says some is the King of America? I'll tell you Friend, he reigns above, and doth not make havoc of mankind like the Royal Brute of Britain. Yet that we may not appear to be defective even in earthly honors, let a day be solemnly set apart for proclaiming the charter; let it be brought forth placed on the divine law, the word of God; let a crown be placed thereon, by which the world may know, that so far as we approve as monarchy, that in America *the law is King*. For as in absolute governments the King is law, so in free countries the law *ought* to be King; and there ought to be no other. But lest any ill use should afterwards arise, let the crown at the conclusion of the ceremony be demolished, and scattered among the people whose right it is.

A government of our own is our natural right: And when a man seriously reflects on the precariousness of human affairs, he will become convinced, that it is infinitely wiser and safer, to form a constitution of our own in a cool deliberate manner, while we have it in our power, than to trust such an interesting event to time and chance. If we omit it now, some, Massanello may hereafter arise, who laying hold of popular disquietudes, may collect together the desperate and discontented, and by assuming to themselves the powers of government, may sweep away the liberties of the continent like a deluge. Should the government of America return again into the hands of Britain, the tottering situation of things, will be a temptation for some desperate adventurer to try his fortune; and in such a case, what relief can Britain give? Ere she could hear the news, the fatal business might be done; and ourselves suffering like the wretched Britons under the oppression of the Conqueror. Ye that oppose independance now, ye know not what ye do; ye are opening a door to eternal tyranny, by keeping vacant the seat of government. ...

O ye that love mankind! Ye that dare oppose, not only the tyranny, but the tyrant, stand forth! Every spot of the old world is overrun with oppression. Freedom hath been hunted round the globe. Asia, and Africa, have long expelled her.—Europe regards her like a stranger, and England hath given her warning to depart. O! receive the fugitive, and prepare in time an asylum for mankind.

Of the Present Ability of America: With Some Miscellaneous Reflections

I have never met with a man, either in England or America, who hath not confessed his opinion, that a separation between the countries would take place one time or other: And there is no instance in which we have shown less judgment, than in endeavoring to describe, what we call, the ripeness or fitness of the continent for independence.

...

Why is it that we hesitate? From Britain we can expect nothing but ruin. If she is once admitted to the government of America again, this Continent will not be worth living in. Jealousies will be always arising; insurrections will be constantly happening; and who will go forth to quell them? Who will venture his life to reduce his own countrymen to a foreign obedience? The difference between Pennsylvania and Connecticut, respecting some unlocated lands, shows the insignificance of a British government, and fully proves that nothing but Continental authority can regulate Continental matters.

Another reason why the present time is preferable to all others is, that the fewer our numbers are, the more land there is yet unoccupied, which, instead of being lavished by the king on his worthless dependents, may be hereafter applied, not only to the discharge of the present debt, but to the constant support of government. No nation under Heaven hath such an advantage as this.

The infant state of the Colonies, as it is called, so far from being against, is an argument in favour of independence. We are sufficiently numerous, and were we more so we might be less united. 'Tis a matter worthy of observation that the more a country is peopled, the smaller their armies are. In military numbers, the ancients far exceeded the moderns; and the reason is evident, for trade being the consequence of population, men became too much absorbed thereby to attend to anything else. Commerce diminishes the spirit both of patriotism and military defence. And history sufficiently informs us that the bravest achievements were always accomplished in the non-age of a nation. With the increase of commerce England hath lost its spirit. The city of London, notwithstanding its numbers, submits to continued insults with the patience of a coward. The more men have to lose, the less willing are they to venture. The rich are in general slaves to fear, and submit to courtly power with the trembling duplicity of a spaniel.

Youth is the seed-time of good habits as well in nations as in individuals. It might be difficult, if not impossible, to form the Continent into one government half a century hence. The vast variety of interests, occasioned by an increase of trade and population, would create confusion. Colony would be against colony. Each being able would scorn each other's assistance; and while the proud and foolish gloried in their little distinctions the wise would lament that the union had not been formed before. Wherefore the present time is the true time for establishing it. The intimacy which is contracted in infancy, and the friendship which is formed in misfortune, are of all others the most lasting and unalterable. Our present union is marked with both these characters; we are young, and we have been distressed; but our concord hath withstood our troubles, and fixes a memorable era for posterity to glory in.

The present time, likewise, is that peculiar time which never happens to a nation but once, viz., the time of forming itself into a government. Most nations have let slip the opportunity, and by that means have been compelled to receive laws from their conquerors, instead of making laws for themselves. First, they had a king, and then a form of government; whereas the articles or charter of government should be formed first, and men delegated to execute them afterwards; but from the errors of other nations let us learn wisdom, and lay hold of the present opportunity—*to begin government at the right end*.

...

To *conclude*, however strange it may appear to some, or however unwilling they may be to think so, matters not, but many strong and striking reasons may be given to show that nothing can settle our affairs so expeditiously as an open and determined declaration for independence. Some of which are,

First. — It is the custom of Nations, when any two are at war, for some other powers, not engaged in the quarrel, to step in as mediators, and bring about the preliminaries of a peace; But while America calls herself the subject of Great Britain, no power, however well disposed she may be, can offer her mediation. Wherefore, in our present state we may quarrel on for ever.

Secondly. — It is unreasonable to suppose that France or Spain will give us any kind of assistance, if we mean only to make use of that assistance for the purpose of repairing the breach, and strengthening the connection between Britain and America; because, those powers would be sufferers by the consequences.

Thirdly. — While we profess ourselves the subjects of Britain, we must, in the eyes of foreign nations, be considered as Rebels. The precedent is somewhat dangerous to their peace, for men to be in arms under the name of subjects; we, on the spot, can solve the paradox; but to unite resistance and subjection requires an idea much too refined for common understanding.

Fourthly. — Were a manifesto to be published, and despatched to foreign Courts, setting forth the miseries we have endured, and the peaceful methods which we have ineffectually used for redress; declaring at the same time that not being able lon-

ger to live happily or safely under the cruel disposition of the British Court, we had been driven to the necessity of breaking off all connections with her; at the same time, assuring all such Courts of our peaceable disposition towards them, and of our desire of entering into trade with them; such a memorial would produce more good effects to this Continent than if a ship were freighted with petitions to Britain.

Under our present denomination of British subjects, we can neither be received nor heard abroad; the custom of all Courts is against us, and will be so, until by an independence we take rank with other nations.

These proceedings may at first seem strange and difficult, but like all other steps which we have already passed over, will in a little time become familiar and agreeable; and until an independence is declared, the Continent will feel itself like a man who continues putting off some unpleasant business from day to day, yet knows it must be done, hates to set about it, wishes it over, and is continually haunted with the thoughts of its necessity.

Appendix to the Third Edition

Since the publication of the first edition of this pamphlet, or rather, on the same day on which it came out, the king's speech made its appearance in this city. Had the spirit of prophecy directed the birth of this production, it could not have brought it forth at a more seasonable juncture, or at a more necessary time. The bloody-mindedness of the one, shows the necessity of pursuing the doctrine of the other. Men read by way of revenge. And the speech, instead of terrifying, prepared a way for the manly principles of independence.

Ceremony, and even silence, from whatever motives they may arise, have a hurtful tendency when they give the least degree of countenance to base and wicked performances, wherefore, if this maxim be admitted, it naturally follows, that the king's speech, *is* being a piece of finished villany, deserved and still deserves, a general execration, both by the Congress and the people.

Yet, as the domestic tranquillity of a nation, depends greatly on the chastity of what might properly be called *national manners*, it is often better to pass some things over in silent disdain, than to make use of such new methods of dislike, as might introduce the least innovation on that guardian of our peace and safety. And, perhaps, it is chiefly owing to this prudent delicacy, that the king's speech hath not before now suffered a public execution. The speech, if it may be called one, is nothing better than a wilful audacious libel against the truth, the common good, and the existence of mankind; and is a formal and pompous method of offering up human sacrifices to the pride of tyrants.

But this general massacre of mankind, is one of the privileges and the certain consequences of kings, for as nature knows them not, they know not her, and although they are beings of our own creating, they know not us, and are become the gods of their creators. The speech hath one good quality, which is, that it is not calculated to deceive, neither can we, even if we would, be deceived by it. Brutality and tyranny appear on the face of it. It leaves us at no loss: And every line convinces, even in the moment of reading, that he who hunts the woods for prey, the naked and untutored Indian, is less savage than the king of Britain. Sir John Dalrymple, the putative father of a whining jesuitical piece, fallaciously called, "The address of the people of England to the inhabitants of America," hath perhaps from a vain supposition that the people here were to be frightened at the pomp and description of a king, given (though very unwisely on his part) the real character of the present one: "But," says this writer, "if you are inclined to pay compliments to an administration, which we do not complain of (meaning the Marquis of Rockingham's at the repeal of the Stamp Act) it is very unfair in you to withhold them from that prince, by whose NOD ALONE they were permitted to do any thing." This is toryism with a witness! Here is idolatry even without a mask: And he who can calmly hear and digest such doctrine, hath forfeited his claim to rationality an apostate from the order of manhood and ought to be considered as one who hath not only given up the proper dignity of man, but sunk himself beneath the rank of animals, and contemptibly crawls through the world like a worm.

However, it matters very little now what the king of England either says or does; he hath wickedly broken through every moral and human obligation, trampled nature and conscience beneath his feet, and by a steady and constitutional spirit of insolence and cruelty procured for himself an universal hatred. It is now the interest of America to provide for herself.

...

I shall conclude these remarks, with the following timely and well-intended hints. We ought to reflect, that there are three different ways by which an independency may hereafter be effected, and that one of those three, will, one day or other, be the fate of America, viz. By the legal voice of the people in Congress; by a military power, or by a mob: It may not always happen that our soldiers are citizens, and the multitude a body of reasonable men; virtue, as I have already remarked, is not hereditary, neither is it perpetual. Should an independency be brought about by the first of those means, we have every opportunity and every encouragement before us, to form the noblest, purest constitution on the face of the earth. We have it in our power to begin the world over again. A situation, similar to the present, hath not happened since the days of Noah until now.

The birthday of a new world is at hand, and a race of men, perhaps as numerous as all Europe contains, are to receive their portion of freedom from the events of a few months. The reflection is awful, and in this point of view, how trifling, how ridiculous, do the little paltry cavilings of a few weak or interested men appear, when weighed against the business of a world.

...

In short, independence is the only bond that tie and keep us together. We shall then see our object, and our ears will be legally shut against the schemes of an intriguing, as well as cruel, enemy. We shall then, too, be on a proper footing to treat with Britain; for there is reason to conclude, that the pride of that court will be less hurt by treating with the American States for terms of peace, than with those, whom she denominates "rebellious subjects," for terms of accommodation. It is our delaying in that, encourages her to hope for conquest, and our backwardness tends only to prolong the war. As we have, without any good effect therefrom, withheld our trade to obtain a redress of our grievances, let us now try the alternative, by independently redressing them ourselves, and then offering to open the trade. The mercantile and reasonable part of England, will be still with us; because, peace, with trade, is preferable to war without it. And if this offer be not accepted, other courts may be applied to.

On these grounds I rest the matter. And as no offer hath yet been made to refute the doctrine contained in the former editions of this pamphlet, it is a negative proof, that either the doctrine cannot be refuted, or, that the party in favor of it are too numerous to be opposed. *wherefore*, instead of gazing at each other with suspicious or doubtful curiosity, let each of us hold out to his neighbor the hearty hand of friendship, and unite in drawing a line, which, like an act of oblivion, shall bury in forgetfulness every former dissension. Let the names of Whig and Tory be extinct; and let none other be heard among us, than those of a good citizen, an open and resolute friend, and a virtuous supporter of the *rights of mankind*, and of the *free and independent States of America*.

GLOSSARY

avarice: greed

barrister: type of lawyer, specifically one who pleads cases in an English court

encomium: wholehearted praise

execration: denunciation; assertion that something is evil

Felo de se: literally, "evildoer with respect to oneself"; something that causes its own destruction

jesuitically: manipulatingly through language

junto: assembly of people with a common purpose

papistical: Roman Catholic; that is, in reference to the role of the pope, authoritarian

Rubicon: a boundary that, when crossed, commits the person to a certain course

toryism: loyalty to the Crown

variance: discord; antagonism

Document Analysis

Paine opens by examining the differences between "society" and "government," with the former termed a "blessing" and the latter "a necessary evil." He details the manner in which a small society would develop into a larger one, eventually entailing the institution of a representative government. This government, Paine notes, is only virtuous in that it precisely serves the interests of *all* the community's people.

Next Paine sets about first denouncing governmental tyranny and then demonstrating that, though well disguised, the British government was a symbol of such tyranny. Paine dismisses the monarchy as "a mere absurdity." Paine reiterates that no government that is directed by a ruler who inherited his position (such as a king) can offer the people true and just representation.

In the section titled "Of Monarchy and Hereditary Succession," Paine focuses further on the illegitimacy of monarchical rule under any circumstances. He laments the fact that kings ever came into existence at all, positing that they have been the ultimate cause of most wars. Then he introduces religion to the discussion, referring to "government by kings" as "the most prosperous invention the Devil ever set on foot for the promotion of idolatry."

Paine notes that even if people choose a first king, they are unjustly constraining their descendants to the rule of that king's descendants. He then points out that even if a king long ago came to power by unjust means, the monarchy could later deceive the people regarding its origins.

In "Thoughts on the Present State of American Affairs," Paine begins by analyzing the American situation, explaining that the wisest course of action would be for the colonies to declare and fight for independence. Paine denounces the possibility of America's maintaining any sort of union with Great Britain, noting that the commercial ties between the two countries are meaningless. Hanover, in modern Germany, was linked to England but was taken by the French in the Seven Years' War; Paine's point is that maintaining exclusive association with a country at war with others would only unnecessarily broaden the extent of that war. Paine seeks to discredit the familial ties that many colonists certainly felt with their "parent" country.

Paine argues that if America remains tied to Great Britain it would find itself dragged unnecessarily into the empire's conflicts. Paine emphasizes that the avoidance of a revolution at that time would be an irresponsible delaying of the inevitable. Paine asserts that the American colonies had grown to the point where dependence on Great Britain was a hindrance to smooth governmental functioning. Above all, Paine notes that the British Parliament would only ever enact laws affecting America in Britain's interest, not in America's interest.

Paine again comments on military matters, noting that engaging in war then would be the only sure way to avoid the continual future loss of life. In hopes of quelling people's fears regarding not just conflict but also the nation's unknown future, he discusses possibilities regarding the government that would take shape after the overthrow of British rule. Paine concludes his analysis of the American situation with a plea for the overthrow of oppression.

In the section titled "Of the Present Ability of America: With Some Miscellaneous Reflections," Paine offers detailed discussion on the advantages the colonies would reap in amassing a naval force; he cites financial figures and dismisses the negative aspects of incurring debt while producing this navy. Paine dismisses the notion that the British would ever offer America sufficient military protection and goes on to cite America's abundance of military resources and its yet-unoccupied land as additional national assets.

Paine proceeds to remark on various aspects of the possibility of independence. He posits that America's youth was a reason for, not against, going to war, as the populace was then energetic and ambitious. Then he mentions the need to avoid being subdued by a conqueror and advocates freedom of religion. He next revisits notions regarding the government to come, mentioning a continental charter and equal representation through a congress.

In this section's conclusion, which constituted the original conclusion to the entire pamphlet, Paine simply summarizes certain points and reiterates his contention that the only rational option for the colonies was to declare independence.

Much of the text in the opening paragraphs of "Appendix to the Third Edition" is devoted to personal criticism of the king. Sir John Dalrymple wrote several political works similar to "The Address of the People of England to the Inhabitants of America"; the author of that work argues that the king should be thanked for the repeal of the Stamp Act since he did not prevent those proceedings. Paine dismisses this praise of the king as "idolatry."

Paine effectively reiterates points that he made throughout the original text in favor of independence over reconciliation. Paine endeavors to convey to his readers the full gravity of the American situation.

Essential Themes

Common Sense was written with an enormous audience in mind: the entire population of North America. By virtue of his life experience, Paine was attuned to the inclinations and desires of both the upper and lower classes, and his pamphlet proved successful largely because of his intent and ability to communicate with the masses. While the tone may seem excessively academic to the modern reader, elongated grammatical constructions were standard in the eighteenth century; thus, in its time, *Common Sense* was considered exceptionally accessible.

With regard to content, Paine catered to common men in part by focusing more on ideas and general concepts than on legislative or political specifics. When he offers formulations regarding the possible shape of the new American government, he does so vaguely and briefly so as not to alienate the less educated with technicalities. Many of his references were to the Bible, with which most any literate person would have been familiar in that era. In *Common Sense*, Paine makes frequent references to nature and the natural order, strengthening the connections that common men, many of whom were farmers, would have felt with his ideas. Overall, forgoing scholarly objectivity, Paine argues quite vehemently that America had no reasonable course to follow but that which would bring about immediate separation from Great Britain.

———*Michael Allen Holmes*

Bibliography and Additional Reading

Bodnar, John E. *Remaking America: Public Memory, Commemoration, and Patriotism in the Twentieth Century*. Princeton, N.J. Princeton University Press, 1991.

Foner, Eric. *Tom Paine and Revolutionary America*. New York: Oxford University Press, 1976.

Fruchtman, Jack, Jr. *Thomas Paine: Apostle of Freedom*. New York: Four Walls Eight Windows, 1994.

Kaye, Harvey J. *Thomas Paine and the Promise of America*. New York: Hill and Wang, 2005.

Nelson, Craig. *Thomas Paine: Enlightenment, Revolution, and the Birth of Modern Nations*. New York: Viking, 2006.

■ Petition against the Excise Tax by Inhabitants of Western Pennsylvania

Date: 1792
Author: Albert Gallatin
Genre: Petition

Summary Overview

While this "Petition against the Excise Tax" was credited to "Inhabitants of Western Pennsylvania," its author was Albert Gallatin. Gallatin's petition frames farmer concerns over the new tax as being contrary to the interests of liberty and property rights. He echoes many themes that would be familiar to Americans familiar with the then-recent war for independence and the chaos (such as Shays's Rebellion) that followed.

Gallatin's appeal to Congress on behalf of his fellow Pennsylvanians also reflects the changing nature of the American economy. In this document, historians can see the early development of divisions and distinctions that would trouble Americans for generations, such as the urban vs. rural, agriculture vs. industry, and more general class divisions are all present in Gallatin's petition.

In addition to the above divisions that were emerging in American society, this document, and the historical context surrounding it also illustrates the growing importance of the west as a source of wealth and land but also conflict. There is also, contained in Gallatin's words, the suspicion of centralized national authority that would characterize American politics for decades to come.

Defining Moment

There are two key pieces to the context surrounding the creation of this petition. First was the fact that the new national government forged by the Constitution in 1789 found itself deeply in debt, without a sound national currency, and in need of steady streams of revenue. New Treasury Secretary Alexander Hamilton made a number of recommendations to Congress during the George Washington Administration. He wanted to, for example, create a national bank and to assume the debts of the various states. He also asked for an excise tax on distilled spirits (of which whiskey was the most popular at the time) to provide funds to reduce this debt. The tax was passed by Congress and signed into law in 1791. The second piece was the legacy of

western, rural uprisings such as Shays's Rebellion of 1786 that had plagued the United States during the 1780s. In this, and similar, events, farmers in western regions of the states took up arms to shut down courthouses and prevent foreclosures, asserting that they were being victimized by both banks and state and local governments.

Following passage of the Whiskey Tax (as it became widely known), farmers in western Pennsylvania began to discuss ways to protest what they saw as an unfair and dangerous imposition by the federal government. Early efforts involved petitioning the Congress, as we see in the document below. By 1794, more radical elements had gained influence threatening violence against tax officials. Members of the Washington administration—particularly Alexander Hamilton—urged a strong, military response to this crisis. Violent resistance eventually collapsed when Washington himself led troops to the area to put down the "rebellion."

Author Biography

Albert Gallatin was born on January 29, 1761 in Geneva. Coming to the United States in the 1780, he lived in Virginia and eventually settled in the western part of Pennsylvania, buying farmland south of Pittsburgh. It was her in western Pennsylvania that he first became involved in politics, being elected to the Pennsylvania General Assembly in 1790. It was during this time that he penned the "Petition against the Excise Tax by Inhabitants of Western Pennsylvania," reflecting the deep dissatisfaction of farmers in the region with the taxation and financial policies of the Washington administration as envisioned by Alexander Hamilton—especially the excise tax on whiskey enacted in 1791.

After a very short term of office in the United States Senate from December 1791 to February 1794 (he was removed from office when Federalists charged he did not meet the citizenship requirement), Gallatin returned home to find anger at the excise tax had not abated. While many were incensed at the tax a group of radicals called for rebellion and threatened violence against tax officials. Gallatin attended a convention to discuss resistance to the tax and served as a voice of moderation. Radical elements persisted, but the but the rebellion eventually collapsed in the face of armed force from the federal government. In 1785, Gallatin was elected to the U.S. House of Representatives, serving until 1801. During his time in Congress, he repeat-

edly stood against Hamilton's policies—especially those measures that he perceived as being favorable to merchants and manufacturers at the expense of farmers.

He later served as Secretary of the Treasury during the Jefferson and Madison administrations and as minister to France (1816-1823) and Great Britain (1826-1827). he died on August 12, 1849.

HISTORICAL DOCUMENT

To the Honorable the Speaker and the House of Representatives of the Congress of the United States

The petition of the subscribers, inhabitants of the western counties of Pennsylvania, most respectfully showeth:

That your Petitioners have been greatly alarmed by law of Congress which imposes a duty on spirituous liquors distilled from produce of the United States. To us that act appears unequal in its operation and immoral in its effects. Unequal in its operation, as a duty laid on the common drink of a nation, instead of taxing the citizens in proportion to their property, falls as heavy on the poorest class as on the rich; immoral in its effect, because the amount of the duty chiefly resting on the oath of the payer, offers, at the expense of the honest part of the community, a premium to perjury and fraud.

Your Petitioners also consider this law as dangerous to liberty; because the powers necessarily vested in the officers for the collection of so odious a revenue are not only unusual, but incompatible with the free enjoyment of domestic peace and private property; because these powers, to prevent evasion of the duty, must pursue the endless subtleties of the human mind, and be almost infinitely increased; and because we are apprehensive that this excise will by degrees be extended to other articles of consumption until everything we eat, drink, or wear be, as in England and other European countries, subjected to heavy duties and the obnoxious inspection of an host of officers.

Destitute of information of the real deficiencies of the revenues of the United States, of the proportion which the probable proceeds of the excise bear to them, and doubtful whether those deficiencies could not have been supplied by other resources

sufficiently productive and less obnoxious and oppressive, we want those motives which alone can reconcile us to the collection of a duty so odious in its nature and dangerous in its tendency.

Our peculiar situation renders this duty still more unequal and oppressive to us. Distant from a permanent market, and separate from the eastern coast by mountains which render the. communication difficult and almost impracticable, we have no means of bringing the produce of our lands to sale either in grain or in meal. We are therefore distillers through necessity, not choice, that we may comprehend the greatest value in the smallest size and weight.

The inhabitants of the eastern side of the mountains can dispose of their grain without the additional labor of distillation at a higher price than we can, after we have bestowed that labor upon it. Yet with this additional labor we must also pay a high duty from which they are exempted, because we have no means of selling our surplus produce but in a distilled state.

Another circumstance which renders this duty ruinous to us is our scarcity of cash. Our commerce is not, as on the eastern coast, carried on so much by absolute sale as by barter, and we believe it to be a fact that there is not among us a quantity of circulating cash sufficient for the payment of this duty alone.

We are not accustomed to complain without reason; we have punctually and cheerfully paid former taxes on our estates and possessions, because they were proportioned to our real wealth. We believe this to be founded on no such equitable principles, and are persuaded that your Honorable House will find on investigation that its amount of duty collected, will be four times as large as any tax which we have hitherto paid on the whole of our lands and other property.

Submitting these considerations to your honourable body, we respectfully apply for a total repeal of the law, or for such modifications thereof as would render its principles more congenial to the nature of a free government, and its operation upon us less unequal and oppressive. And as in duty bound shall forever pray, &c.

GLOSSARY

distillation: The process of producing alcohol from grain

duty: a tax

onerous: something that is needlessly difficult

spiritous liquors: beverage with a high alcohol content, such as whiskey

Document Analysis

Gallatin begins the petition from his fellow farmers by expressing "alarm" at the new duty (tax) on liquor. A key phrase here is that the tax is on liquor "distilled from produce of the United States." Most whiskey at this time was distilled from corn and was a cost effective way for farmers to make money from their crops. Farmers, then, perceived the tax on whiskey as a tax on their very livelihood. he then claims that the tax is "unequal" because it targets the "common drink" of the nation and, because it taxes something common people drink rather than "taxing the citizens in proportion to their property" it disproportionally affects the poor. It is immoral because, as Gallatin describes it, "the amount of the duty chiefly [rests] on the oath of the payer." Meaning, that the unscrupulous could lie about their tax liability, which was based on how much whiskey they produced, pushing the burden to those who are honest.

Gallatin also criticizes the enforcement of the law and collection of the taxes as being "incompatible with the free enjoyment of domestic peace and private property" and expresses fear that the tax could be extended to almost any other food, drink or manufactured item "as in England and other European countries." This reference to England is telling, as the Federalist faction of Washington's government was often criticized as being "monarchical" in its approach to government. This criticism of a system of taxation and the way in which those taxes were collected must have triggered memories for those of the revolutionary generation who sent similar petitions to Parliament. While, at this point, Gallatin and his compatriots are not threatening to engaged in any sort of armed resistance, the development of the Whiskey Rebellion would demonstrate that such militancy was not out of the question.

Further, Gallatin argues that the people paying the tax do not have enough information about the financial state of the country or exactly what their taxes will do to remedy the situation. He suggests that without this information, the public will not know if such a tax is the best way to solve the country's problems. While Gallatin does not explicitly make any accusations against the Federalists in power at the time, but his questioning of, basically, why the people were ill-informed about the overall situation may be an indicator of some important political trends at the time. There was significant suspicion among those opposed to the Washington administration—and especially to Alexander Hamilton's financial policies—that the purpose of the tax might be to harm farmers rather than help the country.

Gallatin also explains that the law is "unequal and oppressive" because of the geographical realities faced by farmers west of the Allegheny mountains.Selling excess grain as whiskey is the only practical way for these farmers to survive, since they cannot easily transport their crops to markets. Grains like corn were bulky and heavy—a full crop, or even part of a crop, would require several wagons to carry. In a region with few developed roads, and almost no roads to speak of in some regions, the production and sale of whiskey was financial necessity. A further example of geographic discrimination in the law is the fact that the taxes must be paid with cash—which was in short supply on the western frontier.

Gallatin closes his petition by explaining that they people of western Pennsylvania have never complained "without reason" and have been diligent in paying the lawful taxes that have always existed, since those have been "proportioned to [their] real wealth." The Whiskey Tax, however, is not "founded...on such equitable principles." The group of farmers who signed the petition then ask for a repeal of the law or, failing that, changes that would make it "congenial to the nature of a free government."

Essential Themes

The last portion of the petition, in which Gallatin seeks a tax law that is "congenial to the nature of a free government," provides an important window into the thought of Gallatin and his fellow Pennsylvania farmers. What was at stake here was more than the tax on their whiskey. The apparatus of government—a government across the mountains, distant from these farmers—threatened to limit their liberty and property in a manner that seemed prejudicial and, possibly, politically motivated. The tax on whiskey targets the livelihood of these men (and others win a similar situation) in a way that was disproportionate. Throughout the petition, Gallatin expresses concerns that this tax, unlike the other taxes the farmers are happy to pay, is not applied equitably or fairly. Gallatin also spends time focusing on the way the taxes are collected—an imperfect system which is open to abuse by the dishonest, resulting in a further burden being placed on those who do not evade the law. Once again, he returns to the idea of fairness and equal treatment.

—— *Aaron Gulyas, MA*

Bibliography and Additional Reading

Boyd, Steven R. "The Whiskey Rebellion, Popular Rights, and the Meaning of the First Amendment." In W. Thomas Mainwaring, ed. *The Whiskey Rebellion and the Trans-Appalachian Frontier*, 73–84. (Washington, Pennsylvania: Washington and Jefferson College, 1994).

Dungan, Nicholas. *Gallatin: America's Swiss Founding Father*. (New York University Press, 2010).

Hogeland, William. *The Whiskey Rebellion: George Washington, Alexander Hamilton, and the Frontier Rebels Who Challenged America's Newfound Sovereignty*. (New York: Scribner, 2006).

Kohn, Richard H. "The Washington Administration's Decision to Crush the Whiskey Rebellion." *Journal of American History* 59 (December 1972), 567–84.

SLAVERY AND ABOLITION

During the early-to-mid-1600s, African slavery was limited in England's North American colonies. A ready supply of indentured servants from England, combined with the comparatively high cost of purchasing and providing care for slaves meant that the institution would grow slowly. The pace of that growth, however, picked up in the late 1600s. African slaves were present in all regions of the colonies, not just the south, and trade in slaves occurred at every major port from Charleston to Boston. Opposition to slavery existed as well, however. This section contains documents that reflect the changing nature of dissent and protest against the institution of slavery in colonial North America and, after the War for Independence, in the United States. These documents may be grouped into three categories.

In the first category are examples of protest by white Americans against the ownership of slaves. Beginning with the Quakers of Pennsylvania and their Minute against Slavery, Addressed to Germantown Monthly Meeting, we see voices raised against the practice of slavery. The era of the American Revolution, with its rhetoric of freedom, inspired citizens of Pennsylvania (who were not content with a law to gradually emancipate slaves) to submit a Petition to the Assembly of Pennsylvania against the Slave Trade. During the nineteenth century, the radical abolition movement demanded immediate and full freedom for slaves. William Lloyd Garrison established the American Anti-Slavery Society and its 1833 Declaration of Sentiments challenged the morality and legitimacy of American slavery. Garrison's message resonated with others such as Lydia Maria Child, who argued in Prejudices against People of Color, and Our Duties in Relation to This Subject for equal rights and treatment for African-Americans in the north. Wendell Phillips, one of the most radical of the abolitionists, in Under the Flag, described his vision of the coming Civil War as the ultimate means for eliminating slavery. John Brown went so far as to

develop plans for a new nation which would be a haven for freed slaves, creating a Provisional Constitution to administer his new land.

The second category consists of testimony from former slaves who escaped their lives of captivity and used their stories to persuade white America about the evils of slavery and to work for emancipation. Prince Hall and his fellow African-American Massachusetts citizens issued a Petition to the Massachusetts General Court seeking freedom. Writers and orators like Richard Allen, Sojourner Truth, Martin Delaney, Solomon North, and Harriet Jacobs each shared stories that varied in details but had one important theme in common: the brutal inhumanity of the institution of slavery.

In the third category, we find accounts of—or calls for—more forceful resistance. Slave rebellions and uprisings were relatively rare—and successful ones almost unheard of, depending on how one defines "success." Georgia founder James Oglethorpe provides An Account of the Negroe Insurrection in South Carolina, about the 1739 Stono Rebellion. Ninety years later, David Walker's Appeal to the Coloured Citizens of the World suggests that armed rebellion might be both effective and desirable. Nat Turner's Confessions, the account of his deadly 1831 insurrection in Virginia, galvanized southern state governments into placing further restrictions on slaves. Osborn P. Anderson, a free African-American and the only survivor of John Brown's raid on Harper's Ferry, Virginia, provides his account of this attempt to liberate the slaves of the south.

The story of slavery and abolitionism in the United States during the 19th century exists in parallel with the story of sectional conflict between north and south, culminating in the Civil War and the era of Reconstruction following the war. It also (especially in the words of Lydia Maria Child) anticipates the ongoing struggle for political, legal, economic, and social equality faced by African-Americans in the twentieth century.

A Minute against Slavery, From the Germantown Monthly Meeting, Addressed to the Monthly Meeting in Dublin

Date: 1688
Authors: Gerhard (signed in the text as Garret) Henderich, Derick Opden Graff (up de Graeff), Francis Daniell Pastorius, and Abram Opden Graff (Abraham up Den graef)
Genre: Essay

Summary Overview

On February 18, 1688, Quakers met in Germantown, Pennsylvania, located about five miles northwest of Philadelphia, and issued the first known statement in British North America proclaiming the evils of slavery and urging the abolition of the institution. The petition, titled "A Minute against Slavery, Addressed to Germantown Monthly Meeting," raised points that would become the basis for eighteenth-century arguments for the abolition of slavery: It violated the Golden Rule, to do unto others as you would have done to you; it was theft; it inspired the growth of vices such as adultery and caused family dissolution; it detracted from the humanity of the owner; and it presented the constant threat of insurrection and rebellion by those enslaved.

The members of the Germantown Monthly Meeting drafted the resolutions in accordance with their interpretations of the belief system governing Quakers throughout the colony. Part of the most radical faction of the Protestant Reformation, Quakers acknowledge the primacy of following the divine presence known as the Inner Light and, as a consequence, relegate man-made dogmas and rites to lesser significance. The group also adheres to the concept of the "brotherhood" of all individuals and the basic equality of all souls. Finally, they agree that individuals can and should work to remove all taint of sin from their souls and their lives while on earth. The significance of their beliefs and their desire to put into practice what they preach is evident in the Germantown Quakers' statements condemning slavery.

Defining Moment

The colony in which the Germantown protesters lived was unique in many ways. Pennsylvania, meaning "Penn's Woods," owed its existence to William Penn (1644–1718) and his plans for a "Holy Experiment." Penn, a member of the English elite and the son of Admiral Sir William Penn, converted to Quakerism at the age of twenty-three. The Religious Society of Friends, or Quakers, emphasized deep personal and spiritual con-

nections to God, the brotherhood of all humans, pacifism, and the possibility that individuals could achieve grace and perfection of the soul while on earth. Like other radical Protestant groups, such as the Anabaptists, Quakers reject Trinitarian doctrines (belief in the unity of three persons in one god), the validity of man-made dogmas and creeds, and an organized clergy. In most places, with the exception of the Netherlands, Anabaptists were deemed heretics and persecuted on that basis.

Penn, who was politically protected by his status and family connections, recognized the vulnerability of those less fortunate than he and sought to provide safe refuge for persecuted believers. In 1681 he used his ties to the British Crown to acquire a proprietary grant for the territory west of the Delaware River in exchange for a debt owed to his father, and on February 28, 1681, Charles II signed the Charter for the Province of Pennsylvania. By 1685 nearly eight thousand religious dissenters had joined Penn's colonial venture. His plan called for broad-based religious toleration and the disestablishment of the church from the state. The disassociation of faith from the structures of governance brought about a colonial system where community morality was adjudicated by civil rather than religious authorities, and individuals were charged with the responsibility of moving their communities toward moral and ethical ideals.

Despite the fact that the residents of Germantown were inhabitants of an Anglo-American colony established by royal charter, the members of their community and their meeting were not English but rather German and Dutch. The immigrants to the community consisted in large part of pietistic Germans recruited by the Frankfort Land Company, established in 1683, and of Germans and Dutch Quakers organized separately from the town of Krefeld, in the Rhineland region, along the border between the German principalities and the Netherlands. The groups' acknowledged leader, Francis Daniel Pastorius, a pietistic Lutheran, represented the Frankfort Land Company as its legal agent and was the

GERMANTOWN FRIENDS' PROTEST AGAINST SLAVERY, 1688.

THIS IS TO Yᴱ MONTHLY MEETING HELD AT RICHARD WORRELL'S.

These are the reasons why we are against the traffick of men-body, as followeth. Is there any that would be done or handled at this manner? viz., to be sold or made a slave for all the time of his life? How fearful and faint-hearted are many on sea, when they see a strange vessel,—being afraid it should be a Turk, and they should be taken, and sold for slaves into Turkey. Now what is this better done, as Turks doe? Yea, rather is it worse for them, which say they are Christians; for we hear that yᵉ most part of such negers are brought hither against their will and consent, and that many of them are stolen. Now, tho they are black, we can not conceive there is more liberty to have them slaves, as it is to have other white ones. There is a saying, that we shall doe to all men like as we will be done ourselves; making no difference of what generation, descent or colour they are. And those who steal or robb men, and those who buy or purchase them, are they not all alike? Here is liberty of conscience, wᶜʰ is right and reasonable; here ought to be likewise liberty of yᵉ body, except of evil-doers, wᶜʰ is an other case. But to bring men hither, or to rob and sell them against their will, we stand against. In Europe there are many oppressed for conscience sake; and here there are those oppressed wᶜʰ are of a black colour. And we who know that men must not comitt adultery,—some do committ adultery, in others, separating wives from their husbands and giving them to others; and some sell the children of these poor creatures to other men. Ah! doe consider well this thing, you who doe it, if you would be done at this manner? and if it is done according to Christianity? You surpass Holland and Germany in this thing. This makes an ill report in all those countries of Europe, where they hear off, that yᵉ Quakers doe here handel men as they handel there yᵉ cattle. And for that reason some have no mind or inclination to come hither. And who shall maintain this your cause, or pleid for it? Truly we can not do so, except you shall inform us better hereof, viz, that Christians have liberty to practise these things. Pray, what thing in the world can be done worse towards us, than if men should rob or steal us away, and sell us for slaves to strange countries; separating housbands from their wives and children. Being now this is not done in the manner we would be done at therefore we contradict and are against this traffic of men-body. And we who profess that it is not lawful to steal, must, likewise, avoid to purchase such things as are stolen, but rather help to stop this robbing and stealing if possible. And such men ought to be delivered out of yᵉ hands of yᵉ robbers, and set free as well as in Europe. Then is Pennsylvania to have a good report, instead it hath now a bad one for this sake in other countries. Especially whereas yᵉ Europeans are desirous to know in what manner yᵉ Quakers doe rule in their province;—and most of them doe look upon us with an envious eye. But if this is done well, what shall we say is done evil?

If once these slaves (wᶜʰ they say are so wicked and stubbern men) should joint themselves,—fight for their freedom,—and handel their masters and mastrisses as they did handel them before; will these masters and mastrisses take the sword at hand and warr against these poor slaves, licke, we are able to believe, some will not refuse to doe; or have these negers not as much right to fight for their fredom, as you have to keep them slaves?

Now consider well this thing, if it is good or bad? And in case you find it to be good to handel these blacks at that manner, we desire and require you hereby lovingly, that you may inform us herein, which at this time never was done, viz., that Christians have such a liberty to do so. To the end we shall be satisfied in this point, and satisfie likewise our good friends and acquaintances in our natif country, to whose it is a terror, or fairful thing, that men should be handeld so in Pennsylvania.

This is from our meeting at Germantown, held yᵉ 18 of the 2 month, 1688, to be delivered to the Monthly Meeting at Richard Worrel's.

Garret henderich
derick up de graeff
Francis daniell Pastorius
Abraham up Den graef.

At our Monthly Meeting at Dublin, yᵉ 30—2 mo., 1688. we having inspected yᵉ matter, above mentioned, and considered of it, we find it so weighty that we think it not expedient for us to meddle with it here, but do rather commit it to yᵉ consideration of yᵉ Quarterly Meeting; yᵉ tenor of it being nearly related to yᵉ Truth. On behalf of yᵉ Monthly Meeting,

Signed, P. Jo. HART.

This, above mentioned, was read in our Quarterly Meeting at Philadelphia, the 4 of yᵉ 4th mo. '88, and was from thence recommended to the Yearly Meeting, and the above said Derick, and the other two mentioned therein, to present the same to yᵉ above said meeting, it being a thing of too great a weight for this meeting to determine.

Signed by order of yᵉ meeting,

ANTHONY MORRIS.

YEARLY MEETING MINUTE ON THE ABOVE PROTEST.

At a Yearly Meeting held at Burlington the 5th day of the 7th month, 1688.

A Paper being here presented by some German Friends Concerning the Lawfulness and Unlawfulness of Buying and keeping Negroes, It was adjudged not to be so proper for this Meeting to give a Positive Judgment in the Case, It having so General a Relation to many other Parts, and therefore at present they forbear It.

only member of the company to venture to Pennsylvania. They had dual goals for their experiment: They sought both to establish a spiritual and physical haven for other radical religious reformers and to ensure the success of their financial investment.

When the Quaker meeting at Germantown issued "A Minute against Slavery, Addressed to Germantown Monthly Meeting" in 1688, the group operated within a societal framework that was for the seventeenth century remarkably flexible and diverse. In Germantown alone, there resided individuals hailing from several distinct German and Dutch communities as well as English immigrants. Virtually all of the inhabitants practiced some form of radical Protestantism; there were German Lutheran Pietists, German Reformists, and Dutch and English Quakers.

Author Biographies

While the antislavery resolutions were intended as a general statement from the Quaker meeting at Germantown, it was signed by four specific members of the group: Gerhard (or as signed in the text, "Garret") Henderich, Derick Opden Graff ("up de Graeff"), Francis Daniel ("daniell") Pastorius, and Abram Opden Graff ("Abraham up Den graef").

Pastorius was born in 1651 and grew up in an urban and commercial atmosphere. He attended four universities and was well traveled. By the 1680s he was practicing law in Frankfurt am Main. Pastorius was familiar with William Penn even before his arrival in Pennsylvania, having frequently served as the liaison between the residents of Germantown and the colony's bureaucratic structures. He also became well acquainted with the colony leaders David Lloyd and James Logan, and he shared their vision of Pennsylvania as a commercial and mercantile venture. Similarly, he recognized the value of Pennsylvania as a refuge for western Europe's most

radical Protestant reformers, the Anabaptists. Pastorius encouraged the inhabitants of Germantown to adapt to their new environment. He suggested that his fellow immigrants learn and practice English, familiarize themselves with English laws and systems of governance, and intermingle with the larger English population of the colony. Pastorius played a leading role in the organization and recognition of the Germantown Monthly Meeting and actively encouraged its correspondence and affiliation with others throughout the region. He continued to serve as spokesperson and promoter for Germantown and the larger colony until his death in 1720.

Derick and Abram Opden Graff were two of three brothers who emigrated from Krefeld to Germantown in July 1683. The brothers were among the original membership of the Germantown Quaker meeting organized later that year and housed by 1686 in the Kirchlein, a log meetinghouse.

Gerhard Henderich is the member of the group about which the littlest is known. He arrived in Germantown in 1685 with a number of other German and Dutch immigrants. Henderich, accompanied by his wife, Mary, and daughter, Sarah, originated in Krisheim, a community near Krefeld on the Dutch side of the border. He was, by 1688, a substantial member of the Germantown community. As a Dutch Quaker, he, too, aligned himself with the heterogeneous Quaker meeting at Germantown. By 1692, Derick and Abram Opden Graff had parted ways as the consequence of a larger religious controversy, the Keithian schism, which debated the corruption of Quakers in Pennsylvania by secular concerns. Abram, aligning with the Keithians, left Germantown for Perkiomen, the Dutch township. In 1704 Abram Opden Graff, as the last surviving of the brothers, sold the remaining 828 acres of land in Germantown. Of Henderich there is little mention after 1693, when he was recorded on a Germantown tax list.

HISTORICAL DOCUMENT

This is to ye Monthly Meeting held at Richard Worrell's

These are the reasons why we are against the traffick of men-body, as foloweth. Is there any that would be done or handled at this manner? viz., to be sold or made a slave for all the time of his life? How

fearful and faint-hearted are many on sea, when they see a strange vessel,—being afraid it should be a Turk, and they should be taken, and sold for slaves into Turkey. Now what is this better done, as Turks doe? Yea, rather it is worse for them, which say they are Christians; for we hear that ye most part of such negers are brought hither against their will and consent, and that many of them are stolen. Now, tho they are black, we can not conceive there is more liberty to have them slaves, as it is to have other white ones. There is a saying that we shall doe to all men like as we will be done ourselves; making no difference of what generation, descent or colour they are. And those who steal or robb men, and those who buy or purchase them, are they not all alike? Here is liberty of conscience wch is right and reasonable; here ought to be liberty of ye body, except of evil-doers, wch is an other case. But to bring men hither, or to rob and sell them against their will, we stand against. In Europe there are many oppressed for conscience sake; and here there are those oppressed who are of a black colour. And we who know that men must not comitt adultery,— some do committ adultery, in separating wives from their husbands and giving them to others; and some sell the children of these poor creatures to other men. Ah! doe consider will this thing, you who doe it, if you would be done at this manner? And if it is done according to Christianity? You surpass Holland and Germany in this thing. This makes an ill report in all those countries of Europe, where they hear of, that ye Quakers doe here handel men as they handel there ye cattle. And for that reason some have no mind or inclination to come hither. And who shall maintain this your cause, or pleid for it. Truly we can not do so, except you shall inform us better hereof, viz., that Christians have liberty to practise these things. Pray, what thing in the world can be done worse towards us, than if men should rob or steal us away, and sell us for slaves to strange countries; separating husbands from their wives and children. Being now that this is not done in the manner we would be done at therefore we contradict and are against this traffic of men-body. And we who profess that it is not lawful to steal, must, likewise, avoid to purchase such things as are stolen, but rather help to stop this robbing and stealing if possible. And such men ought to be delivered out of ye hands of ye robbers, and set free as well as in Europe. Then is Pennsylvania to have a good report, instead it hath now a bad one for this sake in other countries. Especially whereas ye Europeans are de-

sirous to know in what manner ye Quakers doe rule in their province;—and most of them doe look upon us with an envious eye. But if this is done well, what shall we say is done evil?

If once these slaves (wch they say are so wicked and stubbern men) should join themselves,—fight for their freedom,—and handel their masters and mastrisses as they did handel them before; will these masters and mastrisses take the sword at hand and warr against these poor slaves, licke, we are able to believe, some will not refuse to doe; or have these negers not as much right to fight for their freedom, as you have to keep them slaves?

Now consider will this thing, if it is good or bad? And in case you find it to be good to handle these blacks at that manner, we desire and require you hereby lovingly, that you may inform us herein, which at this time never was done, viz., that Christians have such a liberty to do so. To the end we shall be be satisfied in this point, and satisfie likewise our good friends and acquaintances in our natif country, to whose it is a terror, or fairful thing, that men should be handeld so in Pennsylvania.

This is from our meeting at Germantown, held ye18 of the 2 month, 1688, to be delivered to the Monthly Meeting at Richard Worrell's.

Garret henderich
derick up de graeff
Francis daniell Pastorius
Abraham up Den graef.

Monthly Meeting Response

At our Monthly Meeting at Dublin, ye 30–2 mo., 1688, we have inspected ye matter, above mentioned, and considered of it, we find it so weighty that we think it not expedient for us to meddle with it here, but do rather commit it to ye consideration of ye Quarterly Meeting; ye tenor of it being nearly related to ye Truth. On behalf of ye Monthly Meeting,
Signed, P. Jo. Hart.

Quarterly Meeting Response

This, above mentioned, was read in our Quarterly Meeting at Philadelphia, the 4 of ye 4th mo. '88, and was from thence recommended to the Yearly Meeting, and the above said Derick, and the other

two mentioned therein, to present the same to ye above said meeting, it being a thing of too great a weight for this meeting to determine. Signed by order of ye meeting,
  Anthony Morris.

Yearly Meeting Response
At a Yearly Meeting held at Burlington the 5th day of the 7th month, 1688.

A Paper being here presented by some German Friends Concerning the Lawfulness and Unlawfulness of Buying and keeping Negroes, It was adjusted not to be so proper for this Meeting to give a Positive Judgment in the case, It having so General a Relation to many other Parts, and therefore at present they forbear It.

GLOSSARY

mastrisses mistresses

natif native

negers an antique (and not derogatory) form of "Negro," based on the Germanic word for "black."

pleid plead

Turks a reference to the Barbary pirates operating off the north coast of Africa

viz. an abbreviation of the Latin *videlicet,* meaning "that is."

wch which

ye the

Document Analysis

The authors of the Germantown protest—Pastorius, the Opden Graffs, and Henderich—open their statement with the title "A Minute against Slavery, Addressed to Germantown Monthly Meeting." Here, *minute* refers to a formal record of matters of importance to the writers, often for a superior audience and especially in the context of a meeting. Their prefatory statement, "These are the reasons why we are against the traffick of menbody," clearly indicates their intent: They oppose the selling, buying, and use of human beings as slaves.

The first point raised by the Germantown protesters echoes the Golden Rule. They ask their audience, "Is there any that would be done or handled at this manner? viz., to be sold or made a slave for all the time of his life?" In other words, they ask their fellow colonists how many of them would appreciate being taken and sold into permanent bondage without their consent. They remind their readers of the fear inspired by the Turks and their practice of taking Christian captives in eastern Europe and around the Mediterranean basin, and they ask if Africans facing the same danger should feel less terror or believe themselves less wronged. A bit later in the document the authors return to this theme, suggesting that the racial origin of slaves should not be a factor in determining the morality of enslaving others. Thus the Germantowners explicitly invoke the Golden Rule and make reference to issues of race and equality, emphasizing the obligation to treat others, no matter how different, as they themselves would wish to be treated. They return to this point a final time in drawing a very specific comparison between the plight of those abused for the nature of their faiths—"for conscience sake"—in Europe and the plight of "those oppressed who are of a black colour" in America.

In the course of the first paragraph, the authors also worry about the exposure of their brethren to other vices, in particular those associated with the sanctity of marriage and the family. They argue that slavery presents the opportunity for adultery, citing the evils of "separating wives from their husbands and giving them to others." They also refer to the consequences of family dissolution imposed when the offspring of slaves are sold away from their parents. The petitioners warn their audience that Christians ought not do such things, not simply because they are sins but also because those actions damage the image of the colony and threaten the morality of the whole Pennsylvania enterprise.

The Germantown protesters proceed to question both the inhumanity of slavery and the appearance of their colony in the eyes of the larger world should they permit the institution to flourish within their boundaries. They challenge the morality of all who engage in the institution of slavery, condemning not only those who own slaves and profit from their unlawful labors but also those who join in the buying and selling of slaves. The petitioners then point out that Europeans pay attention to the residents of the colonies and judge their behaviors, implying that colonists who participate in slavery exceed the European evils of religious and political oppression through their sinful treatment of their fellow men.

The second paragraph of the protest contains a warning of a different sort, one that is nearly prophetic in its content. It is a statement concerning the ongoing dangers of holding men in bondage against their wills. The Germantowners here assume the slaveholders' arguments and turn them against those who employ slaves. Owners, supporting permanent bondage of Africans, voice the notion that their slaves represent the basest of all human beings and need to be enslaved. The authors thus ask what would stop these "wicked and stubbern men" from aggressively seeking their liberty and thereupon using "their masters and mastrisses as they did handel them before." The authors go on to ask slaveholders if they would then rebel against the injustice of permanent servitude, wondering, "have these negers not as much right to fight for their freedom, as you have to keep them slaves?" These questions touch on the deepest fears of slave owners and foreshadow the slave rebellions brewing on the horizon. The Germantowners are furthermore expressing concerns over the bearing of arms in response to the threat of revolt. Ingrained in the Quaker belief system is a commitment to pacifism. The petitioners question the ability of slave-owning Quakers to resist the temptation of defending themselves, by taking "the sword at hand," in the case of an insurrection.

The argument closes in the third paragraph with a formal request to be informed of the regional meeting's findings concerning their protests. They do not demand that their counterparts support their cause but rather request that the members of the Dublin Meeting search their consciences and report their findings. They note that up to this point no religious authority had defined the Christian legitimacy of slavery; thus, they in Germantown needed guidance and answers to their questions. They also hoped to calm the fears of their brethren back in their "natif country"—that is, both Germany and Holland—"to whose it is a terror, or fairful thing, that men should be handeld so in Pennsylvania."

"A Minute against Slavery" concludes as it begins, by formally addressing the protests to the next regional Monthly Meeting at Worrell's house. The four signers of the document—Henderich, Pastorius, and the two Opden Graff brothers—follow in no particular order and with no reference to rank or status within Germantown. This presentation is very Quakerly, in that it privileges none of the participants and so emphasizes their equality. The four were, perhaps, more important for what they represented about their community. Although not indicated in the document, Pastorius's name carried considerable weight beyond Germantown, and any petition from the community without his support would have been treated with greater suspicion. The other signers represented the diversity of Germantown and its possible factions. The Opden Graffs were German in origin and among the first wave of colonists. Henderich represented the Dutch voices in the meeting and was a fairly recent arrival. Together the men embodied the larger population of their community.

Essential Themes

To the authors, slavery violates the most basic of Christian tenets—treat others as you wish to be treated. The authors emphasize not only that slavery is immoral but, indeed, that it should be actively fought, contending, "And we who profess that it is not lawful to steal, must, likewise, avoid to purchase such things as are stolen, but rather help to stop this robbing and stealing if possible." Here, their argument reaches its most radical and far-reaching point. They continue by suggesting, in accord with Christian obligation, not only that the trafficking of human beings should be stopped but also that the unlawfully enslaved "ought to be delivered out of ye hands of ye robbers, and set free" everywhere. This is a clear denunciation of the slave trade and of slavery in general; it is a call to abolition.

While he immediate impact of "A Minute against Slavery" was negligible, the protest did, however, foreshadow the wider emergence of antislavery sentiments in Pennsylvania's Quaker communities. What is particularly interesting about the Germantown protest is how accurately the members defined what would become the most politically significant arguments against slavery. They drew on their belief system to construct the condemnation of an institution they considered morally and spiritually repugnant. Germantown's Quakers asked their fellow worshippers to acknowledge their own beliefs in the brotherhood of all humanity, in the obligation to strive for moral perfection, and in the Golden Rule. They also warned their audiences of the consequences of failure to join them in renouncing the institution of slavery: slave owners and holders invited and would suffer the approbation of their European counterparts, the burdens and temptations of sin, and the threat of rebellion.

———*Martha Pallante, PhD*

Bibliography and Additional Reading

Articles

Aptheker, Herbert. "The Quakers and Negro Slavery." *Journal of Negro History* 25, no. 3 (July 1940): 331–362.

Binder-Johnson, Hildegard. "The Germantown Protest of 1688 against Negro Slavery." *Pennsylvania Magazine of History and Biography* 65, no. 2 (April 1941): 145–156.

Cadbury, Henry J. "An Early Quaker Anti-Slavery Statement." *Journal of Negro History* 22, no. 4 (October 1937): 488–493.

Eichhoff, Jürgen. "The Three Hundredth Anniversary of the Germantown Protest against Slavery." *Monatshefte* 80, no. 3 (Fall 1988): 265–267.

Pennypacker, Samuel W. "The Settlement of Germantown, and the Causes Which Led to It." *Pennsylvania Magazine of History and Biography* 4, no. 1 (1880): 1–41.

Books

Jordan, Winthrop D. *White over Black: American Attitudes toward the Negro, 1550–1812.* New York: W. W. Norton, 1977.

Shuffelton, Frank, ed. *A Mixed Race: Ethnicity in Early America.* New York: Oxford University Press, 1993.

Tolles, Frederick. *Meeting House and Counting House: The Quaker Merchants of Colonial Philadelphia, 1682–1763.* New York: W. W. Norton, 1948.

Wolf, Stephanie Grauman. *Urban Village: Population, Community, and Family Structure in Germantown, Pennsylvania, 1683–1800.* Princeton, N.J.: Princeton University Press, 1976.

An Account of the Negroe Insurrection in South Carolina

Date: 1739
Author: James Oglethorpe
Genre: Essay

Summary Overview

Slave rebellions in the American south loom large in the history of the United States, with well known conspiracies such as that of Denmark Vesey and Nat Turner's Rebellion being among the most well known. One of the most significant slave uprisings of the colonial era took place in 1739 in South Carolina. The Stono Rebellion killed almost two dozen whites and led to the deaths of many of the rebels.

Although this report (collected in *The Colonial Records of the State of Georgia*) was unsigned, many historians believe it to be the work of James Oglethorpe, British army officer and founder of the Georgia colony, written as a third-person narrative.Oglethorpe's account of the Stono Rebellion gives a good deal of background about the slaves as well as the broader geopolitical picture of the governor of Spanish Florida offering a safe haven for fugitive slaves. In addition to providing background to the event and the broader context of British-Spanish relations, this report of the Stono slave uprising also gives modern readers a window into white attitudes and fears concerning slaves and the possibility of violent insurgency.

Defining Moment

In South Carolina colony, directly north of Oglethorpe's colony of Georgia, slaves made up a majority of the population, with many being brought from the Kingdom of Kongo. Many of these slaves were Roman Catholic, as Catholicism had become popular in the kingdom due to Portuguese influence in the 15th century. Consequently, runaway slaves tended to head south to Spanish Florida. For example, in 1738, the free black settlement of Fort Mose was founded near St. Augustine.

The South Carolinians worked with the neighbors in Georgia to catch fugitive slaves and guard against revolt. In August, 1739, the colony enacted the Security Act, which required all white men carry firearms to church on Sundays, out of fear of a possible slave insurrection. Despite their precautions, a slave named Jemmy and 22 African slaves came to the Stone River south of Charleston, South Carolina on September 9, 1739. Marching down the road with a banner that said "Liberty!" they raided a store, stealing guns and ammu-

nition and killing the two shop employees. They went on to kill three people at the Godfrey household as well as the inhabitants of the another half dozen houses. Slaves—some willingly, some not-joined the rebellion, swelling its ranks to 50.

That afternoon, after killing as many as two dozen white South Carolinians, an armed posse who had been pursuing the rebels caught up with them as the rested in a field. A firefight took place in which about half of the slaves were killed. Eventually, those rebels who fled were caught and executed.

Author Biography

James Oglethorpe was born on December 22, 1690 in England. Raised in an upper class family, Oglethorpe attended Oxford University but left his studies to join the Army, serving as aid-de-camp to Prince Eugene of Savoy, a member of the Hapsburg dynasty that rule the Holy Roman Empire. He served in the war between Austria and the Ottoman Empire from 1716 to 1718.

Later, in 1722, he was elected to Parliament, working to improve conditions for sailors and working for prison reform. In response to the horrible conditions and abuse he witnessed in a number of debtors' prisons in England, he formed a group to pursue the creation of a new colony, Georgia, in North America. It was approved in 1732 and the first ship headed to America in November of that year.

Oglethorpe's plan for Georgia was for it to be based, economically, on small family farms rather than the rice or tobacco plantations more common elsewhere in the southern colonies. Ironically, one of the early experiments in Georgia was in growing cotton which would become the premier plantation crop in the 19th century. Such a plan was also intended to allow the colony to avoid the urban growth of many colonies in the north and south. Colonists would be granted 50 acre lots, including small plots in town for a house and garden, and a 45 acre lot for farming. While indentured servitude would be allowed (and encouraged, with servant-possessing colonists getting more land), Oglethorpe did not want to allow slavery in Georgia.

Eventually, however, cotton planters would force the ban on slavery to end.

Oglethorpe led troops during the War of Jenkins Ear, fought between Georgia and Florida but was criticized for an unsuccessful siege of St. Augustine. He returned to Britain in 1743, continuing to serve in the Army and, eventually leading troops against the Jacobite Rising of 1745. He died in 1785 at the age of 88.

HISTORICAL DOCUMENT

Sometime since there was a Proclamation published at Augustine, in which the King of Spain (then at Peace with Great Britain) promised Protection and Freedom to all Negroes Slaves that would resort thither. Certain Negroes belonging to Captain Davis escaped to Augustine, and were received there. They were demanded by General Oglethorpe who sent Lieutenant Demere to Augustine, and the Governour assured the General of his sincere Friendship, but at the same time showed his Orders from the Court of Spain, by which he was to receive all Run away Negroes. Of this other Negroes having notice, as it is believed, from the Spanish Emissaries, four or five who were Cattel-Hunters, and knew the Woods, some of whom belonged to Captain Macpherson, ran away with His Horses, wounded his Son and killed another Man. These marched f [sic] for Georgia, and were pursued, but the Rangers being then newly reduced [sic] the Countrey people could not overtake them, though they were discovered by the Saltzburghers, as they passed by Ebenezer. They reached Augustine, one only being killed and another wounded by the Indians in their flight. They were received there with great honours, one of them had a Commission given to him, and a Coat faced with Velvet. Amongst the Negroe Slaves there are a people brought from the Kingdom of Angola in Africa, many of these speak Portugueze (which Language is as near Spanish as Scotch is to English,) by reason that the Portugueze have considerable Settlement, and the Jesuits have a Mission and School in that Kingdom and many Thousands of the Negroes there profess the Roman Catholic Religion. Several Spaniards upon diverse Pretences have for some time past been strolling about Carolina, two of them, who will give no account of themselves have been taken up and committed to Jayl in Georgia. The good reception of the Negroes at Augustine was spread about, Several attempted to escape to the Spaniards, & were taken, one of them was hanged at Charles Town. In the latter end of July last Don Pedro, Colonel of the Spanish Horse, went in a Launch to Charles Town under pretence of a message to General Oglethorpe and the Lieutenant Governour.

On the 9th day of September last being Sunday which is the day the Planters allow them to work for themselves, Some Angola Negroes assembled, to the number of Twenty; and one who was called Jemmy was their Captain, they suprized a Warehouse belonging to Mr. Hutchenson at a place called Stonehow [sic—]; they there killed Mr. Robert Bathurst, and Mr. Gibbs, plundered the House and took a pretty many small Arms and Powder, which were there for Sale. Next they plundered and burnt Mr. Godfrey's house, and killed him, his Daughter and Son. They then turned back and marched Southward along Pons Pons, which is the Road through Georgia to Augustine, they passed Mr. Wallace's Tavern towards day break, and said they would not hurt him, for he was a good Man and kind to his Slaves, but they broke open and plundered Mr. Lemy's House, and killed him, his wife and Child. They marched on towards Mr. Rose's resolving to kill him; but he was saved by a Negroe, who having hid him went out and pacified the others. Several Negroes joyned them, they calling out Liberty, marched on with Colours displayed, and two Drums beating, pursuing all the white people they met with, and killing Man Woman and Child when they could come up to them. Collonel Bull Lieutenant Governour of South Carolina, who was then riding along the Road, discovered them, was pursued, and with much difficulty escaped & raised the Countrey. They burnt Colonel Hext's house and killed his Overseer and his Wife. They then burnt Mr. Sprye's house, then Mr. Sacheverell's, and then Mr. Nash's house, all lying upon the

Pons Pons Road, and killed all the white People they found in them. Mr. Bullock got off, but they burnt his House, by this time many of them were drunk with the Rum they had take in the Houses. They increased every minute by new Negroes coming to them, so that they were above Sixty, some say a hundred, on which they halted in a field, and set to dancing, Singing and beating Drums, to draw more Negroes to them, thinking they were now victorious over the whole Province, having marched ten miles & burnt all before them without Opposition, but the Militia being raised, the Planters with great briskness pursued them and when they came up, dismounting; charged them on foot. The Negroes were soon routed, though they behaved boldly several being killed on the Spot, many ran back to their Plantations thinking they had not been missed, but they were there taken and [sic] Shot, Such as were taken in the field also, were after being examined, shot on the Spot, And this is to be said to the honour of the Carolina Planters, that notwithstanding the Provocation they had received from so many Murders, they did not torture one Negroe, but only put them to an easy death. All the [slaves] proved to be forced & were not concerned in the Murders & Burnings were pardoned,

And this sudden Courage in the field, & the Humanity afterwards hath had so good an Effect that there hath been no farther Attempt, and the very Spirit of Revolt seems over. About 30 escaped from the fight, of which ten marched about 30 miles Southward, and being overtaken by the Planters on horseback, fought stoutly for some time and were all killed on the Spot. The rest are yet untaken. In the whole action about 40 Negroes and 20 whites were killed. The Lieutenant Governour sent an account of this to General Oglethorpe, who met the advices on his return from the Indian Nation He immediately ordered a Troop of Rangers to be ranged, to patrole through Georgia, placed some Men in the Garrison at Palichocolas, which was before abandoned, and near which the Negroes formerly passed, being the only place where Horses can come to swim over the River Savannah for near 100 miles, ordered out the Indians in pursuit, and a Detachment of the Garrison at Port Royal to assist the Planters on any Occasion, and published a Proclamation ordering all the Constables &c. of Georgia to pursue and seize all Negroes, with a Reward for any that should be taken. It is hoped these measures will prevent any Negroes from getting down to the Spaniards.

GLOSSARY

Augustine: St. Augustine, a city in Spanish-controlled Florida

colours: flags, especially of a military unit

Stonehow: misspelling of Stono upon diverse Pretences: using various false excuses or reasons

Document Analysis

Oglethorpe begins his report on the Stono slave uprising with a very long paragraph that comprises an extensive discussion on the relationship of fugitive slaves to the Spanish and their position in Florida. He relates that the King of Spain—who, Oglethorpe points out, was "at peace" with Great Britain at that time)—promised that runaway slaves who made their way to Florida would be free and under Spanish protection. Oglethorpe recounts his personal experience with this arrangement with the story of his sending an officer to inquire

of one of his officer's fugitive slaves. The Governor of Florida, while friendly, explained that he was only following the instructions of the Spanish government.

Oglethorpe then tells the story of runaway slaves who assaulted or murdered whites in their escape and entered Georgia and, evading capture, made their way to St. Augustine after skirmishes with Georgia's Native American allies. Oglethorpe places a portion of the blame for these events on the Spanish, saying that the slaves had notice, as it is believed, from the Spanish Emissaries." What he is saying, basically, is that the

Spanish encouraged slaves to leave their masters and abscond to Florida, caring little for the destruction, injuries, or death that these fugitive slaves may have caused. To reinforce his argument on Spanish encouragement of slave violence and flight, Oglethorpe relates rumors that the slaves were greeted warmly by the Spanish and granted a (presumably military) commission along with "a Coat faced with Velvet."

Oglethorpe, connecting the dots for his readers, discusses the origins of some of the slaves, identifying them as being from the "Kingdom of Angola in Africa." This was the one of the names given to the Kingdom of the Kongo during the early modern period. Oglethorpe explains the connection between this kingdom and the "Portugueze," particularly the conversion of the many of the subjects of the kingdom to Catholicism. He also divulges that some Spanish subjects been spotted in South Carolina "upon diverse Pretences" (in other words, giving authorities various stories to explain their presence) and have been imprisoned in "Jayl [jail]" in Georgia. He concludes this lengthy first paragraph by reiterating that slaves had previously attempted to escape their bondage by fleeing to Spanish territory.

The second long paragraph explains the events of September 9, 1739. Oglethorpe explains that on Sundays, plantation owners allow the slaves to work "for themselves"—that is, to cultivate crops for their own use. Taking advantage of this liberty, a number the "Angola" slaves, under the leadership of Jemmy, obtained weapons and ammunition and went on a murderous trek across South Carolina. Oglethorpe's account is fairly straightforward, detailing the victims of the rebellious slaves but not doing so in a particularly melodramatic way.

As they made their way south, presumably heading for Spanish Florida, Oglethorpe reports that the rebels were drunk on stolen rum and that their numbers steadily increased as more slaves rallied to their cause. He is unclear on the exact numbers, stating that there were more than sixty and, according to some, as many as one hundred slaves involved in the uprising. As the rebel slaves rested in a field, "thinking they were now victorious over the whole Province," South Carolina militia troops confronted them, under the command of the the planters. In this face to face conflict, the fugitive slaves were not able to stand against the trained troops, althought "they behaved boldly several being killed on the Spot." The rebellion ended, and Oglethorpe praises the plantation owners for their restraint in dealing with the rebels, with the guilty being "put...to

an easy death" rather than being tortured. Oglethorpe closes with the hope that new, stronger efforts to patrol roads and the country side will prevent more fugitive slaves from "getting down to the Spaniards."

Essential Themes

The colony of Georgia that James Oglethorpe founded existed in a precarious world, attempting to establish itself between the settled planter cult of South Carolina on its northern border and the sometime-enemy territory of Spanish Florida on its southern border. Because of this position as the so-called "buffer colony" of British North America, Georgia was often in the center of intrigue. Spanish encouragement (at least, that's how Oglethorpe portrays it) of slave resistance, rebellion, and flight had a direct effect on the people of Georgia, as any runaway slaves had to make their way through that colony on their way to freedom in Spanish territory. Thus, Oglethorpe's account highlights the geopolitical themes that would absent from the major slave rebellions of the 19th century.

There is also an element of religious conspiracy that parallels the religious aspects of the Denmark Vesey or Nat Turner rebellions of the next century. Oglethorpe, a staunch Anglican, highlights his assumption of the Roman Catholic beliefs of these slaves from the Kingdom of the Kongo. Their connection with the Spanish is not a mere coincidence of geography. Rather, it is the natural outgrowth of their shared religious tradition.

Also worth noting is Oglethorpe's praise of the plantation owners for showing restraint in not torturing the captured rebels. He also makes a point to highlight the bravery of the fugitive slaves.

——*Aaron Gulyas, MA*

Bibliography and Additional Reading

Hoffer, Peter Charles: *Cry Liberty. The Great Stono River Slave Rebellion of 1739.* (New York: Oxford University Press, 2010).

Shuler, Jack. *Calling Out Liberty: The Stono Rebellion and the Universal Struggle for Human Rights.* Jackson, MS: University Press of Mississippi, 2009.

Smith, Mark M., *Stono: Documenting and Interpreting a Southern Slave Revolt*, Columbia, SC: University of South Carolina Press, 2005.

Thornton, John (October 1991). "African Dimensions of the Stono Rebellion". *The American Historical Review*. 4. 96 (4): 1101–1113.

■ Petition of Prince Hall and Other African Americans to the Massachusetts General Court

Date: 1777
Author: Prince Hall, et al
Genre: Petition

Summary Overview

On January 13, 1777, Prince Hall and seven other African American men—most of them probably free—submitted a petition to the Massachusetts General Court, which at that time consisted of the Massachusetts Revolutionary Council and the House of Representatives. This petition sought freedom for "a great number of Negroes who are detained…in the Bowels of a free & Christian Country." The petition was one of several that African Americans in New England submitted during the late eighteenth century. This one was particularly noteworthy because it challenged the Commonwealth of Massachusetts's government to live up to the human rights principles that had been set forth less than a year earlier in the Declaration of Independence. Little is known of Prince Hall before 1780, and there are conflicting stories of his origins, but what we do know of Hall's life points to him as the leader of this effort.

The Massachusetts legislature failed to pass any laws in response to this petition; however, the *Quock Walker v. Jennison* case, in which an African American filed a claim of unjust enslavement, soon resulted in a jury decision in 1781 and an upper-court ruling in 1783 that spelled the end of slavery in Massachusetts. In the coming years, other northern states passed laws that ended slavery gradually and thus avoided what many whites viewed as the socioeconomic chaos that could have been brought on by immediate abolition. While these governmental actions are usually credited with having ended slavery above the Mason-Dixon Line, the petition of January 1777 and similar formal appeals played critical foundational roles in the process. These petitions also to some extent represent the starting point for the establishment of organized African American communities in New England and elsewhere in the North.

Defining Moment

The number of Africans and their descendants in southern New England had risen from about one thousand in 1700 to around eleven thousand by the middle of the eighteenth century, largely because prominent

merchants in the region had become deeply involved in the slave trade. About a third lived in Boston, the region's center of commerce and government.

Although most blacks in colonial New England were slaves, a significant number were free. The situation of blacks in New England, regardless of their status, was markedly different from that of blacks in other colonies. Most lived in port towns and worked in semi-skilled or unskilled jobs for which Anglo-American labor was scarce. The few who resided in rural villages were probably slaves and served as status symbols for their masters. Rural slaves also provided a pool of menial labor for the local elites, particularly ministers. Of those African Americans who already were free, a very few became successful.

While servitude and racism were facts of life in eighteenth-century New England, as elsewhere in colonial America, the region's culture also nurtured a nascent opposition to the slave trade. This opposition was rooted in the Puritan view that permitted the enslaving of war captives but frowned on "man stealing."

Not surprisingly, African Americans became involved the cause for freedom from British rule and the most important embrace by blacks of Revolutionary goals came in a series of petitions that began in 1773. Between that year and wen fighting broke out between British and American forces, a number of petitions went before the colonial government. African Americans also served in the defense of Boston against British attacks and occupation. On March 17, 1776, the British Army evacuated Boston; before they left, On July 4, 1776, Congress declared independence. Five months later, on January 13, 1777, Prince Hall and seven other African Americans submitted a petition to the Massachusetts General Court on behalf of "a great number of Negroes" that called for an end to slavery.

Author Biography

While eight men put their names on the petition of January 13, 1777, there is extensive information about only one signatory, Prince Hall, a leader the African

American Masonic lodge and other black community organizations in Boston after the Revolutionary War. Hall's subsequent speeches and petitions were written in a style similar to that of this petition, which indicates that he may have also been its author.

Hall's life before the American Revolution is somewhat disputed. The Masonic tradition holds that he was born a free man in Barbados on September 12, 1748, and sailed to Boston in March 1765. By the age of twenty-five he owned a soap-making business, had purchased a home, and was qualified to vote in the city. A non-Masonic biographer claims that Hall was born in 1735 and first appeared in Boston in the 1740s as a slave. In 1770 Hall was given freedom by his master one month after the Boston Massacre.

Hall became a leader of the Boston African American community, beginning with the African American Masonic lodge, which provided services to black Bostonians: free firewood, periodic food drives for those in need, weekly "sick dues," and loans for members and their families. It later became known as the Prince Hall Lodge; today there are forty-seven Prince Hall Lodges that have grown out of the original Boston lodge.

In December, 1786, Hall submitted a petition from the African Lodge to the General Court that complained about society's poor treatment of blacks and sought assistance in returning blacks to Africa. In October 1787, Hall submitted a petition that charged that since African Americans paid district taxes their children had the right to be educated in the city's schools. A few months later, he organized a petition signed by twenty-two Masons for the return of three free Boston African Americans who had been kidnapped and subsequently sold as slaves. On March 26, 1788, the General Court responded with an act that banned the slave trade and gained relief for blacks kidnapped from Massachusetts and resold into slavery.

The last public record of Hall's thought was an address to the African Masonic Lodge on June 24, 1797, in which he celebrated the success of the Haitian slave revolt of 1791 and urged his brothers to exercise patience despite their regular abuse in Boston. He died ten years later.

HISTORICAL DOCUMENT

To the Honorable Council & House of Representatives for the State of Massachusetts Bay in General Court assembled January 13, 1777.

The Petition of a great number of Negroes who are detained in a state of Slavery in the Bowels of a free & Christian Country Humbly Shewing

That your Petitioners apprehend that they have, in common with all other Men, a natural & unalienable right to that freedom, which the great Parent of the Universe hath bestowed equally on all mankind, & which they have never forfeited by any compact or agreement whatever. That they were unjustly dragged by the cruel hand of Power, from their dearest friends, & some of them even torn from the embraces of their tender Parents from a populous, pleasant and plentiful Country—& in Violation of the Laws of Nature & of Nation & in defiance of all the tender feelings of humanity, brought hither to be sold like Beasts of Burden, & like them condemned to slavery for Life. Among a People professing the mild Religion of Jesus—A People not insensible of the sweets of rational freedom—Nor without spirit to resent the unjust endeavors of others to reduce them to a State of Bondage & Subjection—Your donors need not to be informed that a Life of Slavery, like that of your petitioners, deprived of every social privilege, of every thing requisite to render Life even tolerable, is far worse than Non-Existence. In imitation of the laudable example of the People of these States, your Petitioners have long & patiently waited the event of Petition after Petition by them presented to the legislative Body of this State, & can not but with grief reflect that their success has been but too similar. They can not but express their astonishment, that it has never been considered, that every principle from which America has acted in the course of their unhappy difficulties with Great-Britain, pleads stronger than a thousand arguments in favor of your Petitioners. They therefore humbly beseech your Honors to give this Petition its due weight & consideration, & cause an Act of the Legislature to be passed whereby they may be restored to the enjoyment of that freedom which is the natural right of all Men—& their Children (who were born in this Land of Liberty) may not be held as Slaves after they arrive at the age of twenty one years. So may the Inhabitants of this State (no longer chargeable with the inconsistency of acting, themselves, the part which they condemn & oppose in others) be prospered in their present glorious struggles for Liberty: & have those blessings secured to them by

Heaven of which benevolent minds can not wish to deprive their fellow Men.

And your Petitioners as in Duty Bound shall ever pray

Lancaster Hill
Peter Bess
Brister Slenser
Prince Hall
Jack Purpont [mark]
Nero Suneto [mark]
Newport Symner [mark]
Job Lark

GLOSSARY

compact: a treaty or written agreement

"great Parent of the Universe": God

"the mild Religion of Jesus": Christianity

"their unhappy difficulties": The Revolutionary War

Document Analysis

Although the document is not divided into sections, it may be considered in three parts. In the first part, the petitioners call forth concepts cherished by political leaders in the state (and country) and condemn the international slave trade as a violation of those values. They declare that blacks have "a natural & unalienable right" to the freedom granted to all humankind, "which they have never forfeited by any compact or agreement." This phrasing is significant not only because of the reference to natural rights but also because the giver of freedom is described not as Christ or God but as the "great Parent of the Universe"—a phrase in tune with Enlightenment notions of the universe as a machine that God created with predictable rules understandable by human beings. The opening perhaps also retains the scent of a reference to the *Somerset* decision. This was a June, 1772 case in which the chief justice of the King's Bench had ruled slavery could not exist in England or its colonies unless it was explicitly established by written law.

The next clause invokes the emerging Euro-American notion of sentimentalism, that citizens in a republic

needed to develop the virtuous and benevolent moral feelings that could be fostered only within a loving family and by the manly bonds of friendship. Thus the petitioners decry the "cruel hand" of the slave traders, who "unjustly dragged" blacks "from their dearest friends," some "even torn from the embraces of their tender Parents." These practices are condemned as being in violation of the "Laws of Nature & of Nation"—a reference to Locke and the *Somerset* ruling—as well as "in defiance of all the tender feelings of humanity." In perhaps the most unexpected clause, the petitioners associate their lost happiness with "a populous, pleasant and plentiful Country," rather than an African continent more usually depicted (even by Phillis Wheatley in her popular poems) as barbaric, savage, and dark.

The next part first offers flowery praise, then bitter criticism. Here, the petition extols New Englanders for "professing the mild Religion of Jesus" (the tone of the word *professing* being perhaps mildly scolding) and being "not insensible of the sweets of rational freedom." By commending the "spirit" by which the American colonists had resisted "the unjust endeavors of others to reduce them to a State of Bondage & Subjection," this section makes the connection between the ideals of the American Revolution and freedom from slavery. The petitioners then pointedly note that the leaders of the state did not have to be "informed" that a life of slavery without any rights was "far worse than Non-Existence"—that is, even harsher than life under British military rule and Parliament's authority. The petitioners voice their bewilderment and "grief" at how, "in imitation of the laudable example" of American democratic practices, they had submitted "Petition after Petition" to the state legislature. Yet their efforts had been to no avail, much as the efforts of colonial American leaders had failed to gain a sympathetic ear in Parliament. There is no indication that this rebuke was meant to threaten a potential uprising by Massachusetts slaves, but it was a veiled hint at the level of their collective frustration. The petitioners then express "their astonishment" that their fellow Americans had not yet conceded that the principles upon which the Revolution was grounded pleaded "stronger than a thousand arguments" in support of freedom for slaves.

The third part of the petition is its most substantive section. It calls on the legislature to pass a measure ending slavery, though the petitioners are willing for their children born in America to remain slaves until the age of twenty-one. They observe that ending slavery would not be giving slaves new rights but restoring them "to the enjoyment of that freedom which is the natural right of all Men." Again, the petitioners call attention to the principle of natural rights. Unlike previous requests, this petition does not propose that any consideration should be given to slave owners. Likewise, it does not ask for land on which former slaves could start farms, nor is there any suggestion that blacks would return to Africa. If the legislature were to grant the petition's request, Prince Hall and the other signatories note, it would free the people of Massachusetts from "the inconsistency of acting, themselves, the part which they condemn & oppose in others." The people of Massachusetts would therefore certainly "be prospered in their present glorious struggles for Liberty."

Essential Themes

The petition of January 1777 begins by stating that it was an appeal on behalf of not only the signatories but also "a great number of Negroes," many then living in a "state of Slavery." The three previous petitions for freedom submitted between January 1773 and May 1774 had begun similarly. But the 1777 petition was

the first effort by African Americans to improve their situation after the country had declared itself free of British rule. The petition relied heavily on concepts that had emerged with the European Enlightenment in the late seventeenth century, particularly the notion first expressed by the English political philosopher John Locke in 1690 that all humans were born with the "natural" rights of life, liberty, and property. Locke and later Enlightenment thinkers also held that government was not something imposed by God on sinful humans but a contract created by people long ago in order to protect their natural rights from greed or passion; if a government violated those rights, the people had the right to change the government. These concepts would become foundations of the American Revolution and were carefully chosen by Thomas Jefferson to open the Declaration of Independence—published just six months before the eight Boston blacks presented their petition for freedom. The petition also critiques the hypocrisy of calling for freedom while allowing slavery to continue. This argument was quite different from that advanced in the other four petitions, all of which made only passing nods at Enlightenment thought and instead emphasized Christian morality, the "unmanly" situations of the petitioners, and the *Somerset* court decision.

———*Daniel R. Mandell, PhD*

Bibliography and Additional Reading

Mandell, Daniel. "Shifting Boundaries of Race and Ethnicity: Indian-Black Intermarriage in Southern New England, 1760–1880." *Journal of American History* 85, no. 2 (September 1998): 466–501.

Butterfield, L. H., et al. eds. *Adams Family Correspondence*. Vol.1: *December 1761–May 1776*. Cambridge: Belknap Press of Harvard University Press, 1963.

Cottrol, Robert J. *The Afro-Yankees: Providence's Black Community in the Antebellum Era*. Westport, Conn. Greenwood Press, 1982.

Holton, Woody, ed. *Black Americans in the Revolutionary Era: A Brief History with Documents*. New York: Bedford/St. Martin's, 2009.

Horton, James Oliver, and Lois E. Horton. *Black Bostonians: Family Life and Community Struggle in the Antebellum North*. New York: Holmes & Meier Publishers, 1979.

———. *In Hope of Liberty: Culture, Community, and Protest among Northern Free Blacks, 1700–1860*. New York: Oxford University Press, 1997.

Kaplan, Sidney, and Emma Nogrady Kaplan. *The Black Presence in the Era of the American Revolution*. Rev. ed. Amherst: University of Massachusetts Press, 1989.

Nash, Gary B. *Race and Revolution*. Lanham, Md. Rowan and Littlefield, 2001.

Moore, George H. *Notes on the History of Slavery in Massachusetts*. New York: D. Appleton, 1866.

Otis, James. *The Rights of British Colonies Asserted and Proved*. Boston: Edes and Gill, 1764. Piersen, William D. *Black Yankees: The Development of an Afro-American Subculture in Eighteenth-Century New England*. Amherst: University of Massachusetts Press, 1988.

Sewall, Samuel. *The Selling of Joseph: A Memorial*. Boston: Green and Allen, 1700.

Shields, John, ed. *The Collected Works of Phillis Wheatley*. New York: Oxford University Press, 1988.

Web Sites

"Petition for Freedom to Massachusetts Governor Thomas Gage, His Majesty's Council, and the House of Representatives, 25 May 1774." Massachusetts Historical Society Web site. http://www.masshist. org/database/549

"Petition for Freedom to Massachusetts Governor Thomas Gage, His Majesty's Council, and the House of Representatives, June 1774." Massachusetts Historical Society Web site. http://www.masshist.org/database/550

Petition to the Assembly of Pennsylvania against the Slave Trade

Date: 1780
Authors: Various
Genre: Petition

Summary Overview

While Pennsylvania made one of the earliest attempts by a state to end slavery in 1780, its petition for gradual emancipation contained several loopholes. The greatest one was that it did not actually free anyone who was currently enslaved in the state. Rather, it ended outright slavery for children born to slaves in the state, along with some other measures. Almost immediately after that law was passed, petitioners began circulating requests to eliminate those exceptions and grant freedom to a broader audience. This petition, from 1780, addressed concerns about the ongoing slave trade in the state.

Defining Moment

From its earliest days, citizens of Pennsylvania had been active in the fight to end slavery. While the impetus for these efforts had originally come from the Society of Friends (Quakers) in the colony, anti-slavery sentiment was not confined to that particular religious sect. Baptists, Methodists, and many German immigrants also opposed slavery. During the American War for Independence, the long-standing religious opposition to slavery was bolstered by those who believed the institution to be incompatible with the revolution's ideal of liberty. In 1780, Pennsylvania became the first state to enact legislation restricting slavery. The law, entitled "An Act for the Gradual Abolition of Slavery" declared all children born to enslaved women to be indentured servants rather than slaves. The children would have to serve their master until age 28. It outlaw bringing new slaves into the state and required slave owners to register their slaves. Those who did not would see their slaves freed as a penalty. Despite this law, slavery still existed in Pennsylvania. Those who were slaves when the law was enacted would remain slaves. During the time Philadelphia was the national capital, members of Congress were exempt from the law. Finally, as this petition explains, the slave trade was still active in Philadelphia. The petition would have an effect, but not an immediate one. In 1788, The Pennsylvania legislation would amend the 1780 law to forbid Pennsylvanians from having any association with the slave trade.

Author Biography

This petition was submitted and signed by over one hundred Pennsylvanians. While, as discussed above, Quakers and others had long opposed slavery, in 1775 residents of the state founded the Society for the Relief of Free Negroes Unlawfully Held in Bondage, the first organized abolition group in the American colonies. While the signers of this petition are not identified specifically as members of the organization, the Society was reorganized in 1784 as the Pennsylvania Abolition Society and continued to lobby government officials for further restrictions on slavery. It is likely that the originators and signers of this petition were connected with the organization.

HISTORICAL DOCUMENT

Petition to Prevent Slaves from Being Fitted Out at the Port of Philadelphia

To the Representatives of the Freemen of the Commonwealth of Pennsylvania, in General Assembly met,

The Representation and Petitions of the SUBSCRIBERS, Citizens of Pennsylvania.

YOUR Petitioners have observed, with great satisfaction, the salutary effects of the Law of this State, passed on the first day of March, 1780, for the "gradual abolition of slavery."—They have also seen, with equal satisfaction, the progress which the humane and just principles of that Law have made in other States.

They, however, find themselves called upon, by the interesting nature of those principles, to suggest to the General Assembly, that vessels have been publicly equipt in this Port for the Slave Trade, and that several other practices have taken place which they conceive to be inconsistent with the spirit of the Law abovementioned; and that these, and other circumstances relating to the afflicted Africans, do, in the opinion of your Petitioners, require the further interposition of the Legislature.

Your Petitioners therefore earnestly request that you will again take this subject into your serious consideration, and that you will make such additions to the said Law as shall effectually put a stop to the Slave Trade being carried on directly or indirectly in this Commonwealth, and to answer other purposes of benevolence and justice to an oppressed part of the human species.

GLOSSARY

benevolence: mercy and generosity

equipt: stocked and provisioned for carrying slaves

interposition: to act on a situation

"the afflicted Africans": slaves

Document Analysis

This very brief petition, weighing in at only 232 words, came soon after the legislation that granted the gradual abolition of slaves in Pennsylvania. After the official salutations at the beginning of the petition, the petitioners express "satisfaction" the March, 1780 abolition law and express "equal satisfaction" that similar laws were progressing in other states. It would take until 1783 for gradual abolition laws to take effect in New Hampshire, for example. A 1783 court decision in Massachusetts ruled slavery illegal under the 1780 state constitution.

While the abolition law is satisfying, the citizens bringing the petition to the Pennsylvania General Assembly are compelled to express concern over the slave trading ships in the port of Philadelphia. The petitioners argue that the existence of the slave trade in their city and state is "inconsistent with the spirit" of the abolition law. The slave trade, and the horrific conditions that accompany it deserve more attention from the state legislature.

In the concluding paragraph, the petitioners ask the assembly to consider a ban on the slave trade in the Pennsylvania—"either directly or indirectly"—and address in other ways the condition of the "oppressed" residents of the state.

Essential Themes

The key concern expressed by the petitioners is that the slave *trade* taking place in the port of Philadelphia is morally and ethically equivalent to the institution of slavery itself. How could Pennsylvania abolish slavery within its own borders while, at the same time, tolerate Pennsylvanians profiting from slavery elsewhere in the United States? If the legislature saw fit to abolish slavery, then logically, they must end their connection with the business of slavery as well.

———Aaron Gulyas, MA

Bibliography and Additional Reading

Berlin, Ira. *Generations of Captivity: A History of African-American Slaves.* (Cambridge: Harvard University Press, 2004).

Bradley, Patricia. *Slavery, Propaganda, and the American Revolution.* (Jackson: University of Mississippi Press, 1999).

Jackson, Maurice and Susan Kozel, eds. *Quakers and Their Allies in the Abolitionist Cause, 1754-1808* (London: Routledge: 2015).

Thomas, Hugh. The Slave Trade: The Story of the Atlantic Slave Trade: 1440 - 1870 (New York: Simon and Schuster, 1999).

An Address to Those Who Keep Slaves, and Approve the Practice

Date: 1794
Author: Richard Allen
Genre: Essay

Summary Overview

The first abolitionist essay authored by the celebrated black activist and minister Richard Allen, "An Address to Those Who Keep Slaves, and Approve the Practice," was among the most important black abolitionist proclamations of the late eighteenth century. Originally published in 1794 as part of a longer document titled *A Narrative of the Proceedings of the Black People, during the Late Awful Calamity in Philadelphia, in the Year 1793*, which he coauthored with his fellow black churchman Absalom Jones, Allen's antislavery address challenged Americans to end both slavery and racial injustice. With his hometown of Philadelphia serving as the nation's temporary governing capital between 1790 and 1800, he believed that he had a unique opportunity to mold antislavery policy and compel American leaders to create a biracial republic that would shine in the eyes of both God and man.

Defining Moment

Philadelphia's yellow fever epidemic of 1793 made race relations a hot topic in Allen's hometown. From August through November, perhaps as many as four to five thousand people died, including roughly four hundred people of color. African Americans, led by Allen, Absalom Jones, and many others, supported civic reform initiatives. Some white citizens complained that African Americans were attempting to transcend their formerly servile status by asking for equal wages for rescue work. The celebrated white printer Mathew Carey turned such complaints into a broad stereotype about alleged black crime and insolence in his best-selling pamphlet history of the epidemic, *A Short Account of the Malignant Fever, Lately Prevalent in Philadelphia*, published at the close of 1793.

Carey's history infuriated Allen, who with Jones published a reply not long after. Their document, *A Narrative of the Proceedings of the Black People, during the Late Awful Calamity in Philadelphia, in the Year 1793: And a Refutation of Some Censures, Thrown upon Them in Some Late Publications*, attempted to set the record straight by describing blacks' heroism in the stricken city. After they published the work in January 1794, Allen took a copy to the federal clerk's office for the state of Pennsylvania and secured what became the first copyright for African American authors in the United States.

Believing that he would soon have the public spotlight, as returning congressmen would learn of black benevolence during the recent crisis, Allen inserted his antislavery address into his yellow fever narrative. He believed that through the skillful use of his pen, he could foment national racial reform. As he put it, the Lord has "from time to time raised up instruments" to spread righteousness throughout the world; as a black leader intent on eradicating slavery from federal politics and society, Allen viewed himself as just such an instrument.

Author Biography

Richard Allen was born a slave on February 14, 1760, probably in Philadelphia. His first master, was the jurist Benjamin Chew, who later sold Allen's family to Stokely Sturgis. In 1780 he struck a freedom agreement with Sturgis, which he paid off early, allowing him to then gain fame preaching on the mid-Atlantic revival circuit. He moved to Philadelphia in 1786 to preach at Saint George's Methodist Church, where he planned to bolster African American membership. Allen helped form the Free African Society, one of the first African American benevolent groups in the early Republic.

Allen was one of the leading black abolitionists in the early Republic. He published three antislavery essays during the 1790s, signed several abolitionist petitions to the federal government, and aided both kidnapped free blacks and fugitive slaves. Although he was fiercely in favor of black rights within the United States, Allen entered a period of profound doubt about the future of American race relations between 1815 and 1830. During these years he supported African, Haitian, and Canadian emigration movements, believing that people of color needed a safety-valve option to escape the withering racism of the urban North. Allen himself never left America, however, and in 1827 he wrote a famous essay in *Freedom's Journal* claiming the United States as African Americans' "mother country." In September 1830, he hosted the first convention of free black activists at Mother Bethel Church in Philadelphia. His autobiography, published in 1833 by his son, explains Allen's spiritual and political journey in American culture and was celebrated as the first memoir of the black founding generation.

When he died on March 26, 1831, Allen was hailed by African Americans throughout the country as a seminal black abolitionist. None other than the former slave Frederick Douglass considered Allen a heroic precursor to the more famous generation of black and white abolitionists to which he belonged.

HISTORICAL DOCUMENT

The judicious part of mankind will think it unreasonable that a superior good conduct is looked for from our race, by those who stigmatize us as men, whose baseness is incurable, and may therefore be held in a state of servitude, that a merciful man would not doom a beast to; yet you try what you can, to prevent our rising from a state of barbarism you represent us to be in, but we can tell you from a degree of experience, that a black man, although reduced to the most abject state human nature is capable of, short of real madness, can think, reflect, and feel injuries, although it may not be with the same degree of keen resentment and revenge, that you who have been, and are our great oppressors would manifest, if reduced to the pitiable condition of a slave. We believe if you would try the experiment of taking a few black children, and cultivate their minds with the same care, and let them have the same prospect in view as to living in the world, as you would wish for your own children, you would find upon the trial, they were not inferior in mental endowments.

I do not wish to make you angry, but excite your attention to consider how hateful slavery is, in the sight of that God who hath destroyed kings and princes, for their oppression of the poor slaves. and his princes with the posterity of king, were destroyed by the protector and avenger of slaves. Would you not suppose the to be utterly unfit for freedom, and that it was impossible for them, to obtain to any degree of excellence? Their history how slavery had debased their spirits. Men must be wilfully blind, and extremely partial, that cannot see the contrary effects of liberty and slavery upon the mind of man; I truly confess the vile habits often acquired in a state of servitude, are not easily thrown off; the example of the Israelites shews, who with all that could do to reclaim them from it, still con-

tinued in their habits more or less; and why will you look for better from us, why will you look for grapes from thorns, or figs from thistles? It is in our posterity enjoying the same privileges with your own, that you ought to look for better things.

When you are pleaded with, do not you reply as Pharaoh did, " and Aaron let the people from their work, behold the people of the land now are many, and you make them rest from their." We wish you to consider, that God himself was the first pleader of the cause of slaves.

That God who knows the hearts of all men, and the propensity of a slave to hate his oppressor, hath strictly forbidden it to his chosen people, "Thou shalt not abhor an Egyptian, because thou wast a stranger in his land." 23.7. The meek and humble Jesus, the great pattern of humanity, and every other virtue that can adorn and dignify men, hath commanded to love our enemies, to do good to them that hate and despitefully use us. I feel the obligations, I wish to impress them on the minds of our colored brethren, and that we may all forgive you, as we wish to be forgiven, we think it a great mercy to have all anger and bitterness removed from our minds; I appeal to your own feelings, if it is not very disquieting to feel yourselves under dominion of wrathful disposition.

If you love your children, if you love your country, if you love the God of love, clear your hands from slaves, burthen not your children or your country with them, my heart has been sorry for the bloodshed of the oppressors, as well as the oppressed, both appear guilty of each others' blood, in the sight of him who hath said, he that sheddeth man's blood, by man shall his blood be shed.

Will you, because you have reduced us to the unhappy condition our color is in, plead our incapacity for freedom, and our contented condition under oppression, as a sufficient cause for keeping us under the grievous yoke? I have shown the cause,—I will also shew why they appear contented; were we to attempt to plead with our masters, it would be deemed insolence, for which cause they appear as contented as they can in your sight, but the dreadful insurrections they have made when opportunity has offered, is enough to convince a reasonable man, that great uneasiness and not contentment, is the

inhabitant of their hearts. God himself hath pleaded their cause, he hath from time to time raised up instruments for that purpose, sometimes mean and contemptible in your sight, at other times he hath used such as it hath pleased him, with whom you have not thought it beneath your dignity to contend. Many have been convinced of their error, condemned their former conduct, and become zealous advocates for the cause of those, whom you will not suffer to plead for themselves.

GLOSSARY

burthens: burdens

Deut. the Christian Old Testament book of Deuteronomy

Israelites: the Jewish people whose history is chronicled in the Christian Old Testament

Moses: the Christian Old Testament leader, prophet, and lawgiver who led the Israelites out of bondage in Egypt

Pharaoh: the ruler of the Egyptians in biblical times

Saul: a king of the Israelites in biblical times

shew: show

Document Analysis

Allen was convinced that both the Bible and the Declaration of Independence were antislavery documents. Indeed, his 1794 address offers several allusions to biblical antislavery. The story of Exodus, he believed, foretold the divine retribution that would accompany unrepentant slaveholding. For just as Egyptian masters faced eternal damnation, so too would recalcitrant American slaveholders invite harsh retribution by a just God. By comparing black bondage to the plight of ancient Israelites, Allen attempts to show that an almighty being would intervene in human affairs. Remember, he argues, "that God himself was the first pleader of the cause of slaves." Allen also focuses on the New Testament book of the Acts of the Apostles, which declares that God "hath made of one blood all nations of men for to dwell on all the face of the earth." Like other early black leaders, Allen believed that this proclamation sanctioned universal equality.

On the secular front, Allen criticizes American slaveholders who refused to concede the contradiction of slavery in a republic devoted to freedom. He observes, "Men must be wilfully blind, and extremely partial, that cannot see the contrary effects of liberty and slavery upon the mind of man." For a country born of revolutionary liberty, Allen concludes, slavery's maintenance is nothing short of hypocritical.

Allen also critiques the psychology of American slaveholders. In particular, he tries to diminish masters' fears of slave vengeance. Many slaveholders, he realized, refused to consider abolitionism because they worried about black retribution. Allen refutes these fears by pointing out that enslaved people would be grateful for liberation. In addition, the increasing number of enslaved Christians in the United States would realize that they were forbidden to retaliate by the same Bible that condemned slaveholding as a sin.

As for secular solutions, Allen asks slaveholders to treat enslaved people not as enemies to be controlled but as family members to be educated. Allen suggests that if slaveholders altered the conditions in which people of color lived, then African Americans would thrive as citizens of the United States. Here, then, Allen offers one of the first and most significant examples of the concept of nurture over nature in American racial sociology.

In confronting doubts about slave emancipation, Allen also attacks the intellectual foundations of bondage, especially those that saw African Americans as brute machines unprepared for liberty. He deconstructs such beliefs by arguing that slaveholders perpetuated black ignorance and therefore generated their own fears about abolitionism. "Will you," Allen wonders, "plead our incapacity for freedom, and our contented condition under oppression, as a sufficient cause for keeping us under the grievous yoke"? When blacks "plead with our masters" for liberty, it is "deemed insolence." Yet when blacks did not rebel en masse, whites believed they were "contented" simpletons. The matter need not be so complicated, Allen concludes. African Americans now offered ample evidence of their desire for freedom, providing sacred and secular justifications for emancipation. Slaveholders should stop delaying and get on with the business of emancipating their Christian brethren.

Allen's antislavery address exemplifies a hallmark of black abolitionism: the belief that racial equality must accompany emancipation. Envisioning the antislavery cause as patriotic and pious, Allen tries to show it to be compatible with American religious and political doctrine. Far from ruining the American Republic, abolitionism would save it by aligning black and white interests in freedom. He states, "It is in our posterity enjoying the same privileges with your own, that you ought to look for better things." White abolitionists, in fact, did not always agree that equality must follow emancipation. The well-respected Pennsylvania Abolition Society believed that former slaves needed the equivalent of a probationary period in freedom, including white guidance and oversight, before gaining access to full political rights. Moreover, the group did not admit black members until the 1840s.

Black abolitionism also diverged stylistically from the elite legal and political maneuvering that often characterized white abolitionism. Whereas members of the Pennsylvania Abolition Society had access to courts of law and political salons, black abolitionists like Allen had to craft printed appeals in the public realm.

Essential Themes
Richard Allen's antislavery address remains striking for its brevity and focus on a few main ideas. Unlike many antebellum African American reformers (most notably Frederick Douglass, whose elaborate speech "What to the Slave Is the Fourth of July?" arguably remains the epitome of nineteenth-century black political commentary), Allen did not train himself in the art of extended rhetorical analysis. As a preacher, he wanted to craft an essay that was direct and calculated to appeal to learned statesmen as well as average Americans. The cogency of his argument notwithstanding (the entire tract being less than a thousand words), Allen's antislavery address had broad relevance in early national reform circles.

Despite the fact that Allen was not a trained rhetorician, his appeal to slave owners is clear and concise in its argument. Slavery, he argues, is incompatible with both Christianity and human reason. Slave masters are modern-day Pharaohs, imprisoning the chosen people and keeping them from their God-given destiny.

———*Richard Newman, PhD*

Bibliography and Additional Reading
Egerton, Douglas. *Death or Liberty: African Americans and Revolutionary America.* (New York: Oxford University Press, 2008).
Gellman, David. *Emancipating New York: The Politics of Slavery and Freedom, 1777–1827.* (Baton Rouge: Louisiana State University Press, 2006).
Nash, Gary B. *Forging Freedom: The Formation of Philadelphia's African American Community, 1720–1840.* (Cambridge, Mass. Harvard University Press, 1991).
Newman, Richard. *Freedom's Prophet: Bishop Richard Allen, the AME Church, and the Black Founding Fathers.* (New York: New York University Press, 2008).
Wolf, Eva Sheppard. *Race and Liberty in the New Nation: Emancipation in Virginia from the Revolution to Nat Turner's Rebellion.* (Baton Rouge: Louisiana State University Press, 2006).

■ Appeal to the Coloured Citizens of the World

Date: 1829
Author: David Walker
Genre: Pamphlet

Summary Overview

David Walker, a free black man living in Boston, Massachusetts, published the first edition of his *Appeal to the Coloured Citizens of the World* in 1829, and the third and last revised edition of the pamphlet in June 1830. In this *Appeal* Walker encouraged his fellow African Americans in the United States, slave and free, to see themselves as human beings and to do something to elevate themselves from their "wretched state." In doing so, the arguments for slavery, racial slavery in particular, would be torn down, thus weakening the power of the slaveholders.

Because Walker was not beyond advocating the use of violence to help free slaves in America, his pamphlet was banned from several states in the South. Even some abolitionists were appalled by the suggestion that violence would be acceptable in the cause of emancipation. Called "incendiary" and "subversive" in the 1830s, the arguments put forth by Walker continued to provide a foundation upon which later generations of workers for abolition and civil rights in America would make their stand.

Walker directly addressed the men and women held in bondage in the South. It can be surmised that he wrote so that the *Appeal* could be read aloud to the many illiterate slaves by those few who could read. In order to put the pamphlet in the hands of his intended audience, Walker relied on a few contacts in the South as well as the sailors who bought used clothing in his shop.

Besides the intended audience, Walker's *Appeal* engaged—or, in the case of southern whites, repelled—a much wider range of readers. Both northerners and southerners read the pamphlet, with a wide range of reactions, from abhorrence to admiration. Walker's message certainly reached more than the enslaved people of the South.

Defining Moment

Slave rebellion in the Americas is as old as slavery itself. Although rebellions were generally planned by word of mouth, by the Revolutionary War period slaves and freedmen even sometimes wrote secret notes to one another about potential revolts. Most revolts were thwarted before they could get started, and some simply failed. Very few got off the ground, and fewer succeeded. Nonetheless, the ones that succeeded struck fear into the hearts of not only slaveholders but also even whites who owned no slaves, all over the American South.

One attempted rebellion, of which author David Walker may have even been part, was Denmark Vesey's 1822 plot in Charleston, South Carolina. Vesey, a former slave, was a relatively prosperous carpenter with some land. Hating slavery and slaveholding society, Vesey read all he could about antislavery arguments and agitated for freedom and equality for his fellow African Americans. He began to assemble a circle of leaders for a massive rebellion. By the time the plan was to go into effect, Vesey had enlisted about nine thousand free and slave blacks in and around Charleston. As with earlier rebellions, however, the scheme was betrayed by a participant, and Vesey was executed, along with thirty-six coconspirators. The reaction of whites was fierce enough to cause many free blacks to flee to the North.

Into this highly charged environment, Walker dropped his *Appeal* in 1829. Because of his own father's enslavement, Walker had seen firsthand the cruelty and barbarity involved in the American slave system. Once Walker left that environment for one where he could be educated and involved with antislavery efforts, he seemed to realize that his voice could count for something among his fellow African Americans. In the resulting pamphlet, he encouraged them to stop at nothing—including violence—to free themselves from slavery. For white southerners, The *Appeal* evoked thoughts of rebellion plots such as Vesey's, the successful slave uprising in Haiti, and the fear of what could happen if the slave population were to act on Walker's ideas.

Author Biography

David Walker was born in Wilmington, North Carolina (in either 1784-85 or 1796-97), to a free mother and a slave father. Because the status of the mother determined the status of the child, Walker was considered a free black. He was, however, fully familiar with slave life in his hometown, since his father was still in bondage.

Early in the 1820s (when, by the later date of birth, he would have been in his twenties), Walker moved to Charleston, South Carolina. Historians speculate that he may have been involved in Denmark Vesey's plot to revolt against slaveholders in 1822. In any event, Walker moved again shortly after the execution of Vesey and his coconspirators—this time to the North, where many African Americans were heading because of the trouble in Charleston.

In Boston, Massachusetts, Walker made a living for himself by running a used clothing store in the Fisherman's Wharf section of the city. It is there that he likely learned to read and write. Walker used his home and shop to provide shelter for fugitive slaves.

He also began writing, and he submitted some of his work to the New York–based black newspaper *Freedom's Journal*.

In 1829, Walker published his *Appeal to the Coloured Citizens of the World*. He rewrote the pamphlet twice, publishing the third and final edition in June 1830. Many southern state governments put a price on Walker's head, offering $3,000 for his head and $10,000 to the one who could bring him to the South alive. His friends entreated him to go to Canada, but he refused. Instead, he used his secondhand clothes shop to help get banned copies of his *Appeal* into the South, sewing the pamphlets into the clothing so that sailors could take them to ports south.

Two months after the third edition of Walker's *Appeal* came out, he died from consumption (tuberculosis), of which his daughter had died a few days earlier.

HISTORICAL DOCUMENT

My dearly beloved Brethren and Fellow Citizens.
From the Preamble

Having travelled over a considerable portion of these United States, and having, in the course of my travels, taken the most accurate observations of things as they exist—the result of my observations has warranted the full and unshaken conviction, that we, (coloured people of these United States,) are the most degraded, wretched, and abject set of beings that ever lived since the world began; and I pray God that none like us ever may live again until time shall be no more. They tell us of the Israelites in Egypt, the Helots in Sparta, and of the Roman Slaves, which last were made up from almost every nation under heaven, whose sufferings under those ancient and heathen nations, were, in comparison with ours, under this enlightened and Christian nation, no more than a cipher—or, in other words, those heathen nations of antiquity, had but little more among them than the name and form of slavery; while wretchedness and endless miseries were reserved, apparently in a phial, to be poured out upon our fathers, ourselves and our children, by *Christian* Americans!

These positions I shall endeavour, by the help of the Lord, to demonstrate in the course of this *Appeal*, to the satisfaction of the most incredulous mind—and may God Almighty, who is the Father of our Lord Jesus Christ, open your hearts to understand and believe the truth.

The *causes*, my brethren, which produce our wretchedness and miseries, are so very numerous and aggravating, that I believe the pen only of a Josephus or a Plutarch, can well enumerate and explain them. Upon subjects, then, of such incomprehensible magnitude, so impenetrable, and so notorious, I shall be obliged to omit a large class of, and content myself with giving you an exposition of a few of those, which do indeed rage to such an alarming pitch, that they cannot but be a perpetual source of terror and dismay to every reflecting mind.

I am fully aware, in making this appeal to my much afflicted and suffering brethren, that I shall not only be assailed by those whose greatest earthly desires are, to keep us in abject ignorance and wretchedness, and who are of the firm conviction that Heaven has designed us and our children to be slaves and *beasts of burden* to them and their children. I say, I do not only expect to be held up to the public as an ignorant, impudent and restless disturber of the public peace, by such avaricious creatures, as well as a mover of insubordination—

and perhaps put in prison or to death, for giving a superficial exposition of our miseries, and exposing tyrants. But I am persuaded, that many of my brethren, particularly those who are ignorantly in league with slave-holders or tyrants, who acquire their daily bread by the blood and sweat of their more ignorant brethren—and not a few of those too, who are too ignorant to see an inch beyond their noses, will rise up and call me cursed—Yea, the jealous ones among us will perhaps use more abject subtlety, by affirming that this work is not worth perusing, that we are well situated, and there is no use in trying to better our condition, for we cannot. I will ask one question here.—Can our condition be any worse?—Can it be more mean and abject? If there are any changes, will they not be for the better, though they may appear for the worst at first? Can they get us any lower? Where can they get us? They are afraid to treat us worse, for they know well, the day they do it they are gone. But against all accusations which may or can be preferred against me, I appeal to Heaven for my motive in writing—who knows that my object is, if possible, to awaken in the breasts of my afflicted, degraded and slumbering brethren, a spirit of inquiry and investigation respecting our miseries and wretchedness in this *Republican Land of Liberty!!!!!!*

The sources from which our miseries are derived, and on which I shall comment, I shall not combine in one, but shall put them under distinct heads and expose them in their turn; in doing which, keeping truth on my side, and not departing from the strictest rules of morality, I shall endeavour to penetrate, search out, and lay them open for your inspection. If you cannot or will not profit by them, I shall have done *my* duty to you, my country and my God.

And as the inhuman system of *slavery*, is the *source* from which most of our miseries proceed, I shall begin with that *curse to nations*, which has spread terror and devastation through so many nations of antiquity, and which is raging to such a pitch at the present day in Spain and in Portugal. It had one tug in England, in France, and in the United States of America; yet the inhabitants thereof, do not learn wisdom, and erase it entirely from their dwellings and from all with whom they have to do. The fact is, the labour of slaves comes so cheap to the avaricious usurpers, and is (as they think) of such great utility to the country where it exists, that those who are actuated by sordid avarice only, overlook the evils, which will as sure as the Lord lives, follow after the good. In fact, they are so happy to keep in ignorance and degradation, and to receive the homage and the labour of the slaves, they forget that God rules in the armies of heaven and among the inhabitants of the earth, having his ears continually open to the cries, tears and groans of his oppressed people; and being a just and holy Being will at one day appear fully in behalf of the oppressed, and arrest the progress of the avaricious oppressors; for although the destruction of the oppressors God may not effect by the oppressed, yet the Lord our God will bring other destructions upon them—for not unfrequently will he cause them to rise up one against another, to be split and divided, and to oppress each other, and sometimes to open hostilities with sword in hand. Some may ask, what is the matter with this united and happy people?—Some say it is the cause of political usurpers, tyrants, oppressors, &c. But has not the Lord an oppressed and suffering people among them? Does the Lord condescend to hear their cries and see their tears in consequence of oppression? Will he let the oppressors rest comfortably and happy always? Will he not cause the very children of the oppressors to rise up against them, and oftimes put them to death? "God works in many ways his wonders to perform."

I will not here speak of the destructions which the Lord brought upon Egypt, in consequence of the oppression and consequent groans of the oppressed—of the hundreds and thousands of Egyptians whom God hurled into the Red Sea for afflicting his people in their land—of the Lord's suffering people in Sparta or Lacaedemon, the land of the truly famous Lycurgus—nor have I time to comment upon the cause which produced the fierceness with which Sylla usurped the title, and absolutely acted as dictator of the Roman people—the conspiracy of Cataline—the conspiracy against, and murder of Caesar in the Senate house—the spirit with which Marc Antony made himself master of the commonwealth—his associating Octavius and Lipidus with himself in power—their dividing the provinces of Rome among themselves—their attack and defeat, on the plains of Philippi, of the last defenders of their liberty, (Brutus and Cassius)—the tyranny of Tiberius, and from him to the final overthrow of Constantinople by the Turkish Sultan, Mahomed II, ad 1453. I say, I shall not take up time to speak of the *causes* which produced so much wretchedness and massacre among those heathen nations, for I am aware that you know too well, that God is just, as well as merciful!—I shall call your attention a few moments to that *Christian* nation, the Spaniards—while I shall leave almost unnoticed, that avaricious and cruel people, the Portuguese, among whom all true hearted Christians and lovers of Jesus Christ, must evidently see the judgments of God displayed. To show the judgments of God upon the Spaniards, I shall occupy but a little time, leaving a plenty of room for the candid and unprejudiced to reflect.

All persons who are acquainted with history, and particularly the Bible, who are not blinded by the God of this world, and are not actuated solely by avarice—who are able to lay aside prejudice long enough to view candidly and impartially, things as they were, are, and probably will be—who are willing to admit that God made man to serve Him *alone*, and that man should have no other Lord or Lords but Himself—that God Almighty is the *sole proprietor* or *master* of the Whole human family, and will not on any consideration admit of a colleague, being unwilling to divide his glory with another—and who can dispense with prejudice long enough to admit that we are *men*, notwithstanding our *improminent noses* and *woolly heads*, and believe that we feel for our fathers, mothers, wives and children, as well as the whites do for theirs.—I say, all who are permitted to see and believe these things, can easily recognize the judgments of God among the Spaniards. Though others may lay the cause of the fierceness with which they cut each other's throats, to some other circumstance, yet they who believe that God is a God of justice, will believe that Slavery *is the principal cause*.

…I ask every man who has a heart, and is blessed with the privilege of believing—Is not God a God of justice to *all* his creatures? Do you say he is?

Then if he gives peace and tranquillity to tyrants, and permits them to keep our fathers, our mothers, ourselves and our children in eternal ignorance and wretchedness, to support them and their families, would he be to us a God of *justice?* I ask, O ye *Christians!!!* who hold us and our children in the most abject ignorance and degradation, that ever a people were afflicted with since the world began—I say, if God gives you peace and tranquillity, and suffers you thus to go on afflicting us, and our children, who have never given you the least provocation—would he be to us *a God of justice?* If you will allow that we are Men, who feel for each other, does not the blood of our fathers and of us their children, cry aloud to the Lord of Sabaoth against you, for the cruelties and murders with which you have, and do continue to afflict us. But it is time for me to close my remarks on the suburbs, just to enter more fully into the interior of this system of cruelty and oppression.

From Article I: Our Wretchedness in Consequence of Slavery

My beloved brethren …all the inhabitants of the earth, (except however, the sons of Africa) are called *men*, and of course are, and ought to be free. But we, (coloured people) and our children are *brutes!!* and of course are, and *ought to be* Slaves to the American people and their children forever!! to dig their mines and work their farms; and thus go on enriching them, from one generation to another with our *blood* and our *tears!!!!*

I promised in a preceding page to demonstrate to the satisfaction of the most incredulous, that we, (coloured people of these United States of America) are the *most wretched, degraded* and *abject* set of beings that *ever lived* since the world began, and that the white Americans having reduced us to the wretched state of *slavery*, treat us in that condition *more cruel* (they being an enlightened and Christian people), than any heathen nation did any people whom it had reduced to our condition. These affirmations are so well confirmed in the minds of all unprejudiced men, who have taken the trouble to read histories, that they need no elucidation from me. But to put them beyond all doubt, I refer you in the first place to the children of Jacob, or of Israel in Egypt, under Pharaoh and his people. Some of my brethren do not know who Pharaoh and the Egyptians were—I know it to be a fact, that some of them take the Egyptians to have been a gang of *devils*, not knowing any better, and that they (Egyptians) having got possession of the Lord's people, treated them *nearly* as cruel as *Christian Americans* do us, at the present day. For the information of such, I would only mention that the Egyptians, were Africans or coloured people, such as we are—some of them yellow and others dark—a mixture of Ethiopians and the natives of Egypt—about the same as you see the coloured people of the United States at the present day.—I say, I call your attention then, to the children of Jacob, while I point out particularly to you his son Joseph, among the rest, in Egypt.

"And Pharoah said unto Joseph, thou shalt be over my house, and according unto thy word shall all my people be ruled: only in the throne will I be greater than thou."

"And Pharoah said unto Joseph, see, I have set thee over all the land of Egypt."

"And Pharoah said unto Joseph, I am Pharaoh, and without thee shall no man lift up his hand or foot in all the land of Egypt."

Now I appeal to heaven and to earth, and particularly to the American people themselves, who cease not to declare that our condition is not *hard*, and that we are comparatively satisfied to rest in wretchedness and misery, under them and their children. Not, indeed, to show me a coloured President, a Governor, a Legislator, a Senator, a Mayor, or an Attorney at the Bar.—But to show me a man of colour, who holds the low office of a Constable, or one who sits in a Juror Box, even on a case of one of his wretched brethren, throughout this great Republic!!—But let us pass Joseph the son of Israel a little farther in review, as he existed with that heathen nation.

"And Pharoah called Joseph's name Zaphnathpaaneah; and he gave him to wife Asenath the daughter of Potipherah priest of On. And Joseph went out over all the land of Egypt."

Compare the above, with the American institutions. Do they not institute laws to prohibit us from marrying among the whites? I would wish, candidly,

however, before the Lord, to be understood, that I would not give a *pinch of snuff* to be married to any white person I ever saw in all the days of my life. And I do say it, that the black man, or man of colour, who will leave his own colour (provided he can get one, who is good for any thing) and marry a white woman, to be a double slave to her, just because she is *white*, ought to be treated by her as he surely will be, viz: as a Niger!!!! It is not, indeed, what I care about inter-marriages with the whites, which induced me to pass this subject in review; for the Lord knows, that there is a day coming when they will be glad enough to get into the company of the blacks, notwithstanding, we are, in this generation, levelled by them, almost on a level with the brute creation: and some of us they treat even worse than they do the brutes that perish. I only made this extract to show how much lower we are held, and how much more cruel we are treated by the Americans, than were the children of Jacob, by the Egyptians.—We will notice the sufferings of Israel some further, under *heathen Pharaoh*, compared with ours under the *enlightened Christians of America*.

"And Pharoah spake unto Joseph, saying, thy father and thy brethren are come unto thee:"

"The land of Egypt is before thee: in the best of the land make thy father and brethren to dwell; in the land of Goshen let them dwell: and if thou knowest any men of activity among them, then make them rulers over my cattle."

I ask those people who treat us so *well*, Oh! I ask them, where is the most barren spot of land which they have given unto us? Israel had the most fertile land in all Egypt. Need I mention the very notorious fact, that I have known a poor man of colour, who laboured night and day, to acquire a little money, and having acquired it, he vested it in a small piece of land, and got him a house erected thereon, and having paid for the whole, he moved his family into it, where he was suffered to remain but nine months, when he was cheated out of his property by a white man, and driven out of door! And is not this the case generally? Can a man of colour buy a piece of land and keep it peaceably? Will not some white man try to get it from him, even if it is in a *mud hole*? I need not comment any farther on a subject, which all, both black and white, will readily admit. But I must, really, observe that in this very city, when a man of colour dies, if he owned any real estate it most generally falls into the hands of some white person. The wife and children of the deceased may weep and lament if they please, but the estate will be kept snug enough by its white possessor.

But to prove farther that the condition of the Israelites was better under the Egyptians than ours is under the whites. I call upon the professing philanthropist, I call upon the very tyrant himself, to show me a page of history, either sacred or profane, on which a verse can be found, which maintains, that the Egyptians heaped the *insupportable insult* upon the children of Israel, by telling them that they were not of the *human family*. Can the whites deny this charge? ...Oh! pity us we pray thee, Lord Jesus, Master.—Has Mr. Jefferson declared to the world, that we are inferior to the whites, both in the endowments of our bodies and of minds? It is indeed surprising, that a man of such great learning, combined with such excellent natural parts, should speak so of a set of men in chains. I do not know what to compare it to, unless, like putting one wild deer in an iron cage, where it will be secured, and hold another by the side of the same, then let it go, and expect the one in the cage to run as fast as the one at liberty. So far, my brethren, were the Egyptians from heaping these insults upon their slaves, that Pharaoh's daughter took Moses, a son of Israel for her own, as will appear by the following.

"And Pharoah's daughter said unto her, [Moses' mother] take this child away, and nurse it for me, and I will pay thee thy wages. And the woman took the child [Moses] and nursed it."

"And the child grew, and she brought him unto Pharaoh's daughter and he became her son. And she called his name Moses: and she said because I drew him out of the water."

In all probability, Moses would have become Prince Regent to the throne, and no doubt, in process of time but he would have been seated on the throne of Egypt. But he had rather suffer shame, with the people of God, than to enjoy pleasures with that wicked people for a season. O! that the coloured people were long since of Moses' excellent

disposition, instead of courting favour with, and telling news and lies to our *natural enemies*, against each other—aiding them to keep their hellish chains of slavery upon us. Would we not long before this time, have been respectable men, instead of such wretched victims of oppression as we are? Would they be able to drag our mothers, our fathers, our wives, our children and ourselves, around the world in chains and hand-cuffs as they do, to dig up gold and silver for them and theirs? This question, my brethren, I leave for you to digest; and may God Almighty force it home to your hearts. Remember that unless you are united, keeping your tongues within your teeth, you will be afraid to trust your secrets to each other, and thus perpetuate our miseries under the *Christians!!!!!* Addition.—

Remember, also to lay humble at the feet of our Lord and Master Jesus Christ, with prayers and fastings. Let our enemies go on with their butcheries, and at once fill up their cup. Never make an attempt to gain our freedom of *natural right*, from under our cruel oppressors and murderers, until you see your way clear*

[*It is not to be understood here, that I mean for us to wait until God shall take us by the hair of our heads and drag us out of abject wretchedness and slavery, nor do I mean to convey the idea for us to wait until our enemies shall make preparations, and call us to seize those preparations, take it away from them, and put every thing before us to death, in order to gain our freedom which God has given us. For you must remember that we are men as well as they. God has been pleased to give us two eyes, two hands, two feet, and some sense in our heads as well as they. They have no more right to hold us in slavery than we have to hold them, we have just as much right, in the sight of God, to hold them and their children in slavery and wretchedness, as they have to hold us, and no more.]

—when that hour arrives and you move, be not afraid or dismayed; for be you assured that Jesus Christ the King of heaven and of earth who is the God of justice and of armies, will surely go before you. And those enemies who have for hundreds of years stolen our *rights*, and kept us ignorant of Him and His divine worship, he will remove. Millions of whom, are this day, so ignorant and avaricious, that they cannot conceive how God can have an attribute of justice, and show mercy to us because it pleased Him to make us black—which colour, Mr. Jefferson calls unfortunate!!!!!! As though we are not as thankful to our God, for having made us as it pleased himself, as they, (the whites,) are for having made them white. They think because they hold us in their infernal chains of slavery, that we wish to be white, or of their color—but they are dreadfully deceived—we wish to be just as it pleased our Creator to have made us, and no avaricious and unmerciful wretches, have any business to make slaves of, or hold us in slavery. How would they like for us to make slaves of, and hold them in cruel slavery, and murder them as they do us?—

But is Mr. Jefferson's assertions true? viz. "that it is unfortunate for us that our Creator has been pleased to make us *black*." We will not take his say so, for the fact. The world will have an opportunity to see whether it is unfortunate for us, that our Creator *has made us* darker than the *whites*.

Fear not the number and education of our *enemies*, against whom we shall have to contend for our lawful right; guaranteed to us by our Maker; for why should we be afraid, when God is, and will continue, (if we continue humble) to be on our side?

The man who would not fight under our Lord and Master Jesus Christ, in the glorious and heavenly cause of freedom and of God—to be delivered from the most wretched, abject and servile slavery, that ever a people was afflicted with since the foundation of the world, to the present day—ought to be kept with all of his children or family, in slavery, or in chains, to be butchered by his *cruel enemies*.

I saw a paragraph, a few years since, in a South Carolina paper, which, speaking of the barbarity of the Turks, it said: "The Turks are the most barbarous people in the world—they treat the Greeks more like *brutes* than human beings." And in the same paper was an advertisement, which said: "Eight well built Virginia and Maryland *Negro fellows* and four *wenches* will positively be *sold* this day, *to the highest bidder!*" And what astonished me still more was, to see in this same *humane* paper!! the cuts of three men, with clubs and budgets on their backs, and an advertisement offering a considerable sum of money for their apprehension and delivery. I declare, it is really so amusing to hear the Southerners and Westerners of this country talk about *barbarity*, that it is positively, enough to make a man *smile*.

...I have been for years troubling the pages of historians, to find out what our fathers have done to the *white Christians of America*, to merit such condign punishment as they have inflicted on them, and do continue to inflict on us their children. But I must aver, that my researches have hitherto been to no effect. I have therefore, come to the immoveable conclusion, that they (Americans) have, and do continue to punish us for nothing else, but for enriching them and their country. For I cannot conceive of any thing else. Nor will I ever believe otherwise, until the Lord shall convince me.

The world knows, that slavery as it existed among the Romans, (which was the primary cause of their destruction) was, comparatively speaking, no more than a *cypher*, when compared with ours under the Americans. Indeed I should not have noticed the Roman slaves, had not the very learned and penetrating Mr. Jefferson said, "when a master was murdered, all his slaves in the same house, or within hearing, were condemned to death."

—Here let me ask Mr. Jefferson, (but he is gone to answer at the bar of God, for the deeds done in his body while living,) I therefore ask the whole American people, had I not rather die, or be put to death, than to be a slave to any tyrant, who takes not only my own, but my wife and children's lives by the inches? Yea, would I meet death with avidity far! far!! in preference to such *servile submission* to the murderous hands of tyrants. Mr. Jefferson's very severe remarks on us have been so extensively argued upon by men whose attainments in literature, I shall never be able to reach, that I would not have meddled with it, were it not to solicit each of my brethren, who has the spirit of a man, to buy a copy of Mr. Jefferson's "Notes on Virginia," and put it in the hand of his son. For let no one of us suppose that the refutations which have been written by our white friends are enough—they are *whites*—we are *blacks*. We, and the world, wish to see the charges of Mr. Jefferson refuted by the blacks *themselves*, according to their chance; for we must remember that what the whites have written respecting this subject, is other men's labours, and did not emanate from the blacks. I know well, that there are some talents and learning among the coloured people of this country, which we have not a chance to develop, in consequence of oppression; but our oppression ought not to hinder us from acquiring all we can. For we will have a chance to develop them by and by. God will not suffer us, always to be oppressed. Our sufferings will come to an *end*, in spite of all the Americans this side of *eternity*. Then we will want all the learning and talents among ourselves, and perhaps more, to govern ourselves.— "Every dog must have its day," the American's is coming to an end.

But let us review Mr. Jefferson's remarks respecting us some further. Comparing our miserable fathers, with the learned philosophers of Greece, he says: "Yet notwithstanding these and other discouraging circumstances among the Romans, their slaves were often their rarest artists. They excelled too, in science, insomuch as to be usually employed as tutors to their master's children; Epictetus, Terence and Phaedrus were slaves,—but they were of the race of whites. It is not their *condition* then, but *nature*, which has produced the distinction."

See this, my brethren!! Do you believe that this assertion is swallowed by millions of the whites? Do you know that Mr. Jefferson was one of as great character as ever lived among the whites? See his writings for the world, and public labours for the United States of America. Do you believe that the assertions of such a man, will pass away into oblivion unobserved by this people and the world? If you do you are much mistaken—See how the American people treat us—have we souls in our bodies? Are we men who have any spirits at all? I know that there are many *swell-bellied* fellows among us, whose greatest object is to fill their stomachs. Such I do not mean—I am after those who know and feel, that we are Men, as well as other people; to them, I say, that unless we try to refute Mr. Jefferson's arguments respecting us, we will only establish them.

But the slaves among the Romans. Every body who has read history, knows, that as soon as a slave among the Romans obtained his freedom, he could rise to the greatest eminence in the State, and there was no law instituted to hinder a slave from buying his freedom. Have not the Americans instituted laws to hinder us from obtaining our freedom? Do any deny this charge? Read the laws of Virginia, North Carolina, &c. Further: have not the Americans instituted laws to prohibit a man of colour from obtaining and holding any office whatever, under the government of the United States of America? Now, Mr. Jefferson tells us, that our condition is not so hard, as the slaves were under the Romans!!!!!!

It is time for me to bring this article to a close. But before I close it, I must observe to my brethren that at the close of the first Revolution in this country, with Great Britain, there were but thirteen States in the Union, now there are twenty-four, most of which are slave-holding States, and the whites are dragging us around in chains and in handcuffs, to their new States and Territories to work their mines and farms, to enrich them and their children—and millions of them believing firmly that we being a little darker than they, were made by our Creator to be an inheritance to them and their children for ever—the same as a parcel of *brutes*.

Are we Men!!—I ask you, O my brethren! are we Men? Did our Creator make us to be slaves to dust and ashes like ourselves? Are they not dying worms as well as we? Have they not to make their appearance before the tribunal of Heaven, to answer for the deeds done in the body, as well as we? Have we any other Master but Jesus Christ alone? Is he not their Master as well as ours?—What right then, have we to obey and call any other Master, but Himself? How we could be so *submissive* to a gang of men, whom we cannot tell whether they are *as good* as ourselves or not, I never could conceive. However, this is shut up with the Lord, and we cannot precisely tell—but I declare, we judge men by their works.

The whites have always been an unjust, jealous, unmerciful, avaricious and blood-thirsty set of beings, always seeking after power and authority.—We view them all over the confederacy of Greece, where they were first known to be any thing, (in consequence of education) we see them there, cutting each other's throats—trying to subject each other to wretchedness and misery—to effect which, they used all kinds of deceitful, unfair, and unmerciful means. We view them next in Rome, where the spirit of tyranny and deceit raged still higher. We view them in Gaul, Spain, and in Britain.—In fine, we view them all over Europe, together with what were scattered about in Asia and Africa, as heathens, and we see them acting more like devils than accountable men. But some may ask, did not the blacks of Africa, and the mulattoes of Asia, go on in the same way as did the whites of Europe. I answer, no—they never were half so avaricious, deceitful and unmerciful as the whites, according to their knowledge.

But we will leave the whites or Europeans as heathens, and take a view of them as Christians, in which capacity we see them as cruel, if not more so than ever. In fact, take them as a body, they are ten times more cruel, avaricious and unmerciful than ever they were; for while they were heathens, they were bad enough it is true, but it is positively a fact that they were not quite so audacious as to go and take vessel loads of men, women and children, and in cold blood, and through devilishness, throw them into the sea, and murder them in all kind of ways. While they were heathens, they were too ignorant for such barbarity. But being Christians, enlightened and sensible, they are completely prepared for such hellish cruelties. Now suppose God were to give them more sense, what would they do? If it were possible, would they not *dethrone* Jehovah and seat themselves upon his throne? I therefore, in the name and fear of the Lord God of Heaven and of earth, divested of prejudice either on the side of my colour or that of the whites, advance my suspicion of them, whether they are *as good by nature* as we are or not. Their actions, since they were known as a people, have been the reverse, I do indeed suspect them, but this, as I before observed, is shut up with the Lord, we cannot exactly tell, it will be proved in succeeding generations.—The whites have had the essence of the gospel as it was preached by my master and his apostles—the Ethiopians have not, who are to have it in its meridian splendor—the Lord will give it to them to their satisfaction. I hope and pray my God, that they will make good use of it, that it may be well with them.

It is my solemn belief, that if ever the world becomes Christianized, (which must certainly take place before long) it will be through the means, under God of the *Blacks*, who are now held in wretchedness, and degradation, by the white *Christians* of the world, who before they learn to do justice to us before our Maker—and be reconciled to us, and reconcile us to them, and by that means have clear consciences before God and man.—Send out Missionaries to convert the Heathens, many of whom after they cease to worship gods, which neither see nor hear, become ten times more the children of Hell, then ever they were, why what is the reason? Why the reason is obvious, they must learn to do justice at home, before they go into distant lands, to display their charity, Christianity, and benevolence; when they learn to do justice, God will accept their offering, (no man may think that I am against Missionaries for I am not, my object is to see justice done at home, before we go to convert the Heathens)....

From Article IV: Our Wretchedness in Consequence of the Colonizing Plan....

A declaration made July 4, 1776.

It says,

"When in the course of human events, it becomes necessary for one people to dissolve the political bands which have connected them with another, and to assume among the Powers of the earth, the separate and equal station to which the laws of nature and of nature's God entitle them. A decent respect for the opinions of mankind requires, that they should declare the causes which impel them to the separation.—We hold these truths to be self evident—that all men are created equal, that they are endowed by their Creator with certain unalienable rights: that among these, are life, liberty, and the pursuit of happiness that, to secure these rights, governments are instituted among men, deriving their just powers from the consent of the governed; that whenever any form of government becomes destructive of these ends, it is the right of the people to alter or to abolish it, and to institute a new government laying its foundation on such principles, and organizing its powers in such form, as to them shall seem most likely to effect their safety and happiness. Prudence, indeed, will dictate, that governments long established should not be changed for light and transient causes; and accordingly all experience hath shewn, that mankind are more disposed to suffer, while evils are sufferable, than to right themselves by abolishing the forms to which they are accustomed. But when a long train of abuses and usurpations, pursuing invariably the same object, evinces a design to reduce them under absolute despotism, it is their right, it is their duty to throw off such government, and to provide new guards for their future security." See your Declaration Americans!!!

Do you understand your own language? Hear your language, proclaimed to the world, July 4th, 1776—"We hold these truths to be self evident—that All Men Are Created Equal!! that they *are endowed by their Creator with certain unalienable rights*; that among these are life, *liberty*, and the pursuit of happiness!!" Compare your own language above, extracted from your Declaration of Independence, with your cruelties and murders inflicted by your cruel and unmerciful fathers and yourselves on our fathers and on us—men who have never given your fathers or you the least provocation!!!!!!

Hear your language further! "But when a long train of abuses and usurpations, pursuing invariably the same object, evinces a design to reduce them under absolute despotism, it is their *right*, it is their *duty*, to throw off such government, and to provide new guards for their future security."

Now, Americans! I ask you candidly, was your sufferings under Great Britain, one hundredth part as cruel and tyrannical as you have rendered ours under you? Some of you, no doubt, believe that we will never throw off your murderous government and "provide new guards for our future security." If Satan has made you believe it, will he not deceive you?…

Do the whites say, I being a black man, ought to be humble, which I readily admit? I ask them, ought they not to be as humble as I? or do they think that they can measure arms with Jehovah? Will not the Lord yet humble them? or will not these very coloured people whom they now treat worse than brutes, yet under God, humble them low down enough? Some of the whites are ignorant enough to tell us, that we ought to be submissive to them, that they may keep their feet on our throats. And if we do not submit to be beaten to death by them, we are bad creatures and of course must be damned, &c. If any man wishes to hear this doctrine openly preached to us by the American preachers, let him go into the Southern and Western sections of this country—I do not speak from hear say—what I have written, is what I have seen and heard myself. No man may think that my book is made up of conjecture—I have travelled and observed nearly the whole of those things myself, and what little I did not get by my own observation, I received from those among the whites and blacks, in whom the greatest confidence may be placed.

The Americans may be as vigilant as they please, but they cannot be vigilant enough for the Lord, neither can they hide themselves, where he will not find and bring them out.

GLOSSARY

Caesar: Julius Caesar, Roman statesman and general of the first century bce

Cataline: Lucius Sergius Catilina, a Roman who conspired to overthrow the Roman Republic

Epictetus: an ancient Stoic philosopher who was probably born a slave

Ethiopians: a term commonly used to refer to non-Egyptian Africans

Helots: the slave class in ancient Sparta

Jacob: the third patriarch of the Jewish people in the Christian Old Testament

Joseph: one of Jacob's sons, sold into slavery in Egypt

Josephus: a Jewish historian of the first century

Lacedaemon: the name the ancient Greeks gave to Sparta

Lord of Sabaoth: God, literally the "Lord of Hosts," or armies

Lycurgus: a legendary law giver of ancient Sparta

Marc Antony: often spelled "Mark Anthony," a Roman politician and general who formed the Second Triumvirate with Octavian ("Octavius" in the document) and Marcus Lepidus

Phaedrus: a writer of ancient Roman fables

plains of Philippi: the site of a battle in northern ancient Greece between Mark Anthony and the Second Triumvirate and Caesar's assassins, Marcus Junius Brutus and Gaius Cassius Longinus

Plutarch: a Greek philosopher of the first and second centuries ce

Sparta: a city-state in ancient Greece

Sylla: Lucius Sylla (more often spelled "Lucius Sulla"), a dictator of ancient Rome

Terence: a playwright in the ancient Roman Republic (whose Roman name was Publius Terentius Afer)

Tiberius: Tiberius Julius Caesar Augustus, a first-century Roman emperor

Document Analysis

The structure of David Walker's *Appeal* consists of a preamble and four articles. The articles' titles reflect their content, each explicating a reason for the "wretchedness" of the slaves' lives and experiences: "Our Wretchedness in Consequence of Slavery," "Our Wretchedness in Consequence of Ignorance," "Our Wretchedness in Consequence of the Preachers of the Religion of Jesus Christ," and "Our Wretchedness in Consequence of the Colonizing Plan." The present volume reproduces only excerpts from the Preamble, Article I, and a small part of Article IV.

In the preamble, Walker addresses what seems to him the most unbearable paradox of the United States: the misery of Walker's brethren comes at the hands of those who call themselves Christians. The causes of slavery are myriad, so much so that Walker states that he will not even try to lay them all out, but he will at least try to examine some of the worst of those causes. Another contradiction in the United States is that of a slaveholding society existing within a *Republican Land of Liberty.* Worse still is the resistance of slaves and free African Americans to change, because they believe that things can only get worse for them.

Next Walker refers to the biblical Exodus of the Hebrew slaves from Egypt and the plagues visited on the Egyptian slaveholders. He then touches on the history of ancient Sparta and of the Roman Empire and how those slaveholding empires, too, eventually met their downfall. He mentions the wars going on in Spain and Portugal—slaveholding empires—where people are slaughtering one another. In Walker's eyes, there can be no question as to the reason for these things: These societies were receiving "the judgments of God" for holding slaves and being oppressors.

In the closing paragraphs, Walker points out that anyone who is not blinded by the prejudices of the avaricious world can see that he and his brethren are *men* with feelings, just as white people have, and that God has them in his care too.

In Article I: Our Wretchedness in Consequence of Slavery, Walker acknowledges that there have been slaves in many parts of the world at many times. His point, however, is that the slaves in the United States are the worst off of them all.

His first example is from the Bible, taken as a history of the Hebrew people and their time of slavery in Egypt. Walker points out that even these heathen Egyptians—Africans—gave the Hebrews fertile land to live on. Unlike the American slaveholders, they never denied that the Hebrews were human beings. In contrast, even the admired Thomas Jefferson, in his *Notes on the State of Virginia*, said that those of African descent were inferior both mentally and physically to white people. The Egyptians did not seem to hold this view, much less voice it, for Pharaoh's daughter even adopted the Hebrew child Moses into the royal household. He might even have attained the throne if he had not decided instead to cast his lot with his own people, groaning under bondage, to help them free themselves.

Walker digresses from his examination of history, exhorting those in chains to pray and watch for the right time to free themselves. He tells them to watch but also to act. This is by no means his most explicit call to action. In Article II, in fact, he presses black people to defend themselves when someone seeks to murder them, saying that they should kill or be killed. He next asks his audience if they wish they were white. He states they should not wish to be anything other than what God made them, even if white people suppose otherwise. And why should whites have any more right to hold black people in bondage than black people should to hold white people? Why could it not be the other way around? Additionally, the audience should not be afraid of their enemies, who happen to be greater in number and more educated. They may have the law on their side, but the wretched slaves of the nation have, if they are humble, God on theirs. Those who would not fight for their freedom should remain in chains.

Walker asks if there is anything that their African fathers had done to deserve being held in perpetual slavery along with their children. Somehow, Walker states, under Christianity white men have become much more brutal and cruel than they ever were before. The barbarians of Europe—Gaul, Britain, Spain—grew worse after becoming Christians. His theory is that heathens who are educated and enlightened learn new ways of being cruel and greedy. African American people, on the other hand, tend to become better people under Christianity, not worse.

Walker's *Appeal* also includes, at the end of Article IV, a portion on the Declaration of Independence. Here he speaks to "Americans," meaning the white population of the United States. He tells them they should take a look at their own Declaration of Independence, which states that "all men are created equal" and are "endowed with unalienable rights." How can white Americans reconcile these words with their actions toward black people? If these white Americans found British rule too much for them, how much worse must African Americans find American slavery in its brutality and oppression? And if it is any surprise to white Americans that African Americans might rise up "to throw off such government, and to provide new guards for their future security," then it must be the devil deceiving them. Walker tells these Americans that if he must be humble, so should they, since both answer to the same God.

Essential Themes

There are a number of themes that pervade Walker's *Appeal*. One is that the United States, because of its embrace of slavery, faced the inevitable judgment of God. White Americans cannot hide from God, no matter how cautious they might be—Walker's use of the history of empires and states that relied on slave labor presents this as an inexorable conclusion. Connected to this is Walkers persistent focus on the shared humanity of slave and slave owner. The slave owner's (and, indeed the American government's) dehumanization of African slaves makes American slavery the worst in human history, according to Walker.

There is also a lack of passivity in the *Appeal*, illustrating a signifiant but rare strand of anti-slavery activism in the United States. Although abolitionist movements began to coalesce at this time, presenting a much stronger front, these groups tended to favor nonviolent ways of destroying the institution of slavery. One of the most prominent advocates for abolition, William Lloyd Garrison, wrote an editorial in his newspaper, *The Liberator*, in January 1831, saying that while he understood and sympathized with Walker's reasoning, he could not condone the author's encouragement of violent behavior from his brethren or his heated prose. Garrison did not want Walker's *Appeal* to be associated with the wider northern abolition movement precisely because its encouragement of hostility and rebellion only hardened slaveholders' hearts against the abolitionist message.

———*Angela M. Alexander*

Bibliography and Additional Reading

Andrews, William L., ed. *The North Carolina Roots of African American Literature: An Anthology.* Chapel Hill: University of North Carolina Press, 2006.

Hinks, Peter P. *To Awaken My Afflicted Brethren: David Walker and the Problem of Antebellum Slave Resistance.* University Park: Pennsylvania State University Press, 1997.

Newman, Richard, et al., eds. *Pamphlets of Protest: An Anthology of Early African-American Protest Literature, 1790–1860.* New York: Routledge, 2001.

Pinn, Anthony B., ed. *Moral Evil and Redemptive Suffering: A History of Theodicy in African-American Religious Thought.* Gainesville: University Press of Florida, 2002.

■ *The Confessions of Nat Turner*

Date: 1831
Authors: Nat Turner with Thomas Ruffin Gray
Genre: Pamphlet

Summary Overview

In late 1831 Thomas Ruffin Gray published *The Confessions of Nat Turner, the Leader of the Late Insurrection in Southampton, Va.* Gray was the court-appointed attorney who represented Nat Turner, the leader of a bloody slave revolt in the summer of that year, at his trial. The pamphlet was based on Gray's own investigations after the revolt and on the interview he conducted with Turner after his arrest in October 1831, and most of the pamphlet purportedly consists of Turner's own words. Gray's pamphlet is the principal surviving document about the revolt and is a primary source of information about Turner's motivations for and activities in launching the revolt.

Following Nat Turner's Rebellion, sometimes called the Southampton Insurrection after the Virginia county in which it took place in August, 1831, most of the participants in the revolt were tried and executed. Turner, was captured in late October. On November 1 he spoke with Gray, narrating events from his point of view before his execution later that month. Gray was immediately able to find a publisher, and the pamphlet came out just days after Turner's execution.

The fear that Turner's rebellion created led to intense curiosity about the pamphlet, and Gray's account in time sold some fifty thousand copies. Newspapers in Virginia promoted the pamphlet, running lengthy excerpts and commenting on its importance.

Before Turner's rebellion, the Virginia General Assembly had debated the issue of slavery. Following the rebellion and the publicity it received from Gray's account, debate began to focus on the question of whether freed slaves should be deported to Africa. Ultimately, the assembly passed strict laws prohibiting slaves from being educated and curtailing the rights of both free and enslaved blacks.

Defining Moment

Nat Turner's Rebellion was the latest in a string of slave revolts, attempted revolts, and conspiracies in the United States and throughout the Americas dating back to the early eighteenth century. Nat Turner's Rebellion began late in the day on August 21, 1831, as Turner and his accomplices began traveling through the woods from house to house, liberating slaves and killing whites, though Turner and his men spared some poor whites who, in Turner's view, did not hold themselves out as superior to blacks. As the hours went by, Turner's force grew to about seventy men. At one home, that of the Waller family, the rebels killed Levi Waller and his wife and decapitated ten of their children, piling their bodies at the front of the house.

As word of the rampage spread, Virginia authorities mobilized local contingents of the state militia. Joining the Virginia militia were detachments from U.S. Navy vessels anchored at Norfolk, Virginia, as well as detachments of militias from other Virginia counties and from North Carolina. Less than forty-eight hours after the revolt began, the rebels were defeated. In the rebellion's aftermath, extralegal retaliation was widespread, accomplishing the violent deaths of at least a hundred African Americans, though the number was likely much higher. Rumors began to spread that the rebellion was not limited to Southampton County but was in fact part of a more general slave revolt, prompting acts of barbarism against blacks in North Carolina and elsewhere throughout the South.

Forty-eight rebels, both men and women, were initially captured and tried on charges of treason, insurrection, and conspiracy; ultimately, fifty-five participants (or alleged participants) in the revolt were executed, while others were banished from the state. A handful of those tried were acquitted. Turner himself eluded capture for over nine weeks, until he was discovered on October 30. He was taken into custody and then tried and convicted in a Southampton County court on November 5. On November 11 he was hanged in Jerusalem (now Courtland), Virginia. Afterward, his body was beheaded and quartered. Shortly thereafter, a firm in Baltimore, Maryland, published Gray's *The Confessions of Nat Turner*.

Author Biographies

The nominal author of the 1831 pamphlet *The Confessions of Nat Turner* was Thomas Ruffin Gray. Not a great deal is known about Gray's life, particularly after the publication of Turner's confessions. Gray was born in 1800, making him the same age as Turner. At the time, he practiced law in Jerusalem, Virginia. When the Turner case arose, Gray seized the opportunity to use it to his advantage by publishing a record of the events surrounding the rebellion.

Most of the words in *The Confessions of Nat Turner* are Turner's own, though it is difficult to assess how accurately Gray transcribed them. Turner was born on October 2, 1800. Nat Turner was able to educate himself and could read from an early age. He came to conduct Baptist services for his fellow slaves. When he was twenty-one years old, he fled from his master, but he returned a month later after, as he said, he received a vision ordering him to do so. He claimed to receive otherreligious visions, convincing him that he was destined for some great purpose.

In 1830 Turner was growing increasingly convinced that his destiny in life was to lead a great slave revolt. He stated that on February 12, 1831, he witnessed a solar eclipse, which he interpreted as a sign from God that it was time for him to take action. In the months that followed he planned an insurrection. On August 13, a disturbance in the atmosphere cast a bluish-green hue over the sun, possibly caused by atmospheric dust from an eruption that year of Mount Saint Helens. Turner interpreted the event as another sign from God that the time had come for his insurrection. Accordingly, he launched the rebellion on the night of August 21, 1831. After the revolt was suppressed, he went into hiding. He was captured on October 30 and, in jail, narrated his account of events to Thomas Gray on November 1. Turner was tried and convicted on November 5 and executed on November 11, 1831.

HISTORICAL DOCUMENT

Agreeable to his own appointment, on the evening he was committed to prison, with permission of the jailer, I visited NAT on Tuesday the 1st November, when, without being questioned at all, commenced his narrative in the following words:—

Sir,—You have asked me to give a history of the motives which induced me to undertake the late insurrection, as you call it—To do so I must go back to the days of my infancy, and even before I was born. I was thirty-one years of age the 2d of October last, and born the property of Benj. Turner, of this county. In my childhood a circumstance occurred which made an indelible impression on my mind, and laid the ground work of that enthusiasm, which has terminated so fatally to many, both white and black, and for which I am about to atone at the gallows. It is here necessary to relate this circumstance—trifling as it may seem, it was the commencement of that belief which has grown with time, and even now, sir, in this dungeon, helpless and forsaken as I am, I cannot divest myself of. Being at play with other children, when three or four years old, I was telling them something, which my mother overhearing, said it had happened before I was I born—I stuck to my story, however, and related somethings which went,

in her opinion, to confirm it—others being called on were greatly astonished, knowing that these things had happened, and caused them to say in my hearing, I surely would be a prophet, as the Lord had shewn me things that had happened before my birth. And my father and mother strengthened me in this my first impression, saying in my presence, I was intended for some great purpose, which they had always thought from certain marks on my head and breast—[a parcel of excrescences which I believe are not at all uncommon, particularly among negroes, as I have seen several with the same. In this case he has either cut them off or they have nearly disappeared]—My grandmother, who was very religious, and to whom I was much attached—my master, who belonged to the church, and other religious persons who visited the house, and whom I often saw at prayers, noticing the singularity of my manners, I suppose, and my uncommon intelligence for a child, remarked I had too much sense to be raised, and if I was, I would never be of any service to any one as a slave—To a mind like mine, restless, inquisitive and observant of every thing that was passing, it is easy to suppose that religion was the subject to which it would be directed, and although this subject principally occupied my thoughts—there was nothing that I saw or heard of to which my attention was not directed—The manner in which I learned to read and write, not only had great influence on my own mind, as I acquired it with the most perfect ease, so much so, that I have no recollection whatever of learning the alphabet—but to the astonishment of the family, one day, when a book was shewn me to keep me from crying, I began spelling the names of different objects—this was a source of wonder to all in the neighborhood, particularly the blacks—and this learning was constantly improved at all opportunities—when I got large enough to go to work, while employed, I was reflecting on many things that would present themselves to my imagination, and whenever an opportunity occurred of looking at a book, when the school children were getting their lessons, I would find many things that the fertility of my own imagination had depicted to me before; all my time, not devoted to my master's service, was spent either in prayer, or in making experiments in casting different things in moulds made of earth, in attempting to make paper, gunpowder, and many other experiments, that although I could not perfect, yet convinced me of its practicability if I had the means. I was not addicted to stealing in my youth, nor have ever been—Yet such was the confidence of the negroes in the neighborhood, even at this early period of my life, in my superior judgment, that they would often carry me with them when they were going on any roguery, to plan for them. Growing up among them, with this confidence in my superior judgment, and when this, in their opinions, was perfected by Divine inspiration, from the circumstances already alluded to in my infancy, and which belief was ever afterwards zealously inculcated by the austerity of my life and manners, which became the subject of remark by white and black. —Having soon discovered to be great, I must appear so, and therefore studiously avoided mixing in society, and wrapped myself in mystery, devoting my time to fasting and prayer—By this time, having arrived to man's estate, and hearing the scriptures commented on at meetings, I was struck with that particular passage which says: "Seek ye the kingdom of Heaven and all things shall be added unto you." I reflected much on this passage, and prayed daily for light on this subject—As I was praying one day at my plough, the spirit spoke to me, saying "Seek ye the kingdom of Heaven and all things shall be added unto you."

Question—what do you mean by the Spirit.

Ans. The Spirit that spoke to the prophets in former days—and I was greatly astonished, and for two years prayed continually, whenever my duty would permit—and then again I had the same revelation, which fully confirmed me in the impression that I was ordained for some great purpose in the hands of the Almighty. Several years rolled round, in which many events occurred to strengthen me in this my belief. At this time I reverted in my mind to the remarks made of me in my childhood, and the things that had been shewn me—and as it had been said of me in my childhood by those by whom I had been taught to pray, both white and black, and in whom I had the greatest confidence, that I had too much sense to be raised, and if I was, I would never be of any use to any one as a slave. Now finding I had arrived to man's estate, and was a slave, and these revelations being made known to me, I began to direct my attention to this great object, to fulfil the purpose for which, by this time, I felt assured I was intended. Knowing the influence I had obtained over the minds of my fellow servants, (not by the means of conjuring and such like tricks—for to them I always spoke of such things with contempt) but by the communion of the Spirit whose revelations I often communicated to them, and they believed and said my wisdom came from God. I now began to prepare them for my purpose, by telling them something was about to happen that would terminate in fulfilling the great promise that had been made to me—About this time I was placed under an overseer, from whom I ran away—and after remaining in the woods thirty days, I returned, to the astonishment of the negroes on the plantation, who thought I had made my escape to some other part of the country, as my father had done before. But the reason of my return was, that the Spirit appeared to me and said I had my wishes directed to the things of this world, and not to the kingdom of Heaven, and that I should return to the service of my earthly master—"For he who knoweth his Master's will, and doeth it not, shall be beaten with many stripes, and thus, have I chastened you." And the negroes found fault, and murmured against me, saying that if they had my sense they would not serve any master in the world. And about this time I had a vision—and I saw white spirits and black spirits engaged in battle, and the sun was darkened—the thunder rolled in the Heavens, and blood flowed in streams—and I heard a voice saying, "Such is your luck, such you are called to see, and let it come rough or smooth, you must surely bare it." I now withdrew myself as much as my situation would permit, from the intercourse of my fellow servants, for the avowed purpose of serving the Spirit more fully—and it appeared to me, and reminded me of the things it had already shown me, and that it would then reveal to me the knowledge of the elements, the revolution of the planets, the operation of tides, and changes of the seasons. After this revelation in the year 1825, and the knowledge of the elements being made known to me, I sought more than ever to obtain true holiness before the great day of judgment should appear, and then I began to receive the true knowledge of faith. And from the first steps of righteousness until the last, was I made perfect; and the Holy Ghost was with me, and said, "Behold me as I stand in the Heavens"—and I looked and saw the forms of men in different attitudes—and there were lights in the sky to which the children of darkness gave other names than what they really were—for they were the lights of the Saviour's hands, stretched forth from east to west, even as they were extended on the cross on Calvary for the redemption of sinners. And I wondered greatly at these miracles, and prayed to be informed of a certainty of the meaning thereof—and shortly afterwards, while laboring in the field, I discovered drops of blood on the corn as though it were dew from heaven—and I communicated it to many, both white and black, in the neighborhood—and I then found on the leaves in the woods hieroglyphic characters, and numbers, with the forms of men in different attitudes, portrayed in blood, and representing the figures I had seen before in the heavens. And now the Holy Ghost had revealed itself to me, and made plain the miracles it had shown me—For as the blood of Christ had been shed on this earth, and had ascended to heaven for

the salvation of sinners, and was now returning to earth again in the form of dew—and as the leaves on the trees bore the impression of the figures I had seen in the heavens, it was plain to me that the Saviour was about to lay down the yoke he had borne for the sins of men, and the great day of judgment was at band. About this time I told these things to a white man, (Etheldred T. Brantley) on whom it had a wonderful effect—and he ceased from his wickedness, and was attacked immediately with a cutaneous eruption, and blood oozed from the pores of his skin, and after praying and fasting nine days, he was healed, and the Spirit appeared to me again, and said, as the Saviour had been baptised so should we be also—and when the white people would not let us be baptised by the church, we went down into the water together, in the sight of many who reviled us, and were baptised by the Spirit—After this I rejoiced greatly, and gave thanks to God. And on the 12th of May, 1828, I heard a loud noise in the heavens, and the Spirit instantly appeared to me and said the Serpent was loosened, and Christ had laid down the yoke he had borne for the sins of men, and that I should take it on and fight against the Serpent, for the time was fast approaching when the first should be last and the last should be first.

Ques. Do you not find yourself mistaken now?

Ans. Was not Christ crucified. And by signs in the heavens that it would make known to me when I should commence the great work—and until the first sign appeared, I should conceal it from the knowledge of men—And on the appearance of the sign, (the eclipse of the sun last February) I should arise and prepare myself, and slay my enemies with their own weapons. And immediately on the sign appearing in the heavens, the seal was removed from my lips, and I communicated the great work laid out for me to do, to four in whom I had the greatest confidence, (Henry, Hark, Nelson, and Sam)—It was intended by us to have begun the work of death on the 4th July last— Many were the plans formed and rejected by us, and it affected my mind to such a degree, that I fell sick, and the time passed without our coming to any determination how to commence—Still forming new schemes and rejecting them, when the sign appeared again, which determined me not to wait longer.

Since the commencement of 1830, I had been living with Mr. Joseph Travis, who was to me a kind master, and placed the greatest confidence in me; in fact, I had no cause to complain of his treatment to me. On Saturday evening, the 20th of August, it was agreed between Henry, Hark and myself, to prepare a dinner the next day for the men we expected, and then to concert a plan, as we had not yet determined on any. Hark, on the following morning, brought a pig, and Henry brandy, and being joined by Sam, Nelson, Will and Jack, they prepared in the woods a dinner, where, about three o'clock, I joined them.

Q. Why were you so backward in joining them.

A. The same reason that had caused me not to mix with them for years before.

I saluted them on coming up, and asked Will how came he there, he answered, his life was worth no more than others, and his liberty as dear to him. I asked him if he thought to obtain it. He said he would, or lose his life. This was enough to put him in full confidence. Jack, I knew, was only a tool in the hands of Hark, it was quickly agreed we should commence at home (Mr. J. Travis') on that night, and until we had armed and equipped ourselves, and gathered sufficient force, neither age nor sex was to be spared, (which was invariably adhered to.) We remained at the feast until about two hours in the night, when we went to the house and found Austin; they all went to the cider press and drank, except myself. On returning to the house, Hark went to the door with an axe, for the purpose of breaking it open, as we knew we were strong enough to murder the family, if they were awaked by the noise; but reflecting that it might create an alarm in the neighborhood, we determined to enter the house secretly, and murder them whilst sleeping. Hark got a ladder and set it against the chimney, on which I ascended, and hoisting a window, entered and came down stairs, unbarred the door, and removed the guns from their places. It was then observed that I must spill the first blood. On which, armed with a hatchet, and accompanied by Will, I entered my master's chamber, it being dark, I could not give a death blow, the hatchet glanced from his head, he sprang from the bed and called his wife, it was his last word, Will laid him dead, with a blow of his axe, and Mrs. Travis shared the same fate, as she lay in bed. The murder of this family, five in number, was the work of a moment, not one of them awoke; there was a little infant sleeping in a cradle, that was forgotten, until we had left the house and gone some distance, when Henry and Will returned and killed it; we got here, four guns that would shoot, and several old muskets, with a pound or two of powder. We remained some time at the barn, where we paraded; I formed them in a line as soldiers, and after carrying them through all the manoeuvres I was master of, marched them off to Mr. Salathul Francis', about six hundred yards distant. Sam and Will went to the door and knocked. Mr. Francis asked who was there, Sam replied, it was him, and he had a letter for him, on which he got up and came to the door, they immediately seized him, and dragging him out a little from the door, he was dispatched by repeated blows on the head; there was no other white person in the family. We started from there for Mrs. Reese's, maintaining the most perfect silence on our march, where finding the door unlocked, we entered, and murdered Mrs. Reese in her bed, while sleeping; her son awoke, but it was only to sleep the sleep of death, he had only time to say who is that, and he was no more. From Mrs. Reese's we went to Mrs. Turner's, a mile distant, which we reached about sunrise, on Monday morning. Henry, Austin, and Sam, went to the still, where, finding Mr. Peebles, Austin shot him, and the rest of us went to the house; as we approached, the family discovered us, and shut the door. Vain hope! Will, with one stroke of his axe, opened it, and we entered and found Mrs. Turner and Mrs. Newsome in the middle of a room, almost frightened to death. Will immediately killed Mrs. Turner, with one blow of his axe. I took Mrs. Newsome by the hand, and with the sword I had when I was apprehended, I struck her several blows over the head, but not being able to kill her, as the sword was dull. Will turning around and discovering it, despatched her also. A general destruction of property and search for money and ammunition always succeeded the murders. By this time my company amounted to fifteen, and nine men mounted, who started for Mrs. Whitehead's, (the other six were to go through a by way to Mr. Bryant's and rejoin us at Mrs. Whitehead's,) as we approached the house we discovered Mr. Richard Whitehead standing in the cotton patch, near the lane fence; we called him over into the lane, and Will, the executioner, was near at hand, with his fatal axe, to send him to an untimely grave. As we pushed on to the house, I discovered some one run round the garden, and thinking it was some of the white family, I pursued them, but finding it was a servant girl belonging to the house, I returned to commence the work of death, but they whom I left, had not been idle; all the family were already murdered, but Mrs. Whitehead and her daughter Margaret. As I came round to the door I saw Will pulling Mrs. Whitehead out of the house, and at the step he nearly severed her head from her body, with his broad axe. Miss Margaret, when I discovered her, had concealed herself in the corner, formed by the projection of the cellar cap from the house; on my approach she fled, but was soon overtaken, and after repeated blows with a sword, I killed her by a blow on the head, with a fence rail. By this time, the six who had gone by Mr. Bryant's, rejoined us, and informed me they had done the work of death assigned them. We again divided, part going to Mr. Richard Porter's, and from thence to Nathaniel Francis', the others to Mr. Howell Harris', and Mr. T. Doyles. On my reaching Mr. Porter's, he had escaped with his family. I understood there, that the alarm had already spread, and I immediately returned to bring up those sent to Mr. Doyles, and Mr. Howell Harris'; the party I left going on to Mr. Francis', having told them I would join them in that neighborhood. I met these sent to Mr. Doyles' and Mr. Harris' returning, having met Mr. Doyle on the road and killed him; and learning from some who joined them, that Mr. Harris was from home, I immediately pursued the course taken by the party gone on before; but knowing they would complete the work of death and pillage, at Mr. Francis' before I could there, I went to Mr. Peter Edwards', expecting to find them there, but they had been here also. I then went to Mr. John T. Barrow's, they had been here and murdered him. I pursued on their track to Capt. Newit Harris', where I found the greater part mounted, and ready to start; the

men now amounting to about forty, shouted and hurrahed as I rode up, some were in the yard, loading their guns, others drinking. They said Captain Harris and his family had escaped, the property in the house they destroyed, robbing him of money and other valuables. I ordered them to mount and march instantly, this was about nine or ten o'clock, Monday morning. I proceeded to Mr. Levi Waller's, two or three miles distant. I took my station in the rear, and as it 'twas my object to carry terror and devastation wherever we went, I placed fifteen or twenty of the best armed and most to be relied on, in front, who generally approached the houses as fast as their horses could run; this was for two purposes, to prevent their escape and strike terror to the inhabitants—on this account I never got to the houses, after leaving Mrs. Whitehead's, until the murders were committed, except in one case. I sometimes got in sight in time to see the work of death completed, viewed the mangled bodies as they lay, in silent satisfaction, and immediately started in quest of other victims—Having murdered Mrs. Waller and ten children, we started for Mr. William Williams'—having killed him and two little boys that were there; while engaged in this, Mrs. Williams fled and got some distance from the house, but she was pursued, overtaken, and compelled to get up behind one of the company, who brought her back, and after showing her the mangled body of her lifeless husband, she was told to get down and lay by his side, where she was shot dead. I then started for Mr. Jacob Williams, where the family were murdered—Here we found a young man named Drury, who had come on business with Mr. Williams—he was pursued, overtaken and shot. Mrs. Vaughan was the next place we visited—and after murdering the family here, I determined on starting for Jerusalem—Our number amounted now to fifty or sixty, all mounted and armed with guns, axes, swords and clubs—On reaching Mr. James W. Parkers' gate, immediately on the road leading to Jerusalem, and about three miles distant, it was proposed to me to call there, but I objected, as I knew he was gone to Jerusalem, and my object was to reach there as soon as possible; but some of the men having relations at Mr. Parker's it was agreed that they might call and get his people. I remained at the gate on the road, with seven or eight; the others going across the field to the house, about half a mile off. After waiting some time for them, I became impatient, and started to the house for them, and on our return we were met by a party of white men, who had pursued our blood-stained track, and who had fired on those at the gate, and dispersed them, which I knew nothing of, not having been at that time rejoined by any of them—Immediately on discovering the whites, I ordered my men to halt and form, as they appeared to be alarmed—The white men, eighteen in number, approached us in about one hundred yards, when one of them fired, (this was against the positive orders of Captain Alexander P. Peete, who commanded, and who had directed the men to reserve their fire until within thirty paces). And I discovered about half of them retreating, I then ordered my men to fire and rush on them; the few remaining stood their ground until we approached within fifty yards, when they fired and retreated. We pursued and overtook some of them who we thought we left dead; (they were not killed) after pursuing them about two hundred yards, and rising a little hill, I discovered they were met by another party, and had halted, and were reloading their guns, (this was a small party from Jerusalem who knew the negroes were in the field, and had just tied their horses to await their return to the road, knowing that Mr. Parker had family were in Jerusalem, but knew nothing of the party that had gone in with Captain Peete; on hearing the firing they immediately rushed to the spot and arrived just in time to arrest the progress of these barbarous villains, and save the lives of their friends and fellow citizens.) Thinking that those who retreated first, and the party who fired on us at fifty or sixty yards distant, had all only fallen back to meet others with ammunition. As I saw them re-loading their guns, and more coming up than I saw at first, and several of my bravest men being wounded, the others became panic struck and squandered over the field; the white men pursued and fired on us several times. Hark had his horse shot under him, and I caught another for him as it was running by me; five or six of my men were wounded, but none left on

the field; finding myself defeated here I instantly determined to go through a private way, and cross the Nottoway river at the Cypress Bridge, three miles below Jerusalem, and attack that place in the rear, as I expected they would look for me on the other road, and I had a great desire to get there to procure arms and ammunition. After going a short distance in this private way, accompanied by about twenty men, I overtook two or three who told me the others were dispersed in every direction. After trying in vain to collect a sufficient force to proceed to Jerusalem, I determined to return, as I was sure they would make back to their old neighborhood, where they would rejoin me, make new recruits, and come down again. On my way back, I called at Mrs. Thomas's, Mrs. Spencer's, and several other places, the white families having fled, we found no more victims to gratify our thirst for blood, we stopped at Maj. Ridley's quarter for the night, and being joined by four of his men, with the recruits made since my defeat, we mustered now about forty strong. After placing out sentinels, I laid down to sleep, but was quickly roused by a great racket; starting up, I found some mounted, and others in great confusion; one of the sentinels having given the alarm that we were about to be attacked, I ordered some to ride round and reconnoiter, and on their return the others being more alarmed, not knowing who they were, fled in different ways, so that I was reduced to about twenty again; with this I determined to attempt to recruit, and proceed on to rally in the neighborhood, I had left.

Dr. Blunt's was the nearest house, which we reached just before day; on riding up the yard, Hark fired a gun. We expected Dr. Blunt and his family were at Maj. Ridley's, as I knew there was a company of men there; the gun was fired to ascertain if any of the family were at home; we were immediately fired upon and retreated, leaving several of my men. I do not know what became of them, as I never saw them afterwards. Pursuing our course back and coming in sight of Captain Harris', where we had been the day before, we discovered a party of white men at the house, on which all deserted me but two, (Jacob and Nat,) we concealed ourselves in the woods until near night, when I sent them in search of Henry, Sam, Nelson, and Hark, and directed them to rally all they could, at the place we had had our dinner the Sunday before, where they would find me, and I accordingly returned there as soon as it was dark and remained until Wednesday evening, when discovering white men riding around the place as though they were looking for some one, and none of my men joining me, I concluded Jacob and Nat had been taken, and compelled to betray me. On this I gave up all hope for the present; and on Thursday night after having supplied myself with provisions from Mr. Travis's, I scratched a hole under a pile of fence rails in a field, where I concealed myself for six weeks, never leaving my hiding place but for a few minutes in the dead of night to get water which was very near; thinking by this time I could venture out, I began to go about in the night and eaves drop the houses in the neighborhood; pursuing this course for about a fortnight and gathering little or no intelligence, afraid of speaking to any human being, and returning every morning to my cave before the dawn of day. I know not how long I might have led this life, if accident had not betrayed me, a dog in the neighborhood passing by my hiding place one night while I was out, was attracted by some meat I had in my cave, and crawled in and stole it, and was coming out just as I returned. A few nights after, two negroes having started to go hunting with the same dog, and passed that way, the dog came again to the place, and having just gone out to walk about, discovered me and barked, on which thinking myself discovered, I spoke to them to beg concealment. On making myself known they fled from me. Knowing then they would betray me, I immediately left my hiding place, and was pursued almost incessantly until I was taken a fortnight afterwards by Mr. Benjamin Phipps, in a little hole I had dug out with my sword, for the purpose of concealment, under the top of a fallen tree. On Mr. Phipps' discovering the place of my concealment, he cocked his gun and aimed at me. I requested him not to shoot and I would give up, upon which he demanded my sword. I delivered it to him, and he brought me to prison. During the time I was pursued, I had many hair breadth escapes, which your time will not permit you to relate.

I am here loaded with chains, and willing to suffer the fate that awaits me.

I here proceeded to make some inquiries of him after assuring him of the certain death that awaited him, and that concealment would only bring destruction on the innocent as well as guilty, of his own color, if he knew of any extensive or concerted plan. His answer was, I do not. When I questioned him as to the insurrection in North Carolina happening about the same time, he denied any knowledge of it; and when I looked him in the face as though I would search his inmost thoughts, he replied, "I see sir, you doubt my word; but can you not think the same ideas, and strange appearances about this time in the heaven's might prompt others, as well as myself, to this undertaking." I now had much conversation with and asked him many questions, having forborne to do so previously, except in the cases noted in parenthesis; but during his statement, I had, unnoticed by him, taken notes as to some particular circumstances, and having the advantage of his statement before me in writing, on the evening of the third day that I had been with him, I began a cross examination, and found his statement corroborated by every circumstance coming within my own knowledge or the confessions of others whom had been either killed or executed, and whom he had not seen nor had any knowledge since 22d of August last, he expressed himself fully satisfied as to the impracticability of his attempt. It has been said he was ignorant and cowardly, and that his object was to murder and rob for the purpose of obtaining money to make his escape. It is notorious, that he was never known to have a dollar in his life; to swear an oath, or drink a drop of spirits. As to his ignorance, he certainly never had the advantages of education, but he can read and write, (it was taught him by his parents,) and for natural intelligence and quickness of apprehension, is surpassed by few men I have ever seen. As to his being a coward, his reason as given for not resisting Mr. Phipps, shews the decision of his character. When he saw Mr. Phipps present his gun, he said he knew it was impossible for him to escape as the woods were full of men; he therefore thought it was better to surrender, and trust to fortune for his escape.

He is a complete fanatic, or plays his part most admirably. On other subjects he possesses an uncommon share of intelligence, with a mind capable of attaining any thing; but warped and perverted by the influence of early impressions. He is below the ordinary stature, though strong and active, having the true negro face, every feature of which is strongly marked. I shall not attempt to describe the effect of his narrative, as told and commented on by himself, in the condemned hole of the prison. The calm, deliberate composure with which he spoke of his late deeds and intentions, the expression of his fiend-like face when excited by enthusiasm, still bearing the stains of the blood of helpless innocence about him; clothed with rags and covered with chains; yet daring to raise his manacled hands to heaven, with a spirit soaring above the attributes of man; I looked on him and my blood curdled in my veins.

I will not shock the feelings of humanity, nor wound afresh the bosoms of the disconsolate sufferers in this unparalleled and inhuman massacre, by detailing the deeds of their fiend-like barbarity. There were two or three who were in the power of these wretches, had they known it, and who escaped in the most providential manner. There were two whom they thought they left dead on the field at Mr. Parker's, but who were only stunned by the blows of their guns, as they did not take time to reload when they charged on them. The escape of a little girl who went to school at Mr. Waller's, and where the children were collecting for that purpose. excited general sympathy. As their teacher had not arrived, they were at play in the yard, and seeing the negroes approach, ran up on a dirt chimney (such as are common to log houses,) and remained there unnoticed during the massacre of the eleven that were killed at this place. She remained on her hiding place till just before the arrival of a party, who were in pursuit of the murderers, when she came down and fled to a swamp, where, a mere child as she was, with the horrors of the late scene before her, she lay concealed until the next day, when seeing a party go up to the house, she came up, and on being asked how she escaped, replied with the utmost simplicity, "The Lord helped her." She was taken up behind a gentleman of the party, and returned to the arms of her weeping mother. Miss Whitehead concealed herself between the bed and the mat that supported it, while they murdered her sister in the same room, without discovering her. She was afterwards carried off, and concealed for protection by a slave of the family, who gave evidence against several of them on their trial. Mrs. Nathaniel Francis, while concealed in a closet heard their blows, and the shrieks of the victims of these ruthless savages; they then entered the closet where she was concealed, and went out without discovering her. While in this hiding place, she heard two of her women in a quarrel about the division of her clothes. Mr. John T. Baron, discovering them approaching his house, told his wife to make her escape, and scorning to fly, fell fighting on his own threshold. After firing his rifle, he discharged his gun at them, and then broke it over the villain who first approached him, but he was overpowered, and slain. His bravery, however, saved from the hands of these monsters, his lovely and amiable wife, who will long lament a husband so deserving of her love. As directed by him, she attempted to escape through the garden, when she was caught and held by one of her servant girls, but another coming to her rescue, she fled to the woods, and concealed herself. Few indeed, were those who escaped their work of death. But fortunate for society, the hand of retributive justice has overtaken them; and not one that was known to be concerned has escaped.

GLOSSARY

Calvary: the site of Christ's Crucifixion

"For he who knoweth his Master's will …": loosely quoted from the biblical book of Luke, Chapter 12, verses 47–48

infancy: childhood, youth

Jerusalem: a nearby town in Virginia

Saviour: Jesus Christ

"Seek ye the kingdom of Heaven ...": loosely quoted from the biblical books of Matthew (Chapter 6, verse 33) and Luke (Chapter 12, verse 31)

shewn: an antique form of "shown"

Document Analysis

Gray asserts at the opening of the document that he visited Turner in his jail cell on November 1, 1831, and that Turner, without prompting, began to narrate the events as he recalled them.

In the long second paragraph, Turner discusses his early life. He emphasizes an incident in his childhood when he told a story to other children based on events that had taken place before he was born. In Turner's view, this was an early indication that he was destined to be a prophet. He goes on to note that his parents confirmed him in the belief that he was destined for great things, and others noted that his uncommon intelligence and powers of observation would make him unsuitable as a slave. A mark of that intelligence was his ability to read and the "most perfect ease" with which he acquired that ability. He discusses the fertility of his imagination and his efforts to use his intelligence to make such things as paper and gunpowder. He also emphasizes that others placed great confidence in his judgment and his ability to plan, so his peers often took him along when they were planning "roguery."

The paragraph continues with Turner describing the role of religion in his life. He discusses the "communion of the Spirit" that he felt when he arrived at young adulthood and began to consider how he might fulfill his destiny. Because of religious visions, he withdrew himself from his fellow slaves; he cites the year 1825 as the time when he experienced numerous such visions, including Christ on the Cross, blood on the corn in the field, and inspiration from the Holy Spirit. A key religious vision occurred on May 12, 1828, when, Turner says, he saw that "Christ had laid down the yoke he had borne for the sins of men, and that I should take it on and fight against the Serpent." At the end of the paragraph, he discusses the solar eclipse in February 1831 and his conviction that it was a sign from God for him to begin his fight. He took four other slaves—

Henry, Hark, Nelson, and Sam—into his confidence, and they planned the rebellion for July 4. The rebellion was delayed, in part because Turner became sick, but another sign from the heavens—an atmospheric disturbance that colored the sun bluish-green on August 13—convinced him that the time to strike had come.

From the standpoint of southern slave owners, paragraph 3 of the document offers crucial revelations. Here Turner notes that by this time he was owned by Joseph Travis, and he acknowledges that Travis treated him kindly and with "confidence." For defenders of slavery, this was proof that Turner acted neither out of desire for revenge against a cruel master nor out of any considered opposition to the slave system. Turner then begins to detail the events of the rebellion, which began with a dinner on August 20, when the conspirators agreed to meet and form their plans.

After the two one-line paragraphs giving Gray's brief question and Turner's initial answer, paragraph 6 is yet another extremely long paragraph, consisting entirely of details of the men's activities once the revolt started. Turner offers a record of the murders he and his men committed, beginning with the five members of the Travis family, including an infant who was killed only after one of the men went back to the house for that purpose. The men continued to the home of Mr. Salathul Francis and then to the home of Mrs. Reese, where they murdered her and her son in their beds. Numerous other victims followed: the Turners, the Whiteheads (including a daughter, Margaret Whitehead—the only person Turner himself killed during the rampage), T. Doyle, the Wallers (including ten children), and others. Turner details how the marauders gathered guns and ammunition as well as any money and other property they could collect.

Still in paragraph 6, Turner records an encounter with militia under the command of Captain Alexander Peete. After a brief skirmish, the men encountered another military contingent, prompting an aside from Gray, who refers to the men as "barbarous villains." As a result of these skirmishes several of Turner's men were wounded, so Turner and a party of twenty men pursued a path that would take them by a back way into the town of Jerusalem. The men paused to rest, but the military was in pursuit and discovered the men's whereabouts. By this point the killings had stopped, and the men were in flight. Turner knew that at least some of his confederates had been captured, and he suspected that they would be forced to betray him. Accordingly, he went into hiding in a hole he dug under a pile of fence rails. The paragraph continues with details about the time Turner spent in hiding, particularly how his hiding place was discovered by a dog that smelled some meat he had. Fearing that he would be captured, Turner found another hiding place but was eventually discovered by a Mr. Benjamin Phipps. Phipps was armed, so Turner quietly surrendered and allowed Phipps to take him to the local jail.

In paragraph 7, Gray recalls intervening to ask Turner whether his rebellion was part of a larger slave revolt—Turner claimed it was not. Gray then questioned Turner about a supposed insurrection in North Carolina, but again Turner denied any knowledge of such an insurrection. Again, these responses were a matter of grave concern to people throughout the South, many of whom believed that Turner's rebellion was part of a more widespread slave revolt. Gray points out that he questioned Turner about various details, and his statements were corroborated by the accounts of others involved in the rebellion. Gray comments on Turner's intelligence and ability to read, suggesting that Turner was not motivated by greed or the desire for money.

In the final paragraph, Gray provides additional details about the revolt, including stories of those who escaped from Turner's men. Gray refers to the revolt as an "unparalleled and inhuman massacre" and cites the men's "fiend-like barbarity." He concludes by saying, "The hand of retributive justice has overtaken them; and not one that was known to be concerned has escaped."

Essential Themes

One of the telling things about *The Confessions of Nat Turner* is the way that its message was variously interpreted by people at the time it was published, with interpretations differing greatly between north and south and—unsurprisingly—between abolitionist and slaveholder.

William Lloyd Garrison, for example, the prominent abolitionist and publisher of *The Liberator* newspaper,

saw the work as a valuable tool in the abolition movement, for it could inspire admiration of Turner and turn him into a hero, leading perhaps to other insurrections. The historian Scot French quotes Garrison as writing that the pamphlet would "only serve to rouse up other black leaders and cause other insurrections, by creating among blacks admiration for the character Nat, and a deep undying sympathy for his cause."

At the same time, The pamphlet attracted considerable attention among southerners. They argued that it offered a "lesson" to northern abolitionists, for it documented what many southerners regarded as the fanaticism of the abolition movement. Further, they used the pamphlet to emphasize that the uprising did not stem from mistreatment on the part of slave owners. Indeed, the pamphlet presented plausible alternative motives for the revolt—Turner's own twisted fanaticism combined with a charisma that enabled him to attract followers. It thus provided the southern slave-owning class with a scapegoat other than the institution of slavery—Nat Turner himself.

—Michael J. O'Neal, PhD

Bibliography and Additional Reading

Fabricant, Daniel S. "Thomas R. Gray and William Styron: Finally, a Critical Look at the 1831 *Confessions of Nat Turner*." *American Journal of Legal History* 37 (July 1993): 332–361.

Aptheker, Herbert. *Nat Turner's Slave Rebellion*. (New York: Humanities Press, 1966).

———. *American Negro Slave Revolts*. 5th ed. New York: International Publishers, 1983).

Brodhead, Richard H. "Millennium, Prophecy and the Energies of Social Transformation: The Case of Nat Turner." In *Imagining the End: Visions of Apocalypse from the Ancient Middle East to Modern America*, eds. Abbas Amanat and Magnus Bernhardsson. (London: I. B. Tauris, 2002).

French, Scot. *The Rebellious Slave: Nat Turner in American Memory*.(Boston: Houghton Mifflin, 2004).

Greenberg, Kenneth S., ed. *Nat Turner: A Slave Rebellion in History and Memory*. (New York: Oxford University Press, 2003(.

Oates, Stephen B. *The Fires of Jubilee: Nat Turner's Fierce Rebellion*. (New York: HarperPerennial, 1990).

Tragle, Henry Irving, ed. *The Southampton Slave Revolt of 1831: A Compilation of Source Material*. (Amherst: University of Massachusetts Press, 1971).

■ Declaration of Sentiments of the American Anti-Slavery Convention

Date: 1833
Author: William Lloyd Garrison
Genre: Public declaration

Summary Overview

It is not an exaggeration to say that William Lloyd Garrison's speeches and writings, including his "Declaration of Sentiments of the American Anti-Slavery Convention" significantly altered the conversation about slavery in the United States. Garrison's brand of radical abolition startled people in the north while terrifying and angering slave owners in the south. This declaration, in particular, sets out some important aspects of Garrison's viewpoint on slavery that would inform the rest of his career. The first is his militancy—he presents the fight against slavery as equal in importance and consequence as the American Revolution. Garrison's militancy, however, is one of spirit rather than of physical force. While Garrison will reject "all carnal weapons," he believes his cause will triumph because, like the American founders, "the honest conviction that Truth, Justice and Right were on their side" would make his movement "invincible."

Garrison also breaks with the common abolitionist sentiment by demanding complete and immediate emancipation, rather than the gradual efforts that characterized most states' emancipation laws. This declaration clearly demonstrates that Garrison is not a leader who will settle for half measures or compromise. He attacks sacred foundations of the American political and social system—in particular, pointing out aspects of the Constitution that privilege slave owners and slave states. Most striking, however, is his eloquence in the defense of African-American slaves as his fellow human beings and his passion to see them free. Garrison, with his passion and his insistence on radical, rapid change, would become the figurehead of radical abolitionism, revered by some, despised by many.

Defining Moment

The decade of the 1830s saw the development of the abolition movement from one that accepted that the end of slavery in the United States was a long-term project, with a common goal being not only the freeing of the slaves but their transport to Africa, to places like the new nation of Liberia, "restoring" the United States as a white nation. Even in the northern states, racial equality was not enshrined in law, nor was it often exhibited in practice. While slavery had been outlawed in a number of states, most of these emancipation measures were gradual in nature, maintaining the slave-status a of a large number of African Americans and condemning their children to decades of indentured servitude before their freedom would be effective.

Events in the early 1830s, however, changed the landscape of both slavery and abolitionism. Nat Turner's violent slave rebellion in Virginia had encouraged southern state legislatures to increase restrictions on slaves—including prohibitions on teaching slaves to read and write—and increase the financial burden on slave owners who desired to free their slaves. In response to these increasingly repressive measures in the south, activists in the North such as William Lloyd Garrison formed new organizations and publications that agitated for immediate full emancipation of slaves and—shockingly—full legal and citizenship rights not only for the freed slaves but for free African-Americans in northern states. Others, like Lydia Maria Child would echo this more radical approach to the abolition of slaves. Garrison's radical approach would be taken further by revolutions like John Brown, further polarizing those who opposed slavery, and those who clung to the institution.

Author Biography

William Lloyd Garrison was born in Newburyport, Massachusetts, on December 10, 1805. In 1831, he published the first issue of his Boston newspaper, the *Liberator*, which until the end of 1865 served as his personal vehicle for broadcasting his many controversial opinions, most notably that slavery must be immediately abolished and that people of all skin colors must be treated as equals. In 1833 he played a major role in the establishment of the American Anti-Slavery Society, which for the first time united black and white reformers of both genders in support of programs of mass agitation to promote immediate abolition and racial equality.

Throughout the 1840s and 1850s Garrison and his small circle continued to espouse a wide-ranging reform agenda through speeches and in the pages of the *Liberator*. In 1859, however, John Brown's insurrectionary raid on the federal armory at Harpers Ferry, Virginia, led Garrison to jettison his pacifism. When the Civil War began in 1861, he quickly became one of its most fervent supporters, demanding that all slaves be freed by force of arms. In 1865, after the ratification of the Thirteenth Amendment, abolishing slavery, Garrison closed the *Liberator* and ended his career. He died on May 24, 1879.

Garrison was perhaps the antebellum era's most innovative editorial agitator. In an era of rapidly expanding print and telegraphic communication, his ceaseless desire to promote himself as the nation's moral censor and his unerring capacity for challenging conventional values made it all but impossible for Americans to deny the moral problem of slavery. He accomplished his goals because of his exceptional talent as a polemicist and his inexhaustible love of ideological conflict. His temperament aligned him closely to the romantic impulses that inspired New England Transcendentalists and utopian reformers who, like him, were deeply suspicious of established institutions and who celebrated intuitive illuminations of God's "truth." In short, he addressed public opinion in idioms it instinctively understood.

HISTORICAL DOCUMENT

Done at Philadelphia, December 6th, A. D. 1833.

The Convention assembled in the city of Philadelphia, to organize a National Anti-Slavery Society, promptly seize the opportunity to promulgate the following Declaration of Sentiments, as cherished by them in relation to the enslavement of one-sixth portion of the American people.

More than fifty-seven years have elapsed, since a band of patriots convened in this place, to devise measures for the deliverance of this country from a foreign yoke. The corner-stone upon which they founded the Temple of Freedom was broadly this—"that all men are created equal; that they are endowed by their Creator with certain inalienable rights; that among these are life, LIBERTY, and the pursuit of happiness." At the sound of their trumpet-call, three millions of people rose up as from the sleep of death, and rushed to the strife of blood; deeming it more glorious to die instantly as freemen, than desirable to live one hour as slaves. They were few in number—poor in resources; but the honest conviction that Truth, Justice and Right were on their side, made them invincible.

We have met together for the achievement of an enterprise, without which that of our fathers is incomplete; and which, for its magnitude, solemnity, and probable results upon the destiny of the world, as far transcends theirs as moral truth does physical force.

In purity of motive, in earnestness of zeal, in decision of purpose, in intrepidity of action, in steadfastness of faith, in sincerity of spirit, we would not be inferior to them.

Their principles led them to wage war against their oppressors, and to spill human blood like water, in order to be free.

Ours forbid the doing of evil that good may come, and lead us to reject, and to entreat the oppressed to reject, the use of all carnal weapons for deliverance from bondage; relying solely upon those which are spiritual, and mighty through God to the pulling down of strong holds.

Their measures were physical resistance—the marshalling in arms—the hostile array—the mortal encounter. Ours shall be such only as the opposition of moral purity to moral corruption—the destruction of error by the potency of truth—the overthrow of prejudice by the power of love—and the abolition of slavery by the spirit of repentance.

Their grievances, great as they were, were trifling in comparison with the wrongs and sufferings of those for whom we plead. Our fathers were never slaves—never bought and sold like cattle—never shut out from the light of knowledge and religion—never subjected to the lash of brutal taskmasters.

But those, for whose emancipation we are striving—constituting at the present time at least one-sixth part of our countrymen—are recognized by law, and treated by their fellow-beings, as marketable commodities, as goods and chattels, as brute beasts; are plundered daily of the fruits of their toil without redress; really enjoy no constitutional nor legal protection from licentious and murderous outrages upon their persons; and are ruthlessly torn asunder—the tender babe from the arms of its frantic mother—the heart-broken wife from her weeping husband—at the caprice or pleasure of irresponsible tyrants. For the crime of having a dark complexion, they suffer the pangs of hunger, the infliction of stripes, the ignominy of brutal servitude. They are kept in heathenish darkness by laws expressly enacted to make their instruction a criminal offence.

These are the prominent circumstances in the condition of more than two millions of our people, the proof of which may be found in thousands of indisputable facts, and in the laws of the slaveholding States.

Hence we maintain—that, in view of the civil and religious privileges of this nation, the guilt of its oppression is unequalled by any other on the face of the earth; and, therefore, that it is bound to repent instantly, to undo the heavy burdens, and to let the oppressed go free.

We further maintain—that no man has a right to enslave or imbrute his brother—to hold or acknowledge him, for one moment, as a piece of merchandise—to keep back his hire by fraud—or to brutalize his mind, by denying him the means of intellectual, social and moral improvement.

The right to enjoy liberty is inalienable. To invade it is to usurp the prerogative of Jehovah. Every man has a right to his own body—to the products of his own labor—to the protection of law—and to the common advantages of society. It is piracy to buy or steal a native African, and subject him to servitude. Surely, the sin is as great to enslave an American as an African.

Therefore we believe and affirm—that there is no difference, in principle, between the African slave trade and American slavery:

That every American citizen, who detains a human being in involuntary bondage as his property, is, according to Scripture, (Ex. xxi. 16,) a man-stealer:

That the slaves ought instantly to be set free, and brought under the protection of law:

That if they had lived from the time of Pharaoh down to the present period, and had been entailed through successive generations, their right to be free could never have been alienated, but their claims would have constantly risen in solemnity:

That all those laws which are now in force, admitting the right of slavery, are therefore, before God, utterly null and void; being an audacious usurpation of the Divine prerogative, a daring infringement on the law of nature, a base over-throw of the very foundations of the social compact, a complete extinction of all the relations, endearments and obligations of mankind, and a presumptuous transgression of all the holy commandments; and that therefore they ought instantly to be abrogated.

We further believe and affirm—that all persons of color, who possess the qualifications which are demanded of others, ought to be admitted forthwith to the enjoyment of the same privileges, and the exercise of the same prerogatives, as others; and that the paths of preferment, of wealth, and of intelligence, should be opened as widely to them as to persons of a white complexion.

We maintain that no compensation should be given to the planters emancipating their slaves:

Because it would be a surrender of the great fundamental principle, that man cannot hold property in man:

Because slavery is a crime, and therefore is not an article to be sold:

Because the holders of slaves are not the just proprietors of what they claim; freeing the slave is not depriving them of property, but restoring it to its rightful owner; it is not wronging the master, but righting the slave—restoring him to himself:

Because immediate and general emancipation would only destroy nominal, not real property; it would not amputate a limb or break a bone of the slaves, but by infusing motives into their breasts, would make them doubly valuable to the masters as free laborers; and

Because, if compensation is to be given at all, it should be given to the outraged and guiltless slaves, and not to those who have plundered and abused them.

We regard as delusive, cruel and dangerous, any scheme of expatriation which pretends to aid, either directly or indirectly, in the emancipation of the slaves, or to be a substitute for the immediate and total abolition of slavery.

We fully and unanimously recognise the sovereignty of each State, to legislate exclusively on the subject of the slavery which is tolerated within its limits; we concede that Congress, under the present national compact, has no right to interfere with any of the slave States, in relation to this momentous subject:

But we maintain that Congress has a right, and is solemnly bound, to suppress the domestic slave trade between the several States, and to abolish slavery in those portions of our territory which the Constitution has placed under its exclusive jurisdiction.

We also maintain that there are, at the present time, the highest obligations resting upon the people of the free States to remove slavery by moral and political action, as prescribed in the Constitution of the United States. They are now living under a pledge of their tremendous physical force, to fasten the galling fetters of tyranny upon the limbs of millions in the Southern States; they are liable to be called at any moment to suppress a general insurrection of the slaves; they authorize the slave owner to vote for three-fifths of his slaves as property, and thus enable him to perpetuate his oppression; they support a standing army at the South for its protection and they seize the slave, who has escaped into their territories, and send him back to be tortured by an enraged master or a brutal driver. This relation to slavery is criminal, and full of danger: IT MUST BE BROKEN UP.

These are our views and principles—these our designs and measures. With entire confidence in the overruling justice of God, we plant ourselves upon the Declaration of our Independence and the truths of Divine Revelation, as upon the Everlasting Rock.

We shall organize Anti-Slavery Societies, if possible, in every city, town and village in our land.

We shall send forth agents to lift up the voice of remonstrance, of warning, of entreaty, and of rebuke.

We shall circulate, unsparingly and extensively, anti-slavery tracts and periodicals.

We shall enlist the pulpit and the press in the cause of the suffering and the dumb.

We shalt aim at a purification of the churches from all participation in the guilt of slavery.

We shall encourage the labor of freemen rather than that of slaves, by giving a preference to their productions: and

We shall spare no exertions nor means to bring the whole nation to speedy repentance.

Our trust for victory is solely in God. We may be personally defeated, but our principles never. Truth, Justice, Reason, Humanity, must and will gloriously triumph. Already a host is coming up to the help of the Lord against the mighty, and the prospect before us is full of encouragement.

Submitting this Declaration to the candid examination of the people of this country, and of the friends of liberty throughout the world, we hereby affix our signatures to it; pledging ourselves that, under the guidance and by the help of Almighty God, we will do all that in us lies, consistently with this Declaration of our principles, to overthrow the most execrable system of slavery that has ever been witnessed upon earth; to deliver our land from its deadliest curse; to wipe out the foulest stain which rests upon our national escutcheon; and to secure to the colored population of the United States, all the rights and privileges which belong to them as men, and as Americans—come what may to our persons, our interests, or our reputation—whether we live to witness the triumph of Liberty, Justice and Humanity, or perish untimely as martyrs in this great, benevolent, and holy cause.

GLOSSARY

dumb: without speech, silent

expatriation: the practice of sending freed slaves back to Africa

imbrute: to lower someone to the level of a brute or animal

marshall: gather

Pharaoh: ancient ruler of Egypt who, in the Hebrew Bible, enslaved the Israelites

Document Analysis

The declaration begins by taking advantage of the convention's Philadelphia location to draw parallels between their work and the work, half a century before, of the Continental Congress that oversaw the establishing of the United States and its independence from Britain. Recalling the words of the Declaration of Independence, Garrison declares that the Americans won that fight because of the moral rightness of their position rather than their numbers or resources. These founders, however, left their job incomplete and so Garrison and the convention must finish the work of liberty and freedom. Unlike the revolutionaries of the 18th century, this movement will rely on spiritual weapons rather than "carnal" ones. Further, Garrison declares the "grievances" of the American founding to be "trifling" in comparison to those of slaves ("those for whom we plead").

Garrison then describes in harsh and emotional terms the conditions American slaves live under. They are legally considered commodities rather than humans, they are exploited and have no legal protection from physical abuse. Families and marriages are destroyed "at the caprice or pleasure of irresponsible tyrants." His characterization of slave owners as "tyrants" is another, harsher, echo of the revolutionary era, with the founders declaring themselves the enemy of the tyrannical British government. Despite the laws that exist, Garrison asserts that humans have no moral right to enslave others. To steal another's liberty is beyond the rightful ability of human beings.

Garrison then begins to list the specific demands and goals of this new Anti—Slavery Society, beginning from the premise that American slavery is the moral equivalent of the African slave trade. By this point, the United States had banned participation in African slave trade. It follows, logically, that slavery in America itself should be illegal as well. Garrison demands that all slaves should be set free "and brought under the protection of law." He dismisses laws that protect slavery as being "null and void" because they in opposition to the "law of nature." Here, Garrison is using the same ideas of

the social contract (or compact) that the founders did and declaring slavery to be a violation of the foundations of human society. Those freed slaves should also be treated in the same way as white citizens.

Garrison then, in a position that is more radical than other abolitionists of the time, demands that slave owners receive no compensation from the government for their freed slaves. Slavery is a crime against nature and it is not morally possible to own another human. Why should a slave owner receive payment for someone he should never have been able to "own" in the first place? What Garrison is say is that to allow for compensation in return for freeing slaves, is to admit that slavery had been proper and legal at one point. Garrison's argument is that the laws that allowed slavery were never valid. Slaves were never "real" property, they were "nominal" property. Any money being given out, he claims, should be given to "the outraged and guiltless slaves" rather than to their oppressors.

He next denounces "any scheme of expatriation"—an attack on the "colonization" movement whose supporters wanted to end slavery, but not allow freed slaves to stay in the United States, instead wanting to send them back to Africa (even if they had been born in the United States).

Garrison, in the final portion of the declaration, moves to the particulars of ending slavery. He acknowledges that Congress cannot ban slavery in individual states, but he does call upon Congress to ban the interstate trade in slaves (which would have had severe financial consequences for the institution as a whole). While Congress cannot ban slavery, the people of free states have an obligation change the political and legal principles that require taxpayers to put down slave insurrections, that require the return of fugitive slaves, and that provides for the three-fifths clause which gives disproportional power to slave owners. Here, Garrison is attacking the constitutional provisions that he sees as supporting the institution of slavery.

In closing, Garrison outlines his organization's plan of action. They will grow their influence across the country and continue to rebuke and warn of the dangers of slavery. They will distribute publications, push their message in churches and the media—and, at the same time work for an end to the "participation in the guilt of slavery" within churches. They will boycott goods produced by slave labor. They will trust solely in God and Garrison boldly proclaims that God is on their side. Finally, Garrison announces that they will "witness the triumph of Liberty" or they will die as martyrs to the cause of abolition.

Essential Themes

Garrison's declaration sets out a number of principles that would come to define the cause of radical abolitionism. one of the most critical to keep in mind is his insistence that there is no legal or moral legitimacy to the institution of slavery as it is practiced in the United States. Contrary to the arguments of slavery's advocates, Garrison characterizes American chattel slavery not as equivalent to Roman or Greek slavery but rather, as falling under the definition of "man stealing," a heinous crime in Old Testament law.

Because he finds no legitimacy for the institution, Garrison is compelled to distance himself from the more moderate anti-slavery activists of the time who tried to find ways to make emancipation palatable to slave owners. Garrison strongly rejects measures such as gradual emancipation, financial compensation for those who free their slaves, and the "colonization" movement which sought to remove freed slaves from the United States (often, whether they wanted to leave or not). To Garrison, to accept any compromise or delay is to acknowledge that there is at least some degree of legitimacy to the institution of slavery. For Garrison, slavery is not only wrong, it has always been wrong, and it always will be wrong, and it must be expunged from the fabric of American society.

———*Aaron Gulyas, MA*
with additional material by James Brewer Stewart, PhD

Bibliography and Additional Reading

Abzug, Robert H. *Cosmos Crumbling: American Reform and the Religious Imagination.* (New York: Oxford University Press, 1994).

Laurie, Bruce *Beyond Garrison.* (New York: Cambridge University Press, 2005).

Mayer, Henry. *All on Fire: William Lloyd Garrison and the Abolition of Slavery.* (New York: St. Martin's Press, 1998).

McDaniel, W. Caleb. *The Problem of Democracy in the Age of Slavery: Garrisonian Abolitionists and Transatlantic Reform.* (Baton Rouge, Louisiana: Louisiana State University Press, 2013).

■ Prejudices against People of Color, and Our Duties in Relation to This Subject

Date: 1833
Author: Lydia Marie Child
Genre: Book excerpt

Summary Overview

This excerpt from Lydia Maria Childs's Prejudices against People of Color, and Our Duties in Relation to This Subject distinguishes itself from other abolitionist writing of the early-to-mid-eighteenth century by virtue of its focus not on slavery itself but, rather, on the racism and discrimination exhibited against the free African-Americans of the North and the moral hypocrisy that is present in the words and actions of those who might oppose slavery but make no effort to work for the betterment of those slaves once freed from their bonds. Child presents several specific examples from Massachusetts and Connecticut—New England states with a long history of support for abolition—that demonstrate the moral and practical need for equality for Americans regardless of race.

In the second section of this excerpt, Child turns to the institution of slavery itself, urging northerners to take action against slavery and criticizing the prevalent moderate concerns about being too forceful against slavery or the southern states and individuals who support it. Child's arguments provide an example of the radicalization of the abolition movement in the 1830s as anti-slavery advocates began to express strong skepticism that the southern states would ever dismantle the slave economy on their own and would need to be pushed in that direction, even though the fabric of the nation itself might be at risk.

Defining Moment

The decade of the 1830s saw the development of the abolition movement from one that accepted that the end of slavery in the United States was a long-term project, with a common goal being not only the freeing of the slaves but their transport to Africa, to places like the new nation of Liberia, "restoring" the United States as a white nation. Even in the northern states, racial equality was not enshrined in law, nor was it often exhibited in practice. While slavery had been outlawed in a number of states, most of these emancipation measures were gradual in nature, maintaining the slave-status of a large number of African Americans and condemning their children to decades of indentured servitude before their freedom would be effective.

Events in the early 1830s, however, changed the landscape of both slavery and abolitionism. Nat Turner's violent slave rebellion in Virginia (see "The Confessions of Nat Turner") had encouraged southern state legislatures to increase restrictions on slaves—including prohibitions on teaching slaves to read and write—and increase the financial burden on slave owners who desired to free their slaves. In response to these increasingly repressive measures in the south, activists in the North such as William Lloyd Garrison (see "Declaration of Sentiments of the American Anti-Slavery Convention") formed new organizations and publications that agitated for immediate full emancipation of slaves and—shockingly—full legal and citizenship rights not only for the freed slaves but for free African-Americans in northern states.

Author Biography

Lydia Maria Child was born on February 11, 1802 was pioneering American activist who was prominent in the abolition, women's rights, and Native American rights movements. She was also an author of fiction and a poet. She was born in Medford, Massachusetts and attended local schools and a seminary for women, eventually studying in preparation to be a teacher. While she did teach for one year, she quickly became a successful writer.

Lydia, along with her husband David Child, began her involvement with the abolition movement in 1831, the year of Nat Turner's rebellion. Child was part of the new, radical wing of the abolition movement almost from the beginning, entering the movement as a result of her exposure to William Lloyd Garrison's writings as well as her personal acquaintance with him. Child, like Garrison, advocated the immediate, rather than gradual, abolition of slavery. She also, echoing Garrison's views, opposed the argument that slave owners should be compensated for the financial value of their slaves as a condition of emancipation. Child also advocated for women to have equal authority and responsibilities in the American Anti-Slavery Society.

While, by 1833, there had been numerous published speeches, tracts, and magazines devoted to the abolitionist cause, Child's Prejudices against People of Color, and Our Duties in Relation to This Subject was the first anti-slavery work to have its original publication be in book form and it gave her significant standing within the abolition movement. Her efforts within the anti-slavery cause continued, writing additional essays and articles on the subject and helping to organize fundraising efforts as well as the 1834 Anti-Slavery Fair, the first of what would become an annual event. She also edited the National Anti-Slavery Standard, the publication of the Anti-Slavery Society. She left this position in a dispute over the use of violence to end slavery, a position she opposed.

HISTORICAL DOCUMENT

While we bestow our earnest disapprobation on the system of slavery, let us not flatter ourselves that we are in reality any better than our brethren of the South. Thanks to our soil and climate, and the early exertions of the Quakers, the form of slavery does not exist among us; but the very spirit of the hateful and mischievous thing is here in all its strength. The manner in which we use what power we have, gives us ample reason to be grateful that the nature of our institutions does not intrust us with more. Our prejudice against colored people is even more inveterate than it is at the South. The planter is often attached to his negroes, and lavishes caresses and kind words upon them, as he would on a favorite hound: but our coldhearted, ignoble prejudice admits of no exception—no intermission.

The Southerners have long continued habit, apparent interest and dreaded danger, to palliate the wrong they do; but we stand without excuse. They tell us that Northern ships and Northern capital have been engaged in this wicked business; and the reproach is true. Several fortunes in this city have been made by the sale of negro blood. If these criminal transactions are still carried on, they are done in silence and secrecy, because public opinion has made them disgraceful. But if the free States wished to cherish the system of slavery forever, they could not take a more direct course than they now do. Those who are kind and liberal on all other subjects, unite with the selfish and the proud in their unrelenting efforts to keep the colored population in the lowest state of degradation; and the influence they unconsciously exert over children early infuses into their innocent minds the same strong feelings of contempt.

The intelligent and well informed have the least share of this prejudice; and when their minds can be brought to reflect upon it, I have generally observed that they soon cease to have any at all. But such a general apathy prevails and the subject is so seldom brought into view, that few are really aware how oppressively the influence of society is made to bear upon this injured class of the community. When I have related facts, that came under my own observation, I have often been listened to with surprise, which gradually increased to indignation. In order that my readers may not be ignorant of the extent of this tyrannical prejudice, I will as briefly as possible state the evidence, and leave them to judge of it, as their hearts and consciences may dictate.

In the first place, an unjust law exists in this Commonwealth, by which marriages between persons of different color is pronounced illegal. I am perfectly aware of the gross ridicule to which I may subject myself by alluding to this particular; but I have lived too long, and observed too much, to be disturbed by the world's mockery. In the first place, the government ought not to be invested with power to control the affections, any more than the consciences of citizens. A man has at least as good a right to choose his wife, as he has to choose his religion. His taste may not suit his neighbors; but so long as his deportment is correct, they have no right to interfere with his concerns. In the second place, this law is a useless disgrace to Massachusetts. Under existing circumstances, none but those whose condition in life is too low to be much affected by public opinion, will form such alliances; and they, when they choose to do so, will make such marriages, in spite of the law. I know two or three instances where women of the laboring class have been united to reputable, industrious colored men. These husbands regularly bring home their wages, and are kind to their families. If by some of the odd chances, which not unfrequently occur in the world, their wives should become heirs to any property, the children may be wronged out of it, because the law pronounces them illegitimate. And while this injustice exists with regard to honest, industrious individuals, who are merely guilty of differing from us in a matter of taste, neither the legislation nor customs of slave-holding States exert their influence against immoral connexions.

...

There is among the colored people an increasing desire for information, and a laudable ambition to be respectable in manners and appearance. Are we not foolish as well as sinful, in trying to repress a tendency so salutary to themselves, and so beneficial to the community? Several individuals of this class are very desirous to have persons of their own color qualified to teach something more than mere reading and writing. But in the public schools, colored children are subject to many discouragements and difficulties; and into the private schools they cannot gain admission. A very sensible and well-informed colored woman in a neighboring town, whose family have been brought up in a manner that excited universal remark and approbation, has been extremely desirous to obtain for her eldest daughter the advantages of a private school; but she has been resolutely repulsed, on account of her complexion. The girl is a very light mulatto, with great modesty and propriety of manners; perhaps no young person in the Commonwealth was less likely to have a bad influence on her associates. The clergyman respected the family, and he remonstrated with the instructer; but while the latter admitted the injustice of the thing, he excused himself by saying such a step would occasion the loss of all his white scholars.

...

The attempt to establish a school for African girls at Canterbury, Connecticut, has made too much noise to need a detailed account in this volume. I do not know the lady who first formed the project, but I am told that she is a benevolent and religious woman. It certainly is difficult to imagine any other motives than good ones, for an undertaking so arduous and unpopular. Yet had the Pope himself attempted to establish his supremacy over that commonwealth, he could hardly have been repelled with more determined and angry resistance.—Town meetings were held, the records of which are not highly creditable to the parties concerned. Petitions were sent to the Legislature, beseeching that no African school might be allowed to admit individuals not residing in the town where said school was established; and strange to relate, this law, which makes it impossible to collect a sufficient number of pupils, was sanctioned by the State. A colored girl, who availed herself of this opportunity to gain instruction, was warned out of town, and fined for not complying; and the instructress was imprisoned for persevering in her benevolent plan.

It is said, in excuse, that Canterbury will be inundated with vicious characters, who will corrupt the morals of the young men; that such a school will break down the distinctions between black and white; and that marriages between people of different colors will be the probable result. Yet they seem to assume the ground that colored people must always be an inferior and degraded class—that the prejudice against them must be eternal; being deeply founded in the laws of God and nature.—Finally, they endeavored to represent the school as one of the incendiary proceedings of the Anti-Slavery Society; and they appeal to the Colonization Society, as an aggrieved child is wont to appeal to its parent.

The objection with regard to the introduction of vicious characters into a village, certainly has some force; but are such persons likely to leave cities for a quiet country town, in search of moral and intellectual improvement? Is it not obvious that the best portion of the colored class are the very ones to prize such an opportunity for instruction? Grant that a large proportion of these unfortunate people are vicious—is it not our duty, and of course our wisest policy, to try to make them otherwise? And what will so effectually elevate their character and condition, as knowledge? I beseech you, my countrymen, think of these things wisely, and in season.

As for intermarriages, if there be such a repugnance between the two races, founded in the laws of nature, methinks there is small reason to dread their frequency.

The breaking down of distinctions in society, by means of extended information, is an objection which appropriately belongs to the Emperor of Austria, or the Sultan of Egypt.

I do not know how the affair at Canterbury is generally considered; but I have heard individuals of all parties and all opinions speak of it—and never without merriment or indignation. Fifty years hence, the black laws of Connecticut will be a greater source of amusement to the antiquarian, than her famous blue laws....

Let us seriously consider what injury a negro college could possible do us. It is certainly a fair presumption that the scholars would be from the better portion of the colored population; and it is an equally, fair presumption that knowledge would improve their characters. There are already many hundreds of colored people in the city of Boston.— In the street they generally appear neat and respectable; and in our houses they do not "come between the wind and our nobility." Would the addition of one or two hundred more even be perceived? As for giving offence to the Southerners by allowing such establishments—they have no right to interfere with our internal concerns, any more than we have with theirs.—Why should they not give up slavery to please us, by the same rule that we must refrain from educating the negroes to please them? If they are at liberty to do wrong, we certainly ought to be at liberty to do right. They may talk and publish as much about us as they please; and we ask for no other influence over them.

It is a fact not generally known that the brave Kosciusko left a fund for the establishment of a negro college in the United States. Little did he think he had been fighting for a people, who would not grant one rood of their vast territory for the benevolent purpose!

...

A fierce excitement prevailed, not long since, because a colored man had bought a pew in one of our churches. I heard a very kindhearted and zealous democrat declare his opinion that "the fellow ought to be turned out by constables, if he dared to occupy the pew he had purchased." Even at the communion-table, the mockery of human pride is mingled with the worship of Jehovah. Again and again have I seen a solitary negro come up to the altar, meekly and timidly, after all the white communicants had retired. One Episcopal clergyman of this city, forms an honorable exception to this remark. When there is room at the altar, Mr —— often makes a signal to the colored members of his church to kneel beside their white brethren; and once, when two white infants and one colored one were to be baptized, and the parents of the latter bashfully lingered far behind the others, he silently rebuked the unchristian spirit of pride, by first administering the holy ordinance to the little dark-skinned child of God.

...

A worthy colored woman, belonging to an adjoining town, wished to come into Boston to attend upon a son, who was ill. She had a trunk with her, and was too feeble to walk. She begged permission to ride in the stage. But the passengers with noble indignation, declared they would get out, if she were allowed to get in. After much entreaty, the driver suffered her to sit by him upon the box. When he entered the city, his comrades began to point and sneer. Not having sufficient moral courage to endure this, he left the poor woman, with her trunk, in the middle of the street, far from the place of her destination; telling her, with an oath, that he would not carry her a step further.

A friend of mine lately wished to have a colored girl admitted into the stage with her, to take care of her babe. The girl was very lightly tinged with the sable hue, had handsome Indian features, and very pleasing manners. It was, however, evident that she was not white; and therefore the passengers objected to her company. This of course, produced a good deal of inconvenience on one side, and mortification on the other. My friend repeated the circumstance to a lady, who, as the daughter and wife of a clergyman, might be supposed to have imbibed some liberality. The lady seemed to think the experiment was very preposterous; but when my friend alluded to the mixed parentage of the girl, she exclaimed, with generous enthusiasm, "Oh, that alters the case, Indians certainly have their rights."

...

The state of public feeling not only makes it difficult for the Africans to obtain information, but it prevents them from making profitable use of what knowledge they have. A colored man, however intelligent, is not allowed to pursue any business more lucrative than that of a barber, a shoe-black, or a waiter. These, and all other employments, are truly respectable, whenever the duties connected with them are faithfully performed; but it is unjust that a man should, on account of his complexion, be prevented from performing more elevated uses in society. Every citizen ought to have a fair chance to try his fortune in any line of business, which he thinks he has ability to transact. Why should not colored men be employed in the manufactories of various kinds? If their ignorance is an objection, let them be enlightened, as speedily as possible. If their moral character is not sufficiently pure, remove the pressure of public scorn, and thus supply them with motives for being respectable. All this can be done. It merely requires an earnest wish to overcome a prejudice, which has "grown with our growth and strengthened with our strength," but which is in fact opposed to the spirit of our religion, and contrary to the instinctive good feelings of our nature. When examined by the clear light of reason, it disappears. Prejudices of all kinds have their strongest holds in the minds of the vulgar and the ignorant. In a community so enlightened as our own, they must gradually melt away under the influence of public discussion. There is no want of kind feelings and liberal

sentiments in the American people; the simple fact is, they have not thought upon this subject.—An active and enterprising community are not apt to concern themselves about laws and customs, which do not obviously interfere with their interests or convenience; and various political and prudential motives have combined to fetter free inquiry in this direction. Thus we have gone on, year after year, thoughtlessly sanctioning, by our silence and indifference, evils which our hearts and consciences are far enough from approving

...

Mr. Garrison was the first person who dared to edit a newspaper, in which slavery was spoken of as altogether wicked and inexcusable. For this crime the Legislature of Georgia have offered five thousand dollars to any one who will "arrest and prosecute him to conviction under the laws of that State."...It is, to say the least, a very remarkable step for one State in this Union to promulgate such a law concerning a citizen of another State, merely for publishing his opinions boldly

...

The palliator of slavery assures the abolitionists that their benevolence is perfectly quixotic—that the negroes are happy and contented, and have no desire to change their lot. An answer to this may, as I have already said, be found in the Judicial Reports of slaveholding States, in the vigilance of their laws, in advertisements for runaway slaves, and in the details of their own newspapers....

The negro's crimes are repeated, but his sufferings are never told. Even in our geographies it is taught that the colored race must always be degraded. Now and then anecdotes of cruelties committed in the slave-holding States are told by individuals who witnessed them; but they are almost always afraid to give their names to the public, because the Southerners will call them "a disgrace to the soil," and the Northerners will echo the sentiment....

We are told that the Southerners will of themselves do away slavery, and they alone understand how to do it.—But it is an obvious fact that all their measures have tended to perpetuate the system; and even if we have the fullest faith that they mean to do their duty, the belief by no means absolves us from doing ours. The evil is gigantic; and its removal requires every heart and head in the community.

It is said that our sympathies ought to be given to the masters, who are abundantly more to be pitied than the slaves. If this be the case, the planters are singularly disinterested not to change places with their bondmen. Our sympathies have been given to the masters—and to those masters who seemed most desirous to remain forever in their pitiable condition. There are hearts at the South sincerely desirous of doing right in this cause; but their generous impulses are checked by the laws of their respective States, and the strong disapprobation of their neighbors. I know a lady in Georgia, who would, I believe, make any personal sacrifice to instruct her slaves, and give them freedom; but if she were found guilty of teaching the alphabet, or manumitting her slaves, fines and imprisonment would be the consequence; if she sold them, they would be likely to fall into hands less merciful than her own. Of such slave-owners we cannot speak with too much respect and tenderness. They are comparatively few in number, and stand in a most perplexing situation; it is a duty to give all our sympathy to them. It is mere mockery to say, what is so often said, that the Southerners, as a body, really wish to abolish slavery. If they wished it, they certainly would make the attempt....

The strongest and best reason that can be given for our supineness on the subject of slavery, is the fear of dissolving the Union. The Constitution of the United States demands our highest reverence. Those who approve, and those who disapprove of particular portions, are equally bound to yield implicit obedience to its authority. But we must not forget that the Constitution provides for any change that may be required for the general good. The great machine is constructed with a safety valve, by which any rapidly increasing evil may be expelled whenever the people desire it.

If the Southern politicians are determined to make a Siamese question of this also—if they insist that the Union shall not exist without slavery—it can only be said that they join two things, which have no affinity with each other, and which cannot permanently exist together.—They chain the living and vigorous to the diseased and dying; and the former will assuredly perish in the infected neighborhood.

The universal introduction of free labor is the surest way to consolidate the Union, and enable us to live together in harmony and peace. If a history is ever written entitled "The Decay and Dissolution of the North American Republic," its author will distinctly trace our downfall to the existence of slavery among us.

GLOSSARY

disapprobation: disapproval or condemnation

quixotic: an adjective meaning noble or idealistic

promulgate: to create and distribute

supineness: the quality of being passive or negligent

Document Analysis

Child opens this piece strongly by arguing that northerners who oppose slavery should be away that they are not "better" than those in the south. The absence of slavery, she asserts, is the product of the environment and "the early exertions of the Quakers" rather than any moral superiority. Despite slavery not existing in the north, racial prejudice does exist and, in Child's words, "is even more inveterate than it is at the South." Her purpose here, then, is not to denounce slavery in the south but to decry the racist attitudes and actions of her fellow northerners. While southerners, she explains have an excuse for their racist attitudes ("long continued habit, apparent interest and dreaded danger") northerners have no such excuse.

One of the causes for racial prejudices in the north is continued ignorance of just how much racial oppression actually exists. Child explains that many northerners are surprised to hear about "the extent of this tyrannical prejudice." Thus, one of her goals is to provide examples of that tyranny to bring the racism of the north to light and let the people respond to it "as their hearts and consciences may dictate."

Child then embarks on a survey of the injustices that exist against African Americans in Massachusetts. The first she discusses is the law against interracial marriage. She argues against this law not only on the grounds of racial equality but also from a more general perspective of individual rights and liberties. Government, she explains, should have no power to "control the affections" of its citizens and likens it to the freedom of religious conscience. In any case, she suspects that interracial marriages only would take place among "those whose condition in life is too low to be much affected by public opinion"—the working class. These people will marry who they wish regardless of what the law might say. Child provides some examples of working class white women who have been "united to reputable, industrious colored men" who have provided well for their families. Child warns of the unjust possibility of the children of these unions being stripped of their inheritance because the law would see them as illegitimate.

Child then moves into the realm of education, noting the desire of African Americans for education and an "ambition to be respectable in manners and appearance." Despite the strong desire for learning, public schools in Massachusetts have not been fully open to these students. Private schools have been just as restrictive, if not more so. and she recounts the case of a woman whose daughter was denied a place in a private school solely because of her race. In another example, Child explains the situation in the town of Canterbury, Connecticut where resident went to extraordinary lengths to prevent the establishment of a school for African American children, being concerned that "vicious characters" might take up residence in the town, that it would lead to intermarriage and "break down the distinctions between black and white." Child dismantles these concerns and predicts that in the future, such

efforts by the town will seem ridiculous. She then tackles the common concerns about education for African Americans, particularly the complaint that southerners will be offended by northern efforts to educate black children. If the south will not give up slavery, Child argues, northerners should not be compelled to give up the dream of education for all members of the community regardless of their race.

Having dealt with discrimination and restrictions in education and marriage, Child turns to other manifestations. She is disturbed by the churches she had seen which treat their African American parishioners as a secondary concern and praises one Episcopal priest who made a point to treat black and white worshippers as equally as possible. Stage coaches, as well, are a venue where refusing to serve customers because of their skin color was troubling to child. In the examples she presents, she makes sure to explain the circumstances carefully enough to ensure the reader knows that the only reason service was refused was on account of race.

In a similar situation to the racial restrictions on education, Child takes aim at regulations and customs that prevent African Americans from participating fully in the economies of their communities. Black residents of Massachusetts and other northern states are limited to menial jobs regardless of their knowledge or skills. She emphasizes that menial jobs are honorable and "truly respectable" but laments the injustice of people being prohibited from exercising their talents to the fullest on account of their race.

In the closing paragraphs, Child turns to the issue of slavery itself, praising William Lloyd Garrison for his honesty in denouncing slavery and pointing out the troubling fact that the state of Georgia had called for his prosecution and conviction for criticizing the institution. In this section, Child rails against the idea that northerners should sympathize with slave masters more than slaves and the argument that—eventually—southerners will end slavery on their own. This will not happen, she argues, as long as those in the south who dare to teach their slaves to read or even free them face persecution and actual legal prosecution.

Child closes this section on an ominous note, taking up the fear that attacking slavery may lead to the end of the union. If, she says, southerners make the issue of slavery "a Siamese question," that is, if southerners refuse to be part of a union that outlaws slavery, then it is the slave owners' choice to end the union, not those who pass laws to eliminate a "rapidly increasing evil."

Essential Themes

As radical as the goal of immediate emancipation might have been in the early 1830s, the argument for fuller political and social inclusion and equality for African-Americans that Child presents here was shockingly progressive for the time. Several aspects of this argument would likely have struck readers at the time. In particular, her argument in favor of lifting prohibitions on interracial marriage. While the racial aspects of her argument were rare for her time, her assertion that a "government ought not to be invested with power to control the affections" of its citizens tended the definition of personal liberty and freedom beyond politics, property, and religion and into the realm of personal relationships. Along with her support for educational and economic opportunities, her position on marriage establishes Child as an advocate for a fuller and more encompassing vision of equality for African-Americans than was common.

Childs's arguments against the institution of slavery itself also represent the emerging radicalization of the abolition movement. This is especially true of her conception of American unity. Radical abolitionists like Child and Garrison were slowly moving away from the idea that the toleration of slavery was necessary to preserve the union. Child, in saying "If the Southern politicians insist that the Union shall not exist without slavery—it can only be said that they join two things, which have no affinity with each other, and which cannot permanently exist together.— They chain the living and vigorous to the diseased and dying; and the former will assuredly perish in the infected neighborhood." While she is not predicting or hoping for the dissolution of the union, Child warns that the continued compromise with such an example of "rapidly increasing evil" would have dire consequences for the nation.

———*Aaron Gulyas, MA*

Bibliography and Additional Reading

Baer, Helene Gilbert *The Heart is Like Heaven: The Life of Lydia Maria Child*. (Philadelphia: University of Pennsylvania Press, 1964).

Ginzberg, Lori D. *Women in Antebellum Reform*. (Hoboken, New Jersey: Wiley-Blackwell, 2000).

Karcher, Carolyn L. *The First Woman in the Republic: A Cultural Biography of Lydia Maria Child*. (Durham: Duke University Press, 1994).

Salerno, Beth A. *Sister Societies: Women's Antislavery Societies in Antebellum America*. (DeKalb, Illinois: Northern Illinois University Press, 2005).

■ "An Address to the Slaves of the United States of America"

Date: 1843
Author: Henry Highland Garnet
Genre: Speech

Summary Overview

Henry Highland Garnet's "Address to the Slaves of the United States of America" was delivered at the National Convention of Colored Citizens in Buffalo, New York, on August 16, 1843. A former slave, Garnet was pastor of the African American Liberty Street Presbyterian Church in Troy, New York, and editor of *The Clarion*, a weekly newspaper that published abolitionist and church-related articles. At age twenty-eight, he was a rising figure among young African American abolitionists, who were increasingly at odds with William Lloyd Garrison and the American Anti-Slavery Society. Garrison and his followers (both white and African American) had essentially abandoned politics in favor of nonviolent moral suasion in their fight against slavery. Garnet first signaled his disaffection with Garrison's position in 1840 as one of the founding members of the American and Foreign Anti-Slavery Society, which advocated political action as the primary way to achieve emancipation. His subsequent newspaper articles and sermons had carried him well beyond mere dissatisfaction, and because he was a gifted speaker with a reputation as a firebrand, most of the seventy delegates from a dozen states came to Buffalo anticipating a stirring address.

Defining Moment

Beginning in 1830 and intermittently to the 1850s black abolitionists (many of them clergymen and teachers) met in National Negro Conventions to discuss matters of mutual interest. Black abolitionist lecturers and writers like Frederick Douglass and Sojourner Truth were in high demand after 1840. In their books and lectures they emphasized the evils of slavery within conventional Christian morality and advocated moral suasion and nonviolent resistance. All that changed when the Mexican-American War, the Compromise of 1850, and the new Fugitive Slave Act of 1850 transformed the nation's moral and political landscapes.

The Buffalo meeting was itself a reason for excitement because, after a lapse of seven years, its convening renewed a convention movement that had begun thirteen years earlier with the National Convention of Colored Citizens in Philadelphia in 1830. Five annual gatherings followed the first, but the 1836 convention divided over doctrinal matters, and no further national meetings were held until the Buffalo convention was called to order on August 15, 1843. The chairman, Samuel H. Davis, a minister and the principal of the local elementary school for black children, struck the gavel. All delegates were aware that groups in Buffalo had fiercely opposed their meeting. Some openly threatened them and their meeting place, the Vine Street American Methodist Episcopal Church, but the proceedings over the next five days took place without any outside interference. Davis, a graduate of Oberlin College, set the tone with his keynote address, "We Must Assert Our Rightful Claims and Plead Our Own Cause." He reminded the delegates that the work of white abolitionists had thus far failed to win the slaves' emancipation or full civil liberties for free blacks. Those goals could be reached, he said, only if African Americans themselves "make known our wrongs to the world and to our oppressors." To leave the goals to others to achieve was a commitment to failure, Davis warned. When his turn came to speak, Henry Highland Garnet carried that message to a far more radical conclusion.

Author Biography

Henry Highland Garnet was born into slavery on a plantation near Chestertown in Kent County, Maryland, on December 23, 1815, to George and Henrietta Trusty. In 1824, following the death of their owner, the Trustys, aided by the Underground Railroad, made their way to the North, where they adopted Garnet as their new name. In 1827 they settled in New York City, and Garnet's father worked as a shoemaker. Henry attended the African Free School until he went to sea in 1828 and later worked as an indentured field hand on Long Island, where in his second year he severely injured a knee. In 1840 the leg was amputated at the hip.

In 1831 Garnet returned to a high school for blacks in New York and in July 1835 entered Noyes Academy in Canaan, New Hampshire, a school founded by abolitionists to serve both black and white students.

Local townspeople, unhappy with the school's racial mix, destroyed the building in August and attacked the house where the black students were living. Early in 1836 Garnet was admitted to the Oneida Institute in Whitesboro, New York, from which he graduated with honors in 1840.

Garnet was named minister of the African American Liberty Street Presbyterian Church in Troy, New York, in 1840. Garnet became active in abolitionist affairs; edited *The Clarion*, a weekly abolitionist newspaper; and taught school. An organizer of the convention movement in New York State, he campaigned briefly for the Liberty Party.

Following his speech in Buffalo, Garnet returned to his pulpit in Troy. During the 1850s, he traveled to Europe speaking against slavery in Britain and Germany. On February 12, 1865, he became the first African American to deliver a sermon to the U.S. House of Representatives. In 1881 President James Garfield appointed Garnet the U.S. minister resident and consul general to Liberia. He died two months after taking up his post in Monrovia, on February 13, 1882.

HISTORICAL DOCUMENT

Brethren and Fellow-Citizens: —Your brethren of the North, East, and West have been accustomed to meet together in National Conventions, to sympathize with each other, and to weep over your unhappy condition. In these meetings we have addressed all classes of the free, but we have never, until this time, sent a word of consolation and advice to you. We have been contented in sitting still and mourning over your sorrows, earnestly hoping that before this day your sacred liberties would have been restored. But, we have hoped in vain. Years have rolled on, and tens of thousands have been borne on streams of blood and tears, to the shores of eternity. While you have been oppressed, we have also been partakers with you; nor can we be free while you are enslaved. We, therefore, write to you as being bound with you.

Many of you are bound to us, not only by the ties of a common humanity, but we are connected by the more tender relations of parents, wives, husbands, children, brothers, and sisters, and friends. As such we most affectionately address you.

Slavery has fixed a deep gulf between you and us, and while it shuts out from you the relief and consolation which your friends would willingly render, it afflicts and persecutes you with a fierceness which we might not expect to see in the fiends of hell. But still the Almighty Father of mercies has left to us a glimmering ray of hope, which shines out like a lone star in a cloudy sky. Mankind are becoming wiser, and better—the oppressor's power is fading, and you, every day, are becoming better informed, and more numerous. Your grievances, brethren, are many. We shall not attempt, in this short address, to present to the world all the dark catalogue of this nation's sins, which have been committed upon an innocent people. Nor is it indeed necessary, for you feel them from day to day, and all the civilized world look upon them with amazement.

Two hundred and twenty-seven years ago, the first of our injured race were brought to the shores of America. They came not with glad spirits to select their homes in the New World. They came not with their own consent, to find an unmolested enjoyment of the blessings of this fruitful soil. The first dealings they had with men calling themselves Christians, exhibited to them the worst features of corrupt and sordid hearts: and convinced them that no cruelty is too great, no villainy and no robbery too abhorrent for even enlightened men to perform, when influenced by avarice and lust. Neither did they come flying upon the wings of Liberty, to a land of freedom. But they came with broken hearts, from their beloved native land, and were doomed to unrequited toil and deep degradation. Nor did the evil of their bondage end at their emancipation by death. Succeeding generations inherited their chains, and millions have come from eternity into time, and have returned again to the world of spirits, cursed and ruined by American slavery.

The propagators of the system, or their immediate ancestors, very soon discovered its growing evil, and its tremendous wickedness, and secret promises were made to destroy it. The gross inconsistency of a people holding slaves, who had themselves "ferried o'er the wave" for freedom's sake, was too apparent to be entirely overlooked. The voice of Freedom cried, "Emancipate your slaves." Humanity supplicated with tears for the deliverance of the children of Africa. Wisdom urged her solemn plea. The bleeding captive pleaded his innocence, and pointed to Christianity who stood weeping at the cross. Jehovah frowned upon the nefarious institution, and thunderbolts, red with vengeance, struggled to leap forth to blast the guilty wretches who maintained it. But all was vain. Slavery had stretched its dark wings of death over the land, the Church stood silently by—the priests prophesied falsely, and the people loved to have it so. Its throne is established, and now it reigns triumphant.

Nearly three millions of your fellow-citizens are prohibited by law and public opinion (which in this country is stronger than law) from reading the Book of Life. Your intellect has been destroyed as much as possible, and every ray of light they have attempted to shut out from your minds. The oppressors themselves have become involved in the ruin. They have become weak, sensual, and rapacious—they have cursed you—they have cursed themselves—they have cursed the earth which they have trod.

The colonists threw the blame upon England. They said that the mother country entailed the evil upon them, and that they would rid themselves of it if they could. The world thought they were sincere, and the philanthropic pitied them. But time soon tested their sincerity. In a few years the colonists grew strong, and severed themselves from the British Government. Their independence was declared, and they took their station among the sovereign powers of the earth. The declaration was a glorious document. Sages admired it, and the patriotic of every nation reverenced the God-like sentiments which it contained. When the power of Government returned to their hands, did they emancipate the slaves? No; they rather added new links to our chains. Were they ignorant of the principles of Liberty? Certainly they were not. The sentiments of their revolutionary orators fell in burning eloquence upon their hearts, and with one voice they cried, *Liberty or Death*. Oh what a sentence was that! It

ran from soul to soul like electric fire, and nerved the arm of thousands to fight in the holy cause of Freedom. Among the diversity of opinions that are entertained in regard to physical resistance, there are but a few found to gainsay that stern declaration. We are among those who do not.

Slavery! How much misery is comprehended in that single word. What mind is there that does not shrink from its direful effects? Unless the image of God be obliterated from the soul, all men cherish the love of Liberty. The nice discerning political economist does not regard the sacred right more than the untutored African who roams in the wilds of Congo. Nor has the one more right to the full enjoyment of his freedom than the other. In every man's mind the good seeds of liberty are planted, and he who brings his fellow down so low, as to make him contented with a condition of slavery, commits the highest crime against God and man. Brethren, your oppressors aim to do this. They endeavor to make you as much like brutes as possible. When they have blinded the eyes of your mind— when they have embittered the sweet waters of life—when they have shut out the light which shines from the word of God—then, and not till then, has American slavery done its perfect work.

To such Degradation it is sinful in the Extreme for you to make voluntary Submission. The divine commandments you are in duty bound to reverence and obey. If you do not obey them, you will surely meet with the displeasure of the Almighty. He requires you to love him supremely, and your neighbor as yourself—to keep the Sabbath day holy—to search the Scriptures—and bring up your children with respect for his laws, and to worship no other God but him. But slavery sets all these at nought, and hurls defiance in the face of Jehovah. The forlorn condition in which you are placed, does not destroy your moral obligation to God. You are not certain of heaven, because you suffer yourselves to remain in a state of slavery, where you cannot obey the commandments of the Sovereign of the universe. If the ignorance of slavery is a passport to heaven, then it is a blessing, and no curse, and you should rather desire its perpetuity than its abolition. God will not receive slavery, nor ignorance, nor any other state of mind, for love and obedience to him. Your condition does not absolve you from your moral obligation. The diabolical injustice by which your liberties are cloven down, *neither God; nor angels, or just men, command you to suffer for a single moment. Therefore it is your solemn and imperative duty to use every means, both moral, intellectual and physical that promises success.* If a band of heathen men should attempt to enslave a race of Christians, and to place their children under the influence of some false religion, surely, Heaven would frown upon the men who would not resist such aggression, even to death. If, on the other hand, a band of Christians should attempt to enslave a race of heathen men, and to entail slavery upon them, and to keep them in heathenism in the midst of Christianity, the God of heaven would smile upon every effort which the injured might make to disenthral themselves.

Brethren, it is as wrong for your lordly oppressors to keep you in slavery, as it was for the man thief to steal our ancestors from the coast of Africa. You should therefore now use the same manner of resistance, as would have been just in our ancestors, when the bloody footprints of the first remorseless soul-thief was placed upon the shores of our fatherland. The humblest peasant is as free in the sight of God as the proudest monarch that ever swayed a sceptre. Liberty is a spirit sent out from God, and like its great Author, is no respecter of persons.

Brethren, the time has come when you must act for yourselves. It is an old and true saying that, "if hereditary bondmen would be free, they must themselves strike the blow." You can plead your own cause, and do the work of emancipation better than any others. The nations of the old world are moving in the great cause of universal freedom, and some of them at least will, ere long, do you justice. The combined powers of Europe have placed their broad seal of disapprobation upon the African slave-trade. But in the slaveholding parts of the United States, the trade is as brisk as ever. They buy and sell you as though you were brute beasts. The North has done much—her opinion of slavery in the abstract is known. But in regard to the South, we adopt the opinion of the New York Evangelist—"We have advanced so far, that the cause apparently waits for

a more effectual door to be thrown open than has been yet." We are about to point you to that more effectual door. Look around you, and behold the bosoms of your loving wives heaving with untold agonies! Hear the cries of your poor children! Remember the stripes your fathers bore. Think of the torture and disgrace of your noble mothers. Think of your wretched sisters, loving virtue and purity, as they are driven into concubinage and are exposed to the unbridled lusts of incarnate devils. Think of the undying glory that hangs around the ancient name of Africa:—and forget not that you are native-born American citizens, and as such, you are justly entitled to all the rights that are granted to the freest. Think how many tears you have poured out upon the soil which you have cultivated with unrequited toil and enriched with your blood; and then go to your lordly enslavers and tell them plainly, that you *are determined to be free.* Appeal to their sense of justice, and tell them that they have no more right to oppress you, than you have to enslave them. Entreat them to remove the grievous burdens which they have imposed upon you, and to remunerate you for your labor. Promise them renewed diligence in the cultivation of the soil, if they will render to you an equivalent for your services. Point them to the increase of happiness and prosperity in the British West Indies since the Act of Emancipation. Tell them in language which they cannot misunderstand, of the exceeding sinfulness of slavery, and of a future judgment, and of the righteous retributions of an indignant God. Inform them that all you desire is *freedom*, and that nothing else will suffice. Do this, and for ever after cease to toil for the heartless tyrants, who give you no other reward but stripes and abuse. If they then commence the work of death, they, and not you, will be responsible for the consequences. You had far better all die—*die immediately*, than live slaves, and entail your wretchedness upon your posterity. If you would be free in this generation, here is your only hope. However much you and all of us may desire it, there is not much hope of redemption without the shedding of blood. If you must bleed, let it all come at once—rather *die freemen, than live to be the slaves.* It is impossible, like the children of Israel, to make a grand exodus from the land of bondage. The Pharaohs are on both sides of the blood-red waters! You cannot move *en masse*, to the dominions of the British Queen—nor can you pass through Florida and overrun Texas, and at last find peace in Mexico. The propagators of American slavery are spending their blood and treasure, that they may plant the black flag in the heart of Mexico and riot in the halls of the Montezumas. In the language of the Rev. Robert Hall, when addressing the volunteers of Bristol, who were rushing forth to repel the invasion of Napoleon, who threatened to lay waste the fair homes of England, "Religion is too much interested in your behalf, not to shed over you her most gracious influences."

You will not be compelled to spend much time in order to become inured to hardships. From the first moment that you breathed the air of heaven, you have been accustomed to nothing else but hardships. The heroes of the American Revolution were never put upon harder fare than a peck of corn and a few herrings per week. You have not become enervated by the luxuries of life. Your sternest energies have been beaten out upon the anvil of severe trial. Slavery has done this to make you subservient to its own purposes; but it has done more than this, it has prepared you for any emergency. If you receive good treatment, it is what you could hardly expect; if you meet with pain, sorrow, and even death, these are the common lot of the slaves.

Fellow-men! patient sufferers! Behold your dearest rights crushed to the earth! See your sons murdered, and your wives, mothers and sisters doomed to prostitution. In the name of the merciful God, and by all that life is worth, let it no longer be a debatable question whether it is better to choose *Liberty or death*.

In 1822, Denmark Veazie, of South Carolina, formed a plan for the liberation of his fellow-men. In the whole history of human efforts to overthrow slavery, a more complicated and tremendous plan was never formed. He was betrayed by the treachery of his own people, and died a martyr to freedom. Many a brave hero fell, but history, faithful to her high trust, will transcribe his name on the same monument with Moses, Hampden, Tell, Bruce and Wallace, Toussaint L'Ouverture, Lafayette and

Washington. That tremendous movement shook the whole empire of slavery. The guilty soul thieves were overwhelmed with fear. It is a matter of fact, that at that time, and in consequence of the threatened revolution, the slave States talked strongly of emancipation. But they blew but one blast of the trumpet of freedom, and then laid it aside. As these men became quiet, the slaveholders ceased to talk about emancipation: and now behold your condition today! Angels sigh over it, and humanity has long since exhausted her tears in weeping on your account!

The patriotic Nathaniel Turner followed Denmark Veazie. He was goaded to desperation by wrong and injustice. By despotism, his name has been recorded on the list of infamy; and future generations will remember him among the noble and brave.

Next arose the immortal Joseph Cinque, the hero of the *Amistad*. He was a native African, and by the help of God he emancipated a whole ship-load of his fellow-men on the high seas. And he now sings of liberty on the sunny hills of Africa and beneath his native palm-trees, where he hears the lion roar and feels himself as free as that king of the forest.

Next arose Madison Washington, that bright star of freedom, and took his station in the constellation of true heroism. He was a slave on board the brig *Creole* of Richmond, bound to New Orleans, that great slave mart, with a hundred and four others. Nineteen struck for liberty or death. But one life was taken, and the whole were emancipated, and the vessel was carried into Nassau, New Providence.

Noble men! Those who have fallen in freedom's conflict, their memories will be cherished by the true-hearted and the God-fearing in all future generations; those who are living, their names are surrounded by a halo of glory.

Brethren, arise, arise! Strike for your lives and liberties. Now is the day and the hour. Let every slave throughout the land do this, and the days of slavery are numbered. You cannot be more oppressed than you have been—you cannot suffer greater cruelties than you have already. *Rather die freemen than live to be slaves*. Remember that you are *four millions*!

It is in your power so to torment the God-cursed slaveholders, that they will be glad to let you go free. If the scale was turned, and black men were the masters and white men the slaves, every destructive agent and element would be employed to lay the oppressor low. Danger and death would hang over their heads day and night. Yes, the tyrants would meet with plagues more terrible than those of Pharaoh. But you are a patient people. You act as though you were made for the special use of these devils. You act as though your daughters were born to pamper the lusts of your masters and overseers. And worse than all, you tamely submit while your lords tear your wives from your embraces and defile them before your eyes. In the name of God, we ask, are you men? Where is the blood of your fathers? Has it all run out of your veins? Awake, awake; millions of voices are calling you! Your dead fathers speak to you from their graves. Heaven, as with a voice of thunder, calls on you to arise from the dust.

Let your motto be resistance! *resistance! resistance!* No oppressed people have ever secured their liberty without resistance. What kind of resistance you had better make, you must decide by the circumstances that surround you, and according to the suggestion of expediency. Brethren, adieu! Trust in the living God. Labor for the peace of the human race, and remember that you are *four millions*.

GLOSSARY

Book of Life: the Bible

British West Indies since the Act of Emancipation: a reference to Great Britain's 1833 Slavery Abolition Act

Children of Israel…Pharaohs: reference to the Old Testament Israelites and their bondage under ancient Egypt

concubinage: the condition of being forced to submit to sexual relations

Denmark Veazie: usually spelled "Vesey"; the leader of a planned slave rebellion in South Carolina in 1822

"ferried o'er the wave": a quotation from William Cowper's 1785 poem "The Task"

Florida…Mexico: a reference to the disputes that arose over slavery as the nation expanded

Hampton…Washington: John Hampden, a leading opponent of King Charles I, who died of wounds sustained in 1643 in the second year of the English Civil War; William Tell, the legendary marksman, leader of a rebellion against the Hapsburg rulers in the fourteenth century; Robert the Bruce and William Wallace, who fought for Scotland against the English in the fourteenth century; Toussaint-Louverture, who successfully freed Haiti from French rule in the 1790s, outlawed slavery, and established native government; the Marquis de Lafayette, famous for his military role in the American and the French revolutions; George Washington, who led the Continental army to victory and America to independence in 1783

Jehovah: God, a name commonly used in the biblical Old Testament

Liberty or Death: an allusion to Patrick Henry's revolutionary statement, "Give me liberty, or give me death"

Montezumas: Aztec emperors in Mexico

Nathaniel Turner: Nat Turner, the leader of a slave rebellion in Virginia in 1831

Robert Hall: a British Baptist minister of the late eighteenth and early nineteenth centuries

Document Analysis

The opening three paragraphs set the tone for the rest of the speech. Garnet uses the word *brethren* dualistically, directing it to both the immediate audience and the absent slaves, who are his real audience. Garnet spells out the connection between free person and slave and, in the third, how the institution of slavery has kept them apart. He also discusses ways the perpetual horrors of slavery reach from generation to generation. He criticizes the silence on slavery from American Christianity—apart from the Quakers—and the means by which both north and south deny education to free and enslaved black Americans.

In paragraph 7, Garnet celebrates the American Revolution and the Declaration of Independence, but he laments the missed opportunity to abolish slavery and the inclusion of protections for slaveholders in the Constitution. He invokes the human need for freedom and equates the slave's failure to openly oppose slavery, even at the risk of death, as a violation of the Ten Commandments and argues that the slaves must themselves bring an end to slavery, asserting that resistance in the name of freedom is right and just and will be blessed by God.

In paragraph 11 Garnet reminds the slaves that they are native-born American citizens. He instructs them to remind their owners that their birthright is freedom, even at the cost of whippings or death. Garnet turns in paragraphs 12 and 13 to the strengths that the slaves possess. He compares them to the American rebels in the Revolution, who endured hardship, and reminds them that hardship is what they have known. Given the abuses to their loved ones, there is no longer a debate over what they must do. To encourage them further, Garnet offers them as exemplars of resistance, in paragraphs 14 through 18, thirteen "noble men" who chose to fight for liberty at the risk of or price of death. Garnet discusses a number of heroes of resistance to slavery, such as Denmark Vesey and Nat Turner, connecting them to historical heroes such as a Moses, William Wallace of Scotland, and the Marquis de Lafayette, French hero of the American Revolution as well As Toussaint-Louverture, who fought to free Haiti from French rule in the 1790s.

In paragraph 16, Garnet praises Joseph Cinqué, a captive African, who on July 2, 1839, led fifty-two fellow Africans in gaining control of the slave ship *La Amistad*, Eventually intercepted by the US Navy, Federal officers then took the Africans to New London, Connecticut, to be sold, in clear violation of the Constitution's ban on importing slaves. Abolitionists quickly came to the blacks' aid. In a dramatic appearance before the Supreme Court, the former president John Quincy Adams argued the abolitionists' position that the Africans had been illegally enslaved, that they were justified in using force to gain their freedom, and that the court should return them to their homeland. On March 9, 1841 (a little over two years before Garnet's speech), the court ruled in favor of the abolitionists and the Africans were set free.

The heroism of Madison Washington, whom Garnet introduces in paragraph 17, followed close on the Court's decision in that case. On the night of November 7, 1841, Washington led a slave revolt on board the *Creole*, a coastal slave ship, carrying him and 134 other slaves from Virginia to New Orleans, where they were to be sold. Washington and eighteen of his fellow slaves overpowered the ship's crew and forced the captain to take them to Nassau in the Bahamas, a British colony. Despite protests from the American government, the British declared the slaves to be free persons. Washington and his partners were briefly imprisoned but ultimately freed.

What Garnet has said to this point is preparation for his call for a slave rebellion that, through violence, would destroy the evils of slavery and bring freedom to African Americans at long last. "Brethren, arise, arise!" Garnet says in paragraph 19, reminding the nation's slaves that they number four million (the number in 1848 was closer to 3.2 million) and that if they join together, they can wipe out a dying institution. They have, he adds, nothing to lose but the restrictions that already were limiting their lives and making their wives and children subject to every cruelty; they cannot be made to suffer more than they already have.

Paragraph 20 is a forceful reminder that the slaves have within their hands the power to awaken the fear that overtook southern whites during the Vesey conspiracy and Nat Turner's Rebellion. In an Old Testament reference well known to his audience, Garnet invokes the ten plagues that Moses promised that God would inflict on Egypt unless the pharaoh freed the Israelites from bondage. What holds slavery together, Garnet says, is the passivity of the slaves, their patience and inaction in the face of daily cruelty and humiliation. It is time for them to awaken. In his conclusion, Garnet reiterates that resistance is the only plausible solution to the slaves' plight.

Essential Themes

In "An Address to the Slaves of the United States of America," Henry Highland Garnet presents his audience with a series of carefully connected themes, woven together in forceful images and powerful language. He begins with a direct appeal to those in bondage to recognize their close ties to those who are free, their common memory of past and present injustices, and their mutual connection to past generations of slaves. He points to heroic rebels as examples of what the slaves themselves must do to secure their freedom, and he urges them to see the strengths that lie in their numbers and their shared consciousness of their condition. He highlights their masters' dependency on slavery and the slave owners' deep-seated fear of a slave insurrection. He tells them in ringing terms that violence is their only recourse if they wish to be free. "An Address to the Slaves of the United States of America" was like a thunderclap to the assembled delegates at the Buffalo convention. The first major abolitionist speech directed to the nation's slaves since David Walker's "Appeal to the Coloured Citizens of the World," its call for armed resistance shocked both the convention audience and the nation at large.

——*Allan L. Damon*

Bibliography and Additional Reading

Stuckey, Sterling. "A Last Stern Struggle: Henry Highland Garnet and Liberation Theory." In *Black Leaders of the Nineteenth Century*, eds. Leon Litwack and August Meier. Chicago: University of Illinois Press, 1988.

"'To the Public.' January 1, 1831." In *William Lloyd Garrison and the Fight against Slavery: Selections from the* Liberator, ed. William E. Cain. New York: Bedford/St. Martins, 1997.

Hutchinson, Earl Ofari. *Let Your Motto Be Resistance: The Life and Thought of Henry Highland Garnet.* Boston: Beacon Press, 1972.

Quarles, Benjamin. *Black Abolitionists.* New York: Da Capo Press, 1991.

Schor, Joel. *Henry Highland Garnet: A Voice of Black Radicalism in the Nineteenth Century.* Westport, Conn. Greenwood Publishing, 1977.

■ "What to the Slave is the Fourth of July?"

Date: 1852
Author: Frederick Douglass
Genre: Speech

Summary Overview

The Fourth of July Speech is the most famous address delivered by the abolitionist and civil rights advocate Frederick Douglass. In the nineteenth century, many American communities and cities celebrated Independence Day with a ceremonial reading of the Declaration of Independence, which was usually followed by an oral address or speech dedicated to the celebration of independence and the heritage of the American Revolution and the Founding Fathers. On July 5, 1852, the Ladies' Anti-Slavery Society of Rochester, New York, invited Douglass to be the keynote speaker for their Independence Day celebration.

The Fourth of July Speech, scheduled for Rochester's Corinthian Hall, attracted a crowd of between five hundred and six hundred, each of whom paid twelve and a half cents admission. The meeting opened with a prayer offered by the Reverend S. Ottman of Rush, New York, followed by a reading of the Declaration of Independence by the Reverend Robert R. Raymond of Syracuse, New York. Douglass then delivered his address, which the local press reported to be eloquent and admirable and which drew much applause. Upon conclusion of the address, the crowd thanked Douglass and called for the speech to be published in pamphlet form. Douglass complied, publishing a widely distributed pamphlet of the address. He also reprinted a text of the speech in his newspaper *Frederick Douglass' Paper* on July 9, 1852.

Defining Moment

The 1850s were a time of rising sectional tensions as slavery became the single most divisive issue in the United States. The U.S. war with Mexico (1846–1848) resulted in the acquisition of a continental United States that stretched from the Atlantic to Pacific oceans. Americans began debating whether slavery should be allowed in California and the New Mexico territories. Southerners in Congress demanded more protection for slavery where it existed, which resulted in the Fugitive Slave Act of 1850. The new law required northerners to assist in returning escaped slaves, leading a number of northern states to pass "personal liberty

laws" that aimed to skirt the act by routing fugitive slave cases through state courts.

The Fugitive Slave Act of 1850 also led many antislavery activists to take a more militant stance against slavery. On numerous occasions in the 1850s, abolitionists planned and executed the escape of fugitive slaves held in custody or liable for capture. If the Fugitive Slave Act served to heighten awareness and prompt physical action against slavery among abolitionists, the March 1852 publication of Harriet Beecher Stowe's *Uncle Tom's Cabin* succeeded in bringing the evils of slavery to the citizens of the northern states.

Douglass's "Fourth of July" Speech came in the early years of the turbulent 1850s, which began with the Fugitive Slave Act of 1850. Advocates and opponents of slavery clashed again in 1854 when the Kansas-Nebraska Act opened up those territories to slavery if the residents so desired. Later, in October 1859, the abolitionist John Brown led a failed slave uprising and raid on the federal arsenal at Harpers Ferry, Virginia. The 1850s ended with a nation more divided than ever before on the issue of slavery and teetering on the edge of civil war.

Author Biography

Frederick Douglass was born into slavery on a Maryland plantation in February 1818—the exact date of his birth cannot be determined. He spent twenty years in bondage—first on a plantation in Talbot County, Maryland, and then in the shipbuilding city of Baltimore. His mother, Harriet Bailey, was a fieldworker, and his father was most likely his first owner, Aaron Anthony.

During his enslavement, Douglass learned the basics of reading from his mistress, Sophia Auld, and later improved his reading and writing on his own. In September 1838 Douglass borrowed the free papers of a friend and boarded a train for the North. This rather uneventful escape from the bonds of slavery marked the beginning of his life as a crusader against the evils of slavery and in favor of civil rights for African Americans and women.

By 1841 Douglass had been hired as a field lecturer for the Massachusetts Anti-Slavery Society and in

1845 the publication of his first autobiography, *Narrative of the Life of Frederick Douglass*, afforded him an international reputation as America's most famous fugitive slave. In 1847 he moved his family to Rochester, New York, where he began publishing an antislavery newspaper called the *North Star*, later renamed *Frederick Douglass' Paper*. In 1852 the Rochester Ladies' Anti-Slavery Society invited Douglass to offer the annual Fourth of July address at their July 5 event.

During and after the Civil War, Douglass was a strong advocate for civil rights. During the war, he recruited African American troops and advised President Abraham Lincoln on the best plan to incorporate blacks into the Union war effort. In 1872 Douglass moved his family to Washington, D.C., where he accepted a post as president of the Freedman's Savings Bank in 1874. In 1877 President Rutherford B. Hayes appointed him U.S. marshal for the District of Columbia, and in 1881 he became recorder of deeds for the District of Columbia. His highest federal post came as U.S. resident minister and consul general (ambassador) to Haiti. He died at Cedar Hill, his home in Washington, D.C., on February 20, 1895.

HISTORICAL DOCUMENT

July 5, 1852

Mr. President, Friends and Fellow Citizens:

He who could address this audience without a quailing sensation, has stronger nerves than I have. I do not remember ever to have appeared as a speaker before any assembly more shrinkingly, nor with greater distrust of my ability, than I do this day. A feeling has crept over me, quite unfavorable to the exercise of my limited powers of speech. The task before me is one which requires much previous thought and study for its proper performance. I know that apologies of this sort are generally considered flat and unmeaning. I trust, however, that mine will not be so considered. Should I seem at ease, my appearance would much misrepresent me. The little experience I have had in addressing public meetings, in country school houses, avails me nothing on the present occasion.

The papers and placards say, that I am to deliver a 4th July oration. This certainly, sounds large, and out of the common way, for me. It is true that I have often had the privilege to speak in this beautiful Hall, and to address many who now honor me with their presence. But neither their familiar faces, nor the perfect gage I think I have of Corinthian Hall, seems to free me from embarrassment.

The fact is, ladies and gentlemen, the distance between this platform and the slave plantation, from which I escaped, is considerable—and the difficulties to be overcome in getting from the latter to the former, are by no means slight. That I am here today, is, to me, a matter of astonishment as well as of gratitude. You will not, therefore, be surprised, if in what I have to say, I evince no elaborate preparation, nor grace my speech with any high sounding exordium. With little experience and with less learning, I have been able to throw my thoughts hastily and imperfectly together; and trusting to your patient and generous indulgence, I will proceed to lay them before you.

This, for the purpose of this celebration, is the 4th of July. It is the birthday of your National Independence, and of your political freedom. This, to you, is what the Passover was to the emancipated people of God. It carries your minds back to the day, and to the act of your great deliverance; and to the signs, and to the wonders, associated with that act that day. This celebration also marks the beginning of another year of your national life; and reminds you that the Republic of America is now 76 years old. I am glad, fellow-citizens, that your nation is so young. Seventy-six years, though a good old age for a man, is but a mere speck in the life of a nation. Three score years and ten is the allotted time for individual men; but nations number their years by thousands. According to this fact, you are, even now only in the beginning of you national career, still lingering in the period of childhood. I repeat, I am glad this is so. There is hope in the thought, and hope is much needed, under the dark clouds which lower above the horizon. The eye of the reformer is met with angry flashes, portending disastrous times; but his heart may well beat lighter at the thought that America is young, and that she is still in the impressible stage of her existence. May he not hope that high lessons of wisdom, of justice and of truth, will yet give direction to her destiny? Were the nation older, the patriot's heart might be sadder, and the reformer's brow heavier. Its future might be shrouded in gloom, and the hope of its prophets go out in sorrow. There is consolation in the thought, that America is young. Great streams are not easily turned from channels, worn deep in the course of ages. They may sometimes rise in quiet and stately majesty, and inundate the land, refreshing and fertilizing the earth with their mysterious properties. They may also rise in wrath and fury, and bear away, on their angry waves, the accumulated wealth of years of toil and hardship. They, however, gradually flow back to the same old channel, and flow on as serenely as ever. But, while the river may not be turned aside, it may dry up, and leave nothing behind but the withered branch, and the unsightly rock, to howl in the abyss-sweeping wind, the sad tale of departed glory. As with rivers so with nations.

Fellow-citizens, I shall not presume to dwell at length on the associations that cluster about this day. The simple story of it is, that, 76 years ago, the people of this country were British subjects. The style and title of your "sovereign people" (in which you now glory) was not then born. You were under the British Crown. Your fathers esteemed the English Government as the home government and England as the fatherland. This home government, you know, although a considerable distance from your home, did, in the exercise of its parental prerogatives, impose upon its colonial children, such restraints, burdens and limitations, as, in its mature judgment, it deemed wise, right and proper.

But, your fathers, who had not adopted the fashionable idea of this day, of the infallibility of government, and the absolute character of its acts, presumed to differ from the home government in respect to the wisdom and the justice of some of those burdens and restraints.

They went so far in their excitement as to pronounce the measures of government unjust, unreasonable, and oppressive, and altogether such as ought not to be quietly submitted to. I scarcely need say, fellow-citizens, that my opinion of those measures fully accords with that of your fathers. Such a declaration of agreement on my part, would not be worth much to anybody. It would, certainly, prove nothing, as to what part I might have taken, had I lived during the great controversy of 1776. To say now that America was right, and England wrong, is exceedingly easy. Everybody can say it; the dastard, not less than the noble brave, can flippantly discant on the tyranny of England towards the American Colonies. It is fashionable to do so; but there was a time when, to pronounce against England, and in favor of the cause of the colonies, tried men's souls. They who did so were accounted in their day, plotters of mischief, agitators and rebels, dangerous men. To side with the right, against the wrong, with the weak against the strong, and with the oppressed against the oppressor! here lies the merit, and the one which, of all others, seems un fashionable in our day. The cause of liberty may be stabbed by the men who glory in the deeds of your fathers. But, to proceed.

Feeling themselves harshly and unjustly treated, by the home government, your fathers, like men of honesty, and men of spirit, earnestly sought redress. They petitioned and remonstrated; they did so in a decorous, respectful, and loyal manner. Their conduct was wholly unexceptionable. This, however, did not answer the purpose. They saw themselves treated with sovereign indifference, coldness and scorn. Yet they persevered. They were not the men to look back.

As the sheet anchor takes a firmer hold, when the ship is tossed by the storm, so did the cause of your fathers grow stronger, as it breasted the chilling blasts of kingly displeasure. The greatest and best of British statesmen admitted its justice, and the loftiest eloquence of the British Senate came to its support. But, with that blindness which seems to be the unvarying characteristic of tyrants, since Pharaoh and his hosts were drowned in the Red sea, the British Government persisted in the exactions complained of.

The madness of this course, we believe, is admitted now, even by England; but, we fear the lesson is wholly lost on our present rulers.

Oppression makes a wise man mad. Your fathers were wise men, and if they did not go mad, they became restive under this treatment. They felt themselves the victims of grievous wrongs, wholly incurable in their colonial capacity. With brave men there is always a remedy for oppression. Just here, the idea of a total separation of the colonies from the crown was born! It was a startling idea, much more so, than we, at this distance of time, regard it. The timid and the prudent (as has been intimated) of that day, were, of course, shocked and alarmed by it.

...

On the 2d of July, 1776, the old Continental Congress, to the dismay of the lovers of ease, and the worshippers of property, clothed that dreadful idea with all the authority of national sanction. They did so in the form of a resolution; and as we seldom hit upon resolutions, drawn up in our day, whose transparency is at all equal to this, it may refresh your minds and help my story if I read it.

Resolved, That these united colonies are, and of right, ought to be free and Independent States; that they are absolved from all allegiance to the British Crown; and that all political connection between them and the State of Great Britain is, and ought to be, dissolved.

Citizens, your fathers Made good that resolution. They succeeded; and today you reap the fruits of their success. The freedom gained is yours; and you, therefore, may properly celebrate this anniversary. The 4th of July is the first great fact in your nation's history—the very ring-bolt in the chain of your yet undeveloped destiny.

...

From the round top of your ship of state, dark and threatening clouds may be seen. Heavy billows, like mountains in the distance, disclose to the leeward huge forms of flinty rocks! That bolt drawn, that chain, broken, and all is lost. Cling to this day—cling to it, and to its principles, with the grasp of a storm-tossed mariner to a spar at midnight.

The coming into being of a nation, in any circumstances, is an interesting event. But, besides general considerations, there were peculiar circumstances which make the advent of this republic an event of special attractiveness.

...

Fellow Citizens, I am not wanting in respect for the fathers of this republic. The signers of the Declaration of Independence were brave men. They were great men too—great enough to give fame to a great age. It does not often happen to a nation to raise, at one time, such a number of truly great men. The point from which I am compelled to view them is not, certainly the most favorable; and yet I cannot contemplate their great deeds with less than admiration. They were statesmen, patriots and heroes, and for the good they did, and the principles they contended for, I will unite with you to honor their memory.

They loved their country better than their own private interests; and, though this is not the highest form of human excellence, all will concede that it is a rare virtue, and that when it is exhibited, it ought to command respect. He who will, intelligently, lay down his life for his country, is a man whom it is not in human nature to despise. Your fathers staked their lives, their fortunes, and their sacred honor, on the cause of their country. In their admiration of liberty, they lost sight of all other interests.

They were peace men; but they preferred revolution to peaceful submission to bondage. They were quiet men; but they did not shrink from agitating against oppression. They showed forbearance; but that they knew its limits. They believed in order; but not in the order of tyranny. With them, nothing was "settled" that was not right. With them, justice, liberty and humanity were "final;" not slavery and oppression. You may well cherish the memory of such men. They were great in their day and generation. Their solid manhood stands out the more as we contrast it with these degenerate times.

How circumspect, exact and proportionate were all their movements! How unlike the politicians of an hour! Their statesmanship looked beyond the passing moment, and stretched away in strength into the distant future. They seized upon eternal principles, and set a glorious example in their defence. Mark them!

Fully appreciating the hardships to be encountered, firmly believing in the right of their cause, honorably inviting the scrutiny of an on-looking world, reverently appealing to heaven to attest their sincerity, soundly comprehending the solemn responsibility they were about to assume, wisely measuring the terrible odds against them, your fathers, the fathers of this republic, did, most deliberately, under the inspiration of a glorious patriotism, and with a sublime faith in the great principles of justice and freedom, lay deep, the corner-stone of the national super-structure, which has risen and still rises in grandeur around you.

Of this fundamental work, this day is the anniversary. ...

Friends and citizens, I need not enter further into the causes which led to this anniversary. Many of you understand them better than I do.

...

I leave, therefore, the great deeds of your fathers to other gentlemen whose claim to have been regularly descended will be less likely to be disputed than mine!

The Present

My business, if I have any here today, is with the present. The accepted time with God and his cause is the ever-living now.

"Trust no future, however pleasant, Let the dead past bury its dead; Act, act in the living present, Heart within, and God overhead."

...

Fellow-citizens, pardon me, allow me to ask, why am I called upon to speak here today? What have I, or those I represent, to do with your national independence? Are the great principles of political freedom and of natural justice, embodied in that Declaration of Independence, extended to us? and am I, therefore, called upon to bring our humble offering to the national altar, and to confess the benefits and express devout gratitude for the blessings resulting from your independence to us?

Would to God, both for your sakes and ours, that an affirmative answer could be truthfully returned to these questions! Then would my task be light, and my burden easy and delightful. For who is there so cold, that a nation's sympathy could not warm him? Who so obdurate and dead to the claims of gratitude, that would not thankfully acknowledge such priceless benefits? Who so stolid and selfish, that would not give his voice to swell the hallelujahs of a nation's jubilee, when the chains of servitude had been torn from his limbs? I am not that man. In a case like that, the dumb might eloquently speak, and the "lame man leap as an hart."

But, such is not the state of the case. I say it with a sad sense of the disparity between us. I am not included within the pale of this glorious anniversary! Your high independence only reveals the immeasurable distance between us. The blessings in which you, this day, rejoice, are not enjoyed in common. The rich inheritance of justice, liberty, prosperity and independence, bequeathed by your fathers, is shared by you, not by me. The sunlight that brought life and healing to you, has brought stripes and death to me. This Fourth July is yours, not mine. You may rejoice, I must mourn. To drag a man in fetters into the grand illuminated temple of liberty, and call upon him to join you in joyous anthems, were inhuman mockery and sacrilegious irony. Do you mean, citizens, to mock me, by asking me to speak today? If so, there is a parallel to your conduct. And let me warn you that it is dangerous to copy the example of a nation whose crimes, towering up to heaven, were thrown down by the breath of the Almighty, burying that nation in irrecoverable ruin! I can today take up the plaintive lament of a peeled and woe-smitten people!

...

Fellow citizens; above your national, tumultuous joy, I hear the mournful wail of millions! whose chains, heavy and grievous yesterday, are, today, rendered more intolerable by the jubilee shouts that reach them. If I do forget, if I do not faithfully remember those bleeding children of sorrow this day, "may my right hand forget her cunning, and may my tongue cleave to the roof of my mouth!" To forget them, to pass lightly over their wrongs, and to chime in with the popular theme, would be treason most scandalous and shocking, and would make me a reproach before God and the world. My subject, then, fellow-citizens, is AMERICAN SLAVERY. I shall see, this day, and its popular characteristics, from the slave's point of view. Standing, there, identified with the American bondman, making his wrongs mine, I do not hesitate to declare, with all my soul, that the character and conduct of this nation never looked blacker to me than on this 4th of July! Whether we turn to the declarations of the past, or to the professions of the present, the conduct of the nation seems equally hideous and revolting. America is false to the past, false to the present, and solemnly binds herself to be false to the future. Standing with God and the crushed and bleeding slave on this occasion, I will, in the name of humanity which is outraged, in the name of liberty which is fettered, in the name of the constitution and the Bible, which are disregarded and trampled upon, dare to call in question and to denounce, with all the emphasis I can command, everything that serves to perpetuate slavery—the great sin and shame of America! "I will not equivocate; I will not excuse;" I will use the severest language I can command; and yet not one word shall escape me that any man, whose judgment is not blinded by prejudice, or who is not at heart a slaveholder, shall not confess to be right and just.

But I fancy I hear some one of my audience say, it is just in this circumstance that you and your brother abolitionists fail to make a favorable impression on the public mind. Would you argue more, and denounce less, would you persuade more, and rebuke less, your cause would be much more likely to succeed. But, I submit, where all is plain there is nothing to be argued. What point in the anti-slavery creed would you have me argue? On what branch of the subject do the people of this country need light? Must I undertake to prove that the slave is a man? That point is conceded already. Nobody doubts it. The slave-holders themselves acknowledge it in the enactment of laws for their government. They acknowledge it when they punish disobedience on the part of the slave. There are seventy-two crimes in the State of Virginia, which, if committed by a black

man (no matter how ignorant he be), subject him to the punishment of death; while only two of the same crimes will subject a white man to the like punishment. What is this but the acknowledgement that the slave is a moral, intellectual and responsible being. The manhood of the slave is conceded. It is admitted in the fact that Southern statute books are covered with enactments forbidding, under severe fines and penalties, the teaching of the slave to read or to write. When you can point to any such laws, in reference to the beasts of the field, then I may consent to argue the manhood of the slave. When the dogs in your streets, when the fowls of the air, when the cattle on your hills, when the fish of the sea, and the reptiles that crawl, shall be unable to distinguish the slave from a brute, then will I argue with you that the slave is a man.

For the present, it is enough to affirm the equal manhood of the negro race. Is it not astonishing that, while we are ploughing, planting and reaping, using all kinds of mechanical tools, erecting houses, constructing bridges, building ships, working in metals of brass, iron, copper, silver and gold; that, while we are reading, writing and cyphering, acting as clerks, merchants and secretaries, having among us lawyers, doctors, ministers, poets, authors, editors, orators and teachers; that, while we are engaged in all manner of enterprises common to other men, digging gold in California, capturing the whale in the Pacific, feeding sheep and cattle on the hillside, living, moving, acting, thinking, planning, living in families as husbands, wives and children, and, above all, confessing and worshipping the Christian's God, and looking hopefully for life and immortality beyond the grave, we are called upon to prove that we are men!

Would you have me argue that man is entitled to liberty? that he is the rightful owner of his own body? You have already declared it. Must I argue the wrongfulness of slavery? Is that a question for Republicans?…There is not a man beneath the canopy of heaven, that does not know that slavery is wrong for him.

What, am I to argue that it is wrong to make men brutes, to rob them of their liberty, to work them without wages, to keep them ignorant of their relations to their fellow men, to beat them with sticks, to flay their flesh with the lash, to load their limbs with irons, to hunt them with dogs, to sell them at auction, to sunder their families, to knock out their teeth, to burn their flesh, to starve them into obedience and submission to their masters? Must I argue that a system thus marked with blood, and stained with pollution, is wrong? No I will not. I have better employment for my time and strength, than such arguments would imply.

What, then, remains to be argued? Is it that slavery is not divine; that God did not establish it; that our doctors of divinity are mistaken? There is blasphemy in the thought. That which is inhuman, cannot be divine! Who can reason on such a proposition? They that can, may; I cannot. The time for such argument is past.

At a time like this, scorching irony, not convincing argument, is needed. O! had I the ability, and could I reach the nation's ear, I would, to day, pour out a fiery stream of biting ridicule, blasting reproach, withering sarcasm, and stern rebuke. For it is not light that is needed, but fire; it is not the gentle shower, but thunder. We need the storm, the whirlwind, and the earthquake. The feeling of the nation must be quickened; the conscience of the nation must be roused; the propriety of the nation must be startled; the hypocrisy of the nation must be exposed; and its crimes against God and man must be proclaimed and denounced.

What, to the American slave, is your 4th of July? I answer: a day that reveals to him, more than all other days in the year, the gross injustice and cruelty to which he is the constant victim. To him, your celebration is a sham; your boasted liberty, an unholy license; your national greatness, swelling vanity; your sounds of rejoicing are empty and heartless; your denunciations of tyrants, brass fronted impudence; your shouts of liberty and equality, hollow mockery; your prayers and hymns, your sermons and thanksgivings, with all your religious parade, and solemnity, are, to him, mere bombast, fraud, deception, impiety, and hypocrisy—a thin veil to cover up crimes which would disgrace a nation of savages. There is not a nation on the earth guilty of practices, more shocking and bloody, than are the people of these United States, at this very hour.

Go where you may, search where you will, roam through all the monarchies and despotisms of the old world, travel through South America, search out every abuse, and when you have found the last, lay your facts by the side of the every day practices of this nation, and you will say with me, that, for revolting barbarity and shameless hypocrisy, America reigns without a rival.

The Internal Slave Trade

Take the American slave-trade, which we are told by the papers, is especially prosperous just now. Ex-Senator Benton tells us that the price of men was never higher than now. He mentions the fact to show that slavery is in no danger. This trade is one of the peculiarities of American institutions. It is carried on in all the large towns and cities in one half of this confederacy; and millions are pocketed every year, by dealers in this horrid traffic. In several states, this trade is a chief source of wealth. It is called (in contradistinction to the foreign slave-trade) "the internal slave-trade." It is, probably, called so, too, in order to divert from it the horror with which the foreign slave-trade is contemplated. That trade has long since been denounced by this government, as piracy. It has been denounced with burning words, from the high places of the nation, as an execrable traffic. To arrest it, to put an end to it, this nation keeps a squadron, at immense cost, on the coast of Africa. Every-where, in this country, it is safe to speak of this foreign slave-trade, as a most inhuman traffic, opposed alike to the laws of God and of man. The duty to extirpate and destroy it, is admitted even by our DOCTORS OF DIVINITY. In order to put an end to it, some of these last have consented that their colored brethren (nominally free) should leave this country, and establish themselves on the western coast of Africa! It is, however, a notable fact, that, while so much execration is poured out by Americans, upon those engaged in the foreign slave-trade, the men engaged in the slave-trade between the states pass without condemnation, and their business is deemed honorable.

Behold the practical operation of this internal slave-trade, the American slave-trade, sustained by American politics and American religion. Here you will see men and women, reared like swine, for the market. You know what is a swine-drover? I will show you a man-drover. They inhabit all our Southern States. They perambulate the country, and crowd the highways of the nation, with droves of human stock. You will see one of these human flesh jobbers, armed with pistol, whip and bowie-knife, driving a company of a hundred men, women, and children, from the Potomac to the slave market at New Orleans. These wretched people are to be sold singly, or in lots, to suit purchasers. They are food for the cotton-field, and the deadly sugar-mill. Mark the sad procession, as it moves wearily along, and the inhuman wretch who drives them. Hear his savage yells and his blood-chilling oaths, as he hurries on his affrighted captives!...The crack you heard, was the sound of the slave-whip; the scream you heard, was from the woman you saw with the babe. Her speed had faltered under the weight of her child and her chains! that gash on her shoulder tells her to move on. Follow this drove to New Orleans. Attend the auction; see men examined like horses; see the forms of women rudely and brutally exposed to the shocking gaze of American slave-buyers. See this drove sold and separated for ever; and never forget the deep, sad sobs that arose from that scattered multitude. Tell me citizens, WHERE, under the sun, you can witness a spectacle more fiendish and shocking. Yet this is but a glance at the American slave-trade, as it exists, at this moment, in the ruling part of the United States.

I was born amid such sights and scenes. To me the American slave-trade is a terrible reality. When a child, my soul was often pierced with a sense of its horrors. I lived on Philpot Street, Fell's Point, Baltimore, and have watched from the wharves, the slave ships in the Basin, anchored from the shore, with their cargoes of human flesh, waiting for favorable winds to waft them down the Chesapeake. There was, at that time, a grand slave mart kept at the head of Pratt Street, by Austin Woldfolk....

The flesh-mongers gather up their victims by dozens, and drive them, chained, to the general depot at Baltimore. When a sufficient number have been collected here, a ship is chartered, for the purpose of conveying the forlorn crew to Mobile, or to New Orleans. From the slave prison to the ship, they are usually driven in the darkness of night; for since the anti-slavery agitation, a certain caution is observed.

In the deep still darkness of midnight, I have been often aroused by the dead heavy footsteps, and the piteous cries of the chained gangs that passed our door. The anguish of my boyish heart was intense; and I was often consoled, when speaking to my mistress in the morning, to hear her say that the custom was very wicked; that she hated to hear the rattle of the chains, and the heart-rending cries. I was glad to find one who sympathized with me in my horror.

Fellow-citizens, this murderous traffic is, to-day, in active operation in this boasted republic. In the solitude of my spirit, I see clouds of dust raised on the highways of the South; I see the bleeding footsteps; I hear the doleful wail of fettered humanity, on the way to the slave-markets, where the victims are to be sold like horses, sheep, and swine, knocked off to the highest bidder. There I see the tenderest ties ruthlessly broken, to gratify the lust, caprice and rapacity of the buyers and sellers of men. My soul sickens at the sight.

"Is this the land your Fathers loved, The freedom which they toiled to win? Is this the earth whereon they moved? Are these the graves they slumber in?"

But a still more inhuman, disgraceful, and scandalous state of things remains to be presented.

By an act of the American Congress, not yet two years old, slavery has been nationalized in its most horrible and revolting form. By that act, Mason & Dixon's line has been obliterated; New York has become as Virginia; and the power to hold, hunt, and sell men, women and children, as slaves, remains no longer a mere state institution, but is now an institution of the whole United States. The power is co-extensive with the star-spangled banner, and American Christianity. Where these go, may also go the merciless slave-hunter. Where these are, man is not sacred. He is a bird for the sportsman's gun. By that most foul and fiendish of all human decrees, the liberty and person of every man are put in peril. Your broad republican domain is hunting ground for men. Not for thieves and robbers, enemies of society, merely, but for men guilty of no crime. Your lawmakers have commanded all good citizens to engage in this hellish sport. Your President, your Secretary of State, your lords, nobles, and ecclesiastics, enforce, as a duty you owe to your free and glorious country, and to your God, that you do this accursed thing. Not fewer than forty Americans, have, within the past two years, been hunted down, and, without a moment's warning, hurried away in chains, and consigned to slavery, and excruciating torture. Some of these have had wives and children, dependent on them for bread; but of this, no account was made. The right of the hunter to his prey, stands superior to the right of marriage, and to all rights in this republic, the rights of God included! For black men there are neither law, justice, humanity, nor religion.

The Fugitive Slave Law makes MERCY TO THEM, A CRIME; and bribes the judge who tries them. An American JUDGE GETS TEN DOLLARS FOR EVERY VICTIM HE CONSIGNS to slavery, and five, when he fails to do so. The oath of any two villains is sufficient, under this hell-black enactment, to send the most pious and exemplary black man into the remorseless jaws of slavery! His own testimony is nothing. He can bring no witnesses for himself. The minister of American justice is bound, by the law to hear but one side; and that side, is the side of the oppressor. Let this damning fact be perpetually told. Let it be thundered around the world, that, in tyrant-killing, king-hating, people-loving, democratic, Christian America, the seats of justice are filled with judges, who hold their offices under an open and palpable bribes, and are bound, in deciding in the case of a man's liberty, to hear only his accusers!

In glaring violation of justice, in shameless disregard of the forms of administering law, in cunning arrangement to entrap the defenceless, and in diabolical intent, this Fugitive Slave Law stands alone in the annals of tyrannical legislation. I doubt if there be another nation on the globe, having the brass and the baseness to put such a law on the statute-book. If any man in this assembly thinks differently from me in this matter, and feels able to disprove my statements, I will gladly confront him at any suitable time and place he may select.

Religious Liberty

I take this law to be one of the grossest infringements of Christian Liberty, and, if the churches and ministers of our country were not stupidly blind, or most wickedly indifferent, they, too, would so regard it.

At the very moment that they are thanking God for the enjoyment of civil and religious liberty, and for the right to worship God according to the dic-

tates of their own consciences, they are utterly silent in respect to a law which robs religion of its chief significance, and makes it utterly worthless to a world lying in wickedness....The fact that the church of our country, (with fractional exceptions,) does not esteem "the Fugitive Slave Law" as a declaration of war against religious liberty, implies that that church regards religion simply as a form of worship, an empty ceremony, and not a vital principle, requiring active benevolence, justice, love and good will towards man. It esteems sacrifice above mercy; psalm-singing above right doing; solemn meetings above practical righteousness. A worship that can be conducted by persons who refuse to give shelter to the houseless, to give bread to the hungry, clothing to the naked, and who enjoin obedience to a law forbidding these acts of mercy, is a curse, not a blessing to mankind. The Bible addresses all such persons as "scribes, pharisees, hypocrites, who pay tithe of mint, anise, and cumin, and have omitted the weightier matters of the law, judgment, mercy and faith."

The Church Responsible

But the church of this country is not only indifferent to the wrongs of the slave, it actually takes sides with the oppressors. It has made itself the bulwark of American slavery, and the shield of American slave-hunters. Many of its most eloquent Divines, who stand as the very lights of the church, have shamelessly given the sanction of religion, and the bible, to the whole slave system. They have taught that man may, properly, be a slave; that the relation of master and slave is ordained of God; that to send back an escaped bondman to his master is clearly the duty of all the followers of the Lord Jesus Christ; and this horrible blasphemy is palmed off upon the world for Christianity.

For my part, I would say, welcome infidelity! welcome atheism! welcome anything! in preference to the gospel, as preached by those Divines! They convert the very name of religion into an engine of tyranny, and barbarous cruelty, and serve to confirm more infidels, in this age, than all the infidel writings of Thomas Paine, Voltaire, and Bolingbroke, put together, have done? These ministers make religion a cold and flinty-hearted thing, having neither principles of right action, nor bowels of compassion. They strip the love of God of its beauty, and leave the throne of religion a huge, horrible, repulsive form. It is a religion for oppressors, tyrants, man-stealers, and thugs. It is not that "pure and undefiled religion" which is from above, and which is "first pure, then peaceable, easy to be entreated, full of mercy and good fruits, without partiality, and without hypocrisy." But a religion which favors the rich against the poor; which exalts the proud above the humble; which divides mankind into two classes, tyrants and slaves; which says to the man in chains, stay there; and to the oppressor, oppress on; it is a religion which may be professed and enjoyed by all the robbers and enslavers of mankind; it makes God a respecter of persons, denies his fatherhood of the race, and tramples in the dust the great truth of the brotherhood of man. All this we affirm to be true of the popular church, and the popular worship of our land and nation—a religion, a church and a worship which, on the authority of inspired wisdom, we pronounce to be an abomination in the sight of God....

The American church is guilty, when viewed in connection with what it is doing to uphold slavery; but it is superlatively guilty when viewed in connection with its ability to abolish slavery.

The sin of which it is guilty is one of omission as well as of commission. Albert Barnes but uttered what the common sense of every man at all observant of the actual state of the case will receive as truth, when he declared that "There is no power out of the church that could sustain slavery an hour, if it were not sustained in it."

Let the religious press, the pulpit, the Sunday school, the conference meeting, the great ecclesiastical, missionary, bible and tract associations of the land array their immense powers against slavery, and slave-holding; and the whole system of crime and blood would be scattered to the winds, and that they do not do this involves them in the most awful responsibility of which the mind can conceive....

Religion in England and Religion in America

One is struck with the difference between the attitude of the American church towards the anti-slavery movement, and that occupied by the churches in England towards a similar movement in that country. There, the church, true to its mission of ameliorating, elevating, and improving the condition of mankind, came forward promptly, bound up the wounds of the West Indian slave, and restored him to his liberty. There, the question of emancipation was a high religious question. It was demanded, in the name of humanity, and according to the law of the living God. The Sharps, the Clarksons, the Wilberforces, the Buxtons, the Burchells and the Knibbs, were alike famous for their piety, and for their philanthropy....

Americans! your republican politics, not less than your republican religion, are flagrantly inconsistent. You boast of your love of liberty, your superior civilization, and your pure Christianity, while the whole political power of the nation, (as embodied in the two great political parties, is solemnly pledged to support and perpetuate the enslavement of three millions of your countrymen. You hurl your anathemas at the crowned headed tyrants of Russia and Austria, and pride yourselves on your Democratic institutions, while you yourselves consent to be the mere tools and body-guards of the tyrants of Virginia and Carolina. You invite to your shores fugitives of oppression from abroad, honor them with banquets, greet them with ovations, cheer them, toast them, salute them, protect them, and pour out your money to them like water; but the fugitives from your own land, you advertise, hunt, arrest, shoot and kill. You glory in your refinement, and your universal education; yet you maintain a system as barbarous and dreadful, as ever stained the character of a nation— a system begun in avarice, supported in pride, and perpetuated in cruelty....You profess to believe "that, of one blood, God made all nations of men to dwell on the face of all the earth," and hath commanded all men, everywhere to love one another; yet you notoriously hate, (and glory in your hatred,) all men whose skins are not colored like your own. You declare, before the world, and are understood by the world to declare, that you "hold these truths to be self evident, that all men are created equal; and are endowed by their Creator with certain, inalienable rights; and that, among these are, life, liberty, and the pursuit of happiness"; and yet, you hold securely, in a bondage, which according to your own Thomas Jefferson, "is worse than ages of that which your fathers rose in rebellion to oppose," a seventh part of the inhabitants of your country.

Fellow-citizens! I will not enlarge further on your national inconsistencies. The existence of slavery in this country brands your republicanism as a sham, your humanity as a base pretence, and your Christianity as a lie. It destroys your moral power abroad it corrupts your politicians at home. It saps the foundation of religion; it makes your name a hissing, and a bye-word to a mocking earth. It is the antagonistic force in your government, the only thing that seriously disturbs and endangers your Union. It fetters your progress; it is the enemy of improvement, the deadly foe of education; it fosters pride; it breeds insolence; it promotes vice; it shelters crime; it is a curse to the earth that supports it; and yet, you cling to it, as if it were the sheet anchor of all your hopes. Oh! be warned! be warned! a horrible reptile is coiled up in your nation's bosom; the venomous creature is nursing at the tender breast of your youthful republic; for the love of God, tear away, and fling from you the hideous monster, and let the weight of twenty millions, crush and destroy it forever!

The Constitution

But it is answered in reply to all this, that precisely what I have now denounced is, in fact, guaranteed and sanctioned by the Constitution of the United States; that, the right to hold, and to hunt slaves is a part of that Constitution framed by the illustrious Fathers of this Republic. Then, I dare to affirm, notwithstanding all I have said before, your fathers stooped, basely stooped. "To palter with us in a double sense: And keep the word of promise to the ear, But break it to the heart."

And instead of being the honest men I have before declared them to be, they were the veriest imposters that ever practiced on mankind. This is the inevitable conclusion, and from it there is no escape; but I differ from those who charge this baseness on the framers of the Constitution of the United States. It is a slander upon their memory, at least, so I believe....

Fellow-citizens! there is no matter in respect to which, the people of the North have allowed themselves to be so ruinously imposed upon, as that of

the pro-slavery character of the Constitution. In that instrument I hold there is neither warrant, license, nor sanction of the hateful thing; but interpreted, as it ought to be interpreted, the Constitution is a GLORIOUS LIBERTY DOCUMENT. Read its preamble, consider its purposes. Is slavery among them? Is it at the gateway? or is it in the temple? it is neither. While I do not intend to argue this question on the present occasion, let me ask, if it be not somewhat singular that, if the Constitution were intended to be, by its framers and adopters, a slave-holding instrument, why neither slavery, slaveholding, nor slave can anywhere be found in it....

Now, take the constitution according to its plain reading, and I defy the presentation of a single pro-slavery clause in it. On the other hand it will be found to contain principles and purposes, entirely hostile to the existence of slavery.

...

Allow me to say, in conclusion, notwithstanding the dark picture I have this day presented, of the state of the nation, I do not despair of this country. There are forces in operation, which must inevitably, work the downfall of slavery. "The arm of the Lord is not shortened," and the doom of slavery is certain.

I, therefore, leave off where I began, with hope. While drawing encouragement from "the Declaration of Independence," the great principles it contains, and the genius of American Institutions, my spirit is also cheered by the obvious tendencies of the age. Nations do not now stand in the same relation to each other that they did ages ago. No nation can now shut itself up, from the surrounding world, and trot round in the same old path of its fathers without interference. The time was when such could be done. Long established customs of hurtful character could formerly fence themselves in, and do their evil work with social impunity. Knowledge was then confined and enjoyed by the privileged few, and the multitude walked on in mental darkness. But a change has now come over the affairs of mankind. Walled cities and empires have become unfashionable. The arm of commerce has borne away the gates of the strong city. Intelligence is penetrating the darkest corners of the globe. It makes its pathway over and under the sea, as well as on the earth. Wind, steam, and lightning are its chartered agents. Oceans no longer divide, but link nations together. From Boston to London is now a holiday excursion. Space is comparatively annihilated. Thoughts expressed on one side of the Atlantic, are distinctly heard on the other.

… In the fervent aspirations of William Lloyd Garrison, I say, and let every heart join in saying it:

> God speed the year of jubilee
> The wide world o'er!
> When from their galling chains set free,
> Th' oppress'd shall vilely bend the knee,
> And wear the yoke of tyranny
> Like brutes no more.
> That year will come, and freedom's
> reign, To man his plundered rights again
> Restore.
> God speed the day when human blood
> Shall cease to flow!
> In every clime be understood,
> The claims of human brotherhood,

> And each return for evil, good, Not blow
> for blow;
> That day will come all feuds to end,
> And change into a faithful friend
> Each foe.
> God speed the hour, the glorious hour,
> When none on earth
> Shall exercise a lordly power,
> Nor in a tyrant's presence cower; But
> all to manhood's stature tower, By equal
> birth!
> THAT HOUR WILL COME, to each,
> to all,
> And from his prison-house, the thrall Go
> forth.
> Until that year, day, hour, arrive,
> With head, and heart, and hand I'll strive,
> To break the rod, and rend the gyve, The
> spoiler of his prey deprive
> So witness Heaven!
> And never from my chosen post,
> Whate'er the peril or the cost,
> Be driven.

GLOSSARY

despotisms: absolute rules

ecclesiastics: priests and ministers

exordium: introduction, especially in a classic or rhetorical text

fettered: shackled or chained together

perambulate: walk around

Document Analysis

Douglass begins by juxtaposing himself as a former slave with those in the audience who he deems the true beneficiaries of the Declaration of Independence. Douglass then compares the abolitionist reformers of the 1850s with the independence-seekers of the founding generation, heaping praise on the achievements of the Revolutionary generation but then transitioning into matters affecting the present state of the nation.

Douglass then turns toward the influence of those achievements in the present. The problem of the present that most concerns Douglass is the existence of slavery in the United States and the inherent contradiction between celebrating American independence while many suffer under the bonds of slavery. Douglass powerfully asks the crowd if it was their intention to mock him by inviting him to speak on the Fourth of July, noting that "The rich inheritance of justice, liberty, prosperity, and independence, bequeathed by your fathers, is shared by you, not by me." Douglass transitions from the celebration of the Fourth of July to a more familiar topic, American slavery. Many in the audience were abolitionist-minded, and most would have anticipated the shift in topic. He argues that the character and conduct of the nation "never looked blacker." Douglass condemns the use of religion and the U.S. Constitution to support slavery and vows to actively oppose slavery in every way he can, taking the quote "I will not equivocate; I will not excuse" from abolitionist William Lloyd Garrison.

Douglass next examines a series of issues commonly found in abolitionists' denunciations of slavery, including the humanity of the enslaved, their entitlement to liberty, and biblical justifications for the institution. He touches on the fact that slavery is neither divinely sanctioned nor created by God. The speech changes course again as Douglass begins a scathing condemnation of the country with the famous title line "What, to the American slave, is your 4th of July?"

Douglass argues that, for enslaved Americans, the Fourth of July is the one day of the year that most represents the "gross injustice and cruelty to which he is the constant victim." He finds that the celebration of liberty and equality is hypocritical while slavery continues to exist in the United States. Finally, he claims that the hypocrisy of the United States is deeper than the abuses of European and other world monarchies and that even the cruelties of South American slavery do not match the cruelty brought about by the contradiction between slavery and freedom in America.

In the next section of the speech, he condemns the slave trade within the United States. These passages offer some details about the ways that the slave trade functioned and of how it affected and dehumanized those who were subjected to sale and movement. Douglass then heartily condemns the Fugitive Slave Act, a law which angered abolitionists and led many who had previously been neutral on the issue of slavery to speak out against the measure. The injustice inherent in this law led many formerly pacifistic abolitionists to take more active roles in helping fugitives to escape, sometimes physically rescuing them from jails and courthouses across the North.

Douglass also places blame on the established churches and denominations of the United States for their failure to condemn the Fugitive Slave Act, arguing that if the matter involved financial benefit or harm to the church, clergy would call for the law's repeal. Douglass provides examples of figures who have opposed slavery and well-known ministers who supported the practice. Douglass concludes this section by reminding the audience that although his words apply to the majority of American ministers, notable exceptions include the Reverend Robert R. Raymond, who also spoke at the Corinthian Hall event.

To draw a clear contrast between the antislavery activism of the British and those in the United States, Douglass names a number of prominent antislavery British activists. Douglass had traveled for a year and a half in Great Britain and Ireland in 1845 to 1847, during which time he met and worked with a number of British reformers. Unlike the U.S. antislavery movement, when Great Britain ended slavery under the Slavery Abolition Act of 1833, the established Anglican Church supported the abolition of slavery in the British West Indies. Douglass contrasts the failure of American clergy to oppose slavery with their sympathy for such foreign causes as the movement of Hungarians to shake off an invasion by Russian and Austrian troops in 1849.

The final section of the speech turns to the constitutionality of slavery. Although Douglass once held the view that the U.S. Constitution was a proslavery document, by 1852 he was committed to using political means to end slavery. In the opening paragraph he paraphrases Shakespeare's *Macbeth* to emphasize the fallacy of those who believe that the Constitution sanctions slavery. He mentions several prominent northerners committed to antislavery politics, each of whom had published works arguing that the Constitution does not support slavery. Douglass outlines the evidence for his argument, pointing especially to the fact that the words *slave* and *slavery* do not appear anywhere in the document. Although some historians argue that slavery was implicitly protected in several articles of the Constitution, Douglass does not see a single proslavery clause.

Douglass turns more hopeful for the speech's conclusion. He believes that slavery will one day be abolished and that the Declaration of Independence will one day apply to all. In the final paragraph, he proclaims that slavery will end when the light of freedom reaches the United States, The essay concludes with the poem "The Triumph of Freedom" authored by the famous abolitionist William Lloyd Garrison.

Essential Themes

Although traditional Fourth of July addresses tended to emphasize the achievements of the American Revolution and its legacy, Douglass's address intends to bring focus to the present. For example, in the introductory section he carefully distances himself from the historical events of the Revolution, preparing the way to contrast the rights white Americans enjoy and the oppression of slavery. He describes the day as one celebrating "your National Independence" and "your political freedom." American institutions were shaped and developed without regard to the vast numbers of slaves in the United States.

Douglass, in this speech, tends to focus his ire and disappointment on institutions rather than individuals. The system that created and enforces the fugitive slave act is more than the work of a single person. Similarly, he seems to attack American Christianity as an institutional whole for its failures to oppose slavery. In both cases, there are brave and worthy individual who fight against unjust systems (in the case of the Fugitive Slave Act) or swim against the tide of their own religious institutions in order to protect the human rights and dignity of the oppressed. These, however, are too few and far between.

———*L. Diane Barnes, PhD*

Bibliography and Additional Reading

Blassingame, John W., et al., eds. *The Frederick Douglass Papers*, Series One: *Speeches, Debates, and Interviews*, Vol. 2: *1847–54*. New Haven, Conn. Yale University Press, 1982.

Colaiaco, James A. *Frederick Douglass and the Fourth of July*. New York: Palgrave Macmillan, 2006.

Douglass, Frederick. *Oration, Delivered in Corinthian Hall, Rochester, July 5, 1852*. Rochester, New York, 1852.

Lampe, Gregory P. *Frederick Douglass: Freedom's Voice*. Rhetoric and Public Affairs Series. East (Lansing: Michigan State University Press, 1998).

McFeely, William S. *Frederick Douglass*. (New York: W.W. Norton, 1991)

■ *The Condition, Elevation, Emigration, and Destiny of the Colored People of the United States, Politically Considered*

Date: 1852
Author: Martin Delany
Genre: Book Excerpt

Summary Overview

Martin Robison Delany's famous 1852 work *The Condition, Elevation, Emigration, and Destiny of the Colored People of the United States, Politically Considered* is an early black nationalist manifesto. Delany was a significant early founder of the philosophy of black nationalism, and over the course of his life he contributed in a variety of ways to the black freedom struggle. He developed a number of practical strategies, including education, to promote black independence, self-determination, and self-sufficiency. To this end, he also strongly supported African emigration. Delany stands at the head of a succession of black leaders known for their staunch advocacy of black nationalism, including Henry McNeal Turner, Marcus Garvey, Malcolm X, and Louis Farrakhan. In his influential work, Delany offers a close examination of the merits of black emigration as a means of elevation to freedom and equality.

Delany's words were addressed to all African Americans in the United States, although many other Americans read and reacted to them, including politicians and abolitionists. Delany was mainly attempting to persuade everyday African Americans that the benefits of emigration made such a prospect a preferable alternative to the race conundrum in the United States. Within the black community, reactions to his proposals differed widely in accord with the variety of political stances adopted by black intellectuals.

Defining Moment

Black nationalists of the late eighteenth and early nineteenth centuries first advanced the Back to Africa movement because of their belief that African Americans could never achieve equality in the United States under the existing oppressive conditions promoted by whites. The Society for the Colonization of Free People of Color of America was officially formed in 1816 at a meeting in Washington, D.C. Although it was nominally an antislavery organization, the American Colonization Society (ACS), as the society was known, was primarily concerned with eliminating the threat of the class of free African Americans deemed dangerous to the maintenance of slavery. In 1821 the ACS established Liberia as a colony for the resettlement of free African Americans.

Most black abolitionists, however, including David Walker, viewed the ACS as a pro-slavery plan to drive African Americans from the United States, diluting abolitionist efforts to end slavery. Thus arose a debate about the sociocultural fit of Africa as a place of settlement for those who had been exposed to slavery in the United States. Put simply, the debate was between the holders of two competing positions. The "integrationists" argued that the United States was their home and sought ways to become more fully integrated into American society. The "nationalists" believed that blacks could achieve freedom and equality only in their own nation. Martin Delany, a contemporary of Frederick Douglass, adopted a culture-centered and independent approach that concentrated on his unique form of black nationalism. In 1852, he wrote the small, yet significant book *The Condition, Elevation, Emigration, and Destiny of the Colored People of the United States, Politically Considered*. In this work, Delany advanced a serious and thoughtful plan of action for the emigration of African Americans. He advocated Central and South America as prime destinations for the race, also supporting the continent of Africa in the book's appendix.

Author Biography

Martin Robison Delany was born on May 6, 1812, in what is now West Virginia, to the enslaved Samuel Delany and Pati Peace Delany, a free woman of color. Delany's grandparents were native Africans, who were brought to the United States as slaves. Delany and his siblings were taught to read by a northern peddler, and, as a result, a white neighbor threatened to imprison Delany's mother. In response to this threat, Pati Delany uprooted her children and took them to Chambersburg, Pennsylvania, just across the Mason-Dixon Line. In 1822, Delany's father bought his freedom and was reunited with his family.

Delany received an elementary education in Chambersburg, where he remained until he was nineteen. He then traveled to Pittsburgh on foot, via the Allegheny Mountains. He began studying medicine with a local white doctor, gaining enough expertise to practice "as a cupper, leecher, and bleeder." Delany soon became a local leader in Pittsburg's black community. While working as an officer with the Pittsburgh Anti-Slavery Society, he worked with the Underground Railroad.

In the early 1840s, Delany launched the newspaper *The Mystery*, which he edited until the paper went out of business in 1847. That year he joined Frederick Douglass's *North Star* newspaper in Rochester, New York. At the same time, he maintained a vigorous speaking schedule. In 1849 he was accepted as a student by Harvard Medical School. In 1854 he led the National Emigration Convention of Colored People in Cleveland, Ohio.

Delany ran an unsuccessful bid for the position of lieutenant governor of the state of South Carolina in 1874. After the attempt, Delany lectured and found support in the areas of medicine and anthropology, selling copies of his 1879 *Principia of Ethnology: The Origin of Races and Color, with an Archeological Compendium of Ethiopian and Egyptian Civilization, from Years of Careful Examination and Enquiry* to attending crowds. During the latter part of 1884, Delany returned to Wilberforce, where he died on January 24, 1885.

HISTORICAL DOCUMENT

V. Means of Elevation

Moral theories have long been resorted to by us, as a means of effecting the redemption of our brethren in bonds, and the elevation of the free colored people in this country. Experience has taught us, that speculations are not enough; that the *practical* application of principles adduced, the thing carried out, is the only true and proper course to pursue.

We have speculated and moralised much about equality—claiming to be as good as our neighbors, and everybody else—all of which, may do very well in ethics—but not in politics. We live in society among men, conducted by men, governed by rules and regulations. However arbitrary, there are certain policies that regulate all well-organized institutions and corporate bodies. We do not intend here to speak of the legal political relations of society, for those are treated on elsewhere. The business and social, or voluntary and mutual policies, are those that now claim our attention. Society regulates itself—being governed by mind, which like water, finds its own level. "Like seeks like," is a principle in the laws of matter, as well as of mind. There is such a thing as inferiority of things, and positions; at least society has made them so; and while we continue to live among men, we must agree to all *just* measures—all those we mean, that do not necessarily infringe on the rights of others. By the regulations of society, there is no equality of persons, where there is not an equality of attainments. By this, we do not wish to be understood as advocating the actual equal attainments of every individual; but we mean to say, that if these attainments be necessary for the elevation of the white man, they are necessary for the elevation of the colored man. That some colored men and women, in a like proportion to the whites, should be qualified in all the attainments possessed by them. It is one of the regulations of society the world over, and we shall have to conform to it, or be discarded as unworthy of the associations of our fellows.

Cast our eyes about us and reflect for a moment, and what do we behold! Every thing that presents to view gives evidence of the skill of the white man. Should we purchase a pound of groceries, a yard of linen, a vessel of crockeryware, a piece of furniture, the very provisions that we eat,—all, all are the products of the white man, purchased by us from the white man, consequently, our earnings and means, are all given to the white man.

Pass along the avenues of any city or town, in which you live—behold the trading shops—the manufactories—see the operations of the various machinery—see the stage-coaches coming in, bringing the mails of intelligence—look at the railroads interlining every section, bearing upon them their mighty trains, flying with the velocity of the swallow, ushering in the hundreds of industrious, enterprising travelers. Cast again your eyes widespread over the ocean—see the vessels in every direction with their white sheets spread to the winds of heaven, freighted with the commerce, merchandise and wealth of many nations. Look as you pass along through the cities, at the great and massive buildings—the beautiful and extensive structures of architecture—behold the ten thousand cupolas, with their spires all reared up towards heaven, intersecting the territory of the clouds—all standing as mighty living monuments, of the industry, enterprise, and intelligence of the white man. And yet, with all these living truths, rebuking us with scorn, we strut about, place our hands akimbo, straighten up ourselves to our greatest height, and talk loudly about being "as good as any body." How do we compare with them? Our fathers are their coachmen, our brothers their cookmen, and ourselves their waiting-men. Our mothers their nurse-women, our sisters their scrubwomen, our daughters their maid-women, and our wives their washer-women. Until colored men, attain to a position above permitting their mothers, sisters, wives, and daughters, to do the drudgery and "menial" offices of other men's wives and daughters; it is useless, it is nonsense, it is pitiable mockery, to talk about equality and elevation in society. The world is looking upon us, with feelings of commiseration, sorrow, and contempt. We scarcely deserve sympathy, if we peremptorily refuse advice, bearing upon our elevation....

White men are producers—we are consumers. They build houses, and we rent them. They raise produce, and we consume it. They manufacture clothes and wares, and we garnish ourselves with them. They build coaches, vessels, cars, hotels, saloons, and other vehicles and places of accommodation, and we deliberately wait until they have got them in readiness, then walk in, and contend with as much assurance for a "right," as though the whole thing was bought by, paid for, and belonged to us. By their literary attainments, they are the contributors to, authors and teachers of, literature, science, religion, law, medicine, and all other useful attainments that the world now makes use of. We have no reference to ancient times—we speak of modern things.

These are the means by which God intended man to succeed; and this discloses the secret of the white man's success with all of his wickedness, over the head of the colored man, with all of his religion.

We have been pointed and plain, on this part of the subject, because we desire our readers to see persons and things in their true position. Until we are determined to change the condition of things, and raise ourselves above the position in which we are now prostrated, we must hang our heads in sorrow, and hide our faces in shame. It is enough to know that these things are so; the causes we care little about. Those we have been examining, complaining about, and moralising over, all our life time. This we are weary of. What we desire to learn now is, how to effect a *remedy*; this we have endeavored to point out. Our elevation must be the result of *self-efforts*, and work of our *own hands*. No other human power can accomplish it. If we but determine it shall be so, it will be so. Let each one make the case his own, and endeavor to rival his neighbor, in honorable competition.

These are the proper and only means of elevating ourselves and attaining equality in this country or any other, and it is useless, utterly futile, to think about going any where, except we are determined to use these as the necessary means of developing our manhood. The means are at hand, within our reach. Are we willing to try them? Are we willing to raise ourselves superior to the condition of slaves, or continue the meanest underlings, subject to the beck and call of every creature bearing a pale complexion? If we are, we had as well remained in the South, as to have come to the North in search of more freedom. What was the object of our parents in leaving the South, if it were not for the purpose of attaining equality in common with others of their fellow citizens, by giving their children access to all the advantages enjoyed by others? Surely this was their object. They heard of liberty and equality here, and they hastened on to enjoy it, and no people are more astonished and disappointed than they, who for the first time, on beholding the position we occupy here in the free North—what is called, and what they expect to find, the free States. They at once tell us, that they have as much liberty in the South as we have in the North—that there as free people, they are protected in their rights—that we have nothing more—that in other respects they have the same opportunity, indeed the preferred opportunity, of being their maids, servants, cooks, waiters, and menials in general, there, as we have here—that had they known for a moment, before leaving, that such was to be the only position they occupied here, they would have remained where they were, and never left. Indeed, such is the disappointment in many cases, that they immediately return back again, completely insulted at the idea, of having us here at the north, assume ourselves to be their superiors. Indeed, if our superior advantages of the free States, do not induce and stimulate us to the higher attainments in life, what in the name of degraded humanity will do it?

VI. The United States Our Country

Our common country is the United States. Here were we born, here raised and educated; here are the scenes of childhood; the pleasant associations of our school going days; the loved enjoyments of our domestic and fireside relations, and the sacred graves of our departed fathers and mothers, and from here will we not be driven by any policy that may be schemed against us.

We are Americans, having a birthright citizenship—natural claims upon the country—claims common to all others of our fellow citizens—natural rights, which may, by virtue of unjust laws, be obstructed, but never can be annulled. Upon these do we place ourselves, as immovably fixed as the decrees of the living God. But according to the economy that regulates the policy of nations, upon which rests the basis of justifiable claims to all freemen's rights, it may be necessary to take another view of, and enquire into the political claims of colored men....

XXIII. Things as They Are

"And if thou boast Truth to utter, Speak, and leave the rest to God."

In presenting this work, we have but a single object in view, and that is, to inform the minds of the colored people at large, upon many things pertaining to their elevation, that but few among us are acquainted with. Unfortunately for us, as a body, we have been taught to believe, that we must have some person to think for us, instead of thinking for ourselves. So accustomed are we to submission and this kind of training, that it is with difficulty, even

among the most intelligent of the colored people, an audience may be elicited for any purpose whatever, if the expounder is to be a colored person; and the introduction of any subject is treated with indifference, if not contempt, when the originator is a colored person. Indeed, the most ordinary white person, is almost revered, while the most qualified colored person is totally neglected. Nothing from them is appreciated.

We have been standing comparatively still for years, following in the footsteps of our friends, believing that what they promise us can be accomplished, just because they say so, although our own knowledge should long since, have satisfied us to the contrary. Because even were it possible, with the present hate and jealousy that the whites have towards us in this country, for us to gain equality of rights with them; we never could have an equality of the exercise and enjoyment of those rights—because, the great odds of numbers are against us. We might indeed, as some at present, have the right of the elective franchise—nay, it is not the elective franchise, because the *elective franchise* makes the enfranchised, *eligible* to any position attainable; but we may exercise the right of *voting* only, which to us, is but poor satisfaction; and we by no means care to cherish the privilege of voting somebody into office, to help to make laws to degrade us.

In religion—because they are both *translators* and *commentators*, we must believe nothing, however absurd, but what our oppressors tell us. In Politics, nothing but such as they promulge; in Anti-Slavery, nothing but what our white brethren and friends say we must; in the mode and manner of our elevation, we must do nothing, but that which may be laid down to be done by our white brethren from some quarter or other; and now, even in the subject of emigration, there are some colored people to be found, so lost to their own interest and self-respect, as to be gulled by slave owners and colonizationists, who are led to believe there is no other place in which they can become elevated, but Liberia, a government of American slaveholders, as we have shown—simply, because white men have told them so.

Upon the possibility, means, mode and manner, of our Elevation in the United States—Our Original

Rights and Claims as Citizens—Our Determination not to be Driven from our Native Country—the Difficulties in the Way of our Elevation—Our Position in Relation to our Anti-Slavery Brethren—the Wicked Design and Injurious Tendency of the American Colonization Society—Objections to Liberia—Objections to Canada—Preferences to South America, &c., &c., all of which we have treated without reserve; expressing our mind freely, and with candor, as we are determined that as far as we can at present do so, the minds of our readers shall be enlightened. The custom of concealing information upon vital and important subjects, in which the interest of the people is involved, we do not agree with, nor favor in the least; we have therefore, laid this cursory treatise before our readers, with the hope that it may prove instrumental in directing the attention of our people in the right way, that leads to their Elevation. Go or stay—of course each is free to do as he pleases—one thing is certain; our Elevation is the work of our own hands. And Mexico, Central America, the West Indies, and South America, all present now, opportunities for the individual enterprise of our young men, who prefer to remain in the United States, in preference to going where they can enjoy real freedom, and equality of rights. Freedom of Religion, as well as of politics, being tolerated in all of these places.

Let our young men and women, prepare themselves for usefulness and business; that the men may enter into merchandise, trading, and other things of importance; the young women may become teachers of various kinds, and otherwise fill places of usefulness. Parents must turn their attention more to the education of their children. We mean, to educate them for useful practical business purposes. Educate them for the Store and the Counting House—to do every-day practical business. Consult the children's propensities, and direct their education according to their inclinations. It may be, that there is too great a desire on the part of parents to give their children a professional education, before the body of the people are ready for it. A people must be a business people, and have more to depend upon than mere help in people's houses and Hotels, before they are either able to support, or capable of properly appreciating the services of

professional men among them. This has been one of our great mistakes—we have gone in advance of ourselves. We have commenced at the superstructure of the building, instead of the foundation—at the top instead of the bottom. We should first be mechanics and common tradesmen, and professions as a matter of course would grow out of the wealth made thereby. Young men and women, must now prepare for usefulness—the day of our Elevation is at hand—all the world now gazes at us—and Central and South America, and the West Indies, bid us come and be men and women, protected, secure, beloved and Free.

The branches of Education most desirable for the preparation of youth, for practical useful every-day life, are Arithmetic and good Penmanship, in order to be Accountants; and a good rudimental knowledge of Geography—which has ever been neglected, and underestimated—and of Political Economy; which without the knowledge of the first, no people can ever become adventurous—nor of the second, never will be an enterprising people. Geography, teaches a knowledge of the world, and Political Economy, a knowledge of the wealth of nations; or how to make money. These are not abstruse sciences, or learning not easily acquired or understood; but simply, common School Primer learning, that every body may get. And, although it is the very Key to prosperity and success in common life, but few know anything about it. Unfortunately for our people, so soon as their children learn to read a Chapter in the New Testament, and scribble a miserable hand, they are pronounced to have "Learning enough"; and taken away from School, no use to themselves, nor community. This is apparent in our Public Meetings, and Official Church Meetings; of the great number of men present, there are but few capable of filling a Secretaryship. Some of the large cities may be an exception to this. Of the multitudes of Merchants, and Business men throughout this country, Europe, and the world, few are qualified, beyond the branches here laid down by us as necessary for business. What did John Jacob Astor, Stephen Girard, or do the millionaires and the greater part of the merchant princes, and mariners, know about Latin and Greek, and the Classics? Precious few of them know any thing. In proof of this, in 1841, during the

Administration of President Tyler, when the mutiny was detected on board of the American Man of War Brig Somers. the names of the Mutineers, were recorded by young S—a Midshipman in Greek. Captain Alexander Slidell McKenzie, Commanding, was unable to read them; and in his despatches to the Government, in justification of his policy in executing the criminals, said that he "discovered some curious characters which he was unable to read," &c.; showing thereby, that that high functionary, did not understand even the Greek Alphabet, which was only necessary, to have been able to read proper names written in Greek.

What we most need then, is a good business practical Education; because, the Classical and Professional education of so many of our young men, before their parents are able to support them, and community ready to patronize them, only serves to lull their energy, and cripple the otherwise, praiseworthy efforts they would make in life. A Classical education, is only suited to the wealthy, or those who have a prospect of gaining a livelihood by it. The writer does not wish to be understood, as underrating a Classical and Professional education; this is not his intention; he fully appreciates them, having had some such advantages himself; but he desires to give a proper guide, and put a check to the extravagant idea that is fast obtaining, among our people especially, that a Classical, or as it is named, a "finished education," is necessary to prepare one for usefulness in life. Let us have an education, that shall practically develop our thinking faculties and manhood; and then, and not until then, shall we be able to vie with our oppressors, go where we may. We as heretofore, have been on the extreme; either no qualification at all, or a Collegiate education. We jumped too far; taking a leap from the deepest abyss to the highest summit; rising from the ridiculous to the sublime; without medium or intermission.

Let our young women have an education; let their minds be well informed; well stored with useful information and practical proficiency, rather than the light superficial acquirements, popularly and fashionably called accomplishments. We desire accomplishments, but they must be useful.

Our females must be qualified, because they are to be the mothers of our children. As mothers are the first nurses and instructors of children; from them children consequently, get their first impressions, which being always the most lasting, should be the most correct. Raise the mothers above the level of degradation, and the offspring is elevated with them. In a word, instead of our young men, transcribing in their blank books, recipes for *Cooking;* we desire to see them making the transfer of *Invoices of Merchandise.* Come to our aid then; the *morning* of our *Redemption* from degradation, adorns the horizon.

In our selection of individuals, it will be observed, that we have confined ourself entirely to those who occupy or have occupied positions among the whites, consequently having a more general bearing as useful contributors to society at large. While we do not pretend to give all such worthy cases, we gave such as we possessed information of, and desire it to be understood, that a large number of our most intelligent and worthy men and women, have not been named, because from their more private position in community, it was foreign to the object and design of this work. If we have said aught to offend, "take the will for the deed," and be assured, that it was given with the purest of motives, and best intention, from a true-hearted man and brother; deeply lamenting the sad fate of his race in this country, and sincerely desiring the elevation of man, and submitted to the serious consideration of all, who favor the promotion of the cause of God and humanity.

XXIV. A Glance at Ourselves—Conclusion

With broken hopes—sad devastation; a race *resigned* to degradation! ...

If we did not love our race superior to others, we would not concern ourself about their degradation; for the greatest desire of our heart is, to see them stand on a level with the most elevated of mankind. No people are ever elevated above the condition of their *females;* hence, the condition of the mother determines the condition of the child. To know the position of a people, it is only necessary to know the *condition* of their females; and despite themselves, they cannot rise above their level. Then what is our condition? Our *best ladies* being washerwomen, chambermaids, children's traveling nurses, and common house servants, and menials, we are all a degraded, miserable people, inferior to any other people as a whole, on the face of the globe.

These great truths, however unpleasant, must be brought before the minds of our people in its true and proper light, as we have been too delicate about them, and too long concealed them for fear of giving offence. It would have been infinitely better for our race, if these facts had been presented before us half a century ago—we would have been now proportionably benefitted by it.

As an evidence of the degradation to which we have been reduced, we dare premise, that this chapter will give offence to many, very many, and why? Because they may say, "He dared to say that the occupation of a *servant* is a degradation." It is not necessarily degrading; it would not be, to one or a few people of a land; but a *whole race of servants* are a degradation to that people.

Efforts made by men of qualifications for the toiling and degraded millions among the whites, neither gives offence to that class, nor is it taken unkindly by them; but received with manifestations of gratitude; to know that they are thought to be, equally worthy of, and entitled to stand on a level with the elevated classes; and they have only got to be informed of the way to raise themselves, to make the effort and do so as far as they can. But how different with us. Speak of our position in society, and it at once gives insult. Though we are servants; among ourselves we claim to be *ladies* and *gentlemen*, equal in standing, and as the popular expression goes, "Just as good as any body"—and so believing, we make no efforts to raise above the common level of menials; because the *best* being in that capacity, all are content with the position. We cannot at the same time, be domestic and lady; servant and gentleman. We must be the one or the other. Sad, sad indeed, is the thought, that hangs drooping in our mind, when contemplating the picture drawn before us. Young men and women, "we write these things unto you, because ye are strong," because the writer, a few years ago, gave unpardonable offence to many of the young people of Philadelphia and other places, because he dared tell them, that he thought too much of them, to be content with seeing them the servants of other people. Surely, she

that could be the mistress, would not be the maid; neither would he that could be the master, be content with being the servant; then why be offended, when we point out to you, the way that leads from the menial to the mistress or the master. All this we seem to reject with fixed determination, repelling with anger, every effort on the part of our intelligent men and women to elevate us, with true Israelitish degradation, in reply to any suggestion or proposition that may be offered, "Who made thee a ruler and judge?"

The writer is no "Public Man," in the sense in which this is understood among our people, but simply an humble individual, endeavoring to seek a livelihood by a profession obtained entirely by his own efforts, without relatives and friends able to assist him; except such friends as he gained by the merit of his course and conduct, which he here gratefully acknowledges; and whatever he has accomplished, other young men may, by making corresponding efforts, also accomplish.

In our own country, the United States, there are *three million five hundred thousand slaves*; and we, the nominally free colored people, are *six hundred thousand* in number; estimating one-sixth to be men, we have *one hundred thousand* able bodied freemen, which will make a powerful auxiliary in any country to which we may become adopted—an ally not to be despised by any power on earth. We love our country, dearly love her, but she doesn't love us—she despises us, and bids us begone, driving us from her embraces; but we shall not go where she desires us; but when we do go, whatever love we have for her, we shall love the country none the less that receives us as her adopted children.

For the want of business habits and training, our energies have become paralyzed; our young men never think of business, any more than if they were so many bondmen, without the right to pursue any calling they may think most advisable. With our people in this country, dress and good appearances have been made the only test of gentleman and ladyship, and that vocation which offers the best opportunity to dress and appear well, has generally been preferred, however menial and degrading, by our young people, without even, in the majority of cases, an effort to do better; indeed, in many instances, refusing situations equally lucrative, and superior in position; but which would not allow as much display of dress and personal appearance. This, if we ever expect to rise, must be discarded from among us, and a high and respectable position assumed.

One of our great temporal curses is our consummate poverty. We are the poorest people, as a class, in the world of civilized mankind—abjectly, miserably poor, no one scarcely being able to assist the other. To this, of course, there are noble exceptions; but that which is common to, and the very process by which white men exist, and succeed in life, is unknown to colored men in general. In any and every considerable community may be found, some one of our white fellow-citizens, who is worth more than all the colored people in that community put together. We consequently have little or no efficiency. We must have means to be practically efficient in all the undertakings of life; and to obtain them, it is necessary that we should be engaged in lucrative pursuits, trades, and general business transactions. In order to be thus engaged, it is necessary that we should occupy positions that afford the facilities for such pursuits. To compete now with the mighty odds of wealth, social and religious preferences, and political influences of this country, at this advanced stage of its national existence, we never may expect. A new country, and new beginning, is the only true, rational, politic remedy for our disadvantageous position; and that country we have already pointed out, with triple golden advantages, all things considered, to that of any country to which it has been the province of man to embark.

Every other than we, have at various periods of necessity, been a migratory people; and all when oppressed, shown a greater abhorrence of oppression, if not a greater love of liberty, than we. We cling to our oppressors as the objects of our love. It is true that our enslaved brethren are here, and we have been led to believe that it is necessary for us to remain, on that account. Is it true, that all should remain in degradation, because a part are degraded? We believe no such thing. We believe it to be the duty of the Free, to elevate themselves in the most speedy and effective manner possible; as the redemption of the bondman depends entirely upon the elevation of the freeman; therefore, to elevate

the free colored people of America, anywhere upon this continent; forebodes the speedy redemption of the slaves. We shall hope to hear no more of so fallacious a doctrine—the necessity of the free remaining in degradation, for the sake of the oppressed. Let us apply, first, the lever to ourselves; and the force that elevates us to the position of manhoods considerations and honors, will cleft the manacle of every slave in the land.

When such great worth and talents—for want of a better sphere—of men like Rev. Jonathan Robinson, Robert Douglass, Frederick A. Hinton, and a hundred others that might be named, were permitted to expire in a barber-shop; and such living men as may be found in Boston, New York, Philadelphia, Baltimore, Richmond, Washington City, Charleston (S.C.), New Orleans, Cincinnati, Louisville, St, Louis, Pittsburg, Buffalo, Rochester, Albany, Utica, Cleveland, Detroit, Milwaukee, Chicago, Columbus, Zanesville, Wheeling, and a hundred other places, confining themselves to barber-shops and waiterships in Hotels; certainly the necessity of such a course as we have pointed out, must be cordially acknowledged; appreciated by every brother and sister of oppression; and not rejected as heretofore, as though they preferred inferiority to equality. These minds must become "unfettered," and have "space to rise." This cannot be in their present positions. A continuance in any position, becomes what is termed "Second Nature"; it begets an *adaptation*, and *reconciliation* of *mind* to such condition. It changes the whole physiological condition of the system, and adapts man and woman to a higher or lower sphere in the pursuits of life. The offsprings of slaves and peasantry, have the general characteristics of their parents; and nothing but a different course of training and education, will change the character.

The slave may become a lover of his master, and learn to forgive him for continual deeds of maltreatment and abuse; just as the Spaniel would couch and fondle at the feet that kick him; because he has been taught to reverence them, and consequently, becomes adapted in body and mind to his condition. Even the shrubbery-loving Canary, and lofty-soaring Eagle, may be tamed to the cage, and learn to love it from habit of confinement. It has been so with us in our position among our oppressors; we have been so prone to such positions, that we have learned to love them. When reflecting upon this all important, and to us, all absorbing subject; we feel in the agony and anxiety of the moment, as though we could cry out in the langauge of a Prophet of old: "Oh that my head were waters, and mine eyes a fountain of tears, that I might weep day and night for the" degradation "of my people! Oh that I had in the wilderness a lodging place of wayfaring men; that I might leave my people, and go from them!"

The Irishman and German in the United States, are very different persons to what they were when in Ireland and Germany, the countries of their nativity. There their spirits were depressed and downcast; but the instant they set their foot upon unrestricted soil; free to act and untrammelled to move; their physical condition undergoes a change, which in time becomes physiological, which is transmitted to the offspring, who when born under such circumstances, is a decidedly different being to what it would have been, had it been born under different circumstances.

A child born under oppression, has all the elements of servility in its constitution; who when bom under favorable circumstances, has to the contrary, all the elements of freedom and independence of feeling. Our children then, may not be expected, to maintain that position and manly bearing; born under the unfavorable circumstances with which we are surrounded in this country; that we so much desire. To use the language of the talented Mr. Whipper, "they cannot be raised in this country, without being stoop shouldered." Heaven's pathway stands unobstructed, which will lead us into a Paradise of bliss. Let us go on and possess the land, and the God of Israel will be our God.

The lessons of every school book, the pages of every history, and columns of every newspaper, are so replete with stimuli to nerve us on to manly aspirations, that those of our young people, who will now refuse to enter upon this great theatre of Polynesian adventure, and take their position on the stage of Central and South America, where a brilliant engagement, of certain and most triumphant success, in the drama of human equality awaits them; then, with the blood of *slaves*, write upon the lintel of every door in sterling Capitals, to be gazed and hissed at by every passer by—

> Doomed by the Creator
> To servility and degradation;
> The SERVANT of the *white man*,
> And despised of every nation!

GLOSSARY

elective franchise: the right to vote

Frederick A. Hinton: the African American proprietor of the Gentleman's Dressing Room in Philadelphia

Israelitish: referring to the people of ancient Israel; Hebrew; Jewish

John Jacob Astor: the nation's first multimillionaire businessman

Jonathan Robinson: a black abolitionist about whom little is known

Mr. Whipper: William Whipper of Pennsylvania, one of the wealthiest African Americans at the time and the leader of the American Moral Reform Society

mutiny: a reference to the "*Somers*' affair," an alleged mutiny aboard the naval ship in 1842, the only shipboard mutiny in American naval history that led to executions of the perpetrators

Robert Douglass: a well-to-do African American barber in Philadelphia

Stephen Girard: a French-born American banker and among the wealthiest Americans at the time

Document Analysis

Delany opens the chapter "Means of Elevation" by questioning "moral theories" as a means of racial empowerment and concentrates his attention on business and social policies. He launches into a discussion about how blacks have become dependent upon the skill of whites. He notes the social circumstance whereby free blacks often function primarily in service-oriented capacities toward whites, such that the latter benefit exclusively and the former remain dependent. He notes his belief that African Americans do not deserve any form of sympathy as long as they refuse to take advice concerning their present dismal condition.

In the fifth paragraph, Delany begins by offering a powerful commentary stating that "white men are producers" and blacks "are consumers," providing several examples. His wake-up call to black America includes a serious indictment of their seeming complacency. It is not enough for black people to be aware of the conditions of their race but only talk about the problems and never do anything to confront or change the conditions themselves. He goes so far as to state that he and many others are weary of this strictly discursive approach.

Delany ends this section with a resounding appeal to embolden the black self, stating that the approach he is outlining represents the only sure means of elevating the race, be it in the United States or in any other country where blacks would settle. He draws out the falsity of the northern black notion of superiority over southern blacks. Delany essentially concludes that African Americans, regardless of where they reside or any small measures of difference in their conditions, share the same experience as an oppressed cultural group in the United States.

In Chapter VI, "The United States Our Country," Delany explains that the United States functions as the common country of every African American. This relates to matters of birth, education, and familial and community relations as well as death and burial, all of which contribute to a common experience familiar to most African Americans. Delany affirms the American birthright of African Americans, relating their rights of citizenship as natural rights that though repeatedly denied "never can be annulled."

"Things as They Are" cites the inability of African Americans to think for themselves as a collective, without a supposed spokesperson speaking for them and telling them what to think. He notes that black inferiority is assumed by many, whereas any ordinary white American gains instant credibility, even reverence, for no other reason than whiteness and its associated privileges and perceived superiority, among blacks as well as whites.

Delany condemns the idea that African Americans should simply follow the path to equality proposed by friends of the race. He doubts that there is any sort of hope among blacks for equality on the horizon. With respect to voting, Delany laments the present circumstance in which some African Americans have the "elective franchise" but cannot run for office, such that they can vote only for whites.

In contrast to the constrained and limited opportunities available to blacks in America and even Liberia, Delany offers alternatives for African Americans in places like Mexico, Central America, the West Indies, and South America. He places a high premium on the education and training African American men and women need in order to take advantage of these opportunities. While acknowledging the importance of a classical or "finished education," Delany bluntly states that "a good business practical Education" is what is most needed for the race.

Delany advocates that young black women receive an education that will provide them with information that is useful and has practical applications and offers a more far-reaching educational philosophy for women than was generally supported during his era in many quarters of the United States.

In Chapter XXIV, "A Glance at Ourselves—Conclusion," Delany returns to the reasons for his black nationalist position. He appeals to race loyalty and love of race as reasons for his insistent urging of emigration for African Americans. He argues that the black race cannot rise any higher than the position and condition of black women. He argues that with black women being subjected persistently to degrading and menial jobs, the entire black race is disgraced across the globe.

Delany positions himself as a humble person who has worked hard to obtain what he has in life, stating that other young men can achieve the same. He cites "consummate poverty" as "one of our great temporal curses." Considering the odds against African Americans in a wide variety of spheres, as demonstrated by their lagging significantly behind white Americans in terms of social, religious, economic, and political indicators and circumstances, Delany suggests that the best option for many—perhaps even for the entire class of free blacks—would be to start fresh in a new country.

Delany concludes by addressing certain concerns and objections to the project of emigration. Among them he cites blacks' attachment to whites as objects of love and admiration along with reluctance to leave loved ones behind. Dismissing those claims and others, Delany argues that free African Americans have a duty to elevate themselves, as the freedom of those enslaved is tied to those who are free and make the most of their freedom.

Essential Themes

Overall, *The Condition, Elevation, Emigration, and Destiny of the Colored People of the United States* has three significant aspects: It provides a unique report on the successes and achievements of black men and women in the United States, a severe indictment of abolitionists for what Delany believed to be a serious lack of consistent effort in fighting for the rights of blacks and gaining for them full integration into American society, and advocacy of emigration as a solution to racial discrimination. Of paramount importance in this book is one of the most compelling concepts to capture the essence of black nationalist philosophy, as coined by Delany—the idea of a nation within a nation. With this key idea, Delany instituted a conceptualization of African America that stands to this very day, having been adopted in various contexts by a num-ber of scholars and race leaders, including E. Franklin Frazier, W. E. B. Du Bois, Albert B. Cleage, Jr., and Darlene Clark Hine.

———Zachery Williams, PhD

Bibliography and Additional Reading

Adeleke, Tunde. "Martin R. Delany's Philosophy of Education: A Neglected Aspect of African American Liberation Thought." *Journal of Negro Education* 63, no. 2 (Spring 1994): 221–236.

Shelby, Tommie. "Two Conceptions of Black Nationalism: Martin Delany on the Meaning of Black Political Solidarity." *Political Theory* 31, no. 5 (October 2003): 664–692.

Adeleke, Tunde. *Without Regard to Race: The Other Martin Robison Delany*. Jackson: University Press of Mississippi, 2003.

Griffith, Cyril E. *The African Dream: Martin R. Delany and the Emergence of Pan-African Thought*. University Park: Pennsylvania State University Press, 1975.

Levine, Robert S., ed. *Martin R. Delany: A Documentary Reader*. Chapel Hill: University of North Carolina Press, 2003.

Sterling, Dorothy. *The Making of an Afro-American: Martin Robison Delany, 1812–1885*. New York: Da Capo Press, 1996.

■ *Twelve Years a Slave: Narrative of Solomon Northup*

Date: 1853
Author: Solomon Northup
Genre: Book

Summary Overview

Solomon Northup's *Twelve Years a Slave*, published in 1853, stands out as an important piece of literature about slavery because it is written from the perspective of a free man who was captured and forced into bondage and who wrote in great detail about this experience after his release twelve years later. Northup's insights into the workings of the southern slave system reveal the spiritual and physical torment slaves endured. Northup's powerful language describing his capture, his life as a slave, and then his release helps explain why *Twelve Years a Slave* became one of the fastest-selling and most popular narratives of the nineteenth century. Although the authenticity and reliability of slave narratives have been frequently challenged, such narratives are recognized as essential sources for the study of American slavery in the antebellum South.

Prior to Solomon Northup's capture in 1841 at the age of thirty-three, he led a relatively quiet life as a free black man in Saratoga Springs, New York. To care for his wife and three children, he worked in a variety of jobs in agriculture, lumbering, and hotel services. He also used his talent for the violin to earn money throughout his life. In 1841 he met two white men, who overheard him playing the violin and offered to travel with him to New York and later Washington, D.C., where they assured him that he would be able to earn money playing music for a traveling circus. Believing that he would be gone only a short while, Northup did not notify his family. Little did he know that this trip, which would end with his enslavement, would be the beginning of the twelve most difficult years of his life.

Defining Moment

The decades before the American Civil War were rife with conflict as sectional discord gripped the nation. Debates over the extension of slavery into newly acquired territory divided the country and would culminate in the secession of the southern states and the war. One development during the 1850s was a new and harsher federal measure called the Fugitive Slave Act, which required federal authorities in the northern states to assist southern slave catchers in returning runaway slaves to their owners. Many northern states responded by enacting personal liberty laws that increased the legal rights of accused fugitives. However, these laws were overturned by the U.S. Supreme Court based on the constitutional premise that federal laws took supremacy over state laws.

While lawmakers and justices debated and decided the fate of slavery and slaves, many individuals embarked on campaigns of their own. Frederick Douglass became one of the most powerful abolitionists and orators of the nineteenth century as he spoke out against the evils of slavery. After spending twenty years in bondage, Douglass published his autobiography, the *Narrative of the Life of Frederick Douglass* (1845), and created an antislavery newspaper titled the *North Star*. Harriet Beecher Stowe's *Uncle Tom's Cabin*, published in 1852, fanned opposition to the Fugitive Slave Act with a graphic story of slavery that evoked empathy and outrage throughout the North.

It was in this context that the story of Solomon Northup unfolded. When he was kidnapped in 1841, Northup was unaware that his twelve-year episode would coincide with an escalation of sectional discord that would tear the nation apart eight years after his release and the publication of his narrative in 1853.

Author Biography

Solomon Northup was born into a free black family in Minerva, New York, in 1808. Northup spent many of his leisure hours playing the violin, which gave him amusement and served as consolation for the limited possibilities for blacks to advance in nineteenth-century America.

In 1829, Solomon Northup married Anne Hampton, a mixed-race woman. Northup purchased part of a farm, which he diligently worked for many years, but he was never satisfied with the income produced by agriculture. During the winters he and his family lived in a variety of hotels, where he worked as a carriage driver and relied upon his violin for additional earnings. In March 1841, he accepted an offer that would result in the loss of his freedom for the next twelve years.

SOLOMON IN HIS PLANTATION SUIT.

While he was working in Saratoga Springs, New York, Northup was approached by two white men, Merrill Brown and Abram Hamilton, who offered him a job playing violin for a circus, which was located in Washington, D.C. Northup accepted the offer and first traveled to New York City, where his soon-to-be captors suggested he acquire papers declaring his status as a free black citizen of New York, since he would be traveling to Washington, D.C., where slavery was legal. Believing they were protecting his freedom and looking out for his best interests, Northup cooperated with Brown and Hamilton and even enjoyed their polite company.

When the three men arrived in Washington, D.C., in April 1841, the decision was made to attend the funeral procession of President William Henry Harrison. That afternoon, the three spent time in a local saloon, which is where Northup believed he was drugged with laudanum. He passed out that evening; when he awoke a few days later, he found himself in chains in a prison cell, having been robbed of his documents, money, and ultimately his freedom. He remained a slave until January 4, 1853. Later, with the help of David Wilson, a local lawyer and legislator, he wrote his narrative so that readers could come to their own conclusions about slavery.

HISTORICAL DOCUMENT

Chapter VI.

The very amiable, pious-hearted Mr. Theophilus Freeman, partner or consignee of James H. Burch, and keeper of the slave pen in New-Orleans, was out among his animals early in the morning. With an occasional kick of the older men and women, and many a sharp crack of the whip about the ears of the younger slaves, it was not long before they were all astir, and wide awake. Mr. Theophilus Freeman bustled about in a very industrious manner, getting his property ready for the sales-room, intending, no doubt, to do that day a rousing business.

In the first place we were required to wash thoroughly, and those with beards, to shave. We were then furnished with a new suit each, cheap, but clean. The men had hat, coat, shirt, pants and shoes; the women frocks of calico, and handkerchiefs to bind about their heads. We were now conducted into a large room in the front part of the building to which the yard was attached, in order to be properly trained, before the admission of customers. The men were arranged on one side of the room, the women on the other. The tallest was placed at the head of the row, then the next tallest, and so on in the order of their respective heights. Emily was at the foot of the line of women.

Freeman charged us to remember our places; exhorted us to appear smart and lively,—sometimes threatening, and again, holding out various inducements. During the day he exercised us in the art of "looking smart," and of moving to our places with exact precision.

After being fed, in the afternoon, we were again paraded and made to dance. Bob, a colored boy, who had some time belonged to Freeman, played on the violin. Standing near him, I made bold to inquire if he could play the "Virginia Reel." He answered he could not, and asked me if I could play. Replying in the affirmative, he handed me the violin. I struck up a tune, and finished it. Freeman ordered me to continue playing, and seemed well pleased, telling Bob that I far excelled him—a remark that seemed to grieve my musical companion very much.

Next day many customers called to examine Freeman's "new lot." The latter gentleman was very loquacious, dwelling at much length upon our several good points and qualities. He would make us hold up our heads, walk briskly back and forth, while customers would feel of our hands and arms and bodies, turn us about, ask us what we could do, make us open our mouths and show our teeth, precisely as a jockey examines a horse which he is about to barter for or purchase. Sometimes a man or woman was taken back to the small house in the yard, stripped, and inspected more minutely. Scars upon a slave's back were considered evidence of a rebellious or unruly spirit, and hurt his sale.

One old gentleman, who said he wanted a coachman, appeared to take a fancy to me. From his conversation with Burch, I learned he was a resident in the city. I very much desired that he would buy me, because I conceived it would not be difficult to make my escape from New-Orleans on some northern vessel. Freeman asked him fifteen hundred dollars for me. The old gentleman insisted it was too much, as times were very hard. Freeman, however, declared that I was sound and healthy, of a good constitution, and intelligent. He made it a point to enlarge upon my musical attainments. The old gentleman argued quite adroitly that there was nothing extraordinary about the nigger, and finally, to my regret, went out, saying he would call again. During the day, however, a number of sales were made. David and Caroline were purchased together by a Natchez planter. They left us, grinning broadly, and in the most happy state of mind, caused by the fact of their not being separated. Lethe was sold to a planter of Baton Rouge, her eyes flashing with anger as she was led away.

The same man also purchased Randall. The little fellow was made to jump, and run across the floor, and perform many other feats, exhibiting his activity and condition. All the time the trade was going on, Eliza was crying aloud, and wringing her hands. She besought the man not to buy him, unless he also bought her self and Emily. She promised, in that case, to be the most faithful slave that ever lived. The man answered that he could not afford it, and then Eliza burst into a paroxysm of grief, weeping plaintively. Freeman turned round to her, savagely, with his whip in his uplifted hand, ordering her to stop her noise, or he would flog her. He would not have such work—such snivelling; and unless she ceased that minute, he would take her to the yard and give her a hundred lashes. Yes, he would take the nonsense out of her pretty quick—if he didn't, might he be dead. Eliza shrunk before him, and tried to wipe away her tears, but it was all in vain. She wanted to be with her children, she said, the little time she had to live. All the frowns and threats of Freeman, could not wholly silence the afflicted mother. She kept on begging and beseeching them, most piteously not to separate the three. Over and over again she told them how she loved her boy. A great many times she repeated her former promises—how very faithful and obedient she would be; how hard she would labor day and night, to the last

moment of her life, if he would only buy them all together. But it was of no avail; the man could not afford it. The bargain was agreed upon, and Randall must go alone. Then Eliza ran to him; embraced him passionately; kissed him again and again; told him to remember her—all the while her tears falling in the boy's face like rain.

Freeman damned her, calling her a blubbering, bawling wench, and ordered her to go to her place, and behave herself; and be somebody. He swore he wouldn't stand such stuff but a little longer. He would soon give her something to cry about, if she was not mighty careful, and that she might depend upon.

The planter from Baton Rouge, with his new purchases, was ready to depart.

"Don't cry, mama. I will be a good boy. Don't cry," said Randall, looking back, as they passed out of the door.

What has become of the lad, God knows. It was a mournful scene indeed. I would have cried myself if I had dared.

That night, nearly all who came in on the brig Orleans, were taken ill. They complained of violent pain in the head and back. Little Emily—a thing unusual with her—cried constantly. In the morning, a physician was called in, but was unable to determine the nature of our complaint. While examining me, and asking questions touching my symptoms, I gave it as my opinion that it was an attack of smallpox—mentioning the fact of Robert's death as the reason of my belief. It might be so indeed, he thought, and he would send for the head physician of the hospital. Shortly, the head physician came—a small, light-haired man, whom they called Dr. Carr. He pronounced it small-pox, whereupon there was much alarm throughout the yard. Soon after Dr. Carr left, Eliza, Emmy, Harry and myself were put into a hack and driven to the hospital a large white marble building, standing on the outskirts of the city. Harry and I were placed in a room in one of the upper stories. I became very sick. For three days I was entirely blind. While lying in this state one day, Bob came in, saying to Dr. Carr that Freeman had sent him over to inquire how we were getting on. Tell him, said the doctor, that Platt is very bad, but that if he survives until nine o'clock, he may recover.

I expected to die. Though there was little in the prospect before me worth living for, the near approach of death appalled me. I thought I could have been resigned to yield up my life in the bosom of my family, but to expire in the midst of strangers, under such circumstances, was a bitter reflection.

There were a great number in the hospital, of both sexes, and of all ages. In the rear of the building coffins were manufactured. When one died, the bell tolled—a signal to the undertaker to come and bear away the body to the potter's field. Many times, each day and night, the tolling bell sent forth its melancholy voice, announcing another death. But my time had not yet come. The crisis having passed, I began to revive, and at the end of two weeks and two days, returned with Harry to the pen, bearing upon my face the effects of the malady, which to this day continues to disfigure it. Eliza and Emily were also brought back next day in a hack, and again were we paraded in the sales-room, for the inspection and examination of purchasers. I still indulged the hope that the old gentleman in search of a coachman would call again, as he had promised, and purchase me. In that event I felt an abiding confidence that I would soon regain my liberty. Customer after customer entered, but the old gentleman never made his appearance.

At length, one day, while we were in the yard, Freeman came out and ordered us to our places, in the great room. A gentleman was waiting for us as we entered, and inasmuch as he will be often mentioned in the progress of this narrative, a description of his personal appearance, and my estimation of his character, at first sight, may not be out of place.

He was a man above the ordinary height, somewhat bent and stooping forward. He was a good-looking man, and appeared to have reached about the middle age of life. There was nothing repulsive in his presence; but on the other hand, there was something cheerful and attractive in his face, and in his tone of voice. The finer elements were all kindly mingled in his breast, as any one could see. He moved about among us, asking many questions, as to what we could do, and what labor we had been accustomed to; if we thought we would like to live with him, and would be good boys if he would buy us, and other interrogatories of like character.

After some further inspection, and conversation touching prices, he finally offered Freeman one thousand dollars for me, nine hundred for Harry, and seven hundred for Eliza. Whether the small-pox had depreciated our value, or from what cause Freeman had concluded to fall five hundred dollars from the price I was before held at, I cannot say. At any rate, after a little shrewd reflection, he announced his acceptance of the offer.

As soon as Eliza heard it, she was in an agony again. By this time she had become haggard and hollow-eyed with sickness and with sorrow. It would be a relief if I could consistently pass over in silence the scene that now ensued. It recalls memories more mournful and affecting than any language can portray. I have seen mothers kissing for the last time the faces of their dead offspring; I have seen them looking down into the grave, as the earth fell with a dull sound upon their coffins, hiding them from their eyes forever; but never have I seen such an exhibition of intense, unmeasured, and unbounded grief, as when Eliza was parted from her child. She broke from her place in the line of women, and rushing down where Emily was standing, caught her in her arms. The child, sensible of some impending danger, instinctively fastened her hands around her mother's neck, and nestled her little head upon her bosom. Freeman sternly ordered her to be quiet, but she did not heed him. He caught her by the arm and pulled her rudely, but she only clung the closer to the child. Then, with a volley of great oaths, he struck her such a heartless blow, that she staggered backward, and was like to fall. Oh! how piteously then did she beseech and beg and pray that they might not be separated. Why could they not be purchased together? Why not let her have one of her dear children? "Mercy, mercy, master!" she cried, falling on her knees. "Please, master, buy Emily. I can never work any if she is taken from me: I will die."

Freeman interfered again, but, disregarding him, she still plead most earnestly, telling how Randall had been taken from her—how she never him see him again, and now it was too bad—oh, God! it was too bad, too cruel, to take her away from Emily—her pride—her only darling, that could not live, it was so young, without its mother!

Finally, after much more of supplication, the purchaser of Eliza stepped forward, evidently affected, and said to Freeman he would buy Emily, and asked him what her price was.

"What is her *price*? *Buy* her?" was the responsive interrogatory of Theophilus Freeman. And instantly answering his own inquiry, he added, "I won't sell her. She's not for sale."

The man remarked he was not in need of one so young—that it would be of no profit to him, but since the mother was so fond of her, rather than see them separated, he would pay a reasonable price. But to this humane proposal Freeman was entirely deaf. He would not sell her then on any account whatever. There were heaps and piles of money to be made of her, he said, when she was a few years older. There were men enough in New-Orleans who would give five thousand dollars for such an extra, handsome, fancy piece as Emily would be, rather than not get her. No, no, he would not sell her then. She was a beauty—a picture—a doll—one of the regular bloods—none of your thick-lipped, bullet-headed, cotton-picking niggers—if she was might he be d—d.

When Eliza heard Freeman's determination not to part with Emily, she became absolutely frantic.

"I will *not* go without her. They shall *not* take her from me," she fairly shrieked, her shrieks commingling with the loud and angry voice of Freeman, commanding her to be silent.

Meantime Harry and myself had been to the yard and returned with our blankets, and were at the front door ready to leave. Our purchaser stood near us, gazing at Eliza with an expression indicative of regret at having bought her at the expense of so much sorrow. We waited some time, when, finally, Freeman, out of patience, tore Emily from her mother by main force, the two clinging to each other with all their might.

"Don't leave me, mama—don't leave me," screamed the child, as its mother was pushed harshly forward; "Don't leave me—come back, mama," she still cried, stretching forth her little arms imploringly. But she cried in vain. Out of the door and into the street we were quickly hurried. Still we could hear her calling to her mother, "Come back—don't leave me—come back, mama," until her infant voice grew faint and still more faint, and gradually died away as distance intervened, and finally was wholly lost.

Eliza never after saw or heard of Emily or Randall. Day nor night, however, were they ever absent from her memory. In the cotton field, in the cabin, always and everywhere, she was talking of them—often *to* them, as if they were actually present. Only when absorbed in that illusion, or asleep, did she ever have a moment's comfort afterwards.

She was no common slave, as has been said. To a large share of natural intelligence which she possessed, was added a general knowledge and information on most subjects. She had enjoyed opportunities such as are afforded to very few of her oppressed class. She had been lifted up into the regions of a higher life. Freedom—freedom for herself and for her offspring, for many years had been her cloud by day, her pillar of fire by night. In her pilgrimage through the wilderness of bondage, with eyes fixed upon that hope-inspiring beacon, she had at length ascended to "the top of Pisgah," and beheld "the land of promise." In an unexpected moment she was utterly overwhelmed with disappointment and despair. The glorious vision of liberty faded from her sight as they led her away into captivity. Now "she weepeth sore in the night, and tears are on her cheeks: all her friends have dealt treacherously with her: they have become her enemies."

GLOSSARY

Pisgah: In the Christian Old Testament book of Deuteronomy, the name of a mountain in Palestine, probably Mount Nebo, from which Moses looks out over the "land of promise"

potter's field: a burial place for criminals, paupers, and indigent people

"she weepeth sore in the night ...": from the Christian Old Testament book of Lamentations, chapter 1, verse 2

Document Analysis

Chapter VI in *Twelve Years a Slave* discusses Northup's experience in going from a slave pen to a slave auction after his kidnapping in Washington, D.C. In the opening paragraph, Northup introduces the reader to Mr. Theophilus Freeman, a partner of James H. Burch and keeper of the slave pen in New Orleans. Burch was the slave dealer who bought Northup in Washington, D.C., destroyed his freedom papers, and beat him when he insisted that he was a free man. Burch was also responsible for assigning him his new name, Platt, along with the story that he was an escaped slave from Georgia.

In the first paragraph of chapter VI, Northup begins with a description of Freeman as amiable and pious-hearted, but he continues with zoo imagery, where Freeman goes "out among his animals" and proceeds to beat them into submission to prepare them to be sold. Northup seems careful to describe the people he encounters. He gives them the benefit of the doubt, by offering both positive and negative descriptions of their behavior toward him and others.

In the third paragraph, Northup describes how he and the rest of those captive in the slave pen are paraded out to impress future owners. He explains how Freeman discovers that Northup can play the violin and then orders him to play so the others might dance. Earlier in the narrative, Northup had described his love for the violin, which he had played since his youth, as a source of amusement, consolation, and income. Now his musical talent is being exploited as part of his own degradation. In later chapters of the narrative, he would explain that once he had settled on the Louisiana plantation, his talent gained him a degree of mobility when he played for dances at neighboring plantations.

In the fourth and fifth paragraphs, Northup portrays the dehumanizing treatment of slaves in the pen and what it felt like to be bartered as someone's property. He describes in detail how they were examined, some of them right down to their naked bodies, and how slave buyers would look for scars on slaves' bodies as a way to gauge their level of rebelliousness. When a gentleman begins bargaining with Freeman, it becomes clear that the more Freeman emphasizes Northup's talents, the higher the price will be for his sale.

The importance of family becomes evident in Northup's description of a mother's response to her children's sale. In the sixth paragraph, we are reintroduced to two children, Randall and Emily, and their mother, Eliza, who are waiting with Northup to be purchased by southern plantation owners. Despite her pleading, Freeman refuses to accommodate her, and Randall is sold off separately. Later, in paragraph 17, with the prospect of the sale of Eliza without Emily, Eliza's "intense, unmeasured, and unbounded grief" causes her to attempt to physically prevent the sale. This action results in Freeman's inflicting "a heartless blow" to Eliza. When the prospective owner agrees to purchase Emily also to keep the family together, Freeman, realizing the desirability of Emily and believing that he could receive more money for Emily, refuses to sell the child. Eliza is sold off, never again to hear from either of her children. Northup's detail in describing Eliza's grief and his depiction of her as "no common slave" with her "natural intelligence" helps the reader understand how powerless slaves were even to protect their young children. In the last paragraph of this chapter, Northup connects lack of freedom with a total loss of hope. Eliza stands for all slave mothers who watched their future generations descend into slavery.

From the moment he realizes he has been kidnapped, Northup understands that survival will be his main concern. In the middle of this chapter, in paragraph 12, he describes his bout with smallpox. Brought to a hospital to receive care, his fear was "to expire in the midst of strangers," but he thought that he "could have been resigned to yield up [his] life in the bosom of [his] family." He dwells on the number of coffins being hauled away to the potters' field, never to be mourned by their loved ones.

Most authors of slave narratives describe religious beliefs, frequently as part of their search for spiritual guidance. Northup accepts religious gospel yet sees the hypocrisy of such gospel being spread by the slaveholders of the Deep South. He feels that religion and freedom go hand in hand and speaks about this topic regularly among his fellow slaves.

Essential Themes

Northup wrote *Twelve Years* to inform the general public about the tragic intricacies of slavery. Northup writes that he wanted to repeat the story of his life so that others could determine whether this "peculiar institution" of slavery should be allowed to continue. Because of his frustration over the eventual release of his captors, he also probably wanted other citizens of the United States to see the injustice in criminal proceedings that involved the rights of free blacks and slaves. His story illustrates quite clearly that the lines between free and slave states were not as clearly defined as most Americans would like to believe. In the wake of the new, stronger Fugitive Slave Act, even those of African descent who had been born free in a state where slavery was banned could be subject to the indignities and loss of liberty that slavery entailed. Slavery, Northup's narrative seems to suggest, cannot simply exist in one place and not another: it was insidious, devious, and would rob even the free of their liberty if given the chance.

Coming on the heels of *Uncle Tom's Cabin* during the "Decade of Crisis" before the Civil War, Northup's slave narrative added more controversy to the disputes between the North and the South. Whereas earlier authors moderated their stories about slavery to gain credibility with white audiences, Northup provided his readers with the honest and open truth about the horrors of slavery. It is easy to understand its popularity in this context.

——*Wendy Thowdis, MA*

Bibliography and Additional Reading

Corrigan, Mary Beth. "Imaginary Cruelties? A History of the Slave Trade in Washington, D.C." *Washington History* 13, no. 2 (Fall/Winter 2001–2002): 4–27.

Nichols, William W. "Slave Narratives: Dismissed Evidence in the Writing of Southern History." *Phylon* 32, no. 4 (1971): 403–409.

Worley, Sam. "Solomon Northup and the Sly Philosophy of the Slave Pen." *Callaloo* 20, no. 1 (Winter 1997): 243–259.

Davis, Charles Twitchell, and Henry Louis Gates. *The Slave's Narrative.* New York. Oxford University Press, 1985.

"A Kidnapped Negro's Wife Petitions for His Freedom, 1852." In *A Documentary History of the Negro People in the United States*, ed. Herbert Aptheker. New York: Citadel Press, 1969.

Osofsky, Gilbert, ed. *Puttin' on Ole Massa: The Slave Narratives of Henry Bibb, William Wells Brown, and Solomon Northup.* New York: Harper & Row, 1969.

■ Provisional Constitution and Ordinances for the People of the United States

Date: 1858
Author: John Brown
Genre: Formal document

Summary Overview

In 1858, when John Brown developed this "Provisional Constitution and Ordinances for the People of the United States," he was already notorious for his and his family's violent actions against pro-slavery forces in "Bleeding Kansas." His doomed attempt to seize the federal arsenal at Harper's Ferry in Virginia, an event that would lead to his arrest, trial, and execution, was still in the future. As he and his followers thought about ways to cleanse the United States of the evil of slavery, Brown made plans for a new system of government that he and his associates would implement when they began to liberate slave territory in the southern states.

This constitution, with a government modeled in many ways on that of the United States, would be a strange curiosity for future historians. During Brown's trial following his failed Harper's Ferry raid, one of his attorneys sought to use the "constitution" as proof that Brown was insane and, thus, not culpable for his allegedly treasonous actions. Brown forbade this line of defense, however. The "provisional constitution" was dismissed by his defense lawyers as insignificant part of Brown's plan; a system for organizing his followers rather than something larger. Because this argument was the one that emerged at the trial, legal scholar Robert L. Tsai argues "the literature depicts him as a terrorist or folk hero, martyr or madman—but rarely as a would-be statesman or founder." The constitution, Tsai argues, gives us a broader view of Brown as an aspiring political leader rather than simply a violent radical.

Defining Moment

Even setting aide the violent activities of militant radicals such as John Brown, the question of slavery's place in the United States was threatening to tear the nation apart in the late 1850s. In southern states, abolitionist publications from the north had been suppressed and often destroyed if found. In May, 1856, a South Carolina Congressman, Preston Brooks, severely beat Massachusetts Senator Charles Sumner in response to an anti-slavery speech Sumner had given. Even after fight-

ing in Kansas abated, controversy over the territory's application for statehood, which attempted to keep Kansas open to slavery while banning new slaves, angered those who saw this as a subversion of the will of the territory's anti-slave majority. But perhaps the most telling incident that informed Brown's provisional constitution and his plans to create a homeland for liberated slaves was the 1857 court case *Dred Scott vs. Sandford*, which Brown refers to in the preamble of the document. In their decision on this case, the court—dominated by pro-slavery southerners, including Chief Justice Roger Taney who wrote the decision—determined that people of African descent were not citizens of the United States and were not intended to be by the framers of the Constitution.

After his activities in Kansas and in the wake of the Dred Scott decision, Brown continued to work against slavery, supporting fugitive slaves and beginning to plan a wide-scale liberation of southern states. On May 10, 1858, Brown and his followers called a "constitutional convention" in Chatam, Ontario. Here, Brown discussed his plans to establish a free settlement (possibly in Kansas). This is where the provisional constitution was presented and signed by the convention, which was made up of 34 black (many escaped slaves) and 12 whites.

Author Biography

John Brown was born in Connecticut in 1800, moving to Ohio in 1805. When he was 16, Brown moved away to school in Plainfield Massachusetts, and later continued his education in Connecticut. Failing to complete his education in ministry due to a lack of money, he retuned to Ohio, opening a tannery. He married, later fathering 11 children who lived past childhood. His business success was sporadic. He moved to Pennsylvania, then back to Ohio. In 1837, when abolitionist publisher Elijah Lovejoy was murdered, Brown declared that he would dedicate his life to ending slavery.

His business fortunes collapsed in 1839 and eventually he and a business partner moved to Springfield, Massachusetts. Brown became involved in the abolitionist movement in Springfield, seeing speakers such as Frederick Douglass and Sojourner Truth. After suffering more business reversals, Brown (along with his son-in-law) moved to the Kansas territory, where his adult sons and their families lived. In Kansas, Brown became involved in the violence between pro- and anti-slavery forces. In late May 1856, angered by the attack on the town of Lawrence, Brown and his abolitionist followers executed five pro-slavery activists near Pottawatamie Creek. In June, pro-slavery forces destroy the Brown's farm, captured two of Brown's sons. The violence continued throughout the summer, with Brown's son Frederick killed in August and Brown's brave defense of anti-slavery settlements was reported in papers throughout the nation.

After leaving Kansas, Brown traveled the United States and Canada, meeting with like-minded radicals and planning for the creation of a territory for liberated slaves. Brown and his closest associates, known as the Secret Six, developed a plan for fighting the slave establishment of the southern states. Eventually, these plans would culminate in Brown's 1859 raid on the federal arsenal at Harper's Ferry and ultimately, Brown's capture, trial, and execution.

HISTORICAL DOCUMENT

PREAMBLE

Whereas slavery, throughout its entire existence in the United States, is none other than a most barbarous, unprovoked, and unjustifiable war of one portion of its citizens upon another portion—the only conditions of which are perpetual imprisonment and hopeless servitude or absolute extermination—in utter disregard and violation of those eternal and self-evident truths set forth in our Declaration of Independence:

Therefore, we, citizens of the United States, and the oppressed people who, by a recent decision of the Supreme Court, are declared to have no rights which the white man is bound to respect, together with all other people degraded by the laws thereof, do, for the time being, ordain and establish for ourselves the following Provisional Constitution and Ordinances, the better to protect our persons, property, lives, and liberties, and to govern our actions

ARTICLE I

Qualifications for membership
All persons of mature age, whether proscribed, oppressed, and enslaved citizens, or of the proscribed and oppressed races of the United States, who shall agree to sustain and enforce the Provisional Constitution and Ordinances of this organization, together with all minor children of such persons, shall be held to be fully entitled to protection under the same.

ARTICLE II

Branches of government
The provisional government of this organization shall consist of three branches, viz: legislative, executive, and judicial.

ARTICLE III

Legislative
The legislative branch shall be a Congress or House of Representative, composed of not less than five nor more than ten members, who shall be elected by all citizens of mature age and of sound mind connected with this organization, and who shall remain in office for three years, unless sooner removed for misconduct, inability, or by death. A majority of such members shall constitute a quorum.

ARTICLE IV

Executive
The executive branch of this organization shall consist of a President and Vice-President, who shall be chosen by the citizens or members of this organization, and each of whom shall hold his office for

three years unless sooner removed by death or for inability or misconduct.

ARTICLE V

Judicial

The judicial branch of this organization shall consist of one Chief Justice of the Supreme Court and of four associate judges of said court, each constituting a circuit court. They shall each be chosen in the same manner as the President, and shall continue in office until their places have been filled in the same manner by election of the citizens. Said court shall have jurisdiction in all civil or criminal causes arising under this constitution, except breaches of the rules of war.

ARTICLE VI

Validity of enactments

All enactments of the legislative branch shall, to become valid during the first three years, have the approbation of the President and of the Commander-in-chief of the army.

ARTICLE VII

Commander-in-chief

A Commander-in-chief of the army shall be chosen by the President, Vice-President, a majority of the Provisional Congress, and of the Supreme Court, and he shall receive his commission from the President, signed by the Vice-President, the Chief Justice of the Supreme Court, and the Secretary of War, and he shall hold his office for three years, unless removed by death or on proof of incapacity or misbehavior. He shall, unless under arrest, (and until his place is actually filled as provided for by this constitution) direct all movements of the army and advise with any allies. He shall, however, be tried, removed, or punished, on complaint of the President, by at least three general officers, or a majority of the House of Representatives, or of the Supreme Court; which House of Representatives, (the President presiding) the Vice-President, and the members of the Supreme Court, shall constitute a

court-martial for his trial; with power to remove or punish, as the case may require, and to fill his place, as above provided.

ARTICLE VIII

Officers

A Treasurer, Secretary of State, Secretary of War, and Secretary of the Treasury, shall each be chosen, for the first three years, in the same way and manner as the Commander-in-chief, subject to trial or removal on complaint of the President, Vice-President, or Commander in-chief, to the Chief Justice of the Supreme Court, or on complaint of the majority of the members of said court or the Provisional Congress. The Supreme Court shall have power to try or punish either of those officers, and their places shall be filled as before.

ARTICLE IX

Secretary of War

The Secretary of War shall be under the immediate direction of the Commander-in-chief, who may temporarily fill his place in case of arrest or of any inability to serve.

ARTICLE X

Congress or House of Representatives

The House of Representatives shall make ordinances providing for the appointment (by the President or otherwise) of all civil officers, excepting those already named; and shall have power to make all laws and ordinances for the general good, not inconsistent with this Constitution and these ordinances.

ARTICLE XI

Appropriation of money, &c.

The Provisional Congress shall have power to appropriate money or other property actually in the hands of the treasurer, to any object calculated to promote the general good, so far as may be consistent with the provisions of this constitution; and may, in certain cases, appropriate for a moderate compensation of agents, or persons not members of this organization, for any important service they are known to have rendered.

ARTICLE XII

Special duties
It shall be the duty of Congress to provide for the instant removal of any civil officer or policeman, who becomes habitually intoxicated, or who is addicted to other immoral conduct, or to any neglect or unfaithfulness in the discharge of his official duties. Congress shall also be a Standing Committee of Safety, for the purpose of obtaining important information; and shall be in constant communication with the Commander-in-chief; the members of which shall each, as also the President, Vice-President, members of the Supreme Court, and Secretary of State, have full power to issue warrants, returnable as Congress shall ordain (naming witnesses, &c.) upon their own information, without the formality of a complaint. Complaint shall be immediately made after arrest, and before trial; the party arrested to be served with a copy at once.

ARTICLE XIII

Trial of President and Other Officers
The President and Vice-President may either of them be tried, removed, or punished, on complaint made to the Chief Justice of the Supreme Court, by a majority of the House of Representatives; which house together with the Associate Judges of the Supreme Court, the whole to be presided over by the Chief Justice in case of the trial of the Vice-President, shall have full power to try such officers, to remove or punish as the case may require, and to fill any vacancy so occurring, the same as in the case of the Commander-in-chief.

ARTICLE XIV

Trial of members of Congress
The members of the House of Representatives may, any and all of them, be tried, and, on conviction, removed or punished, on complaint before the Chief

Justice of the Supreme Court, made by any number of the members of said house exceeding one-third; which house, with the Vice-President and Associate Judges of the Supreme Court, shall constitute the proper tribunal with power to fill such vacancies.

ARTICLE XV

Impeachment of Judges
Any member of the Supreme Court may also be impeached, tried, convicted, or punished by removal or otherwise, Oil complaint to the President, who shall in such case, preside; the Vice-President, House of Representatives, and other members of the Supreme Court, constituting the proper tribunal, (with power to fill vacancies) on complaint of a majority of said House of Representatives, or of the Supreme Court; a majority of the whole having power to decide.

ARTICLE XVI

Duties of President and Secretary of State
The President, with the Secretary of State, shall, immediately upon entering on the duties of their office, give special attention to secure from amongst their own people, men of integrity, intelligence, and good business habits and capacity, and, above an, of first-rate moral and religious character and influence, to act as civil officers of every description and grade, as well as teachers, chaplains, physicians, surgeons, mechanics, agents of every description, clerks, and messengers. They shall make special efforts to induce, at the earliest possible period, persons and families of that description to locate themselves within the limits secured by this organization; and shall, moreover, from time to time, supply the names and residence of such persons to the Congress, for their special notice and information, as among the most important of their duties; and the President is hereby authorized and empowered to afford special aid to such individuals, from such moderate appropriations as the Congress shall be able and may deem advisable to make for that object. The President and Secretary of State, and in all cases of disagreement the Vice-President, shall

appoint all civil officers, but shall not have power to remove any officer. All removals shall be the result of a fair trial, whether civil or military.

ARTICLE XVII

Further duties

It shall be the duty of the President and Secretary of State to find out (as soon as possible) the real friends as well as enemies of this organization in every part of the country; to secure among them innkeepers, private postmasters, private mail contractors, messengers, and agents, through whom may be obtained correct and regular information constantly; recruits for the service, places of deposit and sale, together with all needed supplies; and it shall be matter of special regard to secure such facilities through the northern States.

ARTICLE XVII

Duty of the President

It shall be the duty of the President, as well as the House of Representatives, at all times, to inform the Commander-in-chief of any matter that may require his attention, or that may affect the public safety.

ARTICLE XIX

Duty of President, continued

It shall be the duty of the President to see that the provisional ordinances of this organization, and those made by the Congress, are promptly and faithfully executed; and he may, in cases of great urgency, call on the Commander-in-chief of the army or other officers for aid; it being, however, intended that a sufficient civil police shall always be in readiness to secure implicit obedience to law.

ARTICLE XX

The Vice-President

The Vice-President shall be the presiding officer of the Provisional Congress, and in cases of tie shall give the casting vote.

ARTICLE XXI

Vacancies

In case of the death, removal, or inability of the President, the Vice President, and, next to him, the Chief Justice of the Supreme Court shall be the President during the remainder of the term; and the place of the Chief Justice, thus made vacant, shall be filled by Congress from some of the members of said court; and the places of the Vice-President and Associate Justice, thus made vacant, filled by an election by the united action of the Provisional Congress and members of the Supreme Court. All other vacancies, not heretofore specially provided for, shall, during the first three years, be filled by the united action of the President, Vice-President, Supreme Court, and Commander-in-chief of the army.

ARTICLE XXII

Punishment of crimes

The punishment of crimes not capital, except in case of insubordinate convicts or other prisoners, shall be (so far as may be) by hard labor on the public works, roads, &c.

ARTICLE XXIII

Army appointments

It shall be the duty of all commissioned officers of the army to name candidates of merit, for office or elevation, to the Commander-in-chief, who, with the Secretary of War, and, in. cases of disagreement, the President, shall be the appointing power of the army; and all commissions of military officers shall bear the signatures of the Commander in-chief and the Secretary of War. And it shall be the special duty of the Secretary of War to keep for constant reference of the Commander-in-chief a full list of names of persons nominated for office or elevation by the officers of the army, with the name and rank of the officer nominating, stating distinctly, but briefly, the grounds for such notice or nomination. The Commander-in-chief shall not have power to remove or punish any officer or soldier, but he may order their arrest and trial at any time by court-martial.

ARTICLE XXIV

Courts-martial

Courts-martial for companies, regiments, brigades, &c., shall be called by the chief officer of each command, on complaint to him by any officer, or any five privates in such command, and shall consist of not less than five nor more than nine officers, non-commissioned officers and privates, one half of whom shall not be lower in rank than the person on trial, to be chosen by the three highest officers in the command, which officers shall not be a part of such court. The chief officer of any command shall, of course, be tried by a court-martial of the command above his own. All decisions affecting the lives of persons, or office of persons holding commission, must, before taking full effect, have the signature of the Commander-in-chief, who may also, on the recommendation of at least one third of the members of the court-martial finding any sentence, grant a reprieve or commutation of the same.

ARTICLE XXV

Salaries

No person connected with this organization shall be entitled to any salary, pay, or emolument, other than a competent support of himself and family, unless it be from an equal dividend made of public property, on the establishment of peace, or of special provision by treaty; which provision shall be made for all persons who may have been in any active civil or military service at any time previous to any hostile action for liberty and equality.

ARTICLE XXVI

Treaties of peace

Before any treaty of peace shall take full effect it shall be signed by the President and Vice-President, the Commander-in-chief, a majority of the House of Representatives, a majority of the Supreme Court, and a majority of all the general officers of the army.

ARTICLE XXVII

Duty of the military

It shall be the duty of the Commander-in-chief and all officers and soldiers of the army to afford special protection, when needed, to Congress or any member thereof, to the Supreme Court or any member thereof, to the President, Vice-President, Treasurer, Secretary of State, Secretary of the Treasury, and Secretary of War; and to afford general protection to all civil officers or other persons having right to the same.

ARTICLE XXVIII

Property

All captured or confiscated property and all property the product of the labor of those belonging to this organization and of their families, shall. be held as the property of the whole, equally, without distinction, and may be used for the common benefit, or disposed of for the same object; and any person, officer, or otherwise, who shall improperly retain, secrete, use, or needlessly destroy such property, or property found, captured, or confiscated, belonging to the enemy, or shall willfully neglect to render a full and fair statement of such property by him so taken or held, shall be deemed guilty of a misdemeanor, and, on conviction, shall be punished accordingly.

ARTICLE XXIX

Safety or intelligence fund

All money, plate, watches, or jewelry captured by honorable warfare, found, taken, or confiscated, belonging to the enemy, shall be held sacred to constitute a liberal safety or intelligence fund; and any person who shall improperly retain, dispose of, hide, use, or destroy such money or other article above named, contrary to the provisions and spirit of this article, shall be deemed guilty of theft, and, on conviction thereof, shall be punished accordingly. The treasurer shall furnish the Commander-in-chief at all times with a full statement of the condition of such fund, and its nature.

ARTICLE XXX

The Commander-in-chief and the treasury
The Commander-in-chief shall have power to draw from the treasury the money and other property of the fund provided for in article twenty-ninth; but his orders shall be signed also by the Secretary of War, who shall keep strict account of the same subject to examination by any member of Congress or general officer.

ARTICLE XXXI

Surplus of the safety or intelligence fund
It shall be the duty of the Commander-in-chief to advice the President of any surplus of the safety and intelligence fund, who shall have power to draw such surplus (his order being also signed by the Secretary of State) to enable him to carry out the provisions of article seventeenth.

ARTICLE XXXII

Prisoners
No person, after having surrendered himself or herself a prisoner, and who shall properly demean himself or herself as such, to any officer or private connected with this organization, shall afterward be put to death, or be subject to any corporeal punishment, without first having had the benefit of a fair and impartial trial; nor shall any prisoner be treated with any kind of cruelty, disrespect, insult, or needless severity; but it shall be the duty of all persons, male and female, connected herewith, at all times and under all circumstances, to treat all such prisoners with every degree of respect and kindness that the nature of the circumstances will admit of, and to insist on a like course of conduct from all others, as in the fear of Almighty God, to whose care and keeping we commit our cause.

ARTICLE XXXIII

Voluntaries
All persons who may come forward, and shall voluntarily deliver up their slaves, and have their names registered on the books of the organization, shall, so long as they continue at peace, be entitled to the fullest protection of person and property, though not connected with this organization, and shall be treated as friends and not merely as persons neutral.

ARTICLE XXXIV

Neutrals
The persons and property of all non-slaveholders, who shall remain absolutely neutral, shall be respected so far as the circumstances can allow of it, but they shall not be entitled to any active protection.

ARTICLE XXXV

No needless waste
The needless waste or destruction of any useful property or article by fire, throwing open of fences, fields, buildings, or needless killing of animals, or injury of either, shall not be tolerated at any time or place, but shall be promptly and properly punished.

ARTICLE XXXVI

Property confiscated
The entire personal and real property of all persons known to be acting either directly or indirectly with or for the enemy, or Found in arms with them, or found willfully holding slaves, shall be confiscated and taken whenever and wherever it may be found in either free or slave States.

ARTICLE XXXVII

Desertion
Persons convicted on impartial trial of desertion to the enemy, after becoming members, acting as spies, or of treacherous surrender of property, ammunition, provisions, or supplies of any kind, roads, bridges, persons, or fortifications shall be put to death, and their entire property confiscated.

ARTICLE XXXVIII

Violation of parole of honor
Persons proven to be guilty of taking up arms after having been set at liberty on parole of honor, or, after the same, to have taken any active part with or for the enemy, direct or indirect, shall be put to death, and their entire property confiscated.

ARTICLE XXXIX

All must labor
All persons connected in any way with this organization, and who may be entitled to full protection under it, shall be held as under obligation to labor in some way for the general good; and persons refusing or neglecting so to do, shall, on conviction, receive a suitable and appropriate punishment.

ARTICLE XL

Irregularities
Profane swearing, filthy conversation, indecent behavior, or indecent exposure of the person, or intoxication or quarreling, shall not be allowed or tolerated, neither unlawful intercourse of the sexes.

ARTICLE XLI

Crimes
Persons convicted of the forcible violation of any female prisoner shall be put to death.

ARTICLE XLII

The marriage relation, schools, the Sabbath
The marriage relation shall be at all times respected, and families kept together, as far as possible; and broken families encouraged to reunite, and intelligence offices established for that purpose. Schools and churches established, as soon as may be, for the purpose of religious and other instructions; for the first day of the week, regarded as a day of rest, and appropriated to moral and religious instruction and improvement, relief of the suffering, instruction of the young and ignorant, and the encouragement of personal cleanliness; nor shall any persons be required on that day to perform ordinary manual labor, unless in extremely urgent cases.

ARTICLE XLIII

Carry arms openly
All persons known to be of good character and of sound mind and suitable age, who are connected with this organization, whether male or female, shall be encouraged to carry arms openly.

ARTICLE XLIV

No person to carry concealed weapons
No person within the limits of the conquered territory, except regularly appointed policemen, express officers of the army, mail carriers, or other fully accredited messengers of the Congress, President, Vice President, members of the Supreme Court, or commissioned officers of the army—and those only under peculiar circumstances—shall be allowed at any time to carry concealed weapons; and any person not specially authorized so to do, who shall be found so doing, shall be deemed a suspicious person, and may at once be arrested by any officer, soldier, or citizen, without the formality of a complaint or warrant, and may at once be subjected to thorough search, and shall have his or her case thoroughly investigated, and be dealt with as circumstances on proof shall require.

ARTICLE XLV

Persons to be seized
Persons within the limits of the territory holden by this organization, not connected with this organization, having arms at all, concealed or otherwise, shall be seized at once, or, be taken in charge of some vigilant officer, and their case thoroughly investigated; and it shall be the duty of all citizens and soldiers, as well as officers, to arrest such parties as are named in this and the preceding section or article, without the formality of complaint or warrant; and they shall be placed in charge of some proper officer for examination or for safekeeping.

ARTICLE XLVI

These articles not for the overthrow of government

The foregoing articles shall not be construed so as in any way to encourage the overthrow of any State government, or of the general government of the United States, and look to no dissolution of the Union, but simply to amendment and repeal. And our flag shall be the same that our fathers fought under in the Revolution.

ARTICLE XLVII

No plurality of offices

No two of the offices specially provided for by this instrument shall be filled by the same person at the same time.

ARTICLE XLVIII

Oath

Every officer, civil or military, connected with this organization shall, before entering upon the duties of his office, make solemn oath or affirmation to abide by and support this provisional constitution and these ordinances; also every citizen and soldier, before being fully recognized as such, shall do the same.

Schedule

The president of this convention shall convene, immediately on the adoption of this instrument, a convention of all such persons as shall have given their adherence by signature to the constitution, who shall proceed to fill, by election, all offices specially named in said constitution, the president of this convention presiding, and issuing commissions to such officers elect; all such officers being thereafter elected in the manner provided in the body of this instrument.

GLOSSARY

"a recent decision of the Supreme Court": A reference to the Dred Scott vs. Sanford case

plate: precious metals, such as those in dining services or flatware

real property: property such as land and buildings

viz.: Abbreviation of the Latin word videlicet meaning namely or "that is to say"

Document Analysis

The Preamble begins by denouncing slavery as an act of war by "one portion of…citizens upon another portion" and incompatible with the Declaration of Independence. As a result, American citizens along with slaves ("the oppressed people") are establishing a new government. Some of the language ("ordain and establish" for example) echoes the US Constitution of 1787. The invocation of the rights of "property, lives, and liberties" is a reference to the social contract philosophies of John Locke, and influence on the American founders.

Article I, the "Qualifications for membership" in this new nation are simply being the age of legal majority and willingness to live within the bounds of the constitution. It explicitly includes former slaves and members of "the proscribed and oppressed races of the United States." This forthright extension of citizenship to people regardless of race was a repudiation of the Dred Scott decision which refused to recognize citizenship rights for people of color.

In Articles II-VI, Brown models his new government on that of the United States, with a balanced system of executive, judicial, and legislative branches. One notable innovation is that Supreme Court justices will be "chosen in the same manner as the President," that is, elected rather than appointed. This would prevent the domination of the court by people appointed by the president—a situation that abolitionists believed had led to a Supreme Court bench disproportionately filled with slave owners.

In another innovation, Brown separates the military position of Commander-in-Chief from that of the President (Article VII). There is still a good deal of civilian control over the military, however, as the Commander-in-Chief may be removed upon action by any of the three branches of government.

Articles VIII and IX establish the cabinet officials ("officers") in the new government, outline their duties, and detail the ways in which they may be removed. Here, and in other articles in this constitution, Brown makes extensive provision for the reasons why an official may be removed from office and the way that this can be carried out. This gives the impression of a government where elected and appointed officials would be under constant scrutiny by the citizens and by each other.

Articles X-XII outline the duties of the Congress which, unlike the US Congress, will be a unicameral legislature, consisting only of a House of Representatives.

Articles XIII-XV are further examples of the extensive attention Brown paid to the removal of elected officials. In these sections, the causes for removal are vague, with a "complaint" sufficient to begin removal proceedings.

Brown's constitution, in Articles XVI-XXI, outlines the duties of the President and Vice-President. The most attention is paid to the very important job of finding sufficient people for the new country to ensure that all the various needs of the society are met. Thus, one of the President's tasks is to find men of high moral character to fill just about every occupational need a community might need. This duty is shared with the Secretary of state but the Vice-President's involvement is limited to break ties in Congress and to be the deciding voice in disagreements between the President and Secretary of State.

The first Twenty-one articles deal with the creation of the new government and how it should be organized. Articles XXII-XXXI make it very clear that this new government is going to face many enemies as it establishes itself. They establish how crimes shall be punished (hard labor on public works not only punishes criminals, but ensures that things like roads, bridges, and the like are constructed at low cost), how military officers will be appointed and how disobedient military personnel will be punished, how government officials will be paid and how the government will conclude peace treaties. Once again, in a contrast to the United States, Brown places the Commander-in-Chief of the military in a strong political position, in this case requiring his approval of peace treaties. Articles XXiX through XXXI discusses the creation of a "safety or intelligence fund" to be used by the Commander in Chief for the vaguely described "safety" of the public.

Articles XXXII-XXXVIII lay out the treatment of various enemies of the new nation, including prisoners, those who give up slaves voluntarily and the confiscation of the property of those who remain enemies.

The final large group of articles (XXXIX-XLV) lay out regulations for the behavior of the population of this new nation. All people will be required to work and, if they refuse, will be forced to work. Various kinds of "indecent behavior" are prohibited, including intoxication and "unlawful intercourse." Article XLI makes the rape of a female prisoner a capital crime, but rape in general is not mentioned within this constitution. Marriage, education, and religious observance are enshrined in the constitution. Men and women who are citizens are "encouraged" to openly carry weapons but, apart from some special exceptions, concealed weapons are forbidden. If people within the new nation that are not citizens, they are not allowed to possess weapons of any kind.

Confusingly, considering that Brown sought to establish a new nation on land seized from others, Articles XLVI claims that the new constitution is simply for the purposes of "amendment and repeal" and that this nation will be a continuation of the United States.

Article XLVII stipulates that no person can hold more than one office and Article XLVIII requires officials to swear an oath to support the new constitution and requires the President to convene the new government upon its approval.

Essential Themes

John Brown's provisional constitution lays out his vision for a new American society free from the taint of slavery. The constitution itself reflects the reality that this would be a society under siege, accounting for the fact that a great deal of this plan for government consists of detailed instructions for dealing with the regime's enemies. Another notable feature of the constitution is that the position of President in this system is relatively weak. To supplement this, however, the constitution provides for a commander-in-chief of the military with broad powers. John Brown's followers approved of his appointment to the position himself following the meeting in which this constitution was ratified. While Brown's constitution took the notable step of conferring citizenship on all adults who were part of the community, the greatest impression this document gives is that of setting up a society with a robust military presence, a sharp division between citizens, "neutrals" and conquered enemies and a system of regulations that proclaimed a wide array of moral offensives subject to punishment. This was a plan for a society on the defensive, struggling to maintain its position and serve as an embattled beacon for liberty.

———*Aaron Gulyas, MA*

Bibliography and Additional Reading

Horwitz, Tony. *Midnight Rising: John Brown and the Raid That Sparked the Civil War.* New York: Henry Holt & Co., 2011.

McGinty, Brian. *John Brown's Trial.* (Cambridge, Massachusetts: Harvard University Press, 2009).

McGlone, Robert E. *John Brown's War against Slavery.* (Cambridge, Cambridge University Press, 2009).

Stauffer, John and Zoe Trodd, eds. *The Tribunal: Responses to John Brown and the Harpers Ferry Raid* (Cambridge, Massachusetts, Belknap Press, 2012).

Tsai, Robert L. *John Brown's Constitution*, 51 B.C.L. Rev. 151 (2010). Available online at http://lawdigitalcommons.bc.edu/bclr/vol51/iss1/4

■ *A Voice from Harper's Ferry*

Date: 1861
Author: Osborne P. Anderson
Genre: Pamphlet

Summary Overview

In 1861 Osborne Anderson published *A Voice from Harper's Ferry: A Narrative of Events at Harper's Ferry; With Incidents Prior and Subsequent to Its Capture by Captain Brown and His Men* to present his eyewitness account of events during and revolving around John Brown's raid on the federal arsenal at Harpers Ferry, Virginia (now West Virginia), of October 16–18, 1859. After the capture and execution of the other raiders, Anderson was the only one left alive who had been present in Harpers Ferry during the raid; because he believed that southern accounts were biased, he felt compelled to give an account of the event from the raiders' perspective. The book's publication, accomplished by the author with the aid of antislavery Bostonians, was announced in William Lloyd Garrison's newspaper *The Liberator* on January 11, 1861, and in Frederick Douglass's *Monthly* in the February 1861 issue. Anderson's book seems to have had minimal impact on any general audience in its own day, and indeed it almost disappeared. But it has become a popular source among historians of today who focus on black studies and the abolitionist movement, particularly those seeking to establish proof of participation by local blacks in the raid on Harpers Ferry.

Defining Moment

John Brown was a white man who had always been opposed to slavery, but in November 1837, following the murder of Elijah P. Lovejoy, editor of an antislavery newspaper in Alton, Ohio, Brown publicly declared his personal war on slavery and committed himself to its destruction. He had come to believe that the only way to end slavery was through the use of violence. In 1855, Brown joined with five of his sons in an attempt to help bring the Kansas Territory into the Union as a free state. Brown made himself a legend and a wanted man primarily because of his actions following the sack of Lawrence, Kansas, by proslavery factions on May 21, 1856. To avenge the murders of five Lawrence residents, Brown ordered and carried out the murder of five proslavery men who lived along the banks of the Pottawatomie Creek. This incident came to be known as the Pottawatomie Massacre.

Although a fugitive, Brown became a hero to white and black abolitionists alike. Fleeing to the East, and with the support of other abolitionists in the United States and Canada, Brown planned a slave uprising with weapons gained from a raid on the federal arsenal at Harpers Ferry, Virginia. On October 16, 1859. He then had only twenty-one followers, including five blacks and sixteen whites. He led eighteen of them into Harpers Ferry, and they quickly captured two bridges, the arsenal, the rifle factory, and the engine house. But soon, Brown and his men were cut off from their major escape route. The local militia was later joined by Colonel Robert E. Lee and ninety U.S. marines. On the morning of October 18, Lee's marines attacked the engine house, capturing Brown and those of his men who were still alive. Anderson and Albert Hazlett were the only two men to escape from Harpers Ferry. Hazlett was captured, convicted, and executed.

Anderson was thus the only one of Brown's men to witness the events at Harpers Ferry and live to tell about them.

Author Biography

Osborne Perry Anderson was an abolitionist, author, and political activist and one of five black raiders who followed John Brown in his attack on the arsenal at Harpers Ferry in 1859. He was born free in West Fallowfield, Pennsylvania. His father, Vincent Anderson, moved the family to West Goshen (near West Chester) around 1850. There Anderson met the Shadds, a family of black abolitionists. In the early 1850s he followed them to Chatham, Canada West, one of several Canadian communities in which free blacks and fugitive slaves from the United States could find a haven. Blacks could be full citizens in Canada, and it is estimated that forty to fifty thousand African Americans had moved there by 1850. Anderson lived with the Shadd family and became a printer's apprentice at the *Provincial Freeman*, a newspaper founded by Mary Ann Shadd, the first black woman editor on the continent. Thus, Anderson was in Chatham when Brown planned and held his convention there.

Unlike many other recruits, Anderson paid his own way to the rally point of Chambersburg, Pennsylvania, arriving on September 16, 1859. There, he stayed with a local black barber named Henry Watson, and on September 24 he walked (by night) from Chambersburg to meet Brown near the Kennedy Farm in Maryland, a place that Brown had rented to be used as a staging area for the raid. The raid on the federal arsenal at Harpers Ferry, Virginia, began on October 16, 1859, and ended two days later. Anderson, being the only one of Brown's men to witness the raid and live to tell the story, proceeded to write *A Voice from Harper's Ferry*, which was edited by Shadd, his mentor, and published in 1861. Along with an estimated fifty thousand other Canadians, Anderson went south to the United States when the Civil War began. While some historians believe that he served in the army, there is no record of such service; he did, however, work as a recruiter for the Union army's U.S. Colored Troops.

Following the war, Anderson resided in the United States, where he had trouble supporting himself. He revisited Harpers Ferry a year before his death, pointing out strategic scenes to Richard Hinton, who would author *John Brown and His Men: With Some Account of the Roads They Traveled to Reach Harper's Ferry* (1894). In 1872, Anderson died penniless in Washington, D.C., and was buried in a pauper's grave. Because of his abolitionist activities, Anderson is claimed by Canada as a national hero.

HISTORICAL DOCUMENT

Preface

My sole purpose in publishing the following Narrative is to save from oblivion the facts connected with one of the most important movements of this age, with reference to the overthrow of American slavery. My own personal experience in it, under the orders of Capt. Brown, on the 16th and 17th of October, 1859, as the only man alive who was at Harper's Ferry during the entire time the unsuccessful groping after these facts, by individuals, impossible to be obtained, except from an actor in the scene and the conviction that the cause of impartial liberty requires this duty at my hands alone have been the motives for writing and circulating the little book herewith presented.

I will not under such circumstances, insult nor burden the intelligent with excuses for defects in composition, nor for the attempt to give the facts. A plain unadorned, truthful story is wanted, and that by one who knows what he says, who is known to have been at the great encounter, and to have labored in shaping the same. My identity as a member of Capt. Brown's company cannot be questioned, successfully, by any who are bent upon suppressing the truth; neither will it be by any in Canada or the United States familiar with John Brown and his plans, as those know his men personally, or by reputation, who enjoyed his confidence sufficiently to know thoroughly his plans.

The readers of this narrative will therefore keep steadily in view this main point that they are perusing a story of events which have happened under the eye of the great Captain, or are incidental thereto, and not a compendium of the "plans" of Capt. Brown; for as his plans were not consummated, and as their fulfilment is committed to the future, no one to whom they are known will recklessly expose all of them to the public gaze. Much has been given as true that never happened; much has been omitted that should have been made known; many things have been left unsaid, because, up to within a short time, but two could say them; one of them has been offered up, a sacrifice to the Moloch, Slavery; being that other one, I propose to perform the duty, trusting to that portion of the public who love the right for an appreciation of my endeavor. O.P.A....

Chapter X. The Capture of Harper's Ferry—Col. A. D. Stevens and Party Sally Out To the Plantations—What We Saw, Heard, Did, Etc.

As John H. Kagi and A. D. Stevens entered the bridge, as ordered in the fifth charge, the watchman, being at the other end, came toward them with a lantern in his hand. When up to them, they told him he was their prisoner, and detained him a few minutes, when he asked them to spare his life. They replied, they did not intend to harm him; the object was to free the slaves, and he would have to submit to them for a time, in order that the purpose might be carried out.

Captain Brown now entered the bridge in his wagon, followed by the rest of us, until we reached that part where Kagi and Stevens held their prisoner, when he ordered Watson Brown and Stewart Taylor to take the positions assigned them in order sixth, and the rest of us to proceed to the engine house. We started for the engine house, taking the prisoner along with us. When we neared the gates of the engine-house yard, we found them locked, and the watchman on the inside. He was told to open the gates, but refused, and commenced to cry. The men were then ordered by Captain Brown to open the gates forcibly, which was done, and the watchman taken prisoner. The two prisoners were left in the custody of Jerry Anderson and Adolphus Thompson, and A. D. Stevens arranged the men to take possession of the Armory and rifle factory. About this time, there was apparently much excitement. People were passing back and forth in the town, and before we could do much, we had to take several prisoners. After the prisoners were secured, we passed to the opposite side of the street and took the Armory, and Albert Hazlett and Edwin Coppic were ordered to hold it for the time being.

The capture of the rifle factory was the next work to be done. When we went there, we told the watchman who was outside of the building our business, and asked him to go along with us, as we had come to take possession of the town, and make use of the Armory in carrying out our object. He obeyed the command without hesitation. John H. Kagi and John Copeland were placed in the Armory, and the prisoners taken to the engine house. Following the capture of the Armory, Oliver Brown and William Thompson were ordered to take possession of the bridge leading out of town, across the Shenandoah river, which they immediately did. These places were all taken, and the prisoners secured, without the snap of a gun, or any violence whatever.

The town being taken, Brown, Stevens, and the men who had no post in charge, returned to the engine house, where council was held, after which Captain Stevens, Tidd, Cook, Shields Green, Leary

and myself went to the country. On the road, we met some colored men, to whom we made known our purpose, when they immediately agreed to join us. They said they had been long waiting for an opportunity of the kind. Stevens then asked them to go around among the colored people and circulate the news, when each started off in a different direction. The result was that many colored men gathered to the scene of action. The first prisoner taken by us was Colonel Lewis Washington. When we neared his house, Capt. Stevens placed Leary and Shields Green to guard the approaches to the house, the one at the side, the other in front. We then knocked, but no one answering, although females were looking from upper windows, we entered the building and commenced a search for the proprietor. Col. Washington opened his room door, and begged us not to kill him. Capt. Stevens replied, "You are our prisoner," when he stood as if speechless or petrified. Stevens further told him to get ready to go to the Ferry; that he had come to abolish slavery, not to take life but in self-defence, but that he must go along. The Colonel replied: "You can have my slaves, if you will let me remain." "No," said the Captain, "you must go along too; so get ready." After saying this, Stevens left the house for a time, and with Green, Leary and Tidd proceeded to the "Quarters," giving the prisoner in charge of Cook and myself. The male slaves were gathered together in a short time, when horses were tackled to the Colonel's two-horse carriage and four-horse wagon, and both vehicles brought to the front of the house.

During this time, Washington was walking the floor, apparently much excited. When the Captain came in, he went to the sideboard, took out his whiskey, and offered us something to drink, but he was refused. His fire-arms were next demanded, when he brought forth one double-barreled gun, one small rifle, two horse-pistols and a sword. Nothing else was asked of him. The Colonel cried heartily when he found he must submit, and appeared taken aback when, on delivering up the famous sword formerly presented by Frederic to his illustrious kinsman, George Washington, Capt. Stevens told me to step forward and take it. Washington was secured and placed in his wagon, the women of the family making great outcries, when the party drove forward to Mr. John Allstadt's. After making known our business to him, he went into as great a fever of excitement as Washington had done. We could have his slaves, also, if we would only leave him. This, of course, was contrary to our plans and instructions. He hesitated, puttered around, fumbled and meditated for a long time. At last, seeing no alternative, he got ready, when the slaves were gathered up from about the quarters by their own consent, and all placed in Washington's big wagon and returned to the Ferry.

One old colored lady, at whose house we stopped, a little way from the town, had a good time over the message we took her. This liberating the slaves was the very thing she had longed for, prayed for, and dreamed about, time and again; and her heart was full of rejoicing over the fulfilment of a prophecy which had been her faith for long years. While we were absent from the Ferry, the train of cars for Baltimore arrived, and was detained. A colored man named Haywood, employed upon it, went from the Wager House up to the entrance to the bridge, where the train stood, to assist with the baggage. He was ordered to stop by the sentinels stationed at the bridge, which he refused to do, but turned to go in an opposite direction, when he was fired upon, and received a mortal wound. Had he stood when ordered, he would not have been harmed. No one knew at the time whether he was white or colored, but his movements were such as to justify the sentinels in shooting him, as he would not stop when commanded. The first firing happened at that time, and the only firing, until after daylight on Monday morning.

Chapter XI. The Events of Monday, Oct. 17—Arming The Slaves—Terror. In the Slaveholding Camp—Important Losses to Our Party—The Fate of Kagi—Prisoners Accumulate—Workmen at the Kennedy Farm, Etc.

Monday, the 17th of October, was a time of stirring and exciting events. In consequence of the movements of the night before, we were prepared for commotion and tumult, but certainly not for more than we beheld around us. Gray dawn and yet brighter daylight revealed great confusion, and as the sun arose, the panic spread like wildfire. Men, women and children could be seen leaving their homes in every direction; some seeking refuge among residents, and in quarters further away, others climbing up the hillsides, and hurrying off in various directions, evidently impelled by a sudden fear which was plainly visible in their countenances or in their movements.

Capt. Brown was all activity, though I could not help thinking that at times he appeared somewhat puzzled. He ordered Sherrard Lewis Leary, and four slaves, and a free man belonging in the neighborhood, to join John Henry Kagi and John Copeland at the rifle factory, which they immediately did. Kagi, and all except Copeland, were subsequently killed, but not before having communicated with Capt. Brown, as will be set forth further along.

As fast as the workmen came to the building or persons appeared in the street near the engine house, they were taken prisoners, and directly after sunrise, the detained train was permitted to start for the eastward. After the departure of the train, quietness prevailed for a short time; a number of prisoners were already in the engine house, and of the many colored men living in the neighborhood, who had assembled in the town, a number were armed for the work.

Capt. Brown ordered Capts. Charles P. Tidd, Wm. H. Leeman, John E. Cook, and some fourteen slaves, to take Washington's four-horse wagon, and to join the company under Capt. Owen Brown, consisting of F. J. Merriam and Barclay Coppic, who had been left at the Farm the night previous, to guard the place and the arms. The company, thus reinforced, proceeded, under Owen Brown, to move the arms and goods from the Farm down to the school-house in the mountains, three-fourths of a mile from the Ferry.

Capt. Brown next ordered me to take the pikes out of the wagon in which he rode to the Ferry, and to place them in the hands of the colored men who had come with us from the plantations, and others who had come forward without having had communication with any of our party. It was out of the circumstances connected with the fulfilment of this order, that the false charge against "Anderson" as leader, or "ringleader," of the negroes, grew.

The spectators, about this time, became apparently wild with fright and excitement. The number of prisoners was magnified to hundreds, and the judgment-day could not have presented more terrors, in its awful and certain prospective punishment to the justly condemned for the wicked deeds of a life-time, the chief of which would no doubt be slaveholding, than did Capt. Brown's operations.

The prisoners were also terror-stricken. Some wanted to go home to see their families, as if for the last time. The privilege was granted them, under escort, and they were brought back again. Edwin Coppic, one of the sentinels at the Armory gate, was fired at by one of the citizens, but the ball did not reach him, when one of the insurgents close by put up his rifle, and made the enemy bite the dust.

Among the arms taken from Col. Washington was one double-barrel gun. This weapon was loaded by Leeman with buckshot, and placed in the hands of an elderly slave man, early in the morning. After the cowardly charge upon Coppic, this old man was ordered by Capt. Stevens to arrest a citizen. The old man ordered him to halt, which he refused to do, when instantly the terrible load was discharged into him, and he fell, and expired without a struggle.

After these incidents, time passed away till the arrival of the United States troops, without any further attack upon us. The cowardly Virginians submitted like sheep, without resistance, from that time until the marines came down. Meanwhile, Capt. Brown, who was considering a proposition for release from his prisoners, passed back and forth from the Armory to the bridge, speaking words of comfort and encouragement to his men. "Hold on a little longer, boys," said he, "until I get matters arranged with the prisoners." This tardiness on the part of our brave leader was sensibly felt to be an omen of evil by some us, and was eventually the cause of our defeat. It was no part of the original plan to hold on to the Ferry, or to parley with prisoners; but by so doing, time was afforded to carry the news of its capture to several points, and forces were thrown into the place, which surrounded us.

At eleven o'clock, Capt. Brown dispatched William Thompson from the Ferry up to Kennedy Farm with the news that we had peaceful possession of the town, and with directions to the men to continue on moving the things. He went; but before he could get back, troops had begun to pour in and the general encounter commenced.

Chapter XII. Reception to the Troops—They Retreat to the Bridge—A Prisoner—Death of Dangerfield Newby—William Thompson—The Mountains Alive—Flag of Truce—The Engine House Taken.

It was about twelve o'clock in the day when we were first attacked by the troops. Prior to that, Capt. Brown, in anticipation of further trouble, had girded to his side the famous sword taken from Col. Lewis Washington the night before, and with that memorable weapon, he commanded his men against General Washington's own State.

When the Captain received the news that the troops had entered the bridge from the Maryland side, he, with some of his men, went into the street, and sent a message to the Arsenal for us to come forth also. We hastened to the street as ordered, when he said "The troops are on the bridge, coming into town; we will give them a warm reception." He then walked around amongst us, giving us words of encouragement, in this wise:—"Men! be cool! Don't waste your powder and shot! Take aim, and make every shot count!" "The troops will look for us to retreat on their first appearance; be careful to shoot first." Our men were well supplied with firearms, but Capt. Brown had no rifle at that time; his only weapon was the sword before mentioned.

The troops soon came out of the bridge, and up the street facing us, we occupying an irregular position. When they got within sixty or seventy yards, Capt. Brown said, "Let go upon them!" which we did, when several of them fell. Again and again the dose was repeated.

There was now consternation among the troops. From marching in solid martial columns, they became scattered. Some hastened to seize upon and bear up the wounded and dying,—several lay dead upon the ground. They seemed not to realize, at first, that we would fire upon them, but evidently expected we would be driven out by them without firing. Capt. Brown seemed fully to understand the matter, and hence, very properly and in our defence, undertook to forestall their movements. The consequence of their unexpected reception was, after leaving several of their dead on the field, they beat a confused retreat into the bridge, and there stayed under cover until reinforcements came to the Ferry.

On the retreat of the troops, we were ordered back to our former post. While going, Dangerfield Newby, one of our colored men, was shot through the head by a person who took aim at him from a brick store window, on the opposite side of the street, and who was there for the purpose of firing upon us. Newby was a brave fellow. He was one of my comrades at the Arsenal. He fell at my side, and his death was promptly avenged by Shields Green, the Zouave of the band, who afterwards met his fate calmly on the gallows, with John Copeland. Newby was shot twice; at the first fire, he fell on his side and returned it; as he lay, a second shot was fired, and the ball entered his head. Green raised his rifle in an instant, and brought down the cowardly murderer, before the latter could get his gun back through the sash.

There was comparative quiet for a time, except that the citizens seemed to be wild with terror. Men, women and children forsook the place in great haste, climbing up hillsides and scaling the mountains. The latter seemed to be alive with white fugitives, fleeing from their doomed city. During this time, Wm. Thompson, who was returning from his errand to the Kennedy Farm, was surrounded on the bridge by the railroad men, who next came up, taken a prisoner to the Wager House, tied hand and foot, and, at a late hour of the afternoon, cruelly murdered by being riddled with balls and thrown headlong on the rocks.

Late in the morning, some of his prisoners told Capt. Brown that they would like to have breakfast, when he sent word forthwith to the Wager House to that effect, and they were supplied. He did not order breakfast for himself and men, as was currently but falsely stated at the time, as he suspected foul play; on the contrary, when solicited to have breakfast so provided for him, he refused. Between two and three o'clock in the afternoon. armed men could be seen coming from every direction; soldiers were marching and counter-marching; and on the mountains. a host of blood-thirsty ruffians swarmed, waiting for their opportunity to pounce upon the little band. The fighting commenced in earnest after the arrival of fresh troops. Volley upon volley was discharged, and the echoes from the hills, the shrieks of the townspeople, and the groans of their wounded and dying, all of which filled the air, were truly frightful. The Virginians may well conceal their losses, and Southern chivalry may hide its brazen head, for their boasted bravery was well tested that day, and in no way to their advantage. It is remarkable, that except that one fool-hardy colored man was reported buried, no other funeral is mentioned, although the Mayor and other citizens are known to have fallen. Had they reported the true number, their disgrace would have been more apparent; so they wisely (?) concluded to be silent.

The fight at Harper's Ferry also disproved the current idea that slaveholders will lay down their lives for their property. Col. Washington, the representative of the old hero, stood "blubbering like a great calf at supposed danger"; while the laboring white classes and non-slaveholders, with the marines (mostly gentlemen from "furrin" parts), were the men who faced the bullets of John Brown and his men. Hardly the skin of a slaveholder could be scratched in open fight; the cowards kept out of the way until danger was passed, sending the poor whites into the pitfalls, while they were reserved for the bragging, and to do the safe but cowardly judicial murdering afterwards.

As strangers poured in, the enemy took positions round about, so as to prevent any escape, within shooting distance of the engine house and Arsenal. Capt. Brown, seeing their manouevres, said: "We will hold on to our three positions, if they are unwilling to come to terms, and die like men."

All this time, the fight was progressing; no powder and ball were wasted. We shot from under cover, and took deadly aim. For an hour before the flag of truce was sent out, the firing was uninterrupted, and one and another of the enemy were constantly dropping to the earth.

One of the Captain's plans was to keep up communication between his three points. In carrying out this idea, Jerry Anderson went to the rifle factory, to see Kagi and his men. Kagi, fearing that we would be overpowered by numbers if the Captain delayed leaving, sent word by Anderson to advise him to leave the town at once. This word Anderson communicated to the Captain, and told us also at the Arsenal. The message sent back to Kagi was, to hold out for a few minutes longer, when we would all evacuate the place. Those few minutes proved disastrous, for then it was that the troops before spoken of came pouring in, increased by crowds of men from the surrounding country. After an hour's hard fighting, and when the enemy were blocking up the avenues of escape, Capt. Brown sent out his son Watson with a flag of truce, but no respect was paid to it; he was fired upon, and wounded severely. He returned to the engine house, and fought bravely after that for fully an hour and a half, when he received a mortal wound, which he struggled under until the next day. The contemptible and savage manner in which the flag of truce had been received, induced severe measures in our defence, in the hour and a half before the next one was sent out. The effect of our work was, that the troops ceased to fire at the buildings, as we clearly had the advantage of position.

Capt. A. D. Stevens was next sent out with a flag, with what success I will presently show. Meantime, Jeremiah Anderson, who had brought the message from Kagi previously, was sent by Capt. Brown with another message to John Henrie, but before he got far on the street he was fired upon and wounded. He returned at once to the engine house, where he survived but a short time. The ball, it was found, had entered the right side in such manner that death necessarily ensued speedily.

Capt. Stevens was fired upon several times while carrying his flag of truce, and received severe wounds, as I was informed that day, not being myself in a position to see him after. He was captured, and taken to the Wager House, where he was kept until the close of the struggle in the evening, when he was placed with the rest of our party who had been captured.

After the capture of Stevens, desperate fighting was done by both sides. The marines forced their way inside the engine-house yard, and commanded Capt. Brown to surrender, which he refused to do, but said in reply, that he was willing to fight them, if they would allow him first to withdraw his men to the second lock on the Maryland side. As might be expected, the cowardly hordes refused to entertain such a proposition, but continued their assault, to cut off communication between our several parties. The men at the Kennedy Farm having received such a favorable message in the early part of the day, through Thompson, were ignorant of the disastrous state of affairs later in the day. Could they have known the truth, and come down in time, the result would have been very different; we should not have been captured that day. A handful of determined men, as they were, by taking a position on the Maryland side, when the troops made their attack and retreated to the bridge for shelter, would have placed the enemy between two fires. Thompson's news prevented them from hurrying down, as they otherwise would have done, and thus deprived us of able assistance from Owen Brown, a host in himself, and Tidd, Merriam and Coppic, the brave fellows composing that band.

The climax of murderous assaults on that memorable day was the final capture of the engine house, with the old Captain and his handful of associates. This outrageous burlesque upon civilized warfare must have a special chapter to itself, as it concentrates more of Southern littleness and cowardice than is often believed to be true.

Chapter XIII. The Capture of Captain John Brown at the Engine House.

One great difference between savages and civilized nations is the improved mode of warfare adopted by the latter. Flags of truce are always entitled to consideration, and an attacking party would make a wide departure from military usage, were they not to give opportunity for the besieged to capitulate, or to surrender at discretion. Looking at the Harper's Ferry combat in the light of civilized usage, even where one side might be regarded as insurrectionary, the brutal treatment of Captain Brown and his men in the charge by the marines on the engine house is deserving of severest condemnation, and is one of those blood-thirsty occurrences, dark enough in depravity to disgrace a century.

Captain Hazlett and myself being in the Arsenal opposite, saw the charge upon the engine house with the ladder, which resulted in opening the doors to the marines, and finally in Brown's capture. The old hero and his men were hacked and wounded with indecent rage, and at last brought out of the house and laid prostrate upon the ground, mangled and bleeding as they were. A formal surrender was required of Captain Brown, which he refused, knowing how little favor he would receive, if unarmed, at the hands of that infuriated mob. All of our party who went from the Farm, save the Captain, Shields Green, Edwin Coppic and Watson Brown (who had received a mortal wound some time before), the men at the Farm, and Hazlett and I, were either dead or captured before this time; the particulars of whose fate we learned still later in the day, as I shall presently show. Of the four prisoners taken at the engine house, Shields Green, the most inexorable of all our party, a very Turco in his hatred against the stealers of men, was under Captain Hazlett, and consequently of our little band at the Arsenal; but when we were ordered by Captain Brown to return to our positions, after having driven the troops into the bridge, he mistook the order, and went to the engine house instead of with his own party. Had he remained with us, he might have eluded the vigilant Virginians. As it was, he was doomed, as is well known, and became a free-will offering for freedom, with his comrade, John Copeland. Wiser and better men no doubt there were, but a braver man never lived than Shields Green.

Chapter XIV. Setting for the Reasons Why O.P. Anderson and A. Hazlett Escaped from the Arsenal, Instead of Remaining, When They Had Nothing to Do—Took a Prisoner, and What Resulted to Them, And to this Narrative, Therefrom—Pursuit, When Somebody Got Killed, And Other Bodies Wounded.

Of the men assigned a position in the arsenal by Captain Brown, four were either slain or captured; and Hazlett and myself, the only ones remaining, never left our position until we saw, with feelings of intense sadness, that we could be of no further avail to our commander, he being a prisoner in the hands of the Virginians. We therefore, upon consultation, concluded it was better to retreat while it was possible, as our work for the day was clearly finished, and gain a position where in the future we could work with better success, than to recklessly invite capture and brutality at the hands of our enemies. The charge of deserting our brave old leader and of fleeing from danger has been circulated to our detriment, but I have the consolation of knowing that, reckless as were the half-civilized hordes against whom we contended the entire day, and much as they might wish to disparage his men, they would never have thus charged us. They know better. John Brown's men at Harper's Ferry were and are a unit in their devotion to John Brown and the cause he espoused. To have deserted him would have been to belie every manly characteristic for which Albert Hazlett, at least, was known by the party to be distinguished, at the same time that it would have endangered the future safety of such deserter or deserters. John Brown gave orders; those orders must be obeyed, so long as Captain Brown was in a position to enforce them; once unable to command, from death, being a prisoner, or otherwise, the command devolved upon John Henry Kagi. Before Captain Brown was made prisoner, Captain Kagi had ceased to live, though had he been living, all communication between our post and him had been long cut off. We could not aid Captain Brown by remaining. We might, by joining the men at the Farm, devise plans for his succor; or our experience might become available on some future occasion.

The charge of running away from danger could only find form in the mind of some one unwilling to encounter the difficulties of a Harper's Ferry campaign, as no one acquainted with the out-of-door and in-door encounters of that day will charge anyone with wishing to escape danger, merely. It is well enough for men out of danger, and who could not be induced to run the risk of a scratching, to talk flippantly about cowardice, and to sit in judgment upon the men who went with John Brown and who did not fall into the hands of the Virginians; but to have been there, fought there, and to understand what did transpire there, are quite different. As Capt. Brown had all the prisoners with him, the whole force of the enemy was concentrated there, for a time, after the capture of the rifle factory. Having captured our commander, we knew that it was but little two of us could do against so many, and that our turn to be taken must come; so Hazlett and I went out at the back part of the building, climbed up the wall, and went upon the railway. Behind us, in the Arsenal were thousands of dollars, we knew full well but that wealth had no charms for us, and we hastened to communicate with the men sent to the Kennedy Farm. We traveled up the Shenandoah along the railroad, and overtook one of the citizens. He was armed, and had been in the fight in the afternoon. We took him prisoner, in order to facilitate our escape. He submitted without resistance, and quietly gave up his gun. From him we learned substantially of the final struggle at the rifle factory, where the noble Kagi commanded. The number of citizens killed was, according to his opinion, much larger than either Hazlett or I had supposed, although we knew there were a great many killed and wounded together. He said there must be at least seventy killed, besides wounded. Hazlett had said there must be fifty, taking into account the defence of the three strong positions. I do not know positively, but would not put the figure below thirty killed, seeing many fall as I did, and knowing the "dead aim" principle upon which we defended ourselves. One of the Southern published accounts, it will be remembered, said twenty citizens were killed, another said fifteen. At last it got narrowed down to five, which was simply absurd, after so long an engagement. We had forty rounds apiece when we went to the Ferry, and when Hazlett and I left, we had not more than twenty rounds between us. The rest of the party were as free with their ammunition as we were, if not more so. We had further evidence that the number of dead was larger than published, from the many that we saw lying dead around.

When we had gone as far as the foot of the mountains, our prisoner begged us not to take his life, but to let him go at liberty. He said we might keep his gun; he would not inform on us. Feeling compassion for him, and trusting to his honor, we suffered him to go, when he went directly into town, and finding every thing there in the hands of our enemies, he informed on us, and we were pursued. After he had left us, we crawled or climbed up among the rocks in the mountains, some hundred yards or more from the spot where we left him, and hid ourselves, as we feared treachery, on second thought. A few minutes before dark, the troops came in search of us. They came to the foot of the mountains, marched and counter-marched, but never attempted to search the mountains; we supposed from their movements that they feared a host of armed enemies in concealment. Their air was so defiant, and their errand so distasteful to us, that we concluded to apply a little ammunition to their case, and having a few cartridges on hand, we poured from our excellent position in the rocky wilds, some well-directed shots. It was not so dark but that we could see one bite the dust now and then, when others would run to aid them instantly, particularly the wounded. Some lay where they fell, undisturbed, which satisfied us that they were dead. The troops returned our fire, but it was random shooting, as we were concealed from their sight by the rocks and bushes. Interchanging of shots continued for some minutes, with much spirit, when it became quite dark, and they went down into the town. After their return to the Ferry, we could hear the drum beating for a long time; an indication of their triumph, we supposed. Hazlett and I remained in our position three hours, before we dared venture down.

Chapter XV. The Encounter at the Rifle Factory.

As stated in a previous chapter, the command of the rifle factory was given to Captain Kagi. Under him were John Copeland, Sherrard Lewis Leary, and three colored men from the neighborhood. At an early hour, Kagi saw from his position the danger in remaining, with our small company, until assistance could come to the inhabitants. Hence his suggestion to Captain Brown, through Jeremiah Anderson, to leave. His position, being more isolated than the others, was the first to invite an organized attack with success; the Virginians first investing the factory with their hordes, before the final success at the engine house. From the prisoner taken by us who had participated in the assault upon Kagi's position, we received the sad details of the slaughter of our brave companions. Seven different times during the day they were fired upon, while they occupied the interior part of the building, the insurgents defending themselves with great courage, killing and wounding with fatal precision. At last, overwhelming numbers, as many as five hundred, our informant told us, blocked up the front of the building, battered the doors down, and forced their way into the interior. The insurgents were then forced to retreat the back way, fighting, however, all the time. They were pursued, when they took to the river, and it being so shallow, they waded out to a rock, mid-way, and there made a stand being completely hemmed in, front and rear. Some four or five hundred shots, said our prisoner, were fired at them before they were conquered. They would not surrender into the hands of the enemy, but kept on fighting until every one was killed, except John Copeland. Seeing he could do no more, and that all his associates were murdered, he suffered himself to be captured. The party at the rifle factory fought desperately till the last, from their perch on the rock. Slave and free, black and white, carried out the special injunction of the brave old Captain, to make sure work of it. The unfortunate targets for so many bullets from the enemy, some of them received two or three balls. There fell poor Kagi, the friend and adviser of Captain Brown in his most trying positions, and the cleverest man in the party; and there also fell Sherrard Lewis Leary, generous-hearted and companionable as he was, and in that and other difficult positions, brave to desperation. There fought John Copeland, who met his fate like a man. But they were all "honorable men," noble, noble fellows, who fought and died for the most holy principles. John Copeland was taken to the guard-house, where the other prisoners afterwards were, and thence to Charlestown jail. His subsequent mockery of a trial, sentence and execution, with his companion Shields Green, on the 16th of December—are they not part of the dark deeds of this era, which will assign their perpetrators to infamy, and cause after generations to blush at the remembrance? ...

Chapter XIX. The Behavior of the Slaves—Captain Brown's Opinion.

Of the various contradictory reports made by slave-holders and their satellites about the time of the Harper's Ferry conflict, none were more untruthful than those relating to the slaves. There was seemingly a studied attempt to enforce the belief that the slaves were cowardly, and that they were really more in favor of Virginia masters and slavery, than of their freedom. As a party who had an intimate knowledge of the conduct of the colored men engaged, I am prepared to make an emphatic denial of the gross imputation against them, They were charged especially with being unreliable, with deserting Captain Brown at the first opportunity, and going back to their masters; and with being so indifferent to the work of their salvation from the yoke, as to have to be forced into service by the Captain, contrary to their will.

On the Sunday evening of the outbreak, we visited the plantations and acquainted the slaves with our purpose to effect their liberation, the greatest enthusiasm was manifested by them—joy and hilarity beamed from every countenance, One old mother, white-haired from age and borne down with the labors of many years in bond, when told of the work in hand, replied: "God bless you! God bless you!" She then kissed the party at her house, and requested all to kneel, which we did, and she offered prayer to God for His blessing on the enterprise, and our success. At the slaves' quarters, there was apparently a general jubilee, and they stepped forward manfully, without impressing or coaxing. In one case, only, was there any hesitation. A dark-complexioned free-born man refused to take up arms. He showed the only want of confidence in the movement, and far less courage than any slave consulted about the plan. In fact, so far as I could learn, the free blacks in the South are much less reliable than the slaves, and infinitely more fearful. In Washington City, a party of free colored persons offered their services to the Mayor, to aid in suppressing our movement. Of the slaves who followed us to the Ferry, some were sent to help remove stores, and the others were drawn up in a circle around the engine-house, at one time, where they were, by Captain Brown's order, furnished by me with pikes, mostly, and acted as a guard to the prisoners to prevent their escape, which they did.

As in the war of the American Revolution, the first blood shed was a black man's, Crispus Attuck's, so at Harper's Ferry, the first blood shed by our party, after the arrival of the United States troops, was that of a slave. In the beginning of the encounter, and before the troops had fairly emerged from the bridge, a slave was shot. I saw him fall. Phil, the slave who died in prison, with fear, as it was reported, was wounded at the Ferry, and died from the effects of it. Of the men shot on the rocks, when Kagi's party were compelled to take to the river, some were slaves, and they suffered death before they would desert their companions, and their bodies fell into the waves beneath. Captain Brown, who was surprised and pleased by the promptitude with which they volunteered, and with their manly bearing at the scene of violence, remarked to me, on that Monday morning, that he was agreeably disappointed in the behavior of the slaves; for he did not expect one out of ten to be willing to fight. The truth of the Harper's Ferry "raid," as it has been called, in regard to the part taken by the slaves, and the aid given by colored men generally, demonstrates clearly: First, that the conduct of the slaves is a strong guarantee of the weakness of the institution, should a favorable opportunity occur; and, secondly, that the colored people, as a body, were well represented by numbers, both in the fight, and in the number who suffered martyrdom afterward.

The first report of the number of "insurrectionists" killed was seventeen, which showed that several slaves were killed; for there were only ten of the men that belonged to the Kennedy Farm who lost their lives at the Ferry, namely: John Henri Kagi, Jerry Anderson, Watson Brown, Oliver Brown, Stewart Taylor, Adolphus Thompson, William Thompson, William J. Leeman, all eight whites, and Dangerfield Newby and Sherrard Lewis Leary, both colored. The rest reported dead, according to their own showing, were colored. Captain Brown had but seventeen with him, belonging to the Farm, and when all was over, there were four besides himself taken to Charlestown, prisoners, viz: A. D. Stevens, Ed-

win Coppic, white; John A. Copeland and Shields Green, colored. It is plain to be seen from this, that there was a proper percentage of colored men killed at the Ferry, and executed at Charlestown. Of those that escaped from the fangs of the human bloodhounds of slavery, there were four whites, and one colored man, myself being the sole colored man of those at the Farm.

That hundreds of slaves were ready, and would have joined in the work, had Captain Brown's sympathies not been aroused in favor of the families of his prisoners, and that a very different result would have been seen, in consequence, there is no question. There was abundant opportunity for him and the party to leave a place ill which they held entire sway and possession, before the arrival of the troops. And so cowardly were the slaveholders, proper, that from Colonel Lewis Washington, the descendant of the Father of his Country, General George Washington, they were easily taken prisoners. They had not pluck enough to fight, or to use the well-loaded arms in their possession, but were concerned rather in keeping a whole skin by parleying, or in spilling cowardly tears, to excite pity, as did Colonel Washington, and in that way escape merited punishment. No, the conduct of the slaves was beyond all praise; and could our brave old Captain have steeled his heart against the entreaties of his captives, or shut up the fountain of his sympathies against their families—could he, for the moment, have forgotten them, in the selfish thought of his own friends and kindred, or, by adhering to the original plan, have left the place, and thus looked forward to the prospective freedom of the slave—hundreds ready and waiting would have been armed before twenty-four hours had elapsed. As it was, even the noble old man's mistakes were productive of great good, the fact of which the future historian will record, without the embarrassment attending its present narration. John Brown did not only capture and hold Harper's Ferry for twenty hours, but he held the whole South. He captured President Buchanan and his Cabinet, convulsed the whole country, killed Governor Wise, and dug the mine and laid the train which will eventually dissolve the union between Freedom and Slavery. The rebound reveals the truth. So let it be!

GLOSSARY

Crispus Attuck: Crispus Attucks, an African American killed in the Boston Massacre of 1770 and sometimes regarded as the first casualty of American Revolution

engine house: a structure where train engines are housed and repaired

furrin: dialect pronunciation of "foreign"

Governor Wise: Henry Wise of Virginia, who personally interviewed John Brown after his arrest and, with some reluctance, ordered his execution

Kennedy Farm: a Maryland farm Brown rented as a staging area for the raid

Moloch: an ancient god associated with costly sacrifices, often by fire

parleying: talking, from the French *parler* meaning "to talk" or "to speak"

pike:

pitfalls: in combat, concealed holes in the ground, dug with the purpose of impeding or injuring attacking troops

President Buchanan: James Buchanan, the U.S. President from 1857-1861.

Wager House: a hotel in Harpers Ferry

Zouave: originally, a North African soldier who served with the French army but by the time of the Civil War any soldier who adopted the colorful uniform and elaborate drill maneuvers of the Zouaves

Document Analysis

Anderson establishes his credibility in the Preface by arguing that no one can question the fact that he was one of Brown's raiders; after all, he points out that he is a wanted man. He also notes that he is the only one left alive who can give a true account of what happened from the point of view of the raiders.

In Chapter X, Anderson begins with the entry of the raiders into the town of Harpers Ferry and shows how easily Brown and eighteen of his men captured the two bridges into and out of town, the engine house, the arsenal, and the rifle factory.

Anderson is intent on showing the fear and cowardice of some of the southerners who were taken prisoner and offers numerous examples of this in Chapter X. Anderson also tells his readers that each prisoner was assured by his captors that he would not be harmed. In this chapter, Anderson also discusses encounters with local blacks who were asked to "circulate the news," with the result that "many colored men gathered to the scene of action."

Anderson records the spread of fear among the residents of Harpers Ferry and among the prisoners in Chapter XI. More prisoners were taken, and Brown ordered Anderson to begin arming local slaves with pikes.

As in Chapter X, Anderson dwells on the cowardice of white southerners and discusses the difficulty of deciding what to do with prisoners.

In Chapter XII, Anderson reports on the initial triumph of Brown's men over the armed troops who arrived to put down the insurrection. Brown ordered his men out into the street, and they fired upon the troops, scattering them and notes their hasty retreat to the bridge, where they awaited reinforcements.

Anderson continues to good deal of time in this chapter denigrating the southerners, particularly taking aim at the myth of southern chivalry and the alleged bravery of white plantation owners, pointing out that the white lower classes and marines fought the raiders, while slave owners held back.

In Chapter XIII, Anderson again discusses the lack of honor that he witnessed among the raiders' opponents, especially in regard to the flags of truce. Anderson writes that he "saw the charge upon the engine house with the ladder" leading to "Brown's capture," which he describes in some detail. Anderson pays lofty tribute to Green, one of the black raiders who was captured by the marines.

Anderson attempts to explain why he and Hazlett did not remain in Chapter XIV. Since out of the six men originally stationed at the arsenal, he and Hazlett were the only ones left and felt that they could do nothing, they decided to escape while they still could, in order to fight another day. As they escaped, they captured a prisoner who told them that seventy "citizens" had been killed. Again, Anderson is trying to counter subsequent southern claims—in this instance, that Brown's raiders had killed only twenty southerners.

After their prisoner begged for his life and assured them that he would not inform on them, Hazlett and Anderson let him go—but having second thoughts, they soon concealed themselves. Sure enough, troops pursued them, but the two raiders fought them off, killing a few, and the troops returned to Harpers Ferry. Once more, Anderson records the lack of honor among southerners and the cowardice of the enemy.

Anderson admired the wisdom and courage of John Kagi, Brown's second in command, and although he does not openly criticize Brown in Chapter XV, Anderson notes that Kagi foresaw the danger that they were in and urged Brown early on to leave Harpers Ferry, to no avail. As the man was a participant in the assault on Kagi's position, Anderson learns from the prisoner taken by himself and Hazlett the details of Kagi's death. Anderson describes the courage of the rifle factory's defenders

Anderson saves the most controversial subject for Chapter XIX: the actions of local slaves during the Harpers Ferry raid. In order to counter the claims of southerners "that the slaves were cowardly," he gives numerous examples to prove that they were not. They indeed supported the raid, and Brown told him that he was "agreeably disappointed in the behavior of the slaves; for he did not expect one out of ten to be willing to fight." Anderson projects, based on the examples he gives, "that hundreds of slaves were ready, and would have joined in the work, had Captain Brown's sympathies not been aroused in favor of the families of his prisoners." Again, there is a note of criticism in his appraisal of Brown's actions as commander.

Essential Themes

Brown's raid has often been referred to as the "catalyst of the Civil War" because it widened the breach between the North and South. In the North, the philosopher and essayist Ralph Waldo Emerson and the naturalist and writer Henry David Thoreau spoke out in Brown's defense, justifying his violent acts, labeling him a hero, and comparing him to Christ because he had sacrificed his life for the slaves. Even northerners, who disapproved of Brown's violent means, believed that his end—the destruction of slavery—was ultimately good. Indeed, on the day of Brown's execution, northern church bells tolled for the martyred hero. While Brown's belief that violence was required to destroy slavery had not yet gained universal approval among northerners, his actions and his much-quoted antislavery testimony during the trial had given them food for thought; thus, his ideas began gaining support.

When Anderson's account of the raid was published in early 1861, the connection between violence and the question of slavery's expansion or, even, continued existence was foremost on American minds. The cotton growing states of the deep south had seceded from the union and formed the Confederate States of America and, while peace negotiations were ongoing, Americans viewed the future with uncertainty. Anderson's repeated claims about the cowardice and dishonor of the southerners he encountered—particularly slave owners—and the bravery of Brown's men, including African Americans, served as a form of pre-war propaganda, suggesting that if the struggle between north and south were to be decided in combat, the north and their potential African American allies would have an advantage.

———*Peggy A. Russo, PhD*

Bibliography and Additional Reading

Du Bois, W. E. B. *John Brown*. New York: International Publishers, 1962.

Finkelman, Paul, ed. *His Soul Goes Marching On: Responses to John Brown and the Harpers Ferry Raid*. Charlottesville: University Press of Virginia, 1995.

Hinton, Richard J. *John Brown and His Men: With Some Account of the Roads They Traveled to Reach Harper's Ferry*. 1894. Reprint. New York: Arno Press, 1968.

Libby, Jean. *Black Voices from Harpers Ferry: Osborne Anderson and the John Brown Raid*. Palo Alto, Calif. Libby, 1979.

McCarthy, Timothy P., and John Stauffer, eds. *Prophets of Protest: Reconsidering the History of American Abolitionism*. New York: New Press, 2006.

Oates, Stephen B. *To Purge This Land with Blood: A Biography of John Brown*. 2nd ed. Amherst: University of Massachusetts Press, 1985.

Quarles, Benjamin. *Allies for Freedom: Blacks and John Brown*. New York: Oxford University Press, 1974.

Russo, Peggy A., and Paul Finkelman, eds. *Terrible Swift Sword: The Legacy of John Brown*. Athens: Ohio University Press, 2005.

Sanborn, Franklin B. *The Life and Letters of John Brown: Liberator of Kansas and Martyr of Virginia*. 1885. Reprint. New York: Negro Universities Press, 1969.

Stowe, Harriet Beecher. *Uncle Tom's Cabin*. New York: Signet Classics, 2008.

Villard, Oswald Garrison. *John Brown, 1800–1859: A Biography Fifty Years After*. New York: Alfred A. Knopf, 1943.

■ *Incidents in the Life of a Slave Girl*

Date: 1861
Author: Harriet Jacobs
Genre: Book

Summary Overview

Harriet Jacobs's *Incidents in the Life of a Slave Girl: Written by Herself* (1861) is a personal narrative published as the author was approaching fifty years of age on the cusp of the Civil War. Jacobs was born into slavery in North Carolina, but she managed to escape and gain her freedom as well as the freedom of her two children. While the book is autobiographical, it changes the names of the participants, with Jacobs writing under the pseudonym Linda Brent. Her narrative details her life as a young slave girl, focusing on the unrelenting sexual advances she endured from her master. She surveys the time that she spent as a fugitive, including seven years hiding in her grandmother's attic. In detailing her time spent in the North while she was still a fugitive, she emphasizes her efforts to keep her children, who were born into slavery, out of the hands of slave catchers. Chapter XL of Jacobs's book, "The Fugitive Slave Law," details the effect that the 1850 law had on her, her family, and the black community in New York City.

The book originally began appearing in serial form in the *New York Tribune*, a newspaper run by the abolitionist Horace Greeley. Many of the incidents of sexual abuse, however, as well as Jacobs's out-of-wedlock motherhood, were regarded as too shocking for newspaper readers, so Greeley suspended publication before the narrative was completed. It was eventually published in book form in Boston. The narrative went on to find a wide audience, particularly in England, and ranks with Harriet Beecher Stowe's novel *Uncle Tom's Cabin* (1852) as one of the most moving accounts of the conditions of slavery published prior to the Civil War. The book is classed within the slave narrative genre and as such has earned a place beside other influential slave narratives, including the one published by the famed abolitionist and orator Frederick Douglass, *Narrative of the Life of Frederick Douglass, an American Slave* (1845).

Defining Moment

Jacobs's narrative was published in 1861, the year that the sectional conflict dividing the United States erupted into war. For decades the nation had been grappling with the slavery issue. The events of the 1850s, when Jacobs

gained her freedom and began writing her narrative, thrust the nation toward civil war. A key event was the passage of the Compromise of 1850, a package of legislation that included a new Fugitive Slave Act, which was highly controversial because it required federal authorities in the northern states, as well as citizens, to help southern slave catchers in returning runaway slaves to their owners. In many northern states the response to the Fugitive Slave Act was the enactment of personal liberty laws designed to increase the legal rights of accused fugitives and prevent the kidnapping of free blacks. The U.S. Supreme Court, however, overturned these laws, arguing that federal law took precedence over state laws.

Meanwhile, abolitionist societies had sprung up in the North. While some of them were created and run by African Americans, many were the work of whites, particularly Quakers, who had long had a strong religious aversion to slavery. The abolitionist movement shared many of the goals of the incipient women's rights and suffrage movement, so some women, such as Jacobs's friend Amy Post, played key roles in the opposition to slavery and deliberately flouted the law by hiding escaped slaves and giving them aid.

During this period, many people mounted their own campaigns against slavery. Prominent among them was Frederick Douglass, who became one of the nation's most powerful abolitionists and orators as he railed against the evils of slavery. After spending some twenty years as a slave, Douglass escaped, and seven years later he published an autobiography, *Narrative of the Life of Frederick Douglass* (1845). Fanning the flames of opposition to the Fugitive Slave Act was Harriet Beecher Stowe's 1852 novel *Uncle Tom's Cabin*, a graphic depiction of slavery that evoked sympathy and outrage throughout the North. Stowe's depiction of Tom's enslaved life under his cruel white overseer, Simon Legree, mobilized abolitionists and others who had perhaps until then given little thought to the issue.

Author Biography

Harriet Ann Jacobs was born into slavery in Edenton, North Carolina, in 1813. After her mother's death in about 1819, Harriet Jacobs lived with her mother's mistress, Margaret Horniblow, where she learned to read and write and became an accomplished seamstress. Margaret Horniblow died in 1825, apparently leaving Harriet, now twelve years old, to her five-year-old niece. The result was that the niece's father, Dr. James Norcom, became in effect Jacobs's master—and her tormentor for nearly a decade, alternatively threatening and cajoling her in making advances; he never did resort to using force. Jacobs, in an effort to escape his unwanted attentions, paired herself with a white lawyer, Samuel Sawyer, and the two had two children, Joseph and Louisa. Norcom yet threatened to force the children to work on a plantation as slaves if Jacobs did not submit to him. Determined not to let this happen, Jacobs escaped in 1835, to spend seven years hiding out in the attic of her grandmother, Molly Horniblow, a free black who operated a bakery out of her home. Norcom, as Jacobs had predicted, no longer had any use for the children, so he sold them to Sawyer, who granted them their freedom and then arranged for Jacobs and the children to flee to the North.

In 1842 Jacobs was able to escape to Philadelphia, where members of the Vigilant Committee of Philadelphia, an antislavery group, took her in. In 1845 the group helped her get to New York, where she found work as a nursemaid in the home of a prominent writer, Nathaniel Parker Willis, and his wife, Mary. After Mary died, Jacobs remained with Willis and even traveled with him to England. Upon her return to the United States she left Willis's employment and went first to Boston to be with her children and then to Rochester, New York, to be with her brother, John, who had opened a local antislavery reading room and was an abolitionist lecturer.

When the Fugitive Slave Act was passed in 1850, Jacobs and her brother began to fear for their safety. John decided to join the California gold rush, principally because California was not enforcing the act. Sometime around 1852 or 1853, friends suggested that Jacobs write her life story. Jacobs favored the idea, and over the next several years she wrote while living at the Willis home, named Idlewild, in Cornwall, New York. Finally, the book was published privately in 1861. During the Civil War, Jacobs used her newfound celebrity to raise funds to help southern blacks who had fled the Confederacy. After a stay in Savannah, Georgia, she returned north in 1866, to spend her final decades with her daughter in Cambridge, Massachusetts. She died, having survived into her mid-eighties, on March 7, 1897.

HISTORICAL DOCUMENT

XL: The Fugitive Slave Law

My brother, being disappointed in his project, concluded to go to California; and it was agreed that Benjamin should go with him. Ellen liked her school, and was a great favorite there. They did not know her history, and she did not tell it, because she had no desire to make capital out of their sympathy. But when it was accidentally discovered that her mother was a fugitive slave, every method was used to increase her advantages and diminish her expenses.

I was alone again. It was necessary for me to be earning money, and I preferred that it should be among those who knew me. On my return from Rochester, I called at the house of Mr. Bruce, to see Mary, the darling little babe that had thawed my heart, when it was freezing into a cheerless distrust of all my fellow-beings. She was growing a tall girl now, but I loved her always. Mr. Bruce had married again, and it was proposed that I should become nurse to a new infant. I had but one hesitation, and that was my feeling of insecurity in New York, now greatly increased by the passage of the Fugitive Slave Law. However, I resolved to try the experiment. I was again fortunate in my employer. The new Mrs. Bruce was an American, brought up under aristocratic influences and still living in the midst of them; but if she had any prejudice against color, I was never made aware of it; and as for the system of slavery, she had a most hearty dislike of it. No sophistry of Southerners could blind her to its enormity. She was a person of excellent principles and a noble heart. To me, from that hour to the present, she has been a true and sympathizing friend. Blessings be with her and hers!

About the time that I reentered the Bruce family, an event occurred of disastrous import to the colored people. The slave Hamlin, the first fugitive that came under the new law, was given up by the bloodhounds of the north to the bloodhounds of the south. It was the beginning of a reign of terror to the colored population. The great city rushed on in its whirl of excitement, taking no note of the "short and simple annals of the poor." But while fashionables were listening to the thrilling voice of Jenny Lind in Metropolitan Hall, the thrilling voices of poor hunted colored people went up, in an agony of supplication, to the Lord, from Zion's church. Many families, who had lived in the city for twenty years, fled from it now. Many a poor washerwoman, who, by hard labor, had made herself a comfortable home, was obliged to sacrifice her furniture, bid a hurried farewell to friends, and seek her fortune among strangers in Canada. Many a wife discovered a secret she had never known before—that her husband was a fugitive, and must leave her to insure his own safety. Worse still, many a husband discovered that his wife had fled from slavery years ago, and as "the child follows the condition of its mother," the children of his love were liable to be seized and carried into slavery. Every where, in those humble homes, there was consternation and anguish. But what cared the legislators of the "dominant race" for the blood they were crushing out of trampled hearts?

When my brother William spent his last evening with me, before he went to California, we talked nearly all the time of the distress brought on our oppressed people by the passage of this iniquitous law; and never had I seen him manifest such bitterness of spirit, such stern hostility to our oppressors. He was himself free from the operation of the law; for he did not run from any Slaveholding State, being brought into the Free States by his master. But I was subject to it; and so were hundreds of intelligent and industrious people all around us. I seldom ventured into the streets; and when it was necessary to do an errand for Mrs. Bruce, or any of the family, I went as much as possible through back streets and by-ways. What a disgrace to a city calling itself free, that inhabitants, guiltless of offence, and seeking to perform their duties conscientiously, should be condemned to live in such incessant fear, and have nowhere to turn for protection! This state of things, of course, gave rise to many impromptu vigilance committees. Every colored person, and ev-

ery friend of their persecuted race, kept their eyes wide open. Every evening I examined the newspapers carefully, to see what Southerners had put up at the hotels. I did this for my own sake, thinking my young mistress and her husband might be among the list; I wished also to give information to others, if necessary; for if many were "running to and fro," I resolved that "knowledge should be increased."

This brings up one of my Southern reminiscences, which I will here briefly relate. I was somewhat acquainted with a slave named Luke, who belonged to a wealthy man in our vicinity. His master died, leaving a son and daughter heirs to his large fortune. In the division of the slaves, Luke was included in the son's portion. This young man became a prey to the vices growing out of the "patriarchal institution," and when he went to the north, to complete his education, he carried his vices with him. He was brought home, deprived of the use of his limbs, by excessive dissipation. Luke was appointed to wait upon his bed-ridden master, whose despotic habits were greatly increased by exasperation at his own helplessness. He kept a cowhide beside him, and, for the most trivial occurrence, he would order his attendant to bare his back, and kneel beside the couch, while he whipped him till his strength was exhausted. Some days he was not allowed to wear any thing but his shirt, in order to be in readiness to be flogged. A day seldom passed without his receiving more or less blows. If the slightest resistance was offered, the town constable was sent for to execute the punishment, and Luke learned from experience how much more the constable's strong arm was to be dreaded than the comparatively feeble one of his master. The arm of his tyrant grew weak, and was finally palsied; and then the constable's services were in constant requisition. The fact that he was entirely dependent on Luke's care, and was obliged to be tended like an infant, instead of inspiring any gratitude or compassion towards his poor slave, seemed only to increase his irritability and cruelty. As he lay there on his bed, a mere disgraced wreck of manhood, he took into his head the strangest freaks of despotism; and if Luke hesitated to submit to his orders, the constable was immediately sent for. Some of these freaks were of a nature too filthy to be repeated. When I fled from the house of bondage, I left poor Luke still chained to the bedside of this cruel and disgusting wretch.

One day, when I had been requested to do an errand for Mrs. Bruce, I was hurrying through back streets, as usual, when I saw a young man approaching, whose face was familiar to me. As he came nearer, I recognized Luke. I always rejoiced to see or hear of any one who had escaped from the black pit; but, remembering this poor fellow's extreme hardships, I was peculiarly glad to see him on Northern soil, though I no longer called it *free* soil. I well remembered what a desolate feeling it was to be alone among strangers, and I went up to him and greeted him cordially. At first, he did not know me; but when I mentioned my name, he remembered all about me. I told him of the Fugitive Slave Law, and asked him if he did not know that New York was a city of kidnappers.

He replied, "De risk ain't so bad for me, as 'tis fur you. 'Cause I runned away from de speculator, and you runned away from de massa. Dem speculators vont spen dar money to come here fur a runaway, if dey ain't sartin sure to put dar hans right on him. An I tell you I's tuk good car 'bout dat. I had too hard times down dar, to let 'em ketch dis nigger."

He then told me of the advice he had received, and the plans he had laid. I asked if he had money enough to take him to Canada. "'Pend upon it, I hab," he replied. "I tuk car fur dat. I'd bin workin all my days fur dem cussed whites, an got no pay but kicks and cuffs. So I tought dis nigger had a right to money nuff to bring him to de Free States. Massa Henry he lib till ebery body vish him dead; an ven he did die, I knowed de debbil would hab him, an vouldn't vant him to bring his money 'long too. So I tuk some of his bills, and put 'em in de pocket of his ole trousers. An ven he was buried, dis nigger ask fur dem ole trousers, an dey gub 'em to me." With a low, chuckling laugh, he added, "You see I didn't *steal* it; dey *gub* it to me. I tell you, I had mighty hard time to keep de speculator from findin it; but he didn't git it."

This is a fair specimen of how the moral sense is educated by slavery. When a man has his wages stolen from him, year after year, and the laws sanction and enforce the theft, how can he be expected to have more regard to honesty than has the man who robs him? I have become somewhat enlightened, but I confess that I agree with poor, ignorant, much-abused Luke, in thinking he had a *right* to that money, as a portion of his unpaid wages. He went to Canada forthwith, and I have not since heard from him.

All that winter I lived in a state of anxiety. When I took the children out to breathe the air, I closely observed the countenances of all I met. I dreaded the approach of summer, when snakes and slaveholders make their appearance. I was, in fact, a slave in New York, as subject to slave laws as I had been in a Slave State. Strange incongruity in a State called free!

Spring returned, and I received warning from the south that Dr. Flint knew of my return to my old place, and was making preparations to have me caught. I learned afterwards that my dress, and that of Mrs. Bruce's children, had been described to him by some of the Northern tools, which slaveholders employ for their base purposes, and then indulge in sneers at their cupidity and mean servility.

I immediately informed Mrs. Bruce of my danger, and she took prompt measures for my safety. My place as nurse could not be supplied immediately, and this generous, sympathizing lady proposed that I should carry her baby away. It was a comfort to me to have the child with me; for the heart is reluctant to be torn away from every object it loves. But how few mothers would have consented to have one of their own babes become a fugitive, for the sake of a poor, hunted nurse, on whom the legislators of the country had let loose the bloodhounds! When I spoke of the sacrifice she was making, in depriving herself of her dear baby, she replied, "It is better for you to have baby with you, Linda; for if they get on your track, they will be obliged to bring the child to me; and then, if there is a possibility of saving you, you shall be saved."

This lady had a very wealthy relative, a benevolent gentleman in many respects, but aristocratic and pro-slavery. He remonstrated with her for harboring a fugitive slave; told her she was violating the laws of her country; and asked her if she was aware of the penalty. She replied, "I am very well aware of it. It is imprisonment and one thousand dollars fine. Shame on my country that it *is* so! I am ready to incur the penalty. I will go to the state's prison, rather than have any poor victim torn from *my* house, to be carried back to slavery."

The noble heart! The brave heart! The tears are in my eyes while I write of her. May the God of the helpless reward her for her sympathy with my persecuted people!

I was sent into New England, where I was sheltered by the wife of a senator, whom I shall always hold in grateful remembrance. This honorable gentleman would not have voted for the Fugitive Slave Law, as did the senator in "Uncle Tom's Cabin;" on the contrary, he was strongly opposed to it; but he was enough under its influence to be afraid of having me remain in his house many hours. So I was sent into the country, where I remained a month with the baby. When it was supposed that Dr. Flint's emissaries had lost track of me, and given up the pursuit for the present, I returned to New York.

GLOSSARY

Benjamin: the fictional name Jacobs gives to her son, Joseph

"the child follows the condition of its mother": a reference to the fact that under the law, the children of a slave mother were automatically born as slaves

Dr. Flint: the fictional name Jacobs gives to her master and tormentor, Dr. James Norcom

Fugitive Slave Law: the Fugitive Slave Act of 1850

Jenny Lind: a famous Swedish opera singer

Linda: Linda Brent, the persona Jacobs adopts in her narrative

Mr. Bruce: the fictional name Jacobs gives to Nathanial Parker Willis, the New Yorker who took her in

"running to and fro"…"knowledge should be increased": quotations from the book of Daniel in the King James Bible

"short and simple annals of the poor": a line originally from Thomas Gray's 1751 poem "Elegy Written in a Country Churchyard," later used by Abraham Lincoln to describe his childhood

speculator: a person who purchased the rights to runaway slaves so as to catch them and then sell them to the highest bidder

Uncle Tom's Cabin: the widely read antislavery novel by Harriet Beecher Stowe

wife of a Senator: probably a reference to Robert Rantoul, Jr., an outspoken opponent of the Fugitive Slave Act

William: the fictional name Jacobs gives her brother John

Document Analysis

Chapter XL in *Incidents in the Life of a Slave Girl* is titled "The Fugitive Slave Law" and is the book's penultimate chapter. Earlier chapters detail Jacobs's life from her girlhood in North Carolina through her flight to her grandmother's home, her escape to Philadelphia, her time with the Willis family, her freedom, and other events. Throughout the narration the names of the characters are changed, such that she herself is "Linda Brent," her brother is "William Brent," her children are "Benjamin" (or "Benny") and "Ellen," Dr. Norcom is named "Dr. Flint," Samuel Sawyer is "Mr. Sands," Nathaniel Parker Willis is "Mr. Bruce," and Willis's second wife, who bought Jacobs's freedom, is "Cornelia Bruce."

By the first paragraph of Chapter XL, the narration has reached the time when William Brent decides to head to California to take part in the gold rush and agrees that Benjamin, Linda Brent's son, will go with him. Left alone, the narrator decides to return to New York and to the Bruce family, where she was previously employed. Mr. Bruce has taken a new wife, Cornelia, whom the narrator describes as "aristocratic" but also as heartily opposed to slavery and resistant to any of the "sophistry" used by southerners to defend it. In the third paragraph, the narrator makes reference to an event of "disastrous import to the colored people"—the passage of the Fugitive Slave Act of 1850. She refers to a slave by the name of Hamlin who was hunted down by the "bloodhounds" of the North and South in New York. In describing the impact of the law on New Yorkers, she refers to the "short and simple annals of the poor." This is a line originally from Thomas Gray's famous poem "Elegy Written in a Country Churchyard" (1751) and later used by Abraham Lincoln in 1859 to describe his childhood. The paragraph also makes reference to Jenny Lind, a Swedish opera singer known in America as the "Swedish Nightingale." The narrator makes the point that while "fashionables" were listening to opera, "the thrilling voices of poor hunted colored people went up…from Zion's church," a reference to the city's African Methodist Episcopal Zion Church.

Because of the new law, many blacks who had found homes in the city had little choice but to flee, perhaps to Canada; many wives and husbands discovered that their spouses were fugitive slaves and liable to capture. Making matters worse was the fact that children born to a slave mother were themselves legally slaves, so fathers faced the prospect of losing not only their wives but also their children to slave catchers.

In paragraph 4 the narrator refers to the discussions she and her brother had before he left for California, pointing out his anger at the new law. The narrator then goes on to describe how she and others had to go about the city through back streets and byways, living in constant fear of being taken by slave catchers. Vigilance committees were formed to keep tabs on the activities of slave catchers, and New York's blacks kept their eyes on newspapers that reported the arrival of southerners at the city's hotels. The phrases "running to and fro" and "knowledge should be increased" are from the book of Daniel in the King James Bible.

In paragraphs 5–9, the narrator tells the story of a slave named Luke whom she had known as a child.

Luke had been owned by a particularly cruel master who depended on Luke for his care but beat him constantly—or called on the town constable to do so for him. After the master died, Luke hid some of the man's money in the pocket of the pants in which he would be buried. At the time of the burial, Luke asked for the pants, in this way getting funds that enabled him to flee to New York with the goal of reaching Canada—where he would have joined an estimated twenty thousand New York African Americans who fled to Canada after the law was passed. The narrator encounters Luke in New York and learns of his plans. Luke refers to "speculators," men who purchased the rights to runaway slaves so as to catch them and then sell them to the highest bidder. The narrator concludes this portion of the account by noting that Luke's tale offered an example of how the slave system corrupted morals: "When a man has his wages stolen from him, year after year, and the laws sanction and enforce the theft, how can he be expected to have more regard to honesty than has the man who robs him?"

With paragraph 10, the narrator returns to her own experiences, again stressing how anxious she was that she could be caught, especially with the approach of summer. She reflects on the irony that she was in a "free" state but still felt like a slave. Her anxiety was well advised, for she learned that Dr. Flint was on the hunt for her and had learned from informants about her mode of dress. In point of fact, the real-life Norcom placed newspaper ads in which he offered a reward of $100 for information about her. The ads stressed that "being a good seamstress, she has been accustomed to dress well, has a variety of very fine clothes, made in the prevailing fashion, and will probably appear, if abroad, tricked out in gay and fashionable finery." When she informed Mrs. Bruce of the danger she was in, Mrs. Bruce offered to allow the narrator to carry her daughter about so that if the narrator were caught, the authorities would have to return the Bruce child to her mother. In this way Mrs. Bruce could learn of the capture and take action to help. In paragraph 13 the narrator notes that Mrs. Bruce had a proslavery relative who questioned her decision to harbor a fugitive slave. When he asked her whether she knew the penalty for doing so, she acknowledged that she did but expressed her willingness to go to jail "rather than have any poor victim torn from *my* house, to be carried back to slavery." The narrator concludes the account by noting that she went to the safety of Massachusetts to avoid capture. The

Massachusetts senator referred to by the narrator was probably Robert Rantoul, Jr., an outspoken opponent of the Fugitive Slave Act who provided a legal defense for Thomas Sims, the first purported slave captured under the new act in Massachusetts.

Essential Themes

Jacobs confessed in letters to her friend Post that she felt some reticence about committing her life story to paper, largely because it would deal with the sexual exploitation of slaves and because she would have to make known her own status as an unwed mother. It was for these reasons that she created the fictional persona Linda Brent, who narrates the story. The book differed from other slave narratives of the era in its focus on two major themes regarding the female narrator's life, as that of a "fallen woman" and as that of a heroic woman who keeps her children from falling prey to chattel slavery. Notably, the book accordingly uses two different styles: When Jacobs is discussing her efforts on behalf of her children, she writes in a direct, pointed style. When the subject turns to sexual exploitation and her own sexual history, the style becomes more indirect and elevated, similar to the style of much popular fiction from the time. The fact that Jacobs's narrative was written by a woman was alone a distinguishing factor. The slave narratives of writers such as Frederick Douglass and Solomon Northup focus on the largely solitary efforts of a heroic man. Jacobs, on the other hand, embedded her narrative in more of a social context that includes family relationships and friendships both within and outside the black community.

——*Michael J. O'Neal, PhD*

Bibliography and Additional Reading

Fisch, Audrey, ed. *The Cambridge Companion to the African American Slave Narrative*. Cambridge, U.K. Cambridge University Press, 2007.

Heglar, Charles J. *Rethinking the Slave Narrative: Slave Marriage and the Narratives of Henry Bibb and William and Ellen Craft*. Westport, Conn. Greenwood Press, 2001.

Johnson, Yvonne. *The Voices of African American Women: The Use of Narrative and Authorial Voice in the Works of Harriet Jacobs, Zora Neale Hurston, and Alice Walker*. New York: Peter Lang, 1998.

Washington, Mary Helen. "Meditations on History: The Slave Narrative of Linda Brent." In *Invented Lives: Narratives of Black Women, 1860–1960*, ed. Mary Helen Washington. New York: Doubleday, 1987.

Yellin, Jean Fagan. *Harriet Jacobs: A Life*. Cambridge, Mass. Basic Civitas Books, 2004.

■ "Under the Flag"

Date: 1861
Author: Wendell Phillips
Genre: Speech

Summary Overview

Wendell Phillips's calling was that of the political agitator, and his gifts were those of a compelling public speaker and intellectual. Since his speeches circulated widely in print, his audiences of readers were even more numerous and far-flung than those who heard him in person. His embrace of civil war as a means to annihilate slavery is evident in "Under the Flag" (1861), a speech Phillips delivered in Boston just nine days after Confederate forces fired on a U.S. military installation at Fort Sumter in South Carolina, marking the beginning of the Civil War.

Defining Moment

Phillips delivered this speech just as sectional crisis was merging with the Civil War. Following Abraham Lincoln's election in November 1860, nearly all of the slave states seceded. On April 12, l861, Confederates then U.S. forces attempting to provision Fort Sumter, the federal installation located in Charleston Harbor in South Carolina. This hostile act led Lincoln's call for seventy-five thousand troops to prevent seceding states from leaving the Union. Lincoln's appeal to arms placed Phillips in a difficult position.

For nearly two decades Phillips had been the abolitionists' premier advocate of northern disunion, the doctrine that slavery could be abolished only if the free states dissolved their constitutional ties with the South. Arguing that in 1787 the Founding Fathers had built protections for slavery throughout the Constitution, Phillips had insisted that the institution's survival depended entirely on northern legal and political support. Were this support withdrawn, slavery would collapse either through insurrection or as a result of planters' demoralization. Throughout the crisis of 1861, Phillips had deployed these arguments to urge that the seceding states be allowed to depart in peace. Now, however, Lincoln had declared a war against the slave system that Phillips so hated in order to preserve the Union that Phillips had so long condemned. In this speech Phillips resolves this obvious contradiction by abandoning his northern disunionism while welcoming civil war as the means for forging a new and radically egalitarian American state.

Author Biography

Born in Boston in 1811, Wendell Phillips joined the American Anti-Slavery Society in 1837. Phillips became a highly sought-after public speaker despite his controversial advocacy of immediate emancipation, racial equality, women's rights, and antislavery violence and his denunciations of American politics as irredeemably pro-slavery.

Within the American Anti-Slavery Society, Phillips became the abolitionists' resident intellectual by developing sophisticated justifications for the role of radical agitators in refreshing America's democracy. He also became their leading legal controversialist by attacking the movement's opponents with unmatched vitriol and by developing widely debated claims that the United States Constitution was a pro-slavery document. Phillips had the unique ability to make ordinary Americans respond substantively to the egalitarianism of an otherwise highly unpopular radical abolitionist movement. His extraordinary oratory explains this result, but only when it is recalled that Phillips was steeped in a nationalistic version of American history that touched the memories, fears, and aspirations of his ever-expanding Yankee audiences.

As conflict deepened between North and South during the 1850s, Phillips became a proponent of violent resistance, and when the insurrectionist John Brown invaded Harpers Ferry, Virginia, in 1859, Phillips defended him. He embraced the Civil War as a crusade for black equality and took a prominent role in efforts to achieve these goals during the reconstruction of the postwar South from 1865 to 1870. After the dissolution of the American Anti-Slavery Society in 1870, Phillips continued demanding black equality but also expanded his advocacy to include the labor movement, temperance, women's suffrage, and equal rights for Native Americans and Chinese immigrants. He died on February 2, 1884.

HISTORICAL DOCUMENT

MANY times this winter, here and elsewhere, I have counselled peace,—urged, as well as I knew how, the expediency of acknowledging a Southern Confederacy, and the peaceful separation of these thirty-four States. One of the journals announces to you that I come here this morning to retract those opinions. No, not one of them! I need them all,—every word I have spoken this winter,—every act of twenty-five years of my life, to make the welcome I give this war hearty and hot....

All winter long, I have acted with that party which cried for peace. The antislavery enterprise to which I belong started with peace written on its banner. We imagined that the age of bullets was over; that the age of ideas had come; that thirty millions of people were able to take a great question, and decide it by the conflict of opinions; that, without letting the ship of state founder, we could lift four millions of men into Liberty and Justice. We thought that if your statesmen would throw away personal ambition and party watchwords, and devote themselves to the great issue, this might be accomplished. To a certain extent it has been. The North has answered to the call. Year after year, event by event, has indicated the rising education of the people,—the readiness for a higher moral life, the calm, self-poised confidence in our own convictions that patiently waits—like master for a pupil—for a neighbor's conversion. The North has responded to the call of that peaceful, moral, intellectual agitation which the antislavery idea has initiated. Our mistake, if any, has been that we counted too much on the intelligence of the masses, on the honesty and wisdom of statesmen as a class. Perhaps we did not give weight enough to the fact we saw, that this nation is made up of different ages; not homogeneous, but a mixed mass of different centuries. The North *thinks*,—can appreciate argument,—is the nineteenth century,—hardly any struggle left in it but that between the working class and the money-kings. The South *dreams*,—it is the thirteenth and fourteenth century,—baron and serf,—noble and slave. Jack Cade and Wat Tyler loom over its horizon, and the serf, rising, calls for another Thierry to record his struggle. There the fagot still burns which the Doctors of the Sorbonne called, ages ago, "the best light to guide the erring." There men are tortured for opinions, the only punishment the Jesuits were willing their pupils should look on. This is, perhaps, too flattering a picture of the South. Better call her, as Sumner does, "the Barbarous States." Our struggle, therefore, is between barbarism and civilization. Such can only be settled by arms. The government has waited until its best friends almost suspected its courage or its integrity; but the cannon shot against Fort Sumter has opened the only door out of this hour. There were but two. One was compromise; the other was battle. The integrity of the North closed the first; the generous forbearance of nineteen States closed the other. The South opened this with cannon-shot, and Lincoln shows himself at the door. The war, then, is not aggressive, but in self defence, and Washington has become the Thermopylae at Liberty and Justice. Rather than surrender that Capital, cover every square feet of it with a living body; crowd it with a million of men, and empty every bank vault at the North to pay the cost. Teach the world once for all, that North America belongs to the Stars and Stripes, and under them no man shall wear a chain. In the whole of this conflict, I have looked only at Liberty,—only at the slave....

The noise and dust of the conflict may hide the real question at issue. Europe may think, some of us may, that we are fighting for forms and parchments, for sovereignty and a flag. But really the war is one of opinions: it is Civilization against Barbarism: it is Freedom against Slavery. The cannon-shot against Fort Sumter was the yell of pirates against the DECLARATION OF INDEPENDENCE, the war-cry of the North is the echo of that sublime pledge. The South, defying Christianity, clutches its victim. The North offers its wealth and blood in glad atonement for the selfishness of seventy years. The result is as sure as the throne of God. I believe in the possibility of justice, in the certainty of union. Years hence, when the smoke of this conflict clears away, the world will see under our banner all tongues, all creeds, all races,—one brotherhood,—and on the banks of the Potomac, the Genius of Liberty, robed in light, four and thirty stars for her diadem, broken chains under feet, and an olive-branch in her right hand.

GLOSSARY

diadem: crown

Fort Sumter: the U.S. fort on the coast of South Carolina, site of the first hostilities in the Civil War

Jack Cade: the leader of a revolt in England in 1450

Jesuits: an order of Catholic priests, known historically for their efforts to expose and eliminate heresy, or false church doctrine

olive-branch: a traditional symbol of peace

Potomac: the Potomac River, often used as a figure of speech to refer to the area surrounding Washington, D.C., and the seat of government

Sumner: Charles Sumner, U.S. senator, abolitionist, and one of the leaders of the Radical Republicans during Reconstruction

Thermopylae: the Greek site of the Battle of Thermopylae in 480 BCE

Thierry: nineteenth-century liberal French historian Augustin Thierry

Wat Tyler: leader of the English Peasants' Revolt of 1381

Document Analysis

Phillps begins his speech by explaining that he has, over the chaotic and troubling secession winter of 1861, advised peace and reminds his audience that he has advised the recognition of the Confederacy and a "peaceful separation" of the United States. While some have reported, he claims, that he is planning on retracting his ideas, he denies this. He welcomes the war.

Abolitionism, he explains, had always embraced peace, had hoped that "the age of bullets was over; that the age of ideas had come," and could work for the freedom of slaves without a national catastrophe. The north had responded to "the call of that peaceful, moral, intellectual agitation which the antislavery idea has initiated." The problem, Phillips, explains is not so much that the United States consists of different ideas or policies but that it actually consists of people who live in "a mixed mass of different centuries."

The North, he explains, is rational and logical. It "thinks," in Phillips's words and "can appreciate argument." In this way, the North not only exists in the nineteenth century, but in a way "is" the nineteenth century. Other than the growing conflict between socio-economic classes, it has "hardly any struggle left."

The South, however, does not think—it "dreams." It represents the late medieval period—the thirteenth and fourteenth centuries— and the feudal structure which characterized that era in Europe. Here, Phillips refers to revolutionary figures such as Wat Tyler, a leader in England's fourteenth century peasant uprising. The South, in Phillips's presentation, is a place where people are tortured for their opinions, like the heretics of long ago. He cites Senator Charles Sumner—who was beaten severely on the floor of the Senate in retaliation for comments he made about slaveowners—in calling the South "the Barbarous States." Such a "struggle between "barbarism and civilization" can only, Phillips asserts, be settled by force. With the Confederate attack on Fort Sumter, he explains, this becomes a matter of self defense for the north.

Referring to the ancient war between the Athenians and Persians, Phillips refers to Washington as "the Thermopylae at Liberty and Justice" and urges a strong defense of the nation using hyperbole ("cover every square feet of it with a living body"; "empty every bank vault in the North to pay the cost") to convey the severity of the nation's plight. He then ties the defense of the Union with the abolitionist cause, proclaiming that the United States would "Teach the world once for all, that North America belongs to the Stars and Stripes, and under them no man shall wear a chain."

Phillips, in closing the speech, cautions that the chaos and destruction of the coming war carries with it the danger of hiding "the real question at issue"—the ending of slavery. Here, he raises the issue of "Civilization against Barbarism," explicitly equating that battle to "Freedom against "Slavery." He views the coming losses of men and money in the war to a sacrifice to atone for the existence of slavery since the nation's founding and predicts that, in the end, the nation will be whole and free of slavery.

Essential Themes
Phillips demonstrates throughout this speech the enormous differences that always distinguished his understanding of the Civil War from the views of those who prosecuted it, Lincoln and the Republican Party. For Lincoln and for most Republicans, warfare aimed to reassemble the Union as it had existed prior to 1861, not to remake the nation through social and political revolution. Even when Lincoln issued the Emancipation Proclamation, he made clear that his primary motive was to restore the Union. In this fundamental respect, the "union" to which Phillips swore his allegiance in 1861 was worlds apart from the Constitution that Lincoln maintained.

In this address Phillips makes the revolutionary nature of his expectations clear in his dramatic contrasts between a South mired in the "barbarism" of the "thirteenth and fourteenth century" and a North that "thinks" and is fully involved in the egalitarian "nineteenth century." Warfare between two such antithetical civilizations, "Civilization against Barbarism" must, in Phillips's view, lead to the destruction of the latter and to the complete transformation of the entire nation to lift up "all tongues, all creeds, all races—one brotherhood." Implicit in this prediction are all the specific measures that Phillips and other radical abolitionists demanded during the war and in its immediate aftermath. For Phillips and the other radicals for whom he spoke, final victory would be assured only when the emancipated slaves possessed complete civil rights, occupation of lands confiscated from rebel planters, access to education, and unqualified male suffrage. In this respect, Phillips's "Under the Flag" oration clearly anticipated the epochal struggles for racial equality in the South after emancipation.

——James Brewer Stewart, PhD
with additional material by Aaron Gulyas, MA

Bibliography and Additional Reading
Aisèrithe, A.J. and Donald Yacovone, eds. *Wendell Phillips, Social Justice, and the Power of the Past* (Baton Rouge: Louisiana State University Press, 2016).

Hinks, Peter P, John R. McKivigan, and R. Owen Williams. Encyclopedia of Antislavery and Abolition: Greenwood Milestones in African American History. (Westport, Connecticut: Greenwood Press, 2007).

Osofsky, Gilbert. "Wendell Phillips and the Quest for a New American National Identity" *Canadian Review of Studies in Nationalism* 1973 1(1): 15-46.

Stewart, James B. "Heroes, Villains, Liberty, and License: the Abolitionist Vision of Wendell Phillips" in *Antislavery Reconsidered: New Perspectives on the Abolitionists* (Louisiana State U. Press, 1979): 168-191.

■ Valedictory Editorial of the *Liberator*

Date: 1865
Author: William Lloyd Garrison
Genre: Editorial

Summary Overview

William Lloyd Garrison's self-described roles were those of agitator, moral censor, prophet, and "universal reformer." His gifts were his extraordinary skills as an editorial polemicist and his resolve to follow the implications of his religious illuminations wherever they might lead him. In an age of rapidly multiplying editorial voices, Garrison proved to be a master of making himself (as he put it in his First *Liberator* Editorial) "heard!" When the Thirteenth Amendment was ratified, Garrison ended his thirty-five-year editorship of his abolitionist newspaper. In the Valedictory Editorial of the *Liberator* he explains why, in his view, an organized abolitionist movement was no longer needed. Garrison's vision of the abolition movement was quite literal—the thirteenth amendment ended slavery in the United States but it did not, as events would prove, guarantee the protections of citizenship or civil rights on the newly freed slaves. Garrison's "Valedictory" is, in many ways, about what he saw as *his* victory as much as it is about the victory of freedom over slavery.

Defining Moment

By December 1865, the Civil War between the forces of the Federal government and the rebellious Confederate States of America had ended (in April of that year). The thirteenth amendment to the US Constitution, which prohibited "slavery or involuntary servitude" was passed by the Senate on April 8, 1864, ratified by the required number of states on December 6, 1865, and formally declared to be adopted twelve days later on December 18.

This was not, of course, the first federal measure during the Civil War period to severely limit slavery. In January, 1863, President Abraham Lincoln issued the Emancipation Proclamation which declared that "all persons held as slaves within any State or designated part of a State the people whereof shall then be in rebellion against the United States shall be then, thenceforward, and forever free." The key limitation on the Emancipation Proclamation, however, was that it did not free slaves in those border states that stayed loyal to the union and where slavery was legal (such

as Missouri, Kentucky, Maryland, and Delaware). Lincoln's proclamation provided a firm legal basis for the Union army to free slaves in conquered areas of the Confederacy but it was not a blanket proclamation of slavery's end.

And while the thirteenth amendment ended slavery, it did nothing to confer citizenship on the newly freed slaves. Indeed, in 1857, the Supreme Court ruled (in *Dred Scott v. Sanford*) that even free people of color were not citizens of the United States. Southern states, after the war, quickly enacted laws known as Black Codes which placed restrictions on the freed men and woman's liberty. Abolitionists knew that despite the end of literal slavery in the south, there was still work to do. William Lloyd Garrison—one of the most radical of the abolitionists—had decided, however, to exit the scene and end publication of his groundbreaking paper, the *Liberator*.

Author Biography

William Lloyd Garrison was born in Newburyport, Massachusetts, on December 10, 1805. In 1831, he published the first issue of his Boston newspaper, the *Liberator*, which until the end of 1865 served as his personal vehicle for broadcasting his many controversial opinions, most notably that slavery must be immediately abolished and that people of all skin colors must be treated as equals. In 1833 he played a major role in the establishment of the American Anti-Slavery Society, which for the first time united black and white reformers of both genders in support of programs of mass agitation to promote immediate abolition and racial equality.

Throughout the 1840s and 1850s Garrison and his small circle continued to espouse a wide-ranging reform agenda through speeches and in the pages of the *Liberator*. In 1859, however, John Brown's insurrectionary raid on the federal armory at Harpers Ferry, Virginia, led Garrison to jettison his pacifism. When the Civil War began in 1861, he quickly became one of its most fervent supporters, demanding that all slaves be freed by force of arms. In 1865, after the ratification of the Thirteenth Amendment, abolishing slavery, Garrison closed the *Liberator* and ended his career. He died on May 24, 1879.

Garrison was perhaps the antebellum era's most innovative editorial agitator. In an era of rapidly expanding print and telegraphic communication, his ceaseless desire to promote himself as the nation's moral censor and his unerring capacity for challenging conventional values made it all but impossible for Americans to deny the moral problem of slavery. He accomplished his goals because of his exceptional talent as a polemicist and his inexhaustible love of ideological conflict. His temperament aligned him closely to the romantic impulses that inspired New England Transcendentalists and utopian reformers who, like him, were deeply suspicious of established institutions and who celebrated intuitive illuminations of God's "truth." In short, he addressed public opinion in idioms it instinctively understood.

HISTORICAL DOCUMENT

I began the publication of the *Liberator* without a subscriber, and I end it—it gives me unalloyed satisfaction to say—without a farthing as the pecuniary result of the patronage extended to it during thirty-five years of unremitted labors.

From the immense change wrought in the national feeling and sentiment on the subject of slavery, the *Liberator* derived no advantage at any time in regard to its circulation. The original "disturber of the peace," nothing was left undone at the beginning, and up to the hour of the late rebellion, by Southern slaveholding villainy on the one hand, and Northern pro-slavery malice on the other, to represent it as too vile a sheet to be countenanced by any claiming to be Christian or patriotic; and it always required rare moral courage or singular personal independence to be among its patrons. Never had a journal to look such opposition in the face—never was one so constantly belied and caricatured. If it had advocated all the crimes forbidden by the moral law of God and the statutes of the State, instead of vindicating the sacred claims of oppressed and bleeding humanity, it could not have been more vehemently denounced or more indignantly repudiated. To this day—such is the force of prejudice—there are multitudes who cannot be induced to read a single number of it, even on the score of curiosity, though their views on the slavery question are now precisely those which it has uniformly advocated....Yet no journal has been conducted with such fairness and impartiality; none has granted such freedom in its columns to its opponents; none has so scrupulously and uniformly presented all sides of every question discussed in its pages; none has so readily and exhaustively published, without note or comment, what its enemies have said to its disparagement, and the vilification of its editor; none has vindicated primitive Christianity, in its spirit and purpose—"the higher law," in its supremacy over nations and governments as well as individual conscience—the Golden Rule; in its binding obligation upon all classes—the Declaration of Independence, with its self-evident truths— the rights of human nature, without distinction of race, complexion or sex—more earnestly or more uncompromisingly; none has exerted a higher moral or more broadly reformatory influence upon those who have given it a careful perusal; and none has gone beyond it in asserting the Fatherhood of God and the brotherhood of man. All this may be claimed for it without egotism or presumption....

In this connection, I must be permitted to express my surprise that I am gravely informed, in various quarters, that this is no time to retire from public labor; that though the chains of the captive have been broken, he is yet to be vindicated in regard to the full possession of equal civil and political rights; that the freedmen in every part of the South are subjected to many insults and outrages; that the old slaveholding spirit is showing itself in every available form; that there is imminent danger that, in the hurry of reconstruction and readmission to the Union, the late rebel States will be left free to work any amount of mischief; that there is manifestly a severe struggle yet to come with the Southern "powers of darkness," which will require the utmost vigilance and the most determined efforts on the part of the friends of impartial liberty—&c., &c., &c. Surely, it is not meant by all this that I am therefore bound to continue the publication of the *Liberator*; for that is a matter for me to determine, and no one else. As I commenced its publication with out asking leave of any one, so I claim to be competent to decide when it may fitly close its career.

Again—it cannot be meant, by this presentation of the existing state of things at the South, either to impeach my intelligence, or to impute to me a lack of interest in behalf of that race, for the liberation and elevation of which I have labored so many years! If, when they had no friends, and no hope of earthly redemption, I did not hesitate to make their cause my own, is it to be supposed that, with their yokes broken, and their friends and advocates multiplied indefinitely, I can be any the less disposed to stand by them to the last—to insist on the full Measure of justice and equity being meted out to them—to retain in my breast a lively and permanent interest in all that relates to their present condition and future welfare?…

The object for which the *Liberator* was commenced—the extermination of chattel slavery—having been gloriously consummated, it seems to me specially appropriate to let its existence cover the historic period of the great struggle, leaving what remains to be done to complete the work of emancipation to other instrumentalities (of which I hope to avail myself), under new auspices, with more abundant means, and with millions instead of hundreds for allies.…

BOSTON, DECEMBER 29, 1865.

GLOSSARY

instrumentalities: organizations

late rebel States: former states of the Confederacy

the late rebellion: the Civil War

on the score of: because of

valedictory: a farewell, especially when applied to a speech or, in this case, an essay

without a farthing as the pecuniary result of the patronage extended: without the slightest amount of financial benefit

yokes: restraints designed for keeping captives together in a group

Document Analysis

Garrison begins this "valedictory" editorial by recalling that he began publication of the *Liberator* with no subscribers and, at the end of its decades-long run, still has made no money from the "unremitted labors" of producing it. From the outset, Garrison presents himself as something of a martyr for the cause of abolition. He continues this theme in the second, very long paragraph. Despite the change in public opinion on the question of slavery (and the fact that his *Liberator* was "the original 'disturber of the peace'"), Garrison insists that he "derived no advantage" from the rise and ultimate success of the abolition movement. Garrison goes on to claim that both southern slave owners and "Northern pro-slavery malice" continually turned public opinion against him; those who supported him had "rare moral courage or singular personal independence" and there were no other publications that faced the same difficulties and opposition as Garrison's. He continues in this manner for most of the paragraph. All of this abuse, however, did not dim the *Liberator*'s work. No publication "exerted a higher moral or more broadly reformatory influence" upon readers. Surprisingly, Garrison closes the paragraph by denying any "egotism or presumption."

Garrison then turns to the subject of his retirement from the abolitionist movement, professing to be surprised that some thing it is the wrong time to do so. He recounts the concerns of his fellow abolitionists, particularly that former slaves, while free, have no guarantee of "equal civil and political rights" and that they are subject to "many insults and outrages." Basically, the argument is that the fight if far from over. Despite the fact that those concerns are real, not imagined, Garrison does not believe that the plight of former slaves has any bearing on his decision to end publication of the *Liberator*. After all, he explains, he began its publication without anyone's permission—why should ending it be any different?

Garrison then argues that those who oppose his exit from the public debate over abolition and civil rights cannot think that he is unaware or uninterested in the on-going struggle of African Americans in the south. Here, Garrison promotes his own actions on behalf of slaves saying that "when they had no friends, and no hope of earthly redemption" he "did not hesitate to make their cause" his cause by beginning to publish the *Liberator* (at, he no doubt would like readers to remember) no benefit to himself. He calls into question the assumption that, after all he had done for the cause of ending slavery, he would abandon the freed slaves of the south as they sought full equality.

He closes by explaining that the purpose for which he created the *Liberator*, "the extermination of chattel slavery," has been accomplished. The work will continue, he acknowledges, but he leaves this to future organizations. He does not rule out participation in these "other instrumentalities," and predicts that they will have "millions instead of hundreds" of supporters. In this final sentence, Garrison once again slyly draws attention to the lack of support he received when beginning his radical abolitionist work on the *Liberator*.

Essential Themes

The document demonstrates how much more deeply preoccupied Garrison was with vindicating his own career by ending it in triumph than with continuing the struggle for equality. "Never had a journal to look such opposition in the face—never was one so constantly belied and caricatured," he claimed. And, still, he goes on, "no journal has been conducted with such fairness and impartiality;…none has so readily and exhaustively published, without note or comment, what its enemies have said to its disparagement, and the vilification of its editor." Garrison congratulates himself that "the object for which the *Liberator* was commenced—the extermination of chattel slavery—[has] been gloriously consummated." While he professes an ongoing commitment to the emancipated slaves, he reveals his self-satisfied naïveté when asserting that since the freed people were now being supported by "millions instead of hundreds for allies," an organized abolitionist movement was no longer needed. As the epic political battles to secure black equality played out during Reconstruction, Garrison remained secure in his belief that "his" abolitionist movement had already succeeded.

——*James Brewer Stewart, PhD*
with additional material by Aaron Gulyas, MA

Bibliography and Additional Reading

Abzug, Robert H. *Cosmos Crumbling: American Reform and the Religious Imagination.* (New York: Oxford University Press, 1994).

Laurie, Bruce *Beyond Garrison.* (New York: Cambridge University Press, 2005).

Mayer, Henry. *All on Fire: William Lloyd Garrison and the Abolition of Slavery.* (New York: St. Martin's Press, 1998).

McDaniel, W. Caleb. *The Problem of Democracy in the Age of Slavery: Garrisonian Abolitionists and Transatlantic Reform.* (Baton Rouge, Louisiana: Louisiana State University Press, 2013).

SECTIONAL CONFLICT, CIVIL WAR, AND RECONSTRUCTION

Closely tied to the rising tide of radical abolitionism in the north was the increasing political and cultural conflict between the northern states and southern states. While slavery was the most visible, divisive factor contributing to this animosity, the changing economics as well as the territorial growth of the growing United States were significant reasons for the conflict as well. During the earl 1800s, the northeastern states—especially Massachusetts and New York—began to develop an economic base that increasingly thrived through manufacturing. The southern states, especially after the invention of the cotton gin in the late 1700s, grew dependent on cotton—grown on plantations and cultivated by slaves. Plantation owners in the deep southern states profited from the sale of their cotton, merchants in the upper southern states profited from selling cotton to northern manufacturers and overseas customers. Business owners in the north profited from the sale of thread, fabric, and clothing produced in their factories or sold in their stores or through their catalogs. These two sections were tied to each other.

In 1819, however, the organization of the vast Louisiana Territory into states complicated the relationship between north and south. When Missouri applied for admission to the union as a slave state, a debate erupted over whether or not slavery would exist in the west. Some anti-slavery advocates, believed that if slavery were confined to the south, east of the Mississippi river, it would eventually die out. If it was allowed to expand, it might never vanish.

Compromises such as the Missouri Compromise (which settled the issue of slavery in the Louisiana Purchase lands) and the Compromise of 1850 (which settled the status of the area acquired from Mexico after the Mexican-American War) as well as the policy of admitting states in pairs—one slave, one free—maintained the balance of power between north and south. In 1854, however, the Kansas-Nebraska Act,

which would have repealed parts of the Missouri Compromise, unleashed a firestorm of conflict. Sam Houston, at the time a US Senator from Texas, delivered his Speech Opposing the Kansas-Nebraska Act in which he expressed fears held by many in the north and south: that the Missouri Compromise had been holding the nation together and without it, conflicts would continue to grow.

Those conflicts erupted in 1860 when Illinois Republican Abraham Lincoln was elected President without even appearing on ballots in southern states. Fearing that the Republican Party—which advocated that slavery not be allowed to expand into the west—was, in fact, aiming to eliminate slavery in the south, southern states began to secede from the union, forming a new nation, the Confederate States of America. South Carolina was the first state to do so, issuing its Declaration of Causes of Secession on December 24, 1860. As the new government took shape, elected officials who remained loyal to their states rather than the United States as a nation left their positions to, in many cases, take up similar posts in the Confederacy. Jefferson Davis, Senator from Mississippi and former Secretary of War delivered a Farewell Address to the U.S. Senate in January, 1861. Texas's Sam Houston, however, opposed to secession and not accepting the validity of Texas's decision to join the Confederacy, delivered a Speech on His Refusal to Take the Oath of Loyalty to the Confederacy, giving up his office as governor. The Confederate government itself was similar in many way to that of the United States. Confederate Vice President Alexander Stephens, in his "Cornerstone Speech," details what he sees as the advantages of the Confederate constitution. One of the greatest accomplishments of the new nation, he believes, is its "corner stone": white supremacy and the institution of slavery.

Following the Civil War, the federal government undertook a program of Reconstruction to dismantle slavery and eliminate the vestiges of loyalty to the Confederacy. This era saw a level of African-American presence politics at the local, state and federal levels that would not be matched until well into the twentieth century. The white southern elite, however, through violence and intimidation (aided by the inability or unwillingness of the federal government to consistently pursue its Reconstruction politics) led to African-American politicians being marginalized and driven from office. Henry McNeal Turner's Speech on His Expulsion from the Georgia Legislature and Richard Harvey Cain's speech asking for Equal Laws, Equal Legislation, and Equal Rights illustrate the uphill battle faced by African-Americans at the end of the Reconstruction era.

As an epilogue to the saga of sectional conflict, Civil War, and Reconstruction, we present Confederate President Jefferson Davis's prospective on *The Rise and Fall of the Confederate Government*. Davis maintains the position that the Confederacy was a legitimate government and the secession was both constitutional and justified.

■ South Carolina Ordinance of Nullification

Date: 1832
Author: South Carolina Nullification Convention
Genre: Public declaration

Summary Overview

On November 24, 1832, South Carolina passed the Ordinance of Nullification. The issue that lay behind the Ordinance of Nullification was tariffs, which had been the subject of controversy since 1819, when Congress began to consider tariffs a form of protection for manufacturing rather than purely a revenue-raising measure. When Congress passed the Tariff of 1832, South Carolinians, who had long opposed the tariff, organized a campaign to reject the legislation. Nullifiers rode the issue to victory in the state elections in October, defeating unionists and gaining a two-thirds control of the legislature. In a special session, legislators called for a convention, which convened November 19. A committee drafted an Ordinance of Nullification, authored by William Harper, as well as addresses explaining the ordinance. Convention delegates passed on November 24 the Ordinance of Nullification, which declared the tariffs of 1828 and 1832 null in the state as of February 1, 1833. It pledged that any effort by the federal government to enforce the tariff would be met by secession. President Andrew Jackson responded to the ordinance by issuing the Proclamation to the People of South Carolina regarding Nullification, in which he called South Carolina's ordinance an act of treason and threatened the state with military action if it tried to secede.

Defining Moment

The South Carolina Ordinance of Nullification emerged from a climate of economic and political strain that characterized the state following the War of 1812. Economically, cotton growers in the state suffered from a decline in cotton prices. While state politicians like John C. Calhoun approved of the tariffs passed in 1816, their nationalism was conditional, linked to issues of national defense. With an economy dependent on the export of rice and cotton, South Carolinians generally favored free trade. With the passage of the Tariff of 1824 and the collapse in cotton prices in 1825, public support for economic nationalism declined in the state, while political leaders criticized a tariff policy that benefited northeastern and western manufactur-

ing and threatened South Carolina's export trade with the prospect of foreign retaliation.

Congressional debates over increased woolen duties and colonization kept the tariff and slavery at the forefront of politics in the state. Both issues were important in convincing South Carolina politicians that the state was threatened by the tyranny of the majority. When Congress passed a tariff increase in 1828, to many in South Carolina it seemed that the state was being taxed to benefit northeastern and western interests. Tariff opponents declared the legislation unconstitutional because it destroyed rather than regulated commerce and it illegally promoted industry rather than raising revenue. Calhoun expounded on these theories in an anonymously written pamphlet, arguing that states had the authority to determine the constitutionality of legislation because each state was sovereign before the individual states ratified the Constitution. The Union, therefore, was a compact of individual states.

Knowledge of Calhoun's authorship quickly spread, contributing to the vice president's growing breech with Jackson. Jackson, facing reelection in 1832, had come out in favor of the Tariff of 1832. At the same time, nullifiers in South Carolina had gained control of the state legislature and called for a convention on the tariff issue. The Ordinance of Nullification was passed on November 24.

Author Biography

Governor James Hamilton presided over the South Carolina Nullification Convention. The delegates included nullifiers Robert Hayne (who served as chair of the convention), Robert J. Turnbull, Robert Barnwell, and William Harper. While Harper, former speaker of the South Carolina House of Representatives and judge on the court of appeals, wrote the Ordinance of Nullification, one of the most significant figures at the Nullification Convention was its chair, Robert Hayne.

Robert Hayne, at the time of the Nullification Convention, was one of South Carolina's two United States Senators, a position he held from 1823 to 1832. During his time in the Senate, he consistently opposed tariff measures proposed by Senators from northern states, which were moving to an increasingly industrial economic base. His views on the tariff, but also on restrictions being sought on westward expansion and the nature of the relationship between the states and the federal government, led to a s debates with Massachusetts Senator Daniel Webster. The Webster-Hayne debate took place between January 19 and January 27, 1830. While Webster's speeches, which favored not only the tariffs but also the idea that the states were subject to the authority of the federal government, has become classics of American political oratory, Haynes's are also significant for forthrightly promoting the primacy of the states over the federal government, calling "the independence of the states" as "the very life of our system [of government]." During this debate, Hayne also defended the idea of nullification, basing them in the Kentucky and Virginia Resolutions of 1798 and declaring that individual states, not the federal government, were the sole judges of "when the barriers of the constitution shall be overleaped."

HISTORICAL DOCUMENT

November 24, 1832

An ordinance to nullify certain acts of the Congress of the United States, purporting to be laws laying duties and imposts on the importation of foreign commodities.

Whereas the Congress of the United States by various acts, purporting to be acts laying duties and imposts on foreign imports, but in reality intended for the protection of domestic manufactures and the giving of bounties to classes and individuals engaged in particular employments, at the expense and to the injury and oppression of other classes and individuals, and by wholly exempting from taxation certain foreign commodities, such as are not produced or manufactured in the United States, to afford a pretext for imposing higher and excessive duties on articles similar to those intended to be protected, hath exceeded its just powers under the constitution, which confers on it no authority to afford such protection, and hath violated the true meaning and intent of the constitution, which provides for equality in imposing the burdens of taxation upon the several States and portions of the confederacy: And whereas the said Congress, exceeding its just power to impose taxes and collect revenue for the purpose of effecting and accomplishing the specific objects and purposes which the constitution of the United States authorizes it to effect and accomplish, hath raised and collected unnecessary revenue for objects unauthorized by the constitution.

We, therefore, the people of the State of South Carolina, in convention assembled, do declare and ordain and it is hereby declared and ordained, that the several acts and parts of acts of the Congress of the United States, purporting to be laws for the imposing of duties and imposts on the importation of foreign commodities, and now having actual operation and effect within the United States, and, more especially, an act entitled "An act in alteration of the several acts imposing duties on imports," approved on the nineteenth day of May, one thousand eight hundred and twenty-eight and also an act entitled "An act to alter and amend the several acts imposing duties on imports," approved on the fourteenth day of July, one thousand eight hundred and thirty-two, are unauthorized by the constitution of the United States, and violate the true meaning and intent thereof and are null, void, and no law, nor binding upon this State, its officers or citizens; and all promises, contracts, and obligations, made or entered into, or to be made or entered into, with purpose to secure the duties imposed by said acts, and all judicial proceedings which shall be hereafter had in affirmance thereof, are and shall be held utterly null and void.

And it is further ordained, that it shall not be lawful for any of the constituted authorities, whether of this State or of the United States, to enforce the payment of duties imposed by the said acts within the limits of this State; but it shall be the duty of the legislature to adopt such measures and pass such acts as may be necessary to give full effect to this ordinance, and to prevent the enforcement and arrest the operation of the said acts and parts of acts of the Congress of the United States within the limits of this State, from and after the first day of February next, and the duties of all other constituted authorities, and of all persons residing or being within the limits of this State, and they are hereby required and enjoined to obey and give effect to this ordinance, and such acts and measures of the legislature as may be passed or adopted in obedience thereto.

And it is further ordained, that in no case of law or equity, decided in the courts of this State, wherein shall be drawn in question the authority of this ordinance, or the validity of such act or acts of the legislature as may be passed for the purpose of giving effect thereto, or the validity of the aforesaid acts of Congress, imposing duties, shall any appeal be taken or allowed to the Supreme Court of the United States, nor shall any copy of the record be permitted or allowed for that purpose; and if any such appeal shall be attempted to be taken, the courts of this State shall proceed to execute and enforce their judgments according to the laws and usages of the State, without reference to such attempted appeal, and the person or persons attempting to take such appeal may be dealt with as for a contempt of the court.

And it is further ordained, that all persons now holding any office of honor, profit, or trust, civil or military, under this State (members of the legislature excepted), shall, within such time, and in such manner as the legislature shall prescribe, take an oath well and truly to obey, execute, and enforce this ordinance, and such act or acts of the legislature as may be passed in pursuance thereof, according to the true intent and meaning of the same, and on the neglect or omission of any such person or persons so to do, his or their office or offices shall be forthwith vacated, and shall be filled up as if such person or persons were dead or had resigned; and no person hereafter elected to any office of honor, profit, or trust, civil or military (members of the legislature excepted), shall, until the legislature shall otherwise provide and direct, enter on the execution of his office, or be he any respect competent to discharge the duties thereof until he shall, in like manner, have taken a similar oath; and no juror shall be impaneled in any of the courts of this State, in any cause in which shall be in question this ordinance, or any act of the legislature passed in pursuance thereof, unless he shall first, in addition to the usual oath, have taken an oath that he will well and truly obey, execute, and enforce this ordinance, and such act or acts of the legislature as may be passed to carry the same into operation and effect, according to the true intent and meaning thereof.

And we, the people of South Carolina, to the end that it may be fully understood by the government of the United States, and the people of the co-States, that we are determined to maintain this our ordinance and declaration, at every hazard, do further declare that we will not submit to the application of force on the part of the federal government, to reduce this State to obedience, but that we will consider the passage, by Congress, of any act authorizing the employment of a military or naval force against the State of South Carolina, her constitutional authorities or citizens; or any act abolishing or closing the ports of this State, or any of them, or otherwise obstructing the free ingress and egress of vessels to and from the said ports, or any other act on the part of the federal government, to coerce the State, shut up her ports, destroy or harass her commerce or to enforce the acts hereby declared to be null and void, otherwise than through the civil tribunals of the country, as inconsistent with the longer continuance of South Carolina in the Union; and that the people of this State will henceforth hold themselves absolved from all further obligation to maintain or preserve their political connection with the people of the other States; and will forthwith proceed to organize a separate government, and do all other acts and things which sovereign and independent States may of right do.

Done in convention at Columbia, the twenty-fourth day of November, in the year of our Lord one thousand eight hundred and thirty-two, and in the fifty-seventh year of the Declaration of the Independence of the United States of America.

GLOSSARY

affirmance: affirmation; support

egress: exit; the act of leaving

imposts: taxes or other forms of imposed payments

ingress: the act of entering

Document Analysis

The Ordinance of Nullification opens by claiming that Congress acted unconstitutionally in passing tariff laws that sought to protect certain industries ("domestic manufactures") and individuals at the expense of others. The Constitution gives Congress the power to pass tariffs to raise revenue, but not explicitly for any other purpose, including the protection of domestic manufacturing or for the benefit of particular individuals involved in such industries. In essence, the opening paragraph of the Nullification Ordinance declares tariffs passed for the purpose of supporting domestic manufacturing to be unconstitutional. While determining laws to be within or outside the bounds of the Constitution and, since *Marbury vs. Madison* (1803) been the responsibility of the Supreme Court, the doctrine of nullification argued that states had the authority to determine the constitutionality of laws.

The ordinance proceeds to declare that the tariffs passed on May 19, 1828, and on July 14, 1832, are null and void. It further states that South Carolina and its people are neither bound by these laws nor required to pay the tariffs. Having declared the laws themselves null, the ordinance also declares "all judicial proceedings" that affirmed the laws to also be null and voice. Thus, the Nullification Convention not only assumed the authority to cancel out federal law but also to set aside court decisions regarding that law.

The ordinance then turns to the specific actions the state would take if the legislation was not repealed by February 1, 1833. In this case, the legislature of South Carolina would pass all necessary legislation to "prevent the enforcement and arrest the operation of" the enforcement of the tariff laws In essence, preventing the federal government from collecting tariffs. Any efforts to appeal state court decisions relating to the nullification to the United States Supreme Court were to

be considered in contempt of state courts and, presumably, would be subject to prosecution. The ordinance mandates that all officeholders in the state and jurors, with the exception of the legislators, take an oath to uphold the ordinance or lose their positions. Further, if a court case or a piece of legislation related to the ordinance came under consideration, individuals would have to take an oath to uphold "the true intent and meaning" of the ordinance.

The ordinance closes with a pledge that the people of South Carolina would withstand "every hazard" to enforce the ordinance and resist any federal attempt to enforce the law and, further, to not submit to any force applied to the state by the federal government. The ordinance warns the Congress passed legislation authorizing the federal government to use the army or navy against the state, to close its ports, to interfere with trading vessels, or to enforce the tariff "otherwise than through the civil tribunals of the country"—a condition seemingly at odds with the ordinance's earlier discussions of the judicial system and its judgements.

In concluding the ordinance, the Convention lays out the consequences of any military action the federal government may undertake to enforce the tariff. South Carolina would find such actions as "inconsistent with the longer continuance of South Carolina in the Union." In that event, South Carolina would withdraw from the Union and organize a separate government under their rights as a sovereign state. The language in the final lines echoes that of the 1776 Declaration of Independence. While, unlike at the time of that Declaration, armed hostilities had not yet begun. The threat of secession prefigures the violence to come.

Essential Themes

As discussed above, the nullification crisis was about much more than tariff legislation. This was not the first discussion of the concept of nullification (the aforementioned Kentucky and Virginia resolutions introduced the idea) and it was far from the first inkling of sectional strife between north and south. The Constitutional Convention, the Hartford Convention during the War of 1812, and the events leading to the Missouri Compromise in the early 1820s were all steps on the road to increasing sectional fragmentation.

What the Ordinance of Nullification does (owing much to the speeches and essays that preceded it, including the Webster-Hayne debate) is lay out a practical plan for the defiance of federal law and a very specific set of quite prescient consequences for federal reprisals. Many southern state legislatures rejected the validity of nullification, and national Republicans, including many of Jackson's political opponents, heartily approved of his proclamation denouncing nullification. The crisis did not legitimize nullification but instead strengthened support for states' rights interpretations of the Constitution, the right of secession, and calls to protect the rights of minority, specifically those who had an interest in the institution of slavery, from the majority.

———*Christine Dee, PhD*

Bibliography and Additional Reading

Bolt, William K. "Founding Father and Rebellious Son: James Madison, John C. Calhoun, and the Use of Precedents." *American Nineteenth Century History* 53, no. 3 (Fall 2004): 1–27.

Ericson, David F. "The Nullification Crisis, American Republicanism, and the Force Bill Debate." *Journal of Southern History* 61, no. 2 (1995): 249–270.

Maier, Pauline. "The Road Not Taken: Nullification, John C. Calhoun, and the Revolutionary Tradition in South Carolina." *South Carolina Historical Magazine* 82, no. 1 (1981): 1–19.

Pease, Jane H., and William H. Pease. "The Economics and Politics of Charleston's Nullification Crisis." *Journal of Southern History* 47, no. 3 (August 1981): 335–362.

Ratcliffe, Donald J. "The Nullification Crisis, Southern Discontents, and the American Political Process." *American Nineteenth Century History* 1, no. 2 (Summer 2000): 1.

Wood, W. Kirk. "In Defense of the Republic: John C. Calhoun and State Interposition in South Carolina, 1776–1833." *Southern Studies* 10, nos. 1–2 (2003): 9–48.

Ellis, Richard E. *The Union at Risk: Jacksonian Democracy, States' Rights and the Nullification Crisis.* New York: Oxford University Press, 1987.

Ericson, David F. *The Shaping of American Liberalism: The Debates over Ratification, Nullification, and Slavery.* Chicago: University of Chicago Press, 1993.

Niven, John. *John C. Calhoun and the Price of Union.* Baton Rouge: Louisiana State University Press, 1988.

Peterson, Merrill D. *Olive Branch and Sword: The Compromise of 1833.* Baton Rouge: Louisiana State University Press, 1982.

■ Speech Opposing the Kansas-Nebraska Act

Date: 1843
Author: Sam Houston
Genre: Speech

Summary Overview

Houston was involved in some of the most dramatic events in American history. Aside from his successful military career, he proved to be a passionate and dedicated politician. Unlike many of his southern counterparts, he was sympathetic to Native Americans and firmly believed that secession was a mistake. A charismatic orator and eloquent writer, Houston's writings and speeches often stirred people to action. In his Speech Opposing the Kansas-Nebraska Act, Houston spoke out against the plan of Illinois senator Stephen Douglas to move the issue of slavery from the federal arena to the individual territories, thus easing tensions between the North and South. According to Houston, the plan would jeopardize the rights of Indians within the territory and, moreover, was in direct violation of the 1820 Missouri Compromise, which outlawed slavery north of latitude 36°30′. Calling the compromise a "wall of fire," Houston believed that it remained a binding agreement between North and South that had kept peace for more than thirty years.

Defining Moment

Authored by Senator Stephen Douglas, the Kansas-Nebraska Act was designed to move the issue of slavery from the federal arena to the individual territories, to thereby ease tensions between the North and South because the South would be able to expand slavery while states in the North could still abolish the institution. The act originated with Douglas's desire to see a transcontinental railroad built through his home state of Illinois. But the proposed railroad could follow such a route, and thereby benefit the people of Illinois, only if it could continue westward into what would become Nebraska Territory. This territory, however, would lie north of the dividing line between free and slave states established by the Missouri Compromise.

Accordingly, senators from the southern states opposed its inception. Douglas's bill was intended to be a new compromise; it would divide the territory into two potential states, Nebraska and Kansas, while at the same time repealing the Missouri Compromise line. It was expected that Nebraska, the more northerly territory, would be free territory and that Kansas, the more southerly, would elect to be a slave territory.

Author Biography

Samuel Houston—military hero, governor of two states, president of the Texas Republic, and U.S. senator—was born on March 2, 1793. He lived his early life in Tennessee, where he spent most of his time with the Cherokee and was even adopted into the Cherokee Nation. He later enlisted in the army during the War of 1812, worked as an Indian subagent, and pursued a law career in Tennessee. By 1819 Houston's political career was starting to evolve; he served as adjunct general of the state militia and attorney general for the district of Nashville. With the support of Andrew Jackson, Houston was elected to the U.S. House of Representatives, where he served from 1823 to 1827. Then, in 1827, he ran for and won the governorship of Tennessee, though he resigned on April 16, 1829, heading west into Indian Territory and eventually to Texas.

Once in Texas, Houston became enmeshed in the events unfolding there. He was one of the Texas representatives at the Convention of 1833, through which Texas sought a peaceful independence from Mexico. Hopes for peace were dashed when war broke out in October 1835. As commander in chief of the Texas army, Houston led Texas to victory over Mexican forces in 1836. In September that year, Houston was elected as the first president of the Republic of Texas, serving until December 1838. He was elected again in December 1841, to serve until December 1844. After Texas became a state in 1845, Houston was elected as one of the state's first senators, a post he held for thirteen years.

Without doubt, Houston's most eloquent documents were speeches. In his early days in Tennessee he was known as a gifted orator. While his oratory might be considered flowery in the twenty-first century, in that respect his was little different from that of other great orators of the day. In addition, his speeches, such as his 1836 Inaugural Address, were infused with common sense and gentle humor, and when he spoke, he could attract crowds and move people to action. It was as a senator that Houston delivered two of his most powerful speeches, on the Compromise of 1850 and on the 1854 Kansas-Nebraska Act. In late 1859 Houston became Texas's seventh governor, but he resigned less than two years later over the controversy surrounding his refusal to take the Confederate loyalty oath. Houston retired into private life and died at home on July 26, 1863.

HISTORICAL DOCUMENT

I am aware, Mr. President, that in presenting myself as the advocate of the Indians and their rights, I shall claim but little sympathy from the community at large, and that I shall stand very much alone, pursuing the course which I feel it my imperative duty to adhere to. It is not novel for me to seek to advocate the rights of the Indians upon this floor and elsewhere. A familiar knowledge of them, their manners, their habits, and their intercourse with this Government for the last half century, from my early boyhood through life, have placed within my possession facts, and, I trust, implanted in me a principle enduring as life itself. That principle is to protect the Indian against wrong and oppression, and to vindicate him in the enjoyment of rights which have been solemnly guaranteed to him by this Government; and *that* is the principle, Mr. President, which I shall insist grows out of the course of policy avowed by this Government as far back as 1785. The Hopewell treaty was then negotiated with the Cherokee Indians of Tennessee....

Successive promises were made from 1785 to 1802, during the administration of General Washington; and the pledges of amity and regard that were made to the Indians by him, inured to Mr. Jefferson, for he, in 1809, made solemn promises to them, provided they would migrate west of the Mississippi....They continued there up to 1814, 1816 and 1817, under the promises of the Government, battling against the hostile, wild Indians, and relying upon the pledges of the different Presidents of the United States, their great father, that they should not be molested in their settlement there....After that, the policy of the Government became more stringent upon them; and a disposition arising, owing to pressure from surrounding States, to remove them to Arkansas, it was proposed that the whole nation of Cherokees east of the Mississippi should migrate, and exchange their lands on the east for lands lying to the far west....

These were the suggestions, and the most solemn pledges were made by this Government—that if they would remove to the west of the Mississippi they should never again be surrounded by white men, and that they should have a boundless and interminable outlet, as far as the jurisdiction of the United States extended....I need not rehearse to gentlemen who are familiar with the past, the tragedies that followed, the sanguinary murders and massacres, the mid-night conflagrations—these attest the inharmonious action which arose from this faithless conduct on the part of the Government or its agents. I know this may appear a very harsh assertion to make here, that our Government acts in bad faith with the Indians....Look at the Creeks, at the Choctaws, the Chickasaws; look at every tribe that has ever been within our jurisdiction, and in every instance our intercourse has resulted in their detriment or destruction....

It seems to be a foregone conclusion that the Indians must yield to the progress of the white man—that they must surrender their country—that they must go from place to place, and that there is to be no rest for them. Is not the earth wide enough for all the creatures the Almighty has placed upon it? But they seem not to be regarded in the light of human beings, and are driven like wild beasts; and when their habitation is made in one place, they are only considered as temporary residents, to be transferred at will to some more distant station....

I have a proposition to make, and I will submit it to the intelligence of Senators, though the destruction of the Indians seems to be a foregone conclusion.

Military posts are distributed throughout New Mexico and Texas, along the borders of the Rio Grande, to a great extent. It takes an immense amount of money to supply the various garrisons and to carry on the transportation for the provisioning of the troops....If you appropriate that money to the Indians, you can civilize every Indian east of the Rocky Mountains. Place capable men among them—men who feel higher impulses than a disposition to rob the defenseless—and you will be enabled to collect these people together, and to teach them the arts of agriculture and mechanics. You will civilize them preparatory to their christianization; you can do all this, and yet have a large surplus left out of the money which you are now expending for the support of these garrisons....

I will speak in reference to the Indians, and the advantage which arises when they are justly treated.

Within my recollection, the first missionary, or schoolmaster, went to the Cherokee nation on the Tennessee river; for that was the northern boundary of the nation; and I found myself in boyhood located within six miles of that boundary, and every scene upon the banks of the river and its adjacent tributaries are as familiar to me as my right hand. I had every opportunity of becoming acquainted with them....I was familiar with them then. They were in a savage state; they had no refinement....What are they now? They are a civilized people....

Sir, aid them in their progress....They are not inferior in intellect, sagacity, or moral excellence to any people who are born upon the earth; and though the charge of perfidy has been made against them for ages back, I have lived for many years in connection with them, and, as a strict observer, can bear testimony that I never knew an Indian nation violate a treaty which was made in good faith, and observed by the white man....

Here, Mr. President, I shall terminate my remarks on the subject of the Indians....As my position in relation to the repeal of the Missouri compromise, if unexplained, might not exactly be comprehended, I must speak of it....Although I stood alone in the South, with the exception of a southwestern Senator [Mr. Benton, of Missouri], I expressed my opinion, and voted my principle upon it. I supported the Missouri compromise, Mr. President, in its application to Oregon....Although I had determined to vote against the bill, and the Indian provisions furnished insuperable objections to it, I have not denounced its general features....

I adopt no new course, but have heretofore maintained my present position; and the reasons which I gave on that occasion I will take care, sir, to reassert on this, and will show that it is no new ground to me; that it is one which I have maintained since Texas was annexed to the United States, and since she formed one star of our constellation.

If I voted, Mr. President, on a former occasion, in 1848, for the Missouri Compromise, I voted for it in accordance with the sanction of Texas....Among the conditions expressed in that enactment, to which the consent of the Republic of Texas was peremptorily exacted, as a prerequisite to her admission into the Union, will be found the following. It provides that all new States formed north of 36°30☒, within the limits of Texas, as she then rightfully claimed, slavery should be prohibited; that in all south of that, they could come into the Union with or without slavery, as they might think proper. This was accepted by Texas, with all the sanctity and solemnity that could attach to any compact whatever. She adopted the Missouri compromise....

The Missouri compromise has been repeatedly recognized and acted upon by Congress as a *solemn* compact between the States; and as such, it has received the sanction of each individual member of the Confederacy. I consider that the vital interests of all the States, and *especially of the South*, are dependent, in a great degree, upon the preservation and sacred observance of that compact....*I assert the principle that Congress has no right to legislate upon the subject of slavery in any of our territories of this Union*....

I would oppose to the last by all means of rational resistance the repeal of the Missouri compromise, because I deem it essential to the preservation of this Union, and to the very existence of the South. It has heretofore operated as a wall of fire to us....

I do not wish to be sectional. I do not wish to be regarded as for the South alone. I need not say that I am for the whole country. If I am, it is sufficient without rehearsing it here. But, sir, my all is in the South. My identity is there. My life has been spent there....I claim the Missouri compromise, as it now stands, in behalf of the South. I ask Senators to let its benefits inure to us. I do not want it taken away....

I am now called upon to vote for the repeal of the Missouri compromise, which I esteem everything to the South—under which it has prospered, and in which we have always acquiesced since its adoption—which the South united in applying to Texas when it was admitted into the Union; and even Texas has prospered under the infliction....

Mr. President, in the far distant future I think I perceive those who come after us, who are to be affected by the action of this body upon this bill. Our children have two alternatives here presented. They are either to live in after times in the enjoyment of peace, of harmony, and prosperity, or the alternative remains for them of anarchy, discord, and civil broil. We can avert the last. I trust we shall. At any rate, so far as my efforts can avail, I will resist every attempt to infringe or repeal the Missouri Compromise.

GLOSSARY

compact: an official agreement between parties

Hopewell treaty: three treaties, named for the South Carolina estate where they were signed, between the United States and the Cherokee (November 28, 1785), the Choctaw (January 3, 1786), and the Chicasaw (January 10, 1786)

perfidy: treachery, disloyalty

sagacity: wisdom

Document Analysis

In February 1854, Houston delivered a passionate and dramatic speech to the U.S. Senate opposing the Kansas-Nebraska bill that took almost two complete days. He focused on two main issues that he had with the legislation. The first issue centered on the Native Americans living in the territories in question. Houston begins by acknowledging that as a supporter of the Indians and their rights, he is alone but remains duty bound to advocate for them. He goes on to explain that over his live he has gained "a familiar knowledge of them" and their ways.

At this point he begins referring to and quoting from a series of agreements between the government and various Indian nations starting as far back as 1785 with the Hopewell treaties which was made with the Cherokee, Choctaw, and Chickasaw tribes. He also describes treaty after treaty, skillfully pointing out each broken promise made by the U.S. government. Despite that, as Houston points out, "the destruction of the Indians seems to be a foregone conclusion," he encourages the Senate to civilize and Christianize the Indians, stating, "They seem not be regarded in the light of human beings, and are driven like wild beasts; and when their habitation is made in one place, they are considered as temporary residents." He adds that by civilizing the Indians, the federal government could abandon its forts along the Rio Grande and in Texas and New Mexico, saving money and men for other purposes.

At the point in the speech marking the beginning of the second day, Houston resumes his plea for the Native Americans within the Kansas-Nebraska territory by outlining the advantages he sees gained "when they [the Indians] are justly treated." As an example, he points to the Cherokee in Tennessee. As a boy, he lived with the Cherokee before they had adopted modes of white American civilization; in time, they learned to work as farmers and mechanics and gained education. Houston does not advocate for the preservation of native cultures, but he believes that the country and the Indian nations would be better off working together. He believes that by honoring its treaties, the government could establish meaningful and permanent relationships with native nations.

With his plea on behalf of Native Americans finished, Houston turns his attention to his second issue with the bill, the repeal of the Missouri Compromise. By declaring that the people of the new territories would decide whether to allow slavery by popular sovereignty, the Kansas-Nebraska bill was in direct violation of the 1820 Missouri Compromise, which outlawed slavery north of latitude 36°30'; indeed, the bill included a clause that would repeal the Missouri Compromise. Houston asserts that the continued existence and observance of the Missouri Compromise is crucial to the "interests of all the state, and especially the South." Calling the compromise their "wall of fire," Houston argues that it remained a binding agreement between North and South that had kept peace for more than thirty years and was "essential to the preservation of this Union." The compromise kept the peace by determining where slavery would exist and where it would not. Houston sees a danger to the South, and perhaps to the institution of slavery in the repeal of the Missouri Compromise. Earlier in the speech, he proclaimed his believe that Congress had no authority to pass laws concerning slavery. Eliminating the Missouri Compromise would reopen the door to Congressional debate over slavery.

He emphasizes that the repeal of that compromise would have disastrous consequences for future generations. America's children would be condemned "either to live in after times in the enjoyment of peace, of harmony, and prosperity, or the alternative remains for them of anarchy, discord, and civil broil."

Essential Themes

While he was a southerner, and a slave owner, Sam Houston, as demonstrated in this speech, was primarily a unionist. The Missouri Compromise, he argued, was a boon for the south, for it guaranteed the existence of slavery, keeping Congress from attempting to legislate its will on the matter. The removal of the Compromise would reopen the fault lines in the United States that had been closed for decades, possibly plunging the nation into chaos and conflict.

Houston's views on the relationship between the federal government and Native American tribes is also a significant thread in this speech. As white Americans continue to push westward, that government has violated countless treaties with Native Americans. His suggestion—for the federal government to work toward the goal of "civilizing" and "Christianizing" the natives presages the plans and programs that would become a reality later in the century.

———*Michael J. O'Neal, PhD*

Bibliography and Additional Reading

Etchison, Jessica. *Bleeding Kansas: Contested Liberty in the Civil War Era* (Lawrence: University of Kansas Press, 2004).

Gregory, Jack and Rennard Strickland. *Sam Houston with the Cherokees, 1829-1933*. (Norman: University of Oklahoma Press, 1996).

James, Marquis. *The Raven: A Biography of Sam Houston*. (Austin: University of Texas Press, 1988).

■ South Carolina Declaration of Causes of Secession

Date: 1860
Author: Christopher Memminger
Genre: Government proclamation

Summary Overview

The Declaration of Causes of Secession, adopted on December 24, 1860, represented South Carolina's statement to the South, the nation, and the world that it was compelled to secede from the United States In a detailed explanation, South Carolina presented the southern theory of the Union and the nature of the U.S. Constitution, aired its grievances against the North, and justified its decision to secede. The Declaration of Causes of Secession left no doubt that the precipitating factor behind South Carolina's withdrawal from the Union was the election of Abraham Lincoln to the presidency.

South Carolina's decision to secede encouraged secessionists elsewhere to intensify their opposition to the Union and, in rapid fashion, to persuade their states to follow suit. The justifications for secession were grounded in the compact theory of the Constitution, the view that sovereign states had created the Union and, therefore, in the exercise of their sovereignty, could withdraw from the Union at their pleasure. The declaration sought legitimacy, moreover, through its reference to the causes that impelled the American colonists to declare their independence from England: The rights of the people had been violated by a government grown tyrannical. Those conditions in 1776 and 1860, South Carolina argued, justified the right of the people to create their own government. For South Carolinians, tyranny emerged in the form of Abraham Lincoln, who, they declared, intended to destroy slavery, in violation of southerners' property rights in their slaves. The arguments aroused the passions of the lower southern states and soon put the nation on a war footing. As a result, the United States would never be the same.

Defining Moment

The election of Abraham Lincoln to the presidency in 1860 proved to be the tipping point for South Carolina. Fearful that Lincoln would place the law of slavery on a path toward its extinction, secessionists in South Carolina called for a convention to remove their state from the Union on November 6, the day Lincoln was elected.

Three different positions developed in response to Lincoln's election. The first, held by the "fire-eaters," argued for immediate secession, believing that each state should secede without waiting for a decision from other states. The second group, known as the "cooperationists," argued that states should not act individually, but collectively, in response to Lincoln's victory. The third position, that of the "unconditional unionists," (living principally in the border states: Maryland, Kentucky, Delaware, and Missouri) opposed the idea of secession.

The Lower South was united by its belief in state sovereignty and states' rights, its insistence on a constitutional property right to slaves, and its considerable fear of northern intentions. Lincoln's election unleashed a panoply of fears. South Carolinian secessionists hammered away at a grim future under Lincoln and the Republicans, who, they believed, meant to abolish slavery. Secessionists, for example, pointed to the impact on the South of Republican opposition to the extension of slavery in the western territories. The net result, they argued, would be the incorporation in the Union of additional free states, which would easily outnumber southern states in Congress. Congress would repeal the Fugitive Slave Act, and slaves would engage in a mass migration to the North, depriving the South of its labor pool. Lincoln, it was charged, would appoint Republicans to the U.S. Supreme Court, and the institution that had been long controlled by Southern justices would become a tool of the North. Finally, Congress might employ means of abolishing slavery altogether. In sum, the southern way of life was jeopardized by the ascension of Lincoln. In this context, the secessionists won converts, and South Carolina withdrew from the Union.

Author Biography

Following Abraham Lincoln's election to the presidency, South Carolina state legislator Christopher Gustavus Memminger became a forceful advocate of secession and was the author South Carolina Declaration of Causes of Secession. He was also selected to represent South Carolina as a delegate to the provisional congress that established the Confederate States of America and

CHARLESTON

MERCURY

EXTRA:

Passed unanimously at 1.15 o'clock, P. M. December 20th, 1860.

AN ORDINANCE

To dissolve the Union between the State of South Carolina and other States united with her under the compact entitled "The Constitution of the United States of America."

We, the People of the State of South Carolina, in Convention assembled, do declare and ordain, and it is hereby declared and ordained,

That the Ordinance adopted by us in Convention, on the twenty-third day of May, in the year of our Lord one thousand seven hundred and eighty-eight, whereby the Constitution of the United States of America was ratified, and also, all Acts and parts of Acts of the General Assembly of this State, ratifying amendments of the said Constitution, are hereby repealed; and that the union now subsisting between South Carolina and other States, under the name of "The United States of America," is hereby dissolved.

THE

UNION

IS

DISSOLVED!

chaired the committee that wrote the provisional constitution in just four days.

Memminger was born on January 9, 1803, in Württemberg, Germany. After his father was killed in combat, Memminger immigrated with his mother to Charleston, South Carolina. His mother died from yellow fever in 1807, and Christopher was soon taken into the home of Thomas Bennett, later a governor of South Carolina. Memminger graduated from South Carolina College in 1819 and, after studying law, opened in 1825 what became a highly successful law practice in Charleston.

In 1836 when he won a seat in the South Carolina legislature, where he served until 1852. He returned to the legislature and served from 1854 to 1860. Throughout his political career, Memminger defended slavery. While viewed as moderate among secessionists, at least

until Lincoln's election, he boldly asserted the need for South Carolina to secede and even declared that his state may have to drag others with it. In 1861 the Confederate president Jefferson Davis appointed Memminger secretary of the treasury. Despite his creative efforts to raise money, Memminger was helpless in the face of the depreciation of the currency and the ultimate collapse of Confederate credit, for which he was nonetheless held responsible.

In 1864 he resigned from his post. He received a presidential pardon from President Andrew Johnson in 1866 for his role in the war and retired to Flat Rock, North Carolina, a year later, where he resumed the practice of law. He spent his retirement in service of public education for blacks and whites. He died on March 7, 1888.

HISTORICAL DOCUMENT

December 24, 1860

The people of the State of South Carolina, in Convention assembled, on the 26th day of April, A.D., 1852, declared that the frequent violations of the Constitution of the United States, by the Federal Government, and its encroachments upon the reserved rights of the States, fully justified this State in then withdrawing from the Federal Union; but in deference to the opinions and wishes of the other slaveholding States, she forbore at that time to exercise this right. Since that time, these encroachments have continued to increase, and further forbearance ceases to be a virtue.

And now the State of South Carolina having resumed her separate and equal place among nations, deems it due to herself, to the remaining United States of America, and to the nations of the world, that she should declare the immediate causes which have led to this act.

In the year 1765, that portion of the British Empire embracing Great Britain, undertook to make laws for the government of that portion composed of the thirteen American Colonies. A struggle for the right of self-government ensued, which resulted, on the 4th of July, 1776, in a Declaration, by the Colonies, "that they are, and of right ought to be, FREE AND INDEPENDENT STATES; and that,

as free and independent States, they have full power to levy war, conclude peace, contract alliances, establish commerce, and to do all other acts and things which independent States may of right do."

They further solemnly declared that whenever any "form of government becomes destructive of the ends for which it was established, it is the right of the people to alter or abolish it, and to institute a new government." Deeming the Government of Great Britain to have become destructive of these ends, they declared that the Colonies "are absolved from all allegiance to the British Crown, and that all political connection between them and the State of Great Britain is, and ought to be, totally dissolved."

In pursuance of this Declaration of Independence, each of the thirteen States proceeded to exercise its separate sovereignty; adopted for itself a Constitution, and appointed officers for the administration of government in all its departments—Legislative, Executive and Judicial. For purposes of defense, they united their arms and their counsels; and, in 1778, they entered into a League known as the Articles of Confederation, whereby they agreed to entrust the administration of their external relations to a common agent, known as the Congress of the United States, expressly declaring, in the first Article "that each State retains its sovereignty, freedom and independence, and every power, jurisdiction and right which is not, by this Confederation, expressly delegated to the United States in Congress assembled."

Under this Confederation the war of the Revolution was carried on, and on the 3rd of September, 1783, the contest ended, and a definite Treaty was signed by Great Britain, in which she acknowledged the independence of the Colonies in the following terms: "ARTICLE 1—His Britannic Majesty acknowledges the said United States, viz: New Hampshire, Massachusetts Bay, Rhode Island and Providence Plantations, Connecticut, New York, New Jersey, Pennsylvania, Delaware, Maryland, Virginia, North Carolina, South Carolina and Georgia, to be FREE, SOVEREIGN AND INDEPENDENT STATES; that he treats with them as such; and for himself, his heirs and successors, relinquishes all claims to the government, propriety and territorial rights of the same and every part thereof."

Thus were established the two great principles asserted by the Colonies, namely: the right of a State to govern itself; and the right of a people to abolish a Government when it becomes destructive of the ends for which it was instituted. And concurrent with the establishment of these principles, was the fact, that each Colony became and was recognized by the mother Country a FREE, SOVEREIGN AND INDEPENDENT STATE.

In 1787, Deputies were appointed by the States to revise the Articles of Confederation, and on 17th September, 1787, these Deputies recommended for the adoption of the States, the Articles of Union, known as the Constitution of the United States.

The parties to whom this Constitution was submitted, were the several sovereign States; they were to agree or disagree, and when nine of them agreed the compact was to take effect among those concurring; and the General Government, as the common agent, was then invested with their authority.

If only nine of the thirteen States had concurred, the other four would have remained as they then were—separate, sovereign States, independent of any of the provisions of the Constitution. In fact, two of the States did not accede to the Constitution until long after it had gone into operation among the other eleven; and during that interval, they each exercised the functions of an independent nation.

By this Constitution, certain duties were imposed upon the several States, and the exercise of certain of their powers was restrained, which necessarily implied their continued existence as sovereign States. But to remove all doubt, an amendment was added, which declared that the powers not delegated to the United States by the Constitution, nor prohibited by it to the States, are reserved to the States, respectively, or to the people. On the 23d May, 1788, South Carolina, by a Convention of her People, passed an Ordinance assenting to this Constitution, and afterwards altered her own Constitution, to conform herself to the obligations she had undertaken.

Thus was established, by compact between the States, a Government with definite objects and powers, limited to the express words of the grant. This limitation left the whole remaining mass of power subject to the clause reserving it to the States or to the people, and rendered unnecessary any specification of reserved rights.

We hold that the Government thus established is subject to the two great principles asserted in the Declaration of Independence; and we hold further, that the mode of its formation subjects it to a third fundamental principle, namely: the law of compact. We maintain that in every compact between two or more parties, the obligation is mutual; that the failure of one of the contracting parties to perform a material part of the agreement, entirely releases the obligation of the other; and that where no arbiter is provided, each party is remitted to his own judgment to determine the fact of failure, with all its consequences.

In the present case, that fact is established with certainty. We assert that fourteen of the States have deliberately refused, for years past, to fulfill their constitutional obligations, and we refer to their own Statutes for the proof.

The Constitution of the United States, in its fourth Article, provides as follows: "No person held to service or labor in one State, under the laws thereof, escaping into another, shall, in consequence of any law or regulation therein, be discharged from such service or labor, but shall be delivered up, on claim of the party to whom such service or labor may be due."

This stipulation was so material to the compact, that without it that compact would not have been made. The greater number of the contracting parties held slaves, and they had previously evinced their estimate of the value of such a stipulation by making it a condition in the Ordinance for the government of the territory ceded by Virginia, which now composes the States north of the Ohio River.

The same article of the Constitution stipulates also for rendition by the several States of fugitives from justice from the other States.

The General Government, as the common agent, passed laws to carry into effect these stipulations of the States. For many years these laws were executed. But an increasing hostility on the part of the non-slaveholding States to the institution of slavery, has led to a disregard of their obligations, and the laws of the General Government have ceased to effect the objects of the Constitution. The States of Maine, New Hampshire, Vermont, Massachusetts, Connecticut, Rhode Island, New York, Pennsylvania, Illinois, Indiana, Michigan, Wisconsin and Iowa, have enacted laws which either nullify the Acts of Congress or render useless any attempt to execute them. In many of these States the fugitive is discharged from service or labor claimed, and in none of them has the State Government complied with the stipulation made in the Constitution. The State of New Jersey, at an early day, passed a law in conformity with her constitutional obligation; but the current of anti-slavery feeling has led her more recently to enact laws which render inoperative the remedies provided by her own law and by the laws of Congress. In the State of New York even the right of transit for a slave has been denied by her tribunals; and the States of Ohio and Iowa have refused to surrender to justice fugitives charged with murder, and with inciting servile insurrection in the State of Virginia. Thus the constituted compact has been deliberately broken and disregarded by the non-slaveholding States, and the consequence follows that South Carolina is released from her obligation.

The ends for which the Constitution was framed are declared by itself to be "to form a more perfect union, establish justice, insure domestic tranquility, provide for the common defence, promote the general welfare, and secure the blessings of liberty to ourselves and our posterity."

These ends it endeavored to accomplish by a Federal Government, in which each State was recognized as an equal, and had separate control over its own institutions. The right of property in slaves was recognized by giving to free persons distinct political rights, by giving them the right to represent, and burthening them with direct taxes for three-fifths of their slaves; by authorizing the importation of slaves for twenty years; and by stipulating for the rendition of fugitives from labor.

We affirm that these ends for which this Government was instituted have been defeated, and the Government itself has been made destructive of them by the action of the non-slaveholding States. Those States have assume the right of deciding upon the propriety of our domestic institutions; and have denied the rights of property established in fifteen of the States and recognized by the Constitution; they have denounced as sinful the institution of slavery; they have permitted open establishment among them of societies, whose avowed object is to disturb the peace and to eloign the property of the citizens of other States. They have encouraged and assisted thousands of our slaves to leave their homes; and those who remain, have been incited by emissaries, books and pictures to servile insurrection.

For twenty-five years this agitation has been steadily increasing, until it has now secured to its aid the power of the common Government. Observing the *forms* of the Constitution, a sectional party has found within that Article establishing the Executive Department, the means of subverting the Constitution itself. A geographical line has been drawn across the Union, and all the States north of that line have united in the election of a man to the high office of President of the United States, whose opinions and purposes are hostile to slavery. He is to be entrusted with the administration of the common Government, because he has declared that that "Government cannot endure permanently half slave, half free," and that the public mind must rest in the belief that slavery is in the course of ultimate extinction.

This sectional combination for the submersion of the Constitution, has been aided in some of the States by elevating to citizenship, persons who, by the supreme law of the land, are incapable of becoming citizens; and their votes have been used to inaugurate a new policy, hostile to the South, and destructive of its beliefs and safety.

On the 4th day of March next, this party will take possession of the Government. It has announced that the South shall be excluded from the common territory, that the judicial tribunals shall be made sectional, and that a war must be waged against slavery until it shall cease throughout the United States.

The guaranties of the Constitution will then no longer exist; the equal rights of the States will be lost. The slaveholding States will no longer have the power of self-government, or self-protection, and the Federal Government will have become their enemy.

Sectional interest and animosity will deepen the irritation, and all hope of remedy is rendered vain, by the fact that public opinion at the North has invested a great political error with the sanction of more erroneous religious belief.

We, therefore, the People of South Carolina, by our delegates in Convention assembled, appealing to the Supreme Judge of the world for the rectitude of our intentions, have solemnly declared that the Union heretofore existing between this State and the other States of North America, is dissolved, and that the State of South Carolina has resumed her position among the nations of the world, as a separate and independent State; with full power to levy war, conclude peace, contract alliances, establish commerce, and to do all other acts and things which independent States may of right do.

Adopted December 24, 1860

GLOSSARY

burthening: placing a burden, responsibility, or duty upon

eloign: to remove or carry away, as to conceal

evinced: shown or demonstrated clearly

forbearance: the act of refraining or resisting

General Government: national or federal government

insurrection: the act of rebellion against civil authority

material: relevant

rendition: the act of surrendering a person to another jurisdiction

sovereignty: the location or repository of the supreme power in a country or political entity

Document Analysis

The first two paragraphs express South Carolina's frustration with the federal government. The government, it asserts, has frequently violated the US Constitution, particularly in its encroachments on the rights of states. In fact, South Carolina had come perilously close to seceding from the Union in 1852, the declaration states, but out of respect to sister states, and with hope for improvement, elected to stay in the Union. Still, after years of usurpations and abuses of power, South Carolina had reached the end of its patience. It now had little choice but to secede. It is an exercise of respect for other states, and even for other nations, that it believes it has the duty to identify and explain the causes that have compelled its secession.

In paragraphs 3–7, the South Carolina document reviews the Declaration of Independence, pointing out two key principles: "the right of a State to govern itself" and "the right of a people to abolish a Government." The whole question involved the exercise of its power. What if a state, in the exercise of self-governance, abused its powers? That state would be tyrannical and thus vulnerable to revolution, inviting the second great principle: the right of a people to abolish government when it violates the very tenets that gave birth to it in the first place.

South Carolina's invocation of the Declaration raises questions. For example, was secession legal, or was it an exercise in rebellion? Many secessionists argued that withdrawal was legal and constitutional. The Patriots in 1776 relied on the rhetoric of inalienable rights, such as the right to "abolish" government when it becomes destructive of just ends. The model of 1776 was not as useful if South Carolina had a legal right to secede, and disregard of the rationale for independence in 1776 deprived South Carolinians of the '76 model. Which fork in the road to take?

Most South Carolinians believed that secession was constitutionally protected, arguing that the states were sovereign. At the time of the ratification of the Constitution, the sovereign states had opted to join the Union; it followed that they could leave the Union when they preferred to do so. Other secessionists contended that their action was both legal and revolutionary. They claimed that secession was constitutionally permissible on the basis of the compact theory and, at the same time, believed that a people could abolish a government that was violating their rights. The right of secession was a legal right; the right to abolish government was an exercise of an inalienable right, as claimed by the American colonists.

The South Carolinians aimed to portray the federal government as revolutionary, since it was violating the rights of the southerners, particularly their property rights in slaves. They cite the failure of the North to enforce the Fugitive Slave Act, the passage by northern states of personal liberty laws for blacks, and opposition to the expansion of slavery in the territories asserting that the Union has become the menace to liberty, just as Great Britain had threatened the colonists' liberty a century before.

In paragraphs 8–11, the declaration details the compact theory of the Constitution. The Constitution, it is argued, was submitted to "the states" for ratification. The sovereign states entered into a contract, or compact. Sovereignty was retained by the states.

The compact theory hinges on the claim that the Constitution was submitted to the states as states. However, in the Constitutional Convention of 1787, the framers decided to submit the proposed Constitution to state-ratifying conventions—to the people themselves rather than the state governments. In 1819, in the landmark case of *McCulloch v. Maryland,* Chief Justice John Marshall had rejected the claim of state sovereignty. The people, he observed, were sovereign, not the states. The "people," not the "states," he pointed out, had ratified the Constitution.

In paragraphs 12–18 South Carolina states its case that its right to slave property had been violated by the North and, in particular, the issue of the Union's attack on slavery is addressed in paragraph has 19–23. South Carolina contends that the Union has violated the provisions of the Constitution that maintain slavery, including the duty of states to comply with the Fugitive Slave Act. Since the Union has failed to adhere to its obligations in the Constitution to maintain a "more perfect Union," South Carolina is within its rights to secede. But Lincoln reacted with a sharp rebuke. He reminded the South that dissolution of the Union undermines the Union. The Union cannot be perfect, he argued, if it is destroyed by southern states.

The South Carolina declaration refers, in paragraph 22, to the election of Lincoln as the precipitating factor in its decision to withdraw from the Union. The document assails Lincoln, without naming him, as "a man" who is hostile to slavery and determined to terminate its existence. In the face of such hostility, South Carolina claims (in paragraph 25), states will no longer have equal rights, and the "guaranties of the Constitution will then no longer exist"; states will lose both their rights of self-government and self-protection; and the "Federal Government will have become their enemy." With that grim future, South Carolina declares, it is forced to secede from the Union.

Essential Themes

The South Carolina document explains and justifies the state's secession from the Union. In moving and even passionate terms, the state airs its view of the Union, the location of sovereignty within the United States, and its understanding of the nature of the Constitution. The declaration, moreover, represents a distillation of some of South Carolina's principal grievances against the North, and it explains, in the end, why the state had no choice but to secede. Whatever one's view of the document might be, it provides a window into a theory that ultimately destroyed the Union. The Civil War constituted the gravest crisis in American constitutional history. The fact that the legal crisis stemmed principally from the debate on the repository of sovereignty in the United States brings the South Carolina document center stage, since it articulates a theory of state sovereignty. This was not, however, an abstract debate over political philosophy and practice. The issue of slavery and, in particular, fear that the Lincoln and the northern Republicans would either severely limit or abolish the institution were a crucial part of the secession movement.

———*David Gray Adler, PhD*

Bibliography and Additional Reading

Catton, Bruce. *The Coming Fury*. Vol. 1. Garden City, N.Y. Doubleday, 1961.

Farber, Daniel. *Lincoln's Constitution*. Chicago: University of Chicago Press, 2003.

Hyman, Harold M., and William M. Wiecek. *Equal Justice under Law: Constitutional Development, 1835–1875*. New York: Harper & Row, 1982.

McPherson, James M. *Ordeal by Fire: The Civil War and Reconstruction*. New York:Knopf, 1982.

Potter, David M. *The Impending Crisis, 1848–1861*. New York: Harper & Row, 1976.

Stampp, Kenneth M. *The Imperiled Union: Essays on the Background of the Civil War*. New York: Oxford University Press, 1980.

■ Farewell Address to the U.S. Senate

Date: 1861
Author: Jefferson Davis
Genre: Speech

Summary Overview

Jefferson Davis's Farewell Address to the U.S. Senate was delivered on January 21, 1861, less than two weeks after the Mississippi legislature voted to secede from the Union. To fully understand Davis and his importance during the critical period of the American Civil War, it is important to place him in the context of the time in which he lived and understand what led him and millions of other Americans to support the Confederate cause. For most of the 1850s Davis was the spokesperson for the southern cause in the Senate and a strong supporter of states' rights.

The resolution he offered the Senate on February 20, 1860, represents a last-ditch effort on his part to unequivocally assert the southern cause, articulating positions from which the South would not retreat. These demands marked the death knell of Democratic unity, setting forth demands that were unacceptable to northern Democrats. Upon notification of the vote of the Mississippi legislature that the state formally seceded from the Union, Davis had to make a choice between his state and the Union. He also realized that any hope of an amicable solution was over. His resignation speech demonstrates why he chose to side with his state.

Defining Moment

The sectional conflicts that faced the nation for much of the 1850s culminated in the election of Abraham Lincoln as president on November 6, 1860. The clouds of dissent that gathered over the North and the South as a result of slavery, its expansion, and states' rights cast a long shadow that portended secession and civil war. On December 20, 1860, South Carolina formally seceded from the Union. Although Davis, a moderate on the issue of secession, hoped to test it in the courts or through some constitutional means, on January 5, 1861, he joined senators from other slaveholding states in a resolution stating that as soon as possible their states should set up the necessary convention to organize a confederacy of the seceding states. On January 9, 1861, the Mississippi legislature voted to secede from the Union. Davis received notice of the act of secession while he was on his sickbed suffering from dyspepsia and neuralgia. His condition was so serious that doctors thought that he would be unable to speak.

On his final walk to the Senate, Davis knew that he was entering for the last time the chamber that he loved and had worked in for more than a decade. With the effects of his illness clearly visible to the crowded Senate gallery, Davis bid farewell to the U.S. Senate. The act of the Mississippi legislature had forced him to make a choice between loyalty to his state and loyalty to the Union. To Davis the choice was plain. Holding back tears, Davis made it clear that he was not hostile or bitter. In choosing his state, he recognized that his desire to preserve the Union was no longer viable, that reconciliation between North and South was impossible.

Author Biography

Davis was born on June 3, 1808, in Christian County (now Todd County) Kentucky; he moved with his parents to southwestern Mississippi in 1810. In 1824 he entered the U.S. Military Academy at West Point, but resigned from the army in 1835. In 1845 he was elected to the U.S. House of Representatives, his first political office.

In 1846 Davis resigned his seat in the House to lead a Mississippi unit in the Mexican-American War, during which he won recognition for heroism. Upon his return to civilian life, he was elected to the U.S. Senate and served until 1853, when he became secretary of war. In January 1856 Davis was again elected to the Senate, where he became the primary spokesperson in Congress for states' rights and the southern cause. He served in the Senate until his resignation on January 21, 1861, twelve days after Mississippi seceded from the Union.

After he was officially notified that the Mississippi legislature had voted to secede from the Union, Davis resigned from the Senate. Davis was a leading choice for president of the new Confederate States of America. As president of the Confederacy, he faced the daunting task of forming a central government from a group of states that had left the Union asserting their states' rights; at the same time he had to finance and fight a war against an enemy with superior industrial and military strength.

After the surrender of General Robert E. Lee on April 9, 1865, Davis attempted to maintain his government while on the run, hoping to reestablish it west of the Mississippi. On May 10, 1865, he was arrested by federal troops. He was taken to Fortress Monroe, Virginia, and was ultimately charged with treason, a charge that the U.S. government never successfully prosecuted. In response, Davis sought a trial, holding that secession was not treason—a position that he would maintain for the rest of his life. Davis died on December 6, 1889, in New Orleans.

HISTORICAL DOCUMENT

I rise, Mr. President [John C. Breckinridge], for the purpose of announcing to the Senate that I have satisfactory evidence that the State of Mississippi, by a solemn ordinance of her people in convention assembled, has declared her separation from the United States. Under these circumstances, of course my functions are terminated here. It has seemed to me proper, however, that I should appear in the Senate to announce that fact to my associates, and I will say but very little more. The occasion does not invite me to go into argument; and my physical condition would not permit me to do so if it were otherwise; and yet it seems to become me to say something on the part of the State I here represent, on an occasion so solemn as this.

It is known to Senators who have served with me here, that I have for many years advocated, as an essential attribute of State sovereignty, the right of a State to secede from the Union. Therefore, if I had not believed there was justifiable cause; if I had thought that Mississippi was acting without sufficient provocation, or without an existing necessity, I should still, under my theory of the Government, because of my allegiance to the State of which I am a citizen, have been bound by her action. I, however, may be permitted to say that I do think she has justifiable cause, and I approve of her act. I conferred with her people before that act was taken, counseled them then that if the state of things which they apprehended should exist when the convention met, they should take the action which they have now adopted.

I hope none who hear me will confound this expression of mine with the advocacy of the right of a State to remain in the Union, and to disregard its constitutional obligations by the nullification of the law. Such is not my theory. Nullification and secession, so often confounded, are indeed antagonistic principles.

Nullification is a remedy which it is sought to apply within the Union, and against the agent of the States. It is only to be justified when the agent has violated his constitutional obligation, and a State, assuming to judge for itself, denies the right of the agent thus to act, and appeals to the other States of the Union for a decision; but when the States themselves, and when the people of the States, have so acted as to convince us that they will not regard our constitutional rights, then, and then for the first time, arises the doctrine of secession in its practical application.

A great man who now reposes with his fathers, and who has been often arraigned for a want of fealty to the Union, advocated the doctrine of nullification, because it preserved the Union. It was because of his deep-seated attachment to the Union, his determination to find some remedy for existing ills short of a severance of the ties which bound South Carolina to the other States, that Mr. [John C.] Calhoun advocated the doctrine of nullification, which he proclaimed to be peaceful, to be within the limits of State power, not to disturb the Union, but only to be a means of bringing the agent before the tribunal of the States for their judgment.

Secession belongs to a different class of remedies. It is to be justified upon the basis that the States are sovereign. There was a time when none denied it. I hope the time may come again, when a better comprehension of the theory of our Government, and the inalienable rights of the people of the States, will prevent any one from denying that each State is a sovereign, and thus may reclaim the grants which it has made to any agent whomsoever.

I therefore say I concur in the action of the people of Mississippi, believing it to be necessary and proper, and should have been bound by their action if my belief had been otherwise; and this brings me to the important point which I wish on this last occasion to present to the Senate. It is by this confounding of nullification and secession that the name of a great man, whose ashes now mingle with his mother earth, has been invoked to justify coercion against a seceded State. The phrase "to execute the laws," was an expression which General Jackson applied to the case of a State refusing to obey the laws while yet a member of the Union. That is not the case which is now presented. The laws are to be executed over the United States, and upon the people of the United States. They have no relation to any foreign country. It is a perversion of terms, at least it is a great misapprehension of the case, which cites that expression for application to a State which has withdrawn from the Union. You may make war on a foreign State. If it be the purpose of gentlemen, they may make war against a State which has withdrawn from the Union; but there are no laws of the United States to be executed within the limits of a seceded State. A State finding herself in the condition in which Mississippi has judged she is, in which her safety requires that she should provide for the maintenance of her rights out of the Union, surrenders all the benefits, (and they are known to be many,) deprives herself of the advantages, (they are known to be great,) severs all the ties of affection, (and they are close and enduring,) which have bound her to the Union; and thus divesting herself of every benefit, taking upon herself every burden, she claims to be exempt from any power to execute the laws of the United States within her limits.

I well remember an occasion when Massachusetts was arraigned before the bar of the Senate, and when then the doctrine of coercion was rife and to be applied against her because of the rescue of a fugitive slave in Boston. My opinion then was the same that it is now. Not in a spirit of egotism, but to show that I am not influenced in my opinion because the case is my own, I refer to that time and that occasion as containing the opinion which I then entertained, and on which my present conduct is based. I then said, if Massachusetts, following her through a stated line of conduct, chooses to take the last step which separates her from the Union, it is her right to go, and I will neither vote one dollar nor one man to coerce her back; but will say to her, God speed, in memory of the kind associations which once existed between her and the other States.

It has been a conviction of pressing necessity, it has been a belief that we are to be deprived in the Union of the rights which our fathers bequeathed to us, which has brought Mississippi into her present decision. She has heard proclaimed the theory that all men are created free and equal, and this made the basis of an attack upon her social institutions; and the sacred Declaration of Independence has been invoked to maintain the position of the equality of the races. That Declaration of Independence is to be construed by the circumstances and purposes for which it was made. The communities were declaring their independence; the people of those communities were asserting that no man was born—to use the language of Mr. Jefferson—booted and spurred to ride over the rest of mankind; that men were created equal—meaning the men of the political community; that there was no divine right to rule; that no man inherited the right to govern; that there were no classes by which power and place descended to families, but that all stations were equally within the grasp of each member of the body-politic. These were the great principles they announced; these were the purposes for which they made their declaration; these were the ends to which their enunciation was directed. They have no reference to the slave; else, how happened it that among the items of arraignment made against George III was that he endeavored to do just what the North has been endeavoring of late to do—to stir up insurrection among our slaves? Had the Declaration announced that the negroes were free and equal, how was the Prince to be arraigned for stirring up insurrection among them? And how was this to be enumerated among the high crimes which caused the colonies to sever their connection with the mother country? When our Constitution was formed, the same idea was rendered more palpable, for there we find provision made for that very class of persons as property; they were not put upon the footing of equality with white men—not even upon that of paupers and convicts; but, so far as representation was concerned, were discriminated against as a lower caste, only to be represented in the numerical proportion of three fifths.

Then, Senators, we recur to the compact which binds us together; we recur to the principles upon which our Government was founded; and when you deny them, and when you deny to us the right to withdraw from a Government which thus perverted threatens to be destructive of our rights, we but tread in the path of our fathers when we proclaim our independence, and take the hazard. This is done not in hostility to others, not to injure any section of the country, not even for our own pecuniary benefit; but from the high and solemn motive of defending and protecting the rights we inherited, and which it is our sacred duty to transmit unshorn to our children.

I find in myself, perhaps, a type of the general feeling of my constituents towards yours. I am sure I feel no hostility to you, Senators from the North. I am sure there is not one of you, whatever sharp discussion there may have been between us, to whom I cannot now say, in the presence of my God, I wish you well; and such, I am sure, is the feeling of the people whom I represent towards those whom you represent. I therefore feel that I but express their desire when I say I hope, and they hope, for peaceful relations with you, though we must part. They may be mutually beneficial to us in the future, as they have been in the past, if you so will it. The reverse may bring disaster on every portion of the country; and if you will have it thus, we will invoke the God of our fathers, who delivered them from the power of the lion, to protect us from the ravages of the bear; and thus, putting our trust in God and in our own firm hearts and strong arms, we will vindicate the right as best we may.

In the course of my service here, associated at different times with a great variety of Senators, I see now around me some with whom I have served long; there have been points of collision; but whatever of offense there has been to me, I leave here; I carry with me no hostile remembrance. Whatever offense I have given which has not been redressed, or for which satisfaction has not been demanded, I have, Senators, in this hour of our parting, to offer you my apology for any pain which, in heat of discussion, I have inflicted. I go hence unencumbered of the remembrance of any injury received, and having discharged the duty of making the only reparation in my power for any injury offered.

Mr. President, and Senators, having made the announcement which the occasion seemed to me to require, it only remains to me to bid you a final adieu.

GLOSSARY

adieu: French for "farewell"

arraignment: formal or legal accusation

a great man who now reposes with his fathers: a reference to John C. Calhoun, vice president and senator, who had died in 1860

John C. Breckenridge: vice president to James Buchanan, southern Democratic candidate for the presidency (1860), general and later secretary of war under the Confederacy

lion…bear: a reference to the British and the U.S. government, respectively

nullification: refusal by a U.S. state to enforce the laws of the federal government

ordinance of her people in convention assembled: a formal and legal statement by the people of Mississippi, speaking through their elected representatives

unshorn: without being reduced

a want of fealty: a lack of loyalty

Document Analysis

Davis begins by announcing the Mississippi has seceded from the United States and declaring that, as such, his service in the Senate is at an end. While he does not want to engage in a debate on the issue, he wishes to speak on behalf of Mississippi. He reminds his Senate colleagues that he has been an advocate of individual states' rights to secede from the union. He also asserts that even if he thought Mississippi was mistake in seceding, he would still be "bound by her action." That, however, is not the case. Davis argues that Mississippi is right to secede and that he supports the state's decision.

He then goes on to explain that he believes secession to be fundamentally "antagonistic" to the notion of nullification—the theory that a state has the right to cancel out federal laws which it believes to (in Davis's words) have "violated...constitutional obligation." Nullification, Davis explains, is a method of appealing federal acts. Secession, on the other hand, is necessary when other states and their people "will not regard" the "constitutional rights" of another state.

The "great man" Davis discusses in the fourth paragraph, as revealed later, is South Carolina's John C. Calhoun, one of the key advocates of nullification. In 1832 and 1833, Calhoun supported the South Carolina legislature's decision to nullify a federal tariff and to prohibit federal officials from enforcing it. Davis, nearly three decades later, uses Calhoun's ideas about nullification to further explain how it is distinct from secession, arguing that Calhoun saw nullification as a means to preserve the union by providing a means for states to seek a "peaceful" remedy to unjust actions by the federal government. The relevance of the nullification crisis of 1832-1833 to the secession crisis of 1860-1861 lies in the way in which then-President Andrew Jackson handled the former crisis. Jackson, with the support of Congress, sent troops to "execute the laws," repudiating the notion of nullification. Opponents of secession, Davis explains, use this precedent to "justify coercion against a seceded state." This is a false precedent, he argues, because in the case of nullification, Jackson was attempting to enforce a law in an existing state of the union. In the case of secession, however, there is no law for the Union to enforce because the seceded states are no longer under the jurisdiction of the federal government. To attack a seceded state, he argues, would be an act of war.

Davis then provides an example of his long-standing support for secession, recalling that when Massachusetts had protested the enforcement of the Fugitive Slave Act, he supported the right of a state to secede, saying, "it is her right to go, and I will neither vote one dollar nor one man to coerce her back." It is that attitude, he implies, that northern states should have toward states such as Mississippi.

Davis, having discussed his vision of the legality of secession, turns to the specific reasons Mississippi is justified in leaving the Union. He asserts that the notion that "all men are created equal," as enshrined in the Declaration of Independence has been taken out of its original context and used as "the basis of an attack upon her social institutions"—a euphemism for slavery. Davis argues that "all men" referred to "men of the political community" and that the declaration "has no reference to the slave." He alleges that the north was attempting to incite violent insurrection among slaves, just as the Declaration accused King George III of doing.

Davis, having argued that the Declaration of Independence did not reject the notion of slavery, turns to the Constitution of the United States, arguing that the document contains" provision made for that very class of persons as property." He uses the three-fifths clause (which stipulated that, for the purposes of determining the number of Representatives and Presidential Electors from each state, only three fifths of slaves were to be counted) as evidence that the framers of the Constitution intended there to be inequalities built into the American system. The implication is that attempts to eliminate slavery are contrary to the will of the founders.

Davis concludes his farewell address by assuring his colleagues that he feels "no hostility" towards northern Senators and wishes them well—and asserts that the people of Mississippi likely feel the same toward the citizens of northern states. He expresses his hope for a peaceful future between their peoples, prediction that "the reverse may bring disaster on every portion of the country "and asks forgiveness for any offense he might have inflicted on his colleagues.

Essential Themes

There are two main strands to Davis's farewell address to his fellow Senators. The first is a legal justification for a state's secession from the United States. Davis invokes the "compact" theory of the relationship between the states and the federal government, which asserts that the union is an agreement between sovereign states. Thus, if states agree to join the United States, they can also agree to leave. This is an extreme step, but one than cannot be reversed by the federal government except by making war on the seceded state (since that state would, by definition, now be a foreign nation). Thus, in addition to justifying the legal basis for secession, Davis preemptively positions the northern states as the aggressors in the upcoming Civil War.

The other strand is a justification of Mississippi's reasons for secession which are, for Davis, closely tied to what he perceives as northern efforts to strip the rights from his fellow southerners—in particular, the right to own slaves. Davis compares the northerners who support slave insurrections (such as Ohio's John Brown, executed in 1859 for attempting to seize the federal armory at Harper's Ferry for the purposes of a slave rebellion) to the British at the time of the American Revolution and argues that slavery was enshrined in the Constitution via the three fifths clause.

———*C. Ellen Connally, JD*
with additional material by Aaron Gulyas, MA

Bibliography and Additional Reading

Nichols, Roy F. "United States vs. Jefferson Davis, 1865–1869." *American Historical Review* 31(January 1926): 266–284.

Cashin, Joan E. *First Lady of the Confederacy: Varina Davis's Civil War*. Cambridge, Mass. Belknap Press of Harvard University Press, 2006.

Cooper, William J., Jr. *Jefferson Davis, American*. New York: Knopf, 2000.

———. *Jefferson Davis and the Civil War Era*. Baton Rouge: Louisiana State University Press, 2009.

Davis, Varina. *Jefferson Davis: Ex-President of the Confederate States of America—A Memoir by His Wife*. 1890. Reprinted with an introduction by Craig L. Symonds. Baltimore: Nautical and Aviation Publishing Company of America, 1990.

Davis, William C. *Jefferson Davis: The Man and His Hour*. New York: HarperCollins Publishers, 1991.

Hattaway, Herman, and Richard E. Beringer. *Jefferson Davis: Confederate President*. Lawrence: University Press of Kansas, 2002.

■ Speech on His Refusal to Take the Oath of Loyalty to the Confederacy

Date: 1861
Author: Sam Houston
Genre: Speech

Summary Overview

Sam Houston was involved in some of the most dramatic events in American history. Aside from his successful military career, he proved to be a passionate and dedicated politician. Unlike many of his southern counterparts, he was sympathetic to Native Americans and firmly believed that secession—the decision of southern states to separate from the United States and form their own country, the Confederate States of America—was a mistake. A charismatic orator and eloquent writer, Houston's writings and speeches often stirred people to action. His love of the Union and commitment to peace are evident in the Speech on His Refusal to Take the Oath of Loyalty to the Confederacy, an address he gave to the Texas Secession Convention. The version presented here includes a preface in which Houston provides the context of his remarks.

Defining Moment

Throughout the tumultuous 1850s, Houston advocated for a peaceful solution to the growing discord over whether new states and territories should be admitted to the United States allowing slavery or as free. Houston waited as long as possible to call a special session of his state's legislature to debate secession. The Texas legislature met on January 21, 1861, at which time South Carolina, Mississippi, Georgia, Florida, and Alabama had already seceded. In addressing the legislature, Houston tried to sway the group by pointing out how Texas was different from other southern states. For instance, no other southern state bordered a foreign country or was susceptible to Indian attacks, and Texas relied on the support of the federal government to defend itself.

Ultimately, Houston argued that the people of Texas should decide the issue. The Texas Secession Convention assembled a week later, promptly voted 171 to six in favor of secession, and named a committee to draft an ordinance on which the people of Texas would vote. In a bill titled "An Ordinance: To Dissolve the Union between the State of Texas and the Other States, United under the Compact Styled 'The Constitution of the United States of America,'" the convention explained why it should leave the Union.

In the only case where the people directly voted on the issue of secession, the people of Texas voted to secede. Even though Texas delegates had already traveled to Montgomery, Alabama, to take their seats in the First Confederate Congress, Houston insisted that Texas had merely reclaimed its independence and had not yet agreed to become a part of another government. The members of the Texas Secession Convention were outraged and sent a messenger to Houston's home instructing him to appear the next day to take the Confederate oath of allegiance. During the night, Houston wrote a letter addressed to the people of Texas, which he read to the convention the next day.

Author Biography

Samuel Houston was born on March 2, 1793. He lived his early life in Tennessee and later enlisted in the army during the War of 1812, worked as an Indian subagent, and pursued a law career in Tennessee. By 1819 Houston's political career was starting to evolve; he served as adjunct general of the state militia and attorney general for the district of Nashville. Houston was elected to the U.S. House of Representatives, where he served from 1823 to 1827. Then, in 1827, he ran for and won the governorship of Tennessee, though he resigned on April 16, 1829, heading west, eventually to Texas.

Once in Texas, Houston became enmeshed in the events unfolding there. He was one of the Texas representatives at the Convention of 1833, through which Texas sought a peaceful independence from Mexico. Hopes for peace were dashed when war broke out in October 1835. As commander in chief of the Texas army, Houston led Texas to victory over Mexican forces in 1836. In September that year, Houston was elected as the first president of the Republic of Texas, serving until December 1838. He was elected again in December 1841, to serve until December 1844. After Texas became a state in 1845, Houston was elected as one of the state's first senators, a post he held for thirteen years.

In late 1859 Houston became Texas's seventh governor, but he resigned less than two years later over the controversy surrounding his refusal to take the Confederate loyalty oath. Houston retired into private life and died at home on July 26, 1863.

HISTORICAL DOCUMENT

When on account of the election of Mr. Lincoln to the Presidency of the United States, I was urged to call the Legislature, I refused to do so until such time as I believed the public interests required it....

In the meantime, the Convention had been called....That convention, besides being revolutionary in its character, did not receive the sanction of a majority of the people. As the representative of a minority, however large, it could not claim the right to speak for the people. It was without the pale of the Constitution, and was unknown to the laws which I had sworn to support. While sworn to support the Constitution, it was my duty to stand aloof from all revolutionary schemes calculated to subvert the Constitution. The people who were free from such solemn obligations, might revolutionize and absolve me from mine, my oath only having reference to my acts in the capacity of their Chief Executive; but as a sworn officer, my duty was too plain to be misunderstood....

Fellow Citizens, I have refused to recognize this Convention....

I have declared my determination to stand by Texas in whatever the position she assumes. Her people have declared in favor of a separation from the Union. I have followed her banners before, when an exile from the land of my fathers. I went back into the Union with the people of Texas. I go out from the Union with them; and though I see only gloom before me, I shall follow the "Lone Star" with the same devotion as of yore.

You have withdrawn Texas from her connection with the United States. Your act changes the character of the obligation I assumed at the time of my inauguration. As Your Chief Executive, I am no longer bound to support the Constitution of the United States.

I love Texas too well to bring civil strife and bloodshed upon her. To avert this calamity, I shall make no endeavor to maintain my authority as Chief Executive of this State, except by the peaceful exercise of my functions. When I can no longer do this, I shall calmly withdraw from the scene, leaving the Government in the hands of those who have usurped its authority; but still claiming that I am its Chief Executive.

I protest in the name of the people of Texas against all the acts and doings of this convention, AND I DECLARE THEM NULL AND VOID! I solemnly protest against the act of its members who are bound by no other than themselves, in declaring my office vacant, and I refuse to appear before it and take the oath prescribed.

GLOSSARY

Lone Star: a reference to the Texas state flag, which features a single star

without the pale of the Constitution: outside the bounds of the Constitution, referring to the pickets, or "pales," of a fence

Document Analysis

In his address to the Texas Secession Convention, Houston begins by explaining that he would not take the oath of allegiance because the convention had not obtained its authority from the Texas legislature or people. As he put it, "That convention, besides being revolutionary in its character, did not receive the sanction of a majority of the people." He further notes that the convention had held its meetings in secret and appointed military personnel to operate under its authority. He then states that he refuses to recognize the authority of the convention and declares its actions null and void. At the end he declares, "I solemnly protest against the act of its members who are bound by no other than themselves, in declaring my office vacant, and I refuse to appear before it and take the oath prescribed." As a result of his refusal to take the Confederate oath, Houston was replaced as governor by the lieutenant governor, Edward Clark.

Essential Themes

In 1860, Sam Houston sought the Constitutional Unionist party's nomination for the Presidency, coming in second to candidate John Bell, this address to the Texas Secession Convention features Houston placing his unionist ideals above his own political ambitions, choosing to step aide form the governor's office rather than swear loyalty to a Confederacy of which he did not believe Texas to be a legitimate part. His claims that the convention is without legitimate sanction, or permission, of the people illustrates Houston's devotion to democratic principles. Hous-

ton's unionism was not a recent development—he opposed the Kansas Nebraska act on the grounds that it would reopen sectional conflict that the Missouri Compromise had settled. Houston did not see a conflict between the fact that he was a slave owner and did not believe that slavery should be abolished and his loyalty to the union. While the event of the Civil War sometimes obscure the fact, unionist tendencies in the Confederate states would persist throughout the conflict.

———*Michael J. O'Neal, PhD*
with additional material by Aaron Gulyas, MA

Bibliography and Additional Reading

Baum, Dale. *The Shattering of Texas Unionism: Politics in the Lone Star State during the Civil War Era.* (Boton Rouge: Louisiana State University Press, 1998).

Buenger, Walter L. *Secession and the Union in Texas.* (Austin: University of Texas Press, 1984).

James, Marquis. *The Raven: A Biography of Sam Houston.* (Austin: University of Texas Press, 1988).

Marten, James. *Texas Divided: Loyalty and Dissent in the Lone Star State, 1856-1874.* Lexington: University Press of Kentucky, 1990.

■ "Cornerstone Speech"

Date: 1861
Author: Alexander Stephens
Genre: Speech

Summary Overview

Confederate States of America Vice President Alexander Stephens delivered the "Cornerstone Speech," on March 21, 1861 in Savannah, Georgia. The speech provides an overview of the new Confederate government, a comparison of both the systems of government of the north and the south as well as a comparison of their ideological foundation. It also defended both the southern states secession from the United States as well as the institution of slavery. This new government, in Stephens's view, restored the balance of power between the central government and the states—a balance that had been destroyed in the United States in the face of growing federal power. He also explains the differences in the executive branch and the presidency from those of the United States.

Stephens's defense of the secession of southern states relies upon the "compact" theory of the union and constitution. Most significantly, however, in this speech, Stephens presents race-based slavery as the "cornerstone" of the Confederacy. Crucially, Stephens makes the argument that slavery is necessary and that, for those of African descent, "subordination to the superior race is his natural and normal condition." Coming from the Vice President of this new attempt at a nation, this view cannot be considered a fringe opinion.

Defining Moment

In November, 1860, Illinois Republican Abraham Lincoln was elected President of the United States, entirely by voters in northern states. Between December of that year and February of 1861, the cotton-dependent states of the lower south—Florida, Georgia, Alabama, Mississippi, South Carolina, Louisiana, and Texas withdrew from the United States and declared themselves to be the Confederate States of America and began the process of seizing military assets within their borders and forming a new government.

Often, the waves of secession which began in December, 1860 gets conflated with the onset of Civil War which began in April, 1861. This five months between initial state secession and the outbreak of armed conflict, however, was a crucial period for the formation

of the new Confederate government as well as attempts by moderates in both sections of the United States to reach some kind of compromise that would preserve the union without recourse to violence.

In December, 1860, Kentucky Senator John J. Crittenden proposed a package of measures referred as the "Crittenden Compromise." The package was composed of six Constitutional amendments and four Congressional resolutions that would—among other things—extend the Missouri Compromise line all the way to the Pacific Ocean, prohibited Congressional regulation of the slave trade, and the elimination of "Personal Liberty Laws" (laws in some northern states that prevented enforcement of fugitive slave laws). Crittenden's proposal was tabled and died within a few weeks. In February, 1861, Congress rejected a similar compromise which emerged from the Washington Peace Conference.

Lincoln's March 4th inauguration address clarified that he would not compromise with secession, which he declared to be a legal and constitutional impossibility. Given Lincoln's stance on secession, the Confederacy sent delegates to Washington offering money to pay for seized federal installations as well as a peace treaty. Lincoln refused to meet with the delegation.

As armed conflict appeared to draw closer, Alexander Stephens, now Vice President of the Confederacy, gave this "Cornerstone Speech" on March 12, 1861, in Savannah Georgia.

Author Biography

Alexander Hamilton Stephens was born in Gerorgia on February 11, 1812. Raised on a farm, Stephens became a motivated learner and voracious reader, thanks to his father's large collection of books. He obtained an education thanks to numerous wealthy community members who sponsored his schooling and, after a stint as a school teacher, became a lawyer in 1834.

In 1836, his political career began with his election to the Georgia House of Representatives and, later, to the state Senate. In the 1840s, he entered politics at the national level, a member of Congress, where he would serve until 1858, when he decided against running for re-election. In the early years of his political career he was a member of the Whig party until the early 1850s when he began to believe that Whig goals were not aligned with the interests of southern states.

While, after his exit from Congress father 1858, he remained committed to the right of southerners to own slaves (he himself owned more than 30) Stephens was also firmly opposed to talk of secession. Even as a delegate to the Georgia convention which would determine whether or not that state would leave the union, he urged delegates to be cautious, arguing that even though Republicans controlled the White House, they did not fully control Congress. Despite his caution, he was elected Vice President of the Confederate States of America in February, 1861. He served in this office throughout the Civil War and was one of the delegates in the unsuccessful southern effort to achieve a peace treaty in early 1865. Following the war, after being arrested on May 11, 1865, he eventually returned to Congress in the 1870s. He died in 1883, four months after being sworn in as Governor of Georgia.

HISTORICAL DOCUMENT

...We are passing through one of the greatest revolutions in the annals of the world. Seven States have within the last three months thrown off an old government and formed a new. This revolution has been signally marked, up to this time, by the fact of its having been accomplished without the loss of a single drop of blood.

This new constitution, or form of government, constitutes the subject to which your attention will be partly invited. In reference to it, I make this first general remark: it amply secures all our ancient rights, franchises, and liberties. All the great principles of Magna Charta are retained in it. No citizen is deprived of life, liberty, or property, but by the judgment of his peers under the laws of the land. The great principle of religious liberty, which was the honor and pride of the old constitution, is still maintained and secured. All the essentials of the old constitution, which have endeared it to the hearts of the American people, have been preserved and perpetuated. Some changes have been made. Some of these I should have preferred not to have seen made; but other important changes do meet my cordial approbation. They form great improvements upon the old constitution. So, taking the whole new constitution, I have no hesitancy in giving it as my judgment that it is decidedly better than the old.

Allow me briefly to allude to some of these improvements. The question of building up class interests, or fostering one branch of industry to the prejudice of another under the exercise of the revenue power, which gave us so much trouble under the old constitution, is put at rest forever under the new. We allow the imposition of no duty with a view of giving advantage to one class of persons, in any trade or business, over those of another. All, under our system, stand upon the same broad principles of perfect equality. Honest labor and enterprise are left free and unrestricted in whatever pursuit they may be engaged. This old thorn of the tariff, which was the cause of so much irritation in the old body politic, is removed forever from the new.

Again, the subject of internal improvements, under the power of Congress to regulate commerce, is put at rest under our system. The power, claimed by construction under the old constitution, was at least a doubtful one; it rested solely upon construction. We of the South, generally apart from considerations of constitutional principles, opposed its exercise upon grounds of its inexpediency and injustice. Notwithstanding this opposition, millions of money, from the common treasury had been drawn for such purposes. Our opposition sprang from no hostility to commerce, or to all necessary aids for facilitating it. With us it was simply a question upon whom the burden should fall. In Georgia, for instance, we have done as much for the cause of internal improvements as any other portion of the country, according to population and means. We have stretched out lines of railroads from the seaboard to the mountains; dug down the hills, and filled up the valleys at a cost of not less than $25,000,000. All this was done to open an outlet for our products of the interior, and those to the west of us, to reach the marts of the world. No State was in greater need of such facilities than Georgia, but we did not ask that these works should be made by appropriations out of the common treasury. The cost of the grading, the superstructure, and the equipment of our roads was borne by those who had entered into the enterprise. Nay, more not only the cost of the iron no small item in the aggregate cost was borne in the same way, but we were compelled to pay into the common treasury several millions of dollars for the privilege of importing the iron, after the price was paid for it abroad. What justice was there in taking this money, which our people paid into the common treasury on the importation of our iron, and applying it to the improvement of rivers and harbors elsewhere? The true principle is to subject the commerce of every locality, to whatever burdens may be necessary to facilitate it. If Charleston harbor needs improvement, let the commerce of Charleston bear the burden. If the mouth of the Savannah river has to be cleared out, let the sea-going navigation which is benefited by it, bear the burden. So with the mouths of the Alabama and Mississippi river. Just as the products of the interior, our cotton, wheat, corn, and other articles, have to bear the necessary rates of freight over our railroads to reach the seas. This is again the broad principle of perfect equality and justice, and it is especially set forth and established in our new constitution.

Another feature to which I will allude is that the new constitution provides that cabinet ministers and heads of departments may have the privilege of seats upon the floor of the Senate and House of Representatives and may have the right to participate in the debates and discussions upon the various subjects of administration. I should have preferred that this provision should have gone further, and required the President to select his constitutional advisers from the Senate and House of Representatives. That would have conformed entirely to the practice in the British Parliament, which, in my judgment, is one of the wisest provisions in the British constitution. It is the only feature that saves that government. It is that which gives it stability in its facility to change its administration. Ours, as it is, is a great approximation to the right principle.

Under the old constitution, a secretary of the treasury for instance, had no opportunity, save by his annual reports, of presenting any scheme or plan of finance or other matter. He had no opportunity of explaining, expounding, enforcing, or defending his views of policy; his only resort was through the medium of an organ. In the British parliament, the premier brings in his budget and stands before the nation responsible for its every item. If it is indefensible, he falls before the attacks upon it, as he ought to. This will now be the case to a limited extent under our system. In the new constitution, provision has been made by which our heads of departments can speak for themselves and the administration, in behalf of its entire policy, without resorting to the indirect and highly objectionable medium of a newspaper. It is to be greatly hoped that under our system we shall never have what is known as a government organ.

Another change in the constitution relates to the length of the tenure of the presidential office. In the new constitution it is six years instead of four, and the President rendered ineligible for a re-election. This is certainly a decidedly conservative change. It will remove from the incumbent all temptation to use his office or exert the powers confided to him for any objects of personal ambition. The only incentive to that higher ambition which should move and actuate one holding such high trusts in his hands, will be the good of the people, the advancement, prosperity, happiness, safety, honor, and true glory of the confederacy.

But not to be tedious in enumerating the numerous changes for the better, allow me to allude to one other though last, not least. The new constitution has put at rest, forever, all the agitating questions relating to our peculiar institution African slavery as it exists amongst us the proper status of the negro in our form of civilization. This was the immediate cause of the late rupture and present revolution. Jefferson in his forecast, had anticipated this, as the "rock upon which the old Union would split." He was right. What was conjecture with him, is now a realized fact. But whether he fully comprehended the great truth upon which that rock stood and stands, may be doubted. The prevailing ideas entertained by him and most of the leading statesmen at the time of the formation of the old constitution, were that r; that it was wrong in principle, socially, morally, and politically. It was an evil they knew not well how to deal with, but the general opinion of the men of that day was that, somehow or other in the order of Providence, the institution would be evanescent and pass away. This idea, though not incorporated in the constitution, was the prevailing idea at that time. The constitution, it is true, secured every essential guarantee to the institution while it should last, and hence no argument can be justly urged against the constitutional guarantees thus secured, because of the common sentiment of the day. Those ideas, however, were fundamentally wrong. They rested upon the assumption of the equality of races. This was an error. It was a sandy foundation, and the government built upon it fell when the "storm came and the wind blew."

Our new government is founded upon exactly the opposite idea; its foundations are laid, its cornerstone rests, upon the great truth that the negro is not equal to the white man; that slavery subordination to the superior race is his natural and normal condition. This, our new government, is the first, in the history of the world, based upon this great physical, philosophical, and moral truth. This truth has been slow in the process of its development, like all other truths in the various departments of science. It has been so even amongst us. Many who hear me, perhaps, can recollect well, that this truth was not generally admitted, even within their day. The errors of the past generation still clung to many as late as twenty years ago. Those at the North, who still cling to these errors, with a zeal above knowledge, we justly denominate fanatics. All fanaticism springs from an aberration of the mind from a defect in reasoning. It is a species of insanity. One of the most striking characteristics of insanity, in many instances, is forming correct conclusions from fancied or erroneous premises; so with the anti-slavery fanatics. Their conclusions are right if their premises were. They assume that the negro is equal, and hence conclude that he is entitled to equal privileges and rights with the white man. If their premises were correct, their conclusions would be logical and just but their premise being wrong, their whole argument fails. I recollect once of having heard a gentleman from one of the northern States, of great power and ability, announce in the House of Representatives, with imposing effect, that we of the South would be compelled, ultimately, to yield upon this subject of slavery, that it was as impossible to war successfully against a principle in politics, as it was in physics or mechanics. That the principle would ultimately prevail. That we, in maintaining slavery as it exists with us, were warring against a principle, a principle founded in nature, the principle of the equality of men. The reply I made to him was, that upon his own grounds, we should, ultimately, succeed, and that he and his associates, in this crusade against our institutions, would ultimately fail. The truth announced, that it was as impossible to war successfully against a principle in politics as it was in physics and mechanics, I admitted; but told him that it was he, and those acting with him, who were warring against a principle. They were attempting to make things equal which the Creator had made unequal.

In the conflict thus far, success has been on our side, complete throughout the length and breadth of the Confederate States. It is upon this, as I have stated, our social fabric is firmly planted; and I cannot permit myself to doubt the ultimate success of a full recognition of this principle throughout the civilized and enlightened world.

As I have stated, the truth of this principle may be slow in development, as all truths are and ever have been, in the various branches of science. It was so with the principles announced by Galileo it was so with Adam Smith and his principles of political economy. It was so with Harvey, and his theory of the circulation of the blood. It is stated that not a single one of the medical profession, living at the time of the announcement of the truths made by him, admitted them. Now, they are universally acknowledged. May we not, therefore, look with confidence to the ultimate universal acknowledgment of the truths upon which our system rests? It is the first government ever instituted upon the principles in strict conformity to nature, and the ordination of Providence, in furnishing the materials of human society. Many governments have been founded upon the principle of the subordination and serfdom of certain classes of the same race; such were and are in violation of the laws of nature. Our system commits no such violation of nature's laws. With us, all of the white race, however high or low, rich or poor, are equal in the eye of the law. Not so with the negro. Subordination is his place. He, by nature, or by the curse against Canaan, is fitted for that condition which he occupies in our system. The architect, in the construction of buildings, lays the foundation with the proper material-the granite; then comes the brick or the marble. The substratum of our society is made of the material fitted by nature for it, and by experience we know that it is best, not only for the superior, but for the inferior race, that it should be so. It is, indeed, in conformity with the ordinance of the Creator. It is not for us to inquire into the wisdom of His ordinances, or to question them. For His own purposes, He has made one race to differ from another, as He has made "one star to differ from another star in glory." The great objects of humanity are best attained when there is conformity to His laws and decrees, in the formation of governments as well as in all things else. Our confederacy is founded upon principles in strict conformity with these laws. This stone which was rejected by the first builders "is become the chief of the corner" the real "corner-stone" in our new edifice. I have been asked, what of the future? It has been apprehended by some that we would have arrayed against us the civilized world. I care not who or how many they may be against us, when we stand upon the eternal principles of truth, if we are true to ourselves and the principles for which we contend, we are obliged to, and must triumph.

Thousands of people who begin to understand these truths are not yet completely out of the shell; they do not see them in their length and breadth. We hear much of the civilization and Christianization of the barbarous tribes of Africa. In my judgment, those ends will never be attained, but by first teaching them the lesson taught to Adam, that "in the sweat of his brow he should eat his bread," and teaching them to work, and feed, and clothe themselves.

But to pass on: Some have propounded the inquiry whether it is practicable for us to go on with the confederacy without further accessions? Have we the means and ability to maintain nationality among the powers of the earth? On this point I would barely say, that as anxiously as we all have been, and are, for the border States, with institutions similar to ours, to join us, still we are abundantly able to maintain our position, even if they should ultimately make up their minds not to cast their destiny with us.

That they ultimately will join us be compelled to do it is my confident belief; but we can get on very well without them, even if they should not.

We have all the essential elements of a high national career. The idea has been given out at the North, and even in the border States, that we are too small and too weak to maintain a separate nationality. This is a great mistake. In extent of territory we embrace five hundred and sixty-four thousand square miles and upward. This is upward of two hundred thousand square miles more than was included within the limits of the original thirteen States. It is an area of country more than double the territory of France or the Austrian empire. France, in round numbers, has but two hundred and twelve thousand square miles. Austria, in round numbers, has two hundred and forty-eight thousand square miles. Ours is greater than both combined. It is greater than all France, Spain, Portugal, and Great Britain, including England, Ireland, and Scotland, together. In population we have upward of five millions, according to the census of 1860; this includes white and black. The entire population, including white and black, of the original thirteen States, was less than four millions in 1790, and still less in 76, when the independence of our fathers was achieved. If they, with a less population, dared maintain their independence against the greatest power on earth, shall we have any apprehension of maintaining ours now?

In point of material wealth and resources, we are greatly in advance of them. The taxable property of the Confederate States cannot be less than twenty-two hundred millions of dollars! This, I think I venture but little in saying, may be considered as five times more than the colonies possessed at the time they achieved their independence. Georgia, alone, possessed last year, according to the report of our comptroller-general, six hundred and seventy-two millions of taxable property. The debts of the seven confederate States sum up in the aggregate less than eighteen millions, while the existing debts of the other of the late United States sum up in the aggregate the enormous amount of one hundred and seventy-four millions of dollars. This is without taking into account the heavy city debts, corporation debts, and railroad debts, which press, and will continue to press, as a heavy incubus upon the resources of those States. These debts, added to others, make a sum total not much under five hundred millions of dollars. With such an area of territory as we have-with such an amount of population-with a climate and soil unsurpassed by any on the face of the earth-with such resources already at our command-with productions which control the commerce of the world-who can entertain any apprehensions as to our ability to succeed, whether others join us or not?

It is true, I believe I state but the common sentiment, when I declare my earnest desire that the border States should join us. The differences of opinion that existed among us anterior to secession, related more to the policy in securing that result by co-operation than from any difference upon the ultimate security we all looked to in common.

These differences of opinion were more in reference to policy than principle, and as Mr. Jefferson said in his inaugural, in 1801, after the heated contest preceding his election, that there might be differences of opinion without differences on principle, and that all, to some extent, had been Federalists and all Republicans; so it may now be said of us, that whatever differences of opinion as to the best policy in having a co-operation with our border sister slave States, if the worst came to the worst, that as we were all co-operationists, we are now all for independence, whether they come or not.

In this connection I take this occasion to state, that I was not without grave and serious apprehensions, that if the worst came to the worst, and cutting loose from the old government should be the

only remedy for our safety and security, it would be attended with much more serious ills than it has been as yet. Thus far we have seen none of those incidents which usually attend revolutions. No such material as such convulsions usually throw up has been seen. Wisdom, prudence, and patriotism, have marked every step of our progress thus far. This augurs well for the future, and it is a matter of sincere gratification to me, that I am enabled to make the declaration. Of the men I met in the Congress at Montgomery, I may be pardoned for saying this, an abler, wiser, a more conservative, deliberate, determined, resolute, and patriotic body of men, I never met in my life. Their works speak for them; the provisional government speaks for them; the constitution of the permanent government will be a lasting monument of their worth, merit, and statesmanship.

. . .

As to whether we shall have war with our late confederates, or whether all matters of differences between us shall be amicably settled, I can only say that the prospect for a peaceful adjustment is better, so far as I am informed, than it has been. The prospect of war is, at least, not so threatening as it has been. The idea of coercion, shadowed forth in President Lincoln's inaugural, seems not to be followed up thus far so vigorously as was expected....

The surest way to secure peace, is to show your ability to maintain your rights. The principles and position of the present administration of the United States the republican party present some puzzling questions. While it is a fixed principle with them never to allow the increase of a foot of slave territory, they seem to be equally determined not to part with an inch "of the accursed soil." Notwithstanding their clamor against the institution, they seemed to be equally opposed to getting more, or letting go what they have got. They were ready to fight on the accession of Texas, and are equally ready to fight now on her secession. Why is this? How can this strange paradox be accounted for? There seems to be but one rational solution and that is, notwithstanding their professions of humanity, they are disinclined to give up the benefits they derive from slave labor. Their philanthropy yields to their interest. The idea of enforcing the laws, has but one object, and that is a collection of the taxes, raised by slave labor to swell the fund necessary to meet their heavy appropriations. The spoils is what they are after though they come from the labor of the slave.

That as the admission of States by Congress under the constitution was an act of legislation, and in the nature of a contract or compact between the States admitted and the others admitting, why should not this contract or compact be regarded as of like character with all other civil contracts liable to be rescinded by mutual agreement of both parties? The seceding States have rescinded it on their part, they have resumed their sovereignty. Why cannot the whole question be settled, if the north desire peace, simply by the Congress, in both branches, with the concurrence of the President, giving their consent to the separation, and a recognition of our independence?

GLOSSARY

"a government organ": A newspaper friendly to the political party in power

internal improvements: infrastructure such as bridges, canals, and roads

Magna Charta: Meaning "Great Charter," this was an English document from 1215 that established rights such as a trial by jury and the equality of all before the law.

"our late confederates": Citizens of states that remained loyal to the United States.

Document Analysis

Stephens begins by describing the secession of the southern sates and the formation of the Confederate government as a "revolution" and notes that this revolution has been "accomplished" without violence or bloodshed. He then moves to his first topic of discussion, the new Confederate constitution. He asserts that no rights or liberties have been removed from citizens— the "essentials" of the constitution of the United States ("the old constitution") are all present. The differences between the old constitution and the new make it, according to Stephens, "decidedly better than the old."

He begins his explanation of these improvements by explaining that the Confederate constitution will not favor one branch of industry 'to the prejudice of another" and will not allow the creation of duties or tariffs to support "any trade or business, over those of another." The issue of tariffs had long been a concern for southern states and this measure indicates a devotion to showing no favoritism between industrial and agricultural sectors of the economy. The next, long, paragraph points out how, in a similar way, the issue of national funding for internal improvements (a term meaning infrastructure such as bridges, canals, and roads) has been "put to rest"—meaning that such things are the responsibility of the state without national government support or management. He justifies the state-level management of internal improvements by describing Georgia's efforts in building railroads, and explaining that it making states pay for improvements that benefited the states was an example of this new constitution's "perfect equality and justice."

The next issue Stephens addresses is the differences between the executive branch of the Confederacy and the existing federal government. Perhaps the most striking change is the implementation of a "ministerial" style of government, with cabinet department heads (like the Secretary of the Treasury) having " the privilege of seats upon the floor of the Senate and House of Representatives and may have the right to participate in the debates and discussions upon the various subjects of administration." This is, Stephens points out, similar to way that the British Parliamentary system of government operates. This system, Stephens argues, enables department heads to present and defend their proposals directly to their legislative colleagues, as opposed to through "the indirect and highly objectionable medium of a newspaper." Another change to the executive powers of the government under the Confederacy is that the President was limited to one, six-year term rather than multiple four-year terms as in the United States government.

At this point Stephens moves into the heart of his speech—a defense of slavery's place as an institution within the Confederacy. The new constitution, Stephens explains, has settled the issue of slavery by protecting it. African slavery as it exists amongst us," Stephens says, is "the proper status of the negro in our form of civilization." The framers of the US constitution, he says, erred in thinking that "the enslavement of the African was in violation of the laws of nature" but that, eventually, it would fade away. While he acknowledges that the 1787 constitution did not undermine slavery, he calls the sentiment that slavery was somehow morally flawed "fundamentally wrong." The new confederate government is founded upon the "opposite" notion. The fundamental idea underlying the new nation is "the great truth that the negro is not equal to the white man; that slavery subordination to the superior race is his natural and normal condition." Stephens continues, explains that the government Confederate States of America" is the first, in the history of the world, based upon this great physical, philosophical, and moral truth."

Stephens's argument goes beyond a defense of slavery based on economic grounds or on a constitutional argument that merely asserts that the federal government had no right to interfere in the practice of slavery. Instead, it is a condemnation of the very notion that people of African descent were equal to those of European descent. This is the fundamental error made by abolitionists, according to Stephens, is to assume that this equality exists. If it did, he explains, then slavery would be unjust. However, as Stephens explained to a colleague in Congress anti-slavery advocates, "were attempting to make things equal which the Creator had made unequal." Stephens believes it is only a matter of time until the "civilized and enlightened world" recognizes this fact.

In the next long paragraph, Stephens defense his views on racial inequality by explaining that scientific truths are often doubted at the beginning, but later are "universally acknowledged." He follows this with examples of supposed race-based slavery in Biblical history and it is here that Stephens refers to slavery as the "cornerstone" of the southern government. He follows this by explaining that despite talk of "the civilization and

Christianization of the barbarous tribes of Africa," he does not think this will ever fully occur without teaching them to provide for themselves which, presumably, he believes slavery does.

Following his discussion of the importance of slavery to he southern states and the ultimate rightness of the institution, Stephens goes on to explain that the Confederacy will thrive even without other states joining them, due to "a high national character" as well as a vast quantity of land—more than comprised the original thirteen states as well as a population more than adequate for its needs. The same could be said of taxable property and the forms of wealth. While Stephens wants the other southern and border states to join them, stating that their differences were not of principle, but of policy and could be overcome.

in the lengthy concluding paragraphs (excerpted here), Stephens goes on to explain that he is apprehensive about the future, but that the secession of the lower south was undertaken after serious deliberation. and that—while war is certainly one possible outcome of the secession crisis, a firm dedication to their principles will only help the south. While the northerners, especially Republicans may oppose slavery or its spread, they benefit from the products produced, such as the cotton which provides raw materials for northern textile factories, saying "the spoils is what they are after though they come from the labor of the slave." Stephens concludes by defending the principle of secession.

Essential Themes

The most significant theme of Stephens's "Cornerstone Speech" is the defense of and justification for slavery and his insistence that it is a foundational element of the Confederate States of America and the life of the southern states. This defense relies not on economic data about the value of the work performed by the slaves but rather on the racial and cultural determination that persons of African descent are naturally suited to be slave labor and that they were not equal to white Americans. By Stephens's own admission, this is the only justification for slavery that will withstand the rhetoric of abolitionists for, if non-whites are equal to whites, then slavery is unjustifiable. This slavery, Stephens argues, is essential for the future success of the Confederate states. He also, in making this argument, very consciously and explicitly makes a break with the founding of the United States and the revered figures (such as Thomas Jefferson, himself a slave owner) who loomed large in its early history. This is entirely in keeping with his view that what is occurring is a revolution. The past, and its lingering notion that the enslavement of Africans is shameful and, at best, a necessary evil, is giving away to what he sees as a glorious present and future where slavery is viewed as a positive good and an acknowledgement of a natural racial hierarchy.

———*Aaron Gulyas, MA*

Bibliography and Additional Reading

Davis, William C. *Look Away! A History of the Confederate States of America* (New York: The Free Press, 2002).

———. *The Union that Shaped the Confederacy: Robert Toombs & Alexander H. Stephens* (Lawrence: University Press of Kansas, 2001).

Schott, Thomas E. *Alexander H. Stephens of Georgia: A Biography* (Baton Rogue: Louisiana State University Press, 1988).

Thomas, Emory M. *The Confederate Nation: 1861-1865* (New York: Harper Perennial, 2011).

■ Speech on His Expulsion from the Georgia Legislature

Date: 1868
Author: Henry McNeal Turner
Genre: Speech

Summary Overview

Henry McNeal Turner's speech to the Georgia legislature in September 1868 was a direct response to the expulsion by that body of twenty-seven African American state legislators. In the first elections initiated by Radical Reconstruction in July 1867, three African Americans were elected to the Georgia Senate and twenty-nine to the Georgia House of Representatives. These black legislators represented a Republican Party that hoped to rise to power in the Reconstruction South by creating a coalition among the newly enfranchised freedmen, sympathetic native southern whites, and northern whites who had come to the South seeking economic prosperity and political opportunities. As in most southern states, Georgia Republicans were riven by factional disputes. Democrats, hoping to take advantage of Republican factionalism, sought means to regain political power for conservative whites.

The speech was rooted in the experiment in biracial democracy that underlay Radical Reconstruction. It thus speaks to several important issues in African American political history and in the history of Reconstruction. It sheds light on the nature of black political leadership, the dynamics of Reconstruction politics in the South, and the ideology of African American leaders during Reconstruction.

Years earlier, the former governor Joseph E. Brown had suggested the expulsion of the recently elected black legislators on the ground of constitutional ineligibility. On August 6, 1868, a resolution from the House minority committee declared a mulatto representative ineligible. Soon after that, the Democratic state senator Milton A. Candler presented a motion to investigate the eligibility of African Americans to sit in the legislature. White Republicans in the Georgia legislature faced public pressure to attack the evils of "Negro government." By early September, enough Republicans joined with Georgia Democrats to pass resolutions removing African Americans from the legislature. The Senate voted twenty-four to eleven for these resolutions, specifically expelling the blacks Tunis G. Campbell and George Wallace as "ineligible to seats, on the ground that they are persons of color, and not eligible to

office by the Constitution and laws of Georgia, nor by the Constitution and laws of the United States." White conservative strength was stronger in the state House of Representatives, where the final vote, cast on September 2, 1868, was eighty-three to twenty-three. In all, close to thirty Republicans in the Georgia legislature supported the measure either by voting for it or by abstaining.

The Republican governor Rufus Bullock defended the expelled blacks, claiming that "the framers of the Constitution made no distinction between electors or citizens on account of race or color, and neither can you." Bullock aimed his protest at the nation's capital, where, with support from black leaders in Georgia, Congress passed the Congressional Reorganization Act of 1869, reconvening the Georgia legislature of 1868 and reseating those black members who had been expelled.

Defining Moment

In 1867, the period of Congressional, or Radical, Reconstruction began in the South. This resulted from strong resistance from southern Democratic-party controlled state governments against more lenient reconstruction efforts. They reelected former Confederates to office and passed a series of "Black Codes" that severely compromised the freedom and civil rights of former slaves. State governments were dismantled and the Army was put in charge of voter registration and elections. This spurred the growth of the a Republican Party in the south, where Republicans were an alliance of northern whites, native southern white supporters, and African Americans. Although the extent of black domination of Reconstruction governments was exaggerated by those whites who opposed them, blacks did serve in the U.S. Congress, state executive and legislative positions, and local offices.

State constitutional conventions of 1867–1868 created new Republican governments but over the course of the next decade these Republican regimes would fall. Three major factors were responsible for the end of Radical Reconstruction. First, antiblack and anti-Republican violence seriously crippled Reconstruction efforts. Republican officeholders were attacked and often murdered. Second, conflicts within the Republican coalition hampered their ability to rule effectively. Third, Reconstruction in the South was doomed by a growing lack of support among northern Republicans. Scandals and economic crises led to growing concern with domestic financial issues at the expense of following through with reconstruction efforts in the south.

Reconstruction in Georgia followed this regional pattern. Like other states, internal dissensions within Republican ranks led to their defeat. Particularly challenging was the attempt to appeal to both the freedmen and the former Democrats of north Georgia. Georgia Republicans also had to contend with politically motivated terrorism. In March 1868 the Republican legislator George A. Ashburn was assassinated while visiting Columbus after receiving a warning from the Ku Klux Klan. Radical Reconstruction in Georgia was relatively short lived. And during its heyday, in protest of Congressional Reconstruction that enfranchised African American males, conservative southern white Democrats barred their admission into the Georgia legislature by declaring their ineligibility to holding office both in Georgia and the United States.

Author Biography

Henry McNeal Turner was born in Newberry, South Carolina, to free black parents in 1834. He learned to read and write while working in a law office. Turner joined the African Methodist Episcopal Church in 1848 and became a licensed preacher in 1853. He traveled throughout the South as an itinerant evangelist and, in 1860, took a preaching position at Union Beth-el Church in Baltimore, Maryland. In 1862 he moved to Washington, D.C., and, as pastor of Israel Bethel Church there, became a prominent leader in the black community. During the Civil War, President Abraham Lincoln appointed Turner as chaplain to the First Regiment, U.S. Colored Troops.

Turner moved to Georgia in 1865 and soon became an influential figure in Reconstruction politics in that state. He organized Union Leagues that brought blacks into the Republican Party and served as a delegate to the 1866 Georgia black convention and worked for the Republican Congressional Committee in 1867. Turner was elected to the Georgia constitutional convention of 1867–1868. Voters then chose him for the Georgia House of Representatives in 1868. After his expulsion, Turner was reseated by order of Congress in 1870 and reelected in 1871. As a legislator, he submitted bills for an eight-hour day for laborers and to prohibit discrimination on public transportation (primarily streetcars), yet he was the only black member to support a literacy test for voting. Turner's political activism proved dangerous in Georgia in the late 1860s. Two attempts were made on his life, and his home was often protected by armed guards. In 1871 Turner was appointed by national Republicans as customs inspector in Savannah.

Turner was ordained a bishop in the African Methodist Episcopal Church in 1880 and became chancellor of Morris Brown College, an African American institution in Atlanta. He later joined the Prohibitionist Party. Besides publishing three religious periodicals, he became a leading advocate for black emigration from the United States. He died in Windsor, Canada, in 1915.

HISTORICAL DOCUMENT

Mr. Speaker: Before proceeding to argue this question upon its intrinsic merits, I wish the members of this House to understand the position that I take. I hold that I am a member of this body. Therefore, sir, I shall neither fawn nor cringe before any party, nor stoop to beg them for my rights. Some of my colored fellow members, in the course of their remarks, took occasion to appeal to the sympathies of members on the opposite side, and to eulogize their character for magnanimity. It reminds me very much, sir, of slaves begging under the lash. I am here to demand my rights and to hurl thunderbolts at the men who would dare to cross the threshold of my manhood. There is an old aphorism which says, "fight the devil with fire," and if I should observe the rule in this instance, I wish gentlemen to understand that it is but fighting them with their own weapon.

The scene presented in this House, today, is one unparalleled in the history of the world. From this day, back to the day when God breathed the breath of life into Adam, no analogy for it can be found. Never, in the history of the world, has a man been arraigned before a body clothed with legislative, judicial or executive functions, charged with the offense of being a darker hue than his fellow men. I know that questions have been before the courts of this country, and of other countries, involving topics not altogether dissimilar to that which is being discussed here today. But, sir, never in the history of the great nations of this world—never before—has a man been arraigned, charged with an offense committed by the God of Heaven Himself. Cases may be found where men have been deprived of their rights for crimes and misdemeanors; but it has remained for the state of Georgia, in the very heart of the nineteenth century, to call a man before the bar, and there charge him with an act for which he is no more responsible than for the head which he carries upon his shoulders. The Anglo-Saxon race, sir, is a most surprising one. No man has ever been more deceived in that race than I have been for the last three weeks. I was not aware that there was in the character of that race so much cowardice or so much pusillanimity. The treachery which has been exhibited in it by gentlemen belonging to that race has shaken my confidence in it more than anything that has come under my observation from the day of my birth.

What is the question at issue? Why, sir, this Assembly, today, is discussing and deliberating on a judgment; there is not a Cherub that sits around God's eternal throne today that would not tremble—even were an order issued by the Supreme God Himself—to come down here and sit in judgment on my manhood. Gentlemen may look at this question in whatever light they choose, and with just as much indifference as they may think proper to assume, but I tell you, sir, that this is a question which will not die today. This event shall be remembered by posterity for ages yet to come, and while the sun shall continue to climb the hills of heaven.

Whose legislature is this? Is it a white man's legislature, or is it a black man's legislature? Who voted for a constitutional convention, in obedience to the mandate of the Congress of the United States? Who first rallied around the standard of Reconstruction? Who set the ball of loyalty rolling in the state of Georgia? And whose voice was heard on the hills and in the valleys of this state? It was the voice of the brawny-armed Negro, with the few humanitarian-hearted white men who came to our assistance. I claim the honor, sir, of having been the instrument of convincing hundreds—yea, thousands—of white men, that to reconstruct under the measures of the United States Congress was the safest and the best course for the interest of the state.

Let us look at some facts in connection with this matter. Did half the white men of Georgia vote for this legislature? Did not the great bulk of them fight, with all their strength, the Constitution under which we are acting? And did they not fight against the organization of this legislature? And further, sir, did they not vote against it? Yes, sir! And there are persons in this legislature today who are ready to spit their poison in my face, while they themselves opposed, with all their power, the ratification of this Constitution. They question my right to a seat in this body, to represent the people whose legal votes elected me. This objection, sir, is an unheard-of monopoly of power. No analogy can be found for it, except it be the case of a man who should go into my house, take possession of my wife and children, and then tell me to walk out. I stand very much in the position of a criminal before your bar, because I dare to be the exponent of the views of those who sent me here. Or, in other words, we are told that if black men want to speak, they must speak through white trumpets; if black men want their sentiments expressed, they must be adulterated and sent through white messengers, who will quibble and equivocate and evade as rapidly as the pendulum of a clock. If this be not done, then the black men have committed an outrage, and then representatives must be denied the right, to represent their constituents.

The great question, sir, is this: Am I a man? If I am such, I claim the rights of a man. Am I not a man because I happen to be of a darker hue than honorable gentlemen around me? Let me see whether I am or not. I want to convince the House today that

I am entitled to my seat here. A certain gentleman has argued that the Negro was a mere development similar to the orangoutang or chimpanzee, but it so happens that, when a Negro is examined, physiologically, phrenologically and anatomically, and I may say, physiognomically, he is found to be the same as persons of different color. I would like to ask any gentleman on this floor, where is the analogy? Do you find me a quadruped, or do you find me a man? Do you find three bones less in my back than in that of the white man? Do you find fewer organs in the brain? If you know nothing of this, I do; for I have helped to dissect fifty men, black and white, and I assert that by the time you take off the mucous pigment—the color of the skin—you cannot, to save your life, distinguish between the black man and the white. Am I a man? Have I a soul to save, as you have? Am I susceptible of eternal development, as you are? Can I learn all the arts and sciences that you can? Has it ever been demonstrated in the history of the world? Have black men ever exhibited bravery as white men have done? Have they ever been in the professions? Have they not as good articulative organs as you? Some people argue that there is a very close similarity between the larynx of the Negro and that of the orangoutang. Why, sir, there is not so much similarity between them as there is between the larynx of the man and that of the dog, and this fact I dare any member of this House to dispute. God saw fit to vary everything in nature. There are no two men alike—no two voices alike—no two trees alike. God has weaved and tissued variety and versatility throughout the boundless space of His creation. Because God saw fit to make some red, and some white, and some black, and some brown, are we to sit here in judgment upon what God has seen fit to do? As well might one play with the thunderbolts of heaven as with that creature that bears God's image—God's photograph.

The question is asked, "What is it that the Negro race has done?" Well, Mr. Speaker, all I have to say upon the subject is this: If we are the class of people that we are generally represented to be, I hold that we are a very great people. It is generally considered that we are the children of Canaan; and the curse of a father rests upon our heads, and has rested, all through history. Sir, I deny that the curse of Noah had anything to do with the Negro. We are not the Children of Canaan; and if we are, sir, where should we stand? Let us look a little into history. Melchizedek was a Canaanite; all the Phoenicians—all those inventors of the arts and sciences—were the posterity of Canaan; but, sir, the Negro is not. We are the children of Cush, and Canaan's curse has nothing whatever to do with the Negro. If we belong to that race, Ham belonged to it, under whose instructions Napoleon Bonaparte studied military tactics. If we belong to that race, Saint Augustine belonged to it. Who was it that laid the foundation of the great Reformation? Martin Luther, who lit the light of gospel truth—a light that will never go out until the sun shall rise to set no more; and, long ere then, Democratic principles will have found their level in the regions of Pluto and of Proserpine....

The honorable gentleman from Whitfield [Mr. Shumate], when arguing this question, a day or two ago, put forth the proposition that to be a representative was not to be an officer—"it was a privilege that citizens had a right to enjoy." These are his words. It was not an office; it was a "privilege." Every gentleman here knows that he denied that to be a representative was to be an officer. Now, he is recognized as a leader of the Democratic party in this House, and generally cooks victuals for them to eat; makes that remarkable declaration, and how are you, gentlemen on the other side of the House, because I am an officer, when one of your great lights says that I am *not* an officer? If you deny my right—the right of my constituents to have representation here—because it is a "privilege," then, sir, I will show you that I have as many privileges as the whitest man on this floor. If I am not permitted to occupy a seat here, for the purpose of representing my constituents, I want to know how white men can be permitted to do so. How can a white man represent a colored constituency, if a colored man cannot do it? The great argument is: "Oh, we have inherited" this, that and the other. Now, I want gentlemen to come down to cool, common sense. Is the created greater than the Creator? Is man greater than God? It is very strange, if a white man can occupy on this floor *a seat created by colored votes*, and a black man cannot do it. Why, gentlemen, it is the most short-sighted reasoning in the world. A man can see better than that with half an eye; and even if he had no eye at all, he could forge one, as the Cyclops did, or punch one with his finger, which would enable him to see through that.

It is said that Congress never gave us the right to hold office. I want to know, sir, if the Reconstruction measures did not base their action on the ground that no distinction should be made on account of race, color or previous condition? Was not that the grand fulcrum on which they rested? And did not every reconstructed state have to reconstruct on the idea that no discrimination, in any sense of the term, should be made? There is not a man here who will dare say No. If Congress has simply given me a merely sufficient civil and political rights to make me a mere political slave for Democrats, or anybody else—giving them the opportunity of jumping on my back in order to leap into political power—I do not thank Congress for it. Never, so help me God, shall I be a political slave. I am not now speaking for those colored men who sit with me in this House, nor do I say that they endorse my sentiments, but assisting Mr. Lincoln to take me out of servile slavery did not intend to put me and my race into *political* slavery. If they did, let them take away my ballot—I do not want it, and shall not have it. I don't want to be a mere tool of that sort. I have been a slave long enough already.

I tell you what I would be willing to do: I am willing that the question should be submitted to Congress for an explanation as to what was meant in the passage of their Reconstruction measures, and of the Constitutional Amendment. Let the Democratic party in this House pass a resolution giving this subject that direction, and I shall be content. I dare you, gentlemen, to do it. Come up to the question openly, whether it meant that the Negro might hold office, or whether it meant that he should merely have the right to vote. If you are honest men, you will do it. If, however, you will not do that, I would make another proposition: Call together, again, the convention that framed the constitution under which we are acting; let them take a vote upon the subject, and I am willing to abide by their decision....

These colored men, who are unable to express themselves with all the clearness and dignity and force of rhetorical eloquence, are laughed at in derision by the Democracy of the country. It reminds me very much of the man who looked at himself in a mirror and, imagining that he was addressing another person, exclaimed: "My God, how ugly you are!" These gentlemen do not consider for a moment the dreadful hardships which these people have endured, and especially those who in any way endeavored to acquire an education. For myself, sir, I was raised in the cotton field of South Carolina, and in order to prepare myself for usefulness, as well to myself as to my race, I determined to devote my spare hours to study. When the overseer retired at night to his comfortable couch, I sat and read and thought and studied, until I heard him blow his horn in the morning. He frequently told me with an oath, that if he discovered me attempting to learn, that he would whip me to death, and I have no doubt he would have done so, if he had found an opportunity. I prayed to Almighty God to assist me, and He did, and I thank Him with my whole heart and soul....

So far as I am personally concerned, no man in Georgia has been more conservative than I. "Anything to please the white folks" has been my motto; and so closely have I adhered to that course, that many among my own party have classed me as a Democrat. One of the leaders of the Republican party in Georgia has not been at all favorable to me for some time back, because he believed that I was too "conservative" for a Republican. I can assure you, however, Mr. Speaker, that I have had quite enough, and to spare, of such "conservatism." ...

But, Mr. Speaker, I do not regard this movement as a thrust at me. It is a thrust at the Bible—a thrust at the God of the Universe, for making a man and not finishing him; it is simply calling the Great Jehovah a fool. Why, sir, though we are not white, we have accomplished much. We have pioneered civilization here; we have built up your country; we have worked in your fields and garnered your harvests for two hundred and fifty years! And what do we ask of you in return? Do we ask you for compensation for the sweat our fathers bore for you—for the tears you have caused, and the hearts you have broken, and the lives you have curtailed, and the blood you have spilled? Do we ask retaliation? We ask it not. We are willing to let the dead past bury its dead; but we ask you, now for our *rights*. You have all the elements of superiority upon your side; you have our money and your own; you have our education and your own; and you have our land and your own too. We, who number hundreds of thousands in Georgia, including our wives and families, with not a foot of land to call our own—strangers in the land of our birth; without money, without education, without aid, without a roof to cover us while we live, nor sufficient clay to cover us when we die! It is extraordinary that a race such as yours, professing gallantry and chivalry and education and superiority, living in a land where ringing chimes call child and sire to the church of God—a land where Bibles are read and Gospel truths are spoken, and where courts of justice are presumed to exist; it is extraordinary that, with all these advantages on your side, you can make war upon the poor defenseless black man. You know we have no money, no railroads, no telegraphs, no advantages of any sort, and yet all manner of injustice is placed upon us. You know that the black people of this country acknowledge you as their superiors, by virtue of your education and advantages....

You may expel us, gentlemen, but I firmly believe that you will some day repent it. The black man cannot protect a country, if the country doesn't protect him; and if, tomorrow, a war should arise, I would not raise a musket to defend a country where my manhood is denied. The fashionable way in Georgia, when hard work is to be done, is for the white man to sit at his ease while the black man does the work; but, sir, I will say this much to the colored men of Georgia, as, if I should be killed in this campaign, I may have no opportunity of telling them at any other time: Never lift a finger nor raise a hand in defense of Georgia, until Georgia acknowledges that you are men and invests you with the rights pertaining to manhood. Pay your taxes, however, obey all orders from your employers, take good counsel from friends, work faithfully, earn an honest living, and show, by your conduct, that you can be good citizens.

Go on with your oppressions. Babylon fell. Where is Greece? Where is Nineveh? And where is Rome, the Mistress Empire of the world? Why is it that she stands, today, in broken fragments throughout Europe? Because oppression killed her. Every act that we commit is like a bounding ball. If you curse a man, that curse rebounds upon you; and when you bless a man, the blessing returns to you; and when you oppress a man, the oppression also will rebound. Where have you ever heard of four millions of freemen being governed by laws, and yet have no hand in their making? Search the records of the world, and you will find no example. "Governments derive their just powers from the consent of the governed." How dare you to make laws by which to try me and my wife and children, and deny me a voice in the making of these laws? I know you can establish a monarchy, an autocracy, an oligarchy, or any other kind of *ocracy* that you please; and that you can declare whom you please to be sovereign; but tell me, sir, how you can clothe me with more power than another, where all are sovereigns alike? How can you say you have a republican form of government, when you make such distinction and enact such proscriptive laws?

Gentlemen talk a good deal about the Negroes "building no monuments." I can tell the gentlemen one thing: that is, that we could have built monuments of fire while the war was in progress. We could have fired your woods, your barns and fences, and called you home. Did we do it? No, sir! And God grant that the Negro may never do it, or do anything else that would destroy the good opinion of his friends. No epithet is sufficiently opprobrious for us now. I saw, sir, that we have built a monument of docility, of obedience, of respect, and of self-control, that will endure longer than the Pyramids of Egypt.

We are a persecuted people. Luther was persecuted; Galileo was persecuted; good men in all nations have been persecuted; but the persecutors have been handed down to posterity with shame and ignominy. If you pass this bill, you will never get Congress to pardon or enfranchise another rebel in your lives. You are going to fix an everlasting disfranchisement upon Mr. Toombs and the other leading men of Georgia. You may think you are doing yourselves honor by expelling us from this House; but when we go, we will do as Wickliffe and as Latimer did. We will light a torch of truth that will never be extinguished—the impression that will run through the country, as people picture in their mind's eye these poor black men, in all parts of this Southern country, pleading for their rights. When you expel us, you make us forever your political foes, and you will never find a black man to vote a Democratic ticket again; for, so help me God, I will go through all the length and breadth of the land, where a man of my race is to be found, and advise him to beware of the Democratic party. Justice is the great doctrine taught in the Bible. God's Eternal Justice is founded upon Truth, and the man who steps from Justice steps from Truth, and cannot make his principles to prevail.

I have now, Mr. Speaker, said all that my physical condition will allow me to say. Weak and ill, though I am, I could not sit passively here and see the sacred rights of my race destroyed at one blow. We are in a position somewhat similar to that of the famous "Light Brigade," of which Tennyson says, they had

> *Cannon to right of them,*
> *Cannon to left of them,*
> *Cannon in front of them,*
> *Volleyed and thundered.,*

I hope our poor, downtrodden race may act well and wisely through this period of trial, and that they will exercise patience and discretion under all circumstances.

You may expel us, gentlemen, by your votes, today; but, while you do it, remember that there is a just God in Heaven, whose All-Seeing Eye beholds alike the acts of the oppressor and the oppressed, and who, despite the machinations of the wicked, never fails to vindicate the cause of Justice, and the sanctity of His own handiwork.

GLOSSARY

Anglo-Saxon: a reference to the Germanic tribes that overran Europe prior to the Middle Ages; loosely used to refer to the British people

Canaan: in the Old Testament of the Christian Bible, a region corresponding to portions of the present-day Middle East

Cush: the grandson of Noah in the Bible

Cyclops: in Greek and Roman mythology, a member of a race of early giants with a single eye in the middle of the forehead

Galileo: Galileo Galilei (1564–1642), an Italian scientist, best known for disputing the belief that the earth is the center of the universe

Ham: the son of Noah in the Bible

Latimer: probably a reference to Hugh Latimer, an English Protestant martyr who was burned at the stake in 1555

Martin Luther: the sixteenth-century German priest who initiated the Protestant Reformation

Melchizedek: an Old Testament figure in the Christian Bible, perhaps a king or high priest

Napoleon Bonaparte: the ruler of postrevolutionary France in the late eighteenth and early nineteenth centuries

Nineveh: a city in ancient Assyria destroyed by God

Phoenicians: members of an ancient civilization in northern Canaan, or modern-day Lebanon

Pluto: the Roman god of the underworld

Proserpine: the Roman goddess of springtime and the wife of Pluto

Saint Augustine: Augustine of Hippo, an early father of the Christian church

Tennyson: Alfred Lord Tennyson, a nineteenth-century British poet and author of "The Charge of the Light Brigade"

Wickliffe: probably a reference to John Wycliffe, an early dissident in the Catholic Church and the leader of the Lollards, a persecuted Christian group

Document Analysis

Henry McNeal Turner's speech of September 3, 1868, to the Georgia legislature was essentially an impassioned attack on the injustice of his expulsion—an event he claimed in the first paragraph was "unparalleled in the history of the world." Turner wanted to force his white listeners to look squarely at the fundamental contradiction between the principles of republicanism and racism. Attacking the pillars of white supremacy, he defends (in paragraph 4) the contributions of African Americans: "Who first rallied around the standard of Reconstruction? Who set the ball of loyalty rolling in the state of Georgia?" Turner then pursues the theme of white hypocrisy, pointing out the inconsistency of voting against the Constitution of 1867 while acting as current legislators to remove a black person.

He opens his remarks in an essentially defiant tone. He would be defending his right to a seat in the legislature without apology: "I am here to demand my rights and to hurl thunderbolts at the men who would dare to cross the threshold of my manhood." In the next two paragraphs Turner drives home the novel and momentous nature of his case. Never, he claims, has a man been expelled from a governing body for no other offense than the color of his skin. He next reminds his fellow legislators of the political wisdom of giving former slaves political rights, calling it the "safest and best course for the interest of the state." In the fifth paragraph, he points out the irony that he is being expelled by sitting white legislators, many of whom did not even vote for the Georgia constitutional convention or originally recognize the legitimacy of the Radical government.

In paragraphs 6–8, Turner defends political equality between the races. He asks his listeners to remember the essential humanity of African Americans: "Am I a man?…Have I a soul to save, as you have?" He also counters the old proslavery argument that blacks were of a different species and reminds his audience of the contributions of southern blacks. On the basis of this primary political equality, blacks should be able to speak for themselves: "It is very strange, if a white man can occupy on this floor *a seat created by colored votes*, and a black man cannot do it."

In the following three paragraphs, Turner counters the argument that Congress never gave blacks the right to hold office and insists that a biracial political order was the essence of Reconstruction. If this principle is in doubt, he suggests that the question of a black representative be submitted to the sitting Congress. Moreover, he begins to insist that former slaves deserve this change. White legislators do not realize "the dreadful hardships which these people have endured, and especially those who in any way endeavored to acquire an education."

To appeal to the white legislators, Turner reminds them in paragraphs 12 and 13 that during the Civil War and so far in the postwar period blacks have not behaved in any destructive fashion. He reminds them how few advantages the freed people have had, perhaps appealing to their sympathies as well. In speaking to both African American and white legislators, Turner then insists that black loyalty to the state depends on the state's loyalty to blacks: "Never lift a finger nor raise a hand in defense of Georgia, until Georgia acknowledges that you are men and invests you with the rights pertaining to manhood." Going back to his defense based on essentials (in paragraph 15), Turner argues that his expulsion contradicts a basic premise of republican government—the consent of the governed.

In paragraphs 16 and 17, Turner seems to reassure his audience, who were perhaps anxious about black radicalism. He repeats his earlier point that blacks will act within the boundaries of political behavior. He reminds white listeners that "we have built a monument of docility, of obedience, of respect, and of self-control, that will endure longer than the Pyramids of Egypt." He also presents himself as a political martyr, comparing his plight with other persecuted pioneers like the religious leader Martin Luther and the scientist Galileo.

Finally, Turner warns the legislature that by their action to expel him, they will permanently alienate black voters. In his final paragraphs Turner closes with poetic and religious imagery, comparing the position of blacks to that of the ill-fated British cavalry charge (of October 25, 1854) against Russian forces in the Battle of Balaclava during the Crimean War and warning of providential revenge for "acts of the oppressor."

Essential Themes

In his speech to the Georgia legislature, Turner echoed several themes of African American political thought during Reconstruction. First and primary was the fundamental commitment to Jeffersonian notions of independence and equality. Significantly, Turner quoted the Revolutionary premise that "government derives their just powers from the consent of the governed." A second theme was the use of religious principles and language to defend his cause.

Because God saw fit to make some red, and some white, and some black, and some brown, are we to sit here in judgment upon what God has seen fit to do? As well might one play with the thunderbolts of heaven as with that creature that bears God's image—God's photograph.

Like many Americans in the nineteenth century, Turner saw the scriptures as a political tract that taught the principles of justice.

Turner exhibits a curious mixture of militancy and conciliation in this speech. "I am here to demand my rights," he declares at one point, "and to hurl thunderbolts at the men who would dare to cross the threshold of my manhood." At other points, however, he assures his listeners that the freedman is not seeking retribution: "We are willing to let the dead past bury its dead; but we ask you, now for our *rights*." Turner even urges his fellow freedmen to pay taxes and obey their employers. Turner's ambivalence might be explained by the nature of his audience. He undoubtedly had to appease the Radicals in the Republican ranks. At the same time, Georgia freedmen needed the support of white Republicans, who needed reassurance that Reconstruction would not turn the racial order upside down.

———*Mitchell Snay, PhD*

Bibliography and Additional Reading

Armstrong, Thomas F. "From Task Labor to Free Labor: The Transition along Georgia's Rice Coast, 1820–1880."*Georgia Historical Quarterly* 64 (Fall 1980): 432–447.

Carson, Roberta F. "The Loyalty Leagues in Georgia." *Georgia Historical Society* 20 (June 1936): 125–153.

Cimbala, Paul A. "The Freedmen's Bureau, the Freedmen, and Sherman's Grant in Reconstruction Georgia, 1865–1867."*Journal of Southern History* 55 (November 1989): 597–632.

Coulter, E. Merton "Henry M. Turner: Georgia Negro Preacher-Politician during the Reconstruction Era." *Georgia Historical Quarterly* 48 (December 1964): 371–410.

Gottlieb, Manuel. "The Land Question in Georgia." *Science and Society* 3 (Summer 1939): 356–388.

Matthews, John M. "Negro Republicans in the Reconstruction of Georgia." *Georgia Historical Quarterly* 60 (Summer 1976): 145–164.

Angell, Stephen Ward. *Bishop Henry McNeal Turner and African-American Religion in the South*. Knoxville: University of Tennessee Press, 1992.

Conway, Alan. *The Reconstruction of Georgia*. Minneapolis: University of Minnesota Press, 1966.

Drago, Edmund L. *Black Politicians and Reconstruction in Georgia: A Splendid Failure*. Baton Rouge: Louisiana State University Press, 1982.

Duncan, Russell. *Freedom's Shore: Tunis Campbell and the Georgia Freedman*. Athens: University of Georgia Press, 1986.

Fitzgerald, Michael W. "Reconstruction Politics and the Politics of Reconstruction." In *Reconstructions: New Perspectives of the Postbellum United States*, ed. Thomas J. Brown. New York: Oxford University Press, 2006.

Foner, Eric. *Reconstruction, America's Unfinished Revolution, 1863–1877*. New York: Harper and Row, 1988.

Nathans, Elizabeth S. *Losing the Peace: Georgia Republicans and Reconstruction, 1865–1871*. Baton Rouge: Louisiana State University Press, 1968.

Redkey, Edwin S.*Respect Black: The Writings and Speeches of Henry McNeal Turner*. New York: Arno Press, 1971.

Thompson, C. Mildred. *Reconstruction in Georgia: Economic, Social, Political, 1865–1872*. New York: Columbia University Press, 1915.

"Reconstruction: The Second Civil War." PBS "American Experience" Web site. http://www.pbs.org/wgbh/amex/reconstruction/index.html

■ "All That We Ask Is Equal Laws, Equal Legislation, and Equal Rights"

Date: 1874
Author: Richard Harvey Cain
Genre: Speech

Summary Overview

This speech by South Carolina congressman Richard Harvey Cain to the U.S. House of Representatives on January 10, 1874, was one of two that he made in support of what became the Civil Rights Act of 1875. His plea energized the bill's supporters, and it was approved by the Senate, minus, however, its provision banning discrimination in churches.

Despite its success in the Senate, most observers thought the bill would not get through the House. But impassioned speeches by the seven black members of Congress, including Cain, helped create momentum for the bill. All of the men related instances of personal discrimination against them even after their election to Congress. The oratory of Cain's fellow South Carolina congressman Robert Brown Elliott on behalf of the bill attracted national attention, but the powerful words of Cain's speech of January 1874 were little noticed by the press, even among sympathetic Republican newspapers in his home state. However, Cain's speech, together with the others, had ample impact where it counted. One Republican leader in Congress praised all the black congressmen for being more eloquent than their white brethren. Congress was impressed, and the bill became law on March 1, 1875, though it had been further amended to delete the coverage of public schools. Nevertheless, the bill's passage was a major step forward taken just in time, as soon thereafter a Democratic majority took over the House. The enactment of the public accommodations bill was in many ways the high-water mark for the Reconstruction-era Congress.

Defining Moment

After the Civil War, the United States attempted to reconstruct the war-ravaged South and lay a foundation for the broader democracy that would encompass both black and white citizens. Emancipation would result in long-term economic and social shifts, but how the law would be molded was the most critical question.

Among the many laws proposed to facilitate this was the civil rights bill introduced by Senator Sumner in 1870, which aimed to ban discrimination in all major areas of everyday life—in public accommodations, transportation, jury service, public schools, and churches. Southern whites by and large opposed any civil rights for the former slaves, and their opposition was often violent. Sumner's bill languished for three sessions after its first introduction, but Sumner introduced it in the Senate yet again in December 1873, on the opening day of the second session of the Forty-third Congress. In the House, Congressman Butler did the same. Sumner died on March 11, 1874, and his deathbed request was that his bill be passed. Cain had been elected a U.S. congressman from South Carolina the previous year, and he made an impassioned speech in support of the bill in January 1874. In all, seven black representatives sat in the Forty-third Congress, and all spoke in support of Sumner's civil rights bill.

Speaking in opposition were a number of former Confederate soldiers and officers. Among them was Democratic congressman Robert B. Vance of North Carolina. He asserted that black men were asking for something they had not earned, their civil rights. But his major concern was one that would echo through the halls of Congress for decades. He argued that the bill would force whites to socialize with blacks. He warned that forced socialization would destroy the kind relationship that southern whites had established with their freed slaves and that those former slaves could not survive without the help of their former masters.

Author Biography

Richard Harvey Cain was born on April 12, 1825, of free black parents in Greenbrier County, Virginia (now in West Virginia). In 1831 the family moved to Gallipolis, Ohio. There he obtained an education through church school classes. In 1844 he was ordained in the Methodist Episcopal Church and assigned to Hannibal, Missouri, but the segregationist practices of the Methodists caused him to resign and join the African Methodist Episcopal Church (AME). He served an AME church in Iowa in the 1850s and then attended

Wilberforce University, an AME school in Ohio. When the Civil War broke out, he and other Wilberforce students attempted to enlist but were turned away by the governor of Ohio. From 1861 to 1865, Cain was assigned to a church in Brooklyn, New York. While he was in New York he attended the National Convention of Colored Men, held in Syracuse in 1864.

Following the Civil War, Cain reorganized Emanuel Church in Charleston, South Carolina and become one of the most potent political organizations in the state. He was elected as a delegate to the South Carolina Constitutional Convention of 1868 and elected to the state senate from Charleston in the same year. He was chairman of the Charleston County Republican Party from 1870 to 1871 and a delegate to numerous state Republican conventions from 1867 to 1876. His political power was demonstrated with his election as the at-large representative from South Carolina to the Forty-third Congress, opening March 4, 1873.

In Congress, Cain and other black congressmen gained national attention through their oratory in support of the civil rights bill. Cain was one of seven black members who spoke of their personal experiences with discrimination even as congressmen. Cain was not a candidate for renomination in 1874 but was elected to the Forty-fifth Congress, opening March 4, 1877. Cain's service in Congress ended in March 1879. Cain moved to Washington, D.C., in 1883 and died there on January 18, 1887.

HISTORICAL DOCUMENT

Mr. Speaker, I feel called upon more particularly by the remarks of the gentleman from North Carolina [Mr. Vance] on civil rights to express my views. For a number of days this question has been discussed, and various have been the opinions expressed as to whether or not the pending bill should be passed in its present form or whether it should be modified to meet the objections entertained by a number of gentlemen whose duty it will be to give their votes for or against its passage. It has been assumed that to pass this bill in its present form Congress would manifest a tendency to override the Constitution of the country and violate the rights of the States.

Whether it be true or false is yet to be seen. I take it, so far as the constitutional question is concerned, if the colored people under the law, under the amendments to the Constitution, have become invested with all the rights of citizenship, then they carry with them all rights and immunities accruing to and belonging to a citizen of the United States. If four, or nearly five, million people have been lifted from the thralldom of slavery and made free; if the Government by its amendments to the Constitution has guaranteed to them all rights and immunities, as to other citizens, they must necessarily therefore carry along with them all the privileges enjoyed by all other citizens of the Republic.

Sir, the gentleman from North Carolina [Mr. Vance] who spoke on the question stated some objections, to which I desire to address a few words of reply. He said it would enforce social rights, and therefore would be detrimental to the interests of both the whites and the blacks of the country. My conception of the effect of this bill, if it be passed into a law, will be simply to place the colored men of this country upon the same footing with every other citizen under the law, and will not at all enforce social relationship with any other class of persons in the country whatsoever. It is merely a matter of law. What we desire is that our civil rights shall be guaranteed by law as they are guaranteed to every other class of persons; and when that is done all other things will come in as a necessary sequence, the enforcement of the rights following the enactment of the law.

Sir, social equality is a right which every man, every woman, and every class of persons have within their own control. They have a right to form their own acquaintances, to establish their own social relationships. Its establishment and regulation is not within the province of legislation. No laws enacted by legislators can compel social equality. Now, what is it we desire? What we desire is this: inasmuch as we have been raised to the dignity, to the honor, to the position of our manhood, we ask that the laws of this country should guarantee all the rights and immunities belonging to that proud position, to be enforced all over this broad land.

Sir, the gentleman states that in the State of North Carolina the colored people enjoy all their rights as far as the highways are concerned; that in the hotels, and in the railroad cars, and in the various public places of resort, they have all the rights and all the immunities accorded to any other class of citizens of the United States. Now, it may not have come under his observation, but it has under mine, that such really is not the case; and the reason why I know and feel it more than he does is because my face is painted black and his is painted white. We who have the color—I may say the objectionable color—know and feel all this. A few days ago, in passing from South Carolina to this city, I entered a place of public resort where hungry men are fed, but I did not dare—I could not without trouble—sit down to the table. I could not sit down at Wilmington or at Weldon without entering into a contest, which I did not desire to do. My colleague, the gentleman who so eloquently spoke on this subject the other day, [Mr. Elliott,] a few months ago entered a restaurant at Wilmington and sat down to be served, and while there a gentleman stepped up to him and said, "You cannot eat here." All the other gentlemen upon the railroad as passengers were eating there; he had only twenty minutes, and was compelled to leave the restaurant or have a fight for it. He showed fight, however, and got his dinner; but he has never been back there since. Coming here last week I felt we did not desire to draw revolvers and present the bold front of warriors, and therefore we ordered our dinners to be brought into the cars, but even there we found the existence of this feeling; for, although we had paid a dollar apiece for our meals, to be brought by the servants into the cars, still there was objection on the part of the railroad people to our eating our meals in the cars, because they said we were putting on airs. They refused us in the restaurant, and then did not desire that we should eat our meals in the cars, although we paid for them. Yet this was in the noble State of North Carolina.

Mr. Speaker, the colored men of the South do not want the adoption of any force measure. No; they do not want anything by force. All they ask is that you will give them, by statutory enactment under the fundamental law, the right to enjoy precisely the same privileges accorded to every other class of citizens.

The gentleman, moreover, has told us that if we pass this civil-rights bill we will thereby rob the colored men of the South of the friendship of the whites. Now, I am at a loss to see how the friendship of our white friends can be lost to us by simply saying we should be permitted to enjoy the rights enjoyed by other citizens. I have a higher opinion of the friendship of the southern men than to suppose any such thing. I know them too well. I know their friendship will not be lost by the passage of this bill. For eight years I have been in South Carolina, and I have found this to be the fact, that the higher class, comprising gentlemen of learning and refinement, are less opposed to this measure than are those who do not occupy so high a position in the social scale.

Sir, I think that there will be no difficulty. But I do think this that there will be more trouble if we do not have those rights. I regard it important, therefore, that we should make the law so strong that no man can infringe those rights.

But, says the gentleman from North Carolina, some ambitious colored man will, when this law is passed, enter a hotel or railroad car, and thus create disturbance. If it be his right, then there is no vaulting ambition in his enjoying that right. And if he can pay for his seat in a first-class car or his room in a hotel, I see no objection to his enjoying it. But the gentleman says more. He cited, on the school question, the evidence of South Carolina, and says the South Carolina University has been destroyed by virtue of bringing into contact the white students with the colored. I think not. It is true that a small number of students left the institution, but the institution still remains. The buildings are there as erect as ever; the faculty are there as attentive to their duties as ever they were; the students are coming in as they did before. It is true, sir, that there is a mixture of students now; that there are colored and white students of law and medicine sitting side by side; it is true, sir, that the prejudice of some of the professors was so strong that it drove them out of the institution; but the philanthropy and good sense of others were such that they remained; and thus we have still the institution going on, and because some students have left, it cannot be reasonably argued that the usefulness of the institution has been destroyed. The University of South Carolina has not been destroyed.

But the gentleman says more. The colored man cannot stand, he says, where this antagonism exists, and he deprecates the idea of antagonizing the races. The gentleman says there is no antagonism on his part. I think there is no antagonism so far as the country is concerned. So far as my observation extends, it goes to prove this: that there is a general acceptance upon the part of the larger and better class of the whites of the South of the situation, and that they regard the education and the development of the colored people as essential to their welfare, and the peace, happiness, and prosperity of the whole country. Many of them, including the best minds of the South, are earnestly engaged in seeking to make this great system of education permanent in all the States. I do not believe, therefore, that it is possible there can be such an antagonism. Why, sir, in Massachusetts there is no such antagonism. There the colored and the white children go to school side by side. In Rhode Island there is not that antagonism. There they are educated side by side in the high schools. In New York, in the highest schools, are to be found, of late, colored men and colored women. Even old democratic New York does not refuse to give the colored people their rights, and there is no antagonism. A few days ago, when in New York, I made it my business to find out what was the position of matters there in this respect. I ascertained that there are, I think, seven colored ladies in the highest school in New York, and I believe they stand No. 1 in their class, side by side with members of the best and most refined families of the citizens of New York, and without any objection to their presence.

I cannot understand how it is that our southern friends, or a certain class of them, always bring back this old ghost of prejudice and of antagonism.

There was a time, not very far distant in the past, when this antagonism was not recognized, when a feeling of fraternization between the white and the colored races existed, that made them kindred to each other. But since our emancipation, since liberty has come, and only since—only since we have stood up clothed in our manhood, only since we have proceeded to take hold and help advance the civilization of this nation—it is only since then that this bugbear is brought up against us again. Sir, the progress of the age demands that the colored man of this country shall be lifted by law into the enjoyment of every right, and that every appliance which is accorded to the German, to the Irishman, to the Englishman, and every foreigner, shall be given to him; and I shall give some reasons why I demand this in the name of justice.

For two hundred years the colored men of this nation have assisted in building up its commercial interests. There are in this country nearly five millions of us, and for a space of two hundred and forty-seven years we have been hewers of wood and drawers of water; but we have been with you in promoting all the interests of the country. My distinguished colleague, who defended the civil rights of our race the other day on this floor, set this forth so clearly that I need not dwell upon it at, this time.

I propose to state just this: that we have been identified with the interests of this country from its very foundation. The cotton crop of this country has been raised and its rice-fields have been tilled by the hands of our race. All along as the march of progress, as the march of commerce, as the development of your resources has been widening and expanding and spreading, as your vessels have gone on every sea, with the stars and stripes waving over them, and carried your, commerce everywhere, there the black man's labor has gone to enrich your country and to augment the grandeur of your nationality. This was done in the time of slavery. And if, for the space of time I have noted, we have been hewers of wood and drawers of water; if we have made your cotton-fields blossom as the rose; if we have made your rice-fields wave with luxuriant harvests; if we have made your corn-fields rejoice; if we have sweated and toiled to build up the prosperity of the whole country by the productions of our labor, I submit, now that the war has made a change, now that we are free—I submit to the nation whether it is not fair and right that we should come in and enjoy to the fullest extent our freedom and liberty.

A word now as to the question of education. Sir, I know that, indeed, some of our republican friends are even a little weak on the school clause of this bill; but, sir, the education of the race, the education of the nation, is paramount to all other considerations. I regard it important, therefore, that the colored people should take place in the educational march of this nation, and I would suggest that there should be no discrimination. It is against discrimination in this particular that we complain.

Sir, if you look over the reports of superintendents of schools in the several States, you will find, I think, evidences sufficient to warrant Congress in passing the civil-rights bill as it now stands. The report of the commissioner of education of California shows that, under the operation of law and of prejudice, the colored children of that State are practically excluded from schooling. Here is a case where a large class of children are growing up in our midst in a state of ignorance and semi-barbarism. Take the report of the superintendent of education of Indiana, and you will find that while efforts have been made in some places to educate the colored children, yet the prejudice is so great that it debars the colored children from enjoying all the rights which they ought to enjoy under the law. In Illinois, too, the superintendent of education makes this statement: that, while the law guarantees education to every child, yet such are the operations among the school trustees that they almost ignore, in some places, the education of colored children.

All we ask is that you, the legislators of the nation, shall pass a law so strong and so powerful that no one shall be able to elude it and destroy our rights under the Constitution and laws of our country. That is all we ask.

But, Mr. Speaker, the gentleman from North Carolina [Mr. Vance] asks that the colored man shall place himself in an attitude to receive his rights. I ask, what attitude can we assume? We have tilled your soil, and during the rude shock of war, until our hour came, we were docile during that long, dark night, waiting patiently the coming day. In the Southern States during that war our men and women stood behind their masters; they tilled the soil, and there were no insurrections in all the broad lands of the South; the wives and daughters of the slaveholders were as sacred then as they were before; and the history of the war does not record a single event, a single instance, in which the colored people were unfaithful, even in slavery; nor does the history of the war record the fact that on the other side, on the side of the Union, there were any colored men who were not willing at all times to give their lives for their country. Sir, upon both sides we waited patiently. I was a student at Wilberforce University, in Ohio, when the tocsin of war was sounded, when Fort Sumter was fired upon, and I never shall forget the thrill that ran through my soul when I thought of the coming consequences of that shot. There were one hundred and fifteen of us, students at that university, who, anxious to vindicate the stars and stripes, made up a company, and offered our services to the governor of Ohio; and, sir, we were told that this was a white man's war and that the negro had nothing to do with it. Sir, we returned—docile, patient, waiting, casting our eyes to the heavens whence help always comes. We knew that there would come a period in the history of this nation when our strong black arms would be needed. We waited patiently; we waited until Massachusetts, through her noble governor, sounded the alarm, and we hastened then to hear the summons and obey it.

Sir, as I before remarked, we were peaceful on both sides. When the call was made on the side of the Union we were ready; when the call was made for us to obey orders on the other side, in the confederacy, we humbly performed our tasks, and waited patiently. But, sir, the time came when we were called for; and, I ask, who can say that when that call was made, the colored men did not respond as readily and as rapidly as did any other class of your citizens. Sir, I need not speak of the history of this bloody war. It will carry down to coming generations the valor of our soldiers on the battle-field. Fort Wagner will stand forever as a monument of that valor, and until Vicksburgh shall be wiped from the galaxy of battles in the great contest for human liberty that valor will be recognized.

And for what, Mr. Speaker and gentlemen was the great war made! The gentleman from North Carolina [Mr. Vance] announced before he sat down, in answer to an interrogatory by a gentleman on this side of the House, that they went into the war conscientiously before God. So be it. Then we simply come and plead conscientiously before God that those are our rights, and we want them. We plead conscientiously before God, believing that these are our rights by inheritance, and by the inexorable decree of Almighty God.

We believe in the Declaration of Independence, that all men are born free and equal, and are endowed by their Creator with certain inalienable rights, among which are life, liberty, and the pursuit of happiness. And we further believe that to secure those rights governments are instituted. And we further believe that when governments cease to subserve those ends the people should change them.

I have been astonished at the course which gentlemen on the other side have taken in discussing this bill. They plant themselves right behind the Constitution, and declare that the rights of the State ought not to be invaded. Now, if you will take the history of the war of the rebellion, as published by the Clerk of this House, you will see that in 1860 the whole country, each side, was earnest in seeking to make such amendments to the Constitution as would forever secure slavery and keep the Union together under the circumstances. The resolutions passed, and the sentiments expressed in speeches at that time, if examined by gentlemen, will be found to bear out all that I have indicated. It was felt in 1860 that anything that would keep the "wayward sisters" from going astray was desirable. They were then ready and willing to make any amendments.

And now, when the civil rights of our race are hanging upon the issue, they on the other side are not willing to concede to us such amendments as will guarantee them; indeed, they seek to impair the force of existing amendments to the Constitution of the United States, which would carry out the purpose,

I think it is proper and just that the civil-rights bill should be passed. Some think it would be better to modify it, to strike out the school clause, or to so modify it that some of the State constitutions should not be infringed. I regard it essential to us and the people of this country that we should be secured in this if in nothing else. I cannot regard that our rights will be secured until the jury-box and the school-room, these great palladiums of our liberty, shall have been opened to us. Then we will be willing to take our chances with other men.

We do not want any discriminations to be made. If discriminations are made in regard to schools, then there will be accomplished just what we are fighting against. If you say that the schools in the State of Georgia, for instance, shall be allowed to discriminate against colored people, then you will have discriminations made against us. We do not want any discriminations. I do not ask any legislation for the colored people of this country that is not applied to the white people. All that we ask is equal laws, equal legislation, and equal rights throughout the length and breadth of this land.

The gentleman from North Carolina [Mr. Vance] also says that the colored men should not come here begging at the doors of Congress for their rights. I agree with him. I want to say that we do not come here begging for our rights. We come here clothed in the garb of American citizenship. We come demanding our rights in the name of justice. We come, with no arrogance on our part, asking that this great nation, which laid the foundations of civilization and progress more deeply and more securely than any other nation on the face of the earth, guarantee us protection from outrage. We come here, five millions of people—more than composed this whole nation when it had its great tea-party in Boston Harbor, and demanded its rights at the point of the bayonet—asking that unjust discriminations against us be forbidden. We come here in the name of justice, equity, and law, in the name of our children, in the name of our country, petitioning for our rights.

Our rights will yet be accorded to us, I believe, from the feeling that has been exhibited on this floor of the growing sentiment of the country. Rapid as the weaver's shuttle, swift as the lightning's flash, such progress is being made that our rights will be accorded to us ere long. I believe the nation is perfectly willing to accord this measure of Justice, if only those who represent the people here would say the word. Let it be proclaimed that henceforth all the children of this land shall be free; that the stars and stripes, waving over all, shall secure to every one equal rights, and the nation will say "amen."

Let the civil-rights bill be passed this day, and five million black men, women, and children, all over the land, will begin a new song of rejoicing, and the thirty-five millions of noble-hearted Anglo-Saxons will join in the shout of joy. Thus will the great mission be fulfilled of giving to all the people equal rights.

Inasmuch as we have toiled with you in building up this nation; inasmuch as we have suffered side by side with you in the war; inasmuch as we have together passed through affliction and pestilence, let there be now a fulfillment of the sublime thought of our fathers—let all men enjoy equal liberty and equal rights.

In this hour, when you are about to put the capstone on the mighty structure of government, I ask you to grant us this measure, because it is right. Grant this, and we shall go home with our hearts filled with gladness. I want to "shake hands over the bloody chasm." The gentleman from North Carolina has said he desires to have forever buried the memory of the recent war. I agree with him. Representing a South Carolina constituency, I desire to bury forever the tomahawk. I have voted in this House with a free heart to declare universal amnesty. Inasmuch as general amnesty has been proclaimed, I would hardly have expected there would be any objection on this floor to the civil-rights bill, giving to all men the equal rights of citizens. There should be no more contest. Amnesty and civil rights should go together. Gentlemen on the other side will admit that we have been faithful; and now, when we propose to bury the hatchet, let us shake hands upon this measure of justice; and if heretofore we have been enemies, let us be friends now and forever.

Our wives and our children have high hopes and aspirations; their longings for manhood and womanhood are equal to those of any other race. The same sentiment of patriotism and of gratitude, the same spirit of national pride that animates the hearts of other citizens, animates theirs. In the name of the dead soldiers of our race, whose bodies lie at Petersburgh and on other battle-fields of the South; in the name of the widows and orphans they have left behind; in the name of the widows of the confederate soldiers who fell upon the same fields, I conjure you let this righteous act be done. I appeal to you in the name of God and humanity to give us our rights, for we ask nothing more.

GLOSSARY

Anglo-Saxons: the early Germanic tribes that subdued the British Isles; used loosely to refer to white northern Europeans

Fort Wagner: a fort in South Carolina, the scene of an 1863 assault led by the Fifty-fourth Massachusetts Volunteer Infantry, one of the Union's first black units

Mr. Elliott: Robert Brown Elliott, a congressional representative from South Carolina

Mr. Vance: Democratic congressman Robert B. Vance of North Carolina

Petersburgh: Petersburg, a city in Virginia, scene of one of the final campaigns of the Civil War

tocsin: a warning bell

Vicksburgh: Vicksburg, a city in Mississippi, the site of a major Civil War battle in 1863

Document Analysis

In the second paragraph Cain argues that the Thirteenth, Fourteenth, and Fifteenth Amendments stand for the proposition that black people are "invested with all the rights of citizenship." Next, he addresses Vance's allegation that the civil rights bill would impose social relations. Cain retorts that the bill would simply place African Americans on the same level as whites. He counters Vance's claim that civil rights were already enjoyed by all people in North Carolina by using his own and other blacks' personal experiences there.

Next Cain responds to Vance's argument that if the bill were to pass, the black man in the South would lose the friendship of the region's whites and exhibits optimism about the country and the age. In some of his most eloquent words, Cain states in paragraph 26, "Rapid as the weaver's shuttle, swift as the lightning's flash, such progress is being made that our rights will be accorded to us ere long."

Vance had claimed that desegregation had destroyed the state university in South Carolina. But Cain easily repels this attack, explaining that the university was still thriving. He again asserts that the better class of whites in the South support African American equality, here declaring that they see the value of education for his people. Cain recognizes that the right to an education is the most paramount civil right. At the end of his speech, Cain briefly returns to the subject of education to cite it as a device critical to civil rights and to declare his belief that the educational system ought not to discriminate against anyone.

Another argument utilized effectively by Cain is a call for civil rights as a matter of economic justice, providing examples of patient service and sacrifice by his people for the nation. He reminds the assembly of the costs incurred by black men in the ranks of the Union army, especially citing their bravery on the battlefields of Fort Wagner, in South Carolina, and Vicksburg, Mississippi. Cain also adapts Vance's defensive affirmation that he had gone to war on behalf of the Confederacy "conscientiously before God" to offer his own prayer to "Almighty God" to grant "our rights by inheritance." Then Cain points out the clarion call of the Declaration of Independence whereby "all men...are endowed by their Creator with certain inalienable rights, among which are life, liberty, and the pursuit of happiness."

Cain next moves to respond to the critics of the bill who claimed it would usurp the rights of the states. He expresses astonishment that these congressmen could place states' rights above the rights of individuals. He points out that these same men had joined efforts to pass legislation in Congress in 1860 to save the Union and preserve slavery. Without explicitly stating as much, Cain makes the point that since the war for states' rights had already been lost and the war for civil rights had been won, the patriotic course of action would be to concede that the Reconstruction Amendments were the law of the land. These amendments and the Civil War should compel these "gentlemen" to accept civil rights for all people.

It is in paragraph 24 that Cain's most famous line, lending the speech its title, is uttered: "All that we ask is equal laws, equal legislation, and equal rights throughout the length and breadth of this land." Then Cain responds to Vance's remark that "the colored men" were begging Congress for their rights. Cain denies this by recasting the circumstances, asserting, "We come demanding our rights in the name of justice."

In concluding, Cain expresses an optimism that justice will prevail. Cain calls on the nation's five million black people to sing a song of rejoicing, and he again emphasizes the toil and sacrifice they have made on behalf of the nation. Before his final words, Cain cites his own support for amnesty for former Confederates; in giving the speech, he turned to Vance and offered to shake hands as he affirmed his "desire to bury forever the tomahawk." Cain then turns his offer into a memorial for the "widows and orphans" of North and South and urges that in their name Congress "let this righteous act be done. I appeal to you in the name of God and humanity to give us our rights, for we ask nothing more."

Essential Themes

The chief theme of Cain's speech is that the black man merely wants "equal laws, equal legislation, and equal rights." While the speech was responsive to one by Representative Vance, it was independently a powerful and assertive oration on behalf of the civil rights bill. Cain made clear that African Americans had "come demanding our rights in the name of justice." In his speech, Cain identifies a number of difference aspects of "civil rights" and equality that go beyond political rights. Access to education of equal quality, alongside whites as well as economic opportunity and justice are crucial parts of Cain's vision for a new south.

It is this new south that Cain is promoting in opposition to Vance's vision of a south where black peoples' deference to whites is a defining characteristic of society. Vance and other white southern elites believed that a continued master-servant relationship—in fact, if not in law—was necessary for the south to continue to function. Cain refutes this, providing numerous examples to demonstrate that black Americans have earned the right to be seen as social equals as well as political ones.

———*W. Lewis Burke, PhD*

Bibliography and Additional Reading

Bailey, N. Louise, et al. *Biographical Directory of the South Carolina Senate, 1776–1985.* (Columbia: University of South Carolina Press, 1986).

Black Americans in Congress, 1870–2007. (Washington, D.C. U.S. Government Printing Office, 2008).

Foner, Eric. *Reconstruction: America's Unfinished Revolution, 1863–1877.* (New York: Harper & Row, 1988).

Franklin, John Hope. "The Enforcement of the Civil Rights Act of 1875." In *African Americans and the Emergence of Segregation, 1865–1900,* ed. Donald G. Nieman. (New York: Garland, 1994).

Simmons, William J. *Men of Mark: Eminent, Progressive and Rising.* 1887. Reprint. (New York: Arno Press, 1968).

■ Preface to *The Rise and Fall of the Confederate Government*

Date: 1881
Author: Jefferson Davis
Genre: Chapter

Summary Overview

Jefferson Davis's Preface to *The Rise and Fall of the Confederate Government* presents the former Confederate president's essential arguments in favor of the Confederate cause. To fully understand Davis and his importance during the critical period of the American Civil War, it is important to place him in the context of the time in which he lived and understand what led him and millions of other Americans to support the Confederate cause. For most of the 1850s Davis was the spokesperson for the southern cause in the Senate and a strong supporter of states' rights. The resolution he offered the Senate on February 20, 1860, represents a last-ditch effort on his part to unequivocally assert the southern cause, articulating positions from which the South would not retreat. These demands marked the death knell of Democratic unity, setting forth demands that were unacceptable to northern Democrats. Upon notification of the vote of the Mississippi legislature that the state formally seceded from the Union, Davis had to make a choice between his state and the Union. He also realized that any hope of an amicable solution was over. His resignation speech demonstrates why he chose to side with his state. Unlike other Civil War generals and politicians, who quickly published memoirs of the war, Davis waited until 1881 to speak. His Preface to *The Rise and Fall of the Confederate States* reiterates many of the basic convictions Davis held before the war, the main themes being his firm belief in states' rights, a lifelong faith in the compact theory of the Union, and his undying support for the Confederate cause, even after its military defeat by the North. The memoir establishes him as the quintessential unreconstructed Confederate.

Defining Moment

that had cost more than 620,000 lives and in the South as the man who bore the blame for southern defeat. But as he languished in a federal prison for 720 days and the legal proceedings charging him with treason dragged on, the image of Davis changed, and sympathy for him began to increase. In 1866, while Davis was still a prisoner, one of the physicians who attended him

during his incarceration, Dr. John J. Craven, published *The Prison Life of Jefferson Davis*. The work did much to make Davis a tragic hero and influenced public opinion regarding leniency toward Davis and other former Confederates.

Davis believed that he had acted legally and constitutionally in 1861, and if he had been right in 1861 in his position that secession was not treason, the same was true after the war. He saw himself as a patriot who stood up for the cause of the South and fought a war of self-defense to protect the sovereign rights of the State of Mississippi, not to protect slavery.

Believing both in the righteousness of his cause and that Davis had been maligned by Craven's book, Varina Davis urged her husband to write an account of his life and the war immediately after his release from prison. It was not until 1876 that he actually entered into an agreement with a publishing company to commence work on the project.

Author Biography

Davis was born on June 3, 1808, in Christian County (now Todd County) Kentucky; he moved with his parents to southwestern Mississippi in 1810. In 1824 he entered the U.S. Military Academy at West Point, but resigned from the army in 1835. In 1845 he was elected to the U.S. House of Representatives, his first political office.

In 1846 Davis resigned his seat in the House to lead a Mississippi unit in the Mexican-American War, during which he won recognition for heroism. Upon his return to civilian life, he was elected to the U.S. Senate and served until 1853, when he became secretary of war. In January 1856 Davis was again elected to the Senate, where he became the primary spokesperson in Congress for states' rights and the southern cause. He served in the Senate until his resignation on January 21, 1861, twelve days after Mississippi seceded from the Union.

After he was officially notified that the Mississippi legislature had voted to secede from the Union, Davis resigned from the Senate. Davis was a leading choice for president of the new Confederate States of America. As president of the Confederacy, he faced the daunting task of forming a central government from a group of states that had left the Union asserting their states' rights; at the same time he had to finance and fight a war against an enemy with superior industrial and military strength.

After the surrender of General Robert E. Lee on April 9, 1865, Davis attempted to maintain his govern- ment while on the run, hoping to reestablish it west of the Mississippi. On May 10, 1865, he was arrested by federal troops. He was taken to Fortress Monroe, Virginia, and was ultimately charged with treason, a charge that the U.S. government never successfully prosecuted. In response, Davis sought a trial, hold- ing that secession was not treason—a position that he would maintain for the rest of his life. Davis died on December 6, 1889, in New Orleans.

HISTORICAL DOCUMENT

The object of this work has been from historical data to show that the Southern States had rightfully the power to withdraw from a Union into which they had, as sovereign communities, voluntarily entered; that the denial of that right was a violation of the letter and spirit of the compact between the States; and that the war waged by the Federal Government against the seceding States was in disregard of the limitations of the Constitution, and destructive of the principles of the Declaration of Independence.

The author, from his official position, may claim to have known much of the motives and acts of his countrymen immediately before and during the war of 1861–65, and he has sought to furnish material for the future historian, who, when the passions and prejudices of the day shall have given place to rea- son and sober thought, may, better than a contem- porary, investigate the causes, conduct, and results of the war.

The incentive to undertake the work now offered to the public was the desire to correct misapprehen- sions created by industriously circulated misrepre- sentations as to the acts and purposes of the people and the General Government of the Confederate States. By the reiteration of such inappropriate terms as "rebellion" and "treason," and the asservera- tion that the South was levying war against the Unit- ed States, those ignorant of the nature of the Union, and of the reserved powers of the States, have been led to believe that the Confederate States were in the condition of revolted provinces, and that the United States were forced to resort to arms for the preservation of their existence. To those who knew that the Union was formed for specific enumerated purposes, and that the States had never surrendered

their sovereignty it was a palpable absurdity to ap- ply to them, or to their citizens when obeying their mandates, the terms "rebellion" and "treason"; and, further, it is shown in the following pages that the Confederate States, so far from making war or seek- ing to destroy the United States, as soon as they had an official organ, strove earnestly, by peaceful recog- nition, to equitably adjust all questions growing out of the separation from their late associates.

Another great perversion of truth has been the arraignment of the men who participated in the for- mation of the Confederacy and who bore arms in its defense, as the instigators of a controversy leading to disunion. Sectional issues appear conspicuously in the debates of the Convention which framed the Federal Constitution, and its many compromises were designed to secure an equilibrium between the sections, and to preserve the interests as well as the liberties of the several States. African ser- vitude at that time was not confined to a section, but was numerically greater in the South than in the North, with a tendency to its continuance in the former and cessation in the latter. It therefore thus early presents itself as a disturbing element, and the provisions of the Constitution, which were known to be necessary for its adoption, bound all the States to recognize and protect that species of property. When at a subsequent period there arose in the Northern States an antislavery agitation, it was a harmless and scarcely noticed movement un- til political demagogues seized upon it as a means to acquire power. Had it been left to pseudo-philan- thropists and fanatics, most zealous where least in- formed, it never could have shaken the foundations of the Union and have incited one section to carry fire and sword into the other. That the agitation was political in its character, and was clearly developed as early as 1803, it is believed has been established in these pages. To preserve a sectional equilibrium and to maintain the equality of the States was the effort on one side, to acquire empire was the manifest purpose on the other. This struggle began before the men of the Confederacy were born; how it arose and how it progressed it has been attempted briefly to show. Its last stage was on the question of territorial governments; and, if in this work it has not been demonstrated that the position of the South was justified by the Constitution and the equal rights of the people of all the States, it must be because the author has failed to present the subject with a sufficient degree of force and clearness.

In describing the events of the war, space has not permitted, and the loss of both books and papers has prevented, the notice of very many entitled to consideration, as well for the humanity as the gallantry of our men in the unequal combats they fought. These numerous omissions, it is satisfactory to know, the official reports made at the time and the subsequent contributions which have been and are being published by the actors, will supply more fully and graphically than could have been done in this work.

Usurpations of the Federal Government have been presented, not in a spirit of hostility, but as a warning to the people against the dangers by which their liberties are beset. When the war ceased, the pretext on which it had been waged could no longer be alleged. The emancipation proclamation of Mr. Lincoln, which, when it was issued, he humorously admitted to be a nullity, had acquired validity by the action of the highest authority known to our institutions—the people assembled in their several State Conventions. The soldiers of the Confederacy had laid down their arms, had in good faith pledged themselves to abstain from further hostile operations, and had peacefully dispersed to their homes; there could not, then, have been further dread of them by the Government of the United States. The plea of necessity could, therefore, no longer exist for hostile demonstration against the people and States of the deceased Confederacy. Did vengeance, which stops at the grave, subside? Did real peace and the restoration of the States to their former rights and positions follow, as was promised on the restoration of the Union? Let the recital of the invasion of the reserved powers of the States, or the people, and the perversion of the republican form of government guaranteed to each State by the Constitution, answer the question. For the deplorable fact of the war, for the cruel manner in which it was waged, for the sad physical and yet sadder moral results it produced, the reader of these pages, I hope, will admit that the South, in the forum of conscience, stands fully acquitted.

Much of the past is irremediable; the best hope for a restoration in the future to the pristine purity and fraternity of the Union, rests on the opinions and character of the men who are to succeed this generation: that they may be suited to that blessed work, one, whose public course is ended, invokes them to draw their creed from the fountains of our political history, rather than from the lower stream, polluted as it has been by self-seeking place-hunters and by sectional strife.

GLOSSARY

arraignment: formal or legal accusation

asseveration: declaration

the author: Davis himself

nullity: an act that has no legal force or validity

pseudo-philanthropists: persons who falsely claim to be helping others

sovereignty: self-rule

Document Analysis

Jefferson begins his Preface to *The Rise and Fall of the Confederate government* by asserting that it is a work based on "historical data" to successfully argue that "the Southern States had rightfully the power to withdraw from a Union into which they had, as sovereign communities, voluntarily entered." This, in brief describes the "compact" theory of the United States Constitution, which asserts that the union was an agreement between sovereign states. Thus, if states agreed to join the United States, they could agree to leave. Jefferson also, in this first paragraph, places blame for the Civil War on the North, characterizing it as a "war waged by the Federal Government…in disregard of the limitations of the Constitution."

He claims, in the second paragraph that he knows the motives of Confederate leaders "before and during" the period of secession and Civil War and wishes to present the real story for future historians who will be examining the issue without the "passions and prejudice" of Davis's time. Davis goes on, in the third paragraph, to discuss his motives for writing the book. He claims it is to correct "misapprehensions" and "misrepresentations" about the Confederate cause. He rejects the terms rebellion and treason as being inappropriate and incorrect ways to characterize the secession of southern states from the Union. Here he invokes the compact theory of the Constitution once again by maintaining that the individual states had never surrendered their sovereignty. Logically since they were sovereign states, in Jefferson's view, for them to leave the union would not be treason or rebellion. He also claims that the confederacy did not seek to destroy the United States but rather to simply separate from them.

In the fourth paragraph, Davis seeks to correction "another great perversion of truth." Davis argues that the confederacy did not, in fact, instigate the war. That's diction belongs to the people in the north he describes as fanatics. In particular, abolitionists who found themselves taken advantage of "political demagogues." Davis goes on to emphasize that contentions between sections of the country had been present since the founding of the nation (hence compromises in the Constitution such as the three-fifths clause). Jefferson Davis ends this paragraph by again claiming that the southern states were acting within the bounds of the Constitution.

At this point, Davis points out that his history of the Confederacy Will not concern itself with individual stories of bravery. This is largely due to the loss of his own books and papers as a result of the war.

The next paragraph gets further to the heart of Davis's motivations for writing this history of the Confederacy. He proclaims his work to be "a warning to the people against the dangers by which their liberties are beset, arguing that "when the war ceased, the pretext on which it had been waged could no longer be alleged." When Davis uses the word "pretext" he is saying that the federal government's position was false and that its reasons for using military force against South were based on a false premise—a reference to Davis's belief that secession was a lawful, constitutional act rather than rebellion or treason.

With the war over, he asserts, the federal government should've left the southern states in peace. This did not, however, happen. Rather, there has been an "invasion of the reserved powers of the States, or the people" and a "perversion of the republican form of government guaranteed to each State by the Constitution." As noted above Davis began writing this book in 1876. This is a year before the end of the Reconstruction period. Davis's references to a "perversion" of republican government area reference to the state governments of the south that have been dominated by votes and politicians of the Republican party—the party that, in the eyes of many former Confederates, was primarily responsible for northern aggression in the early 1860s. These Republican dominated state governments included not only southerners who had defected to the Republican party (known as "scalawags") but also northerners who had moved to the south ("carpet baggers") and newly enfranchised, free African American voters and politicians. Furthermore, this new order had been enforced with military rule, under laws which authorized the U.S. Army to conduct voter registration and elections.

Davis closes his preface with the prediction that future generations will work to fully restored the union. He hopes that this future generation is influenced by "the fountains of our political history." That is to say, that Jefferson hopes that future generations will accept his—and the Confederacy's—interpretation of the nature of the Constitution and the United States rather than be influenced by conflict between north and south and by "self-seeking place-hunters"—a reference to the scalawags and carpet baggers that dominated Reconstruction era southern politics.

Essential Themes

The Rise and Fall of the Confederate Government remains a monument to Davis's tenacity and determination to vindicate the cause of the South. Although it is read in its entirety by only the most serious scholars, the essential arguments made by Davis and the tenor of the work can be gleaned from this preface He rejects the terms *rebellion* and *treason* in reference to the Confederate cause. He argues that the war was not fought to protect slavery but rather to protect states' rights. Crucially, he presents this largely as a legal argument aimed at those he characterizes as "ignorant of the nature of the Union, and of the reserved powers of the States." In many ways—and Davis as much admits this—his history of the Confederacy presents arguments that have been settled by the war and the changes that had taken place in the country since. The book, which covers more than twelve hundred pages, was not a financial success, and the national press took little notice of it.

——*C. Ellen Connally, JD*
with additional material by Aaron Gulyas, MA

Bibliography and Additional Reading

Nichols, Roy F. "United States vs. Jefferson Davis, 1865–1869." *American Historical Review* 31 (January 1926): 266–284.

Cashin, Joan E. *First Lady of the Confederacy: Varina Davis's Civil War.* Cambridge, Mass. Belknap Press of Harvard University Press, 2006.

Cooper, William J., Jr. *Jefferson Davis, American.* New York: Knopf, 2000.

———. *Jefferson Davis and the Civil War Era.* Baton Rouge: Louisiana State University Press, 2009.

Davis, Varina. *Jefferson Davis: Ex-President of the Confederate States of America—A Memoir by His Wife.* 1890. Reprinted with an introduction by Craig L. Symonds. Baltimore: Nautical and Aviation Publishing Company of America, 1990.

Davis, William C. *Jefferson Davis: The Man and His Hour.* New York: HarperCollins Publishers, 1991.

Hattaway, Herman, and Richard E. Beringer. *Jefferson Davis: Confederate President.* Lawrence: University Press of Kansas, 2002.

NATIVE AMERICAN DISSENT

From the moment in 1607 when English settlers established their first permanent colony in North America, colonial population growth and need for land put pressure on Native American tribes. Deadly disease, brutal military operations, and disruption of traditional life ways contributed to this pressure and diminished the Native population of English North America. As England came into conflict with other European colonial powers on the continent—particularly France—Native Americans were either caught in the cross-fire or found themselves on the losing side of wars such as the French and Indian War. After the establishment of the United States, westward migration of white Americans led to formal and informal military conflict and a recurring cycle of treaty making and treaty breaking that increased Native American dispossession and desperation.

The Historical Documents in this section examine Native American response and resistance to the increasing white American presence on their lands throughout the nineteenth century. The selection of documents begins with the Shawnee leader Tecumseh. His 1811 Appeal to Choctaws and Chickasaws, he presented his argument for a unified Native American confederation to tribes of the southern United States. Tecumseh's ultimate goal was military and political force that could not only successfully resist further white expansion but would have the ability to push back American settlement and reclaim Native land.

Tecumseh's dreams of Indian unification and military triumph were cut down during the War of 1812 and white settlement increased its pace. One aspect of Federal policy toward Native Americans in the early republic was to encourage tribes to "civilize" and to adopt American ways of life in order to survive. This is a theme that recurs several times over the decades of the nineteenth century. The Cherokee tribe of the southeastern United States attempted to fulfill this directive but, despite their assimilation of American religion, law, and economics, the discovery of gold on their territory put them firmly in the path of a surge of settlement. Cherokee Chief John Ross's 1829 Memorial to Congress prove no match for the Federal government's and the state of Georgia's desire to push the Cherokee of their land.

In the years after the American Civil War, migration across the Mississippi, into the Great Plains and other western areas led to renewed conflict. As demonstrated by the Editorials and Congressional Testimony surrounding the Battle of Sand Creek (also known as the Sand Creek Massacre), the combination of Native tribes, white settlers, and American soldiers was a volatile one. Open warfare between western tribes and the United States took place during the 1860s and 1870s and the Treaty of Fort Laramie is just one example of the many treaties concluded between the two parties throughout this era. The treaty contains provisions for rewarding Native Americans with land and resources in exchange for renouncing their tribal allegiance. This policy was applied more broadly in the 1887 Dawes Severalty Act. While these documents are not examples of Native American dissent, we present them as striking examples of the geographical and cultural conquest which Native Americans resisted. The Ghost Dance Movement was one example of this resistance. The Statements and Eyewitness Accounts of the Wounded Knee Massacre illustrate the desperation of many of he Native Americans as well as the drastic overreaction of the American military forces to the events.

Decades later, driven by the desperately inadequate conditions on Native American reservations and inspired by the wave of protest, civil disobedience, and activism that exploded during the 1960s, a group of young Native Americans physically occupied the island of Alcatraz in San Francisco Bay, claiming it for the Indians of All Tribes. While the occupation would not be permanent, but it brought much needed attention to the plight of Native Americans on the reservations nearly a century after the close of the frontier wars of the nineteenth century.

■ Appeal to Choctaws and Chickasaws

Date: 1811
Author: Tecumseh
Genre: Speech

Summary Overview

In 1811, Tecumseh, leader of the Shawnee tribe, addressed the Choctaw and Chickasaw tribes which held lands in the what was then the southwestern portion of the United States. This was one of several speeches that Tecumseh delivered on his mission to establish a confederacy (a political and military alliance) of several western Native American tribes in an effort to halt the surging waves of white settlement that threatened to engulf the Ohio Valley and the lower Great Lakes region (particularly Ohio and what would become Indiana and Michigan). The text of this speech was recorded by John Pitchlynn, who was the head of the Choctaw Agency, the US government office that managed diplomatic and trade relations with the Choctaw tribe. One of Pitchlynn's main duties was to serve as an interpreter, which meant that his command of the Choctaw language was advanced enough to understand Tecumseh's speech. Pitchlynn would later report that he had never seen a larger group of Native American leaders gathered together.

Tecumseh's attempt to persuade these two tribes to join his cause rested on two crucial points. First was an effort to shame the tribes' leaders into fighting; highlighting the relative ease of their lives while their fellow natives fought and died to resist American settlers. The second point Tecumseh sought to make was the inevitably of white settlement penetrating even the far corners of the west. The fight was coming, he argued, whether the southwestern tribes wanted it to or not.

Defining Moment

The "Indian Policy" of the early United States, that is to say the federal government's official plan of action toward various Native American tribes, underwent a number of changes very rapidly during the late 18th and early 19th centuries. The initial policy was developed in the 1790s by President George Washington and his Secretary of War, Henry Knox. Their plan was to encourage tribes to become "civilized" (emphasizing such things as individual—rather than collective—ownership of property and adoption of Christianity and the English language) with the goal of eventually assim-

ilating them into the broader fabric of American life. At the same time, the US government was also engaging in open warfare against tribes in the Northwest Territory and negotiating treaties in which tribes agreed to give up some of their land to white settlers. By the early 1800s, the increasing pace of white migration westward (which happened much more quickly than anyone had anticipated) led to new policy of coercing tribes to cede (or give up) portions of their territory. As a result, Native tribes migrated westward, hoping to keep ahead of white settlers. Following the 1795 Treaty of Greenville, leaders such as the Shawnee's Black Hoof and the Miami's Little Turtle urged cooperation with the United States and participated in further treaties that recognized American control of more and more native lands.

After the 1809 Treaty of Fort Wayne resulted in the loss of millions more acres of land, Shawnee leader Tecumseh began to advance the idea that tribes did not own land but, rather, that all Native land was owned in common. Thus, it was not right that a particular chief could sign away what rightfully belonged to all. Tecumseh, based in Prophetstown (on the Wabash River in the Indiana Territory) began to urge fellow Natives to created a confederacy of all tribes and argued that this was the only way to resist American domination of their lands. After tense meetings between Tecumseh and Indiana Governor William Henry Harrison in 1810 and 1811, Tecumseh moved south, hoping to build support for his confederacy.

Author Biography

Tecumseh was born in March, 1768 and spent his youth in southern Ohio. During the 1770s, a number of conflicts, including Lord Dunmore's War, were fought between white settlers and the Native Americans of the Ohio River Valley. During the American Revolution, the Shawnee were allies of the British and fought a number of battles in the areas that would become Ohio and Kentucky. After the Revolutionary War, Tecumseh and other Shawnee attacked settlers who were migrating into the area from Pennsylvania. After a brief time spent fighting alongside the Cherokee in Tennessee, Tecumseh returned to Ohio and took part in the pivotal

Battle of Fallen Timbers in 1794. The native loss in that battle led to the Treaty of Greenville (which Tecumseh refused to sign), ending the Northwest Indian Wars and opening vast areas of the region to white settlement.

Tecumseh and his brother, Tenskwatawa or "The Shawnee Prophet," lived in Ohio. Tenskwatawa urged the Shawnee to return to the way of life they had practiced before the arrival of the whites, rejecting alcohol, Christianity, and other trappings of Euro-American life and culture. As Tenskwatawa's movement grew, Tecumseh began to enter into negotiations with American officials as a result of increasing tensions between natives and white settlers. Tecumseh, Tenskwatawa, and their followers moved west, settling at Prophetstown in pres-

ent-day Indiana. It was at this time, around 1808, that Tecumseh began the work of building his broad Native American confederacy.

Open conflict broke out in 1811 between the Shawnee and American forces in the Indiana territory. At the same time Tecumseh was attempting (mostly unsuccessfully) to persuade southern tribes to join him, Indiana governor William Henry Harrison attacked Prophetstown. The suspicion that the British were supporting the Natives was one of the factors that led to the 1812 war between Britain and the United States. During this war, Tecumseh and his allies fought alongside the British. Tecumseh was killed on October 5, 1813 in Ontario at the Battle of the Thames.

HISTORICAL DOCUMENT

In view of questions of vast importance, have we met together in solemn council tonight. Nor should we here debate whether we have been wronged and injured, but by what measures we should avenge ourselves; for our merciless oppressors, having long since planned out their proceedings, are not about to make, but have and are still making attacks upon our race who have as yet come to no resolution. Nor are we ignorant by what steps, and by what gradual advances, the whites break in upon our neighbors. Imagining themselves to be still undiscovered, they show themselves the less audacious because you are insensible. The whites are already nearly a match for us all united, and too strong for any one tribe alone to resist; so that unless we support one another with our collective and united forces; unless every tribe unanimously combines to give check to the ambition and avarice of the whites, they will soon conquer us apart and disunited, and we will be driven away from our native country and scattered as autumnal leaves before the wind.

But have we not courage enough remaining to defend our country and maintain our ancient independence? Will we calmly suffer the white intruders and tyrants to enslave us? Shall it be said of our race that we knew not how to extricate ourselves from the three most dreadful calamities—folly, inactivity and cowardice? But what need is there to speak of the past? It speaks for itself and asks, Where today is the Pequod? Where the Narragansetts, the

Mohawks, Pocanokets, and many other once powerful tribes of our race? They have vanished before the avarice and oppression of the white men, as snow before a summer sun. In the vain hope of alone defending their ancient possessions, they have fallen in the wars with the white men.

Look abroad over their once beautiful country, and what see you now? Naught but the ravages of the pale face destroyers meet our eyes. So it will be with you Choctaws and Chickasaws! Soon your mighty forest trees, under the shade of whose wide spreading branches you have played in infancy, sported in boyhood, and now rest your wearied limbs after the fatigue of the chase, will be cut down to fence in the land which the white intruders dare to call their own.

Soon their broad roads will pass over the grave of your fathers, and the place of their rest will be blotted out forever. The annihilation of our race is at hand unless we unite in one common cause against the common foe. Think not, brave Choctaws and Chickasaws, that you can remain passive and indifferent to the common danger, and thus escape the common fate. Your people, too, will soon be as falling leaves and scattering clouds before their blighting breath. You, too, will be driven away from your native land and ancient domains as leaves are driven before the wintry storms.

Sleep not longer, O Choctaws and Chickasaws, in false security and delusive hopes. Our broad domains are fast escaping from our grasp. Every year our white intruders become more greedy, exacting, oppressive and overbearing. Every year contentions spring up between them and our people and when blood is shed we have to make atonement whether right or wrong, at the cost of the lives of our greatest chiefs, and the yielding up of large tracts of our lands. Before the palefaces came among us, we enjoyed the happiness of unbounded freedom, and were acquainted with neither riches, wants nor oppression. How is it now? Wants and oppression are our lot; for are we not controlled in everything, and date we move without asking, by your leave? Are we not being stripped day by day of the little that remains of our ancient liberty? Do they not even kick and strike us as they do their black-faces? How long will it be before they will tie us to a post and whip us, and make us work for them in their corn fields as they do them? Shall we wait for that moment or shall we die fighting before submitting to such ignominy?

Have we not for years had before our eyes a sample of their designs, and are they not sufficient harbingers of their future determinations? Will we not soon be driven from our respective countries and the graves of our ancestors? Will not the bones of our dead be plowed up, and their graves be turned into fields? Shall we calmly wait until they become so numerous that we will no longer be able to resist oppression? Will we wait to be destroyed in our turn, without making an effort worthy of our race? Shall we give up our homes, our country, bequeathed to us by the Great Spirit, the graves of our dead, and everything that is dear and sacred to us, without a struggle? I know you will cry with me: Never! Never! Then let us by unity of action destroy them all, which we now can do, or drive them back whence they came. War or extermination is now our only choice. Which do you choose? I know your answer. Therefore, I now call on you, brave Choctaws and Chickasaws, to assist in the just cause of liberating our race from the grasp of our faithless invaders and heartless oppressors. The white usurpation in our common country must be stopped, or we, its rightful owners, be forever destroyed and wiped out as a race of people. I am now at the head of many warriors backed by the strong arm of English soldiers. Choctaws and Chickasaws, you have too long borne with grievous usurpation inflicted by the arrogant Americans. Be no longer their dupes. If there be one here tonight who believes that his rights will not sooner or later be taken from him by the avaricious American pale faces, his ignorance ought to excite pity, for he knows little of the character of our common foe.

And if there be one among you made enough to undervalue the growing power of the white race among us, let him tremble in considering the fearful woes he will bring down upon our entire race, if by his criminal indifference he assists the designs of our common enemy against our common country. Then listen to the voice of duty, or honor, of nature and of your endangered country. Let us form one body, one heart, and defend to the last warrior our country, our homes, our liberty, and the graves of our fathers.

Choctaws and Chickasaws, you are among the few of our race who sit indolently at ease. You have indeed enjoyed the reputation of being brave, but will you be indebted for it more from report than fact? Will you let the whites encroach upon your domains even to your very door before you will assert your rights in resistance? Let no one in this council imagine that I speak more from malice against the pale face Americans than just grounds of complaint. Complaint is just toward friends who have failed in their duty; accusation is against enemies guilty of injustice. And surely, if any people every had, we have good and just reasons to believe we have ample grounds to accuse the Americans of injustice; especially when such great acts of injustice have been committed by them upon our race, of which they seem to have no manner of regard, or even to reflect. They are a people fond of innovations, quick to contrive and quick to put their schemes into effectual execution no matter how great the wrong and injury to us; while we are content to preserve what we already have. Their designs are to enlarge their possessions by taking yours in turn; and will you, can you longer dally, O Choctaws and Chickasaws?

Do you imagine that that people will not continue longest in the enjoyment of peace who timely prepare to vindicate themselves right whenever they are wronged? Far otherwise. Then haste to the relief of our common cause, as by consanguinity of blood you are bound; lest the day be not far distant when you will be left single-handed and alone to the cruel mercy of our most inveterate foe.

GLOSSARY

consanguinity: The condition of being descended from a common ancestor; related by blood

indolent: lazy

ignominy: Deep public shame

inveterate: consistent and seemingly permanent

"The Pequod...Narragansetts...Mohawks...Pocanokets": Eastern Native American tribes that had been subjugated and displaced by white settlers

Document Analysis

In the first paragraph, Tecumseh begins by claiming that there is no reason for debating or arguing about whether or not the native tribes have been "wronged and injured" by the whites but, rather, how they should respond in the face of continuing assaults by their "merciless oppressors." Tecumseh relates the ways in which the whites make "gradual advances" on native territory and asserts that they are strong because they are "all united." Until and unless the tribes combine their forces to oppose "the ambition and avarice of the whites," the natives will be scattered and destroyed.

In the second paragraph, we see the first instance of Tecumseh challenging the courage of the Choctaw and Chickasaw tribes, highlighting the history of white/native relations rhetorically asking "Where today is the Pequod? Where the Narragansetts, the Mohawks, Pocanokets, and many other once powerful tribes of our race?" and answering that "they have vanished before the avarice and oppression of the white men, as snow before a summer sun." Over the next two paragraphs, Tecumseh continues to warn of the dangers of white encroachment, leading to the despoilment of their sacred lands. The only hope is for the tribes to unite as one.

After painting this picture of what the future might hold for the tribes of the southwest, Tecumseh issues a call to action, urging the tribes not to "sleep...in false security and delusive hopes." They tribes are losing their land and the whites are becoming increasingly threatening. The pace of violence is increasing. Before the whites came, the tribes enjoyed "unbounded freedom" and "were acquainted with neither riches, wants nor oppression." That is no longer the case. Every day

lands and freedom are lost. Tecumseh also asserts that the whites "kick and strike us as they do their blackfaces," drawing a parallel between the condition of Native Americans and that of African American slaves and warning that they might suffer the same fate. He closes this paragraph by once again challenging the leaders and warriors to fight back rather than "submitting" to white dominance. The next paragraph continues this theme, reminding his audience that they are fully aware of the plans that the whites have for the Native tribes' lands. The time, Tecumseh asserts, has come for resistance before the Americans become too powerful to overcome. "War or extermination" are, he argues, the only two options available to the natives. Tecumseh then reveals that the not only has a number of native warriors at his side but also "the strong arm of English soldiers." This alliance between western tribes and British forces was deeply troubling to western political and military leaders and was, in fact, one of the factors which led to the War of 1812.

Tecumseh moves toward his conclusion by ramping up the pressure on Chickasaw and Choctaw leaders to not be the reason that the whites finally displace Native peoples and tribes. He warns against those who would "undervalue" the strength and numbers of white Americans, asserting that those who underestimate the enemy will bring ruin upon the "entire race." To not oppose the enemy, he argues, is to support the enemy. He repeats his call to "form one body, one heart, and defend to the last warrior our country, our homes, our liberty, and the graves of our fathers." In the next-to-last paragraph, Tecumseh continues to impugn the bravery of the Choctaw and Chickasaw, pointing out that they have had relatively few hardships compared to the tribes in the northern and eastern portions in the United States. While they have a "reputation of being brave," now is the time for them to prove that reputation. Tecumseh argues that it is better for the Choctaw and Chickasaw to take the fight to the enemy rather than to wait until they arrive at their "very door." Tecumseh backs off from this criticism of his audience to reassure them that he is not speaking out of personal animosity toward the Americans but rather from his knowledge of the nation's unjust actions toward Natives of all tribes.

Tecumseh ends his appeal by those who take vengeance on those who wrong them are those who will eventually experience peace. He calls on the leaders of these two tribes to honor the commitment they have to their fellow natives. The alternative, Tecumseh explains, will mean that they are left alone to defend themselves when the Americans ("our most inveterate foe") inevitably take their land.

Essential Themes

Two critical ideas come to the fore in Tecumseh's speech to the Choctaw and Chickasaw leaders: courage and inevitability. Tecumseh appeals to the pride of the Choctaw an Chickasaw leaders and warriors, warning them of the dangers of "folly, inactivity and cowardice" in the face of near constant assault and invasion by white settlers and the military forces they bring with them. In nearly every paragraph, Tecumseh make a reference to either some aspect of bravery and courage as well as, on the other hand, of cowardice, laziness, or ignorance of the danger which the people face. He appeals to the the Choctaw's and Chickasaw's sense of honor both in terms of military prowess and in terms of their cultural significance.

This courage will be necessary because, as Tecumseh repeatedly points out in this address, the onslaught of white settlement is not going to go away. Several times he refers to the "ignorance" of these southwestern tribes as to the danger presented by continued American migration. He also points out that the Choctaw and Chickasaw "are among the few of our race who sit indolently at ease." The harsh battles faced by tribes in Ohio and Indiana have not yet come to the southwest. But they will. Tecumseh warns against those who would "undervalue" the strength of the oncoming white Americans as well as those who forget the fate of other tribes (he mentions the Mohawks, Narragansetts, and others) who have failed to stop the whites. In the face of this united force of American settlers, all the tribes must join together as well to resist them.

———*Aaron Gulyas, MA*

Bibliography and Additional Reading

Dowd, Gregory Evans. *A Spirited Resistance: The North American Indian Struggle for Unity, 1745-1815*. (Baltimore: Johns Hopkins University Press, 1992).

Eckert, Allan. *A Sorrow in Our Hearts: The Life of Tecumseh.* (New York: Bantam Books, 1992).

Edmunds, R. David. *Tecumseh and the Quest for Indian Leadership*. (Boston: Little Brown, 1984).

——(December 1987 – January 1988). "The Thin Red Line. Tecumseh, The Prophet, and Shawnee Resistance." *Timeline*. Ohio Historical Society. 4 (6): 3.

Rugeley, Terry (1989). "Savage and Statesman: Changing Historical Interpretations of Tecumseh". *Indiana Magazine of History*. 85 (4): 289–311.

■ Memorial to Congress

Date: 1829
Author: John Ross
Genre: Message to Congress

Summary Overview

Chief John Ross held the Cherokee Nation together through its greatest crisis, the expulsion of the tribe from its homeland in the Southeastern United States. In the 1820s, politicians in Georgia began demanding that the Cherokee leave the state due to westward expansion as well as the 1829 discovery of gold on Cherokee lands. For the more than a decade,4 Ross fiercely opposed the United States' efforts to appease Georgia and remove the Cherokee. Chief John Ross authored numerous speeches and personal communications as he guided the Cherokee Nation through the crisis of their removal from the state of Georgia in the 1820s and 1830s. They reveal much about Ross's personality and political tactics, showing him to have been an optimistic pragmatist and a skilled politician. He was an ardent advocate for his nation and a reassuring but candid communicator to its citizens. His 1829 Memorial to Congress demonstrates his rhetorical and political skills in his effort to forestall the removal of the Cherokee.

Defining Moment

In the late 1780s the U.S. government developed a national Indian relations policy that treated the Indian tribes as sovereign nations, dealt with them through diplomatic treaties, and pay them for their lands. The United States would teach Native Americans how to farm, speak, live, and worship like Anglo-Americans. Indians would no longer need all of the lands that they had heretofore used as hunting grounds. The United States could then buy these lands and distribute them to American citizens. Later, the government would persuade tribes to move across the Mississippi River to the Louisiana Territory that his administration had just purchased from France.

The year before the Louisiana Purchase, Jefferson's government had negotiated the Compact of 1802. In the compact, Georgia surrendered its claims to its western lands in exchange for a promise from the federal government that it would extinguish the land titles of the Cherokee and Creek as soon as it could be managed peacefully and on a reasonable basis. In the 1820s

Georgia began demanding that the federal government complete the compact and remove the two tribes from the state. Presidents James Monroe and John Quincy Adams agreed with the general idea of removing the tribes to the Louisiana Territory but insisted that the Indians consent to any relocation. The Creek relented in 1826 in the Treaty of Washington and departed from the state, but the Cherokee refused to submit.

The Cherokee refused to accede to Georgia's demands that they surrender their land and leave the state. By the early 1820s the Cherokee government was adamant that it would never again give up any of its territory.

The Cherokee's insistence that they were a sovereign nation holding complete title to their national territory antagonized pro-removal advocates in Georgia. The Georgia legislature, frustrated with federal inaction, took matters into its own hands when, in 1827, it passed a law annexing Cherokee territory into existing Georgian counties. In 1828 it passed another law that extended its legal jurisdiction over the Cherokee people and purported to abolish the Cherokee's government, laws, and courts. That same year, John Ross was elected principal chief of the Cherokee Nation.

Author Biography

John Ross was born along the Coosa River in present-day Alabama on October 3, 1790. Ross was a Cherokee by virtue of his descent from his Cherokee grandmother. His maternal side of the family introduced him to Cherokee culture, and his father, a trader from Scotland, ensured that he received a formal education. By the time he was a young man, John Ross was comfortable in both the Cherokee and Anglo-American worlds and was prepared to assume a leadership role in his tribe. He became a successful planter and businessman, establishing a trading post and ferry service with his brother, Lewis. After fighting on the side of Andrew Jackson's army in the Creek Civil War (1813–1814)—a conflict between traditionalist Creek who resisted American encroachment into their territory and more accomodationist Creek who wanted to adopt aspects of Anglo-American culture and maintain peaceful relations—Ross assumed the responsibilities of clerk to the Cherokee chief Pathkiller. He was elected to the Cherokee national council in 1817 and from 1818 to 1827 presided over the committee that handled the nation's day-to-day affairs. Ross became principal chief pro tem upon Pathkiller's death in 1827. That same year he was elected to the committee that drafted the Cherokee national constitution. In 1828 the Cherokee elected Ross as their first principal chief under the new constitution, a position he held until his death in 1866.

HISTORICAL DOCUMENT

We, the undersigned, Representatives of the Cherokee nation, beg leave to present before your honorable bodies a subject of the deepest interest to our nation, as involving the most sacred rights and privileges of the Cherokee People. The Legislature of Georgia, during its late session, passed an act to add a large portion of our Territory to that State, and to extend her jurisdiction over the same, and declaring "all laws and usages, made and enforced in said Territory by the Indians, to be null and void after the first of June, 1830. No Indian, or descendent of an Indian, to be a competent witness, or a party to any suit to which a white man is a party." This act involves a question of great magnitude and of serious import, and which calls for the deliberation and decision of Congress. It is a question upon which the salvation and happiness or the misery and destruction of *a nation* depends, therefore it should not be trifled with. The anxious solicitude of Georgia to obtain our lands through the United States by treaty was known to us, and after having accommodated her desires (with that of other States bordering on our territory) by repeated cession of lands, until no more can be reasonably spared, it was not conceived, much less believed, that *a State*, proud of *Liberty*, and tenacious of the *rights of man*, would condescend to have placed herself before the world, in the imposing attitude of a usurper of the most sacred rights and privileges of a weak, defenceless, and innocent nation of people, who are in perfect peace with the United States, and to whom the faith of the United States is solemnly pledged to protect and defend them against the encroachments of their citizens.

In acknowledgment for the protection of the United States and the consideration of guaranteeing to our nation forever the security of our lands &c., the Cherokee nation ceded by treaty a large tract of country to the United States, and stipulated that the said Cherokee nation "will not hold any treaty with any *foreign power, individual State*, or with *individuals of any State*." These stipulations on our part have been faithfully observed, and ever shall be.

The right of regulating our own internal affairs is a right which we have inherited from the Author of our existence, which we have always exercised, and have never surrendered. Our nation had no voice in the formation of the Federal compact between the States; and if the United States have involved themselves by an agreement with Georgia relative to the purchase of our lands, and have failed to comply with it in the strictest letter of their compact, it is a matter to be adjusted between themselves; and on no principle of justice can an innocent people, who were in no way a party to that compact, be held responsible for its fulfilment; consequently they should not be oppressed, in direct violation of the solemn obligations pledged by treaties for their protection.

It is with pain and deep regret we have witnessed the various plans which have been advised within a few years past by some of the officers of the General Government, and the measures adopted by Congress in conformity to those plans, with the view of effecting the removal of our nation beyond the Mississippi, for the purpose, as has been expressed to promote our interest and permanent happiness, and save us from the impending fate which has swept others into oblivion....

We cannot but believe, that, if the same zeal and exertion were to be used by the General Government and the State of Georgia, to effect a mutual compromise in the adjustment of their compact, as [it] has been, and is now, using to effect our removal, it could be done to the satisfaction of the people of Georgia, and without any sacrifice to the United

States. We should be wanting in liberal and charitable feelings were we to doubt the virtue and magnanimity of the People of Georgia, and we do believe that there are men in that State whose moral and religious worth stands forth inferior to none within the United States. Why, then, should the power that framed the Constitution of Georgia and made the compact with the United States be not exercised for the honor of the country and the peace, happiness, and preservation of a people, who were the original proprietors of a large portion of the country now in the possession of that State? And whose title to the soil they now occupy, is lost in the ages of antiquity, whose interests are becoming identified with those of the United States, and at whose call they are ever ready to obey in the hour of danger....

We cannot admit that Georgia has the right to extend her jurisdiction over our territory, nor are the Cherokee people prepared to submit to her persecuting edict. We would therefore respectfully and solemnly protest, in behalf of the Cherokee nation, before your honorable bodies, against the extension of the laws of Georgia over any part of our Territory, and appeal to the United States' Government

for justice and protection. The great Washington advised a plan and afforded aid for the general improvement of our nation, in agriculture, science, and government. President Jefferson followed the noble example....

This kind and generous policy to meliorate our condition, has been blessed with the happiest results: our improvement has been without a parallel in the history of all Indian nations. Agriculture is every where pursued, and the interests of our citizens are permanent in the soil. We have enjoyed the blessings of Christian instruction; the advantages of education and merit are justly appreciated, a Government of regular law has been adopted, and the nation, under a continuance of the fostering care of the United States, will stand forth as a living testimony, that all Indian nations are not doomed to the fate which has swept many from the face of the earth. Under the parental protection of the United States, we have arrived at the present degree of improvement, and they are now to decide whether we shall continue as a people or be abandoned to destruction.

GLOSSARY

General Government: The national, or federal government

meliorate: to improve or make better

solicitude: care or concern

"the Author of our existence": God

Document Analysis

In his 1829 memorial, Ross, writing on behalf of the Cherokee leadership, appealed to Congress to protect his nation from Georgia's attacks.

Ross was an artful debater, and he used several tactics to try to persuade congressmen to his view. First, he appeals to the legislators' sense of justice. Ross describes Georgia's extension legislation, explains how it encroaches upon the sovereignty of the Cherokee Nation, and pleads for Congress to intervene on behalf of the Cherokee. Ross states that their nation had always

respected the provisions of the treaties it had signed with the United States and had met American demands with "repeated cession of lands, until no more can be reasonably spared." He criticizes Georgia for trying to impose its will on a "weak, defenceless, and innocent nation of people" and for requiring the Cherokee to call upon the United States to come to its aid. Later in the memorial, he thanks the Congress for encouraging the Cherokee to become a civilized people, notes how much progress they had made on the road to civilization, and then suggests how unfair it would be for the

United States to remove them after they had been so successful in their transformation. He points out that the Cherokee had not been a party to the Compact of 1802 and contends that they should not be forced to suffer the consequences of an agreement to which they were not a party.

Ross's memorial is also defiant. He asserts that the Cherokee rejected the plans for removal and ridicules the claim that a relocation west of the Mississippi would benefit the Indians. The Cherokee, Ross writes, wanted to remain where they were, in a place where they were prosperous and happy. The chief declares that "the right of regulating our own internal affairs is a right which we have inherited from the Author of our existence, which we have always exercised, and have never surrendered." Ross understood that antagonistic feelings on the part of the Cherokee would undermine any chance of compromise, and he typically put the best light on the Cherokee's adversaries and publicly gave them the benefit of the doubt in their intentions. Despite all that the Georgia leadership had done to the Cherokee up to this point, Ross said that he did not doubt "the virtue and magnanimity of the People of Georgia."

Essential Themes

Chief John Ross's memorial to Congress takes both the federal government and the government of the state of Georgia to task for their attempts to subvert the sovereignty of the Cherokee nation. One important aspect of this to notice is the careful way in which Ross uses the set of the treaties and laws to demonstrate that this is not really a matter of interpretation—Georgia is overstepping its bounds and the Cherokee have diligently upheld their endow the mutual obligations between their nation and the United States. Ross also demonstrates that the Cherokee have done what they have done to appease the Georgian state government, with

the Cherokee "having accommodated [Georgia's] desires (with that of other States bordering on our territory) by repeated cession of lands, until no more can be reasonably spared." Furthermore, Ross speculates that, given a sufficient amount of desire, the federal government and the Georgia could work with the Cherokee "to effect a mutual compromise." Ross's implication here—and throughout the message—is that both the federal and state governments do not have that desire to compromise and are committed to seizing the Cherokee lands regardless of law or treaty.

The final paragraph of the message is also significant. Ross revisits the earlier federal policy to "Americanize" the native tribes, explaining that the Cherokee have done all hat has been asked of them, developing agriculture, adopting Christianity and education, and creating written laws. Ross closes by presenting this as evidence that not all the native tribes are "doomed to the fate which has swept many from the face of the earth." Whether or not that will be the case, however, depends on the continued "parental protection" of the United States.

——*Tim Alan Garrison, PhD*
and Kristin Teigen

Bibliography and Additional Reading

Hicks, Brian. *Toward the Setting Sun: John Ross, the Cherokees, and the Trail of Tears.* New York: Atlantic Monthly Press, 2011.

Inskeep, Steve. *Jacksonland: President Andrew Jackson, Cherokee Chief John Ross, and a Great American Land Grab.* Penguin Press, 2015.

Moulton, Gary E. *John Ross Cherokee Chief.* Athens: The University of Georgia Press, 1978.

Williams, David. *The Georgia Gold Rush: Twenty-Niners, Cherokees, and Gold Fever.* Columbia: University of South Carolina Press, 1993.

■ Battle of Sand Creek: Editorials and Congressional Testimony

Date: 1864-1865
Authors: Anonymous editorial writers, John S. Smith, John M. Chivington
Genre: Editorials, Congressional testimony

Summary Overview

The Battle of Sand Creek prompted editorials and congressional testimony as Americans reacted to the events of November 29, 1864. That morning, a unit of the Colorado militia, about seven hundred cavalry troops under the command of Colonel John M. Chivington, attacked an encampment of five hundred to seven hundred Cheyenne and Arapaho Indians near Sand Creek in Colorado Territory. Throughout the morning, the militia brutally slaughtered the Indians, including old men, women, and children, leaving hundreds dead and numerous others injured; the remaining members of the band managed to escape. The soldiers committed numerous atrocities, and when they returned to Denver, they displayed scalps and other body parts from the defeated Indians. Reproduced here are four documents. The first two are unsigned editorials from the *Rocky Mountain News* dated December 17, 1864 and December 30, 1864 and present the battle at Sand Creek as a crucial victory of the heroic soldiers over the brutal natives who had terrorized settlers in the area. The Congressional testimony is from John S. Smith, a federal official and John M. Chivington himself and represent an attempt by government leaders to arrive at a fuller understanding of the events in the west. These editorials and congressional testimony help paint a portrait of differing views of relations with Indians during the late nineteenth century, particularly between western settlers and eastern politicians.

Defining Moment

Earlier in the nineteenth century, the United States considered the entire area west of the Mississippi River to be one immense Indian reservation. As miners and settlers moved westward, however, the policy of the U.S. government changed to what was called "concentration," or assigning definite boundaries to each tribe. Many Indians, though, refused to stay within their assigned lands, and as settlers arrived in places like Colorado, they demanded that the government protect them against Indian attacks. By 1864 the Cheyenne and

Arapaho in Colorado, who had been at war with each other, grew weary of fighting and wanted peace. To that end, they banded together and camped at Sand Creek, about forty miles away from Fort Lyon. They believed that this pacific gesture would show the U.S. government they wanted peace and were placing themselves under government protection. On the morning of the attack, their leader, Black Kettle, even raised an American flag and a white flag of peace, but to no avail.

Initially, the Battle of Sand Creek was reported in the press as a great victory for the soldiers against a force of Indians who put up a brave defense. Two editorials from the *Rocky Mountain News* reproduced here, are suggestive of the attitudes of white settlers in the West to the Indian tribes and efforts to subdue them. Soon, however, witnesses began to come forward, testifying to the brutality of the raid. Americans were shocked, and Congress appointed a committee to investigate the affair. Later, the government concluded a treaty with the two tribes in which it condemned the "wanton outrages" of the attack. Many of the escaped Cheyenne devoted themselves to war with the United States, and some of them got their revenge in 1876 at the Battle of the Little Bighorn ("Custer's Last Stand") in Montana Territory.

Author Biographies

While the authors of the editorials are anonymous, the *Rocky Mountain News* was the first newspaper in Colorado, beginning publication even before Colorado was incorporated as an independent territory (at the time it was part of the Kansas Territory). By 1864, when these editorials were published, the paper was published on a daily basis.

Most of what we know of Congressional committee witness John S. Smith comes from his testimony. He was a trapper and hunter as well as an interpreter employed by government and military officials in the Trans-Mississippi west. He had spent, according to his testimony, 27 years living among the Cheyenne and other tribes and had at least one son, Jack, who was of mixed ancestry. While we often think of white settlement of the west being an easily measured process whereby easterners suddenly move into a territory all at once, often there were whites—such as Smith—who operated very much on their own, establishing relationships with native leaders and learning their languages.

At least partly because of the notoriety gained during the Battle of Sand Creek, we know much more about Lieutenant Colonel John M. Chivington. He was born in Ohio in 1821 and following his ordination as a Methodist minister in 1844, served as a missionary and pastor in a number of posts, moving further and further westward as the years went on. From Illinois, he moved to Kansas, then Nebraska, and finally Colorado, where he retired from church work.

When the Civil War erupted in 1861, Chivington was granted a commission as a Major in the 1st Colorado Volunteers. He became well known for his actions during the Battle of Glorieta Pass, in which his troops attacked a Confederate supply train—effectively nullified the Confederate victory and ended the threat of Confederate incursion. He was subsequently promoted to Colonel and placed in command of the 1st Colorado, a position he still held during the incident at Sand Creek.

HISTORICAL DOCUMENTS

Rocky Mountain News Editorials
December 17, 1864

Among the brilliant feats of arms in Indian warfare, the recent campaign of our Colorado volunteers will stand in history with few rivals, and none to exceed it in final results. We are not prepared to write its history, which can only be done by some one who accompanied the expedition, but we have gathered from those who participated in it and from others who were in that part of the country, some facts which will doubtless interest many of our readers.

The people of Colorado are well aware of the situation occupied by the third regiment during the great snow-storm which set in the last of October. Their rendezvous was in Bijou Basin, about eighty miles southeast of this city, and close up under the foot of the Divide. That point had been selected as the base for an Indian campaign. Many of the companies reached it after the storm set in; marching for days through the driving, blinding clouds of snow and deep drifts. Once there, they were exposed for weeks to an Arctic climate, surrounded by a treeless plain covered three feet deep with snow. Their animals suffered for food and with cold, and the men fared but little better. They were insufficiently supplied with tents and blankets, and their sufferings were intense. At the end of a month the snow had settled to the depth of two feet, and the command set out upon its long contemplated march. The rear guard left the Basin on the 23rd of November. Their course was southeast, crossing the Divide and thence heading for Fort Lyon. For one hundred miles the snow was quite two feet in depth, and for the next hundred it ranged from six to twelve inches. Beyond that the ground was almost bare and the snow no longer impeded their march.

On the afternoon of the 28th the entire command reached Fort Lyon, a distance of two hundred and sixty miles, in less than six days, and so quietly and expeditiously had the march been made that the command at the fort was taken entirely by surprise. When the vanguard appeared in sight in was reported that a body of Indians were approaching, and precautions were taken for their reception. No one upon the route was permitted to go in advance of the column, and persons who it was suspected would spread the news of the advance were kept under surveillance until all danger from that source was past.

At Fort Lyon the force was strengthened by about two hundred and fifty men of the first regiment, and at nine o'clock in the evening the command set out for the Indian village. The course was due north, and their guide was the Polar star. As daylight dawned they came in sight of the Indian camp, after a forced midnight march of forty-two miles, in eight hours, across the rough, unbroken plain. But little time was required for preparation. The forces had been divided and arranged for battle on the march, and just as the sun rose they dashed upon the enemy with yells that would put a Comanche army to blush. Although utterly surprised, the savages were not unprepared, and for a time their defense told terribly against our ranks. Their main force rallied and formed in line of battle on the bluffs beyond the creek, where they were protected by rudely constructed rifle-pits, from which they maintained a steady fire until the shells from company C's (third regiment) howitzers began dropping among them, when they scattered and fought each for himself in genuine Indian fashion. As the battle progressed the field of carriage widened until it extended over not less than twelve miles of territory. The Indians who could escaped or secreted themselves, and by three o'clock in the afternoon the carnage had ceased. It was estimated that between three and four hundred of the savages got away with their lives. Of the balance there were neither wounded nor prisoners. Their strength at the beginning of the action was estimated at nine hundred.

Their village consisted of one hundred and thirty Cheyenne and with Arapahoe lodges. These, with their contents, were totally destroyed. Among their effects were large supplies of flour, sugar, coffee, tea, &c. Women's and children's clothing were found; also books and many other articles which must have been taken from captured trains or houses. One white man's scalp was found which had evidently been taken but a few days before. The Chiefs fought with unparalleled bravery, falling in front of their men. One of them charged alone against a force of two or three hundred, and fell pierced with balls far in advance of his braves.

Our attack was made by five battalions. The first regiment, Colonel Chivington, part of companies C, D, E, G, H and K, numbering altogether about two hundred and fifty men, was divided into two battalions; the first under command of Major Anthony, and the second under Lieutenant Wilson, until the latter was disabled, when the command devolved upon Lieutenant Dunn. The three battalions of the third, Colonel Shoup, were led, respectively, by Lieutenant Colonel Bowen, Major Sayr, and Captain Cree. The action was begun by the battalion of Lieutenant Wilson, who occupied the right, and by a quick and bold movement cut off the enemy from their herd of stock. From this circumstance we gained our great advantage. A few Indians secured horses, but the great majority of them had to fight or fly on foot. Major Anthony was on the left, and the third in the centre.

Among the killed were all the Cheyenne chiefs, Black Kettle, White Antelope, Little Robe, Left Hand, Knock Knee, One Eye, and another, name unknown. Not a single prominent man of the tribe remains, and the tribe itself is almost annihilated. The Arapahoes probably suffered but little. It has been reported that the chief Left Hand, of that tribe, was killed, but Colonel Chivington is of the opinion that he was not. Among the stock captured were a number of government horses and mules, including the twenty or thirty stolen from the command of Lieutenant Chase at Jimmy's camp last summer.

The Indian camp was well supplied with defensive works. For half a mile along the creek there was an almost continuous chain of rifle-pits, and another similar line of works crowned the adjacent bluff. Pits had been dug at all the salient points for miles. After the battle twenty-tree dead Indians were taken from one of these pits and twenty-seven from another.

Whether viewed as a march or as a battle, the exploit has few, if any, parallels. A march of 260 miles in but a fraction more than five days, with deep snow, scanty forage, and no road, is a remarkable feat, whilst the utter surprise of a large Indian village is unprecedented. In no single battle in North America, we believe, have so many Indians been slain.

It is said that a short time before the command reached the scene of battle of an old squaw partially alarmed the village by reporting that a great herd of buffalo were coming. She heard the rumbling of the artillery and tramp of the moving squadrons, but her people doubted. In a little time the doubt was dispelled, but not by buffaloes.

A thousand incidents of individual daring and the passing events of the day might be told, but space forbids. We leave the task for eye-witnesses to chronicle. All acquitted themselves well, and Colorado soldiers have again covered themselves with glory.

December 30, 1964

The issue of yesterday's News, containing the following dispatch, created considerable of a sensation in this city, particularly among the Thirdsters and others who participated in the recent campaign and the battle on Sand creek.

Washington, December 20, 1864

"The affair at Fort Lyon, Colorado, in which Colonel Chivington destroyed a large Indian village, and all its inhabitants, is to be made the subject of congressional investigation. Letters received from high officials in Colorado say that the Indians were killed after surrendering, and that a large proportion of them were women and children."

Indignation was loudly and unequivocally expressed, and some less considerate of the boys were very persistent in their inquiries as to who those "high officials" were, with a mild intimation that they had half a mind to "go for them." This talk about "friendly Indians" and a "surrendered" village will do to "tell to marines," but to us out here it is all bosh.

The confessed murderers of the Hungate family—a man and wife and their two little babes, whose scalped and mutilated remains were seen by all our citizens—were "friendly Indians," we suppose, in the eyes of these "high officials." They fell in the Sand creek battle.

The confessed participants in a score of other murders of peaceful settlers and inoffensive travelers upon our borders and along our roads in the past six months must have been friendly, or else the "high officials" wouldn't say so.

The band of marauders in whose possession were found scores of horses and mules stolen from government and from individuals; wagon loads of flour, coffee, sugar and tea, and rolls of broad cloth, calico, books, &c., robbed from freighters and emigrants on the plains; underclothes of white women and children, stripped from their murdered victims, were probably peaceably disposed toward some of those "high officials," but the mass of our people "can't see it."

Probably those scalps of white men, women and children, one of them fresh, not three days taken, found drying in their lodges, were taken in a friendly, playful manner; or possibly those Indian saddle-blankets trimmed with the scalp's of white women, and with braids and fringes of their hair, were kept simply as mementos of their owners' high affection for the pale face. At any rate, these delicate and tasteful ornaments could not have been taken from the heads of the wives, sisters or daughters of these "high officials."

That "surrendering" must have been the happy thought of an exceedingly vivid imagination, for we can hear of nothing of the kind from any of those who were engaged in the battle. On the contrary, the savages fought like devils to the end, and one of our pickets was killed and scalped by them the next day after the battle, and a number of others were fired upon. In one instance a party of the vidette pickets were compelled to beat a hasty retreat to save their lives, full twenty-four hours after the battle closed. This does not look much like the Indians had surrendered.

But we are not sure that an investigation may not be a good thing. It should go back of the "affair at Fort Lyon," as they are pleased to term it down east, however, and let the world know who were making money by keeping those Indians under the sheltering protection of Fort Lyon; learn who was interested in systematically representing that the Indians were friendly and wanted peace. It is unquestioned and undenied that the site of the Sand creek battle was the rendezvous of the thieving and marauding bands of savages who roamed over this country last summer and fall, and it is shrewdly suspected that somebody was all the time making a very good thing out of it. By all means let there be an investigation, but we advise the honorable congressional committee, who may be appointed to conduct it, to get their scalps insured before they pass Plum creek on their way out

Congressional Testimony of Mr. John S. Smith, Washington, March 14, 1865

Mr. John S. Smith sworn and examined.

By Mr. Gooch:

Question. Where is your place of residence?

Answer. Fort Lyon, Colorado

Question. What is your occupation?

Answer. United States Indian interpreter and special Indian agent.

Question. Will you state to the committee all that you know in relation to the attack of Colonel Chivington upon the Cheyenne and Arapahoe Indians in November last?

Answer. Major Anthony was in command at Fort Lyon at the time. Those Indians had been induced to remain in the vicinity of Fort Lyon, and were promised protection by the commanding officer at Fort Lyon. The commanding officer saw proper to keep them some thirty or forty miles distant from the fort, for fear of some conflict between them and the soldiers or the traveling population, for Fort Lyon is on a great thoroughfare. He advised them to go out on what is called Sand creek, about forty miles, a little east of north from Fort Lyon. Some days after they had left Fort Lyon when I had just recovered from a long spell of sickness, I was called on by Major S.G. Colley, who asked me if I was able and willing to go out and pay a visit to these Indians, ascertain their numbers, their general disposition toward the whites, and the points where other bands might be located in the interior.

Question. What was the necessity for obtaining that information?

Answer. Because there were different bands which were supposed to be at war; in fact, we knew at the time that they were at war with the white population in that country; but this band had been in and left the post perfectly satisfied. I left to go to this village of Indians on the 26th of November last. I arrived there on the 27th and remained there the 28th. On the morning of the 29th, between daylight and sunrise—nearer sunrise than daybreak—a large number of troops were discovered from three-quarters of a mile to a mile below the village. The Indians, who discovered them, ran to my camp, called me out, and wanted to me to go and see what troops they were, and what they wanted. The head chief of the nation, Black Kettle, and head chief of the Cheyennes, was encamped there with us. Some years previous he had been presented with a fine American flag by Colonel Greenwood, a commissioner, who had been sent out there. Black Kettle ran this American flag up to the top of his lodge, with a small white flag tied right under it, as he had been advised to do in case he should meet with any troops out on the prairies. I then left my own camp and started for that portion of the troops that was nearest the village, supposing I could go up to the m. I did not know but they might be strange troops, and thought my presence and explanations could reconcile matters. Lieutenant Wilson was in command of the detachment to which I tried to make my approach; but they fired several volleys at me, and I returned back to my camp and entered my lodge.

Question. Did these troops know you to be a white man?

Answer. Yes, sir; and the troops that went there knew I was in the village.

Question. Did you see Lieutenant Wilson or were you seen by him?

Answer. I cannot say I was seen by him; but his troops were the first to fire at me.

Question. Did they know you to be a white man?

Answer. They could not help knowing it. I had on pants, a soldier's overcoat, and a hat such as I am wearing now. I was dressed differently from any Indian in the country. On my return I entered my lodge, not expecting to get out of it alive. I had two other men there with me: one was David Louderbach, a soldier, belonging to company G, 1st Colorado cavalry; the other, a man by the name of Watson, who was a hired hand of Mr. DD Coolly, the son of Major Coolly, the agent.

After I had left my lodge to go out and see what was going on, Colonel Chivington rode up to within fifty or sixty yards of where I was camped; he recognized me at once. They all call me Uncle John in that country. He said, "Run here, Uncle John; you are all right." I went to him as fast as I could. He told me to get in between him and his troops, who were then coming up very fast; I did so; directly another officer who knew me—Lieutenant Baldwin, in command of a battery - tried to assist me to get a horse; but there was no loose horse there at the time. He said, "Catch hold of the caisson, and keep up with us."

By this time the Indians had fled; had scattered in every direction. The troops were some on one side of the river and some on the other, following up the Indians. We had been encamped on the north side of the river; I followed along, holding on the caisson, sometimes running, sometimes walking. Finally, about a mile above the village, the troops had got a parcel of the Indians hemmed in under the bank of the river; as soon as the troops overtook them, they commenced firing on them; some troops had got above them, so that they were completely surrounded. There were probably a hundred Indians hemmed in there, men, women, and children; the most of the men in the village escaped.

By the time I got up with the battery to the place where these Indians were surrounded there had been some considerable firing. Four or five soldiers had been killed, some with arrows and some with bullets. The soldiers continued firing on these Indians, who numbered about a hundred, until they had almost completely destroyed them. I think I saw altogether some seventy dead bodies lying there; the greater portion women and children. There may have been thirty warriors, old and young; the rest were women and small children of different ages and sizes.

The troops at that time were very much scattered. There were not over two hundred troops in the main fight, engaged in killing this body of Indians under the bank. The balance of the troops were scattered in different directions, running after small parties of Indians who were trying to make their escape. I did not go so see how many they might have killed outside of this party under the bank of the river. Being still quite weak from my last sickness, I returned with the first body of troops that went back to the camp.

The Indians had left their lodges and property; everything they owned. I do not think more than one-half of the Indians left their lodges with their arms. I think there were between 800 and 1,000 men in this command of United States troops. There was a part of three companies of the 1st Colorado, and the balance were what were called 100 days men of the 3rd regiment. I am not able to say which party did the most execution on the Indians, because it was very much mixed up at the time.

We remained there that day after the fight. By 11 o'clock, I think, the entire number of soldiers had returned back to the camp where Colonel Chivington had returned. On their return, he ordered the soldiers to destroy all the Indian property there, which they did, with the exception of what plunder they took away with them, which was considerable.

Question. How many Indians were there there?

Answer. There were 100 families of Cheyennes, and some six or eight lodges of Arapahoes.

Question. How many persons in all, should you say?

Answer. About 500 we estimate them at five to a lodge.

Question. 500 men, women and children?

Answer. Yes, sir.

Question. Do you know the reason for that attack on the Indians?

Answer. I do not know any exact reason. I have heard a great many reasons given. I have heard that that whole Indian war had been brought on for selfish purposes. Colonel Chivington was running for Congress in Colorado, and there were other things of that kind; and last spring a year ago he was looking for an order to go to the front, and I understand he had this Indian war in view to retain himself and his troops in that country, to carry out his electioneering purposes.

Question. In what way did this attack on the Indians further the purpose of Colonel Chivington?

Answer. It was said—I did not hear him say it myself, but it was said that he would do something; he had this regiment of three-months men, and did not want them to go out without doing some service. Now he had been told repeatedly by different persons—by myself, as well as others—where he could find the hostile bands.

The same chiefs who were killed in this village of Cheyennes had been up to see Colonel Chivington in Denver but a short time previous to this attack. He himself told them that he had no power to treat with them; that he had received telegrams from General Curtis directing him to fight all Indians he met with in that country. Still he would advise them, if they wanted any assistance from the whites, to go to their nearest military post in their country, give up their arms and the stolen property, if they had any, and then they would receive directions in what way to act. This was told them by Colonel Chivington and by Governor Evans, of Colorado. I myself interpreted for them and for the Indians.

Question. Did Colonel Chivington hold any communication with these Indians, or any of them, before making the attack upon them?

Answer. No, sir, not then. He had some time previously held a council with them at Denver city. When we first recovered the white prisoners from the Indians, we invited some of the chiefs to go to Denver, inasmuch as they had sued for peace, and were willing to give up these white prisoners. We promised to take the chiefs to Denver, where they had an interview with men who had more power than Major Wynkoop had, who was the officer in command of the detachment that went out to recover these white prisoners. Governor Evans and Colonel Chivington were in Denver, and were present at this council. They told the Indians to return with Major Wynkoop, and whatever he agreed on doing with them would be recognized by them.

I returned with the Indians to Fort Lyon. There we let them go out to their villages to bring in their families, as they had been invited through the proclamation or circular of the governor during the month of June, I think. They were gone some twelve or fifteen days from Fort Lyon, and then they returned with their families. Major Wynkoop had made them one or two issues of provisions previous to the arrival of Major Anthony there to assume command. Then Major Wynkoop, who is now in command at Fort Lyon, was ordered to Fort Leavenworth on some business with General Curtis, I think.

Then Major Anthony, through me, told the Indians that he did not have it in his power to issue rations to them, as Major Wynkoop had done. He said that he had assumed command at Fort Lyon, and his orders were positive from headquarters to fight the Indians in the vicinity of Fort Lyon, or at any other point in the Territory where they could find them. He said that he had understood that they had been behaving very badly. But on seeing Major Wynkoop and others there at Fort Lyon, he was happy to say that things were not as had been presented, and he could not pursue any other course than that of Major Wynkoop except the issuing rations to them. He then advised them to out to some near point, where there was buffalo, not too far from Fort Lyon or they might meet with troops from the Platte, who would not know them from the hostile bands. This was the southern band of Cheyennes; there is another band called the northern band. They had no apprehensions in the world of any trouble with the whites at the time this attack was made.

Question. Had there been, to your knowledge, any hostile act or demonstration on the part of these Indians or any of them?

Answer. Not in this band. But the northern band, the band known by the name of Dog soldiers of Cheyennes, had committed many depredations on the Platte.

Question. Do you know whether or not Colonel Chivington knew the friendly character of these Indians before he made the attack upon them?

Answer. It is my opinion that he did.

Question. On what is that opinion based?

Answer. On this fact, that he stopped all persons from going on ahead of him. He stopped the mail, and would not allow any person to go on ahead of him at the time he was on his way from Denver city to Fort Lyon. He placed a guard around old Colonel Bent, the former agent there; he stopped a Mr. Hagues and many men who were on their way to Fort Lyon. He took the fort by surprise, and as soon as he got there he posted pickets all around the fort, and then left at 8 o'clock that night for this Indian camp.

Question. Was that anything more than the exercise of ordinary precaution in following Indians?

Answer. Well, sir, he was told that there were no Indians in the vicinity of Fort Lyon, except Black Kettle's band of Cheyennes and Left Hand's band of Arapahoes.

Question. How do you know that?

Answer. I was told so.

By Mr. Buckalew:

Question. Do you know it of your own knowledge?

Answer. I cannot say I do.

Question. You did not talk with him about it before the attack?

Answer. No, sir.

By Mr. Gooch:

Question. When you went out to him, you had no opportunity to hold intercourse with him?

Answer. None whatever; he had just commenced his fire against the Indians.

Question. Did you have any communication with him at any time while there?

Answer. Yes, sir.

Question. What was it?

Answer. He asked me many questions about a son of mine, who was killed there afterwards. He asked me what Indians were there, what chiefs; and I told him as fully as I knew.

By Mr. Buckalew:

Question. When did you talk with him?

Answer. On the day of the attack. He asked me many questions about the chiefs who were there, and if I could recognize them if I saw them. I told him it was possible I might recollect the principal chiefs. They were terribly mutilated, lying there in the water and sand; most of them in the bed of the creek, dead and dying, making many struggles. They were so badly mutilated and covered with sand and water that it was very hard for me to tell one from another. However, I recognized some of them - among them the chief One Eye, who was employed by our government at $125 a month and rations to remain in the village as a spy. There was another called War Bonnet, who was here two years ago with me. There was another by the name of Standing-in-the-Water, and I supposed Black Kettle was among them, but it was not Black Kettle. There was one there of his size and dimensions in every way, but so tremendously mutilated that I was mistaken in him. I went out with Lieutenant Colonel Bowen, to see how many I could recognize.

By Mr. Gooch:

Question: Did you tell Colonel Chivington the character and disposition of these Indians at any time during your interviews on this day?

Answer. Yes, sir.

Question. What did he say in reply?

Answer. He said he could not help it; that his orders were positive to attack the Indians.

Question. From whom did he receive these orders?

Answer. I do not know; I presume from General Curtis.

Question. Did he tell you?

Answer. Not to my recollection.

Question. Were the women and children slaughtered indiscriminately, or only so far as they were with the warriors?

Answer. Indiscriminately.

Question. Were there any acts of barbarity perpetrated there that came under your own observation?

Answer. Yes, sir; I saw the bodies of those lying there cut all to pieces, worse mutilated than any I ever saw before; the women cut all to pieces.

By Mr. Buckalew:

Question. How cut?

Answer. With knives; scalped; their brains knocked out; children two or three months old; all ages lying there, from sucking infants up to warriors.

By Mr. Gooch:

Question. Did you see it done?

Answer. Yes, sir; I saw them fall.

Question. Fall when they were killed?

Answer. Yes, sir.

Question. Did you see them when they were mutilated?

Answer. Yes, sir.

Question. By whom were they mutilated?

Answer. By the United States troops.

Question. Do you know whether or not it was done by the direction or consent of any of the officers.

Answer. I do not; I hardly think it was.

By Mr. Buckalew:

Question. What was the date of that massacre?

Answer. On the 29th of November last.

Question. Did you speak of these barbarities to Colonel Chivington?

Answer. No sir; I had nothing at all to say about it, because at that time they were hostile towards me, from the fact of my being there. They probably supposed that I might be compromised with them in some way or other.

Question. Who called on you to designate the bodies of those who were killed?

Answer. Colonel Chivington himself asked me if I would ride out with Lieutenant Colonel Bowen, and see how many chiefs or principal men I could recognize.

Question. Can you state how many Indians were killed - how many women and how many children?

Answer. Perhaps one-half were men, and the balance were women and children. I do not think that I saw more than 70 lying dead then, as far as I went. But I saw parties of men scattered in every direction, pursuing little bands of Indians.

Question. What time of day or night was this attack made?

Answer. The attack commenced about sunrise, and lasted until between 10 and 11 o'clock.

Question. How large a body of troops?

Answer. I think that probably there may have been about 60 or 70 warriors who were armed and stood their ground and fought. Those that were unarmed got out of the way as they best could.

Question. How many of our troops were killed and how many wounded?

Answer. There were ten killed on the ground, and thirty-eight wounded; four of the wounded died at Fort Lyon before I came on east.

Question. Were there any other barbarities or atrocities committed there other than those you have mentioned, that you saw?

Answer. Yes, sir; I had a half-breed son there, who gave himself up. He started at the time the Indians fled; being a half-breed he had but little hope of being spared, and seeing them fire at me, he ran away with the Indians for the distance of about a mile. During the fight up there he walked back to my camp and went into the lodge. It was surrounded by soldiers at the time. He came in quietly and sat down; he remained there that day, that night, and the next day in the afternoon; about four o'clock in the evening, as I was sitting inside the camp, a soldier came up outside of the lodge and called me by name. I got up and went out; he took me by the arm and walked towards Colonel Chivington's camp, which was about sixty yards from my camp. Said he, "I am sorry to tell you, but they are going to kill your son Jack." I knew the feeling towards the whole camp of Indians, and that there was no use to make any resistance. I said, "I can't help it." I then walked on towards where Colonel Chivington was standing by his camp-fire; when I had got within a few feet of him I heard a gun fired, and saw a crowd run to my lodge, and they told me that Jack was dead.

Question. What action did Colonel Chivington take in regard to that matter?

Answer. Major Anthony, who was present, told Colonel Chivington that he had heard some remarks made, indicating that they were desirous of killing Jack; and that he (Colonel Chivington) had it in his power to save him, and that by saving him he might make him a very useful man, as he was well acquainted with all the Cheyenne and Arapahoe country, and he could be used as a guide or interpreter. Colonel Chivington replied to Major Anthony, as the Major himself told me, that he had no orders to receive and no advice to give. Major Anthony is now in this city.

By Mr. Buckalew:

Question. Did Chivington say anything to you, or you to him about the firing?

Answer. Nothing directly; there were a number of officers sitting around the fire, with the most of whom I was acquainted.

By Mr. Gooch:

Question. Were there any other Indians or half-breeds there at that time?

Answer. Yes, sir; Mr. Bent had three sons there; one employed as a guide for these troops at the time, and two others living there in the village with the Indians; and a Mr. Gerry had a son there.

Question. Were there any other murders after the first day's massacre?

Answer. There was none, except of my son.

Question. Were there any other atrocities which you have no mentioned?

Answer. None that I saw myself. There were two women that white men had families by ; they were saved from the fact of being in my lodge at the time. One ran to my lodge; the other was taken prisoner by a soldier who knew her and brought her to my lodge for safety. They both had children. There were some small children, six or seven years old, who were taken prisoners near the camp. I think there were three of them taken to Denver with these troops.

Question. Were the women and children that were killed, killed during the fight with the Indians?

Answer. During the fight, or during the time of the attack.

Question. Did you see any women or children killed after the fight was over?

Answer. None.

Question. Did you see any Indians killed after the fight was over?

Answer. No, sir.

By Mr. Buckalew:

Question. Were the warriors and women and children all huddled together when they were attacked?

Answer. They started and left the village altogether, in a body, trying to escape.

By Mr. Gooch:

Question. Do you know anything as to the amount of property that those Indians had there?

Answer. Nothing more than their horses. They were supposed to own ten horses and mules to a lodge; that would make about a thousand head of horses and mules in that camp. The soldiers drove off about six hundred head.

Question. Had they any money?

Answer. I understood that some of the soldiers found some money, but I did not see it. Mr. D. D. Colley had some provisions and goods in the village at the time, and Mr. Louderback and Mr. Watson were employed by him to trade there. I was to interpret for them, direct them, and see that they were cared for in the village. They had traded for one hundred and four buffalo robes, one fine mule, and two horses. This was all taken away from them. Colonel Chivington came to me and told me that I might rest assured that he would see the goods paid for. He had confiscated these buffalo robes for the dead and wounded; and there was also some sugar and coffee and tea taken for the same purpose.

I would state that in his report Colonel Chivington states that after this raid on Sand creek against the Cheyenne and Arapahoe Indians he traveled northeast some eighty miles in the direction of some hostile bands of Sioux Indians. Now that is very incorrect, according to my knowledge of matters; I remained with Colonel Chivington's camp, and returned on his trail towards Fort Lyon from the camp where he made this raid. I went down with him to what is called the forks of the Sandy. He then took a due south course for the Arkansas river, and I went to Fort Lyon with the killed and wounded, and an escort to take us in. Colonel Chivington proceeded down the Arkansas river, and got within eleven miles of another band of Arapahoe Indians, but did not succeed in overtaking them. He then returned to Fort Lyon, re-equipped, and started immediately for Denver.

Question. Have you spent any considerable portion of your life with the Indians?

Answer. The most of it.

Question. How many years have you been with the Indians?

Answer. I have been twenty-seven successive years with the Cheyennes and Arapahoes. Before that I was in the country as a trapper and hunter in the Rocky mountains.

Question. For how long time have you acted as Indian interpreter?

Answer. For some fifteen or eighteen years.

Question. By whom have you been so employed?

Answer. By Major Fitzpatrick, Colonel Bent, Major Colley, Colonel J.W. Whitfield, and a great deal of the time for the military as guide and interpreter.

By Mr. Buckalew:

Question. How many warriors were estimated in Colonel Chivington's report as having been in this Indian camp?

Answer. About nine hundred.

Question. How many were there?

Answer. About two hundred warriors; they average about two warriors to a lodge, and there were about one hundred lodges.

Testimony of Colonel J. M. Chivington, April 26, 1865

Interrogatories propounded to John M. Chivington by the Joint Committee on the Conduct of the War, and answers thereto given by said Chivington reduced to writing, and subscribed and sworn to before Alexander W. Atkins, notary public, at Denver, in the Territory of Colorado.

1st Question. What is your place of residence, your age and profession?

Answer. My place of residence is Denver, Colorado; my age, forty-five years; I have been colonel of 1st Colorado cavalry, and was mustered out of the service on or about the eighth day of January last, and have not been engaged in any business since that time.

2d question. Were you in November, 1864, in any employment, civil or military, under the authority of the United States; and if so, what was that employment, and what position did you hold?

Answer. In November, 1864, I was colonel of 1st Colorado cavalry, and in command of the district of Colorado.

3d question. Did you, as colonel in command of Colorado troops, about the 29th of November, 1864, make an attack on an Indian village or camp at a place known as Sand creek? If so, state particularly the number of men under your command; how armed and equipped; whether mounted or not; and if you had any artillery, state the number of guns, and the batteries to which they belonged.

Answer. On the 29th day of November, 1864, the troops under my command attacked a camp of Cheyenne and Arapaho Indians at a place known as Big Bend of Sandy, about forty miles north of Fort Lyon, Colorado Territory. There were in my command at that time about (500) five hundred men of the 3d regiment Colorado cavalry, under the immediate command of Colonel George L. Shoup, of said 3d regiment, and about (250) two hundred and fifty men of the 1st Colorado cavalry; Major Scott J. Anthony commanded one battalion of said 1st regiment, and Lieutenant Luther Wilson commanded another battalion of said 1st regiment. The 3d regiment was armed with rifled muskets, and Star's and Sharp's carbines. A few of the men of that regiment had revolvers. The men of the 1st regiment were armed with Star's and Sharp's carbines and revolvers. The men of the 3d regiment were poorly equipped; the supply of blankets, boots, hats, and caps was deficient. The men of the 1st regiment were well equipped; all these troops were mounted. I had four 12-pound mountain howitzers, manned by detachments from cavalry companies; they did not belong to any battery company.

4th question. State as nearly as you can the number of Indians that were in the village or camp at the time the attack was made; how many of them were warriors; how many of them were old men, how many of them were women, and how many of them were children?

Answer. From the best and most reliable information I could obtain, there were in the Indian camp, at the time of the attack, about eleven (11) or twelve (12) hundred Indians: of these about seven hundred were warriors, and the remainder were women and children. I am not aware that there were any old men among them. There was an unusual number of males among them, for the reason that the war chiefs of both nations were assembled there evidently for some special purpose.

5th question. At what time of the day or night was the attack made? Was it a surprise to the Indians? What preparation, if any, had they made for defence or offence?

Answer. The attack was made about sunrise. In my opinion the Indians were surprised; they be-

gan, as soon as the attack was made, to oppose my troops, however, and were soon fighting desperately. Many of the Indians were armed with rifles and many with revolvers; I think all had bows and arrows. They had excavated trenches under the bank of Sand creek, which in the vicinity of the Indian camp is high, and in many places precipitous. These trenches were two to three feet deep, and, in connexion with the banks, were evidently designed to protect the occupants from the fire of an enemy. They were found at various points extending along the banks of the creek for several miles from the camp; there were marks of the pick and shovel used in excavating them; and the fact that snow was seen in the bottoms of some of the trenches, while all snow had disappeared from the surface of the country generally, sufficiently proved that they had been constructed some time previously. The Indians took shelter in these trenches as soon as the attack was made, and from thence resisted the advance of my troops.

6th question. What number did you lose in killed, what number in wounded, and what number in missing?

Answer. There were seven men killed, forty-seven wounded, and one was missing.

7th question. What number of Indians were killed; and what number of the killed were women, and what number were children?

Answer. From the best information I could obtain, I judge there were five hundred or six hundred Indians killed; I cannot state positively the number killed, nor can I state positively the number of women and children killed. Officers who passed over the field, by my orders, after the battle, for the purpose of ascertaining the number of Indians killed, report that they saw but few women or children dead, no more than would certainly fall in an attack upon a camp in which they were. I myself passed over some portions of the field after the fight, and I saw but one woman who had been killed, and one who had hanged herself; I saw no dead children. From all I could learn, I arrived at the conclusion that but few women or children had been slain. I am of the opinion that when the attack was made on the Indian camp the greater number of squaws and children made their escape, while the warriors remained to fight my troops.

8th question. State, as nearly as you can, the number of Indians that were wounded, giving the number of women and the number of children among the wounded.

Answer. I do not know that any Indians were wounded that were not killed; if there were any wounded, I do not think they could have been made prisoners without endangering the lives of soldiers; Indians usually fight as long as they have strength to resist. Eight Indians fell into the hands of the troops alive, to my knowledge; these, with one exception, were sent to Fort Lyon and properly cared for.

9th question. What property was captured by the forces under your command? State the number of horses, mules and ponies, buffalo robes, blankets, and also all other property taken, specifying particularly the kinds, quality, and value thereof.

Answer. There were horses, mules, and ponies captured to the number of about six hundred. There were about one hundred buffalo robes taken. Some of this stock had been stolen by the Indians from the government during last spring, summer and fall, and some of the stock was the property of private citizens from whom they had been stolen during the same period. The horses that belonged to the government were returned to the officers responsible for them; as nearly as could be learned, the horses and mules that were owned by private citizens were returned to them on proof of ownership being furnished; such were my orders at least. The ponies, horses, and mules for which no owner could be found, were put into the hands of my provost marshal in the field, Captain J.J. Johnson, of company E, 3d Colorado cavalry, with instructions to drive them to Denver and turn them over to the acting quartermaster as captured stock, taking his receipt therefor. After I arrived in Denver I again directed Captain Johnson to turn these animals over to Captain Gorton, assistant quartermaster, as captured stock, which I presume he did. Colonel Thos. Moonlight relieved me of the command of the district soon after I arrived in Denver, that is to say, on the _____ day of _____, A.D. 186-, and I was mustered out of the service, the term of service

of my regiment having expired. My troops were not fully supplied with hospital equipage, having been on forced marches. The weather was exceedingly cold, and additional covering for the wounded became necessary; I ordered the buffalo robes to be used for that purpose. I know of no other property of value being captured. It is alleged that groceries were taken from John Smith, United States Indian interpreter for Upper Arkansas agency, who was in the Indian camp at the time of the attack, trading goods, powder, lead, cap, &c., to the Indians. Smith told me that these groceries belonged to Samuel G. Colby, United States Indian agent. I am not aware that these things were taken; I am aware that Smith and D.D. Colby, son of the Indian agent, have each presented claims against the government for these articles. The buffalo robes mentioned above were also claimed by Samuel G. Colby, D.D. Colby and John Smith. One bale of Buffalo robes was marked S. S. Soule, 1st Colorado cavalry, and I am informed that one bale was marked Anthony, Major Anthony being in command of Fort Lyon at that time. I cannot say what has been done with the property since I was relieved of the command and mustered out of service. There was a large quantity of Indian trinkets taken at the Indian camp which were of no value. The soldiers retained a few of these as trophies; the remainder with the Indian lodges were destroyed.

10th question. What reason had you for making the attack? What reasons, if any, had you to believe that Black Kettle or any other Indian or Indians in the camp entertained feelings of hostility towards the whites? Give in detail the names of all Indians so believed to be hostile, with the dates and places of their hostile acts, so far as you may be able to do so.

Answer. My reason for making the attack on the Indian camp was, that I believed the Indians in the camp were hostile to the whites. That they were of the same tribes with those who had murdered many persons and destroyed much valuable property on the Platte and Arkansas rivers during the previous spring, summer and fall was beyond a doubt. When a tribe of Indians is at war with the whites it is impossible to determine what party or band of the tribe or the name of the Indian or Indians belonging to the tribe so at war are guilty of the acts of hostility. The most that can be ascertained is that Indians of the tribe have performed the acts. During the spring, summer and fall of the year 1864, the Arapaho and Cheyenne Indians, in some instances assisted or led on by Sioux, Kiowas, Comanches and Apaches, had committed many acts of hostility in the country lying between the Little Blue and the Rocky mountains and the Platte and Arkansas rivers. They had murdered many of the whites and taken others prisoners, and had destroyed valuable property, probably amounting to $200,000 or $300,000. Their rendezvous was on the headwaters of the Republican, probably one hundred miles from where the Indian camp was located. I had every reason to believe that these Indians were either directly or indirectly concerned in the outrages which had been committed upon the whites. I had no means of ascertaining what were the names of the Indians who had committed these outrages other than the declarations of the Indians themselves; and the character of Indians in the western country for truth and veracity, like their respect for the chastity of women who may become prisoners in their hands, is not of that order which is calculated to inspire confidence in what they may say. In this view I was supported by Major Anthony, 1st Colorado cavalry, commanding at Fort Lyon, and Samuel G. Colby, United States Indian agent, who, as they had been in communication with these Indians, were more competent to judge of their disposition towards the whites than myself. Previous to the battle they expressed to me the opinion that the Indians should be punished. We found in the camp the scalps of nineteen (19) white persons. One of the surgeons informed me that one of these scalps had been taken from the victim's head not more than four days previously. I can furnish a child captured at the camp ornamented with six white women's scalps; these scalps must have been taken by these Indians or furnished to them for their gratification and amusement by some of their brethren, who, like themselves, were in amity with the whites.

11th question. Had you any, and if so, what reason, to believe that Black Kettle and the Indians with him, at the time of your attack, were at peace with the whites, and desired to remain at peace with them?

Answer. I had no reason to believe that Black Kettle and the Indians with him were in good faith at peace with the whites. The day before the attack Major Scott J. Anthony, 1st Colorado cavalry, then in command at Fort Lyon, told me that these Indians were hostile; that he had ordered his sentinels to fire on them if they attempted to come into the post, and that the sentinels had fired on them; that he was apprehensive of an attack from these Indians, and had taken every precaution to prevent a surprise. Major Samuel G. Colby, United States Indian agent for these Indians, told me on the same day that he had done everything in his power to make them behave themselves, and that for the last six months he could do nothing with them; that nothing but a sound whipping would bring a lasting peace with them. These statements were made to me in the presence of the officers of my staff whose statements can be obtained to corroborate the foregoing.

12th question. Had you reason to know or believe that these Indians had sent their chief and leading men at any time to Denver city in order to take measure in connection with the superintendent of Indian affairs there, or with any other person having authority, to secure friendly relations with the whites?

Answer. I was present at an interview between Governor Evans on the part of the whites, and Black Kettle and six other Indians, at Camp Weldmar, Denver, about 27th of September, 1864, in which the Indians desired peace, but did not propose terms. General Curtis, by telegraph to me, declined to make peace with them, and said that there could be no peace without his consent. Governor Evans declined to treat with them, and as General Curtis was then in command of the department, and, of course, I could not disobey his instructions. General Curtis's terms of peace were to require all bad Indians to be given by the Indians for their good conduct. The Indians never complied with these terms.

13th question. Were those Indians, to your knowledge, referred by the superintendent of Indian affairs to the military authorities, as the only power under the government to afford them protection?

Answer. Governor Evans, in the conference mentioned in my last answer, did not refer the Indians to the Military authorities for protection, but for terms of peace. He told the Indians "that he was the peace chief, that they had gone to war, and, therefore, must deal with the war chiefs." It was at this time I gave them the terms of General Curtis, and they said they had not received power to make peace on such terms, that they would report to their young men and see what they would say to it; they would like to do it, but if their young men continued the war they would have to go with them. They said there were three or four small war parties of their young men out on the war path against the whites at that time. This ended the talk.

14th question. Did the officer in command of Fort Lyon, to your knowledge, at any time extend the protection of our flag to Black Kettle and Indians with him, and direct them to encamp upon the reservation of the fort?

Answer. Major E.W. Wynkoop, 1st cavalry, Colorado, did, as I have been informed, allow some of these Indians to camp at or near Fort Lyon, and did promise them the protection of our flag. Subsequently he was relieved of the command of Fort Lyon, and Major Anthony placed in command at that post, who required the Indians to comply with General Curtis's terms, which they failed to do, and thereupon Major Anthony drove them away from the post.

15th question. Were rations ever issued to those Indians either as prisoners of war or otherwise?

Answer. I have been informed that Major Wynkoop issued rations to the Indians encamped near Fort Lyon while he was in command, but whether as prisoners of war I do not know. I think that Major Anthony did not issue any rations.

16th question. And did those Indians remove, in pursuance of the directions, instructions, or suggestions of the commandant at Fort Lyon, to the place on Sand creek, where they were attacked by you?

Answer. I have been informed that Major Anthony, commandant at Fort Lyon, did order the Indians to remove from that post, but I am not aware that they were ordered to go to the place where the battle was fought, or to any other place.

17th question. What measures were taken by you, at any time, to render the attack on those Indians a surprise?

Answer. I took every precaution to render the attack upon the Indians a surprise, for the reason that we had been able to catch them, and it appeared to me that the only way to deal with them was to surprise them in their place of rendezvous. General Curtis, in his campaign against them, had failed to catch them; General Mitchel had met with no better success; General Blunt had been surprised by them, and his command nearly cut to pieces.

18th question. State in detail the disposition made of the various articles of property, horses, mules, ponies, buffalo robes, &c., captured by you at the time of this attack and by what authority was such disposition made?

Answer. The horses and mules that had been stolen from the government were turned over to the officer who had been responsible for the same; and the animals belonging to Atzins was returned to them upon proof being made of such ownership. The animals not disposed of in this way were turned over to Captain S.J. Johnson, 3d regiment Colorado cavalry, with instructions to proceed with the same to Denver, and turn them into the quartermaster's department. After the command arrived in Denver, I again directed Captain Johnson to turn over the stock to Captain C.L. Gorton, assistant quartermaster, at that place. The buffalo robes were turned into the hospital for use of the wounded as before stated.

19th question. Make such further statement as you may desire, or which may be necessary to a full understanding of all matters relating to the attack upon the Indians at Sand creek.

Answer. Since August, 1863, I had been in possession of the most conclusive evidence of the alliance, for the purposes of hostility against the whites, of the Sioux, Cheyennes, Arapahoes, Comanche River, and Apache Indians. Their plan was to interrupt, or, if possible, entirely prevent all travel on the routes along the Arkansas and Platte rivers from the States to the Rocky mountains, and thereby depopulate this country. Rebel emissaries were long since sent among the Indians to incite them against the whites, and afford a medium of communication between the rebels and the Indians; among whom was Gerry Bent, a half-breed Cheyenne Indian, but educated, and to all appearances a white man, who, having served under Price in Missouri, and afterwards becoming a bushwacker, being taken prisoner, took the oath of allegiance, and was paroled, after which he immediately joined the Indians, and has ever since been one of their most prominent leaders in all depredations upon the whites. I have been reliably informed that this half-breed, Bent, in order to incite the Indians against the whites, told them that the Great Father at Washington having all he could do to fight his children at the south, they could now regain their country.

When John Evans, governor of Colorado Territory, and ex officio superintendent of Indian affairs, visited by appointment the Cheyenne Indians on the Republican fork of the Kansas river, to talk with them in regard to their relations with the government, the Indians would have nothing to say to him, nor would they receive the presents sent them by the government, but immediately on his arrival at the said point the Indians moved to a great distance, all their villages appearing determined not to have any intercourse with him individually or as the agent of the government.

This state of affairs continued for a number of months, during which time white men who had been trading with the Indians informed me that the Indians had determined to make war upon the whites as soon as the grass was green, and that they were making preparations for such an event by the large number of arrows they were making and the quantity of arms and ammunition they were collecting; that the settlers along the Platte and Arkansas rivers should be warned of the approaching danger; that the Indians had declared their intention to prosecute the war vigorously when they commenced. With very few troops at my command I could do but little to protect the settlers except to collect the latest intelligence from the Indians' country, communicate it to General Curtis, commanding department of Missouri, and warn the settlers of relations existing between the Indians and the whites, and the probability trouble, all of which I did.

Last April, 1864, the Indians, Cheyennes, Arapahoes, and others, commenced their depredations upon the whites by entering their isolated habitations in the distant parts of this territory, taking therefrom everything they desired, and destroying the balance; driving off their stock, horses, mules and cattle. I sent a detachment of troops after the Indians to recover the stolen property, when the stock &c., being demanded of them they (the Indians) refused to surrender the property so taken from the whites, and stated that they wanted to fight the troops. Again, when a few weeks after the country along the Platte river, near Fremont's orchard, became the theatre of their depredations, one Ripley, a ranchman, living on the Bijon creek, near camp Sanborn, came into camp and informed Captain Sanborn, commanding, that his stock had all been stolen by the Indians, requesting assistance to recover it. Captain Sanborn ordered Lieutenant Clark Dunn, with a detachment of troops, to pursue the Indians and recover the stock; but, if possible, to avoid a collision with them. Upon approaching the Indians, Lieutenant Dunn dismounted, walked forward alone about fifty paces from his command, and requested the Indians to return the stock, which Mr. Ripley had recognized as his; but the Indians treated him with contempt, and commenced firing upon him, which resulted in four of the troops being wounded and about fifteen Indians being killed and wounded, Lieutenant Dunn narrowly escaping with his life. Again, about one hundred and seventy-five head of cattle were stolen from Messrs. Irwin and Jackman, government freighters, when troops were sent in pursuit toward the headwaters of the Republican. They were fired upon by the Indians miles from where the Indians were camped. In this encounter the Indians killed one soldier and wounded another. Again, when the troops were near the Smoky Hill, after stock, while passing through a canon, about eighty miles from Fort Larned, they were attacked by these same Cheyenne Indians, and others, and almost cut to pieces, there being about fifteen hundred Indians. Again, when on a Sunday morning the Kiowas and Camanches were at Fort Larned, to obtain the rations that the commanding officer, on behalf of the government, was issuing to them, they, at a preconcerted signal, fired upon the sentinels at the fort, making a general attack upon the unsuspecting garrison, while the balance of the Indians were driving off the stock belonging to the government, and then as suddenly departed, leaving the garrison afoot excepting about thirty artillery horses that were saved; thus obtaining in all about two hundred and eighty head of stock, including a small herd taken from the suttler at that post.

Again, a few days after this, the Cheyennes and Arapahoes Indians, with whom I had the fight at Sand creek, meeting a government train bound for New Mexico, thirty miles east of Fort Larned, at Walnut creek, who, after manifesting a great deal of friendship by shaking hands, &c., with every person in the train, suddenly attacked them, killing fourteen and wounding a number more scalping and mutilating in the most inhuman manner those they killed, while they scalped two of this party alive, one a boy about fourteen years of age, who has since become an imbecile. The two persons that were scalped alive I saw a few days after this occurred within sight of Fort Zarah, the officer commanding considered his command entirely inadequate to render any assistance. But we think we have related enough to satisfy the most incredulous of the determined hostility of these Indians; suffice it to say that during the spring, summer, and fall such atrocious acts were of almost daily occurrence along the Platte and Arkansas routes, till the Indians becoming so bold that a family, consisting of a man, woman, and two children, by the name of Hungate, were brutally murdered and scalped within fifteen miles of Denver, the bodies being brought to Denver for interment. After seeing which, any person who could for a moment believe that these Indians were friendly, to say the least, must have strange ideas of their habits. We could not see it in that light.

This last atrocious act was referred to by Governor Evans in his talk with the Cheyennes and Arapahoes Indians on about the 27th day of September, 1864, at Denver, Colorado Territory. The Indians then stated that it had been dome by members of their tribe, and that they never denied it. All these things were promptly reported to Major General S. R. Curtis, commanding department, who repeatedly ordered me, regardless of district lines, to appropriately chastise the Indians, which I always endeav-

ored to do. Major General S. R. Curtis himself and Brigadeer General R. B. Mitchell made campaigns against the Indians, but could not find them; the Indians succeeded in keeping entirely from their view. Again, Major General J. P. Blunt made a campaign against the Indians; was surprised by them, and a portion of his command nearly cut to pieces.

Commanding only a district with very few troops under my control, with hundreds of miles between my headquarters and rendezvous of the Indians, with a large portion of the Sante Fe and Platte routes, besides the sparsely settled and distant settlements of this Territory, to protect, I could not do anything till the 3d regiment was organized and equipped, when I determined to strike a blow against this savage and determined foe. When I reached Fort Lyon, after passing over from three to five feet of snow, and greatly suffering from the intensity of the cold, the thermometer ranging from 28 to 30 degrees below zero, I questioned Major Anthony in regard to the whereabouts of hostile Indians. He said there was a camp of Cheyennes and Arapahoes about fifty miles distant; that he would have attacked before, but did not consider his force sufficient; that these Indians had threatened to attack the post, &c., and ought to be whipped, all of which was concurred in by Major Colley, Indian agent for the district of the Arkansas, which information, with the positive orders from Major General Curtis, commanding the department, to punish these Indians, decided my course, and resulted in the battle of Sand Creek, which has created such a sensation in Congress through the lying reports of interested and malicious parties.

On my arrival at Fort Lyon, in all my conversations with Major Anthony, commanding the post, and Major Colley, Indian agent, I heard nothing of this recent statement that the Indians were under the protection of the government, &c., but Major Anthony repeatedly stated to me that he had at different times fired upon these Indians, and that they were hostile, and, during my stay at Fort Lyon, urged the necessity of any immediately attacking the Indians before they could learn of the number of troops at Fort Lyon, and so desirous was Major Colly, Indian agent, that I should find and also attack the Arapahoes, that he sent a messenger after the fight at Sand creek, nearly forty miles, to inform me where I could find the Arapahoes and Kiowas; yet, strange to say, I have learned recently that these men, Anthony and Colly, are the most bitter in their denunciations of the attack upon the Indians at Sand creek. Therefore, I would, in conclusion, most respectfully demand, as an act of justice to myself and the brave men whom I have had the honor to command in one of the hardest campaigns ever made in this country, whether against white men or red, that we be allowed that right guaranteed to every American citizen, of introducing evidence in our behalf to sustain us in what we believe to have been an act of duty to ourselves and to civilization.

We simply ask to introduce as witnesses men that were present during the campaign and know all the facts.

J.M. CHIVINGTON,
Lieu't Col. 1st Cavalry of Colerado [sic], Com'd'g Dist. of Colerado [sic].
Sworn and subscribed to before me this 26th day of April, 1865.
ALEXANDER W. ATKINS,
Notary Public.

GLOSSARY

bosh: Nonsense, a ridiculous falsehood

depredations: Violent attacks usually involving plundering and theft

pickets: A small group of soldiers placed on the edge of an area to act as an advance guard and provide warning of enemy activities

Document Analysis

The editorial offends modern sensibilities, for it boasts about the victory. The opening sentence refers to "brilliant feats of arms in Indian warfare." The editorial goes on to narrate recent events concerning the movements of the Colorado militia and its arrival at Fort Lyon. It then presents a thoroughly one-sided description of the battle, even to the extent of suggesting that the Indians mounted a credible defense "that told terribly against our ranks" and that the chiefs "fought with unparalleled bravery." The editorial concludes that the "Colorado soldiers have again covered themselves with glory." Significantly, the author claims that, due to the number of chiefs supposedly killed, that the Cheyenne tribe "is almost annihilated."

The second editorial, again from the *Rocky Mountain News* and dated December 30, 1864, indignantly responds to calls for a congressional investigation of the massacre. The newspaper states that any talk of "friendly Indians" is "all bosh." The editorial calls attention to the murders of white settlers at the hands of Indians, and it rejects the notion that the Indians were trying to surrender. Sand Creek, the editorial says, was the "rendezvous of the thieving and marauding bands of savages who roamed over this country last summer and fall." The author's sarcastic tone tells us a great deal of the attitudes of westerners—many of whom saw themselves as being in significant danger—toward politicians in the eastern part of the country, particularly those in power in Washington. The author also implies that those attempting to portray the natives as friendly had some sort of financial benefit in doing so, hinting at a conspiracy.

The third document is from the congressional testimony of John S. Smith on March 14, 1865. Smith, as an Indian interpreter and special Indian agent, was a witness to the attack, having arrived at Sand Creek the previous day. In sober language, he describes what he witnessed. At one point, he says, a band of about a hundred Indians were surrounded: "The soldiers continued firing on these Indians, who numbered about a hundred, until they had almost completely destroyed them. I think I saw altogether some seventy dead bodies lying there; the greater portion women and children." Smith then discusses the events that led up to the attack and to the presence of the Indians at Sand Creek. Smith reports that when Chivington asked him to identify the chiefs who were attacked, he could not:

"They were terribly mutilated, lying there in the water and sand; most of them in the bed of the creek, dead and dying, making many struggles. They were so badly mutilated and covered with sand and water that it was very hard for me to tell one from another." He says that the Indians were killed "indiscriminately" and details acts of barbarism and mutilation. Smith's own teenage son, Jack, who was half Cheyenne, was murdered on the night of the massacre. The members of the committee who question Smith do draw attention to the fact that, in some cases, his testimony relied on hearsay.

The final document consists of written answers Chivington gave to questions submitted to him by the congressional committee. Chivington's responses create a very different picture from that of Smith. He describes the campaign from the point of view of a military man planning and executing a military operation with the support of his superiors. When asked what motivated the attack, he responds that the Indians "were of the same tribes with those who had murdered many persons and destroyed much valuable property on the Platte and Arkansas rivers during the previous spring, summer and fall." He later writes that "since August, 1863, I had been in possession of the most conclusive evidence of the alliance, for the purposes of hostility against the whites, of the Sioux, Cheyennes, Arapahoes, Comanche River, and Apache Indians." In his view, and in the view of many Coloradans, the attack was justified and a necessary step in the effort to quell Indian violence.

Essential Themes

One of the key concepts that is laid out very well in this selection of documents is the story of American westward expansion is often considerably more complex than traditional narratives presented. Far from being a simple story of settlers versus Native Americans, the historical evidence presents a narrative that is, honestly, complex and often confusing. Settlers exploited rivalries between Native tribes for their own benefit; some settlers felt threatened by the (often very real) threat of violence against them by Natives, while other whites sought not military domination but commercial exploitation of both settlers and Natives (as demonstrated by the conspiratorial tone of the second *Rocky Mountain News* editorial). Chivington's testimony illustrates the ambiguous position of many military leaders—charged with protecting white settlers from Native attacks, they also had within that a broader responsibility to keep the peace. Too often, however, this "peace" was defined as the elimination of Native opposition.

To add to the complexity of the situation, the west did not exist in a vacuum. Political and business leaders (eyeing prospects for railroad expansion, mining and agriculture) had a vested interest in promoting some kind of stability on the "frontier" resulting in the previously discussed ambiguous position in which many soldiers and officers found themselves.

Regardless of the complexity of the situation in the American west, these documents also illustrate the racism and bloodlust that was key factor in white settlement. The *Rocky Mountain News* editorials, in particular, stubbornly refuse to acknowledge the nuance of the situation, implying that anyone who believed the victims at Sand Creed to be friendly was either ignorant, a liar, or corrupt.

———*Michael J. O'Neal, PhD*

Bibliography and Additional Reading

Brown, Dee. *Bury My Heart at Wounded Knee: An Indian History of the American West.* (New York: Picador, 2007)

Hine, Robert V. and John Mack Faragher. *The American West: A New Interpretive History.* (New Haven, Connecticut: Yale University Press, 2000)

Kelman, Ari. *A Misplaced Massacre: Struggling Over the Memory of Sand Creek.* (Cambridge, MA: Harvard University Press, 2013).

Michno, Gregory. *The Three Battles of Sand Creek: The Cheyenne Massacre in Blood, in Court, and as the End of History.* (El Dorado Hills, California: Savas Beatie, 2017).

■ Treaty of Fort Laramie

Date: 1868
Author: Indian Peace Commission
Genre: Treaty

Summary Overview

The Treaty of Fort Laramie (1868) was an agreement between the United States and various bands of Lakota Sioux, Yanktonai Sioux, Santee Sioux, and Arapaho. The treaty ended Red Cloud's War (1866–1867), established the boundaries of the Great Sioux Reservation, and protected Sioux hunting grounds and the sacred Black Hills from white encroachment. Other provisions of the Treaty of Fort Laramie served as agents of assimilation by trying to induce the Indians to take up farming, wear non-Indian clothing, and educate their children.

The Treaty of Fort Laramie was one of the last great treaties signed between the American government and the Plains Indians. Despite the peaceful intentions of the treaty, the unwillingness of the federal government to live up to its stipulations and the inability of the signing tribes to enforce the treaty on all their members resulted in the Great Sioux War (also known as the Black Hills War) of 1876–1877 and the eventual removal of the Black Hills from Lakota ownership.

Defining Moment

The United States acquired the Great Plains via the Louisiana Purchase of 1803. The region was largely ignored until the 1840s. Beginning in the 1840s, however, overland emigrants began traveling through Plains Indian hunting grounds. The discovery of gold in California in 1848 opened the floodgates, and over the next few decades almost 500,000 people traversed the plains on their way to the Pacific Coast. The Plains Indians felt this increased traffic through the depletion of vital resources such as bison. More tragically, epidemic diseases such as cholera and smallpox were spread to the Plains Indians. Naturally, tribes such as the Lakota and Cheyenne attempted to protect their homeland.

By the summer of 1867 American civilian and military authorities were at odds over what had become known as the "Indian problem." Military leaders such as General William Tecumseh Sherman firmly believed that the warring tribes must be militarily subdued and that only a thorough defeat of the Plains Indians would bring peace. On the other hand, an emerging reform movement that would evolve into President Ulysses S. Grant's "peace policy" began placing the blame for hostilities on the federal government and therefore sought a negotiated peace rather than the forced peace the military preferred.

After treating with the Southern Plains tribes, the commission moved back to negotiations with the Northern Plains tribes at Fort Laramie. On April 29, 1868, twenty-five chiefs and headmen of the Brulé Lakota signed the Treaty of Fort Laramie. A month later, thirty leaders among the Oglala also signed the treaty. Red Cloud, however, refused to come in and talk, and without his signature the work of the commission would have been considered a failure. Finally, when Red Cloud received word that the Bozeman Trail would be closed and the Powder River military posts would be abandoned, he, along with Lakota chiefs from the Hunkpapa, Blackfeet, Cuthead, Two Kettle, and Sans Arc tribes signed the Treaty of Fort Laramie. Noticeably missing were the signatures of the staunch Lakota nationalists Crazy Horse of the Oglala and Sitting Bull of the Hunkpapa. The failure to obtain the signatures of all Lakota leaders would create friction in the near future.

Author Biography

Members of the Indian Peace Commission most likely authored the Treaty of Fort Laramie. A government investigation into Indian affairs in the wake of the Fetterman massacre concluded that the recent hostilities were the result of flagrant treaty violations by the government. As a consequence, Congress interjected itself and created the Indian Peace Commission in July 1867. President Andrew Johnson ordered the commission to negotiate with the warring tribes, bring an end to hostilities, and concentrate the tribes on one of several large reservations in the western half of modern-day South Dakota and Oklahoma. The commission was headed by the commissioner of Indian affairs Nathaniel G. Taylor, who was also a Methodist minister, lawyer, and close personal friend of President Johnson's. It would be his job to rein in the veteran military officers who also served on the commission:

General Sherman along with the generals William S. Harney, Alfred H. Terry, and C. C. Auger. Other civilian members included Samuel F. Tappan, a leading reformer and former abolitionist; John B. Sanborn; and J. B. Henderson. The commission was headed by Commissioner of Indian Affairs Nathaniel G. Taylor and included three other civilians: Samuel F. Tappan, a leading reformer and former abolitionist; John B. Sanborn; and J. B. Henderson. Sanborn stood out among the Sioux as being an important part of the treaty negotiations. The military was represented by four veteran officers: generals William T. Sherman, William S. Harney, Alfred H. Terry, and C. C. Auger. Harney was well known to the Lakota. Known as "Mad Bear" in Lakota culture, Harney had attacked Little Thunder's Brulé village in 1855.

HISTORICAL DOCUMENT

Articles of a Treaty Made and Concluded by and between Lieutenant General William T. Sherman, General William S. Harney, General Alfred H. Terry, General O. O. Augur, J. B. Henderson, Nathaniel G. Taylor, John G. Sanborn, and Samuel F. Tappan, duly appointed commissioners on the part of the United States, and the different bands of the Sioux Nation of Indians, by their chiefs and headmen, whose names are hereto subscribed, they being duly authorized to act in the premises.

Article I.

From this day forward all war between the parties to this agreement shall for ever cease. The government of the United States desires peace, and its honor is hereby pledged to keep it. The Indians desire peace, and they now pledge their honor to maintain it.

If bad men among the whites, or among other people subject to the authority of the United States, shall commit any wrong upon the person or property of the Indians, the United States will, upon proof made to the agent, and forwarded to the Commissioner of Indian Affairs at Washington city, proceed at once to cause the offender to be arrested and punished according to the laws of the United States, and also reimburse the injured person for the loss sustained.

If bad men among the Indians shall commit a wrong or depredation upon the person or property of nay one, white, black, or Indian, subject to the authority of the United States, and at peace therewith, the Indians herein named solemnly agree that they will, upon proof made to their agent, and notice by him, deliver up the wrongdoer to the United States, to be tried and punished according to its laws, and, in case they willfully refuse so to do, the person injured shall be reimbursed for his loss from the annuities, or other moneys due or to become due to them under this or other treaties made with the United States; and the President, on advising with the Commissioner of Indian Affairs, shall prescribe such rules and regulations for ascertaining damages under the provisions of this article as in his judgment may be proper, but no one sustaining loss while violating the provisions of this treaty, or the laws of the United States, shall be reimbursed therefor.

Article II.

The United States agrees that the following district of country, to wit, viz: commencing on the east bank of the Missouri river where the 46th parallel of north latitude crosses the same, thence along low-water mark down said east bank to a point opposite where the northern line of the State of Nebraska strikes the river, thence west across said river, and along the northern line of Nebraska to the 104th degree of longitude west from Greenwich, thence north on said meridian to a point where the 46th parallel of north latitude intercepts the same, thence due east along said parallel to the place of beginning; and in addition thereto, all existing reservations of the east back of said river, shall be and the same is, set apart for the absolute and undisturbed use and occupation of the Indians herein named, and for such other friendly tribes or individual Indians as from time to time they may be willing, with the consent of the United States, to admit amongst them; and the United States now solemnly agrees that no persons, except those herein designated and authorized so to do, and except such officers, agents, and employees of the government as may be authorized to enter upon Indian reservations in discharge of duties enjoined by law, shall ever be permitted to pass over, settle upon, or reside in the territory described in this article, or in such territory as may be added to this reservation for the use of said Indians, and henceforth they will and do hereby relinquish all claims or right in and to any portion of the United States or Territories, except such as is embraced within the limits aforesaid, and except as hereinafter provided.

Article III.

If it should appear from actual survey or other satisfactory examination of said tract of land that it contains less than 160 acres of tillable land for each person who, at the time, may be authorized to reside on it under the provisions of this treaty, and a very considerable number of such persons shall be disposed to commence cultivating the soil as farmers, the United States agrees to set apart, for the use of said Indians, as herein provided, such additional quantity of arable land, adjoining to said reservation, or as near to the same as it can be obtained, as may be required to provide the necessary amount.

Article IV.

The United States agrees, at its own proper expense, to construct, at some place on the Missouri river, near the centre of said reservation where timber and water may be convenient, the following buildings, to wit, a warehouse, a store-room for the use of the agent in storing goods belonging to the Indians, to cost not less than $2,500; an agency building, for the residence of the agent, to cost not exceeding $3,000; a residence for the physician, to cost not more than $3,000; and five other buildings, for a carpenter, farmer, blacksmith, miller, and engineer-each to cost not exceeding $2,000; also, a school-house, or mission building, so soon as a sufficient number of children can be induced

by the agent to attend school, which shall not cost exceeding $5,000.

The United States agrees further to cause to be erected on said reservation, near the other buildings herein authorized, a good steam circular saw-mill, with a grist-mill and shingle machine attached to the same, to cost not exceeding $8,000.

Article V.

The United States agrees that the agent for said Indians shall in the future make his home at the agency building; that he shall reside among them, and keep an office open at all times for the purpose of prompt and diligent inquiry into such matters of complaint by and against the Indians as may be presented for investigation under the provisions of their treaty stipulations, as also for the faithful discharge of other duties enjoined on him by law. In all cases of depredation on person or property he shall cause the evidence to be taken in writing and forwarded, together with his findings, to the Commissioner of Indian Affairs, whose decision, subject to the revision of the Secretary of the Interior, shall be binding on the parties to this treaty.

Article VI.

If any individual belonging to said tribes of Indians, or legally incorporated with them, being the head of a family, shall desire to commence farming, he shall have the privilege to select, in the presence and with the assistance of the agent then in charge, a tract of land within said reservation, not exceeding three hundred and twenty acres in extent, which tract, when so selected, certified, and recorded in the "Land Book" as herein directed, shall cease to be held in common, but the same may be occupied and held in the exclusive possession of the person selecting it, and of his family, so long as he or they may continue to cultivate it.

Any person over eighteen years of age, not being the head of a family, may in like manner select and cause to be certified to him or her, for purposes of cultivation, a quantity of land, not exceeding eighty acres in extent, and thereupon be entitled to the exclusive possession of the same as above directed.

For each tract of land so selected a certificate, containing a description thereof and the name of the person selecting it, with a certificate endorsed thereon that the same has been recorded, shall be delivered to the party entitled to it, by the agent, after the same shall have been recorded by him in a book to be kept in his office, subject to inspection, which said book shall be known as the "Sioux Land Book."

The President may, at any time, order a survey of the reservation, and, when so surveyed, Congress shall provide for protecting the rights of said settlers in their improvements, and may fix the character of the title held by each. The United States may pass such laws on the subject of alienation and descent of property between the Indians and their descendants as may be thought proper. And it is further stipulated that any male Indians over eighteen years of age, of any band or tribe that is or shall hereafter become a party to this treaty, who now is or who shall hereafter become a resident or occupant of any reservation or territory not included in the tract of country designated and described in this treaty for the permanent home of the Indians, which is not mineral land, nor reserved by the United States for special purposes other than Indian occupation, and who shall have made improvements thereon of the value of two hundred dollars or more, and continuously occupied the same as a homestead for the term of three years, shall be entitled to receive from the United States a patent for one hundred and sixty acres of land including his said improvements, the same to be in the form of the legal subdivisions of the surveys of the public lands. Upon application in writing, sustained by the proof of two disinterested witnesses, made to the register of the local land office when the land sought to be entered is within a land district, and when the tract sought to be entered is not in any land district, then upon said application and proof being made to the Commissioner of the General Land Office, and the right of such Indian or Indians to enter such tract or tracts of land shall accrue and be perfect from the date of his first improvements thereon, and shall continue as long as be continues his residence and improvements and no longer. And any Indian or Indians receiving a patent for land

under the foregoing provisions shall thereby and from thenceforth become and be a citizen of the United States and be entitled to all the privileges and immunities of such citizens, and shall, at the same time, retain all his rights to benefits accruing to Indians under this treaty.

Article VII.

In order to insure the civilization of the Indians entering into this treaty, the necessity of education is admitted, especially of such of them as are or may be settled on said agricultural reservations, and they, therefore, pledge themselves to compel their children, male and female, between the ages of six and sixteen years, to attend school, and it is hereby made the duty of the agent for said Indians to see that this stipulation is strictly complied with; and the United States agrees that for every thirty children between said ages, who can be induced or compelled to attend school, a house shall be provided, and a teacher competent to teach the elementary branches of an English education shall be furnished, who will reside among said Indians and faithfully discharge his or her duties as a teacher. The provisions of this article to continue for not less than twenty years.

Article VIII.

When the head of a family or lodge shall have selected lands and received his certificate as above directed, and the agent shall be satisfied that he intends in good faith to commence cultivating the soil for a living, he shall be entitled to receive seeds and agricultural implements for the first year, not exceeding in value one hundred dollars, and for each succeeding year he shall continue to farm, for a period of three years more, he shall be entitled to receive seeds and implements as aforesaid, not exceeding in value twenty-five dollars. And it is further stipulated that such persons as commence farming shall receive instruction from the farmer herein provided for, and whenever more than one hundred persons shall enter upon the cultivation of the soil, a second blacksmith shall be provided, with such iron, steel, and other material as may be needed.

Article IX.

At any time after ten years from the making of this treaty, the United States shall have the privilege of withdrawing the physician, farmer, blacksmith, carpenter, engineer, and miller herein provided for, but in case of such withdrawal, an additional sum thereafter of ten thousand dollars per annum shall be devoted to the education of said Indians, and the Commissioner of Indian Affairs shall, upon careful inquiry into their condition, make such rules and regulations for the expenditure of said sums as will best promote the education and moral improvement of said tribes.

Article X.

In lieu of all sums of money or other annuities provided to be paid to the Indians herein named under any treaty or treaties heretofore made, the United States agrees to deliver at the agency house on the reservation herein named, on or before the first day of August of each year, for thirty years, the following articles, to wit:

For each male person over 14 years of age, a suit of good substantial woollen clothing, consisting of coat, pantaloons, flannel shirt, hat, and a pair of home-made socks.

For each female over 12 years of age, a flannel shirt, or the goods necessary to make it, a pair of woollen hose, 12 yards of calico, and 12 yards of cotton domestics.

For the boys and girls under the ages named, such flannel and cotton goods as may be needed to make each a suit as aforesaid, together with a pair of woollen hose for each.

And in order that the Commissioner of Indian Affairs may be able to estimate properly for the articles herein named, it shall be the duty of the agent each year to forward to him a full and exact census of the Indians, on which the estimate from year to year can be based.

And in addition to the clothing herein named, the sum of $10 for each person entitled to the beneficial effects of this treaty shall be annually appropriated for a period of 30 years, while such persons roam and hunt, and $20 for each person who engages in farming, to be used by the Secretary of the Interior in the purchase of such articles as from time to time the condition and necessities of the Indians may indicate to be proper. And if within the 30 years, at any time, it shall appear that the amount of money needed for clothing, under this article, can be appropriated to better uses for the Indians named herein, Congress may, by law, change the appropriation to other purposes, but in no event shall the amount of the appropriation be withdrawn or discontinued for the period named. And the President shall annually detail an officer of the army to be present and attest the delivery of all the goods herein named, to the Indians, and he shall inspect and report on the quantity and quality of the goods and the manner of their delivery. And it is hereby expressly stipulated that each Indian over the age of four years, who shall have removed to and settled permanently upon said reservation, one pound of meat and one pound of flour per day, provided the Indians cannot furnish their own subsistence at an earlier date. And it is further stipulated that the United States will furnish and deliver to each lodge of Indians or family of persons legally incorporated with the, who shall remove to the reservation herein described and commence farming, one good American cow, and one good well-broken pair of American oxen within 60 days after such lodge or family shall have so settled upon said reservation.

Article XI.

In consideration of the advantages and benefits conferred by this treaty and the many pledges of friendship by the United States, the tribes who are parties to this agreement hereby stipulate that they will relinquish all right to occupy permanently the territory outside their reservations as herein defined, but yet reserve the right to hunt on any lands north of North Platte, and on the Republican Fork of the Smoky Hill river, so long as the buffalo may range thereon in such numbers as to justify the chase. And they, the said Indians, further expressly agree:

1st. That they will withdraw all opposition to the construction of the railroads now being built on the plains.

2d. That they will permit the peaceful construction of any railroad not passing over their reservation as herein defined.

3d. That they will not attack any persons at home, or travelling, nor molest or disturb any wagon trains, coaches, mules, or cattle belonging to the people of the United States, or to persons friendly therewith.

4th. They will never capture, or carry off from the settlements, white women or children.

5th. They will never kill or scalp white men, nor attempt to do them harm.

6th. They withdraw all pretence of opposition to the construction of the railroad now being built along the Platte river and westward to the Pacific ocean, and they will not in future object to the construction of railroads, wagon roads, mail stations, or other works of utility or necessity, which may be ordered or permitted by the laws of the United States. But should such roads or other works be constructed on the lands of their reservation, the government will pay the tribe whatever amount of damage may be assessed by three disinterested commissioners to be appointed by the President for that purpose, one of the said commissioners to be a chief or headman of the tribe.

7th. They agree to withdraw all opposition to the military posts or roads now established south of the North Platte river, or that may be established, not in violation of treaties heretofore made or hereafter to be made with any of the Indian tribes.

Article XII.

No treaty for the cession of any portion or part of the reservation herein described which may be held in common, shall be of any validity or force as against the said Indians unless executed and signed by at least three-fourths of all the adult male Indians occupying or interested in the same, and no cession by the tribe shall be understood or construed in such manner as to deprive, without his consent, any individual member of the tribe of his rights to any tract of land selected by him as provided in Article VI of this treaty.

Article XIII.

The United States hereby agrees to furnish annually to the Indians the physician, teachers, carpenter, miller, engineer, farmer, and blacksmiths, as herein contemplated, and that such appropriations shall be made from time to time, on the estimate of the Secretary of the Interior, as will be sufficient to employ such persons.

Article XIV.

It is agreed that the sum of five hundred dollars annually for three years from date shall be expended in presents to the ten persons of said tribe who in the judgment of the agent may grow the most valuable crops for the respective year.

Article XV.

The Indians herein named agree that when the agency house and other buildings shall be constructed on the reservation named, they will regard said reservation their permanent home, and they will make no permanent settlement elsewhere; but they shall have the right, subject to the conditions and modifications of this treaty, to hunt, as stipulated in Article XI hereof.

Article XVI.

The United States hereby agrees and stipulates that the country north of the North Platte river and east of the summits of the Big Horn mountains shall be held and considered to be unceded. Indian territory, and also stipulates and agrees that no white person or persons shall be permitted to settle upon or occupy any portion of the same; or without the consent of the Indians, first had and obtained, to pass through the same; and it is further agreed by the United States, that within ninety days after the conclusion of peace with all the bands of the Sioux nation, the military posts now established in the territory in this article named shall be abandoned, and that the road leading to them and by them to the settlements in the Territory of Montana shall be closed.

Article XVII.

It is hereby expressly understood and agreed by and between the respective parties to this treaty that the execution of this treaty and its ratification by the United States Senate shall have the effect, and shall be construed as abrogating and annulling all treaties and agreements heretofore entered into between the respective parties hereto, so far as such treaties and agreements obligate the United States to furnish and provide money, clothing, or other articles of property to such Indians and bands of Indians as become parties to this treaty, but no further.

In testimony of all which, we, the said commissioners, and we, the chiefs and headmen of the Brule band of the Sioux nation, have hereunto set our hands and seals at Fort Laramie, Dakota Territory, this twenty-ninth day of April, in the year one thousand eight hundred and sixty-eight.

GLOSSARY

abrogating: repealing or canceling

alienation: the transference of property such as land to another

annulling: voiding, nullifying, or canceling

cession: the act of surrendering or transferring

Greenwich: Greenwich, England, located on the prime meridian

Land Book: a book held by the government agent that listed the legal boundaries of all allotments taken out by Indian farmers

lodge: a household or family unit among the Plains Indians

meridian: an imaginary line passing through the poles at right angles to the equator

Document Analysis

Article I ended Red Cloud's War. In an attempt to guarantee peace, the United States agreed to arrest and prosecute any whites who violated the person or property of the Indians. Had the government lived up to the provisions of this treaty and had the signing tribes been able to enforce the treaty on all its members, warfare might have been avoided. Unfortunately, the discovery of gold in the Black Hills would spark warfare just eight years later.

Article II created and delineated the boundaries of the Great Sioux Reservation. Non-Indians, except for government agents, civilian employees, and military officials in the discharge of duty, were prohibited from entering or settling on the reserve. Finally, the tribes signing this treaty agreed to "relinquish all claims" to territories not outlined in Article II.

Article III provided for the expansion of the Great Sioux Reservation if not enough land was available for every qualified Indian to have 160 acres of tillable land.

Articles IV-IX were designed to promote the development of American-style family farms among the Native American tribes of the plains. By providing land to those who wanted it (land that would be removed from control of the tribe), the federal government was able to weaken the cohesion of these tribes. Article VII provided for public education for children, however, eventually, the Indians were induced to send their children to off-reservation boarding schools in faraway locales, such as Carlisle Indian Industrial School in Pennsylvania.

In what would become a contentious requirement outlined in Article X, the government agent was required to conduct an annual census. The government desired a census in order to provide an accurate count for annuity-distribution purposes. The Indians, however, viewed the census as a means to reduce their annuities.

Article XI was one of the most important, and misunderstood, parts of the treaty. The Indians signing the treaty agreed to surrender their rights to all land outside the stipulated reservation boundaries. The wording, however, linked this to a sufficient amount of game. With the buffalo all but extinct by the late 1870s, the Lakota became trapped within the boundaries of the reservation. The article also eliminated native opposition to railroads and they agreed to halt violence to people or property of the United States.

Article XII would cause the federal government some misgivings in the future. This article required that any future land cession would need the signatures of at least three-fourths of all adult Indian males. When the federal government wanted to remove the Black Hills from the Great Sioux Reservation in the aftermath of the Sioux War of 1876–1877, commissioners could not get the requisite number of signatures and, in fact, did not even try. Using graft, or simply ignoring Article XII, a federal commission obtained the signatures of several chiefs and headmen among the Oglala and Brulé Lakota bands and simply removed the Black Hills from the Great Sioux Reservation in 1877.

In Article XII the federal government agreed to provide and fund for the agency the positions of blacksmith, carpenter, engineer, farmer, miller, teachers, and physician. The men and women who filled these positions were intended to introduce Indians to and teach them the necessary skills to become "Americanized."

Article XIV was used as an incentive to induce Indians to take up farming. Each year for a period of three years, $500 in presents would be distributed among the ten most productive farmers, as selected by the agent.

Article XV reinforced Article XI by stating that once the agency headquarters and related buildings were constructed, the Indians would consider the reservation their permanent home.

Lakota leaders such as Red Cloud probably found Article XVI the most satisfying. To get Red Cloud to sign the treaty, the federal government agreed that within ninety days of the signing of the treaty, all the military forts in this region and along the Bozeman Trail would be abandoned. In many ways, Article XVI recognized the Lakota as victors in Red Cloud's War. They went to war with the United States with the purpose of closing emigration through the Powder River country and getting rid of the hated military posts. In this, Red Cloud and the Lakota succeeded. Many historians point to this victory as the only war won by Native Americans in the long history of Indian-American conflict. Article XVI also reiterates the boundaries of

the unceded hunting grounds. The land north of the North Platte River and east of the summits of the Bighorn Mountains (including the Black Hills) would be reserved Indian hunting grounds. Moreover, all white persons were forbidden to enter this territory without the permission of Indians.

Finally, Article XVII nullified all existing treaty stipulations in relation to the payment of moneys, food, clothing, and annuities. The Treaty of Fort Laramie of 1868 superseded all other agreements.

Essential Themes

With the Treaty of Fort Laramie, the federal government wanted to end Red Cloud's War and protect American interests such as the transcontinental railroad. In order to get the required signatures, treaty commissioners agreed to provisions they never really intended to uphold. The government probably never intended that the Lakota Sioux would always own the entire Great Sioux Reservation. Thus, it was always necessary to break treaties or amend old treaties. In short, the federal government never viewed a treaty signed with Indians in the same way as it would a treaty signed with a foreign nation. The treaty was an agreement between unequals that could be changed, altered, or abrogated at the federal government's expediency.

Despite the regrettably fluid nature of the the boundaries of Indian land under the Treaty of Fort Laramie and other treaties like it, portions of the treaty would have significance in coming years. This treaty was only one step in the quest by the federal government to disrupt and, ultimately, end the tribal way of life practiced by the plains tribes. The treaty provisions that granted individual plots of land, offered prize money for the most efficient farms and allowed for the education of the tribes' children would be expanded on in the future.

———*Mark R. Ellis, PhD*

Bibliography and Additional Reading

DeMallie, Raymond J. "Touching the Pen: Plains Indian Treaty Councils in Ethnohistorical Perspective." In *Ethnicity on the Great Plains*, ed. Frederick C. Luebke. Lincoln: University of Nebraska Press, 1980.

White, Richard. "The Winning of the West: The Expansion of the Western Sioux in the Eighteenth and Nineteenth Centuries." *Journal of American History* 65 (September 1978): 319–343.

Hoig, Stan. *White Man's Paper Trail: Grand Councils and Treaty-Making on the Central Plains.* Boulder: University of Colorado Press, 2006.

Kappler, Charles J., ed. *Indian Treaties.* New York: Interland, 1972.

Olson, James C. *Red Cloud and the Sioux Problem.* Lincoln: University of Nebraska Press, 1965.

Ostler, Jeffrey. *The Plains Sioux and U.S. Colonialism from Lewis and Clark to Wounded Knee.* New York: Cambridge University Press, 2004.

Prucha, Francis Paul. *The Great Father: The United States Government and the American Indian.* 2 vols. Lincoln: University of Nebraska Press, 1995.

Weeks, Philip. *Farewell, My Nation: The American Indian and the United States, 1820–1890.* Arlington Heights, Ill. Harlan Davidson, 1990.

Wunder, John R. *"Retained by the People": A History of American Indians and the Bill of Rights.* New York: Oxford University Press, 1994.

Web Sites

Kappler, Charles J., ed. "Indian Affairs: Laws and Treaties." Oklahoma State University Library Web site. http://digital.library.okstate.edu/KAPPLER/index.htm. Accessed on January 21, 2017.

"New Perspectives on the West." Public Broadcasting System Web Site. http://www.pbs.org/weta/thewest/. Accessed on January 21, 2017.

■ Dawes Severalty Act

Date: 1887
Authors: Henry L. Dawes and others
Genre: Law

Summary Overview

Named after the Massachusetts senator Henry L. Dawes, who headed the U.S. Senate's Committee on Indian Affairs, the Dawes Severalty Act of 1887 was the culmination of decades of policy work designed to free up western land for white settlers and acculturate American Indians to American values and practices. The Dawes Severalty Act broke the land of most remaining reservations into parcels to be farmed by individual American Indians or nuclear American Indian families. Partitioning Indian land in this manner, Congress hoped, would force native peoples to give up communal living and to adopt American farming practices. Eventually, policy makers reasoned, American Indians would embrace all American cultural norms and become integrated into U.S. society.

When the Dawes Act passed in 1887, Americans' views of native peoples varied considerably. Some groups, particularly evangelicals, dedicated themselves to both the religious and the cultural conversion of American Indians. Viewing themselves as benevolent teachers, they believed that they had a duty to acculturate American Indians. Others thought that American Indians were inassimilable, racially inferior savages who were destined for extinction. Few felt that Indian tribes deserved to be treated as sovereign nations as they had been in the past. While the crafters of the Dawes Act believed themselves to have the best interests of American Indians at heart, the act ultimately hurt native peoples, dispossessing them of their lands and further marginalizing them. People unsympathetic to American Indians manipulated the Dawes Act for their own financial gain, resulting in the massive displacement of native peoples. As a consequence, by 1900 the American Indian population had fallen to its lowest point in U.S. history.

Defining Moment

Following the Civil War, Americans had a reinvigorated interest in western migration. Transnational railroads made western migration safer and faster than it had been in the past. Americans were determined to pursue the dream of owning and farming their own land. The federal government aided potential homesteaders by passing the Homestead Act in 1862, providing land grants to hundreds of thousands of Americans.

White American migration into the West did not occur without opposition. Those who posed the greatest obstacle to American homesteaders were the Plains Indians. Primarily semi-sedentary people, the Plains Indians subsisted mainly by hunting buffalo. Homesteaders impeded their ability to survive by breaking land into parcels protected as private property, preventing both the buffalo and the Plains Indians from roaming freely. In many cases Native Americans responded violently in an effort to deter settlers. Homesteaders in turn complained that the government should protect them from Indian attacks. The situation in the West was exacerbated because businessmen, homesteaders, and railroad companies also wanted to remove the American Indians living on reservations in the West. Although the federal government had initially set up reservations in areas considered undesirable for white settlement, as land grew scarcer, the appeal of reservation land increased. In addition, in some cases, such as in the Dakota Territory, valuable natural resources like gold were discovered on Indian lands.

Throughout the second half of the nineteenth century, Native Americans responded to white settlers in a number of ways. Many tribal leaders appealed to U.S. politicians to recognize their equality as men and to appreciate tribal sovereignty. Those who made treaties with the federal government or received promises of land rights lacked recourse when the agreements were ignored or forgotten. Consequently, many Native Americans escalated attacks on American settlers and troops in an effort to protect their way of life. However, even protracted Indian wars, such as that waged by the Apache in the Southwest, eventually resulted in Indian surrender. Indian victories, such as the Sioux and Cheyenne defeat of General George Armstrong Custer and his troops at Little Bighorn, resulted in harsher retribution by American settlers and troops. By the 1880s many Native Americans saw acquiescence to U.S. policies as their best chance for survival.

INDIAN LAND FOR SALE

GET A HOME

OF

YOUR OWN

❀

EASY PAYMENTS

PERFECT TITLE

❀

POSSESSION

WITHIN

THIRTY DAYS

FINE LANDS IN THE WEST

IRRIGATED
IRRIGABLE

GRAZING

AGRICULTURAL
DRY FARMING

IN 1910 THE DEPARTMENT OF THE INTERIOR SOLD UNDER SEALED BIDS ALLOTTED INDIAN LAND AS FOLLOWS:

Location.	Acres.	Average Price per Acre.	Location.	Acres.	Average Price per Acre.
Colorado	5,211.21	$7.27	Oklahoma	34,664.00	$19.14
Idaho	17,013.00	24.85	Oregon	1,020.00	15.43
Kansas	1,684.50	33.45	South Dakota	120,445.00	16.53
Montana	11,034.00	9.86	Washington	4,879.00	41.37
Nebraska	5,641.00	36.65	Wisconsin	1,069.00	17.00
North Dakota	22,610.70	9.93	Wyoming	865.00	20.64

FOR THE YEAR 1911 IT IS ESTIMATED THAT **350,000** ACRES WILL BE OFFERED FOR SALE

For information as to the character of the land write for booklet, "INDIAN LANDS FOR SALE," to the Superintendent U. S. Indian School at any one of the following places:

CALIFORNIA:
Hoopa.
COLORADO:
Ignacio.
IDAHO:
Lapwai.
KANSAS:
Horton.
Nadeau.

MINNESOTA:
Onigum.
MONTANA:
Crow Agency.
NEBRASKA:
Macy.
Santee.
Winnebago.

NORTH DAKOTA:
Fort Totten.
Fort Yates.
OKLAHOMA:
Anadarko.
Cantonment.
Colony.
Darlington.
Muskogee,
Pawnee.

OKLAHOMA—Con.
Sac and Fox Agency.
Shawnee.
Wyandotte.
OREGON:
Klamath Agency.
Pendleton.
Roseburg.
Siletz.

SOUTH DAKOTA:
Cheyenne Agency.
Crow Creek.
Greenwood.
Lower Brule.
Pine Ridge.
Rosebud.
Sisseton.

WASHINGTON:
Fort Simcoe.
Fort Spokane.
Tekoa.
Tulalip.

WISCONSIN:
Oneida.

WALTER L. FISHER,
Secretary of the Interior.

ROBERT G. VALENTINE,
Commissioner of Indian Affairs.

Author Biography

Crafted by the U.S. Congress, the Dawes Act was based on the contribution of many individuals, although it is primarily credited to Senator Henry L. Dawes of Massachusetts, who chaired the Senate's Indian Affairs Committee. Dawes was initially skeptical about attempts to acculturate American Indians through land allotment but was persuaded by advocates to promote the act. Dawes made an exceptional candidate because he both chaired the Indian Affairs Committee and represented the state with the largest contingent of participants in the Indian reform movement.

Henry Laurens Dawes was born in Cummington, Massachusetts, on October 30, 1816. Trained as a lawyer, Dawes entered politics at a young age. As the Republican candidate, he was elected to the Massachusetts House of Representatives at age thirty-two and continued his political career in the Massachusetts state senate followed by the U.S. House of Representatives and the U.S. Senate. During the 1850s, 1860s, and 1870s Dawes adamantly supported antislavery and Reconstruction policies. During the 1880s he became an advocate for Indian reform groups in the Senate. The meetings held by groups sympathetic to the plight of American Indians at Lake Mohonk, New York, particularly influenced Dawes. Dawes increasingly advocated allotment of reservation lands to acculturate American Indians and to integrate them into American society. He remained an active advocate for Indian rights until his death on February 5, 1903.

HISTORICAL DOCUMENT

Be it enacted by the Senate and House of Representatives of the United States of America in Congress assembled, That in all cases where any tribe or band of Indians has been, or shall hereafter be, located upon any reservation created for their use, either by treaty stipulation or by virtue of an act of Congress or executive order setting apart the same for their use, the President of the United States be, and he hereby is, authorized, whenever in his opinion any reservation or any part thereof of such Indians is advantageous for agricultural and grazing purposes, to cause said reservation, or any part thereof, to be surveyed, or resurveyed if necessary, and to allot the lands in said reservation in severalty to any Indian located thereon in quantities as follows:

To each head of a family, one-quarter of a section;

To each single person over eighteen years of age, one-eighth of a section;

To each orphan child under eighteen years of age, one-eighth of a section; and

To each other single person under eighteen years now living, or who may be born prior to the date of the order of the President directing an allotment of the lands embraced in any reservation, one-sixteenth of a section:

Provided, That in case there is not sufficient land in any of said reservations to allot lands to each individual of the classes above named in quantities as above provided, the lands embraced in such reservation or reservations shall be allotted to each individual of each of said classes pro rata in accordance with the provisions of this act: And provided further, That where the treaty or act of Congress setting apart such reservation provides the allotment of lands in severalty in quantities in excess of those herein provided, the President, in making allotments upon such reservation, shall allot the lands to each individual Indian belonging thereon in quantity as specified in such treaty or act: And provided further, That when the lands allotted are only valuable for grazing purposes, an additional allotment of such grazing lands, in quantities as above provided, shall be made to each individual.

Sec. 2. That all allotments set apart under the provisions of this act shall be selected by the Indians, heads of families selecting for their minor children, and the agents shall select for each orphan child, and in such manner as to embrace the improvements of the Indians making the selection. where the improvements of two or more Indians have been made on the same legal subdivision of land, unless they shall otherwise agree, a provisional line may be run dividing said lands between them, and the amount to which each is entitled shall be equalized in the assignment of the remainder of the land to which they are entitled under his act: Provided, That if any one entitled to an allotment shall fail to make a selection within four years after the President shall direct that allotments may be made on a particular reservation, the Secretary of the Interior may direct the agent of such tribe or band, if such there be, and if there be no agent, then a special agent appointed for that purpose, to make a selection for such Indian, which selection shall be allotted as in cases where selections are made by the Indians, and patents shall issue in like manner.

Sec. 3. That the allotments provided for in this act shall be made by special agents appointed by the President for such purpose, and the agents in charge of the respective reservations on which the allotments are directed to be made, under such rules and regulations as the Secretary of the Interior may from time to time prescribe, and shall be certified by such agents to the Commissioner of Indian Affairs, in duplicate, one copy to be retained in the Indian Office and the other to be transmitted to the Secretary of the Interior for his action, and to be deposited in the General Land Office.

Sec. 4. That where any Indian not residing upon a reservation, or for whose tribe no reservation has been provided by treaty, act of Congress, or executive order, shall make settlement upon any surveyed or unsurveyed lands of the United States not otherwise appropriated, he or she shall be entitled, upon application to the local land-office for the district in which the lands arc located, to have the same allotted to him or her, and to his or her children, in quantities and manner as provided in this act for Indians residing upon reservations; and when such settlement is made upon unsurveyed lands, the grant to such Indians shall be adjusted upon the survey of the lands so as to conform thereto; and patents shall be issued to them for such lands in the manner and with the restrictions as herein provided. And the fees to which the officers of such local land-office would have been entitled had such lands been entered under the general laws for the disposition of the public lands shall be paid to them, from any moneys in the Treasury of the United States not otherwise appropriated, upon a statement of an account in their behalf for such fees by the Commissioner of the General Land Office, and a certification of

such account to the Secretary of the Treasury by the Secretary of the Interior.

Sec. 5. That upon the approval of the allotments provided for in this act by the Secretary of the Interior, he shall cause patents to issue therefor in the name of the allottees, which patents shall be of the legal effect, and declare that the United States does and will hold the land thus allotted, for the period of twenty-five years, in trust for the sole use and benefit of the Indian to whom such allotment shall have been made, or, in case of his decease, of his heirs according to the laws of the State or Territory where such land is located, and that at the expiration of said period the United States will convey the same by patent to said Indian, or his heirs as aforesaid, in fee, discharged of said trust and free of all charge or incumbrance whatsoever: Provided, That the President of the United States may in any case in his discretion extend the period. And if any conveyance shall be made of the lands set apart and allotted as herein provided, or any contract made touching the same, before the expiration of the time above mentioned, such conveyance or contract shall be absolutely null and void: Provided, That the law of descent and partition in force in the State or Territory where such lands are situate shall apply thereto after patents therefor have been executed and delivered, except as herein otherwise provided; and the laws of the State of Kansas regulating the descent and partition of real estate shall, so far as practicable, apply to all lands in the Indian Territory which may be allotted in severalty under the provisions of this act: And provided further, That at any time after lands have been allotted to all the Indians of any tribe as herein provided, or sooner if in the opinion of the President it shall be for the best interests of said tribe, it shall be lawful for the Secretary of the Interior to negotiate with such Indian tribe for the purchase and release by said tribe, in conformity with the treaty or statute under which such reservation is held, of such portions of its reservation not allotted as such tribe shall, from time to time, consent to sell, on such terms and conditions as shall be considered just and equitable between the United States and said tribe of Indians, which purchase shall not be complete until ratified by Congress, and the form and manner of executing such release prescribed by

Congress: Provided however, That all lands adapted to agriculture, with or without irrigation so sold or released to the United States by any Indian tribe shall be held by the United States for the sale purpose of securing homes to actual settlers and shall be disposed of by the United States to actual and bona fide settlers only tracts not exceeding one hundred and sixty acres to any one person, on such terms as Congress shall prescribe, subject to grants which Congress may make in aid of education: And provided further, That no patents shall issue therefor except to the person so taking the same as and homestead, or his heirs, and after the expiration of five years occupancy therof as such homestead; and any conveyance of said lands taken as a homestead, or any contract touching the same, or lieu thereon, created prior to the date of such patent, shall be null and void. And the sums agreed to be paid by the United States as purchase money for any portion of any such reservation shall be held in the Treasury of the United States for the sole use of the tribe or tribes Indians; to whom such reservations belonged; and the same, with interest thereon at three per cent per annum, shall be at all times subject to appropriation by Congress for the education and civilization of such tribe or tribes of Indians or the members thereof. The patents aforesaid shall be recorded in the General Land Office, and afterward delivered, free of charge, to the allottee entitled thereto. And if any religious society or other organization is now occupying any of the public lands to which this act is applicable, for religious or educational work among the Indians, the Secretary of the Interior is hereby authorized to confirm such occupation to such society or organization, in quantity not exceeding one hundred and sixty acres in any one tract, so long as the same shall be so occupied, on such terms as he shall deem just; but nothing herein contained shall change or alter any claim of such society for religious or educational purposes heretofore granted by law. And hereafter in the employment of Indian police, or any other employees in the public service among any of the Indian tribes or bands affected by this act, and where Indians can perform the duties required, those Indians who have availed themselves of the provisions of this act and become citizens of the United States shall be preferred.

Sec. 6. That upon the completion of said allotments and the patenting of the lands to said allottees, each and every member of the respective bands or tribes of Indians to whom allotments have been made shall have the benefit of and be subject to the laws, both civil and criminal, of the State or Territory in which they may reside; and no Territory shall pass or enforce any law denying any such Indian within its jurisdiction the equal protection of the law. And every Indian born within the territorial limits of the United States to whom allotments shall have been made under the provisions of this act, or under any law or treaty, and every Indian born within the territorial limits of the United States who has voluntarily taken up, within said limits, his residence separate and apart from any tribe of Indians therein, and has adopted the habits of civilized life, is hereby declared to be a citizen of the United States, and is entitled to all the rights, privileges, and immunities of such citizens, whether said Indian has been or not, by birth or otherwise, a member of any tribe of Indians within the territorial limits of the United States without in any manner affecting the right of any such Indian to tribal or other property.

Sec. 7. That in cases where the use of water for irrigation is necessary to render the lands within any Indian reservation available for agricultural purposes, the Secretary of the Interior be, and he is hereby, authorized to prescribe such rules and regulations as he may deem necessary to secure a just and equal distribution thereof among the Indians residing upon any such reservation; and no other appropriation or grant of water by any riparian proprietor shall permitted to the damage of any other riparian proprietor.

Sec. 8. That the provisions of this act shall not extend to the territory occupied by the Cherokees, Creeks, Choctaws, Chickasaws, Seminoles, and Osage, Miamies and Peorias, and Sacs and Foxes, in the Indian Territory, nor to any of the reservations of the Seneca Nation of New York Indians in the State of New York, nor to that strip of territory in the State of Nebraska adjoining the Sioux Nation on the south added by executive order.

Sec. 9. That for the purpose of making the surveys and resurveys mentioned in section two of this act, there be, and hereby is, appropriated, out of any moneys in the Treasury not otherwise appropriated, the sum of one hundred thousand dollars, to be repaid proportionately out of the proceeds of the sales of such land as may be acquired from the Indians under the provisions of this act.

Sec. 10. That nothing in this act contained shall be so construed to affect the right and power of Congress to grant the right of way through any lands granted to an Indian, or a tribe of Indians, for railroads or other highways, or telegraph lines, for the public use, or condemn such lands to public uses, upon making just compensation.

Sec. 11. That nothing in this act shall be so construed as to prevent the removal of the Southern Ute Indians from their present reservation in Southwestern Colorado to a new reservation by and with consent of a majority of the adult male members of said tribe.

Approved, February, 8, 1887.

GLOSSARY

allot: to allocate a portion (in this case, of land)

embrace: to contain

riparian: relating to a body of water

severalty: the quality of being distinct or autonomous

Document Analysis

Section 1 of the Dawes Act states the main purpose of the act. The act provides the president of the United States with the right to survey and divide reservation lands among individual American Indians and American Indian families. It also stipulates the manner in which the land will be divided, providing every head of household with one-quarter section of land, every single person over age eighteen or orphan under age eighteen with one-eighth section of land, and all other unmarried people under the age of eighteen with one-sixteenth section of land. Section 1 does not specify the actual size of a section but suggests that sections will be determined based on government survey of reservations and the size of the Indian population living on each. If an American Indian receives an allotment suitable only for ranching and not for agriculture, the act guarantees that he will get an additional allotment.

Section 2 guarantees the right of each American Indian to choose the area of land that will become his allotment. Heads of household are charged with choosing plots in the name of their minor children, and Bureau of Land Management agents are responsible for choosing land on behalf of orphaned children. If two people entitled to allotments want the same tract of land, the parcel will be divided between them, and they will receive from another area the remainder of land due to them. After Indians make their selections, agents are responsible for drawing preliminary boundaries, which they are to revise after resurveying the land and adding or subtracting from the various plots to standardize their size.

Section 2 also anticipates potential problems arising from the act. It insists that the agents responsible for choosing land on behalf of orphaned children choose land based on the best interests of those children. Suspecting some resistance to land division and allotment, Section 2 states that if an American Indian entitled to a portion of the newly divided reservations does not stake his claim to a partition of land within four years, the secretary of the interior should have a land agent choose a parcel on behalf of that Indian and issue a patent to the Indian in question for the plot of land in his name.

The purpose of Section 3 is to establish the manner in which allotments will be made, who will make them, who will appoint the officers who grant allotments, and how allotments will be documented. It states that the president will assign agents responsible for overseeing the allotment process. Records of allotment will be stored in both the Indian Office and the General Land Office.

Section 4 explains how the system of allotment will apply to American Indians who do not live on reservations. It states that an Indian residing off a reservation has the right to an allotment parcel equal to that of a native living on a reservation and that he can choose a parcel from any area of unsettled land. Although American Indians can choose their allotment from areas of unsurveyed land, the allotments will be adjusted once the land is surveyed. Section 4 also explains that the U.S. Treasury will compensate local land offices for the land settled by Indians.

Section 5 specifies the requirements for American Indians to gain ownership of their allotments. It states that once American Indians choose their plots of lands, those plots will be patented to them but held in trust by the U.S. government for twenty-five years. During those twenty-five years American Indians cannot sell the land. Furthermore, Section 5 nullifies any sale of allotted land prior to the end of the twenty-five-year period. If an allottee dies during the period in which the government holds his land in trust, his heirs will inherit the right to the land.

Additionally, Section 5 discusses options for reservation land not allotted to individuals under the provision of the act. It states that the federal government can negotiate with tribes to purchase unallotted reservation land but that land purchased from tribes can be used only to encourage actual settlers. Settlers will be restricted to land grants no larger than 160 acres per person. Religious organizations engaged in converting or educating native people are also entitled to tracts of land of no more than 160 acres. Like American Indians living on allotments, non-native settlers will have their land held in trust by the federal government, but only for five years.

The fees paid by homesteaders for tracts of former Indian land are relegated to the American Indians who had previously held the rights to the land in question. The money can be used by Congress for educating or otherwise "civilizing" the American Indians from the reservation in question. Section 5 concludes by stating that American Indians who have taken advantage of the allotment policy as well as those who have become U.S. citizens will have preference in the hiring of public employees working in American Indian communities.

Section 6 deals with the legal and citizenship status of American Indians who participate in the allotment program. All American Indians who receive allotments, it states, will become American citizens and have all of the rights of American citizens. It stipulates that no

local or state government can pass laws denying equal protection by law to American Indians who have taken part in the allotment program. In addition, Section 6 specifies that all American Indians who take part in the allotment process will become subject to the laws of the state or territory in which they reside.

Section 7 endows the secretary of the interior with the authority to regulate water resources, if they are needed to make reservation land fertile for agricultural use. The secretary is charged with equitably distributing water among the American Indians living on a reservation. Section 7 also forbids giving water rights to one individual if doing so would hurt another.

Section 8 excludes certain tribes (Cherokee, Creek, Choctaw, Chickasaw, Fox, Osage, Miami, Peoria, Sac, and Seminole) and certain regions (Seneca Nation of New York reservations and Sioux Nation territory in Nebraska) from the provisions of the act.

Section 9 states that the cost of surveying lands authorized by the act will be paid out of a $100,000 account in the Treasury. The $100,000 will be repaid to the Treasury from the sale of land acquired from American Indians based on the standards set forth by the act.

Section 10 protects the federal government's right to exercise eminent domain over land allotted to American Indians.

Section 11 certifies that the act cannot be used to halt the relocation of the Southern Ute Indians from their current reservation in southwestern Colorado to a new reservation.

Essential Themes

Within the dry, legislative language of the Dawes Act is the core of a very old America ideal: that of the independent yeoman farmer. The same ideal that inspired the Homestead Act of 1862 played a role in this law. The language is technical and verbose, but also pointedly specific. The drafters of the act, who saw themselves as friends of the American Indian, attempted to draft an act so specific that those wishing to use the new policy to displace American Indians would not be able to do so. Notably, the initial act was drafted so seamlessly that speculators had difficulty obtaining legal rights to Native allotments until after the Dawes Act was amended in 1891. The Dawes Act was written with the understanding that employees of the General Land Office and the Bureau of Indian Affairs would frequently refer to it. For that reason these employees are specifically addressed throughout the act, and their actions are strictly proscribed. The act frequently warns agents against attempting to use their position for personal gain, stating, for example, that agents choosing plots of land for orphaned children must consider the best interests of the children and that tribes agreeing to sell reservation land to the government must be fairly compensated.

However, these ideals and the precise legal language which sought to implement them would be imperfectly executed. Within the first decade of the Dawes Act's inception, state and local governments found loopholes allowing outsiders to purchase American Indian allotments. Once speculators and businesses gained ownership of Indian lands, American Indians felt the effects of the Dawes Act swiftly. Fences went up, restricting the movement of Indians as well as the game they hunted. Key resources, such as rivers and forests, were relegated to private, non-Indian owners, often eliminating the subsistence ability of American Indians. Thus one of the key ideals—the promotion of independent farms to supplant communal, "tribal" life did not come to fruition. The continued exploration of the Native Americans and their land would be paired with the "education and civilization" aspects of the law, leading to so-called "Indian Schools" where the cultural and linguistic assimilation of Native American children would be undertaken.

———*G. Mehera Gerardo, PhD*

Bibliography and Additional Reading

Carlson, Leonard A. "The Dawes Act and Indian Farming." *Journal of Economic History* 38, no. 1 (March 1978): 274–276.

Cotroneo, Ross R., and Jack Dozier. "A Time of Disintegration: The Coeur d'Alene and the Dawes Act." *Western Historical Quarterly* 5, no. 4 (October 1974): 405–419.

Hauptman, Laurence M., and L. Gordon McLester, III. *The Oneida Indians in the Age of Allotment, 1860–1920.* (Norman: University of Oklahoma Press, 2006).

Johnston, Robert D., and Catherine McNicol Stock, eds. *The Countryside in the Age of the Modern State: Political Histories of Rural America.* (Ithaca, N.Y. Cornell University Press, 2001).

Leibhardt, Barbara. "Allotment Policy in an Incongruous Legal System: The Yakima Indian Nation as a Case Study, 1887–1934." *Agricultural History* 65, no. 4 (Autumn 1991): 78–103

McDonnell, Janet A. *The Dispossession of the American Indian, 1887–1934.* (Bloomington: Indiana University Press, 1991).

Otis, D. S. *The Dawes Act and the Allotment of Indian Lands,* ed. Francis Paul Prucha. (Norman: University of Oklahoma Press, 1973).

■ Wounded Knee Massacre: Statements and Eyewitness Accounts

Date: 1891
Author: Various
Genre: Testimony

Summary Overview

The Wounded Knee Massacre of December, 1890 marked the end of organized resistance to federal domination of Native American tribes and the Reservation system that would keep Tribes confined to strictly defined geographical regions. It was also—as may be clear from these selections for the great number of statements and testimonials from the disaster—a direct result of the careless, haphazard, and damaging way these policies were implemented and subsequently enforced. Even the testimony of government officials involved in the massacre acknowledge that the policies they had been ordered to enforce contributed to the situation that, ultimately, erupted in violence. The Native Americans who speak about their experiences convey a deep sense of betrayal by a government whose policies and regulations they tried to obey.

There is also, within the testimonies of Valentine T. McGillycuddy and General Nelson Miles, attempts to explain the situation and, especially, to affix blame for the loss of life that occurred on that cold December day at Wounded Knee Creek. From inexperienced government officials to supposed "natural race antagonism," there is no shortage of culpable parties. Pay attention, also, to the Sioux interviewed and the divisions within their community that they discuss as a contributing factor.

Defining Moment

The incident at Wounded Knee—commonly referred to as the Wounded Knee massacre—took place near Wounded Knee Creek on the Pine Ridge Indian Reservation in South Dakota on December 29, 1890. Although the exact number of casualties is the subject of controversy, as are many facts about the incident, at least 150 men, women, and children of the Lakota Sioux tribe were killed by soldiers of the U.S. Seventh Cavalry. Wounded Knee took place at a time when the United States was finalizing its plan of assimilation of the Sioux and all Indian tribes onto reservations such as Pine Ridge.

Into this turbulent atmosphere came the "Paiute Messiah" Wovoka, who created the Ghost Dance ceremony, which promised the return of Indian spirits and the departure of the white man from Indian lands. The Ghost Dance movement was seen by whites as a threat, one that could unite the various tribes and lead to renewed wars between Indians and whites. Another significant figure was Chief Sitting Bull, who whites saw as a figurehead who could help unite Indians around the Ghost Dance. A group of Indian police were dispatched to his home to arrest him. Violence ensued, and Sitting Bull and eight of his men were killed on December 15, 1890.

Fearing additional violence, a group of Lakota Sioux Indians led by Chief Spotted Elk, sought shelter in Pine Ridge. On December 28 some 350 Lakota (including 230 were women and children) were intercepted by the Seventh Cavalry and directed to Wounded Knee Creek. During the night the soldiers surrounded the camp and set up four Hotchkiss guns. At dawn the Indians were ordered to surrender their weapons and told they would be taken to waiting trains to be shipped away from the area. Due, possibly to misunderstanding of the instructions, both sides opened fire. Accounts differ, but it has been argued that women and children were deliberately targeted and that those attempting to flee were run down by soldiers on horseback. Many of the twenty-five dead cavalry were believed to have died from "friendly fire" during the hour-long battle. In the aftermath, soldiers loaded fifty-one surviving Indians onto wagons and sent them to Pine Ridge.

Author biographies

While there is no single author in this collection of testimony about the Wounded Knee Massacre, a brief sketch of the careers of Valentine T. McGillycuddy and General Nelson A. Miles is valuable for our understanding of the relationship between American political and military forces and the Native American tribes of the Great Plains.

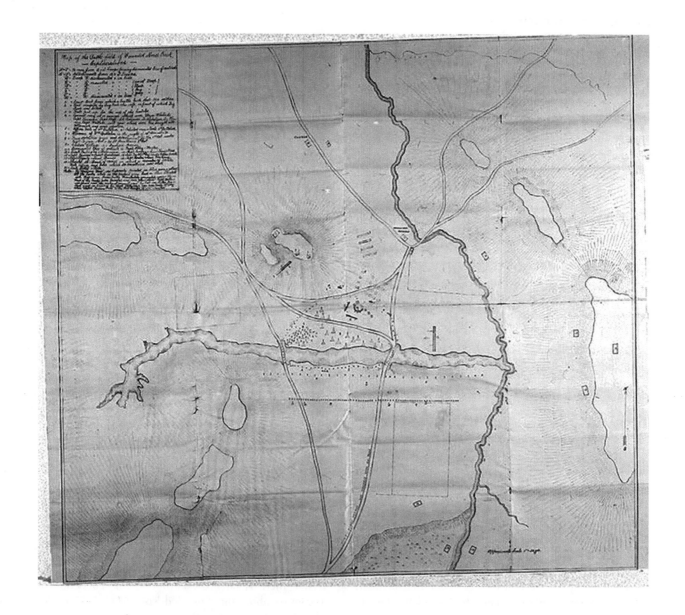

Valentine T. McGillycuddy was born on Valentine's Day, 1849, in Wisconsin. After attending medical school in Detroit, he worked in the city for a year before heading west to indulge his desire to live in less developed parts of the country. He worked for several years as a topographer and surgeon for the expedition that surveyed the border between the US and Canada and on other surveying assignments. He was, later, attached as a surgeon to military forces in the Dakotas, where he came into contact with various native American groups. McGillycuddy treated the gunshot wounds of Native leader Crazy Horse and, after Crazy Horse's death appealed to officials in Washington for more merciful treatment of Native prisoners at western forts. In 1879, he received an appointment as the Indian Agent at Pine Ridge. Despite contentious relationships with leaders such as Red Cloud, McGillycuddy found ways to maintain peace and order on the reservations without the use of Army intervention, establishing a native police force. He also worked to establish a boarding school on the reservation.

The career of General Nelson A. Miles spanned decades, from the Civil War to the Spanish-American War. His role in the wars on the western frontier began in 1866 as the commander of the 5th Infantry Regiment, having an active role in most of the major campaigns against the Great Plains tribes through the subjugation of Geronimo and the Apache in the 1880s. At the time of the Wounded Knee Massacre, Miles was the commander of the Division of the Missouri, overseeing military operations across the Great Plains. Though not present at the scene of the massacre, Miles was affected by the event, describing it to his wife in a letter as an "abominable criminal military blunder."

HISTORICAL DOCUMENT

Former Pine Ridge Agent Valentine T. McGillycuddy's Letter to General Leonard W. Colby (January 15)

Sir: In answer to your inquiry of a recent date, I would state that in my opinion to no one cause can be attributed the recent so-called outbreak on the part of the Sioux, but rather to a combination of causes gradually cumulative in their effect and dating back through many years—in fact to the inauguration of our practically demonstrated faulty Indian policy.

There can be no question but that many of the treaties, agreements, or solemn promises made by our government with these Indians have been broken. Many of them have been kept by us technically, but as far as the Indian is concerned have been misunderstood by him through a lack of proper explanation at time of signing, and hence considered by him as broken.

It must also be remembered that in all of the treaties made by the government with the Indians, a large portion of them have not agreed to or signed the same. Noticeably was this so in the agreement secured by us with them the summer before last, by which we secured one-half of the remainder of the Sioux reserve, amounting to about 16,000 square miles. This agreement barely carried with the Sioux nation as a whole, but did not carry at Pine Ridge or Rosebud, where the strong majority were against it; and it must be noted that wherever there was the strongest opposition manifested to the recent treaty, there, during the present trouble, have been found the elements opposed to the government.

The Sioux nation, which at one time, with the confederated bands of Cheyennes and Arapahos, controlled a region of country bounded on the north by the Yellowstone, on the south by the Arkansas, and reaching from the Missouri river to the Rocky mountains, has seen this large domain, under the various treaties, dwindle down to their now limited reserve of less than 16,000 square miles, and with the land has disappeared the buffalo and other game. The memory of this, chargeable by them to the white man, necessarily irritates them.

There is back of all this the natural race antagonism which our dealings with the aborigine in connection with the inevitable onward march of civilization has [sic] in no degree lessened. It has been our experience, and the experience of other nations, that defeat in war is soon, not sooner or later, forgotten by the coming generation, and as a result we have a tendency to a constant recurrence of outbreak on the part of the weaker race. It is now sixteen years since our last war with the Sioux in 1876—a time when our present Sioux warriors were mostly children, and therefore have no memory of having felt the power of the government. It is but natural that these young warriors, lacking in experience, should require but little incentive to induce them to test the bravery of the white man on the war path, where the traditions of his people teach him is the only path to glory and a chosen seat in the "happy hunting grounds." For these reasons every precaution should be adopted by the government to guard against trouble with its disastrous results. Have such precautions been adopted? Investigation of the present trouble does not so indicate.

Sitting Bull and other irreconcilable relics of the campaign of 1876 were allowed to remain among their people and foment discord. The staple article of food at Pine Ridge and some of the other agencies had been cut down below the subsisting point, noticeably the beef at Pine Ridge, which from an annual treaty allowance of 6,250,000 pounds gross was cut down to 1,000,000 pounds. The contract on that beef was violated, insomuch as that contract called for northern ranch beef, for which was substituted through beef from Texas, with an unparalleled resulting shrinkage in winter, so that the Indians did not actually receive half ration of this food in winter—the very time the largest allowance of food is required. By the fortunes of political war, weak agents were placed in charge of some of the agencies at the very time that trouble was known to be brewing. Noticeably was this so at Pine Ridge, where a notoriously weak and unfit man was placed in charge. His flight, abandonment of his agency, and his call for troops have, with the horrible results of the same, become facts in history.

Now, as for facts in connection with Pine Ridge, which agency has unfortunately become the theater of the present "war," was there necessity for troops? My past experience with those Indians does not so indicate. For seven long years, from 1879 to 1886, I, as agent, managed this agency without the presence of a soldier on the reservation, and none nearer than 60 miles, and in those times the Indians were naturally much wilder than they are to-day. To be sure, during those seven years we occasionally had exciting times, when the only thing lacking to

cause an outbreak was the calling for troops by the agent and the presence of the same. As a matter of fact, however, no matter how much disturbed affairs were, no matter how imminent an outbreak, the progressive chiefs, with their following, came to the front enough in the majority, with the fifty Indian policemen, to at once crush out all attempts at rebellion against the authority of the agent and the government.

Why was this? Because in those times we believed in placing confidence in the Indians; in establishing, as far as possible, a home-rule government on the reservation. We established local courts, presided over by the Indians, with Indian juries; in fact, we believed in having the Indians assist in working out their own salvation. We courted and secured the friendship and support of the progressive and orderly element, us against the mob element. Whether the system thus inaugurated was practicable, was successful, comparison with recent events will decide.

When my Democratic successor took charge in 1886, he deemed it necessary to make general changes in the system at Pine Ridge, i.e., a Republican system. All white men, half-breeds, or Indians who had sustained the agent under the former administration were classed as Republicans and had to go. The progressive chiefs, such as Young Man Afraid, Little Wound, and White Bird, were ignored, and the backing of the element of order and progress was alienated from the agent and the government, and in the place of this strong backing that had maintained order for seven years was substituted Red Cloud and other nonprogressive chiefs, sustainers of the ancient tribal system.

If my successor had been other than an amateur, or had had any knowledge or experience in the inside Indian politics of an Indian tribe, he would have known that if the element he was endeavoring to relegate to the rear had not been the balance of power, I could not for seven years have held out against the mob element which he now sought to put in power. In other words, he unwittingly threw the balance of power at Pine Ridge against the government, as he later on discovered to his cost. When still later he endeavored to maintain order and suppress the ghost dance, the attempt resulted in a most dismal failure.

The Democratic agent was succeeded in October last by the recently removed Republican agent, a gentleman totally ignorant of Indians and their peculiarities; a gentleman with not a qualification in his make-up calculated to fit him for the position of agent at one of the largest and most difficult agencies in the service to manage; a man selected solely as a reward for political services. He might possibly have been an average success as an Indian agent at a small, well-regulated agency. He endeavored to strengthen up matters, but the chiefs and leaders who could have assisted him in so doing had been alienated by the former agent. They virtually said among themselves, "We, after incurring the enmity of the bad element among our people by sustaining the government, have been ignored and ill-treated by that government, hence this is not our affair." Being ignorant of the situation, he had no one to depend on. In his first clash with the mob element he discovered that the Pine Ridge police, formerly the finest in the service, were lacking in discipline and courage, and, not being well supplied with those necessary qualities himself, he took the bluff of a mob for a declaration of war, abandoned his agency, returned with troops—and you see the result.

As for the ghost dance, too much attention has been paid to it. It was only the symptom or surface indication of deep-rooted, long-existing difficulty; as well treat the eruption of smallpox as the disease and ignore the constitutional disease.

As regards disarming the Sioux, however desirable it may appear, I consider it neither advisable nor practicable. I fear that it will result as the theoretical enforcement of prohibition in Kansas, Iowa, and Dakota; you will succeed in disarming the friendly Indians, because yon can, and you will not so succeed with the mob element, because you can not. If I were again to be an Indian agent and had my choice, I would take charge of 10,000 armed Sioux in preference to a like number of disarmed ones; and, furthermore, agree to handle that number, or the whole Sioux nation, without a white soldier.

Respectfully, etc, V. T. Mcgillycuddy.

P. S.—I neglected to state that up to date there has been neither a Sioux outbreak nor war. No citizen in Nebraska or Dakota has been killed, molested, or can show the scratch of a pin, and no property has been destroyed off the reservation.

Statement of General Nelson A. Miles

Cause of Indian dissatisfaction.—The causes that led to the serious disturbance of the peace in the northwest last autumn and winter were so remarkable that an explanation of them is necessary in order to comprehend the seriousness of the situation. The Indians assuming the most threatening attitude of hostility were the Cheyennes and Sioux. Their condition may be stated as follows: For several years following their subjugation in 1877, 1878, and 1879 the most dangerous element of the Cheyennes and the Sioux were under military control. Many of them were disarmed and dismounted; their war ponies were sold and the proceeds returned to them in domestic stock, farming utensils, wagons, etc. Many of the Cheyennes, under the charge of military officers, were located on land in accordance with the laws of Congress, but after they were turned over to civil agents and the vast herds of buffalo and large game had been destroyed their supplies were insufficient, and they were forced to kill cattle belonging to white people to sustain life.

The fact that they had not received sufficient food is admitted by the agents and the officers of the government who have had opportunities of knowing. The majority of the Sioux were under the charge of civil agents, frequently changed and often inexperienced. Many of the tribes became rearmed and remounted. They claimed that the government had not fulfilled its treaties and had failed to make large enough appropriations for their support; that they had suffered for want of food, and the evidence of this is beyond question and sufficient to satisfy any unprejudiced intelligent mind. The statements of officers, inspectors, both of the military and the Interior departments, of agents, of missionaries, and civilians familiar with their condition, leave no room for reasonable doubt that this was one of the principal causes. While statements may be made as to the amount of money that has been expended by the government to feed the different tribes, the manner of distributing those appropriations will furnish one reason for the deficit.

The unfortunate failure of the crops in the plains country during the years of 1889 and 1890 added to the distress and suffering of the Indians, and it was possible for them to raise but very little from the ground for self-support; in fact, white settlers have been most unfortunate, and their losses have been serious and universal throughout a large section of that country. They have struggled on from year to year; occasionally they would raise good crops, which they were compelled to sell at low prices, while in the season of drought their labor was almost entirely lost. So serious have been their misfortunes that thousands have left that country within the last few years, passing over the mountains to the Pacific slope or returning to the east of the Missouri or the Mississippi.

The Indians, however, could not migrate from one part of the United States to another; neither could they obtain employment as readily as white people, either upon or beyond the Indian reservations. They must remain in comparative idleness and accept the results of the drought— an insufficient supply of food. This created a feeling of discontent even among the loyal and well disposed and added to the feeling of hostility of the element opposed to every process of civilization....

Indian Reports to the Commissioner of Indian Affairs: The Indian Story of Wounded Knee

Turning Hawk, Pine Ridge (Mr Cook, interpreter). Mr Commissioner, my purpose to-day is to tell what I know of the condition of affairs at the agency where I live. A certain falsehood came to our agency from the west which had the effect of a fire upon the Indians, and when this certain fire came upon our people those who had farsightedness and could see into the matter made up their minds to stand up against it and fight it. The reason we took this hostile altitude to this fire was because we believed that you yourself would not be in favor of this particular mischief-making thing; but just as we expected, the people in authority did not like this thing and we were quietly told that we must give up or have nothing to do with this certain movement. Though this is the advice from our good friends in the east, there were, of course, many silly young men who were longing to become identified with the movement,

although they knew that there was nothing absolutely bad, nor did they know there was anything absolutely good, in connection with the movement.

In the course of time we heard that the soldiers were moving toward the scene of trouble. After awhile some of the soldiers finally reached our place and we heard that a number of them also reached our friends at Rosebud. Of course, when a large body of soldiers is moving toward a certain direction they inspire a more or less amount of awe, and it is natural that the women and children who see this large moving mass are made afraid of it and be put in a condition to make them run away. At first we thought that Pine Ridge and Rosebud were the only two agencies where soldiers were sent, but finally we heard that the other agencies fared likewise. We heard and saw that about half our friends at Rosebud agency, from fear at seeing the soldiers, began the move of running away from their agency toward ours (Pine Ridge), and when they had gotten inside of our reservation they there learned that right ahead of them at our agency was another large crowd of soldiers, and while the soldiers were there, there was constantly a great deal of false rumor flying back and forth. The special rumor I have in mind is the threat that the soldiers had come there to disarm the Indians entirely and to take away all their horses from them. That was the oft-repeated story.

So constantly repeated was this story that our friends from Rosebud, instead of going to Pine Ridge, the place of their destination, veered off and went to some other direction toward the "Bad Lands." We did not know definitely how many, but understood there were 300 lodges of them, about 1,700 people. Eagle Pipe, Turning Bear, High Hawk, Short Bull, Lance, No Flesh, Pine Bird, Crow Dog, Two Strike, and White Horse were the leaders.

Well, the people after veering off in this way, many of them who believe in peace and order at our agency, were very anxious that some influence should be brought upon these people. In addition to our love of peace we remembered that many of these people were related to us by blood. So we sent out peace commissioners to the people who were thus running away from their agency.

I understood at the time that they were simply going away from fear because of so many soldiers.

So constant was the word of these good men from Pine Ridge agency that finally they succeeded in getting away half of the party from Rosebud, from the place where they took refuge, and finally were brought to the agency at Pine Ridge. Young-Man-Afraid-of-his-Horses, Little Wound, Fast Thunder, Louis Shangreau, John Grass, Jack Red Cloud, and myself were some of these peacemakers.

The remnant of the party from Rosebud not taken to the agency finally reached the wilds of the Bad Lands. Seeing that we had succeeded so well, once more we sent to the same party in the Bad Lands and succeeded in bringing these very Indians out of the depths of the Bad Lands and were being brought toward the agency. When we were about a day's journey from our agency we heard that a certain party of Indians (Big Foot's band) from the Cheyenne River agency was coming toward Pine Ridge in flight....

When we heard that these people were coming toward our agency we also heard this. These people were coming toward Pine Ridge agency, and when they were almost on the agency they were met by the soldiers and surrounded and finally taken to the Wounded Knee creek, and there at a given time their guns were demanded. When they had delivered them up, the men were separated from their families, from their tipis, and taken to a certain spot. When the guns were thus taken and the men thus separated, there was a crazy man, a young man of very bad influence and in fact a nobody, among that bunch of Indians fired his gun, and of course the firing of a gun must have been the breaking of a military rule of some sort, because immediately the soldiers returned fire and indiscriminate killing followed.

Spotted Horse. This man shot an officer in the army; the first shot killed this officer. I was a voluntary scout at that encounter and I saw exactly what was done, and that was what I noticed; that the first shot killed an officer. As soon as this shot was fired the Indians immediately began drawing their knives, and they were exhorted from all sides to desist, but this was not obeyed. Consequently the firing began immediately on the part of the soldiers.

Turning Hawk. All the men who were in a bunch were killed right there, and those who escaped that first fire got into the ravine, and as they went along up the ravine for a long distance they were pursued on both sides by the soldiers and shot down, as the dead bodies showed afterwards. The women were standing off at a different place from where the men were stationed, and when the firing began, those of the men who escaped the first onslaught went in one direction up the ravine, and then the women, who were bunched together at another place, went entirely in a different direction through an open field, and the women fared the same fate as the men who went up the deep ravine.

American Horse. The men were separated, as has already been said, from the women, and they were surrounded by the soldiers. Then came next the village of the Indians and that was entirely surrounded by the soldiers also. When the firing began, of course the people who were standing immediately around the young man who fired the first shot were killed right together, and then they turned their guns, Hotchkiss guns, etc., upon the women who were in the lodges standing there under a flag of truce, and of course as soon as they were fired upon they fled, the men fleeing in one direction and the women running in two different directions. So that there were three general directions in which they took flight.

There was a woman with an infant in her arms who was killed as she almost touched the flag of truce, and the women and children of course were strewn all along the circular village until they were dispatched. Right near the flag of truce a mother was shot down with her infant; the child not knowing that its mother was dead was still nursing, and that especially was a very sad sight. The women as they were fleeing with their babes were killed together, shot right through, and the women who were very heavy with child were also killed. All the Indians fled in these three directions, and after most all of them had been killed a cry was made that all those who were not killed or wounded should come forth and they would be safe. Little boys who were not wounded came out of their places of refuge, and as soon as they came in sight a number of soldiers surrounded them and butchered them there.

Of course we all feel very sad about this affair. I stood very loyal to the government all through those troublesome days, and believing so much in the government and being so loyal to it, my disappointment was very strong, and I have come to Washington with a very great blame on my heart. Of course it would have been all right if only the men were killed; we would feel almost grateful for it. But the fact of the killing of the women, and more especially the killing of the young boys and girls who are to go to make up the future strength of the Indian people, is the saddest part of the whole affair and we feel it very sorely.

I was not there at the time before the burial of the bodies, but I did go there with some of the police and the Indian doctor and a great many of the people, men from the agency, and we went through the battlefield and saw where the bodies were from the track of the blood.

Turning Hawk. I had just reached the point where I said that the women were killed. We heard, besides the killing of the men, of the onslaught also made upon the women and children, and they were treated as roughly and indiscriminately as the men and boys were.

Of course this affair brought a great deal of distress upon all the people, but especially upon the minds of those who stood loyal to the government and who did all that they were able to do in the matter of bringing about peace. They especially have suffered much distress and are very much hurt at heart. These peacemakers continued on in their good work, but there were a great many fickle young men who were ready to be moved by the change in the events there, and consequently, in spite of the great fire that was brought upon all, they were ready to assume any hostile attitude. These young men got themselves in readiness and went in the direction of the scene of battle so they might be of service there. They got there and finally exchanged shots with the soldiers. This party of young men was made up from Rosebud, Ogalalla (Pine Ridge), and members of any other agencies that happened to be there at the time. While this was going on in the neighborhood of Wounded Knee—the Indians and soldiers exchanging shots—the agency, our home, was also fired into by the Indians. Matters went on in this strain until the evening came on, and then the Indians went off down by White Clay creek. When the agency was fired upon by the Indians from the hillside, of course the shots were returned by the Indian police who were guarding the agency buildings.

Although fighting seemed to have been in the air, yet those who believed in peace were still constant at their work. Young-Man-Afraid-of-his-Horses, who had been on a visit to some other agency in the north or northwest, returned, and immediately went out to the people living about White Clay creek, on the border of the Bad Lands, and brought his people out. He succeeded in obtaining the consent of the people to come out of their place of refuge and return to the agency. Thus the remaining portion of the Indians who started from Rosebud were brought back into the agency. Mr Commissioner, during the days of the great whirlwind out there, those good men tried to hold up a counteracting power, and that was "Peace." We have now come to realize that peace has prevailed and won the day. While we were engaged in bringing about peace our property was left behind, of course, and most of us have lost everything, even down to the matter of guns with which to kill ducks, rabbits, etc, shotguns, and guns of that order. When Young-Man-Afraid brought the people in and their guns were asked for, both men who were called hostile and men who stood loyal to the government delivered up their guns.

GLOSSARY

aborigine: original inhabitants; the Native American tribes

allotments: individual grants of land

falsehood: a lie

"the Messiah delusion": a reference to the Ghost Dance movement

Document Analysis

Former Pine Ridge Agent Valentine T. McGillycuddy's Letter to General Leonard W. Colby (January 15)

McGillycuddy begins his statement by saying that there is no single cause for the "so-called" aggression by the Sioux. Instead, the events were the result of years of the "faulty" US policy toward Native American tribes, with "many" of the nation's treaties with tribes having been broken. McGillycuddy presses this point, reminding his audience that many treaties were not signed with the consent of the tribe as a whole. The Sioux, in particular, had seen their possessions shrink drastically.

McGillycuddy then shifts to the "natural race antagonism" that he believes exists between the Native and white peoples. He explains that there is a pattern of successive generations forgetting the horrors of war and that the current generation of Sioux warriors were children during the last outbreak of hostilities in 1876, which is one of the reasons that conflict had broken out. The leaders the old generation have influenced the young people. Compounding this was the fact that food supplies at Pine Ridge were low and the government had not kept its agreements on things like beef deliveries. As conflict grew, McGillycuddy argues that the "notoriously weak and unfit man" in charge precipitated the crisis by calling for troops. He goes on to explain that while he was agent, he did his job with no military presence for 60 miles around. No matter how fraught the situation became, he was able to keep the peace with the assistance of "progressive chiefs" and "Indian policemen." The difference lies in the new agent, appointed by the Democratic administration in 1886. Relations with the natives worsened under his control. Subsequent agents were just as incompetent. Conditions worsened and even without the Ghost Dance (which McGillycuddy dismisses as a symptom of larger issues).

Statement of General Nelson A. Miles

Miles places blame for the conflict on a long series of incidents rooted in the aftermath of the 1876 conflict. While the Natives were disarmed and given land and farming supplies, the destruction of buffalo and other large hunting game meant that the supplies the possessed were "insufficient," leading the natives to target cattle herds owned by whites. Miles points out that most of the Indian Agents were "frequently changed and often inexperienced" and tribes began to rearm. Food and supplies continued to be in short supply.

Crop failures in 1889 and 1890 made conditions worse. While white settlers could migrate out of the area (as many had) the natives were unable to do so, leading to feelings of "discontent" that contributed to existing hostility.

Indian Reports to the Commissioner of Indian Affairs: The Indian Story of Wounded Knee

Turning Hawk discusses the coming of the Ghost Dance movement to the reservation (the "certain falsehood" he mentions). While some at the reservation took a stand against this movement, others were enthralled by it. He then discusses the number of soldiers that came through the area, driving scared women and children to Pine Ridge from other reservations. There was a rumor that the troops were going to disarm the natives and take their horses. The rumor became widespread and, eventually, a large number of natives came to Pine Ridge. Troops rounded up Natives and took them to Wounded Knee, demanding their weapons and separating men from their families. A "crazy man" fired his gun and the soldiers fired back "and indiscriminate killing followed."

Spotted Horse testified that the "crazy man" shot an officer and the soldiers gave the natives a chance to "desist" that was refused before the firing started.

Turning Hawk continued his testimony explaining that some men escaped the first volley of fire, going down into a ravine. Soldiers were able to fire down into the ravine. Women were also shot by the soldiers at this time.

American Horse recounts that the soldiers used Hotchkiss guns against the women who had presented a flag of truce, which should have protected them against such actions and, in fact, were fired upon as they attempted to escape American Horse describes in great detail the killing of women carrying children. The solders also killed the young children of dead parents in cold blood. American Horse explains that he had always been supportive of the government despite the deprivations that the tribes had suffered during the late 1880s. The killing of innocent women and children, however, has motivated him to come to Washington to testify against the soldiers. The children, he explained, were "the future strength of the Indian people." He finishes his testimony by explaining that he was able to tell the position of the bodies "from the track of the blood."

Turning Hawk echoes some of these sentiments, explaining that the massacre had been the most difficult for those who had been loyal to the government and had worked the hardest for a continuing peace. Young men, especially, wanted to fight but peach eventually prevailed. As a result of this peace, however, they have lost their property, including the guns with which they would hunt.

Essential Themes

Cursory, thumbnail sketches of the Wounded Knee Massacre (and, indeed, of the entire history of the interactions between Native Americans and the American settlers, soldiers, and government officials in the Trans-Mississippi west) often tend to reduce the complexity of the narratives and of the parties involved. We hear of two forces in opposition to each other: "Whites" and "Native Americans." Each of these blocks, in this too-simplified approach, are uniform in their motivations, beliefs, and goals. The truth of such things, as demonstrated by the testimony from McGillycuddy, Miles, Turning Hawk, Spotted Horse, and American Horse, is much more complex. Within the "white" or "American" side, tensions exist between political appointees of different approaches and levels of experience (as we see in McGillycuddy's complaints about his successors) and between military officials and civilian officials. Officials pledged to work for the welfare of those on the reservation for which they're responsible come into conflict with officers and soldiers who have their own agendas. Within the "Native American" side, generational conflicts between those who wish to work for the best possible life under the American regime and those who urge resistance and join with outlawed movement illustrate that the story of the Wounded Knee Massacre—and the story of the relationships between different populations in the American west—are far more complex than they first appear.

———*Aaron Gulyas, MA*
with additional material by Keith E. Sealing, JD

Bibliography and Additional Reading

Andersson, Rani-Henrik. *The Lakota Ghost Dance of 1890* (Lincoln, NE: University of Nebraska Press, 2009).

Coleman, William S.E. *Voices of Wounded Knee* (Lincoln: University of Nebraska Press, 2000).

Greene, Jerome A. *American Carnage: Wounded Knee, 1890* (Norman, OK: University of Oklahoma Press, 2014).

Utley, Robert M. *The Indian Frontier 1846–1890.* (Albuquerque: University of New Mexico Press, 2003).

■ Indians of All Tribes Occupation of Alcatraz: Proclamation

Date: 1969
Authors: Richard Oakes and Indians of All Tribes
Genre: Public declaration

Summary Overview

Most people are familiar with Alcatraz, an island in San Francisco Bay, because for three decades the island served as a federal prison—where, for example, the notorious gangster Al Capone was incarcerated. It had also served as the site of a fort and of a lighthouse. As a prison, "the Rock" was closed in 1963. In November 1969 a group of Native American rights activists issued a proclamation in connection with their occupation of Alcatraz Island. This proclamation, attributed to "Indians of All Tribes," had a dual purpose. One goal was to highlight the impoverished and desperate conditions faced by Native Americans on the many reservations in the United States. Unemployment, the lack of an effective education system, disproportionately high rates of alcoholism and suicide, and other issues drove protesters to publicize these situations. Another goal of this declaration is to promote the culture and history of the original inhabitants of North America.

Defining Moment

On November 9, 1969, a group of American Indians led by Richard Oakes symbolically claimed the island as Indian land. On November 20 the group began an occupation of Alcatraz Island that lasted until June 11, 1971. The occupiers, initially about eighty-nine of them (though the number later grew to about a hundred), were from various tribes, so the proclamation was issued in the name of "Indians of All Tribes." This was not the first time Indians had occupied Alcatraz. A similar event had taken place in 1964, but the occupation lasted just four hours and was designed to raise the public's awareness of the plight of American Indians. The 1969–1971 occupation in effect launched what came to be known as the Red Power Movement. The goal of the movement was to assert the right of Indian self-determination and to preserve Indian culture rather than allow it to be absorbed into the larger white culture and. The Red Power Movement would later give rise to such events as the 1972 occupation of the Bureau of Indian Affairs in Washington, D.C., and the seizure of the town of Wounded Knee, South Dakota, in 1973.

Over the nineteen months of the occupation, divisions began to develop. Some groups opposed the leadership of Richard Oakes. A number of the occupiers, including Oakes himself, returned to the mainland. Hippies and elements of the drug culture began to move to the island. Meanwhile, the federal government, after initially demanding that the occupiers leave, adopted a hands-off policy, although power and water to the island were cut off. The lack of leadership meant that the government had no one with whom to negotiate. To raise money, the occupiers stripped the facility of copper wire and sold it. Finally, on June 10, 1971, federal agents forcibly removed the small number of people left on the island, and by the next day the occupation had ended. Nevertheless, the occupation had achieved its symbolic goals in eliciting support for government policies that would improve the lot of American Indians.

Author Biography

While the declaration was composed with input from a number of the 89 activists who occupied Alcatraz, the group was led by Richard Oakes. The tone and content of the declaration reflects his beliefs about the important of sovereignty for Native American nations—including control over their land and their cultural legacies.

Oakes was born in New York in 1942. He worked as a construction worker, specializing in dangerous work such as constructing bridges. In the late 1960s, Oakes abandoned his family in the northeast and moved to San Francisco, coming into contact with members of the "Red Power" community in the Bay area. As a student at San Francisco State University, Oakes helped develop what would be one of the first Native American Studies departments in the United States.

In 1969, he led the Alcatraz occupation, an operation that would last until 1971. Initially, Oakes's leadership and the establishment of rules about security, child care, and other necessary tasks enabled the the occupying community to lay the foundation for a long term occupation and, eventually, the establishment of the educational and cultural facilities and institutions described in their declaration. Oakes himself, however, left the island in 1970 after his stepdaughter fell, striking her head and dying. Lacking Oakes's leadership—and because other occupiers left the island along with him—leadership disputes and the arrival of non-native activists derailed the goals of the occupation and the final protesters were evicted by the US Government in the summer of 1971.

Oakes continued his work on behalf of Native American tribes until his death from a gunshot wound in 1972.

HISTORICAL DOCUMENT

To the Great White Father and All His People:

We, the native Americans, re-claim the land known as Alcatraz Island in the name of all American Indians by right of discovery.

We wish to be fair and honorable in our dealings with the Caucasian inhabitants of this land, and hereby offer the following treaty:

We will purchase said Alcatraz Island for twenty-four dollars ($24) in glass beads and red cloth, a precedent set by the white man's purchase of a similar island about 300 years ago. We know that $24 in trade goods for these 16 acres is more than was paid when Manhattan Island was sold, but we know that land values have risen over the years. Our offer of $1.24 per acre is greater than the 47 cents per acre the white men are now paying the California Indians for their land.

We will give to the inhabitants of this island a portion of that land for their own, to be held in trust by the American Indian Government — for as long as the sun shall rise and the rivers go down to the sea — to be administered by the Bureau of Caucasian Affairs (BCA).

We will further guide the inhabitants in the proper way of living. We will offer them our religion, our education, our life-ways, in order to help them achieve our level of civilization and thus raise them and all their white brothers up from their savage and unhappy state.

We offer this treaty in good faith and wish to be fair and honorable in our dealings with all white men.

We feel that this so-called Alcatraz Island is more than suitable for an Indian Reservation, as determined by the white man's own standards. By this we mean that this place resembles most Indian reservations, in that:

1. It is isolated from modern facilities, and without adequate means of transportation.

2. It has no fresh running water.

3. It has inadequate sanitation facilities.

4. There are no oil or mineral rights.

5. There is no industry so unemployment is great.

6. There are no health care facilities.

7. The soil is rocky and non-productive; and the land does not support game.

8. There are no educational facilities.

9. The population has always exceeded the land base.

10. The population has always been held as prisoners and kept dependent upon others.

Further, it would be fitting and symbolic that ships from all over the world, entering the Golden Gate, would first see Indian land, and thus be reminded of the true history of this nation. This tiny island would he a symbol of the great lands once ruled by free and noble Indians.

Use To Be Made of Alcatraz Island

What use will be made of this land?

Since the San Francisco Indian Center burned down, there is no place for Indians to assemble and carry on our tribal life here in the white man's city. Therefore, we plan to develop on this island several Indian institutes:

1. A Center for Native American Studies will be developed which will train our young people in the best of our native cultural arts and sciences, as well as educate them to the skills and knowledge relevant to improve the lives and spirits of all Indian peoples. Attached to this center will be traveling universities, managed by Indians, which will go to the Indian Reservations in order to learn the traditional values from the people, which are now absent in the Caucasian higher educational system.

2. An American Indian Spiritual center will be developed which will practice our ancient tribal religious ceremonies and medicine. Our cultural arts

will be featured and our young people trained in music, dance, and medicine.

3. An Indian Center of Ecology will be built which will train and support our young people in scientific research and practice in order to restore our lands and waters to their pure and natural state. We will seek to de-pollute the air and the water of the Bay Area. We will seek to restore fish and animal life, and to revitalize sea life which has been threatened by the white man's way. Facilities will be developed to desalt sea water for human use.

4. A Great Indian Training School will be developed to teach our peoples how to make a living in the world, improve our standards of living, and end hunger and unemployment among all our peoples. This training school will include a center for Indian arts and crafts, and an Indian Restaurant serving native foods and training Indians in culinary arts. This center will display Indian arts and offer the Indian foods of all tribes to the public, so they all may know of the beauty and spirit of the traditional Indian ways.

5. Some of the present buildings will be taken over to develop an American Indian Museum, which will depict our native foods and other cultural contributions we have given to all the world. Another part of the Museum will present some of the things the white man has given to the Indians, in return for the land and the life he took: disease, alcohol, poverty, and cultural decimation (as symbolized by old tin cans, barbed wire, rubber tires, plastic containers, etc.). Part of the museum will remain a dungeon, to symbolize both Indian captives who were incarcerated for challenging white authority, and those who were imprisoned on reservations. The Museum will show the noble and the tragic events of Indian history, including the broken treaties, the documentary of the Trail of Tears, the Massacre of Wounded Knee, as well as the victory over Yellow-Hair Custer and his army.

In the name of all Indians, therefore, we re-claim this island for Indian nations, for all these reasons. We feel this claim is just and proper, and that this land should rightfully be granted to us for as long as the rivers shall run and the sun shall shine.

SIGNED, INDIANS OF ALL TRIBES
November 1969 San Francisco, California

GLOSSARY

Bureau of Caucasian Affairs (BCA): an ironic reference to the Bureau of Indian Affairs, which established and regulated, among other things, Indian reservations

game: animals that are hunted for food

Document Analysis

The document begins by claiming Alcatraz for all American Indians "by right of discovery." The proclamation then alludes to the Dutch purchase of Manhattan in 1626, allegedly for goods worth about $24. The proclamation offers a treaty by which the Indians will buy the island for an equivalent amount. The declaration then offers to train and educate the people of the island in Indian religion, culture and history, "and thus raise them and all their white brothers up from their savage and unhappy state." This is a reversal of the tradition American policy toward Native American tribes, which aimed to "civilize" them by training them in American ways of life and conversion to Christianity. The proc-lamation then says that the island would be appropriate as an Indian reservation because it has many of the characteristics of other Indian reservations, including lack of modern facilities, industry, medical care, educational facilities, inadequate healthcare, overcrowding, and other significant concerns. This list of ten grievances about the conditions of Indian reservations illustrates the shift in tone from the clever irony of the early part of the declaration to a serious protest. The final statement of this first part of the declaration asserts the need for the world to understand "the true history" of the United States.

The proclamation then lists the uses that Indians would make of the island. The Indians would develop a number of "institutes," including a Center for Native American Studies, an American Indian spiritual center, an ecology center, a training school for Indians, and a museum. Much of the proclamation is highly ironic. For example, the museum would display "the things the white man has given to the Indians, in return for the land and the life he took: disease, alcohol, poverty, and cultural decimation." The museum would also memorialize such events as the Trail of Tears, when Indians were forcibly removed from their lands east of the Mississippi River in 1838 and 1839 and moved to Oklahoma under President Andrew Jackson's Indian removal policy; the Massacre of Wounded Knee, the 1890 battle that essentially ended the Indian wars; and the defeat of General George Armstrong Custer and his forces by the combined forces of Lakota Sioux and Cheyenne at the Battle of the Little Bighorn in Montana Territory in 1876. Most aspects of this list of possible uses for Alcatraz, however, are not intended to be ironic. The goals of the ecology center to reverse environmental damage. The other plans are deeply concerned with establishing and developing institutions of education, pride, and self-determination for a Native American population that has languished for decades in the oppressive reservation system. The proclamation concludes with the statement that the island should be granted to Indians for their use "for as long as the rivers shall run and the sun shall shine"—a phrase that often appeared in treaties between the United States and Native American tribes and that, by the 1960s, history had shown to be a false promise.

Essential Themes

The 1969 declaration of the activists who occupied Alcatraz island is a notable artifact of the era. This is not only because it serves as an example of the way in which they adopted and adapted tactics and goals of the civil rights movement but also because of the cultural and historical symbolism that Richard Oakes and his fellow protesters employed during the course of their occupation and the crafting of their declaration. References to the purchase of Manhattan Island and the corresponding offer to purchase Alcatraz for $24 in beads and cloth reverses the somewhat cliched historical episode in order to highlight both the absurdity and injustice of the uneven relationship between Native tribes and white colonizers and their descendants. Likewise, their announcement that they will grant "the inhabitants of this island a portion of that land for their own, to be held in trust by the American Indian Government" satirizes and inverts the relationship between the Federal government and Native American tribes, again illustrating absurdity and inequality. The detailed breakdown of the resemblance of Alcatraz to reservations and the group's plans for turning the island into a site for cultural revitalization combines the expressing of physical grievances with a nuanced critique of the way that Native cultures had been subjugated over the centuries.

——*Michael J. O'Neal, PhD*

Bibliography and Additional Reading

Johnson, Troy R. "Roots of Contemporary Native American Activism," *American Indian Culture and Research Journal*, 20(2):127–154.

——. *The Occupation of Alcatraz Island: Indian Self-determination and the Rise of Indian Activism* (University of Illinois Press, 1996).

Kelly, Casey Ryan (2014). "Détournement, Decolonization, and the American Indian Occupation of Alcatraz Island (1969–1971)". *Rhetoric Society Quarterly*. 44 (2): 168.

Smith, Paul Chaar and Robert Allen Warrior. *Like a Hurricane: The Indian Movement from Alcatraz to Wounded Knee* (New York: The New Press, 1996)

■ Summary of Letter Requesting Further Review of the Dakota Access Pipeline (DAPL)

Date: October 10, 2016
Authors: Sierra Club, Honor the Earth, and the Indigenous Environmental Network
Genre: Formal document

Summary Overview

In this document, a coalition of Native American and environmental activists petitioned the U.S. Army Corps of Engineers to reevaluate the potential environmental risks and impact of the Dakota Access Pipeline (DAPL), a multi-state petroleum pipeline controversially passing under the Missouri River just upstream of the Lake Oahe at the border of South and North Dakota. Further, the letter alleges that the company responsible for construction of the pipeline purposefully destroyed recent archaeological discoveries suggesting a Native American burial ground in the area set aside for construction of the pipeline.

Defining Moment

The Dakota Access Pipeline (DAPL) controversy, also called the Standing Rock Sioux protest, was a combined Indigenous rights/environmental protest in opposition to the DAPL construction project near lands occupied by the Standing Rock Sioux tribe. From a conservation/environmentalist perspective, the protest movement could be seen as part of a broader effort to limit petroleum development in general and fracking or oil shale harvesting in particular. Further, environmental and human rights activists were concerned that the proposed path for the pipeline posed a danger to the drinking water used by the Standing Rock Sioux population Finally, the Standing Rock Sioux and other indigenous rights activists accused the Army Corps of Engineers of violating treaties between the United States and the Standing Rock Sioux, which can be seen as part of a much older debate regarding governmental exploitation of Native Americans.

Depending on one's perspective, the 2010s could be seen as a pivotal time in the history of US environmental policy and the future of the petroleum industry. The DAPL project involves "fracking," or "hydraulic fracturing," which is a controversial method used to extract oil from sandstone, limestone, and shale. Opponents of fracking have argued that the process is more expensive, produces more waste, and poses a unique health threat to communities around areas where fracking occurs be-

cause of the increased potential for water and soil pollution. In addition, opponents of fracking argue that further land development to support petroleum exploration of any kind will deepen the climate change problem and potentially divert resources and attention that might otherwise go to developing renewable energy projects such as wind, solar, geothermal, and wave/tidal energy. Supporters of fracking are typically motivated by the potential profits from continued oil development and argue that fracking leads to less greenhouse gas emissions than traditional coal mining and is therefore a cleaner alternative.

While the Obama administration, responding to environmental and economic studies and public sentiment, abandoned another pipeline project, Keystone XL, in 2015, the DAPL project controversy peaked during the 2016 election. Electoral vote winner Donald Trump, during his campaign, pledged to support petroleum exploration, including revitalizing abandoned projects like the Keystone XL pipeline, and to revitalize the coal industry. The Standing Rock Sioux protests therefore also drew in support from individuals concerned about the Trump administration's overall stance on environmental politics. Trump, for instance, has refuted the findings of climate change scientists, and has personal investments in two of the companies involved in the DAPL project, Energy Transfer Partners and Sunoco.

The most complicated issue surrounding DAPL involves the federal government's claim of "eminent domain," in which a government can claim privately owned land for public as long as the government provides fair compensation to the original land owners. Part of the land set aside for DAPL falls into the Black Hills of North Dakota, a sacred site to the Sioux of the region. Much of the territory was given to the Sioux by the 1868 Treaty of Fort Laramie. However, after the Sioux Wars, the government forced the Sioux to accept a new agreement in which much of their original land returned to government control. In 1980, after a long legal battle, the courts ruled that the land had been taken unjustly and ordered the government to compensate the Sioux. The government offered payment, but the Sioux tribe declined and continues to lobby for the return of the sacred Black Hills land. The Standing Rock Sioux claim that the government has no right to grant the corporations use of their ancestral land, and this is part of a much older debate regarding the ownership of land that once belonged to Native American tribes. During an emergency archaeological survey of land within the construction area, conducted by Sioux archaeologist Tim Mentz, archeological artifacts indicating a potential Sioux burial site were allegedly discovered. However, the Standing Rock Sioux alleges that the company purposefully destroyed the alleged artifacts before they could be studied in an effort to remove evidence of archaeological significance that would likely have necessitated postponing construction.

Author Biography

The Sierra Club is one of the oldest environmental organizations in the United States, having been founded in 1892 by pioneer conservationist John Muir. The Sierra Club has been instrumental in passing key US environmental legislation, including the Clean Air Act, the Clean Water Act, and the Endangered Species Act. In the 21st century, the Sierra Club has gravitated towards environmental lobbying for green energy and opposition to petroleum industry expansion. In 2017, three of the organization's major campaigns were the Beyond Coal, Beyond Natural Gas, and Beyond Oil campaigns, which seek to educate the public about the economic and environmental benefits of alternative energy and about the dangers of fossil fuel consumption, including climate change, pollution, and related effects on public health.

Honor the Earth is a Minneapolis, Minnesota based activist organization that focuses on environmental issues facing indigenous populations. The organization was founded in 1993 by musicians Amy Ray and Emily Saliers and activist Winona LaDuke of the Ojibwe Nation. LaDuke, who serves as the organization's executive director, was a two-time vice-presidential candidate with Green Party candidate Ralph Nader in 1996 and 2000 and received an electoral college vote for vice president in 2016, become the first Native American woman to receive a vice presidential electoral vote. Among other issues, Honor the Earth supports Native American voting efforts and has been involved in campaigns to protect indigenous sacred and archaeological sites, as well as getting involved in campaigns to promote renewable energy and other anti-petroleum power initiatives.

The Indigenous Environmental Network (IEN) is an alliance of indigenous individuals and groups dedicated to protecting indigenous culture and rights and working towards renewable energy and environmental conservation. The organization was founded in 1990, and is currently led by executive director Tom Goldtooth, a U.S. Army veteran and member of the Navajo nation who was a prominent organization for Native American rights after the Vietnam Conflict. The IEN is one of the organization that spearheaded the fight against the proposed Keystone XL Pipeline, a project initiated by a Canadian company extending from the Canadian Oil Sands to the Gulf Coast of the United States. In November 2016, the Obama administration rejected the pipeline project, citing climate change concern in addition to analyses indicating that the project would not benefit U.S. consumers, create meaningful job growth, or increase U.S. energy security.

HISTORICAL DOCUMENT

"They arrived immediately after the sites were identified with security guards wielding attack dogs and pepper spray." Summary of Letter Requesting Further Review of the Dakota Access Pipeline (DAPL)
October 10, 2016
Sierra Club, Honor the Earth, and Indigenous Environmental Network requested that the Corps take the following actions with respect to the DAPL:

1. Investigate whether DAPL intentionally destroyed sacred and culturally-significant sites as prohibited by the National Historic Preservation Act (NHPA).

- Section 110(k) of the NHPA prohibits the U.S. Army Corps of Engineers (Corps) from granting any additional permits to DAPL if it has if it has intentionally destroyed historic-eligible sites. 54 U.S.C. § 306113 ("Anticipatory Demolition"). The Corps is evaluating whether to grant a permit and easement for DAPL to cross Corps jurisdictional areas under and adjacent to Lake Oahe in North Dakota. The Corps must investigate whether DAPL intentionally destroyed historic-eligible sites and deny the Lake Oahe permits if it finds in the affirmative.

- On September 2, 2016, the Standing Rock Sioux Tribe (Standing Rock) submitted detailed findings of its archaeologist, Tim Mentz, describing an unusually dense collection of cultural and historic sites located on the pipeline route, including five stone features and 27 grave sites. Mentz described it as "one of the most significant archeological finds in North Dakota in many years." The archaeologist Thomas F. King, Ph.D. confirmed that Mentz possesses all the qualifications to inform his studies of the site and that his observations are derived from a lifelong immersion in the traditional culture of Standing Rock.

- Early the next morning, DAPL arrived at the exact 2-mile location described by Standing Rock in their filing and bulldozed the sites that Standing Rock had identified. As court filings explain, many factors suggest this was intentional. For example, the work crews normally proceed in a linear fashion, but had not previously been working within 20 miles of that site. They arrived immediately after the sites were identified with security guards wielding attack dogs and pepper spray.

2. Prepare an environmental impact statement (EIS) or supplemental EIS (SEIS) for the Corps' approval of the Lake Oahe crossing (and/or an SEIS for NWP 12 as it applies to DAPL).

- The National Environmental Policy Act ("NEPA") requires agencies to supplement their NEPA analyses if "[t]here are significant new circumstances or information relevant to environmental concerns and bearing on the proposed action or its impacts." 40 C.F.R. §1502.9. Similarly, the Corps cannot authorize a project under Nationwide Permit 12 (NWP 12) if information shows the project would have more than "minimal adverse environmental effects." 33 U.S.C. § 1344(e)(1). If projects exceed this threshold, or if further review would serve the public interest, they must undergo an individual CWA §404 permit process and attendant NEPA analysis, even if the Corps has already approved a project under NWP 12. See, e.g., 33 C.F.R. § 330.1(d) (discussing the modification, revocation, or suspension of NWP authorizations).

- The Corps has never devoted a single page of analysis to the risks of oil spills and leaks from DAPL, which is alarming considering that contamination of waterways is among the most controversial aspects of DAPL. New information on oil pipeline spills, many of which have occurred since the Corps' EA was published, demonstrate: (a) the frequency and impacts of pipeline accidents; (b) the inability of pipeline operators to detect and respond to spills; (c) the number of spills that are detected and reported by citizens; and (d) the inability of federal agencies to regulate pipelines once they are constructed. For example, in September 2016, a passerby reported a 336,000 gallon pipeline spill in Alabama; and in June of 2016, a resident of Ventura, CA reported a 30,000 gallon spill of crude oil near his home. On September 30, 2016, Reuters reported that PHMSA data shows that out of 466 pipeline spills in the last six years, more spills were detected by the public (21%) than by the monitoring system DAPL would use (19%).

- Nor has the Corps ever analyzed greenhouse gas emissions associated with DAPL. On August 1, 2016, the Council on Environmental Quality (CEQ) released its Final Guidance on Greenhouse Gases and Climate Change, which instructs agencies to take a comprehensive, broad approach in analyzing the climate impacts of federal actions. The Corps' EA for Lake Oahe makes absolutely no attempt to quantify the greenhouse gas emissions associated with the operation of DAPL, which are significant. For example, an analysis published by Oil Change International on September 12, 2016 estimates that the pipeline would result in an additional 101.4 million metric tons of CO_2 emissions per year, which is equivalent to 30 coal fired power plants or over 21 million U.S. passenger vehicles. An increasing body of scientific literature, including a September 26, 2016 study in Nature Climate Change, indicates that expanding fossil fuel infrastructure like DAPL will jeopardize our ability to meet our climate reductions targets agreed to in the Paris climate accord.

- The Corps must evaluate the environmental justice implications of DAPL as required by Executive Order 12898 and other directives, including whether the pipeline would disproportionately impact Native American communities. On August 18, 2016, the Bismarck Tribune revealed that DAPL originally considered routing the pipeline through Bismarck, but declined to do so over fears that the pipeline could contaminate the city's drinking water supply. Instead, DAPL chose a route that passes directly under Lake Oahe near Standing Rock's drinking water supply over the objections of EPA. The EA fails to address these glaring inequities, and the Corps must do so in an EIS. On September 23, 2016, the United Nations special envoy for the rights of indigenous people called on the U.S. government to halt construction due to threats to the drinking water supplies and sacred sites of Standing Rock and other indigenous nations.

3. Revoke and/or suspend approvals in federal jurisdictional areas pending the preparation of an EIS and/or an individual §404 permit

- NEPA requires the Corps and other agencies to suspend all approvals in federal jurisdictional areas along DAPL while an EIS is being prepared. Otherwise, the entire 1,168-miles of the pipeline will be already constructed up to the edges of Lake Oahe, which will unduly prejudice the outcome and limit the Corps' choice among alternatives.

- First, NEPA prohibits agencies from segmenting their approval of a project, as it requires all "connected" actions to be analyzed together unless they would have independent utility. See 40 C.F.R. § 1508.25 (a)(1). None of the federally-approved parts of DAPL meet the independent utility test, and thus must be considered in a single EIS. Those include, but are not limited to: the Corps' consideration of the Lake Oahe permits; the Corps' grant of §408 permits for pipeline segments in Illinois; the Fish and Wildlife Service's grant of easements across federal grasslands and wetlands in North and South Dakota; and the Corps' Omaha, Rock Island, and St. Louis districts' issuance of verifications of DAPL's water crossings under NWP 12.

- Second, where more than one federal agency is "involved in the same action" or are "involved in a group of actions directly related to each other because of their functional interdependence or geographical proximity," the agencies shall select a lead agency to "supervise the preparation of an environmental impact statement." 40 C.F.R. § 1501.5(a). The Fixing America's Surface Transportation Act further requires the selection of a lead agency to identify all federal approvals and coordinate them in a single NEPA review.

- Third, NEPA prohibits agencies from approving component parts of an interrelated project before the NEPA review is complete, because piecemeal approval and construction would limit the choice among project alternatives and exert undue pressure on the final decision-maker. Until the final approval of a project, agencies cannot take any actions that would "[h]ave an adverse environmental impact" or "[l]imit the choice of reasonable alternatives." 40 C.F.R. § 1506.1(a).

- Therefore, the Corps, FWS, and other federal agencies should suspend or revoke all permits or approvals of DAPL in federal jurisdictional areas, and notify DAPL that it cannot proceed with construction in those areas until the agencies can select a lead agency and prepare an EIS that encompasses all federal aspects of the connected project.

GLOSSARY

pepper spray: chemical agents that irritates the eyes and causes pain and temporary blindness.

easement: the right to cross over or use land belonging to another person or entity for a specific purpose.

NEPA: the National Environmental Policy Act established in 1970 that requires federal agencies to assess the environmental effects of proposed actions.

CORPS: United States Army Corps of Engineers, U.S. federal agency under the Department of Defense responsible public engineering and land management.

DAPL: Dakota Access Pipeline, or Bakken pipeline, an underground oil pipeline project connecting shale oil fields in North Dakota to an oil tank farm in Patoka, Illinois.

Standing Rock: Native American reservation located in North Dakota occupied by members of the Sioux ethnolinguistic group.

EIS: Environmental Impact Statement, a legal document required by NEPA for describing the positive and negative environmental impacts of various actions.

Lake Oahe: large reservoir of the Missouri River in portions of North and South Dakota.

eminent domain: the right of a government to claim land that is part of private property for public use, with compensation.

Document Analysis

In October of 2016, members of the Sierra Club, Honor the Earth and the Indigenous Environmental Network drafted a letter to the U.S. Army Corps of Engineers outlining the concerns of all three organizations regarding the DAPL project and asking the Corps of Engineers to investigate misconduct on the part of the companies involved, to commit to a comprehensive environmental study of the potential impacts of the project, and to either revoke or suspend the Corps approval for use of the lands petitioned by the companies involved in the project. While many journalistic and popular accounts of the DAPL debate were written in the fall and winter of 2016, the Sierra Club, Honor the Earth, and Indigenous Environmental Network letter is a legal response to actions taken by DAPL and the Corps of Engineers that allegedly violated environmental and historical preservation laws.

The first part of the letter concerns the rights of Native American peoples and accuses the companies leading the DAPL of violating the National Historic Preservation Act (NHPA), a 1966 public law that protects areas with historical or archaeological significance. According to the official statement, the Standing Rock

Sioux Tribe submitted detailed findings regarding the discovery of an "unusually dense collection of cultural and historic sites," located along the planned route of the pipeline, including at least 27 grave sites and five stone features. The findings had been discovered by Sioux archaeologist Tim Mentz and became part of the U.S. District Court case *Standing Rock Sioux Tribe v. U.S. Army Corps of Engineers*. According to official court documents, Mentz submitted details of his findings to the courts on and the State Historic Preservation Office on September 2, 2016. Among other findings, Mentz described a large stone chiseled with a representation of the constellation Big Dipper, known to the Sioux as Iyokaptan Tanka, which Mentz argued indicated that the site might contain the remains of a former chief. Mentz and the Standing Rock Sioux argued DAPL's survey of the area, which found no evidence of archaeological remains, was based on a 1985 survey of the area, which had failed to uncover the remains that Mentz discovered. The tribe further argued that, according to North Dakota Tribal Reinternment Committee law, the tribe would have the right to excavate and rebury any remains in the era. Mentz further declared his belief that the bodies would have been buried in shallow graves covered in rock cairns and that the burial sites would therefore be vulnerable to even superficial disturbance.

According to the contributors to the letter, on the morning of September 3rd, DAPL arrived at the 2-mile location where Mentz found archaeological remains and bulldozed the exact sites that had been mentioned in the tribe's official statement to the Historic Preservation Office. Standing Rock and allies officially filed a court complaint accusing DAPL of purposefully destroying the site to destroy evidence of archaeological findings that might have led to a legal challenge against DAPL. As evidence, the letter claims that the work crews that arrived at the site the following day had moved more than 20 miles from where the crews had been working the day before. Further, the letter alleges that, just after the historical sites had been discovered, DAPL security arrived with dogs and pepper spray to chase protestors away from the contested, potential historical sites.

In the second section of the official request, the Standing Rock Sioux tribe and allies formally request that the Army Corps of Engineers conduct an immediate study to produce an environmental impact statement (EIS). Specifically, the authors want the Corps of Engineers to study potential effects of a pipeline rupture or spill under the Missouri River and how this might affect the waters of Lake Oahe that provides a water supply for the Standing Rock Sioux. The letter asserts that the National Environmental Policy Act (NEPA) requires an analysis if new circumstances arise indicating additional environmental concerns, and the authors argue further that federal laws prohibit the continuation of the project until an official EIS finds that the project would have "minimal adverse environmental effects."

In their letter, the coalition argues that the Corps of Engineers never published or submitted any information specifically addressing the risks of oil spills and leaks and argued that past projects managed by Energy Transfer Partners resulted in leaks with significant environmental consequences. To justify this claim, the letter specifies that new information had been revealed since the Corps released their initial environmental analysis indicating that oil spills and accidents were more common than previously believed, that current safety systems were inadequate to detect leaks, and that federal agencies could not effectively manage pipelines once constructed. The letter cites a September 2016 discovery of a pipeline spill reported by a citizen in Alabama, which reportedly released more than

336,000 gallons into the surrounding area. Further, the letter cites a *Reuters* news study indicating that there had been 466 pipeline spills in the six years prior to 2016 and that more than 21 percent had been detected by members of the public, versus only 19 percent detected by the safety system that would be used to monitor the DAPL. The authors further claim that another company involved in the project, Sunoco Logistics, has been responsible for more oil spills than any other oil exploration firm. Data collected from the national disaster management system by *Reuters* estimated that Sunoco was responsible for 203 leaks since 2010, while information from the U.S. National Response Data on projects managed by Energy Transfer Partners revealed at least 69 accidents in 2 years polluting water supplies in 4 states, with more than half of the accidents resulting from ruptures in a petroleum pipeline.

Further, the authors argued that the Corps of Engineers failed to analyze the potential greenhouse gas emissions that would result from the DAPL project, and cited a September 2016 report from Oil Change International indicating that DAPL may result in as much as 101.4 million metric tons of CO2 emissions annually, which the authors note is the equivalent of 21 million passenger vehicles and 30 coal-based power plants. The authors then go on to cite a widely publicized discovery that the project had been moved from its original course, traveling closer to Bismarck, North Dakota, due to concerns that the pipeline might threaten water supplies in the region. The evidence behind this claim became part of a widely-circulated fake news item asserting that DAPL had decided to move the pipeline project away from Bismarck because the plan had been rejected by white property owners in the area. The fake news version of the story then suggested that the decision to move the pipeline closer to Native American settlements represented racism on the part of the executives involved. Later evidence showed that DAPL abandoned an initial plan to pass close to Bismarck because it would have extended the pipeline length and because construction would have been close to residential areas. The white citizens of Bismarck did not reject the project, however, as the news item claimed.

Lastly, the authors of the letter ask the Corps of Engineers to suspend any easements granting DAPL the right to construct on the disputed territory until an environmental analysis was completed. The third argument draws heavily on provisions of NEPA that prohibit construction on any part of a planned project until the impact of the entire project has been assessed. In essence, the third part of the letter reframes the environmental arguments made earlier, drawing on existing NEPA regulations, and asks that the Corps of Engineers postpone construction and establish a lead agency, of the various agencies involved, to coordinate efforts for a full environmental impact study.

Essential Themes

Much like the effort to defeat the Keystone XL pipeline project in 2015, the opposition to the DAPL project drew support from both indigenous rights activists and environmental activists. Like the Keystone XL project, the anti-DAPL movement demonstrated how the goals of indigenous peoples and environmental activists overlap on issues of conservation and environmental protection. While some supporters of DAPL criticized environmentalists for "using" the Native Americans at Standing Rock to promote their agenda, both groups shared legitimate interests. The effort to preserve aspects of Native American culture from erosion, necessarily involves, and has long involved, the need to preserve remnants of American biospheres. This occurs because indigenous culture, by its nature, is linked to the environment in ways that imported European-American culture is not. Teaching traditional skills and passing on information about the history and cultural legacy of indigenous people is dependent on the ability to preserve areas with cultural/spiritual significance.

The timing of the DAPL protests, occurring in the midst of the 2016 presidential election, played a major role in how the protest movement developed. Given Donald Trump's personal investments in petroleum and statements pledging to expand petroleum development, participants on both sides recognized that the outcome of the election would likely have a dramatic influence on the future of DAPL specifically, and potentially, oil exploration in general. As reported by numerous news agencies, Donald Trump was a personal stockholder in the Texas-based Energy Transfer Partners, owning between $15,000 and $50,000 in stock according to federal disclosure forms, as well as between $100,000 and $250,000 in Phillips 66, a petroleum distribution chain with a ¼ share of the project. This personal financial stake, coupled with Trump's stance on climate change and environmental legislation, helped garner unprecedented levels of support for the Standing Rock Sioux and the DAPL Project.

The fight against DAPL took place simultaneously in the courts and on the ground, in the area around the construction site, where thousands gathered in makeshift camps to protest the project. Actress Shailene Woodley and Green Party Presidential Candidate Jill Stein were among the celebrities and public figures who took part in the protests. In a turning point, a group of Armed Forced Veterans, led by Native American veterans, visited the Standing Rock camps where they intended to shield civilian protestors from security guards who had reportedly been using water cannons, pepper spray, and other violent means to disperse the protestors. While the protests continued, garnering more and more public interest, legal representatives took the case to court to obtain a legal remedy. On September 9th, 2016 U.S. District Court Judge James Boasberg denied the Standing Rock Sioux request to halt construction, thus dealing a major blow to the effort. However, the Department of Justice and Department of the Interior announced that construction under Lake Oahe would not proceed until a further evaluation could be completed.

On November 21st, law enforcement agents at the Standing Rock camp used tear gas and fire hose to disperse protestors, despite the fact that the temperature had dropped below freezing, leading to higher levels of public outrage over the issue. The Army Corps of engineers ordered protestors to leave the campsites due to concerns over the weather, but hundreds remained. Then on December 4th, a temporary victory for the DAPL opponents as the Army Corps of Engineers issues a statement saying that it will halt construction of the pipeline pending a full EIS before approving construction of the section crossing Lake Oahe. Despite what many felt was a victory, on January 24th, Trump signed an executive memorandum instructing the Corps of Engineers to expedite the approval process. Trump also expressed his intention to revive the defunct Keystone XL project. The Army Corps of Engineers granted a land-use easement on February 7th and rescinded earlier statements that they would invite public comment and prepare and environmental impact assessment. Despite a Feb 9th, legal challenge by the Cheyenne River Sioux and the Standing Rock Sioux, requests for an injunction were denied by District Judge Boasberg.

As of March 2017, the effort to stop DAPL had been a failure. While the environmental implications of the pipeline remain unknown, due to the Army Corps refusal to prepare an environmental impact study, the controversy also had important implications for Native American rights. Sioux tribes have long contested government ownership of the Black Hills of North Dakota, which has been considered a sacred site by the Sioux people for thousands of years. Despite government efforts to compensate tribal members for what the courts determined had been an unlawful seizure, members of the Sioux nations have refused to accept the payment and, instead, want the land that was seized form them unlawfully through eminent domain. Supporters of the pipeline and conservative media attempted to frame the situation as one in which a group of environmentalists were attempting to oppose energy infrastructure expansion and, in doing so, obfuscated one of the most important issues of the controversy, government treatment of Native Americans and the continuing effort of Native American people to control essential part of the land that long belonged to their ancestors.

——*Micah Issitt*

Bibliography and Additional Reading

Chow, Lorraine. "Company Behind DAPL Reported 69 Accidents, Polluting Rivers in 4 States in Last Two Years." *Ecowatch*, EcoWatch. Feb 14 2017. Web. 14 Mar 2017.

Daly, Matthew. "Trump's Stock in Dakota Access Oil Pipeline Company Raises Concern." *Bloomberg*, Bloomberg Inc. Nov 25 2016. Web. 14 Mar 2017.

"Declaration of Tim Mentz, Sr. In Support of Motion for Temporary Restraining Order." *AFSC*, American Friends Service Committee. Sep 4, 2016. Web. 14 Mar 2017.

Hampton, Liz. "Sunoco, behind protested Dakota pipeline, tops U.S. crude spill charts." *Reuters*, Reuters Inc. Sep 23 2016. Web. 14 Mar 2017.

Hersher, Rebecca. "Key Moments in the Dakota Access Pipeline Fight." *NPR*, National Public Radio. Feb 22 2017. Web. 14 Mar 2017.

LaCapria, Kim. "Mind Your Own Bismarck." *Snopes*, Snopes Inc. Nov 30 2016. Web. 17 Mar 2017.

Meyer, Robinson. "The Legal Case for Blocking the Dakota Access Pipeline." *The Atlantic,* Atlantic Monthly Group. Sep 9 2016. Web. 14 Mar 2017.

"Plaintiff's Motion for Leave to File Supplemental Declaration." *Sierra Club*, Sierra Club. Sep 2 2016. Pdf. 14 Mar 2017.

Worland, Justin. "What do Know About the Dakota Access Pipeline Protests." *Time*, Time Inc. Oct 28 2016. Web. 14 Mar 2017.